Paige Baltzan

Daniels College of Business, University of Denver

Amy Phillips

Daniels College of Business, University of Denver

Brian Detlor

DeGroote School of Business, McMaster University

Business Driven Information Systems

McGraw-Hill
Ryerson

Toronto   Montréal   Boston   Burr Ridge, IL   Dubuque, IA   Madison, WI   New York   San
Francisco   St. Louis   Bangkok   Bogotá   Caracas   Kuala Lumpur   Lisbon   London   Madrid
Mexico City   Milan   New Delhi   Santiago   Seoul   Singapore   Sydney   Taipei

BUSINESS DRIVEN INFORMATION SYSTEMS

CANADIAN EDITION

ISBN-13: 978-0-07-078051-4
ISBN-10: 0-07-078051-X

1 2 3 4 5 6 7 8 9 10 TCP 0 9 8

Printed and bound in Canada

Care has been taken to trace ownership of copyright material contained in this text; however, the publisher will welcome any information that enables them to rectify any reference or credit for subsequent editions.

Editorial Director: Joanna Cotton
Senior Sponsoring Editor: Rhondda McNabb
Marketing Manager: Matthew Busbridge
Developmental Editor: Sarah Fulton
Senior Editorial Associate: Christine Lomas
Supervising Editor: Graeme Powell
Copy Editor: Erin Moore
Senior Production Coordinator: Madeleine Harrington
Cover Design: Dave Murphy
Cover Image: Man Hiking © Noel Hendrickson/Masterfile
Interior Design: Dave Murphy
Page Layout: Aptara, Inc.
Printer: Transcontinental Interglobe

Library and Archives Canada Cataloguing in Publication

Baltzan, Paige
    Business driven information systems / Paige Baltzan, Amy

Phillips, Brian Detlor. — 1st Canadian ed.

Includes index.
ISBN 978-0-07-078051-4
    1. Industrial management—Data processing. 2. Information technology—Management. I. Detlor, Brian
      II. Phillips, Amy (Amy L.) III. Title.

HD30.2.B34 2007   658.4'038011   C2007-904511-1

To Tony, Hannah, Sophie, and Gus
What do you always remember?
That I Love You!
That I'm Proud of You!

Paige

To my colleagues, Jill, David, Hans, Don, Dick, Paul, KED, Dan, Paige, and Deborah with respect. You are an exceptional group of professionals and friends. Thank you very much for making Daniels a wonderful place to park my bike.

Amy

To my parents, Lorne and Julie Detlor. Now you have something else to display on your coffee table!

Brian

Paige Baltzan

Paige Baltzan teaches in the Department of Information Technology and Electronic Commerce at the Daniels College of Business at the University of Denver. She holds a B.S.B.A. specializing in MIS/Accounting from Bowling Green State University and an M.B.A. specializing in MIS from the University of Denver. She is a coauthor on several books including *Business Driven Technology*, I-Series, and a contributor to *Management Information Systems for the Information Age*.

Prior to joining the Daniels College faculty in 1999, Paige spent several years working for a large telecommunications company and an international consulting firm where she participated in client engagements in the United States as well as South America and Europe. Paige lives in Lakewood, Colorado, with her husband, Tony, and daughters, Hannah and Sophie.

Amy Phillips

Amy Phillips is a professor in the Department of Information Technology and Electronic Commerce in the Daniels College of Business at the University of Denver. Amy's main teaching and research areas involve Internet and mobile technologies. With her MCT certification, Amy works with developing training material for Microsoft's Web Services platform, .NET. With more than 22 years teaching experience, Amy has coauthored several textbooks, including *Management Information Systems for the Information Age*, 6/e, *Business Driven Technology, Business Driven Information Systems, Internet Explorer 6.0* and *PowerPoint 2003*.

Brian Detlor

Brian Detlor is an associate professor of Information Systems at the DeGroote School of Business at McMaster University in Hamilton, Ontario. Brian specializes in research concerning Web information seeking, information literacy, knowledge management, and the adoption and use of portals across organizational, government, and community domains. He teaches a large introductory information systems course to undergraduate Commerce students, as well as a course on management issues in electronic business. With over 10 years of computer industry experience, Brian has published scholarly articles in several leading journals, including the *Communications of the ACM*, the *Journal of Business Research*, and the *Information Systems Journal*, and has authored/co-authored two books: *Towards Knowledge Portals* and *Web Work*. Recently, Brian has served as a visiting professor in the College of Commerce at DePaul University in Chicago, USA.

BRIEF CONTENTS

CONTENTS

PREFACE

Business Driven Information Systems discusses various business initiatives first and how technology supports those initiatives second. The premise for this unique approach is that business initiatives should drive technology choices. Every discussion first addresses the business needs and then addresses the technology that supports those needs. This text provides the foundation that will enable students to achieve excellence in business, whether they major in operations management, manufacturing, sales, marketing, finance, human resources, accounting, or virtually any other business discipline. *Business Driven Information Systems* is designed to give students the ability to understand how information technology can be a point of strength for an organization.

Common business goals associated with information technology projects include reducing costs, improving productivity, customer satisfaction and loyalty, creating competitive advantages, streamlining supply chains, global expansion, and so on. Achieving these results is not easy. Implementing a new accounting system or marketing plan is not likely to generate long-term growth or reduce costs across an entire organization. Businesses must undertake enterprisewide initiatives to achieve broad general business goals such as reducing costs. Information technology plays a critical role in deploying such initiatives by facilitating communication and increasing business intelligence. Any individual anticipating a successful career in business, whether it is in accounting, finance, human resources, or operations management, must understand the basics of information technology that can be found in this text.

FORMAT, FEATURES, AND HIGHLIGHTS

Business Driven Information Systems is state-of-the-art in its discussions, presents concepts in an easy-to-understand format, and allows students to be active participants in learning. The dynamic nature of information technology requires all students, more specifically business students, to be aware of both current and emerging technologies. Students are facing complex subjects and need a clear, concise explanation to be able to understand and use the concepts throughout their careers. By engaging students with numerous case studies, exercises, projects, and questions that reinforce concepts, *Business Driven Information Systems* creates a unique learning experience for both faculty and students.

- **Audience.** *Business Driven Information Systems* is designed for use in undergraduate or introductory MBA courses in Management Information Systems, which are required in many Business Administration or Management programs as part of the common body of knowledge for all business majors.

- **Logical Layout.** Students and faculty will find the text well organized with the topics flowing logically from one chapter to the next. The definition of each term is provided before it is covered in the chapter and an extensive glossary is included at the back of the text. Each chapter offers a comprehensive opening case study, a section explaining the relevance of the topic to business students, an introduction, learning outcomes, closing case studies, key terms, summary of key themes, and making business decision questions. The plug-ins, available on the Online Learning Centre, follow the same pedagogical elements with the exception of the exclusion of opening and closing case studies.

- **Thorough Explanations.** Complete coverage is provided for each topic that is introduced. Explanations are written so that students can understand the ideas presented and relate them to other concepts.

- **Solid Theoretical Base.** The text relies on current theory and practice of information systems as they relate to the business environment. Current academic and professional journals cited throughout the text are found in the

Notes at the end of the book—a roadmap for additional, pertinent readings that can be the basis for learning beyond the scope of the chapters or plug-ins.

- **Material to Encourage Discussion.** All chapters contain a diverse selection of case studies and individual and group problem-solving activities as they relate to the use of information technology in business. Three comprehensive cases at the end of each chapter reinforce content. These cases encourage students to consider what concepts have been presented and then apply those concepts to a situation they might find within an organization. Different people in an organization can view the same facts from different points of view and the cases will force students to consider some of those views.

- **Integrative Themes.** Several integrative themes recur throughout the text which adds comprehensiveness to the material. Among these themes are value added techniques and methodologies, ethics and social responsibility, globalization, and gaining a competitive advantage. Such topics are essential to gaining a full understanding of the strategies that a business must recognize, formulate, and in turn implement. In addition to addressing these in the chapter material, many illustrations are provided for their relevance to business practice.

Changes to the Canadian Edition

As a result of extensive reviews of the U.S. version of this textbook by professors teaching introductory Management Information Systems courses at colleges and universities throughout Canada, several changes were made. These changes include the following:

- Incorporating new material on information privacy, with special attention to privacy laws and principles from a Canadian perspective.

- Utilizing numerous examples throughout the chapters concerning Canadian organizations and businesses.

- Updating many of the opening and closing cases to showcase Canadian examples and organizations.

- Incorporating sections to help delineate and organize related material. This involved:
  - creating an initial section that illustrates the "big picture" of how information systems are used in and for business;
  - grouping chapters that cover SCM, CRM, and ERP, with ERP having its own separate chapter;
  - forming an entire section that focuses on the "information" side of information technology and its use in business; and
  - grouping technical chapters together at the end of the textbook.

- Expanding the original material on Collaboration Systems into its own separate chapter concerning how information technology helps organizations access, share, and use information. This includes detailed coverage on enterprise portals.

- Reducing the coverage on Project Management and Outsourcing and incorporating this material into the chapter on Systems Development.

- Including a short write-up at the beginning of each section that describes the purpose of the section and how the chapters within it relate to that purpose.

- Incorporating an explanation at the beginning of each chapter called "Why Do I Need to Know This?" emphasizing each chapter's importance and message.

- Adding a "Summary of Key Themes" at the end of each chapter to recap the major lessons and themes presented in the chapter.

- Including a short description at the start of each closing case to illustrate how the case pertains to the chapter's content.

ACKNOWLEDGMENTS

I would like to acknowledge the hard work of my co-authors who gave me an excellent base on which to build for this Canadian adaptation. I am especially grateful to the good people at McGraw-Hill Ryerson, particularly Rhondda McNabb and Sarah Fulton, who made the job so much easier than it would have been otherwise. To my colleagues at the DeGroote School of Business I am grateful; special thanks goes to Rita Cossa who offered very practical and sage advice on how to write a textbook. I also owe gratitude to Stephen Smith and Shannon McKay who helped contribute valuable material used in some of the new case material for this Canadian adaptation.

Reviewers for the Canadian Edition

Franca Giacomelli
Humber College

Robert Goldstein
University of British Columbia

Mary-Liz Grise
Dalhousie University

Michael Haughton
Wilfrid Laurier University

M. Gordon Hunter
University of Lethbridge

Sherrie Komiak
Memorial University of Newfoundland

Michael A. Malazdrewicz
Brandon University

Hosein Marzi
St. Francis Xavier University

Francisco Moro
Odette School of Business, University of Windsor

David Parker
George Brown College

Al Pilcher
Sprott School of Business Carleton University

Ylber Ramadani
George Brown College

Stephen Rochefort
Red Deer College

Robert Riordan
Sprott School of Business, Carleton University

Harold Smith
Algonquin College

Chris Street
University of Manitoba

John H. Walker
Brock University

Reviewers for the U.S. Edition

Kamal Nayan Agarwal
Howard University

Marvin Albin
University of Southern Indiana

Sunny Baker
California State University – San Bernardino

Cynthia Barnes
Lamar University

Ozden Bayazit
Central Washington University

Jack Becker
University of North Texas

Queen Booker
Minnesota State University – Mankato

Ralph Caputo
Manhattan College

Judith Carlisle
Dowling College

Jerry Carvalho
University of Utah – Salt Lake City

Casey Cegielski
Auburn University

Robert Chi
California State University – Long Beach

Tony Coulson
California State University – San Bernardino

David Dulany
Aurora University

Lauren Eder
Rider University

Frederic Fisher
Florida State University – Tallahassee

Linda Fried
University of Colorado – Denver

James Frost
Idaho State University

John Gerdes
University of California – Riverside

Rajni Goel
Howard University

Robert Gordon
Hofstra University

Lorraine Greenwald
SUNY – Farmingdale

John Gudenas
Aurora University

Roslin Hauck
Illinois State University

Bashorat Ibragimova
University of North Texas

Rex Karsten
University of Northern Iowa

Chung Kim
Southwest Missouri State

Donald Kalmey
Indiana University Southeast

Virginia Kleist
West Virginia University

Chang Koh
University of North Texas

Al Lederer
University of Kentucky

Mark Lewis
Regis College

Stephen Loy
Eastern Kentucky University

Joan Lumpkin
Wright State University

Jane Mackay
Texas Christian University

Don McCubbrey
University of Denver

Nina McGarry
George Washington University

Bernard Merkle
California Lutheran University

Phillip Musa
University of Alabama –
Birmingham

Bijayananda Naik
University of South Dakota

Michael Pangburn
University of Oregon

Barry Pasternack
California State University –
Fullerton

Alan Graham Peace
West Virginia University

Richard Peterson
Montclair State University

John Powell
University of South Dakota

Leonard Presby
William Patterson University

Mahesh Raisinghani
Texas Women's University

Kirsten Rosacker
University of South Dakota

Marcos Schniederjans
University of Nebraska – Lincoln

Ken Sears
University of Texas – Arlington

Ganesan Shankaranarayanan
Boston University

Stephen Shao
Tennessee State University

K. David Smith
Cameron University

Ray Tsai
St. Cloud State University

Richard Turley
University of Northern Colorado

Karen Williams
University of Texas – San Antonio

James Yao
Montclair State University

Randall Young
University of North Texas

Yue Zhang
California State University–
Northridge

WALKTHROUGH

Why Do I Need to Know This? and Learning Outcomes

Why Do I Need to Know This? Located on the first page of each chapter, the author clearly explains to students how the material to be covered in the chapter is relevant to *them* as business students

ment

Why Do I Need To Know This ?

This chapter elaborates upon the concept of customer relationship management (CRM), first introduced in Chapter 3, and discusses how information technology can be used to support firms in their interactions with customers. At the simplest level, organizations implement CRM to gain a better understanding of customer needs and behaviours, and information technology provides companies with a new channel to communicate with customers beyond those traditionally used by organizations such as face-to-face or paper-based methods.

Learning Outcomes. These outcomes focus on what students should learn and be able to answer upon completion of the chapter.

LEARNING OUTCOMES

4.1.	List and describe the five components of a typical supply chain.
4.2.	Define the relationship between information technology and the supply chain.
4.3.	Identify the factors driving supply chain management.
4.4.	Summarize the best practices for implementing a successful supply chain management system.

Chapter Opening Case and Opening Case Study Questions

Chapter Opening Case. To enhance student interest, each chapter begins with an opening case study that highlights an organization that has been time-tested and value proven in the business world. This feature serves to fortify concepts with relevant examples of outstanding companies. Discussion of the case is threaded throughout the chapters.

opening case study

Shell Canada Fuels Productivity with ERP

Shell Canada is one of the nation's largest integrated petroleum companies and is a leading manufacturer, distributor, and marketer of refined petroleum products. The company, headquartered in Calgary, produces natural gas, natural gas liquids, and bitumen. Shell Canada is also the country's largest producer of sulphur. There is a Canada-wide network of 1,809 Shell-branded retail gasoline stations and convenience food stores from coast-to-coast.

Opening Case Study Questions. Located at the end of each section, thought provoking questions connect the Chapter Opening Case Study with important chapter concepts.

OPENING CASE QUESTIONS

Shell Canada Fuels Productivity with ERP

1. How did ERP help improve business operations at Shell Canada?
2. How important was training in helping roll out the system to Shell Canada personnel?
3. How could extended ERP components help improve business operations at Shell Canada?

Projects and Case Studies

Case Studies. The text is packed with 48 case studies illustrating how a variety of prominent organizations and businesses have successfully implemented many of this text's concepts. All cases are timely and promote critical thinking. Company profiles are expecially appealing and relevant to your students, helping to stir classroom discussion and interest. For a full list of cases explored in *Business Driven Information Systems,* turn to the inside front cover.

Apply Your Knowledge. On the Online Learning Centre for this text (available at www.mcgrawhill.ca/olc/baltzan), there is a set of 50 projects aimed at reinforcing the business initiatives explored in the text. These projects help to develop the application and problem-solving skills of your students through challenging and creative business-driven scenarios.

Project 6:
Setting Boundaries

Even the most ethical people sometimes face difficult choices. Acting ethically means behaving in a principled fashion and treating other people with respect and dignity. It is simple to say, but not so simple to do since some situations are complex or ambiguous. The important role of ethics in our lives has long been recognized. As far back as 44 B.C., Cicero said that ethics are indispensable to anyone who wants to have a good career. Having said that, Cicero, along with some of the greatest minds over the centuries, struggled with what the rules of ethics should be.

Our ethics are rooted in our history, culture, and religion, and our sense of ethics may shift over time. The electronic age brings with it a new dimension in the ethics debate—the amount of personal information that we can collect and store, and the speed with which we can access and process that information.

Project Focus

In a team, discuss how you would react to the following situations:

Making Business Decisions. These small scenario-driven projects help students focus individually on decision making as they relate to the topical elements in the chapters.

MAKING BUSINESS DECISIONS

1. **Competitive analysis**

   Cheryl O'Connell is the owner of a small, high-end retailer of women's clothing called Excelus. Excelus's business has been successful for many years, largely because of Cheryl's ability to anticipate the needs and wants of her loyal customer base and provide them with personalized service. Cheryl does not see any value in IT and does not want to invest any capital in something that will not directly affect her bottom line. Develop a proposal describing the potential IT-enabled competitive opportunities or threats Cheryl might be missing by not embracing IT. Be sure to include a Porter's Five Forces analysis and discuss which one of the three generic strategies Cheryl should pursue.

End-of-Chapter Elements

Each chapter contains complete pedagogical support in the form of:

Summary of Key Themes. These brief bulleted sections offer a tidy recap of the chapter's most important ideas, and their relevance to business.

SUMMARY OF KEY THEMES

The purpose of this chapter was to provide you, the business student, with a detailed overview of the various telecommunications technologies employed by organizations today. This included discussion on:

- Network types (LAN, WAN, MAN),
- Network architectures (peer-to-peer, client/server),

Key Terms. ey terms are displayed at the end of each chapter with page numbers referencing where they are discussed in the text.

KEY TERMS

Application service provider (ASP)   43
Associate program (affiliate program)   49
Blog   49
Brick-and-mortar business   46
Business-to-business

Electronic data interchange (EDI)   50
Electronic marketplace (e-marketplace)   44
E-mall   46
Encryption   52
E-procurement   51

Online ad (banner ad)   49
Online service provider (OSP)   43
Personalization   49
Podcasting   49
Pop-under ad   49
Pop-up ad   49

Three Closing Case Studies. These case studies reinforce important concepts with prominent examples from businesses and organizations. Discussion uestions follow each case study.

CLOSING CASE ONE

Fighting Cancer with Information

This case shows how one organization used a CRM solution to solve information issues.
   "The mission of the American Cancer Society (ACS) is to cure cancer and relieve the pain
and suffe
officer, A
   The A
eliminatin

CLOSING CASE TWO

Calling All Canadians

This case shows how other factors, beyond strictly information technology ones, affect CRM success.
   Wi
panie
fashio
consi
money
outso
   For

CLOSING CASE THREE

Revving Up Customer Relationships at Harley-Davidson

This case showcases how information technology can be used to improve customer relations.
   There is a mystique associated with a Harley-Davidson motorcycle. No other motor-

About the Plug-Ins

Located on the Online Learning Centre (www.mcgrawhill.ca/olc/baltzan), the overall goal of the plug-ins is to provide an alternative for faculty who find themselves in the situation of having to purchase an extra book to support Microsoft Office. The plug-ins presented here offer integration with the core chapters and provide critical knowledge using essential business applications, such as Microsoft Excel, Microsoft Access, and Microsoft FrontPage. Each plug-in uses hands-on tutorials for comprehension and mastery.

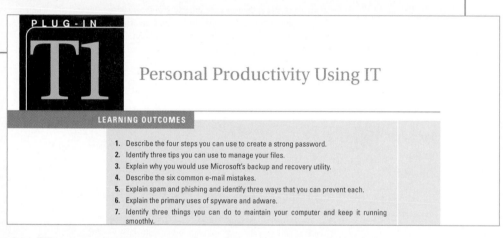

PLUG-IN

T1

Personal Productivity Using IT

LEARNING OUTCOMES

1. Describe the four steps you can use to create a strong password.
2. Identify three tips you can use to manage your files.
3. Explain why you would use Microsoft's backup and recovery utility.
4. Describe the six common e-mail mistakes.
5. Explain spam and phishing and identify three ways that you can prevent each.
6. Explain the primary uses of spyware and adware.
7. Identify three things you can do to maintain your computer and keep it running smoothly.

End-of-Plug-In Elements

Each plug-in contains complete pedagogical support in the form of:

Plug-In Summary. Revisits the plug-in highlights in summary format.

Making Business Decisions. Small scenario-driven projects that help students focus individually on decision making as they relate to the topical elements in the chapters.

★ PLUG-IN SUMMARY

Microsoft Excel is a general-purpose electronic spreadsheet used to organize, calculate, and analyze data. The tasks you can perform with Excel range from preparing a simple invoice to managing an accounting ledger for a business.

Six areas in Excel were covered in this plug-in:

1. Workbooks and worksheets.
2. Working with cells and cell data.
3. Printing worksheets.
4. Formatting worksheets.
5. Formulas.
6. Working with charts and graphics.

★ MAKING BUSINESS DECISIONS

1. Stock Watcher

   Mark Martin has created a basic stock watcher worksheet that he uses to report on gains or losses from when he purchased the stock and the last recorded date and price. Mark has given you a snapshot of his spreadsheet (see Figure T2.29) that you can use to recreate this spreadsheet for yourself. Here are some basic steps to follow:

   1. Create a new workbook.
   2. Enter all the information provided in Figure T2.29.
   3. Apply the currency format to the respective columns.

Supplements for the Students

iStudy

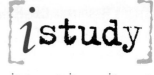

Available 24/7: providing instant feedback when you want, how you want, and where you want. This online *i*Study space was developed to help you master the concepts and achieve better grades with all the learning tools you've come to expect, including tips on what you really need to know, relevant videos, an audio glossary, matching exercises and quizzes. *i*Study offers the best, most convenient way to interact, learn, and succeed.

*i*Study can be purchased through the online Student Success Centre or by purchasing a PIN code card through the campus bookstore. Instructors: Please contact your *i*Learning Sales Specialist for more information on how to make *i*Study part of your students' success.

Online Learning Centre

Available at www.mcgrawhill.ca/olc/baltzan, the Online Learning Centre provides a range of resources to help you succeed in your studies, including a searchable glossary, self-study quizzes, Technology Plug-Ins, and Apply Your Knowledge projects.

MISource

MISource provides animated tutorials and simulated practice of the core skills in Microsoft Excel, Access, and PowerPoint. MISource also animates 47 important computer concepts. Please contact your *i*Learning Sales Specialists for more information about this CD-ROM.

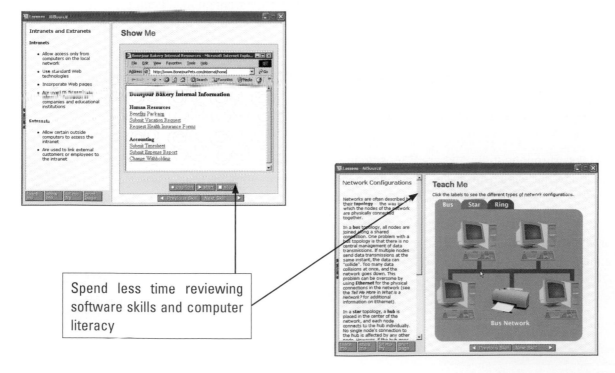

Spend less time reviewing software skills and computer literacy

Supplements for Instructors

INSTRUCTOR'S RESOURCE CD-ROM

The following resources are available on the Instructor's Resource CD. With the exception of the Computerized Test Bank, these resources can also be accessed in the password protected Instructor's Centre on the Online Learning Centre at www.mcgrawhill.ca/olc/baltzan.

Test Bank. This computerized package allows instructors to custom design, save, and generate tests. The test program permits instructors to edit, add, or delete questions from the test bank; analyze test results; and organize a database of tests and students' results.

Instructor's Manual. The instructor's manual includes suggestions for designing the course and presenting the material. Each chapter is supported by answers to end-of-chapter questions and problems, and suggestions concerning the discussion topics and cases. Also available in the instructor's manual are over 50 engaging classroom exercises that challenge students to apply the material they are learning.

PowerPoint Presentations. A set of PowerPoint slides for each chapter features bulleted items that provide a lecture outline, plus key figures and tables from the text, and detailed teaching notes on each slide.

Multiple Data and Solution Files. For appropriate problems, there are multiple data and solution files allowing instructors to assign the same base problem with different data files.

ADDITIONAL RESOURCES, ONLINE LEARNING CENTRE, INSTRUCTOR'S CENTRE

These additional resources can be accessed in the Instructor's Centre of the Online Learning Centre at www.mcgrawhill.ca/olc/baltzan.

Sample Syllabi. Several syllabi have been developed according to different course lengths, as well as different course concentrations, such as a business emphasis or a technology focus.

Image Library. Text figure and tables, as permission allows, are provided.

Captivate Files. A complete set of narrated solution files for all Excel, Access, and Web development projects provide narrated step-by-step detail for each project. These are a great aid to help instructors quickly understand questions and can be posted for students to review, saving instructor time with case reviews.

Internet Links. Throughout the text are Web site addresses where related material can be obtained from the World Wide Web. These Web locations provide valuable information that, when used with the text material, provides a complete, up-to-date coverage of information technology and business.

Additional Material PowerPoints. *Business Driven Information Systems* also offers PowerPoint slides on additional lecture material (i.e. NetFlix' supply chain, or Eddie Bauer's customer relationship management) not found in the text.

The Big Picture

Most organizations today rely heavily on the use of information technologies to run various aspects of their business. Whether it is to order and ship goods, interact with customers, or conduct some other business activity, information technology is often the underlying infrastructure used to perform such work. Information technology enables companies to perform a variety of tasks both efficiently and effectively. Moreover, information technology allows organizations to remain competitive in today's fast-paced world. This is especially true when one considers the burgeoning trend and popularity of conducting business over the Internet.

Organizations that fail to take advantage of information technology run the risk of falling behind others who adopt information technology solutions. Firms are aware that they must adapt to technological advances and innovations to keep pace with today's rapidly changing environment. Their competitors certainly will!

Though technology can be quite an exciting phenomenon on its own, as a business student you should understand that successful organizations do not utilize technology for the sake of technology itself. There must be a business reason. Using a technological solution just because it is available is not reason enough to adopt the technology.

One purpose of this section of the textbook is to raise awareness to this point. Business strategies and processes drive the decision to utilize technology. Although sometimes awareness of an emerging technology can lead to new strategic directions, information technologies, for the most part, do not drive business initiatives. This is an important distinction.

Another purpose of this section is to introduce the concept of electronic business and explain the importance of using the Internet and wireless technologies to conduct business as a means of helping organizations reach their goals and objectives.

1
CHAPTER

Information Systems in Business

Why Do I Need To Know This ?

This chapter sets the stage for the textbook. It starts from ground zero by providing you with a clear description of what information technology is and how it fits into business practice and organizational activities. The chapter then provides an overview of how organizations operate in competitive environments and how firms need to constantly define and redefine their business strategies in order to create competitive advantage. Doing so allows organizations to survive and thrive. Importantly, information technology is shown as a key enabler to help organizations operate successfully in such competitive environments.

As a business student, you need to know this since it does two important things. First, it positions information technology within the larger context of business initiatives and strategies. Second, it raises awareness of information technology's role in daily business life.

Organizational workers need to acquire a solid foundation of information system fundamentals in order to understand technology's potential, its contribution to an organization's business strategy, and how it can be ultimately leveraged to help organizations be competitive and successful. This chapter will help you reach this goal.

Apple—Merging Technology, Business, and Entertainment

Apple Inc., back from near oblivion, is setting the pace in the digital world with innovation and creativity that had been missing from the company for the past 20 years. Introduction of the iPod, a brilliant merger of technology, business, and entertainment, catapulted Apple back into the mainstream.

Capitalizing on New Trends

In 2000, Steve Jobs was fixated on developing video editing software for the Macintosh. But then he realized millions of people were using computers and CD burners to make audio CDs and to download digital songs called MP3s from illegal online services like Napster. Jobs was worried that he was looking in the wrong direction and had missed the MP3 bandwagon.

Jobs moved fast. He began by purchasing SoundStep from Jeff Robbin, a 28-year-old software engineer and former Apple employee. SoundStep was developing software that simplified the importing and compression of MP3 songs. Robbin and a couple of other programmers began writing code from scratch and created the first version of iTunes for the Mac in less than four months. This powerful and ingenious database could quickly sort tens of thousands of songs in a multitude of ways and find particular tracks in nanoseconds.

Jobs next challenged the team to make iTunes portable. He envisioned a Walkman-like player that could hold thousands of songs and be taken anywhere. The idea was to modify iTunes and build a tiny new system for what was basically a miniature computer, along with a user interface that could sort and navigate music files with the same sophistication as iTunes on the Mac. The iPod was born nine months later.

Jobs noticed that one last key element was missing, an online store for buying downloadable songs. Such a store would need an e-business infrastructure that could automatically deliver songs and track billing and payments for conceivably millions of purchases. In the spring of 2003, 18 months after the launch of the iPod, Apple's iTunes Music Store opened for business. The company's goal was to sell 1 million songs in the first six months. It hit this goal in six days.

Capitalizing on the iPod

Consumers purchased more than 14 million iPod devices during the 2005 holiday season, allowing Apple to exceed $1 billion in sales through its retail stores. Apple has now sold more than 40 million iPods. The groundbreaking product has transformed Apple from a niche computer maker into the leading purveyor of digital media.

With millions of iPods in the hands of consumers, other companies are noticing the trend and finding ways to capitalize on the product. John Lin created a prototype of a remote control for the iPod. Lin took his prototype to Macworld, where he found success. A few months later, Lin's company had Apple's blessing and a commitment for shelf space in its retail stores. "This is how Apple supports the iPod economy," Lin said.

In the iPod-dominated market, hundreds of companies have been inspired to develop more than 500 accessories—everything from rechargers for the car to $1,500 Fendi bags. Eric Tong, vice president at Belkin, a cable and peripheral manufacturer, believes that 75 percent of all iPod owners purchase at least one accessory—meaning that 30 million accessories have been sold. With most of the products priced between $10 and $200 that puts the iPod economy well over $300 million and perhaps as high as $6 billion. Popular iPod accessories include:

- Altec Lansing Technologies—iPod speakers and recharger dock ($175).
- Belkin—TuneCast mobile FM transmitter ($47).
- Etymotic Research—high-end earphones ($175).
- Griffin Technology—iTrip FM transmitter ($40).
- Kate Spade—Geneva faux-croc mini iPod holder ($65).
- Apple—socks set in six colours, green, purple, blue, orange, pink, and grey ($34).
- Apple—digital camera connector ($34).

Capitalizing on the Future

The latest iPod packs music, audiobooks, podcasts, photos, video, contacts, calendars, games, clocks, and locks in a design up to 45 percent slimmer than the original iPod. It also boasts stamina (up to 20 hours of battery life), generous capacity (30 GB or 60 GB of storage), a great personality (intuitive, customizable menus), and a touch of genius (the Apple Click Wheel). The latest features include:

- **Videos**—Choose from over 2,000 music videos at the iTunes Music Store or purchase ad-free episodes of a favourite ABC or Disney television show and watch them on the go.
- **Podcasts**—The iTunes Podcast Directory features thousands of free podcasts, or radio-style shows, including favourites from such big names as ABC News, Adam Curry, ESPN, KCRW, and WGBH.

- **Audiobooks**—The digital shelves of the iTunes Music Store are stocked with more than 11,000 audiobooks, including such exclusives as the entire Harry Potter series.
- **Photos**—With storage for up to 25,000 photos, iPod users can view photo slide shows—complete with music—on an iPod or on a TV via the optional video cable.

iPod's Impact on the Music Business

In the digital era, the unbundling of CDs through the purchase of individual tracks lets consumers pay far less to get a few of their favourite songs rather than buying an entire album. Many analysts predicted that the iPod's success coupled with the consumer's ability to choose individual song downloads would lead to increased revenues for music businesses. However, the industry is seeing individual downloads cannibalizing album profits and failing to attract new music sales. "I've still never bought a download," said Eneka Iriondo-Coysh, a 21-year-old graphic-design student in London who has owned a 10,000 song-capacity iPod for more than two years. "I do it all from my CDs," mostly hip-hop and soul.

The global music industry has been under siege for years amid declining sales. Record companies suffer from piracy, including billions of dollars in lost revenue due to bootlegged CDs. At the same time, music faces new competition for consumer time and money from video games, DVDs, and mobile phones. At traditional record stores, DVDs and games are taking an increasing amount of shelf space, squeezing out CDs. The music download numbers suggest that the iPod's iconic success is not translating into new music sales the way the evolution from vinyl albums to cassettes and then CDs did. For many users, the portable devices are just another way of stocking and listening to music, not an incentive to buy new music.

Global CD sales fell 6.7 percent to $14.5 billion in the first half of 2005, according to the London-based International Federation of the Phonographic Industry. The evidence indicates that digital downloads are not good for the music business.[1]

INFORMATION TECHNOLOGY'S ROLE IN BUSINESS

S tudents frequently ask, "Why do we need to study information technology?" The answer is simple: Information technology is everywhere in business. Understanding information technology provides great insight to anyone learning about business.

It is easy to demonstrate information technology's role in business by reviewing a copy of popular business magazines such as *Canadian Business* or *Profit*. Placing a marker (such as a Post-it Note) on each page that contains a technology-related article or advertisement indicates that information technology is everywhere in business (see Figure 1.1). These are *business* magazines, not *technology* magazines, yet they are filled with technology. Students who understand technology have an advantage in business.

These magazine articles typically discuss such topics as databases, customer relationship management, Web services, supply chain management, security, ethics, business intelligence, and so on. They also focus on companies such as Siebel, Oracle, Microsoft, and IBM. This text explores these topics in detail, along with reviewing the associated business opportunities and challenges.

Information Technology's Impact on Business Operations

Figure 1.2 highlights the business functions receiving the greatest benefit from information technology, along with the common business goals associated with information technology projects, according to *CIO* magazine.

Achieving the results outlined in Figure 1.2, such as reducing costs, improving productivity, and generating growth, is not easy. Implementing a new accounting system or marketing plan is not likely to generate long-term growth or reduce costs across an entire organization. Businesses must undertake enterprisewide initiatives to achieve broad general business goals such as reducing costs. Information technology plays a critical role in deploying such initiatives by facilitating communication and increasing business intelligence. For example, e-mail and cell phones allow people across an organization to communicate in new and innovative ways.

Understanding information technology begins with gaining an understanding of how businesses function and IT's role in creating efficiencies and effectiveness across the organization. Typical businesses operate by functional areas (often called functional silos). Each area undertakes a specific core business function (see Figure 1.3).

FIGURE 1.1

Technology in *Canadian Business* and *Profit*

FIGURE 1.2

Business Benefits and Information Technology Project
Goals

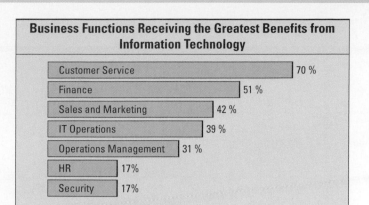

Business Functions Receiving the Greatest Benefits from Information Technology

Customer Service	70 %
Finance	51 %
Sales and Marketing	42 %
IT Operations	39 %
Operations Management	31 %
HR	17%
Security	17%

Information Technology Project Goals

Reduce Costs/Improve Productivity	81 %
Improve Customer Satisfaction/Loyalty	71 %
Create Competitive Advantage	66 %
Generate Growth	54 %
Streamline Supply Chain	37 %
Global Expansion	16%

Functional areas are anything but independent in a business. In fact, functional areas are *interdependent* (see Figure 1.4). Sales must rely on information from operations to understand inventory, place orders, calculate transportation costs, and gain insight into product availability based on production schedules. For an organization to succeed, every department or functional area must work together sharing common information and not be a "silo." Information technology can enable departments to more efficiently and effectively perform their business operations.

Individuals anticipating a successful career in business, whether it is in accounting, finance, human resources, or operation management, must understand information technology including:

- Information technology basics.
- Roles and responsibilities in information technology.
- Measuring information technology's success.

INFORMATION TECHNOLOGY BASICS

Information technology (IT) is any computer-based tool that people use to work with information and support the information and information-processing needs of an organization. Information technology can be an important enabler of business success and innovation. This is not to say that IT *equals* business success and innovation or that IT *represents* business success and innovation. Information technology is most useful when it leverages the talents of people. Information technology in and of itself is not useful unless the right people know how to use and manage it effectively.

Management information systems is a business function just as marketing, finance, operations, and human resources management are business functions. Formally defined, *management information systems (MIS)* is the function that plans for, develops, implements, and maintains IT hardware, software, and applications that people use to support the goals of an organization. To perform the MIS function effectively, almost all organizations today, particularly large and medium-sized ones, have an internal IT department, often called Information Technology (IT),

FIGURE 1.3

Departmental Structure of a
Typical Organization

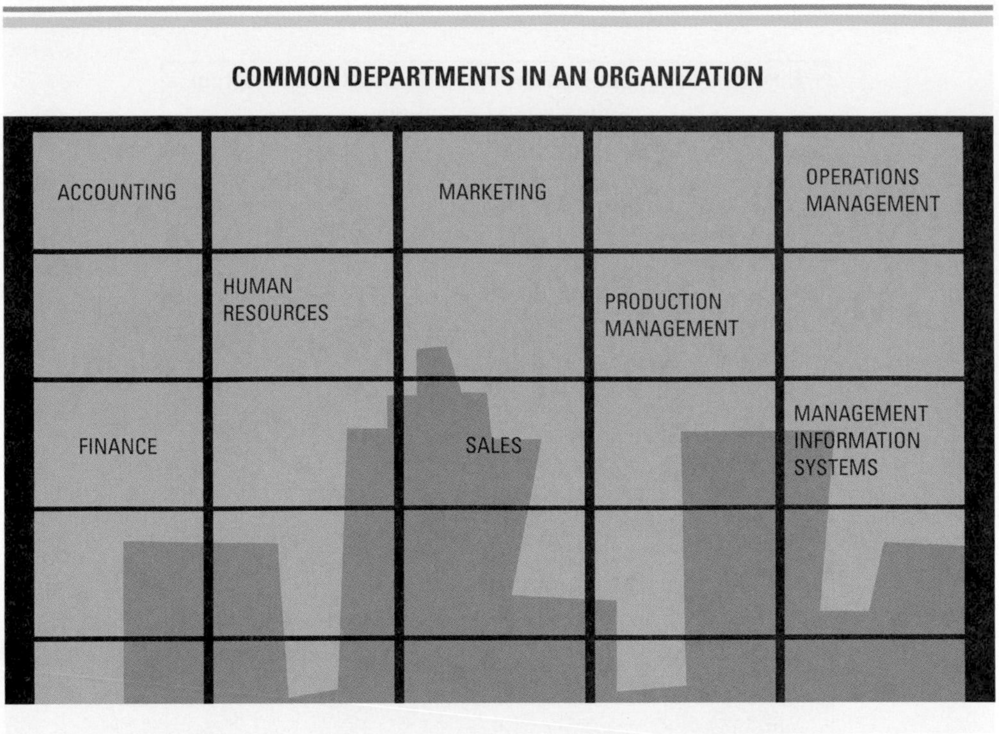

COMMON DEPARTMENTS IN AN ORGANIZATION

- **Accounting** provides quantitative information about the finances of the business including recording, measuring, and describing financial information.

- **Finance** deals with the strategic financial issues associated with increasing the value of the business, while observing applicable laws and social responsibilities.

- **Human resources (HR)** includes the policies, plans, and procedures for the effective management of employees (human resources).

- **Sales** is the function of selling a good or service and focuses on increasing customer sales, which increases company revenues.

- **Marketing** is the process associated with promoting the sale of goods or services. The marketing department supports the sales department by creating promotions that help sell the company's products.

- **Operations management** (also called **production management**) includes the methods, tasks, and techniques organizations use to produce goods and services. Transportation (also called logistics) is part of operations management.

- **Management information systems (MIS)** is the function that plans for, develops, implements, and maintains IT hardware, software, and the portfolio of applications that people use to support the goals of an organization.

Information Systems (IS), or Management Information Systems (MIS). When beginning to learn about information technology it is important to understand:

- Information
- IT resources
- IT cultures

Information

It is important to distinguish between data, information, and knowledge. **Data** are raw facts that describe the characteristics of an event. Characteristics for a sales

FIGURE 1.4

Marketing Working with
Other Organizational
Departments

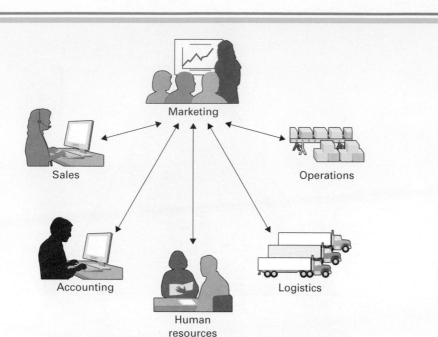

Functional organization—Each functional area has its own systems
and communicates with every other functional area (diagram
displays Marketing communicating with all other functional areas
in the organization).

event could include the date, item number, item description, quantity ordered, customer name, and shipping details. *Information* is data converted into a meaningful and useful context. Information from sales events could include best-selling item, worst-selling item, best customer, and worst customer. Information becomes **knowledge** when information can be enacted upon. In this sense, knowledge is "actionable information" (see Chapter 8).

IT Resources

The plans and goals of the IT department must align with the plans and goals of the organization. Information technology can enable an organization to increase efficiency in manufacturing, retain key customers, seek out new sources of supply, and introduce effective financial management.

It is not always easy for managers to make the right choices when using IT to support (and often drive) business initiatives. Most managers understand their business initiatives well, but are often at a loss when it comes to knowing how to use and manage IT effectively in support of those initiatives. Managers who understand what IT is, and what IT can and cannot do, are in the best position for success. In essence,

- *People* use
- *information technology* to work with
- *Information* (see Figure 1.5).

Those three key resources—people, information, and information technology (in that order of priority)—are inextricably linked. If one fails, they all fail. Most important, if one fails, then chances are the business will fail.

IT Cultures

An organization's culture plays a large role in determining how successfully it will share information. Culture will influence the way people use information (their information behaviour) and will reflect the importance that company leaders

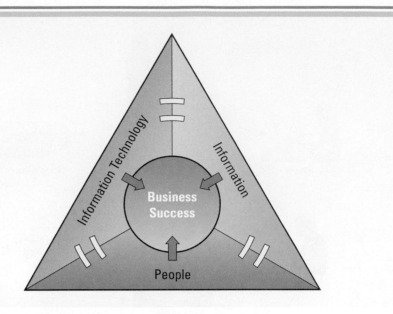

FIGURE 1.6

Different Information Cultures
Found in Organizations

Organizational Information Cultures	
Information-Functional Culture	Employees use information as a means of exercising influence or power over others. For example, a manager in sales refuses to share information with marketing. This causes marketing to need the sales manager's input each time a new sales strategy is developed.
Information-Sharing Culture	Employees across departments trust each other to use information (especially about problems and failures) to improve performance.
Information-Inquiring Culture	Employees across departments search for information to better understand the future and align themselves with current trends and new directions.
Information-Discovery Culture	Employees across departments are open to new insights about crisis and radical changes and seek ways to create competitive advantages.

attribute to the use of information in achieving success or avoiding failure. Four common information-sharing cultures exist in organizations today: information-functional, information-sharing, information-inquiring, and information-discovery (see Figure 1.6 above).[2]

An organization's IT culture can directly affect its ability to compete in the global market. If an organization operates with an information-functional culture, it will have a great degree of difficulty operating. Getting products to market quickly and creating a view of its end-to-end (or entire) business from sales to billing will be a challenge. If an organization operates with an information-discovery culture it will be able to get products to market quickly and easily see a 360-degree view of its entire organization. Employees will be able to use this view to better understand the market and create new products that offer a competitive advantage.

ROLES AND RESPONSIBILITIES IN INFORMATION TECHNOLOGY

Information technology is a relatively new functional area, having been around formally in most organizations only for about 40 years. Job titles, roles, and responsibilities often differ from organization to organization. Nonetheless, clear trends are developing toward elevating some IT positions within an organization to the strategic level.

Most organizations maintain positions such as chief executive officer (CEO), chief financial officer (CFO), and chief operations officer (COO) at the strategic level. Recently there are more IT-related strategic positions such as chief information officer (CIO), chief technology officer (CTO), chief security officer (CSO), chief privacy officer (CPO), and chief knowledge officer (CKO). Note that these roles are not necessarily mutually exclusive. For instance, someone may be both CSO and CPO for a firm.

The *chief information officer (CIO)* is an executive-level position that involves high-level strategic planning and management of technologies and processes pertaining to the creation, storage, and use of information by a business. The chief information officer is responsible for (1) overseeing all uses of information technology and (2) ensuring the strategic alignment of IT with business goals and objectives. As such, the CIO must have a deep understanding of both technology and business; the need for in-depth technology knowledge enables the CIO to understand how technology can help business. This requires that a CIO possess a solid understanding of every aspect of an organization coupled with tremendous insight into the capability of IT. Importantly, the CIO must be able to communicate to others in the organization how technology can be used for the benefit of the enterprise; for example, how technology can enable the development of new products and services and yield greater returns on investment for the company. Further, the CIO must be able to successfully implement and make use of the technology to reach such goals.

Due to the strategic importance of this role, more and more CIOs are playing a key role on companies' boards of directors. Though currently there is a low number of CIOs who sit on Fortune 1,000 boards, as the role of CIO becomes more established within organizations, the CIO will quickly become a key and vital position on most organizations' boards of directors in the near future. This prediction is supported by recent trends in CIO compensation levels. In two separate surveys of CIO executives, the highest paid CIOs receive multiple millions of dollars per year in terms of financial compensation, with most seeing significant increases to their pay cheques over the last few years, especially those at small and mid-sized companies. It is predicted that CIO compensation will increase faster than the rate of inflation. Higher CIO compensation levels were seen at organizations that view technology as pivotal to their operations and success. Further, CIOs who possess a hybrid combination of IT and business backgrounds were shown to be paid significantly more than those coming from strictly IT backgrounds.[3] Broad roles of a CIO include:

- *Manager*—ensure the delivery of all IT projects, on time and within budget.
- *Leader*—ensure the strategic vision of IT is in line with the strategic vision of the organization.
- *Communicator* —advocate and communicate the IT strategy by building and maintaining strong executive relationships.

Though all CIO positions contain aspects of these three broad roles, it is interesting to note that the CIO role can differ internationally in terms of how CIOs manage their time and the hurdles CIOs face, and the impact CIOs have on their organizations. For example, both Canadian and American CIOs indicate that the bulk of their time is spent meeting with company executives and working with IT vendors and non-IT business partners. However, when polled, American CIOs also state that a large chunk of their time is concentrated on planning out strategy. CIOs from both Canada and the United States identify alignment between corporate strategy and IT as a key management priority. Canadians, however, appear to be further ahead in getting business counterparts to share accountability for IT investments, which should have a direct positive effect on alignment. American CIOs rate unrealistic or unknown expectations from business and inadequate budgets as top hurdles to CIO effectiveness. In contrast, German CIOs list unrealistic or unknown expectations from business and shortage of time as their biggest barrier to effectiveness. In

Southeast Asia, CIOs rate risk and uncertainty due to volatile economic conditions as one of their top three hurdles to effectiveness. When spearheading business initiatives, Southeast Asian CIOs are less likely to take risks themselves compared to American CIOs. However, finding time for strategic thinking and planning is less of a struggle for Southeast Asian CIOs; this category was rated near the bottom in their list of 10 barriers to CIO effectiveness. Australian CIOs report that their budgets are largely determined by the organizational business units that leads Australian CIOs to focus their use of IT to generate revenue.[4]

Although CIO is considered a position within IT, CIOs must be concerned with more than just IT. According to an industry survey (see Figure 1.7), most CIOs ranked "enhancing customer satisfaction" ahead of their concerns for any specific aspect of IT. We should applaud CIOs who possess the broad business view that customer satisfaction is more crucial and critical than specific aspects of IT.

The *chief technology officer (CTO)* is responsible for ensuring the throughput, speed, accuracy, availability, and reliability of an organization's information technology. CTOs have direct responsibility for ensuring the efficiency of IT systems throughout the organization. Most CTOs possess well-rounded knowledge of all aspects of IT, including hardware, software, and telecommunications. CTO's typically report to the CIO. The role of CTO is similar to CIO, except that CIO must take on the additional responsibility of ensuring that IT aligns with the organization's strategic initiatives.

The *chief security officer (CSO)* is responsible for ensuring the security of IT systems and developing strategies and IT safeguards against attacks from hackers and viruses. The role of a CSO has been elevated in recent years because of the number of attacks from hackers and viruses. Most CSOs possess detailed knowledge of networks and telecommunications because hackers and viruses usually find their way into IT systems through networked computers.

The *chief privacy officer (CPO)* is responsible for ensuring the ethical and legal use of information within an organization. CPOs are the newest senior executive position in IT. Recently, 150 of the Fortune 500 companies added the CPO position to their list of senior executives. Many CPOs are lawyers by training, enabling them to understand the often complex legal issues surrounding the use of information.

The *chief knowledge officer (CKO)* is responsible for collecting, maintaining, and distributing the organization's knowledge. The CKO designs programs and systems that make it easy for people to reuse knowledge. These systems create repositories of organizational documents, methodologies, tools, and practices, and they establish methods for filtering the information. The CKO must continuously encourage employee contributions to keep the systems up-to-date. The CKO can contribute directly to the organization's bottom line by reducing the learning curve for new employees or employees taking on new roles.

FIGURE 1.7

What Concerns CIOs the Most?

CIO's Concerns	Percentage
Enchancing customer satisfaction	94%
Security	92
Technology evaluation	89
Budgeting	87
Staffing	83
ROI analysis	66
Building new applications	64
Outsourcing hosting	45

Studies conducted at the Institute for Intellectual Capital Research in Hamilton, Ontario, indicate that the CKO position will soon become commonplace. The Institute surveyed 53 executive search firms in Canada and the United States about their perceptions regarding CKO placements. Almost three-quarters of survey respondents expected that searches for CKO placements will increase significantly.[5]

One CKO is Dirk Ramhorst who in 2001 was promoted to the role of CKO with the responsibility for finding knowledge management solutions with return on investment for business departments within Siemens. Siemens Business Services is a global IT service provider based in Munich, Germany, with customers in a wide range of industries including mobile communications, energy, automotive, and transportation. Ramhorst reports to the chief financial officer of the company. This reporting relationship (from CKO to CFO) helps mitigate initial skepticism about the knowledge management function from dissenters in the organization and adds credence to Ramhorst's mantra that knowledge sharing can lead to direct tangible financial benefits.[6]

All the above IT positions and responsibilities are critical to an organization's success. While many organizations may not have a different individual for each of these positions, they must have leaders taking responsibility for all these areas of concern. The individuals responsible for enterprisewide IT and IT-related issues must provide guidance and support to the organization's employees. Figure 1.8 displays the personal skills pivotal for success in an executive IT role.

The Gap Between Business Personnel and IT Personnel

One of the greatest challenges today is effective communication between business personnel and IT personnel. Figure 1.8 clearly demonstrates the importance of communication for IT executives. Business personnel possess expertise in functional areas such as marketing, accounting, sales, and so forth. IT personnel have the technological expertise. Unfortunately, a communications gap often exists between the two. Business personnel have their own vocabularies based on their experience and expertise. IT personnel have their own vocabularies consisting of acronyms and technical terms. Effective communication between business and IT personnel should be a two-way street with each side making the effort to understand each other (including written and oral communication).

Improving Communication Business personnel must seek to increase their understanding of IT. Although they do not need to know every technical detail, it is beneficial to understand what IT can and cannot accomplish. Business managers and leaders should read business-oriented IT magazines, such as *InformationWeek* and *CIO*, to increase their IT knowledge.

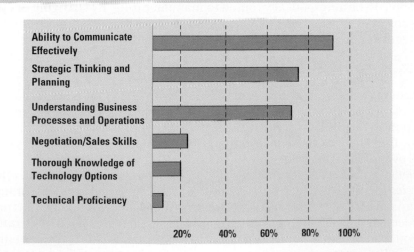

FIGURE 1.8

Skills Pivotal for Success in Executive IT Roles

At the same time, an organization must develop strategies for integrating its IT personnel into the various business functions. Too often, IT personnel are left out of strategy meetings because of the belief they do not understand the business so they will not add any value. That is a dangerous position to take. IT personnel must understand the business if the organization is going to determine which technologies can benefit (or hurt) the business. With a little effort to communicate, IT personnel might provide information on the functionality available in an information system, which could add tremendous value to a meeting about how to improve customer service. Working together, business and IT personnel have the potential to create competitive advantages, reduce costs, and streamline business processes.

It is the CIO's responsibility to ensure effective communications between business and IT personnel. While the CIO assumes the responsibility on an enterprisewide level, it is each employee's responsibility to communicate effectively on a personal level.

MEASURING INFORMATION TECHNOLOGY'S SUCCESS

To offer detailed information to all layers of management, General Electric Co. (GE) invested $1.75 billion in employee time, hardware, software, and other technologies to implement a real-time operations monitoring system. GE's executives use the new system to monitor sales, inventory, and savings across the company's 13 global business operations every 15 minutes. This allows GE to respond to changes, reduce cycle times, and improve risk management on an hourly basis instead of waiting for monthly or quarterly reports. GE estimates the $1.75-billion investment will provide a 33-percent return over five years.[7]

IT professionals know how to install and maintain information systems. Business professionals know how to run a successful business. But how does a company decide if an information system helps make a business successful?

The answer lies in the metrics. Designing metrics requires an expertise that neither IT nor business professionals usually possess. Metrics are about neither technology nor business strategy. The questions that arise in metrics design are almost philosophical: How do you define success? How do you apply quantifiable measures to business processes, especially qualitative ones such as customer service? What kind of information best reflects progress, or the lack of it?

Key performance indicators (KPIs) are the measures that are tied to business drivers. Metrics are the detailed measures that feed those KPIs. Performance metrics fall into a nebulous area of business intelligence that is neither technology- nor business-centred, but this area requires input from both IT and business professionals to find success. Cisco Systems implemented a cross-departmental council to create metrics for improving business process operations. The council developed metrics to evaluate the efficiency of Cisco's online order processing and discovered that due to errors, more than 70 percent of online orders required manual input and were unable to be automatically routed to manufacturing. By changing the process and adding new information systems, within six months the company doubled the percentage of orders that went directly to manufacturing.[8]

Efficiency and Effectiveness Metrics

Organizations spend enormous sums of money on IT to compete in today's fast-paced business environment. Some organizations spend up to 50 percent of their total capital expenditures on IT. To justify these expenditures, an organization must measure the payoff of these investments, their impact on business performance, and the overall business value gained.

Efficiency and effectiveness metrics are two primary types of IT metrics. *Efficiency IT metrics* measure the performance of the IT system itself such as throughput, speed, and availability. *Effectiveness IT metrics* measure the impact IT has on business processes and activities including customer satisfaction, conversion rates, and sell-through increases. Peter Drucker offers a helpful distinction between efficiency and effectiveness. Drucker states that managers "Do things right" and/or "Do the right things." Doing things right addresses efficiency—getting the most from each resource. Doing the right things addresses effectiveness—setting the right goals and objectives and ensuring they are accomplished.[9]

Efficiency focuses on the extent to which an organization is using its resources in an optimal way, while effectiveness focuses on how well an organization is achieving its goals and objectives. The two—efficiency and effectiveness—are definitely interrelated. However, success in one area does not necessarily imply success in the other.

Benchmarking—Baseline Metrics

Regardless of what is measured, how it is measured, and whether it is for the sake of efficiency or effectiveness, there must be *benchmarks,* or baseline values the system seeks to attain. *Benchmarking* is a process of continuously measuring system results, comparing those results to optimal system performance (benchmark values), and identifying steps and procedures to improve system performance.

Consider online government services (e-government) as an illustration of benchmarking efficiency IT metrics and effectiveness IT metrics (see survey results in Figure 1.9). From an effectiveness point of view, Canada ranks number one in terms of e-government satisfaction of its citizens. The survey, sponsored by Accenture, also included such attributes as customer-service vision, initiatives for identifying services for individual citizen segments, and approaches to offering e-government services through multiple-service delivery channels. These are all benchmarks at which Canada's government excels.[10]

In contrast, the *United Nations Division for Public Economics and Public Administration* ranks Canada sixth in terms of efficiency IT metrics. This particular ranking, based purely on efficiency IT metrics, includes benchmarks such as the number of computers per 100 citizens, the number of Internet hosts per 10,000 citizens, and the percentage of the citizen online population. Therefore, while Canada lags behind in IT efficiency, it is the premier e-government provider in terms of effectiveness.[11]

Governments hoping to increase their e-government presence would benchmark themselves against these sorts of efficiency and effectiveness metrics. There is a high degree of correlation between e-government efficiency and effectiveness, although it is not absolute.

The Interrelationship Between Efficiency and Effectiveness IT Metrics

Efficiency IT metrics focus on the technology itself. Figure 1.10 highlights the most common types of efficiency IT metrics.

Efficiency	Effectiveness
1. United States (3.11)	1. Canada
2. Australia (2.60)	2. Singapore
3. New Zealand (2.59)	3. United States
4. Singapore (2.58)	4. Denmark
5. Norway (2.55)	5. Australia
6. Canada (2.52)	6. Finland
7. United Kingdom (2.52)	7. Hong Kong
8. Netherlands (2.51)	8. United Kingdom
9. Denmark (2.47)	9. Germany
10. Germany (2.46)	10. Ireland

FIGURE 1.9

E-Government Ranking for Efficiency and Effectiveness

FIGURE 1.10

Common Types of Efficiency
IT Metrics

Efficiency IT Metrics	
Throughput	The amount of information that can travel through a system at any point in time.
Transaction speed	The amount of time a system takes to perform a transaction.
System availability	The number of hours a system is available for users.
Information accuracy	The extent to which a system generates the correct results when executing the same transaction numerous times.
Web traffic	Includes a host of benchmarks such as the number of page views, the number of unique visitors, and the average time spent viewing a Web page.
Response time	The time it takes to respond to user interactions such as a mouse click.

While these efficiency metrics are important to monitor, they do not always guarantee effectiveness. Effectiveness IT metrics are determined according to an organization's goals, strategies, and objectives. Here, it becomes important to consider the strategy an organization is using, such as a broad cost leadership strategy (Wal-Mart, for example), as well as specific goals and objectives such as increasing new customers by 10 percent or reducing new-product development cycle times to six months. Figure 1.11 displays the broad, general effectiveness IT metrics.

In the private sector, eBay constantly benchmarks its information technology efficiency and effectiveness. In 2005, eBay posted impressive year-end results with revenues increasing 72 percent while earnings grew 125 percent. Maintaining constant Web site availability and optimal throughput performance is critical to eBay's success.[12]

Jupiter Media Metrix ranked eBay as the Web site with the highest visitor volume (efficiency) in 2005 for the fourth year in a row, with an 80-percent growth from the previous year. The auction Web site averaged 8 million unique visitors during each week of the holiday season that year with daily peaks exceeding 12 million visitors. To ensure constant availability and reliability of its systems, eBay implemented

FIGURE 1.11

Common Types of Effectiveness IT Metrics

Effectiveness IT Metrics	
Usability	The ease with which people perform transactions and/or find information. A popular usability metric on the Internet is degrees of freedom, which measures the number of clicks required to find desired information.
Customer satisfaction	Measured by such benchmarks as satisfaction surveys, percentage of existing customers retained, and increases in revenue dollars per customer.
Conversion rates	The number of customers an organization "touches" for the first time and persuades to purchase its products or services. This is a popular metric for evaluating the effectiveness of banner, pop-up, and pop-under ads on the Internet.
Financial	Such as return on investment (the earning power of an organization's assets), cost-benefit analysis (the comparison of projected revenues and costs including development, maintenance, fixed, and variable), and break-even analysis (the point at which constant revenues equal ongoing costs).

ProactiveNet, a performance measurement and management-tracking tool. The tool allows eBay to monitor its environment against baseline benchmarks, which helps the eBay team keep tight control of its systems. The new system has resulted in improved system availability with a 150-percent increase in productivity as measured by system uptime.[13]

Be sure to consider the issue of security while determining efficiency and effectiveness IT metrics. When an organization offers its customers the ability to purchase products over the Internet, it must implement the appropriate security. It is actually inefficient for an organization to implement security measures for Internet-based transactions as compared to processing nonsecure transactions. However, an organization will probably have a difficult time attracting new customers and increasing Web-based revenue if it does not implement the necessary security measures. Purely from an efficiency IT metric point of view, security generates some inefficiency. From an organization's business strategy point of view, however, security should lead to increases in effectiveness metrics.

Figure 1.12 depicts the interrelationships between efficiency and effectiveness. Ideally, an organization should operate in the upper right-hand corner of the graph, realizing both significant increases in efficiency and effectiveness. However, operating in the upper left-hand corner (minimal effectiveness with increased efficiency) or the lower right-hand corner (significant effectiveness with minimal efficiency) may be in line with an organization's particular strategies. In general, operating in the lower left-hand corner (minimal efficiency and minimal effectiveness) is not ideal for the operation of any organization.

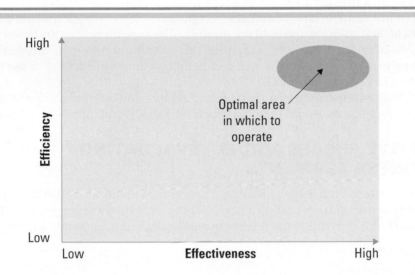

FIGURE 1.12

The Interrelationships Between Efficiency and Effectiveness

OPENING CASE QUESTIONS

Apple—Merging Technology, Business, and Entertainment

1. What might have happened to Apple if its top executives had not supported investment in iPods?

2. Formulate a strategy for how Apple can use efficiency IT metrics to improve its business.

3. Formulate a strategy for how Apple can use effectiveness IT metrics to improve its business.

4. Why would it be unethical for Apple to sell its iTunes customer information to other businesses?

5. Evaluate the effects on Apple's business if it failed to secure its customer information and all of it was accidentally posted to an anonymous Web site.

IDENTIFYING COMPETITIVE ADVANTAGES

To survive and thrive, an organization must create a competitive advantage. A *competitive advantage* is a product or service that an organization's customers place a greater value on than similar offerings from a competitor. Unfortunately, competitive advantages are typically temporary because competitors often seek ways to duplicate the competitive advantage. In turn, organizations must develop a strategy based on a new competitive advantage.

When an organization is the first to market with a competitive advantage, it gains a first-mover advantage. The *first-mover advantage* occurs when an organization can significantly impact its market share by being first to market with a competitive advantage. FedEx created a first-mover advantage by creating its customer self-service software, which allows people and organizations to request parcel pick-ups, print mailing slips, and track parcels online. Other parcel delivery companies quickly began creating their own online services. Today, customer self-service on the Internet is a standard for doing business in the parcel delivery business.

As organizations develop their competitive advantages, they must pay close attention to their competition through environmental scanning. *Environmental scanning* is the acquisition and analysis of events and trends in the environment external to an organization. Information technology has the opportunity to play an important role in environmental scanning.

Frito-Lay, a premier provider of snack foods such as Cracker Jacks and Cheetos, does not just send its representatives into grocery stores to stock shelves; they carry handheld computers and record the product offerings, inventory, and even product locations of competitors. Frito-Lay uses this information to gain business intelligence on everything from how well competing products are selling to the strategic placement of its own products.

Organizations use three common tools to analyze and develop competitive advantages: (1) Five Forces Model, (2) three generic strategies, and (3) value chain analysis.

THE FIVE FORCES MODEL—EVALUATING BUSINESS SEGMENTS

Michael Porter's Five Forces Model is a useful tool to aid organizations facing the challenging decision of entering a new industry or industry segment. The *Five Forces Model* helps determine the relative attractiveness of an industry and includes:

1. Buyer power.
2. Supplier power.
3. Threat of substitute products or services.
4. Threat of new entrants.
5. Rivalry among existing competitors (see Figure 1.13).

Buyer Power

Buyer power in the Five Forces Model is high when buyers have many choices of whom to buy from and low when their choices are few. To reduce buyer power (and create a competitive advantage), an organization must make it more attractive for customers to buy from it instead of its competition. One of the best IT-based examples is the loyalty programs that many organizations offer.

Loyalty programs reward customers based on the amount of business they do with a particular organization. The travel industry is famous for its loyalty programs such as frequent-flyer programs for airlines and frequent-guest programs for hotels. Keeping track of the activities and accounts of many thousands or millions of customers covered by loyalty programs is not practical without large-scale IT systems.

FIGURE 1.13

Porter's Five Forces Model

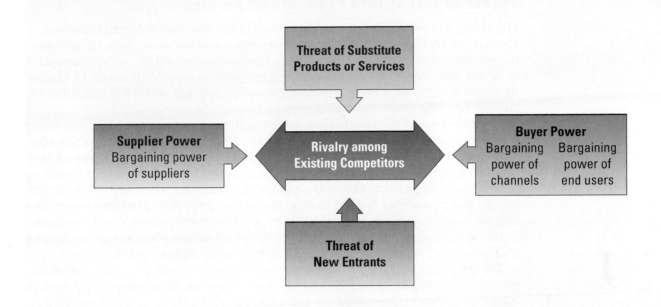

Loyalty programs are a good example of using IT to reduce buyer power; because of the rewards (e.g., free airline tickets, upgrades, or hotel stays) travellers receive, they are more likely to be loyal to or give most of their business to a single organization.

Supplier Power

Supplier power in the Five Forces Model is high when buyers have few choices of whom to buy from and low when their choices are many. Supplier power is the converse of buyer power: A supplier organization in a market will want buyer power to be low. A ***supply chain*** consists of all parties involved, directly or indirectly, in the procurement of a product or raw material. In a typical supply chain, an organization will probably be both a supplier (to customers) and a customer (of other supplier organizations) (see Figure 1.14).

As a buyer, the organization can create a competitive advantage by locating alternative supply sources. IT-enabled business-to-business (B2B) marketplaces can help. A ***business-to-business (B2B) marketplace*** is an Internet-based service that brings together many buyers and sellers (discussed in detail in Chapter 2). One important variation of the B2B marketplace is a private exchange. A ***private exchange*** is a B2B marketplace in which a single buyer posts its needs and then opens the bidding to any supplier who would care to bid. Bidding is typically carried out through a reverse auction. A ***reverse auction*** is an auction format in which increasingly lower bids are solicited from organizations willing to supply the desired product or service at an increasingly

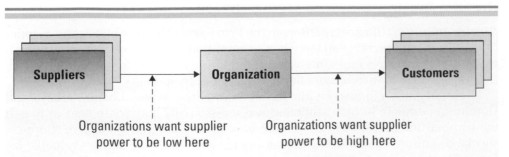

Organizations want supplier power to be low here   Organizations want supplier power to be high here

FIGURE 1.14

An Organization within the Supply Chain

lower price. As the bids get lower and lower, more and more suppliers drop out of the auction. Ultimately, the organization with the lowest bid wins. Internet-based reverse auctions are an excellent example of the way that information technology can reduce supplier power for an organization and create a competitive advantage.

Threat of Substitute Products or Services

The *threat of substitute products or services* in the Five Forces Model is high when there are many alternatives to a product or service and low when there are few alternatives from which to choose. Ideally, an organization would like to be in a market in which there are few substitutes for the products or services it offers. Of course, that is seldom possible today, but an organization can still create a competitive advantage by using switching costs.

Switching costs are costs that can make customers reluctant to switch to another product or service. A switching cost need not have an associated *monetary* cost. Amazon.ca offers an example. As customers purchase products at Amazon.ca over time, Amazon develops a profile of their shopping and purchasing habits, enabling Amazon to offer products tailored to a particular customer based on the customer's profile. If the customer decides to shop elsewhere, there is an associated switching cost because the new site will not have the profile of the customer's past purchases. In this way, Amazon has reduced the threat of substitute products or services by creating a "cost" to the consumer to switch to another online retailer.

The cell phone industry offers another good example of switching costs. Cell phone providers want to keep their customers as long as possible. Many cell phone providers offer their customers free phones or unlimited minutes if they will sign a one- or two-year contract. This creates a switching cost for the customers if they decide to change providers because they will be required to pay a penalty for breaking their contract. Another switching cost for the cell phone customer was losing the actual cell phone number; however, this switching cost has been removed with the implementation of *local number portability (LNP)* or the ability to "port" cell phone numbers to new providers. Within the context of Porter's Five Forces Model, eliminating this switching cost creates a greater threat of substitute products or services for the supplier. That is, customers can now expect to see more new cell phone providers cropping up over the next several years. They will compete on price, quality, and services with the big-name cell phone providers such as Rogers, Fido, and Bell Mobility because cell phone numbers can be moved from one provider to another. When businesses reduce or eliminate switching costs, the consumer gains more power.

Threat of New Entrants

The *threat of new entrants* in the Five Forces Model is high when it is easy for new competitors to enter a market and low when there are significant entry barriers to entering a market. An entry barrier is a product or service feature that customers have come to expect from organizations in a particular industry and must be offered by an entering organization to compete and survive. For example, a new bank must offer its customers an array of IT-enabled services, including ATM use, online bill paying, and account monitoring. These are significant barriers to entering the banking market. At one time, the first bank to offer such services gained a valuable first-mover advantage, but only temporarily, as other banking competitors developed their own IT systems.

Rivalry Among Existing Competitors

Rivalry among existing competitors in the Five Forces Model is high when competition is fierce in a market and low when competition is more complacent. Although competition is always more intense in some industries than in others, the overall trend is toward increased competition in almost every industry.

The retail grocery industry is intensively competitive. While Loblaws, Sobeys, and Dominion compete in many different ways, essentially they try to beat or match the competition on price. Most of them have loyalty programs that give shoppers special discounts. Customers get lower prices while the store gathers valuable information on buying habits to create pricing strategies. In the future, expect to see grocery stores using wireless technologies to track customer movement throughout the store and match it to products purchased to determine product placement and pricing strategies. Such a system will be IT-based and a huge competitive advantage to the first store to implement it.

Since margins are low in the retail grocery market, grocers build efficiencies into their supply chains, connecting with their suppliers in IT-enabled information partnerships such as the one between Wal-Mart and its suppliers. Communicating with suppliers over telecommunications networks rather than using paper-based systems makes the procurement process faster, cheaper, and more accurate. That equates to lower prices for customers and increased rivalry among existing competitors.

THE THREE GENERIC STRATEGIES—CREATING A BUSINESS FOCUS

Once the relative attractiveness of an industry is determined and an organization decides to enter that market, it must formulate a strategy for entering the new market. An organization can follow Porter's three generic strategies when entering a new market: (1) broad cost leadership, (2) broad differentiation, or (3) focused strategy. Broad strategies reach a large market segment, while focused strategies target a niche market. A focused strategy concentrates on either cost leadership or differentiation. Trying to be all things to all people, however, is a recipe for disaster, since it is difficult to project a consistent image to the entire marketplace. Porter suggests that an organization is wise to adopt only one of the three generic strategies.

To illustrate the use of the three generic strategies, consider Figure 1.15. The matrix shown demonstrates the relationships among strategies (cost leadership versus differentiation) and market segmentation (broad versus focused).

- **Hyundai** is following a broad cost leadership strategy. Hyundai offers low-cost vehicles, in each particular model stratification, that appeal to a large audience.
- **Audi** is pursuing a broad differentiation strategy with its Quattro models available at several price points. Audi's differentiation is safety, and it prices

FIGURE 1.15

Porter's Three Generic Strategies in the Auto Industry

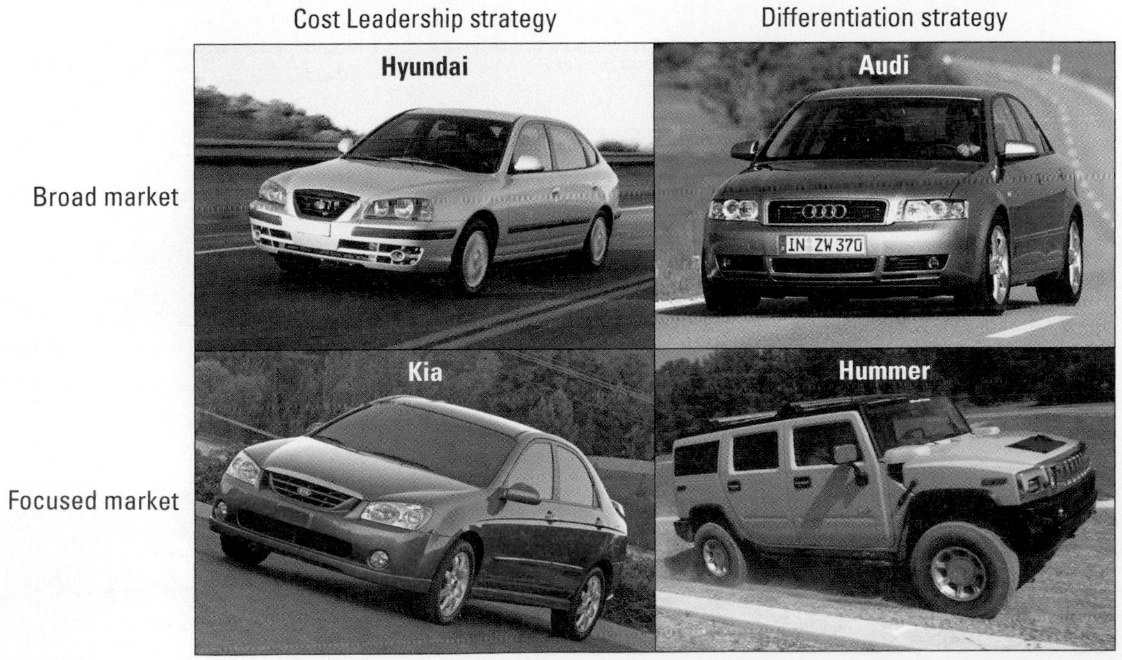

its various Quattro models (higher than Hyundai) to reach a large, stratified audience.

- **Kia** has a more focused cost leadership strategy. Kia mainly offers low-cost vehicles in the lower levels of model stratification.
- **Hummer** offers the most focused differentiation strategy of any in the industry (including Mercedes-Benz).

VALUE CHAIN ANALYSIS—TARGETING BUSINESS PROCESSES

Once an organization enters a new market using one of Porter's three generic strategies, it must understand, accept, and successfully execute its business strategy. Every aspect of the organization contributes to the success (or failure) of the chosen strategy. The business processes of the organization and the value chain they create play an integral role in strategy execution.

Value Creation

A ***business process*** is a standardized set of activities that accomplish a specific task, such as processing a customer's order. To evaluate the effectiveness of its business processes, an organization can use Michael Porter's value chain approach. An organization creates value by performing a series of activities that Porter identified as the value chain. The ***value chain*** approach views an organization as a series of processes, each of which adds value to the product or service for each customer. To create a competitive advantage, the value chain must enable the organization to provide unique value to its customers. In addition to the firm's own value-creating activities, the firm operates in a value system of vertical activities including those of upstream suppliers and downstream channel members. To achieve a competitive advantage, the firm must perform one or more value-creating activities in a way that creates more overall value than do competitors. Added value is created through lower costs or superior benefits to the consumer (differentiation).

Organizations can add value by offering lower prices or by competing in a distinctive way. Examining the organization as a value chain (actually numerous distinct but inseparable value chains) leads to identifying the important activities that add value for customers and then finding IT systems that support those activities. Figure 1.16 depicts a value chain. Primary value activities, shown at the bottom

FIGURE 1.16

The Value Chain

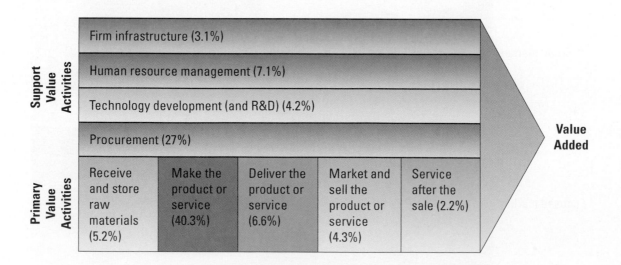

of the graph, acquire raw materials and manufacture, deliver, market, sell, and provide after-sales services. Support value activities, along the top of the graph, such as firm infrastructure, human resource management, technology development, and procurement, support the primary value activities.

The goal is to survey the customers and ask them the extent to which they believe each activity adds value to the product or service. This generates a quantifiable metric, displayed in percentages in Figure 1.16, for how each activity adds value (or reduces value). The competitive advantage decision then is to (1) target high value-adding activities to further enhance their value, (2) target low value-adding activities to increase their value, or (3) perform some combination of the two.

Organizations should attempt to use information technology to add value to both primary and support value activities. One example of a primary value activity facilitated by IT is the development of a marketing campaign management system that could target marketing campaigns more efficiently, thereby reducing marketing costs. The system would also help the organization better pinpoint target market needs, thereby increasing sales. One example of a support value activity facilitated by IT is the development of a human resources system that could more efficiently reward employees based on performance. The system could also identify employees who are at risk of leaving their jobs, allowing the organization to find additional challenges or opportunities that would help retain these employees and thus reduce turnover costs.

Value chain analysis is a highly useful tool in that it provides hard and fast numbers for evaluating the activities that add value to products and services. An organization can find additional value by analyzing and constructing its value chain in terms of Porter's Five Forces (see Figure 1.17). For example, if an organization

FIGURE 1.17

The Value Chain and Porter's Five Forces

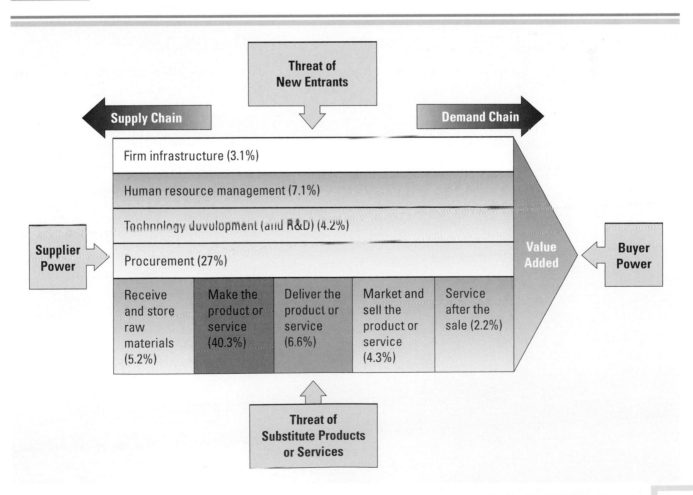

wants to decrease its buyer's or customer's power, it can construct its value chain activity of "service after the sale" by offering high levels of quality customer service. This will increase the switching costs for its customers, thereby decreasing their power. Analyzing and constructing its support value activities can help an organization decrease the threat of new entrants. Analyzing and constructing its primary value activities can help an organization decrease the threat of substitute products or services.

A company can implement its selected strategy by means of programs, budgets, and procedures. Implementation involves organization of the firm's resources and motivation of the employees to achieve objectives. How the company implements its chosen strategy can have a significant impact on its success. In a large company, the personnel implementing the strategy are usually different from those formulating the strategy. For this reason, proper communication of the strategy is critical. Failure can result if the strategy is misunderstood or if lower-level managers resist its implementation because they do not understand the process for selecting the particular strategy.

An organization must continually adapt to its competitive environment, which can cause its business strategy to change. To remain successful, an organization should use Porter's Five Forces, the three generic strategies, and value chain analysis to adopt new business strategies.

OPENING CASE QUESTIONS

Apple—Merging Technology, Business, and Entertainment

6. Did Apple gain a competitive advantage from its decision to invest in an online music business?

7. How can Apple use environmental scanning to gain business intelligence?

8. Using Porter's Five Forces Model, analyze Apple's buyer power and supplier power.

9. Which of the three generic strategies is Apple following?

10. Which of Porter's Five Forces did Apple address through its introduction of the iPod?

The purpose of this chapter was two-fold:

1. To provide you with an introduction to information systems in business.
   - Information technology basics were explained,
   - Roles and responsibilities in information technology were described, and
   - Ways of measuring information technology's success were discussed.

2. To raise awareness of information technology's ability to enable companies to sustain competitive advantage.
   - Businesses must be aware of the various forces that determine whether organizations should enter a new industry or segment and how information technology can be used to reduce or enhance the strength of those forces.
   - Firms need to set strategies and recognize how information technology can be used to add value to those activities that help organizations reach their strategic goals.

KEY TERMS

CLOSING CASE ONE

Say "Charge It" with Your Cell Phone

This case looks at the competitive advantage of using a specific technology (cell phones).

Wireless operators, credit card companies, and retailers are working on a technology that allows customers to purchase items by using their cell phones. For example, a customer could purchase a can of soda by dialing a telephone number on the dispensing machine and have the charge for the soda show up on the customer's cell phone bill. Working prototypes are currently in use in South Korea, Japan, and Europe.

The ability to charge items to a cell phone has significant business potential because credit cards are not nearly as popular in other countries as they are in Canada and the United States. In Japan and China, for example, people are much more likely to have a cell phone than a credit card. Japanese consumers use credit cards for only 5.6 percent of their personal spending compared with 33 percent of North American consumer spending.

The payoff for credit card companies and cell phone operators from this technology could be enormous. By associating a credit card with a cell phone, banks and credit card companies hope to persuade consumers to buy products, such as soda, with their cell phones instead of pocket change. Of course, they will reap transaction fees for each transaction. Mobile phone operators see the technology as a way to increase traffic on their networks as well as to position cell phones as an even more useful and, thus, essential device for consumers. Retailers envision easier transactions also leading to more sales.

MasterCard International and Nokia are currently testing a cell phone credit card for the North American market. The phones have a special chip programmed with the user's credit card information and a radio frequency transmitting circuit. Consumers can simply tap their phone on a special device at a checkout counter equipped with a receiving device that costs the retailer about $95. Betsy Foran-Owens, vice president for Product Services at MasterCard International, commented that with this technology, "You don't even have to get off your phone to pay. You can just tap this thing down at the register." She also noted, "If you're not going to carry cash around, what are you going to carry? Your mobile phone."

The only players who might not look favourably on the technology are the traditional telephone companies, who must certainly view the technology as just one more threat to their traditional telephone business.[14]

Questions

1. Do you view this technology as a potential threat to traditional telephone companies? If so, what counterstrategies could traditional telephone companies adopt to prepare for this technology?
2. Using Porter's Five Forces describe the barriers to entry and switching costs for this new technology.
3. Which of Porter's three generic strategies is this new technology following?
4. Describe the value chain of using cell phones as a payment method.
5. What types of regulatory issues might occur due to this type of technology?

CLOSING CASE TWO

Innovative Business Managers

This case looks at various examples of successful business strategies led by innovative managers.

Industry has recognized several innovative managers in Canada and abroad who have demonstrated talent, vision, and the ability to identify excellent opportunities (see Figure 1.18).

Bruce Poon Tip, G.A.P. Adventures

Back in 1990, Bruce Poon Tip launched G.A.P. Adventures (www.gapadventures.com) with the belief that other travellers would share his desire to experience authentic adventures in the real world. G.A.P. Adventures is a tour operator in more than 100 countries and specializes in small group adventures. It boasts revenues of $100 million a year. The business started out of Poon Tip's Toronto apartment and since has grown from a one-man show to a company of over 300, and from a handful of trips in Latin America to hundreds of adventures on all seven continents. Poon Tip's commitment to in-house information technology, bold acquisitions like the purchase of an Antarctica expedition ship, strong industry partnerships, and innovative marketing strategies has led him to carve out a unique market niche. G.A.P. Adventures takes advantage of serving the

FIGURE 1.18

Innovative Business
Managers

Innovative Managers	
Bruce Poon Tip, G.A.P. Adventures	■ Grew a one-man shop to a $100-million-a-year revenue generator ■ Recognized a market segment (adventure seekers) with needs under-served by the travel industry ■ Took advantage of Web information technologies to market the business and conduct business transactions
Jeffrey Immelt, General Electric (GE)	■ Repositioned GE's portfolio with major acquisitions in health care, entertainment, and commercial finance ■ Created a more diverse, global, and customer-driven culture
Steve Reinemund, PepsiCo	■ Developed strong and diverse leadership that helped PepsiCo tap new markets ■ Attained consistent double-digit growth through productive innovation and smart marketing
Alain Bédard, TransForce Income Fund	■ Pursued a classic expansion strategy for the business that acquires successful companies and gives them the leverage to scale accordingly ■ Diversification across all segments of the trucking industry buffers the company against localized downturns
Philip Knight, Nike	■ Transformed a volatile, fad-driven marketing and design icon into a more shareholder-friendly company

needs of an untapped market through Web technologies that allow customers to customize their trips via a personalized trip planner and to browse trip opportunities through an innovative search tool that classifies trips by destination, activity (e.g., culture, biking, kayaking, hiking, rafting), trip style (e.g., active, comfort, exploratory, family, gourmet), duration, and dates.[15]

Jeffrey Immelt, General Electric (GE)

When Jeffrey Immelt took over as CEO of General Electric, he had big shoes to fill. The former CEO, Jack Welch, had left an unprecedented record as one of the top CEOs of all time. Immelt proved his ability to run the company by creating a customer-driven global culture that spawns innovation and embraces technology.[16]

Steven Reinemund, PepsiCo

Steven Reinemund has turned PepsiCo into a $32-billion food and beverage giant. "To be a leader in consumer products, it's critical to have leaders who represent the population we serve," said Reinemund, who created a diverse leadership group that defines the strategic vision for the company. Reinemund also takes a major role in mentoring and teaching his employees and demands that all senior executives do the same. The payoff: consistent double-digit earnings and solid sales at a time when many of the company's staple products—potato chips and soft drinks—are under attack for fears about childhood obesity and health concerns.[17]

Alain Bédard, TransForce Income Fund

Since 1996, TransForce (www.transforce.ca) has created value for its unit holders by managing and investing in a growing network of independent operating companies. Based in Saint-Laurent, Quebec, Transforce's strategy is simple: acquire successful operating companies and support their drive for constant improvement by leaving their management teams intact and offering these new divisions some benefits of scale. The man behind this strategy is Alain Bédard and his devotion to this strategy has paid off. Today, the Fund, through its subsidiaries, is the leader in Canada's transportation and logistics industry. Specifically, TransForce is the country's leader in less-than-truckload trucking; eastern Canada's leader in parcel business-to-business transportation and truckload operations; Quebec's leader in specialized truckload and waste management; and western Canada's third-largest in oilfield energy services. According to Desjardins Securities, Bédard's acquisition strategy has been central to management's growth plan and has differentiated itself from other competitors by offering services across all segments of the trucking industry. Though the trucking industry is cyclical and vulnerable to economic changes, diversification across all segments of the trucking industry buffers the company against localized downturns.[18]

Philip Knight, Nike

Philip Knight, who got his start by selling Japanese sneakers from the trunk of his car, built the $14-billion sports behemoth Nike. Knight and his team transformed high-performance sports equipment into high-fashion gear and forever changed the rules of sports marketing with huge endorsement contracts and in-your-face advertising. Then, just as suddenly, Nike lost focus. In early 2000, kids stopped craving the latest sneaker, the company's image took a huge hit from its labour practices, sales slumped, and costs soared.

Thus began Knight's second act. He revamped management and brought in key outsiders to oversee finances and apparel lines. Knight devoted more energy to developing new information systems. Today, Nike's earnings are less volatile and less fad-driven. In 2004, Nike's earnings increased $1.2 billion.[19]

Questions

1. Choose one of the companies listed above and explain how it could use a chief information officer (CIO), chief technology officer (CTO), and chief privacy officer (CPO) to improve business.

2. Why is it important for all of G.A.P. Adventures' functional business areas to work together? Provide an example of what might happen if the G.A.P. Adventures' marketing department failed to work with its sales department.

3. Why is information technology important to an organization like G.A.P. Adventures?

4. Which of Porter's Five Forces is most important to Nike's business?

5. Which of the three generic strategies is PepsiCo following? Which strategy is TransForce following?

6. Explain the value chain and how a company like GE can use it to improve operations.

CLOSING CASE THREE

The World Is Flat—Thomas Friedman

This case showcases technology's powerful impact in changing how businesses operate on a global scale.

In his book, *The World is Flat,* Thomas Friedman describes the unplanned cascade of technological and social shifts that effectively levelled the economic world, and "accidentally made Beijing, Bangalore, and Bethesda next-door neighbours." Chances are good that Bhavya in Bangalore will read your next X-ray, or as Friedman learned first-hand, "Grandma Betty in her bathrobe" will make your plane reservation from her home.

Friedman believes this is Globalization 3.0. "In Globalization 1.0, which began around 1492, the world went from size large to size medium. In Globalization 2.0, the era that introduced us to multinational companies, it went from size medium to size small. And then around 2000 came Globalization 3.0, in which the world went from being small to tiny. There is a difference between being able to make long-distance phone calls cheaper on the Internet and walking around Riyadh with a PDA where you can have all of Google in your pocket. It is a difference in degree that's so enormous it becomes a difference in kind," Friedman stated. Figure 1.19 displays Friedman's list of "flatteners."

Friedman writes these flatteners converged around the year 2000 and "created a flat world: a global, Web-enabled platform for multiple forms of sharing knowledge and work, irrespective of time, distance, geography, and increasingly, language." At the very moment this platform emerged, three huge economies materialized—those of India, China, and the former Soviet Union—"and 3 billion people who were out of the game, walked onto the playing field." A final convergence may determine the fate of existing leading economies, such as the United States, in this chapter of globalization. A "political perfect storm," as Friedman describes it—the dot-com bust, the attacks of 9/11, and the Enron scandal—"distracts [the United States] completely as a country." Just when the United States needs to face the fact of globalization and the need to compete in a new world, the country is looking "totally elsewhere," Friedman explains.

Friedman believes that the next great breakthrough in bioscience could come from a 5-year-old who downloads the human genome in Egypt. Bill Gates's view is similar: "20 years ago, would you rather have been a B-student in Poughkeepsie or a genius in Shanghai? Twenty years ago you'd rather be a B-student in Poughkeepsie. Today, it is not even close. You'd much prefer to be the genius in Shanghai because you can now export your talents anywhere in the world."[20]

Questions

1. Do you agree or disagree with Friedman's assessment that the world is flat? Be sure to justify your answer.
2. What are the potential impacts of a flat world for a student performing a job search?
3. What can students do to prepare themselves for competing in a flat world?
4. Identify a current flattener not mentioned on Friedman's list.

Friedman's 10 Forces That Flattened the World	
1. **Fall of the Berlin Wall**	The events of November 9, 1989, tilted the worldwide balance of power toward democracies and free markets.
2. **Netscape IPO**	The August 9, 1995, offering sparked massive investment in fibre-optic cables.
3. **Work flow software**	The rise of applications from PayPal to VPNs enabled faster, closer coordination among far-flung employees.
4. **Open sourcing**	Self-organizing communities, such as Linux, launched a collaborative revolution.
5. **Outsourcing**	Migrating business functions to India saved money *and* a Third World economy.
6. **Offshoring**	Contract manufacturing elevated China to economic prominence.
7. **Supply chaining**	Robust networks of suppliers, retailers, and customers increased business efficiency.
8. **In-sourcing**	Logistics giants took control of customer supply chains, helping mom-and-pop shops go global.
9. **Informing**	Power searching allowed everyone to use the Internet as a "personal supply chain of knowledge."
10. **Wireless**	Wireless technologies pumped up collaboration, making it mobile and personal.

FIGURE 1.19

Thomas Friedman's 10 Forces That Flattened the World

1. Competitive analysis

Cheryl O'Connell is the owner of a small, high-end retailer of women's clothing called Excelus. Excelus's business has been successful for many years, largely because of Cheryl's ability to anticipate the needs and wants of her loyal customer base and provide them with personalized service. Cheryl does not see any value in IT and does not want to invest any capital in something that will not directly affect her bottom line. Develop a proposal describing the potential IT-enabled competitive opportunities or threats Cheryl might be missing by not embracing IT. Be sure to include a Porter's Five Forces analysis and discuss which one of the three generic strategies Cheryl should pursue.

2. Applying the three generic strategies

This chapter discussed several examples of companies that pursue differentiated strategies so that they are not forced into positions where they must compete solely based on price. In a team, choose an industry and find and compare two companies, one that is competing based on price and another that is pursuing a differentiated strategy enabled by the creative use of IT. Some industries you may want to consider are clothing retailers, grocery stores, airlines, and personal computers. Prepare a presentation for the class on the ways that the company is using IT to help it differentiate and compete against the low-cost provider. Before you begin, spend some class time to make sure each team selects a different industry.

3. Using efficiency and effectiveness metrics

You are the CEO of a 500-bed acute care general hospital. Your internal IT department is responsible for running applications that support both administrative functions (e.g., patient accounting) as well as medical applications (e.g., medical records). You need assurance that your IT department is a high-quality operation in comparison to similar hospitals. What metrics should you ask your CIO to provide to give the assurance you seek? Provide the reasoning behind each suggested metric. Also, determine how the interrelationship between efficiency metrics and effectiveness metrics can drive your business's success.

4. Building Business Relationships

Synergistics Inc. is a start-up company that specializes in helping businesses build successful internal relationships. You have recently been promoted to senior manager of the Business and IT Relationship area. Sales for your new department have dwindled over the last two years for a variety of reasons including the burst of the technological stock bubble, recent economic conditions, and a poorly communicated business strategy. Your first task on the job is to prepare a report detailing the following:

- Fundamental reasons for the gap between IT and the business.
- Strategies you can take to convince the business this is an area that is critical to success.
- Strategies the business can follow to ensure synergies exist between the two sides.

5. Determining IT Organizational Structures

You are the chief executive officer for a start-up telecommunications company. The company currently has 50 employees and plans to ramp up to 3,000 by the end of the year. Your first task is to determine how you are going to model your organization. You decide to address the IT department's organizational structure first. You need to consider if you want to have a CIO, CPO, CSO, CTO, and CKO and if so, what the reporting structure will look like and why. You also need to determine the responsibilities for each executive position. Once you have compiled this information, put together a presentation describing your IT department's organizational structure.

E-Business

2
CHAPTER

Why Do I Need To Know This ❓

This chapter discusses the importance of doing business on the Internet. You need to know this since the Internet has revolutionized the way businesses operate today. The Internet offers companies new opportunities for growth and brand new ways of doing things. More than just giving organizations a means of conducting transactions over the Web, electronic business provides companies with the ability to develop and maintain relationships with customers and supply partners, as well as exchange business information between and within enterprises—all with the support of electronic technologies.

You, as a business student, should understand the fundamental impact the Internet has had on business. As future managers and organizational knowledge workers, you need to understand what benefits electronic business can offer an organization. In addition, you need to understand the challenges that come along with adoption of Web technologies. You need to be aware of the various strategies organizations can use to deploy electronic business, as well as recent trends and methods of measuring electronic business performance. This chapter will give you this knowledge and help prepare you for success in today's electronic business world.

Amazon.com—Not Your Average Bookstore

Jeffrey Bezos, CEO and founder of Amazon.com, is running what some people refer to as the "world's biggest bookstore." The story of Bezos's virtual bookstore teaches many lessons about online business. Out of nowhere, this digital bookstore turned an industry upside down. What happened here was more than just creating a Web site. Bezos conceived and implemented an intelligent, global digital business. Its business is its technology; its technology is its business. Shocking traditional value chains in the bookselling industry, Amazon opened thousands of virtual bookstores in its first few months of operation.

Bezos graduated from Princeton and was the youngest vice president at Banker's Trust in New York. He had to decide if he would stay and receive his 1994 Wall Street bonus or leave and start a business on the Internet. "I tried to imagine being 80 years old, looking back on my life. I knew that I would hardly regret having missed the 1994 Wall Street bonus. But having missed being part of the Internet boom—that would have really hurt," stated Bezos. One evening he compiled a list of 20 products he believed would sell on the Internet. Books, being small-ticket items that are easy and inexpensive to ship, were on the top of the list. It was also apparent that no bookstore could conceivably stock more than a fraction of the 5 million books published annually. Bezos, who had never sold a book in his life, developed a strategic plan for selling books on the Internet. Amazon launched three years later. In the fall of 1994, Amazon filled its first book order—personally packaged by Bezos and his wife.

Amazon's E-Business Strategy

Amazon does not operate any physical stores. All of its sales occur through its Web site. It is consistently pushing the technological envelope in its search to provide a satisfying, personalized experience for its customers. What started as a human-edited list of product suggestions morphed into a sophisticated computer-generated recommendation engine. The company captures the comments and recommendations of buyers for site visitors to read—similar to the friendly salesperson in a store offering advice on which books to buy. The Web site tracks customer traffic, the number of visitors who access the site, how long they stay, what pages they click on, and so forth. The company uses the information to evaluate buying and selling patterns and the success of promotions. Amazon has quickly become a model success story for e-businesses around the globe.

Amazon retains customers with Web site features such as personalized recommendations, online customer reviews, and "1-click ordering"—the creation of a true one-stop shopping establishment where customers can find anything they want to buy online. Through the Amazon.com Auctions, zShops (independent third-party sellers), and more recently the Amazon.com Marketplace (where customers can sell used items), the company is able to offer its customers almost everything.

Shaping Amazon's Future

Amazon released a free Web service that enables its business partners (whom Amazon calls "associates") to interact with its Web site. More specifically, this Web service allows its partners to access catalogue data, to create and populate an Amazon.com shopping cart, and even to initiate the checkout process. In 16 months, the company has inspired 30,000 associates to invent new ways to extend Amazon's visibility on the Internet. With over 30 million customers, Amazon has become a household brand.[1]

INTRODUCTION

One of the biggest forces changing business is the Internet. Technology companies such as Intel and Cisco were among the first to seize the Internet to overhaul their operations. Intel deployed Web-based automation to liberate its 200 salesclerks from tedious order-entry positions. Instead, salesclerks concentrate on customer relationship management functions such as analyzing sales trends and pampering customers. Cisco handles 75 percent of its sales online, and 45 percent of online orders never touch employees' hands. This type of Internet-based ordering has helped Cisco hike productivity by 20 percent over the past two years.[2]

E-business is the conducting of business on the Internet, not only buying and selling, but also serving customers and collaborating with business partners. Organizations realize that putting up simple Web sites for customers, employees, and partners does not create an e-business. E-business Web sites must create a buzz, much as Amazon has done in the bookselling industry. E-business Web sites must be innovative, add value, and provide useful information. In short, the site must build a sense of community and collaboration, eventually becoming the port of entry for business. Understanding e-business begins with understanding:

- Disruptive technology.
- Evolution of the Internet.
- Accessing Internet information.
- Providing Internet information.

DISRUPTIVE TECHNOLOGY

Polaroid, founded in 1937, produced the first instant camera in the late 1940s. The Polaroid camera was one of the most exciting technological advances the photography industry had ever seen. By using a Polaroid camera, customers no longer had to depend on others to develop their pictures. The technology was innovative and the product was high-end. The company eventually went public, becoming one of Wall Street's most prominent enterprises, with its stock trading above $70 in 1997. In 2002, the stock was down to 8 cents and the company declared bankruptcy.[3]

How could a company like Polaroid, which had innovative technology and a captive customer base, go bankrupt? Perhaps company executives failed to use Porter's Five Forces to analyze the threat of substitute products or services. If they had, would they have noticed the two threats, one-hour film processing and digital cameras, that eventually stole Polaroid's market share? Would they have understood that their customers, people who want instant access to their pictures without having a third party involved, would be the first to use one-hour film processing and the first to purchase digital cameras? Could the company have found a way to compete with one-hour film processing and the digital camera to save Polaroid?

Most organizations face the same dilemma as Polaroid—the criteria an organization uses to make business decisions for its present business could possibly create issues for its future business. Essentially, what is best for the current business could ruin it in the long term. Some observers of our business environment have an ominous vision of the future—digital Darwinism. *Digital Darwinism* implies that organizations which cannot adapt to the new demands placed on them for surviving in the information age are doomed to extinction.[4]

Disruptive versus Sustaining Technology

A *disruptive technology* is a new way of doing things that initially does not meet the needs of existing customers. Disruptive technologies tend to open new markets and destroy old ones. A *sustaining technology*, on the other hand, produces an improved product customers are eager to buy, such as a faster car or larger hard drive. Sustaining technologies tend to provide us with better, faster, and cheaper products in established markets. Incumbent companies most often lead sustaining technology to market, but virtually never lead in markets opened by disruptive technologies. Figure 2.1 displays companies that are expecting future growth to occur from new investments (disruptive technology) and companies that are expecting future growth to occur from existing investments (sustaining technology).

Disruptive technologies typically cut into the low end of the marketplace and eventually evolve to displace high-end competitors and their reigning technologies. Sony is a perfect example of a company that entered the low end of the marketplace and eventually evolved to displace its high-end competitors. Sony started as a tiny company that built portable, battery-powered transistor radios people could carry around with them. The sound quality of Sony's transistor radios was poor because the transistor amplifiers were of lower quality than traditional vacuum tubes, which produce a better sound. But, customers were willing to overlook sound quality for the convenience of portability. With the experience and revenue stream from the portables, Sony improved its technology to produce cheap, low-end transistor amplifiers that were suitable for home use and invested those revenues to improve the technology further, which produced better radios.[5]

The *Innovator's Dilemma*, a book by Clayton M. Christensen, discusses how established companies can take advantage of disruptive technologies without hindering existing relationships with customers, partners, and stakeholders. Xerox, IBM, Sears, and DEC all listened to existing customers, invested aggressively in

Fortune 500 Rank	Company	Expected Returns on New Investment	Expected Returns on Existing Investments
53	Dell Computer	78%	22%
47	Johnson & Johnson	66	34
35	Procter & Gamble	62	38
6	General Electric	60	40
77	Lockheed Martin	59	41
1	Wal-Mart	50	50
65	Intel	49	51
49	Pfizer	48	52
9	IBM	46	54
24	Merck	44	56
92	Cisco Systems	42	58
18	Home Depot	37	63
16	Boeing	30	70
11	Verizon	21	79
22	Kroger	13	87
32	Sears Roebuck	8	92
37	AOL Time Warner	8	92
3	General Motors	5	95
81	Phillips Petroleum	3	97

FIGURE 2.1

Disruptive versus Sustaining Technology

FIGURE 2.2

Companies That Capitalized
on Disruptive Technology

Company	Disruptive Technology
Charles Schwab	Online brokerage
Hewlett-Packard	Microprocessor-based computers; ink-jet printers
IBM	Minicomputers; personal computers
Intel	Low-end microprocessors
Intuit	QuickBooks software; TurboTax software; Quicken software
Microsoft	Internet-based computing; operating system software; SQL and Access database software
Oracle	Database software
Quantum	3.5-inch disks
Sony	Transistor-based consumer electronics

technology, had their competitive antennae up, and still lost their market-dominant positions. Christensen states that these companies may have placed too much emphasis on satisfying customers' current needs, while neglecting to adopt new disruptive technology that will meet customers' future needs, thus causing the companies to eventually lose market share. Figure 2.2 above highlights several companies that launched new businesses by capitalizing on disruptive technologies.[6]

The Internet—Business Disruption

When the Internet was in its early days, no one had any idea how massive it would become. Computer companies did not think it would be a big deal; neither did the phone companies or cable companies. Difficult to access and operate, it seemed likely to remain an arcane tool of the U.S. Defense Department and academia. However, the Internet grew, and grew, and grew. It began with a handful of users in the mid-1960s and reached 1 billion by 2005 (see Figure 2.3). Estimates predict there

FIGURE 2.3

Worldwide Internet Usage Statistics

Internet Usage Statistics—The Big Picture World Internet Users and Population Statistics						
Region	Population (2006)	% of World Population	Internet Users	Internet Penetration (% of Population)	% of World Usage	Usage Growth. 2000–2005
Africa	915,210,928	14.1%	22,737,500	2.5%	2.2%	403.7%
Asia	3,667,774,066	56.4	364,270,713	9.9	35.7	218.7
Europe	807,289,020	12.4	290,121,957	35.9	28.5	176.1
Middle East	190,084,161	2.9	18,203,500	9.6	1.8	454.2
North America	331,473,276	5.1	225,801,428	68.1	22.2	108.9
Latin America/ Caribbean	553,908,632	8.5	79,033,597	14.3	7.8	337.4
Oceania/ Australia	33,956,977	0.5	17,690,762	52.9	1.8	132.2
WORLD TOTAL	**6,499,697,060**	**100%**	**1,017,859,457**	**15.7%**	**100%**	**182%**

will be more than 3 billion Internet users by 2010. Already, villages in Indonesia and India have Internet access before they have electricity.[7] Figure 2.4 displays several ways the Internet is changing business.

EVOLUTION OF THE INTERNET

During the Cold War in the mid-1960s, the U.S. military decided it needed a bombproof communications system, and thus the concept for the Internet was born. The system would link computers throughout the country, allowing messages to get though even if a large section of the country was destroyed. In the early days, the only linked computers were at government think tanks and a few universities. The Internet was essentially an emergency military communications system operated by the U.S. Department of Defense's Advanced Research Project Agency (ARPA) and called ARPANET. Formally defined, the **Internet** is a global public network of computer networks that pass information from one to another using common computer protocols. **Protocols** are standards that specify the format of data as well as the rules to be followed during transmission.

In time, every university in the United States that had defence-related funding installed ARPANET computers. Gradually, the Internet moved from a military pipeline to a communications tool for scientists. As more scholars came online, system administration transferred from ARPA to the National Science Foundation. Years later, businesses began using the Internet, and the administrative responsibilities were once again transferred. Today, no one party operates the Internet; however, several entities oversee the Internet and set standards including:

- Internet Engineering Task Force (IETF): The protocol engineering and development arm of the Internet.
- Internet Architecture Board (IAB): Responsible for defining the overall architecture of the Internet, providing guidance and broad direction to the IETF.
- Internet Engineering Steering Group (IESG): Responsible for technical management of IETF activities and the Internet standards process.

FIGURE 2.4

The Internet's Impact on Business

Industry	Business Changes Due to Technology
Travel	Travel site Expedia.ca is one of Canada's biggest leisure travel agencies. Thirteen percent of traditional travel agencies closed in 2002 because of their inability to compete with online travel.
Entertainment	The music industry has kept Napster and others from operating, but $40 billion annual online downloads are wrecking the traditional music business. Music unit sales are down 20 percent since 2000. The next big entertainment industry to feel the effects of e-business will be the $78-billion movie business.
Electronics	Using the Internet to link suppliers and customers, Dell dictates industry profits. Its operating margins have risen from 7.3 percent in 2002 to 8 percent in 2003, even as it takes prices to levels where rivals cannot make money.
Financial services	Nearly every public e-finance company left, such as RBC Financial Group, makes money. Processing online mortgage applications is now 40 percent cheaper for customers.
Retail	Less than 5 percent of retail sales occur online. eBay is on track this year to become one of Canada's top retailers. Wal-Mart's e-business strategy is forcing rivals to make heavy investments in technology.
Automobiles	The cost of producing vehicles is down because of SCM and Web-based purchasing. eBay has become the leading Canadian used-car dealer, and most major car sites are profitable.
Education and training	Cisco saved $154 million last year by moving training sessions to the Internet.

Evolution of the World Wide Web

People often interchange the terms *Internet* and the *World Wide Web*, but these terms are not synonymous. Throughout the 1960s, 1970s, and 1980s, the Internet was primarily used by the U.S. Department of Defense to support activities such as e-mail and transferring files. The Internet was restricted to noncommercial activities, and its users included government employees, researchers, university professors, and students. The World Wide Web changed the purpose and use of the Internet.

The **World Wide Web (WWW)** is a global hypertext system that uses the Internet as its transport mechanism. **Hypertext transport protocol (HTTP)** is the Internet standard that supports the exchange of information on the WWW. By defining universal resource locators (URLs) and how they can be used to retrieve resources anywhere on the Internet, HTTP enables Web authors to embed hyperlinks in Web documents. HTTP defines the process by which a Web client, called a browser, originates a request for information and sends it to a Web server, a program designed to respond to HTTP requests and provide the desired information. In a hypertext system, users navigate by clicking a hyperlink embedded in the current document. The action displays a second document in the same or a separate browser window. The Web has quickly become the ideal medium for publishing information on the Internet and serves as the platform for the electronic economy. Figure 2.5 displays the reasons for the popularity and growth in the WWW.

The WWW remained primarily text-based until 1991 when two events occurred that would forever change the Web and the amount and quality of information available (see Figure 2.6). First, Tim Berners-Lee built the first Web site on August 6, 1991 (http://info.cern.ch/—the site has been archived). The site provided details about the World Wide Web including how to build a browser and set up a Web server. It also housed the world's first Web directory, since Berners-Lee later maintained a list of other Web sites apart from his own.[8]

Second, Marc Andreesen developed a new computer program called the NCSA Mosaic (National Center for Supercomputing Applications at the University of Illinois) and gave it away! The browser made it easier to access the Web sites that had started to appear. Soon Web sites contained more than just text; they also had sound and video files (see Figure 2.7). These pages, written in the hypertext markup language (HTML), have links that allow the user to quickly move from one document to another, even when the documents are stored in different computers. Web browsers read the HTML text and convert it into a Web page.[9]

By eliminating time and distance, the Internet makes it possible to perform business in ways not previously imaginable. The **digital divide** is when those with access to technology have great advantages over those without access to technology. People living in the village of Siroha, India, must bike 8 kilometres to find a telephone. For over 700 million rural people living in India, the digital divide was a way of life,

FIGURE 2.5

Reasons for World Wide Web Growth

Reasons for Growth of the World Wide Web
■ The microcomputer revolution made it possible for an average person to own a computer.
■ Advancements in networking hardware, software, and media made it possible for business PCs to be inexpensively connected to larger networks.
■ Browser software such as Microsoft's Internet Explorer and Netscape Navigator gave computer users an easy-to-use graphical interface to find, download, and display Web pages.
■ The speed, convenience, and low cost of e-mail have made it an incredibly popular tool for business and personal communications.
■ Basic Web pages are easy to create and extremely flexible.

FIGURE 2.6

The Internet's Impact on Information

Internet's Impact on Information	
Easy to compile	Searching for information on products, prices, customers, suppliers, and partners is faster and easier when using the Internet.
Increased richness	*Information richness* refers to the depth and breadth of information transferred between customers and businesses. Businesses and customers can collect and track more detailed information when using the Internet.
Increased reach	*Information reach* refers to the number of people a business can communicate with, on a global basis. Businesses can share information with numerous customers all over the world.
Improved content	A key element of the Internet is its ability to provide dynamic relevant content. Buyers need good content descriptions to make informed purchases, and sellers use content to properly market and differentiate themselves from the competition. Content and product description establish the common understanding between both parties to the transaction. As a result, the reach and richness of that content directly affects the transaction.

FIGURE 2.7

File Formats Offered over the WWW

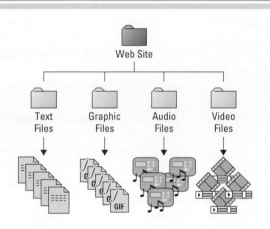

until recently. Media Lab Asia sells telephony and e-mail services via a mobile Internet kiosk mounted on a bicycle, which is known as an "info-thelas." The kiosk has an onboard computer equipped with an antenna for Internet service and a specially designed all-day battery. In 2005, over 2,000 villages had purchased the kiosk for $1,400, and another 600,000 villages were interested.[10]

ACCESSING INTERNET INFORMATION

Organizations use the Internet to share and access information. Consider the case of Atomic Energy of Canada Ltd. (AECL), the makers of CANDU nuclear reactors. In order to help realize the company's goals of making every one of its employees an ambassador of nuclear energy and the company, the Canadian Crown corporation deployed a new intranet solution to improve communications among the roughly 4,000 AECL employees scattered over multiple locations. Prior to the project, the company suffered from communication problems typical of most large organizations: ongoing news and information was not communicated in a timely and consistent manner; business objectives and priorities were not clearly communicated; there was too much reliance on e-mail as the primary method of communication; information on the existing intranet was not current or relevant, was hard to find, and required users to have technical skills to publish; and the existing intranet lacked a formal and comprehensive governance structure to manage intranet changes and to incorporate multiple-stakeholder perspectives. According to CIO André Roillard, the success of the new intranet's roll-out in improving communications at AECL only occurred since the intranet was not viewed as a piece of technology, but rather as a "business system that supported the business." As such, plans for improvements to the intranet had to be part of a larger communications strategy for the company—one that addressed e-mail communications, people and manager communications, as well as the intranet.[11]

Four common tools for accessing Internet information include:

- Intranet
- Extranet
- Portal
- Kiosk

Intranet

An *intranet* is an internalized portion of the Internet, protected from outside access, that allows an organization to provide access to information and application software to only its employees. An intranet is an invaluable tool for presenting organizational information as it provides a central location where employees can find information. It can host all kinds of company-related information such as benefits, schedules, strategic directions, and employee directories. At many companies, each department has its own Web page on the intranet for departmental information sharing. An intranet is not necessarily open to the external Internet and enables organizations to make internal resources available using familiar Internet clients, such as Web browsers, newsreaders, and e-mail.

Intranet publishing is the ultimate in electronic publishing. Companies realize significant returns on investment (ROI) simply by publishing information, such as employee manuals or telephone directories, on intranets rather than printed media.

Bell Canada created an intranet for its employees to facilitate information access, creation, sharing, and use across the enterprise. The Canadian telecommunications giant uses its intranet for a variety of business purposes. For example, customer service representatives use the intranet to retrieve rate plan information, phone specifications, and promotions details, improving the speed and accuracy of the service they provide to customers. To ensure the information shared with customers is accurate and current, approximately 500 Bell Canada employees are able to update content on the intranet. The intranet's content management system language translation capabilities allow Bell Canada to offer content in both French and English. Bell Canada's intranet is accessible to customer service representatives across four divisions, improving communication among approximately 13,000 users.[12]

Extranet

An *extranet* is an intranet that is available to strategic allies (such as customers, suppliers, and partners). Many companies are building extranets as they begin to realize the benefit of offering individuals outside the organization access to intranet-based information and application software such as order processing. Having a common area where employees, partners, vendors, and customers access information can be a major competitive advantage for an organization.

Wal-Mart created an extranet for its suppliers, which can view detailed product information at all Wal-Mart locations. Suppliers log on to Wal-Mart's extranet and view metrics on products such as current inventory, orders, forecasts, and marketing campaigns. This helps Wal-Mart's suppliers maintain their supply chains and ensure Wal-Mart never runs out of products.[13]

Portal

Portal is a very generic term for what is in essence a technology that provides access to information. A *portal* is a Web site that offers a broad array of resources and services, such as e-mail, online discussion groups, search engines, and online shopping malls. There are general portals and specialized or niche portals. Leading general portals include Yahoo!, Netscape, Microsoft, and Canoe. Examples of niche portals include Garden.com (for gardeners), Fool.com (for investors), and SearchNetworking.com (for network administrators).

Pratt & Whitney, one of the largest aircraft-engine manufacturers in the world, has saved millions of dollars with its field service portal initiative. Pratt & Whitney's sales and service field offices are geographically scattered around the globe and were connected via expensive dedicated lines. The company saved $3 million annually by replacing the dedicated lines with high-speed Internet access to its field service portal. Field staff can find information they need in a fraction of the time it took before. The company estimates this change will save another $9.3 million per year in "process and opportunity" savings.[14]

Kiosk

A *kiosk* is a publicly accessible computer system that has been set up to allow interactive information browsing. In a kiosk, the computer's operating system has been hidden from view, and the program runs in a full-screen mode, which provides a few simple tools for navigation.

Indigo Books & Music Inc., Canada's largest books retail chain, offers in-store customers access to Web kiosks as part of its commitment to providing a stress-free, service-driven approach to satisfying book and music lovers. The Web kiosks allow customers to search and buy books, DVDs, videos, gifts, and music, as well as to choose home or store delivery, and find out about upcoming events at stores. The company operates over 600 kiosks across Canada in its Indigo and Chapters stores. As means of improving the customer experience, Indigo is constantly updating its browser-based kiosks with new functionality, such as incorporating more product lines, creating category pages and boutiques such as Oprah's Picks and Harry Potter items, and allowing customers to use discount cards, as well as review and manage their personal accounts.[15]

INTERNET PROVIDERS

Many companies use service providers to supply access to Internet information. For example, British Airways, the $13.8-billion airline, outsourced the automation of its FAQ (frequently asked questions) Web pages. The airline needed to automatically develop, manage, and post different sets of FAQs for British Airway's loyalty program customers, allowing the company to offer special promotions based on the customer's loyalty program status (gold, silver, bronze). The company outsourced the project to application service provider RightNow Technologies. The new system is helping British Airways create the right marketing programs for the appropriate customer tier.[16]

There are three common forms of service providers including:

1. Internet service provider (ISP).
2. Online service provider (OSP).
3. Application service provider (ASP).

Internet Service Provider

An *Internet service provider (ISP)* is a company that provides individuals and other companies access to the Internet along with additional related services, such as Web site building. An ISP has the equipment and the telecommunication line access required to have a point of presence on the Internet for different geographic areas. Larger ISPs have their own high-speed leased lines so they are less dependent on telecommunication providers and can deliver better service to their customers. Among the largest national and regional ISPs are Bell Sympatico, Shaw, Telus, Rogers, Vidéotron Ltee, and Cogeco.

Navigating the different options for an ISP can be daunting and confusing. There are more than 350 ISPs in Canada; some are large with household names, and

FIGURE 2.8

Common ISP Services

Common ISP Services
■ **Web hosting.** Housing, serving, and maintaining files for one or more Web sites is a widespread offering.
■ **Hard-disk storage space.** Smaller sites may need only 300 to 500 MB (megabytes) of Web site storage space, whereas other e-business sites may need at least 10 GB (gigabytes) of space or their own dedicated Web server.
■ **Availability.** To run an e-business, a site must be accessible to customers 24/7. ISPs maximize the availability of the sites they host using techniques such as load balancing and clustering many servers to reach 100 percent availability.
■ **Support.** A big part of turning to an ISP is that there is limited worry about keeping the Web server running. Most ISPs offer 24/7 customer service.

others are literally one-person operations. Although Internet access is viewed as a commodity service, in reality features and performance can differ tremendously among ISPs. Figure 2.8 above highlights common ISP features.

Another member of the ISP family is the ***wireless Internet service provider (WISP)***, an ISP that allows subscribers to connect to a server at designated hotspots or access points using a wireless connection. This type of ISP offers access to the Internet and the Web from anywhere within the zone of coverage provided by an antenna. This is usually a region with a radius of approximately one kilometre. Figure 2.9 displays a brief overview of how this technology works.

One example of a WISP is T-Mobile International, a U.S. company that provides access to wireless laptop users in more than 2,000 locations including airports, airline clubs, Starbucks coffeehouses, and Borders Books. A wireless service called T-Mobile HotSpot allows customers to access the Internet and T-Mobile's corporate intranet via a wireless network from convenient locations away from their home or office. T-Mobile International is the first mobile communications company to extend service on both sides of the Atlantic, offering customers the advantage of using their wireless services when travelling worldwide.[17]

FIGURE 2.9

Wireless Access Diagram

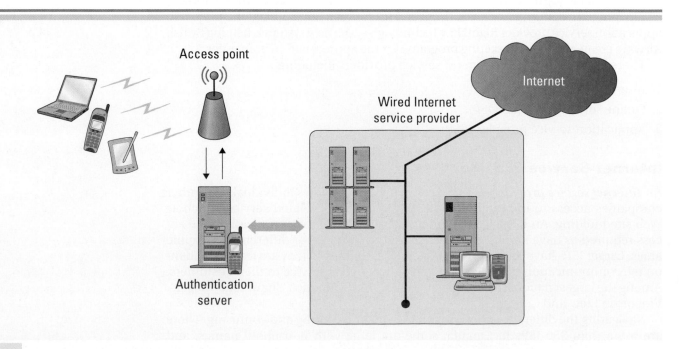

Online Service Provider

An *online service provider (OSP)* offers an extensive array of unique services such as its own version of a Web browser. The term *online service provider* helps to distinguish ISPs that offer Internet access and their own online content, such as America Online (AOL), from ISPs that simply connect users directly with the Internet, such as EarthLink. Connecting to the Internet through an OSP is an alternative to connecting through a national ISP, such as Bell Sympatico, or a regional or local ISP.

Application Service Provider

An *application service provider (ASP)* is a company that offers an organization access over the Internet to systems and related services that would otherwise have to be located in personal or organizational computers. Employing the services of an ASP is essentially outsourcing part of a company's business logic. Hiring an ASP to manage a company's software allows the company to hand over the operation, maintenance, and upgrade responsibilities for a system to the ASP.

One of the most important agreements between the customer and the ASP is the service level agreement. *Service level agreements (SLAs)* define the specific responsibilities of the service provider and set the customer expectations. SLAs include such items as availability, accessibility, performance, maintenance, backup/recovery, upgrades, equipment ownership, software ownership, security, and confidentiality. For example, an SLA might state that the ASP must have the software available and accessible from 7:00 a.m. to 7:00 p.m. Monday through Friday. It might also state that if the system is down for more than 60 minutes, there will be no charge for that day. Most industry analysts agree that the ASP market is growing rapidly. International Data Corporation (IDC) estimates the worldwide ASP market will grow from around $13 billion in 2005 to $23 billion by 2008.[18]

OPENING CASE QUESTIONS

Amazon.com—Not Your Average Bookstore

1. How has Amazon used technology to revamp the bookselling industry?

2. Is Amazon using disruptive or sustaining technology to run its business?

3. How is Amazon using intranets and extranets to run its business?

4. How could Amazon use kiosks to improve its business?

2.2 E-BUSINESS

E-BUSINESS BASICS

In 2003, Tom Anderson and Chris DeWolf started MySpace, a social networking Web site that offers its members information about the independent music scene around the United States representing both Internet culture and teenage culture. Musicians sign up for free MySpace home pages where they can post tour dates, songs, and lyrics. Fans sign up for their own Web pages to link to favourite bands and friends. As of February 2006, MySpace was the world's fifth most popular English-language Web site with over 60 million users.[19] Another popular social networking site is Facebook, which was originally developed for college and university students, but has since been made available to anyone with an e-mail address. As of February 2007, Facebook had the largest number of registered users among college and university focused Web sites.

One of the biggest benefits of the Internet is its ability to allow organizations to perform business with anyone, anywhere, anytime. *E-commerce* is the buying and selling of goods and services over the Internet. E-commerce refers only to online transactions. E-business, derived from the term e-commerce, is the conducting of business on the Internet, not only buying and selling, but also serving customers and collaborating with business partners. The primary difference between e-commerce and e-business is that e-business also refers to online exchanges of information. For example, a manufacturer allowing its suppliers to monitor production schedules or a financial institution allowing its customers to review their banking, credit card, and mortgage accounts.

In the past few years, e-business seems to have permeated every aspect of daily life. Both individuals and organizations have embraced Internet technologies to enhance productivity, maximize convenience, and improve communications globally. From banking to shopping to entertainment, the Internet has become integral to daily life. Figure 2.10 provides examples of a few of the industries using e-business.

E-BUSINESS MODELS

A *e-business model* is an approach to conducting electronic business on the Internet. E-business transactions take place between two major entities—businesses and consumers. All e-business activities happen within the framework of two types of business relationships: (1) the exchange of products and services between businesses (business-to-business, or B2B) and (2) the exchange of products and services with consumers (business-to-consumer, or B2C) (see Figure 2.11).

The primary difference between B2B and B2C are the customers; B2B customers are other businesses while B2C markets to consumers. Overall, B2B relations are more complex and have higher security needs; plus B2B is the dominant e-business force, representing 80 percent of all online business.[20] Figure 2.12 illustrates all the e-business models: Business-to-business, business-to-consumer, consumer-to-consumer, and consumer-to-business.

Business-to-Business (B2B)

Business-to-business (B2B) applies to businesses buying from and selling to each other over the Internet. Online access to data, including expected shipping date, delivery date, and shipping status, provided either by the seller or a third-party provider is widely supported by B2B models. Electronic marketplaces represent a new wave in B2B e-business models. *Electronic marketplaces*, or *e-marketplaces*, are interactive business communities providing a central market where multiple

FIGURE 2.10

Overview of Several Industries Using E-Business

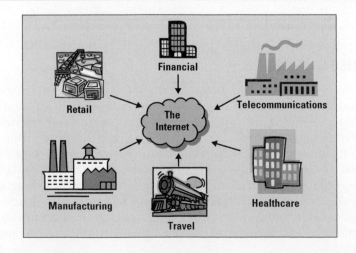

FIGURE 2.11

Basic E-Business Models

E-Business Term	Definition
Business-to-business (B2B)	Applies to businesses buying from and selling to each other over the Internet.
Business-to-consumer (B2C)	Applies to any business that sells its products or services to consumers over the Internet.
Consumer-to-business (C2B)	Applies to any consumer that sells a product or service to a business over the Internet.
Consumer-to-consumer (C2C)	Applies to sites primarily offering goods and services to assist consumers interacting with each other over the Internet.

	Business	**Consumer**
Business	B2B	B2C
Consumer	C2B	C2C

FIGURE 2.12

E-Business Models

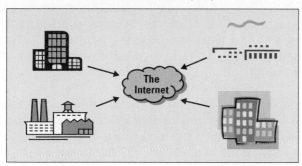
Business-to-Business (B2B)

Business-to-Consumer (B2C)

Consumer-to-Business (C2B)

Consumer-to-Consumer (C2C)

buyers and sellers can engage in e-business activities (see Figure 2.13). They present structures for conducting commercial exchange, consolidating supply chains, and creating new sales channels. Their primary goal is to increase market efficiency by tightening and automating the relationship between buyers and sellers. Existing e-marketplaces allow access to various mechanisms in which to buy and sell almost anything, from services to direct materials.

FIGURE 2.13

Business-to-Business
E-Marketplace Overview

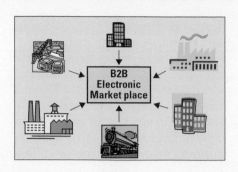

Business-to-Consumer (B2C)

Business-to-consumer (B2C) applies to any business that sells its products or services to consumers over the Internet. Cyberflowers.com, an e-business Canadian success story headquartered in Bolton, Ontario, is an Internet retailer of flowers and speciality gifts selling directly to consumers. Cyberflowers utilizes a network of florists for order fulfillment for same-day delivery anywhere in the United States and Canada and two-business day turn-around for worldwide delivery. The company's Web site provides customers with an online floral and specialty gift store. As a means of creating the Web's "most desirable online floral and gift community," the Web site is primed for easy navigation and the provision of interesting and target content. For example, Cyberflowers helps customers send ideal gifts to important people in their lives by offering a large selection of products, information about the latest trends and concepts, personalized service, and reasonable prices.[21] Cellie Gonsalves, owner of Cyberflowers, says "the Internet is full of untapped opportunities for florists . . . the medium fits with the flower purchaser's needs." For example, consumers can view flower arrangements on their computer screens to help them decide which one they prefer, these arrangements can be viewed day or night, prices in both American and Canadian dollars can be displayed, and shoppers can sign up for e-mail reminders for upcoming holidays and anniversaries.[22]

E-Shop   An *e-shop*, sometimes referred to as an *e-store* or *e-tailer*, is a version of a retail store where customers can shop at any hour of the day without leaving their home or office. These online stores sell and support a variety of products and services. The online businesses channelling their goods and services via the Internet only, such as Amazon.ca, are called pure plays. The others are an extension of traditional retail outlets that sell online as well as through a traditional physical store. They are generally known as "bricks and clicks" or "click and mortar" organizations, such as Sears Canada (www.sears.ca) and Canadian Hickory Farms (www.hickoryfarms.ca) (see Figure 2.14).

E-Mall   An *e-mall* consists of a number of e-shops; it serves as a gateway through which a visitor can access other e-shops. An e-mall may be generalized or specialized depending on the products offered by the e-shops it hosts. Revenues for

FIGURE 2.14

Types of Businesses

	Business Types
Brick-and-mortar business	A business that operates in a physical store without an Internet presence.
Pure-play (virtual) business	A business that operates on the Internet only without a physical store. Examples include Amazon.ca and Expedia.ca.
Click-and-mortar business	A business that operates in a physical store and on the Internet. Examples include Henry Birks and Sons (www.birks.com) and Future Shop.

e-mall operators include membership fees from participating e-shops, advertising, and possibly a fee on each transaction if the e-mall operator also processes payments. E-shops in e-malls benefit from brand reinforcement and increased traffic as visiting one shop on the e-mall often leads to browsing "neighbouring" shops. An example of an e-mall is Montreal-based Emall.ca.

Consumer-to-Business (C2B)

Consumer-to-business (C2B) applies to any consumer that sells a product or service to a business over the Internet. One example of this e-business model is Priceline.com where bidders (or customers) set their prices for items such as airline tickets or hotel rooms, and a seller decides whether to supply them. The demand for C2B e-business will increase over the next few years due to customer's desire for greater convenience and lower prices. The C2B business model is a complete reversal of the traditional business model where companies offer goods and services to consumers.

Consumer-to-Consumer (C2C)

Consumer-to-consumer (C2C) applies to sites primarily offering goods and services to assist consumers interacting with each other over the Internet. eBay, the Internet's most successful C2C online auction Web site, links like-minded buyers and sellers for a small commission. Figure 2.15 displays the different types of online auctions.

C2C online communities, or virtual communities, interact via e-mail groups, Web-based discussion forums, or chat rooms. C2C business models are consumer-driven and opportunities are available to satisfy most consumers' needs, ranging from finding a mortgage to job hunting. They are global swap shops based on customer-centred communication. One C2C community, Kazaa, allows users to download MP3 music files, enabling users to exchange files. Figure 2.16 highlights the different types of C2C communities that are thriving on the Internet.

ORGANIZATIONAL STRATEGIES FOR E-BUSINESS

To be successful in e-business, an organization must master the art of electronic relationships. Traditional means of customer acquisition such as advertising,

Online Auctions	
Electronic Auction (e-auction)	Sellers and buyers solicit consecutive bids from each other and prices are determined dynamically.
Forward Auction	An auction that sellers use as a selling channel to many buyers and the highest bid wins.
Reverse Auction	An auction that buyers use to purchase a product or service, selecting the seller with the lowest bid.

FIGURE 2.15

Online Auctions

C2C Communities
■ **Communities of interest**—People interact with each other on specific topics, such as golfing and stamp collecting.
■ **Communities of relations**—People come together to share certain life experiences, such as cancer patients, senior citizens, and car enthusiasts.
■ **Communities of fantasy**—People participate in imaginary environments, such as fantasy football teams and playing one-on-one with Michael Jordan.

FIGURE 2.16

C2C Communities

promotions, and public relations are just as important with a Web site. Primary business areas taking advantage of e-business include:

- Marketing/sales
- Financial services
- Procurement
- Customer service
- Intermediaries

Marketing/Sales

Direct selling was the earliest type of e-business and has proven to be a stepping-stone to more complex commerce operations. Successes such as eBay, Chapters, Dell Inc., and Travelocity have sparked the growth of this segment, proving customer acceptance of e-business direct selling. Marketing and sales departments are initiating some of the most exciting e-business innovations (see Figure 2.17).

For example, Sears Canada installed on one of its properties a stand-alone, full-colour outdoor LED digital billboard as a means of generating advertising revenue for the retail chain and promoting the individual store's own products and services. The digital billboard utilizes an advanced electronic display system with modular construction, high-quality LED clarity and brightness, wide-viewing angles, and a wide assortment of 16.7 million colours.[23]

Digital billboards are much more expensive than today's billboards, costing between $250,000 and $700,000 versus the $25,000 and $70,000 price tags on non-digital billboards. However, the new billboards offer operators money-saving advantages, including easily changed ad copy; avoiding print and set-up costs; and ad copy's ability to change to pertain to a certain time of day. Each board holds about eight ads, which run six seconds each, allowing operators to sell more ads on the same sign.[24] Eventually customers will be able to buy billboard sign time in hour or minute increments. Current costs to share a digital billboard are $40,000 a month, compared with $10,000 for one standard billboard.[25]

E-business provides an easy way to penetrate a new geographic territory and extend global reach. Large, small, or specialized businesses can use their online sales sites to sell on a worldwide basis with little extra cost. This ability to tap into expanded domestic or even international markets can be an immediate revenue boost to artists, jewellery makers, wineries, and the like, for initial orders and especially for reorders.

The Hotel Gatti (www.hotel-gatti.com) is a small hotel in northern Italy catering primarily to Italian travellers. By introducing its own Web site with English-language options, it significantly extended its geographic reach. Now, at very little cost, the hotel communicates with and takes reservations from potential customers in Canada and the United States and other English-speaking countries. The bottom line is that e-business now allows any company to market and sell products globally, regardless of its size.[26]

Financial Services

Financial services Web sites are enjoying rapid growth as they help consumers, businesses, and financial institutions distribute information with greater convenience and richness than is available in other channels. Consumers in e-business markets pay for products and services using a credit card or one of the methods outlined in Figure 2.18. Online business payments differ from online consumer payments because businesses tend to make large purchases (from thousands to millions of dollars) and typically do not pay with a credit card. Businesses make online payments using electronic data interchange (EDI) (see Figure 2.19). Transactions between businesses are complex and typically require a level of system integration between the businesses.

Many organizations are now turning to providers of electronic trading networks for enhanced Internet-based network and messaging services. Electronic trading networks are service providers that manage network services. They support

FIGURE 2.17

Generating Revenue on the Internet through Marketing and Sales Departments

Marketing and Sales E-Business Innovations
■ An *online ad* is a box running across a Web page that is often used to contain advertisements. The banner generally contains a link to the advertiser's Web site. Web-based advertising services can track the number of times users click the banner, generating statistics that enable advertisers to judge whether the advertising fees are worth paying. *Banner ads* are like living, breathing classified ads.
■ A *pop-up ad* is a small Web page containing an advertisement that appears on the Web page outside of the current Web site loaded in the Web browser. A *pop-under ad* is a form of a pop-up ad that users do not see until they close the current Web browser screen.
■ *Associate programs (affiliate programs)* allow businesses to generate commissions or royalties from an Internet site. For example, a business can sign up as an associate of a major commercial site such as Amazon. The business then sends potential buyers to the Amazon site using a code or banner ad. The business receives a commission when the referred customer makes a purchase on Amazon.
■ *Viral marketing* is a technique that induces Web sites or users to pass on a marketing message to other Web sites or users, creating exponential growth in the message's visibility and effect. One example of successful viral marketing is Hotmail, which promotes its service and its own advertisers' messages in every user's e-mail notes. Viral marketing encourages users of a product or service supplied by an e-business to encourage friends to join. Viral marketing is a word-of-mouth type advertising program.
■ *Mass customization* is the ability of an organization to give its customers the opportunity to tailor its products or services to the customers' specifications. For example, customers can order M&M's with customized sayings such as "Marry Me."
■ *Personalization* occurs when a Web site can know enough about a person's likes and dislikes that it can fashion offers that are more likely to appeal to that person. Personalization involves tailoring a presentation of an e-business Web site to individuals or groups of customers based on profile information, demographics, or prior transactions. Amazon uses personalization to create a unique portal for each of its customers.
■ A *blog* (the contraction of the phrase "Web log") is a Web site in which items are posted on a regular basis and displayed in reverse chronological order. Like other media, blogs often focus on a particular subject, such as food, politics, or local news. Some blogs function as online diaries. A typical blog combines text, images, and links to other blogs, Web pages, and other media related to its topic. Since its appearance in 1995, blogging has emerged as a popular means of communication, affecting public opinion and mass media around the world.
■ *Real simple syndications (RSS)* is a family of Web feed formats used for Web syndication of programs and content. RSS is used by (among other things) news Web sites, blogs, and podcasting, which allows consumers and journalists to have news constantly fed to them instead of searching for it. In addition to facilitating syndication, RSS allows a Web site's frequent readers to track updates on the site.
■ *Podcasting* is the distribution of audio or video files, such as radio programs or music videos, over the Internet to play on mobile devices and personal computers. Podcasting's essence is about creating content (audio or video) for an audience that wants to listen when they want, where they want, and how they want. Podcasters' Web sites also may offer direct download of their files, but the subscription feed of automatically delivered new content is what distinguishes a podcast from a simple download or real-time streaming. Usually, the podcast features one type of show with new episodes either sporadically or at planned intervals such as daily, weekly, etc.
■ *Search engine optimization (SEO)* is a set of methods aimed at improving the ranking of a Web site in search engine listings. Search engines display different kinds of listings in the search engine results pages (SERPs), including: pay-per-click advertisements, paid inclusion listings, and organic search results. SEO is primarily concerned with advancing the goals of Web sites by improving the number and position of organic search results for a wide variety of relevant keywords. SEO strategies can increase the number of visitors and the quality of visitors, where quality means visitors who complete the action the site intends (e.g., purchase, sign up, learn something).   SEO, or "white hat SEO," is distinguished from "black hat SEO," or spamdexing, by methods and objectives. *Spamdexing* uses a variety of deceptive techniques in an attempt to manipulate search engine rankings, whereas legitimate SEO focuses on building better sites and using honest methods of promotion. What constitutes an honest, or ethical, method is an issue that has been the subject of numerous debates.

FIGURE 2.18

Types of Online Consumer
Payments

Online Consumer Payments	
Financial cybermediary	A *financial cybermediary* is an Internet-based company that facilitates payments over the Internet. PayPal is the best-known example of a financial cybermediary.
Electronic cheque	An *electronic cheque* is a mechanism for sending a payment from a chequing or savings account. There are many implementations of electronic cheques, with the most prominent being online banking.
Electronic bill presentment and payment (EBPP)	An *electronic bill presentment and payment (EBPP)* is a system that sends bills over the Internet and provides an easy-to-use mechanism (such as clicking on a button) to pay the bill. EBPP systems are available through local banks or online services such as Checkfree and Quicken.
Digital wallet	A *digital wallet* is both software and information—the software provides security for the transaction and the information includes payment and delivery information (for example, the credit card number and expiration date).

business-to-business integration information exchanges, improved security, guaranteed service levels, and command centre support (see Figure 2.20). As electronic trading networks expand their reach and the number of Internet businesses continues to grow, so will the need for managed trading services. Using these services allows organizations to reduce time to market and the overall development, deployment, and maintenance costs associated with their integration infrastructures.

Traders at U.S. Vanguard Petroleum Corporation spent most days on the phone, patrolling the market for pricing and volume information in order to strike the best possible deal. The process was slow and tied up traders on one negotiation at a time, making it inherently difficult to stay on top of quickly changing prices. One winter, for example, the weather got cold and stayed cold, causing propane prices to increase dramatically. The price was moving so fast that Vanguard was missing opportunities to buy, sell, and execute deals since it was able to complete only one deal at a time.

To bridge these shortcomings and speed the process, Vanguard became one of the first users of Chalkboard, a commodity markets electronic trading network that is now part of ChemConnect, a B2B e-marketplace. Vanguard uses Chalkboard to put bids and offers in front of hundreds of traders and complete various trades at multiple delivery points simultaneously. Vanguard now completes deals in real-time and is able to access a broader audience of buyers and sellers.[27]

Procurement

Web-based procurement of maintenance, repair, and operations (MRO) supplies is expected to reach more than $200 billion worldwide by the year 2009. *Maintenance, repair, and operations (MRO) materials* (also called *indirect materials*)

FIGURE 2.19

Types of Online Business
Payments

Online Business Payments
Electronic data interchange (EDI) is a standard format for exchanging business data. One way an organization can use EDI is through a value-added network. A *value-added network (VAN)* is a private network, provided by a third party, for exchanging information through a high-capacity connection. VANs support electronic catalogues (from which orders are placed), EDI-based transactions (the actual orders), security measures such as encryption, and EDI mailboxes.
Financial EDI (financial electronic data interchange) is a standard electronic process for B2B market purchase payments. National Cash Management Systems is an automated clearinghouse in the United States that supports the reconciliation of the payments.

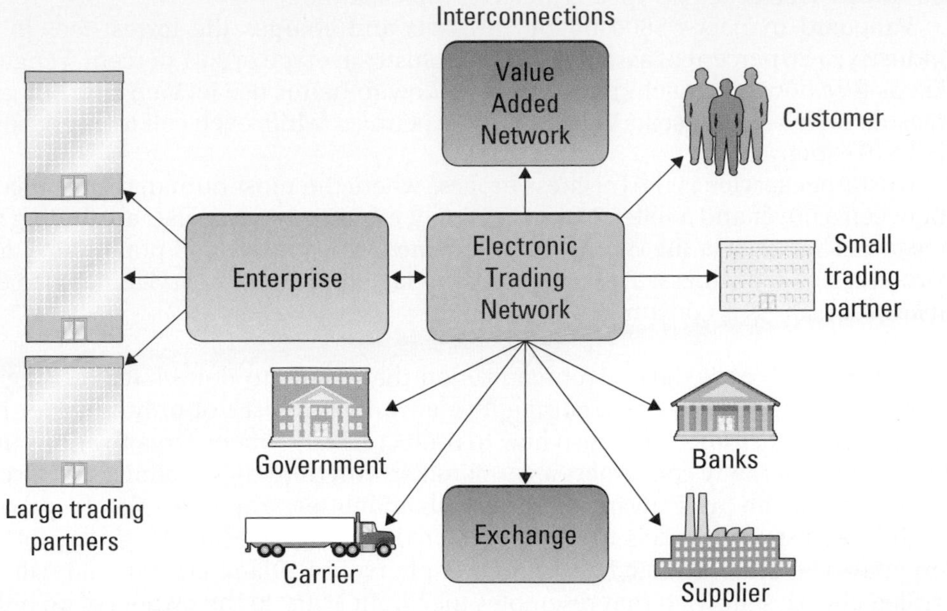

FIGURE 2.20

Diagram of an Electronic
Trading Network

are materials necessary for running an organization but do not relate to the company's primary business activities. Typical MRO goods include office supplies (such as pens and paper), equipment, furniture, computers, and replacement parts. In the traditional approach to MRO purchasing, a purchasing manager would receive a paper-based request for materials. The purchasing manager would need to search a variety of paper catalogues to find the right product at the right price. Not surprisingly, the administrative cost for purchasing indirect supplies often exceeded the unit value of the product itself. According to the Organization for Economic Cooperation and Development (OECD), companies with more than $500 million in revenue spend an estimated $85 to $175 to process a single purchase order for MRO supplies.[28]

E-Procurement *E procurement* is the B2B purchase and sale of supplies and services over the Internet. The goal of many e-procurement applications is to link organizations directly to preapproved suppliers' catalogues and to process the entire purchasing transaction online. Linking to electronic catalogues significantly reduces the need to check the timeliness and accuracy of supplier information.

An *electronic catalogue* presents customers with information about goods and services offered for sale, bid, or auction on the Internet. Some electronic catalogues manage large numbers of individual items, and search capabilities help buyers navigate quickly to the items they want to purchase. Other electronic catalogues emphasize merchandise presentation and special offers, much as a retail store is laid out to encourage impulse or add-on buying. As with other aspects of e-business, it is important to match electronic catalogue design and functionality to a company's business goals.

Customer Service

E-business enables customers to help themselves by combining the communications capability of a traditional customer response system with the content richness only the Web can provide—all available and operating 24/7. As a result, conducting business via the Web offers customers the convenience they want while freeing key support staff to tackle more complex problems. The Web also allows an organization to provide better customer service through e-mail, special messages, and private password-Web access to special areas for top customers.

Vanguard manages $800 billion in assets and charges the lowest fees in the industry: 0.26 percent of assets versus an industry average of 0.81 percent. Vanguard keeps fees down by teaching its investors how to better use its Web site. For good reason: A Web log-on costs Vanguard mere pennies, while each call to a service rep is a $10 expense.[29]

Customer service is the business process where the most human contact occurs between a buyer and a seller. Not surprisingly, e-business strategists are finding that customer service via the Web is one of the most challenging and potentially lucrative areas of e-business. The primary issue facing customer service departments using e-business is consumer protection.

Consumer Protection An organization that wants to dominate by using superior customer service as a competitive advantage must not only consider how to service its customers, but also how to protect its customers. Organizations must recognize that many consumers are unfamiliar with their digital choices, and some e-businesses are well aware of these vulnerabilities. For example, 17-year-old high school senior Francis Cornworth offered his "Young Man's Virginity" for sale on eBay. The offer attracted a $11-million phony bid. Diana Duyser sold half of a grilled cheese sandwich that resembles the Virgin Mary to the owners of an online casino for US$28,000 on eBay. Figure 2.21 highlights the different protection areas for consumers.[30]

Regardless of whether the customers are other businesses or end consumers, one of their greatest concerns is the security level of their financial transactions. This includes all aspects of electronic information, but focuses mainly on the information associated with payments (e.g., a credit card number) and the payments themselves, that is, the "electronic money." An organization must consider such issues as encryption, secure socket layers (SSL), and secure electronic transactions (SET), as explained in Figure 2.22.

FIGURE 2.21

Consumer Protection

Issues for Consumer Protection
■ Unsolicited goods and communication
■ Illegal or harmful goods, services, and content
■ Insufficient information about goods or their suppliers
■ Invasion of privacy
■ Cyberfraud

FIGURE 2.22

E-Business Security

E-Business Security
Encryption scrambles information into an alternative form that requires a key or password to decrypt the information. Encryption is achieved by scrambling letters, replacing letters, replacing letters with numbers, and other ways.
A *secure socket layer (SSL)* (1) creates a secure and private connection between a client and server computer, (2) encrypts the information, and (3) sends the information over the Internet. SSL is identified by a Web site address that includes an "s" at the end—http**s**.
A *secure electronic transaction (SET)* is a transmission security method that ensures transactions are secure and legitimate. Similar to SSL, SET encrypts information before sending it over the Internet. However, SET also enables customer authentication for credit card transaction. SETs are endorsed by major e-commerce players including MasterCard, Visa, Netscape, and Microsoft.

Intermediaries

Intermediaries are agents, software, or businesses that bring buyers and sellers together that provide a trading infrastructure to enhance e-business. With the introduction of e-commerce there was much discussion about disintermediation of middle people/organizations; however, recent developments in e-business have seen more reintermediation. *Reintermediation* refers to using the Internet to reassemble buyers, sellers, and other partners in a traditional supply chain in new ways. One example is BidNavigator.com, a Canadian online marketplace that enables suppliers providing various goods and services to locate bid opportunities from various Canadian government agencies. Government agencies in Canada spend $100 billion annually on various products and services and post over 1,000 of these opportunities on BidNavigator.com at any given time. The marketplace notifies registered suppliers in BidNavigator about new bids through daily alerts. The system not only helps government agencies find the most competitive bids from suppliers who have registered as pre-qualified vendors with them, it also allows suppliers to know about potential bid opportunities they otherwise may miss out on. This is important since governmental bid opportunities typically are open only for two to three weeks.[31] Figure 2.23 lists intermediaries and their functions.

MEASURING E-BUSINESS SUCCESS

Traffic on the Internet retail site for Wal-Mart has grown 66 percent in the last year. The site receives over 500,000 visitors daily (6.5 million per week), downloads 2 million Web pages daily, and averages 60,000 users logged on simultaneously. Wal-Mart's primary concern is maintaining optimal performance for

FIGURE 2.23

Types of Intermediaries

Type of Intermediary	Description	Example
Internet service providers	Make money selling a service, not a product	Vidéotron.com, Telus.com, Bell Sympatico (bell.ca)
Portals	Central hubs for online content	Yahoo.com, MSN.com, Google.com
Content providers	Use the Internet to distribute copyrighted content	wsj.com, cnn.com, espn.com canadiancontent.net
Online brokers	Intermediaries between buyers and sellers of goods and services	charlesschwab.com, fidelity.ca, tradefreedom.com
Market makers	Aggregate three services for market participants: a place, rules, and infrastructure	amazon.com, ebay.com, pricelinc.com
Online service providers	Extensive online array of services	xdrive.com, lawinfo.com
Intelligent agents	Software applications that follow instructions and learn independently	Sidestep.com, WebSeeker.com, iSpyNOW.com
Application service providers	Sell access to Internet-based software applications to other companies	ariba.com, commerceone.com, ibm.com
Infomedianies	Provide specialized information on behalf of producers of goods and services and their potential customers	autobytel.com, BizRate.com

online transactions. A disruption to the Web site directly affects the company's bottom line and customer loyalty. The company monitors and tracks the hardware, software, and network running the company's Web site to ensure high quality of service.[32]

The Yankee Group reports that 66 percent of companies determine Web site success solely by measuring the amount of traffic. Unfortunately, large amounts of Web site traffic does not necessarily indicate large sales. Many Web sites with lots of traffic have minimal sales. The best way to measure a Web site's success is to measure such things as the revenue generated by Web traffic, the number of new customers acquired by Web traffic, any reductions in customer service calls resulting from Web traffic.[33]

Web Site Metrics

Figure 2.24 displays a few metrics an organization can use to measure Web site effectiveness.

To help understand advertising effectiveness, interactivity measures are tracked and monitored. *Interactivity* measures the visitor interactions with the target ad. Such interaction measures include the duration of time the visitor spends viewing the ad, the number of pages viewed, and even the number of repeat visits to the target ad. Interactivity measures are a giant step forward for advertisers, since traditional advertising methods—newspapers, magazines, radio, and television—provide few ways to track effectiveness metrics. Interactivity metrics measure actual consumer activities, something that was impossible to do in the past, and provide advertisers with tremendous amounts of business intelligence.

The ultimate outcome of any advertisement is a purchase. Tying purchase amounts to Web site visits makes it easy to communicate the business value of the Web site. Organizations use metrics to tie revenue amounts and new customer creation numbers directly back to the Web sites or banner ads. Organizations can observe through *clickstream data* the exact pattern of a consumer's navigation through a site. Clickstream data can reveal a number of basic data points on how consumers interact with Web sites. Figure 2.25 displays different types of clickstream metrics.

Marc Barach is the co-inventor and chief marketing officer of Ingenio, a start-up company that specializes in connecting people in real-time. When the Internet first emerged, banner ads were the prevalent marketing tools. Next came pay-per-click where the company pays the search engine each time its Web site is accessed from a search. Today 35 percent of online spending occurs through pay-per-clicks. Unfortunately, pay-per-clicks are not suitable for all businesses. Roofers, plumbers, auto repair people, and cosmetic surgeons rarely have Web sites and

FIGURE 2.24

Web Site Effectiveness Metrics

Effectiveness Web Site Metrics
■ *Cookie*—a small file deposited on a hard drive by a Web site containing information about customers and their Web activities. Cookies allow Web sites to record the comings and goings of customers, usually without their knowledge or consent.
■ *Click-through*—a count of the number of people who visit one site and click on an advertisement that takes them to the site of the advertiser. Tracking effectiveness based on click-throughs guarantees exposure to target ads; however, it does not guarantee that the visitor liked the ad, spent any substantial time viewing the ad, or was satisfied with the information contained in the ad.
■ A *banner ad*—advertises the products and services of another business, usually another dot-com business. Advertisers can track how often customers click on banner ads resulting in a click-through to their Web site. Often the cost of the banner ad depends on the number of customers who click on the banner ad. Tracking the number of banner ad clicks is one way to understand the effectiveness of the ad on its target audience.

FIGURE 2.25

Clickstream Data Metrics

Clickstream Data Metrics
■ The number of page views (i.e., the number of times a particular page has been presented to a visitor).
■ The pattern of Web sites visited, including most frequent exit page and most frequent prior Web site.
■ Length of stay on the Web site.
■ Dates and times of visits.
■ Number of registrations filled out per 100 visitors.
■ Number of abandoned registrations.
■ Demographics of registered visitors.
■ Number of customers with shopping carts.
■ Number of abandoned shopping carts.

do not generate business via pay-per-clicks. Barach believes that the next line of Internet advertising will be pay-per-call, and Ingenio has invested five years and $50 million in building the platform to run the business. Here is how pay-per-call works:

- The user types a keyword into a search engine.
- The search engine passes the keyword to Ingenio.
- Ingenio determines the category and sends back the appropriate merchant's unique, traceable 800 telephone number.
- The 800 number routes through Ingenio's switches, and Ingenio charges the merchant when a customer calls.

A Jupiter Research study discovered that businesses were willing to pay between $2 and $40 for each call lead.[34]

Figure 2.26 provides definitions of common metrics based on clickstream data. To interpret such data properly, managers try to benchmark against other companies. For instance, consumers seem to visit their preferred Web sites regularly, even checking back to the Web site multiple times during a given session. Consumers tend to become loyal to a small number of Web sites, and they tend to revisit those Web sites a number of times during a particular session.

E-BUSINESS BENEFITS AND CHALLENGES

According to an NUA Internet Survey, the Internet links more than 1 billion people worldwide. Experts predict that global Internet usage will nearly triple between 2006 and 2010, making e-business a more significant factor in the global economy. As e-business improves, organizations will experience benefits and challenges alike. Figure 2.27 details e-business benefits for an organization.

The Internet is forcing organizations to refocus their information systems from the inside out. A growing number of companies are already using the Internet to streamline their business processes, procure materials, sell products, automate customer service, and create new revenue streams. Although the benefits of e-business systems are enticing, developing, deploying, and managing these systems is not always easy. Unfortunately, e-business is not something a business can just go out and buy. Figure 2.28 details the challenges facing e-business.

A key element of e-marketplaces is their ability to provide not only transaction capabilities but also dynamic, relevant content to trading partners. The original e-business Web sites provided shopping cart capabilities built around product

FIGURE 2.26

Definitions of Web Site Metrics

Visitor	Visitor Metrics
Unidentified visitor	A visitor is an individual who visits a Web site. An "unidentified visitor" means that no information about that visitor is available.
Unique visitor	A unique visitor is one who can be recognized and counted only once within a given period of time. An accurate count of unique visitors is not possible without some form of identification, registration, or authentication.
Session visitor	A session ID is available (e.g., cookie) or inferred by incoming address plus browser type, which allows a visitor's responses to be tracked within a given visit to a Web site.
Tracked visitor	An ID (e.g., cookie) is available which allows a user to be tracked across multiple visits to a Web site. No information, other than a unique identifier, is available for a tracked visitor.
Identified visitor	An ID is available (e.g., cookie or voluntary registration), which allows a user to be tracked across multiple visits to a Web site. Other information (name, demographics, possibly supplied voluntarily by the visitor) can be linked to this ID.
Exposure	**Exposure Metrics**
Page exposures (page-views)	The number of times a particular Web page has been viewed by visitors in a given time period, without regard to duplication.
Site exposures	The number of visitor sessions at a Web site in a given time period, without regard to visitor duplication.
Visit	**Visit Metrics**
Stickiness (visit duration time)	The length of time a visitor spends on a Web site. Can be reported as an average in a given time period, without regard to visitor duplication.
Raw visit depth (total Web pages exposure per session)	The total number of pages a visitor is exposed to during a single visit to a Web site. Can be reported as an average or distribution in a given time period, without regard to visitor duplication.
Visit depth (total unique Web pages exposure per session)	The total number of unique pages a visitor is exposed to during a single visit to a Web site. Can be reported as an average or distribution in a given time period, without regard to visitor duplication.
Hit	**Hit Metrics**
Hits	When visitors reach a Web site, their computer sends a request to the site's computer server to begin displaying pages. Each element of a requested page (including graphics, text, interactive items) is recorded by the Web site's server log file as a "hit."
Qualified hits	Exclude less important information recorded in a log file (such as error messages, etc.).

catalogues. As a result of the complex e-marketplace that must support existing business processes and systems, content is becoming even more critical for e-marketplaces. Buyers need good content description to make informed purchases, and sellers use content to properly market and differentiate themselves from the competition. Content and product description establish the common understanding between both parties to the transaction. As a result, the accessibility, usability, accuracy, and richness of that content directly affect the transaction. Figure 2.29 displays the different benefits and challenges of various e-marketplace revenue models.

FIGURE 2.27

E-Business Benefits

E-Business Benefits	
Highly Accessible	Businesses can operate 24 hours a day, 7 days a week, 365 days a year.
Increased Customer Loyalty	Additional channels to contact, respond to, and access customers helps contribute to customer loyalty.
Improved Information Content	In the past, customers had to order catalogues or travel to a physical facility before they could compare price and product attributes. Electronic catalogues and Web pages present customers with updated information in real-time about goods, services, and prices.
Increased Convenience	E-business automates and improves many of the activities that make up a buying experience.
Increased Global Reach	Business, both small and large, can reach new markets.
Decreased Cost	The cost of conducting business on the Internet is substantially smaller than traditional forms of business communication.

FIGURE 2.28

E-Business Challenges

E-Business Challenges	
Protecting Consumers	Consumers must be protected against unsolicited goods and communication, illegal or harmful goods, insufficient information about goods or their suppliers, invasion of privacy, and cyberfraud.
Leveraging Existing Systems	Most companies already use information technology to conduct business in non-Internet environments, such as marketing, order management, billing, inventory, distribution, and customer service. The Internet represents an alternative and complementary way to do business, but it is imperative that e-business systems integrate existing systems in a manner that avoids duplicating functionality and maintains usability, performance, and reliability.
Increasing Liability	E-business exposes suppliers to unknown liabilities because Internet commerce law is vaguely defined and differs from country to country. The Internet and its use in e-business have raised many ethical, social, and political issues, such as identity theft and information manipulation.
Providing Security	The Internet provides universal access, but companies must protect their assets against accidental or malicious misuse. System security, however, must not create prohibitive complexity or reduce flexibility. Customer information also needs to be protected from internal and external misuse. Privacy systems should safeguard the personal information critical to building sites that satisfy customer and business needs. A serious deficiency arises from the use of the Internet as a marketing means. Sixty percent of Internet users do not trust the Internet as a payment channel. Making purchases via the Internet is considered unsafe by many. This issue affects both the business and the consumer. However, with encryption and the development of secure Web sites, security is becoming less of a constraint for e-businesses.
Adhering to Taxation Rules	The Internet is not yet subject to the same level of taxation as traditional businesses. While taxation should not discourage consumers from using electronic purchasing channels, it should not favour Internet purchases over store purchases either. Instead, a tax policy should provide a level playing field for traditional retail businesses, mail-order companies, and Internet-based merchants. The Internet marketplace is rapidly expanding, yet it remains mostly free from traditional forms of taxation.

Revenue Models	Advantages	Limitation
Transaction fees	■ Can be directly tied to savings (both process and price savings) ■ Important revenue source when high level of liquidity (transaction volume) is reached	■ If process savings are not completely visible, use of the system is discouraged (incentive to move transactions offline) ■ Transaction fees likely to decrease with time
Licence fees	■ Creates incentives to do many transactions ■ Customization and back-end integration leads to lock-in of participants	■ Up front fee is a barrier to entry for participants ■ Price differentiation is complicated
Subscription fees	■ Creates incentives to do transactions ■ Price can be differentiated ■ Possibility to build additional revenue from new user groups	■ Fixed fee is a barrier to entry for participants
Fees for value-added services	■ Service offering can be differentiated ■ Price can be differentiated ■ Possibility to build additional revenue from established and new user groups (third parties)	■ Cumbersome process for customers to continually evaluate new services
Advertising fees	■ Well-targeted advertisements can be perceived as value-added content by trading participants ■ Easy to implement	■ Limited revenue potential ■ Overdone or poorly targeted advertisements can be disturbing elements on the Web site

NEW TRENDS IN E-BUSINESS: E-GOVERNMENT AND M-COMMERCE

Recent business models that have arisen to enable organizations to take advantage of the Internet and create value are within e-government. *E-government* involves the use of strategies and technologies to transform government(s) by improving the delivery of services and enhancing the quality of interaction between the citizen-consumer within all branches of government (refer to Figure 2.30).

One example of an e-government portal, www.canada.gc.ca, the official Canadian gateway to all federal government information, is the catalyst for a growing electronic government. Its powerful search engine and ever-growing collection of topical and customer-focused links connect citizens and businesses, as well as visitors and people immigrating to Canada, to millions of Web pages from the federal government. Figure 2.31 highlights specific e-government models.

M-Commerce

In a few years, Internet-enabled mobile devices will outnumber PCs. *Mobile commerce*, or *m-commerce*, is the ability to purchase goods and services through a wireless Internet-enabled device. The emerging technology behind m-commerce is a mobile device equipped with a Web-ready micro-browser. To take advantage of the m-commerce market potential, handset manufacturers Nokia, Ericsson, Motorola, and Qualcomm are working with telecommunication carriers AT&T Wireless and Sprint to develop smartphones. Using new forms of technology, smartphones offer fax, e-mail, and phone capabilities all in one, paving the way for m-commerce to be accepted by an increasingly mobile workforce. Figure 2.32 gives a visual overview of m-commerce.

FIGURE 2.30

Extended E-Business Models

	Business	Consumer	Government
Business	B2B canbiotech.com	B2C canadiantire.ca	B2G lockheedmartin.com
Consumer	C2B priceline.com	C2C ebay.ca	C2G hamiltoncatch.org
Government	G2B canadabusiness.gc.ca	G2C servicecanada.gc.ca	G2G aupe.org

FIGURE 2.31

E-Government Models

E-Government Models	
Consumer-to-government (C2G)	C2G mainly constitutes the areas where a consumer (or citizen) interacts with the government. It includes community spaces where people themselves can post information and opinions about government and talk to politicians and government decision-makers directly.
Government-to-business (G2B)	This model includes all government interaction with business enterprises whether it is procurement of goods and services from suppliers or information regarding legal and business issues that is transmitted electronically.
Government-to-consumer (G2C)	Governments around the world are now dealing with consumers (or citizens) electronically, providing them with updated information. Governments are also processing applications for visas, renewal of passports and driver's licences, advertising of tender notices, and other services online.
Government-to-government (G2G)	Governments around the world are now dealing with other governments electronically. Still at an inception stage, this e-business model will enhance international trade and information retrieval, for example, on criminal records of new migrants. At the provincial level, information exchange and processing of transactions online will enable enhanced efficiencies.

Amazon.com has collaborated with Nokia to pioneer a new territory. With the launch of its Amazon.com Anywhere service, it has become one of the first major online retailers to recognize and do something about the potential of Internet-enabled wireless devices. As content delivery over wireless devices becomes faster, more secure, and scalable, m-commerce will surpass landline e-business (traditional telephony) as the method of choice for digital commerce transactions. According to the research firm Strategy Analytics, the global m-commerce market was expected to be worth more than $200 billion by 2005, with some 350 million customers generating almost 14 billion transactions annually. Additionally, information activities like e-mail, news, and stock quotes will progress to personalized transactions, "one-click" travel reservations, online auctions, and video-conferencing.[35]

FIGURE 2.32

M-Commerce Technology Overview

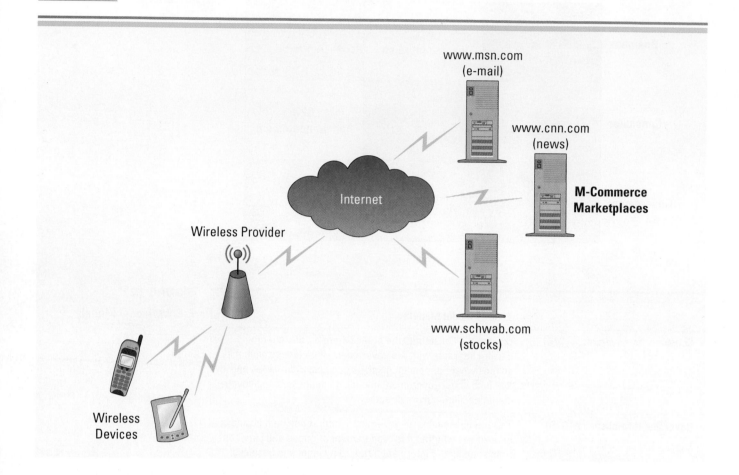

Organizations face changes more extensive and far reaching in their implications than anything since the modern industrial revolution occurred in the early 1900s. Technology is a primary force driving these changes. Organizations that want to survive must recognize the immense power of technology, carry out required organizational changes in the face of it, and learn to operate in an entirely different way.

OPENING CASE QUESTIONS

Amazon.com—Not Your Average Bookstore

5. What is Amazon's e-business model?

6. How can Amazon use m-commerce to influence its business?

7. Which metrics could Amazon use to assess the efficiency and effectiveness of Amazon's Web site?

8. What are some of the business challenges facing Amazon?

The purpose of this chapter was to provide you with an overview of doing business on the Internet. The following key themes were covered:

- Web-based technologies have revolutionized the way organizations conduct business today.

- Internet technologies have not only improved (and sometimes replaced) traditional ways of doing business, but also have introduced new business opportunities and ventures.

By providing this overview, you should now have a better understanding of:

- the benefits and challenges afforded by the Internet channel,

- recent trends that have and are occurring in the marketplace, and

- the various strategies and models organizations use to deploy electronic business.

Armed with this knowledge, you, the business student, should be better prepared to place the material presented in the remainder of this textbook in context of the larger e-business picture.

KEY TERMS

Application service provider (ASP) 43
Associate program (affiliate program) 49
Blog 49
Brick-and-mortar business 46
Business-to-business (B2B) 44
Business-to-consumer (B2C) 46
Clickstream data 54
Click-and-mortar business 46
Click-through 54
Consumer-to-business (C2B) 47
Consumer-to-consumer (C2C) 47
Cookie 54
Digital Darwinism 34
Digital divide 38
Digital wallet 50
Disruptive technology 34
E-business 34
E-business model 44
E-commerce 44
E-government 58
Electronic bill presentment and payment (EBPP) 50
Electronic catalogue 51
Electronic cheque 50

Electronic data interchange (EDI) 50
Electronic marketplace (e-marketplace) 44
E-mall 46
Encryption 52
E-procurement 51
E-shop (e-store, e-tailer) 46
Extranet 40
Financial cybermediary 50
Financial EDI (financial electronic data interchange) 50
Hypertext transport protocol (HTTP) 38
Information reach 39
Information richness 39
Interactivity 54
Intermediary 53
Internet 37
Internet service provider (ISP) 41
Intranet 40
Kiosk 41
Maintenance, repair, and operation (MRO) material (indirect material) 50
Mass customization 49
Mobile commerce, or m-commerce 58

Online ad (banner ad) 49
Online service provider (OSP) 43
Personalization 49
Podcasting 49
Pop-under ad 49
Pop-up ad 49
Portal 40
Protocol 37
Pure-play (virtual) business 46
Real simple syndication (RSS) 49
Reintermediation 53
Search engine optimization (SEO) 49
Secure electronic transaction (SET) 52
Secure socket layer (SSL) 52
Service level agreement (SLA) 43
Spamdexing 49
Sustaining technology 34
Value-added network (VAN) 50
Viral marketing 49
Wireless Internet service provider (WISP) 42
World Wide Web (WWW) 38

eBay—The Ultimate E-Business

This case illustrates how Web-based technologies have revolutionized the way organizations conduct business.

Pierre Omidyar was just 28 when he sat down over a long holiday weekend to write the original computer code for what eventually became an Internet super brand—the auction site eBay. Omidyar viewed auctions as a fair mechanism for Internet commerce where sellers could set their minimum prices, and buyers could then determine an item's market value by bidding up to what they were willingly to pay. A novel feedback system could allow buyers and sellers to rate each other, helping minimize fraud by enabling the community to police itself. "I really wanted to give the individual the power to be a producer as well. It was letting the users take responsibility for building the community," Omidyar would later explain.

The site launched on Labour Day, September 4, 1995, under the title of Auction Web, soon to be renamed after the site's domain name—ebay.com (a shortening of Echo Bay, Omidyar's consulting firm). The service was free at first, but started charging to cover Internet service provider costs.

A National Marketplace

Omidyar's auction Web site, eBay.com, took off. It provided something novel that its users craved: an efficient national marketplace with a strong community built on fairness and trust. A photography student looking for a used camera could choose from models across the nation and trust the timely delivery of the product. The owner of a vintage clothing store could sell to collectors nationwide. The community would expose a deceptive or fraudulent user and ban them from the marketplace.

Entrepreneurs in record numbers began setting up shop on eBay. According to a survey conducted for eBay by ACNielsen International Research, in 2005 more than 724,000 people supported themselves by selling items on eBay, up from 75,000 in 2002. In addition to these professional eBay sellers, another 1.5 million individuals supplement their income by selling on eBay. In the first six months of 2005, Americans sold merchandise worth about US$10.6 billion through eBay.

The stock market value of Omidyar's innovative company grew to US$2 billion in just three years, and his site's staying power as an economic engine was evident. Jeffrey Skoll, a Stanford MBA, joined the company in 1996 after the site was already profitable. In March 1998, Meg Whitman took over as president and CEO. In September 1998, eBay launched a successful public offering, making both Omidyar and Skoll billionaires—three years after Omidyar created eBay. As of 2005, Omidyar's 214 million eBay shares were worth about US$8 billion.

Collaborating with eBay

This e-business is collaborating with marketplace, payment, and communication companies that add value for its customers.

Marketplace—The U.S. Postal Service

People who sell items on eBay all have one thing in common: They need to ship their goods to their customers. To support this growing economic force, eBay and the U.S. Postal Service created an innovative economic and educational opportunity.

The U.S. Postal Service's bread and butter—first-class mail—is beset by rising costs and falling use. E-mail and faxes have reduced the amount of mail sent each day, but the Postal Service still bears the cost of delivering to every business and home, six days a week. Package shipping, however, remains a profitable and booming business, as evidenced by the number and earnings of private shippers in the market.

The Postal Service offers free boxes and heavy-duty envelopes for shippers using overnight or priority mail. To make it easier for those in the vanguard of the new, digital economy, the Postal Service will pick up shipments from the sender, and its Web site sells mailing labels with postage included that can be printed out from a home computer. Over 20 million shipping labels with postage were printed via the eBay/Postal Service link in 2005. Customers can also link to the United Parcel Service site, but eBay does not have a formal relationship with Federal Express.

Payment—PayPal

Founded in 1998, PayPal, an eBay company, enables any individual or business with an e-mail address to securely, easily, and quickly send and receive payments online. PayPal's service builds on the existing financial infrastructure of bank accounts and credit cards and utilizes the world's most advanced proprietary fraud prevention systems to create a safe, global, real-time payment solution.

PayPal has quickly become a global leader in online payment solutions with 96 million account members worldwide. Buyers and sellers on eBay, online retailers, online businesses, as well as traditional off-line businesses are transacting with PayPal, available in 55 countries.

Communication—Skype

Skype, a global Internet communications company, allows people everywhere to make free, unlimited, superior quality voice calls via its innovative peer-to-peer software. Since its launch in August 2003, Skype has been downloaded more than 163 million times in 225 countries and territories. Fifty-four million people are registered to use Skype's free services, with over 3 million simultaneous users on the network at any one time. Skype adds about 150,000 users a day.

In September 2005, eBay acquired Skype for approximately US$2.6 billion, anticipating that Skype will streamline and improve communications between buyers and sellers as it is integrated into the eBay marketplace. Buyers will gain an easy way to talk to sellers quickly and get the information they need, and sellers can more easily build relationships. The auction company hopes the acquisition will strengthen its global marketplace and payments platform, while opening several new lines of business and creating significant new opportunities for the company.

Unforeseen Dangers of Collaboration

"Communications is at the heart of e-commerce and community," said Meg Whitman. "By combining the two leading e-commerce franchises, eBay and PayPal, with the leader in Internet voice communications, Skype, we will create an extraordinarily powerful environment for business on the Net."

In October 2005, one month after eBay's acquisition of Skype, a press release discussed two critical flaws in Skype's software, one of which could allow malicious hackers to take control of compromised systems and another that could allow attackers to crash the client software. While fixes for the issues were being addressed, businesses asked their users to refrain from using voice services based on proprietary protocols like Skype while on corporate networks because of network security issues. Perhaps Skype might not be the collaborative tool of choice for eBay.[36]

Questions

1. eBay is one of the only major Internet "pure plays" to consistently make a profit from its inception. What is eBay's e-business model and why has it been so successful?

2. Other major Web sites, like Amazon.com and Yahoo!, have entered the e-marketplace with far less success than eBay. How has eBay been able to maintain its dominant position?

3. eBay has long been an e-marketplace for used goods and collectibles. Today, it is increasingly a place where major businesses come to auction their wares. Why would a brand name vendor set up shop on eBay?

4. What are the three different types of online auctions and which one is eBay using?

5. What are the different forms of online payment methods for consumers and business? How might eBay's customer benefit from the different payment methods?

6. Which metrics would you use if you were hired to assess the efficiency and effectiveness of eBay's Web site?

CLOSING CASE TWO

Hamilton's GIS-Enhanced Web Site

This case shows how Web technologies can improve the traditional way of doing business.

The City of Hamilton, Ontario, utilizes a GIS or "geographic information system" in almost every one of its departments for sewer, water, and road projects; urban and regional planning; emergency planning preparedness and dispatch; economic development; taxation; municipal elections; and even tracking of public health risks such as the West Nile Virus. A GIS contains a computer database that stores both digital mapping and descriptive text information about geographic features. Public uses of this GIS is through a Web site (www.map. hamilton.ca). The Web site allows the public to do a variety of tasks, such as locating municipal services, verifying the location of a particular address, viewing aerial photos for land use, measuring distances and areas, investigating tax and other property information, etc. For example, the Web site can be used by parents to locate child care centre information within the City of Hamilton (see Figure 2.33). Businesses can use this site to show customers where they are and what other services are in close proximity. Developers around the world can utilize the information at www.map.hamilton.ca to assist in finding appropriate development opportunities.[37]

Hamilton's GIS-enhanced Web site renders more that 78,000 maps per month. To accomplish this task without the aid of a Web site would be a large drain on human resources and time by city staffers. The Web site thus provides a great cost savings to the city as literally thousands of citizens can access the maps they need at their convenience. The strategic

FIGURE 2.33

Finding Child Care Centre Information on map.hamilton.ca

goals in providing citizens with these maps and associated services (e.g., giving citizens access to thematic maps of property taxes showing tax impacts and reassessments along with tools for looking up assessment values and taxes payable) are to spend money more wisely and to use technology to improve business processes. The City of Hamilton's GIS solutions are doing just that by improving customer service, aiding economic development, and helping staff members work in a more efficient manner. For example, the maps are a convenient way for staff and constituents to communicate and collaborate on issues—when solving problems over the phone or online, city staffers and citizens can be looking at the same map or picture on the Web. Plans for future map-based Web services include "Where's my bus?", "Where's my snow plow?", and tools for finding a given location such as the closest library, park, or other municipal service.[38]

The use of a GIS-enhanced Web site is part and parcel of the City of Hamilton's vision to provide citizens, tourists, and potential businesses and individuals looking to relocate to Hamilton, a super site (www.myhamilton.ca). Uniquely, myhamilton integrates the Web sites of the municipal government, the public library and several community databases and content areas. Through myhamilton, the City of Hamilton and its partners are benefiting from a shared content management and collaboration infrastructure while providing citizens with one place to look for local information. The success of myhamilton has been based on the ability of several community partners to come together, develop a shared vision, and then work collaboratively to achieve that vision. The site was launched in September 2005. Now that the site is "live," effort is now being directed toward engaging new partners to ensure there is an even broader range of community participation in the site. Key features and functions include integrated municipal and library services, personalization and single sign-on for secure transactions, comprehensive events listings, and extensive search capabilities. Also included are collaboration spaces and tools including surveys, discussion forums and document sharing, as well as Web casting capabilities.[39]

Questions

1. How is technology being used by the City of Hamilton to support its strategic goals and improve business processes?
2. What barriers likely exist in rolling out these technologies and securing their successful use and adoption?
3. How can the City of Hamilton leverage its GIS functionality for m-commerce?
4. What performance metrics should the City of Hamilton collect to assess the viability and robustness of its maps Web site (map.hamilton.ca)? Its super site (myhamilton.ca)?
5. What problems likely result in building a single community Web site that integrates the Web sites of the municipal government, the public library, and several community databases and content areas?
6. In your opinion, is the City of Hamilton's super site an exemplar model for other municipal government sites to adopt? Why or why not?

CLOSING CASE THREE

How Do You Value Friendster?

This case illustrates how Internet technologies have introduced new business opportunities and ventures.

Jonathan Abrams is keeping quiet about how he is going to generate revenue from his Web site, Friendster, which specializes in social networking. Abrams is a 33-year-old

Canadian software developer whose experiences include being laid off by Netscape and then moving from one start-up to another. In 2002, Abrams was unemployed, not doing well financially, and certainly not looking to start another business when he developed the idea for Friendster. He quickly coded a working prototype and watched in amazement as his Web site took off.

The buzz around social networking start-ups has been on the rise. A number of high-end venture capital firms, including Sequoia and Mayfield, have invested more than $46 million into social networking start-ups such as LinkedIn, Spoke, and Tribe Networks. Friendster received over $15 million in venture capital from Kleiner, Perkins, Caufield, Byers, and Benchmark Capital, which reportedly valued the company at $62 million—a startling figure for a company that had yet to generate even a single dime in revenue.

A year after making its public debut, Friendster was one of the largest social networking Web sites, attracting over 5 million users and receiving more than 50,000 page views per day. The question is how do efficiency metrics, such as Web traffic and page views, turn into cash flow? Everyone is wondering how Friendster is going to begin generating revenue.

The majority of Abrams's competitors make their money by extracting fees from their subscribers. Friendster is going to continue to let its subscribers meet for free but plans to charge them for premium services such as the ability to customize their profile page. The company also has plans to extend beyond social networking to an array of value-added services such as friend-based job referrals and classmate searches. Abrams is also looking into using his high-traffic Web site to tap into the growing Internet advertising market.

Abrams does not appear concerned about generating revenue or about potential competition. "Match.com has been around eight years, has 12 million users, and has spent many millions of dollars on advertising to get them," he said. "We're a year old, we've spent zero dollars on advertising, and in a year or less, we'll be bigger than them—it's a given."

The future of Friendster is uncertain. Google offered to buy Friendster for $35 million even though there are signs, both statistical and anecdotal, that Friendster's popularity may have peaked.[40]

Questions

1. How could you use e-business metrics to place a value on Friendster?
2. Why would a venture capital company value Friendster at $62 million when the company has yet to generate any revenue?
3. Why would Google be interested in buying Friendster for $35 million when the company has yet to generate any revenue?
4. Identify Friendster's e-business model and explain how the company can generate revenue.
5. Explain the e-business benefits and challenges facing Friendster.

MAKING BUSINESS DECISIONS

1. Leveraging the competitive value of the Internet

Physical inventories have always been a major cost component of business. Linking to suppliers in real time dramatically enhances the classic goal of inventory "turn." The Internet provides a multitude of opportunities for radically reducing the costs of designing, manufacturing, and selling goods and services. E-mango.com, a fruit e-marketplace, must take advantage of these opportunities or find itself at a significant competitive disadvantage.

Identify the disadvantages that confront E-mango.com if it does not leverage the competitive value of the Internet.

2. Implementing an e-business model

The Genius is a revolutionary mountain bike with full-suspension and shock-adjustable forks that is being marketed via the Internet. The Genius needs an e-business solution that will easily enable internal staff to deliver fresh and relevant product information throughout its Web site. To support its large audience, the company also needs the ability to present information in multiple languages and serve over 1 million page views per month to visitors in North America and Europe. Explain what e-business model you would use to market The Genius on the Internet.

3. Assessing Internet capabilities

Sports Rentals is a small privately owned business that rents sports equipment in Calgary, Alberta. The company specializes in winter rentals including ski equipment, snowboarding equipment, and snowmobile equipment. The company has been in business for 20 years and, for the first time, it is experiencing a decline in rentals. The company's owner is puzzled by the recent decreases. The snowfall for the last two years has been outstanding, and the ski resorts have opened earlier and closed later than most previous years. Reports say tourism in Alberta is up, and the invention of loyalty programs has significantly increased the number of local skiers. Overall, business should be booming. The only reason for the decrease in sales might be the fact that big retailers such as Wal-Mart and SportChek are now renting winter sports equipment. The company's owner would like your team's help in determining how he can use the Internet to help his company increase sales and decrease costs to compete with these big retailers.

4. Online auction sites

You are working for a new Internet start-up company, eMart.com, an online marketplace for the sale of goods and services. The company offers a wide variety of features and services that enable online members to buy and sell their goods and services quickly and conveniently. The company's mission is to provide a global trading platform where anyone can trade practically anything. Suggest some ways that eMart.com can extend its market reach beyond that of its competitor, eBay.com.

5. Everybody needs an Internet strategy

An Internet strategy addresses the reasons businesses want to "go online." "Going online" because it seems like the right thing to do now or because everyone else is doing it is not a good enough reason. A business must decide how it will best utilize the Internet for its particular needs. It must plan for where it wants to go and how best the Internet can help shape that vision. Before developing a strategy a business should spend time on the Internet, see what similar businesses have grown, and what is most feasible, given a particular set of resources. Think of a new online business opportunity and answer the following questions:

1. Why do you want to put your business online?
2. What benefits will going online bring?
3. What effects will being connected to the Internet have on your staff, suppliers, and customers?

6. Analyzing Web Sites

Stars Inc. is a large clothing corporation that specializes in reselling clothes worn by celebrities. The company's four Web sites generate 75 percent of its sales. The remaining 25 percent of sales occur directly through the company's warehouse. You have recently been hired as the director of sales. The only information you can find on the success of the four Web sites follows:

Web Site	Classic	Contemporary	New Age	Traditional
Traffic analysis	5,000 hits/day	200 hits/day	10,000 hits/day	1,000 hits/day
Stickiness (average)	20 min.	1 hr.	20 min.	50 min.
Number of abandoned shopping carts	400/day	0/day	5,000/day	200/day
Number of unique visitors	2,000/day	100/day	8,000/day	200/day
Number of identified visitors	3,000/day	100/day	2,000/day	800/day
Average revenue per sale	$1,000	$1,000	$50	$1,300

You decide that maintaining four separate Web sites is expensive and adds little business value. You want to propose consolidating to one Web site. Create a report detailing the business value gained by consolidating to a single Web site, along with your recommendation for consolidation. Be sure to include your Web site profitability analysis.

Business Information Systems

Organizations utilize various types of information systems to help run their daily operations. These systems are primarily transactional systems that concentrate on the management and flow of low-level data items pertaining to basic business processes such as purchasing and order delivery. This data is often rolled-up and summarized into higher-level decision support systems to help firms understand what is happening in their organizations and how best to respond. In order to achieve seamless handling of this data, organizations must ensure that their business information systems are tightly integrated across the enterprise. Doing so allows organizations to manage and process basic business processes as efficiently and effectively as possible and to make better informed decisions.

The purpose of this section of the textbook is to highlight the various types of business information systems found in organizations and how they relate to one another. The chapters found within this section speak to various types of business information systems and their role in helping firms reach their strategic goals. Though each chapter is devoted to a specific type of business information system (e.g., those used for strategic decision making, supply chain management, customer relationship management, and enterprise resource planning), bear in mind that these systems must work in tandem with each other so that organizations will be better prepared to meet their strategic business goals and outperform their competitors.

3

CHAPTER

Strategic Decision Making

LEARNING OUTCOMES

3.1. Explain the difference between transactional information and analytical information. Be sure to provide an example of each.

3.2. Define TPS, DSS, and EIS and explain how an organization can use these systems to make decisions and gain competitive advantages.

3.3. Describe the three quantitative models typically used by decision support systems.

3.4. Describe the relationship between digital dashboards and executive information systems.

3.5. Identify the four types of artificial intelligence systems.

3.6. Describe the four basic components of supply chain management.

3.7. Explain customer relationship management and the benefits it can provide to an organization.

3.8. Define enterprise resource planning and explain its importance to an organization.

3.9. Identify how an organization can use business process reengineering to improve its business.

Why Do I Need To Know This ?

This chapter describes various types of business information systems found across the enterprise used to run basic business operations and used to facilitate sound and proper decision making. An overview is given first on decision-making information systems and then later on the various kinds of enterprise systems typically found in organizations.

As a business student, you need to know what types of information systems exist in an enterprise as a first step towards understanding how to utilize these systems to improve organizational performance. From this chapter, you will gain an appreciation for the various kinds of information systems employed by organizations and how they can be utilized to help organizations make strategically informed decisions.

Better yet, you will get a taste of the complexity and importance of integrating these various systems together. As a business student, you should recognize the importance of integrating various types of business information systems to help improve organizational decision making. This chapter should help pave the way.

Information Systems are Central at Grocery Gateway

Grocery Gateway is Canada's leader in online retailing of home and office delivered groceries. Founded by a group of entrepreneurs who had the idea that people had better things to do in life than grocery shop, Grocery Gateway started out with only a handful of employees and a couple of rental trucks. In 2004, Grocery Gateway was acquired by Longo Brothers Fruit Market Inc., a family-owned independent grocery business that has operated physical groceries stores since 1956.[1] Today, Grocery Gateway has successfully secured the business of literally over 100,000 registered customers throughout the Greater Toronto Area. Quite a bit of growth for a start-up company founded only in 1997 by a bunch of classmates and rugby mates in a basement of a house.

Like other online grocers, Grocery Gateway's strategy is all about the last mile of service. Online grocers sell groceries over the Internet and deliver them directly to the door. In this sense, groceries are used to initiate the customer relationship and create a pipeline to the home. The online grocer then leverages this pipeline to introduce complimentary products to the consumer.[2]

What is attractive to consumers is that the online grocery store is open 24 hours, 7 days a week, and that there is greater simplicity in clicking a mouse to get the food you want over that of trekking down to a physical store and pushing a grocery cart. Though prices are competitive with supermarkets, price is not the value proposition for the online grocery shopper. Rather, for the consumer, shopping online for groceries is a time-saver. Consumers —generally busy people with not enough time on their hands—are looking to find easier and quicker ways to do chores, like grocery shopping. Also, people who find it physically challenging to do grocery shopping (such as the elderly and the disabled), as well as those who choose not to own a car, find the service that Grocery Gateway provides to be quite beneficial.

Information Systems are the Heart of the Business

Online grocers realize the critical role information systems play in the health and viability of their electronic business. Technology is used to host a Web site that supports online merchandising, single item picking, home delivery operations, and customer service. For example, Grocery Gateway has built in several key features in its Web site to attract and retain its customers. This includes offering an online shopping demo, a getting-started tutorial, and e-mail customer support. Moreover, the Web site offers a full suite of electronic commerce functionality that allows consumers to browse or find grocery items, see pictures and descriptions of product items (including their price), and to select items in a shopping basket and to check out those items for delivery.[3] To work effectively, the various functions built into the Web site, such as item searching, grocery ordering, customer profiling, electronic payments, and delivery scheduling must be tightly integrated and coordinated with one another in order for the Web site to function as a cohesive whole.

Using Information Systems to Manage Logistics

A key information system utilized by online grocers is their underlying logistics management systems. For example, Grocery Gateway is well aware that what will make or break this company is the logistics of quick delivery. As such, the company has turned to Cube Route, an on-demand logistics management solutions provider, to optimize Grocery Gateway's selection of delivery routes. The goal is to maximize efficiency in route selection by incorporating historical delivery data with real-time information into route selection determination. Real-time data is achieved through a combination of sophisticated routing, tracking, planning, and dispatching functionality. The technology allows Grocery Gateway to guarantee its customers a specific 90-minute window of delivery of groceries to their doors. This 90-minute window is much narrower than other retail delivery operations.

Imagine the complexity of coordinating the delivery of groceries. With thousands of active customers, Grocery Gateway delivery trucks make roughly 500 stops to customer homes and offices per day. Cube Route's logistic management software ensures that these orders are delivered within the 90-minute window. To do so, the software needs to take into account unpredictable delays, such as traffic jams and road accidents, as well as last minute customer requests or cancellations. GPS-enabled mobile phones allow the logistics software to know the exact position and location of Grocery Gateway drivers to make the best decisions on routes for drivers to follow.

The use of Cube Route's software has improved the bottom line. Since deploying the Cube Route solution, Grocery Gateway has improved its on-time delivery performance by 14 percent and is exceeding its yearly stops per paid hour by 12.4 percent.[4]

The Effective Use of Information Systems Will Enable Online Grocers to Succeed

Online grocers face significant challenges. A recent electronic commerce research study suggests that the challenge for online grocery retailers is to convey the specific benefits of shopping online to the public and to offer potential customers more reasons to use the channel.[5] Of relevance, the study suggests that online grocery retailers should be looking to improve ordering processes and delivery mechanisms as means to secure a solid and repeating customer base. With Grocery Gateway's strategy to offer customers a fully-enabled electronic commerce interface and to utilize state-of-the art logistics management software, the company is taking the right steps to succeed.

Decision-making and problem-solving abilities are now the most sought-after traits in up-and-coming executives, according to a recent survey of 1,000 executives. To put it mildly, decision makers and problem solvers have limitless career potential.[6]

Decision making and problem solving in today's electronic world encompass large-scale, opportunity-oriented, strategically focused solutions. The traditional "cookbook" approach to decision making simply will not work. This chapter focuses on technology to help make decisions, solve problems, and find new innovative opportunities. The chapter also highlights how to bring people together with the best IT processes and tools in complete, flexible solutions that can seize business opportunities and combat business challenges (see Figure 3.1).

DECISION MAKING

What is the value of information? The answer to this important question varies. Karsten Solheim would say the value of information is its ability to lower a company's handicap. Solheim, an avid golfer, invented a putter, one with a "ping," that led to a successful golf equipment company and the PING golf clubs. PING Inc., a privately held corporation, was the first to offer customizable golf clubs. The company prides itself on being a just-in-time manufacturer that depends on flexible information systems to make informed production decisions. PING's production systems scan large amounts of information and pull orders that meet certain criteria such as order date (this week), order priority (high), and customer type (Gold). PING then manufactures the appropriate products,

FIGURE 3.1

Examples of Decision-Making Systems

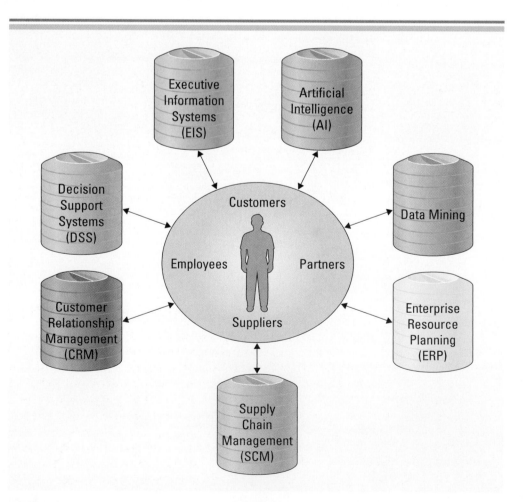

allowing it to carry less than 5 percent of inventory in its warehouse. PING depends on its flexible information systems for production decision support and thanks information technology for the explosion of its business over the past decade.[7]

Business is accelerating at a breakneck pace. The more information a business acquires, the more difficult it becomes to make decisions. The amount of information people must understand to make good decisions is growing exponentially. In the past, people could rely on manual processes to make decisions because they had limited amounts of information to process. Today, with massive volumes of available information it is almost impossible for people to make decisions without the aid of information systems. Highly complex decisions—involving far more information than the human brain can comprehend—must be made in increasingly shorter time frames. Figure 3.2 highlights the primary reasons dependence on information systems to make decisions is growing and will continue to grow.

A *model* is a simplified representation or abstraction of reality. Models can calculate risks, understand uncertainty, change variables, and manipulate time. Decision-making information systems work by building models out of organizational information to lend insight into important business issues and opportunities. Figure 3.3 displays three common types of decision-making information systems used in organizations today—transaction processing systems, decision support systems, and executive information systems. Each system uses different models to assist in decision making, problem solving, and opportunity capturing.

Though each system uses different models, it is important to understand that these various decision-making information systems need to be tightly integrated

Reasons for Growth of Decision-Making Information Systems
1. **People need to analyze large amounts of information**—Improvements in technology itself, innovations in communication, and globalization have resulted in a dramatic increase in the alternatives and dimensions people need to consider when making a decision or appraising an opportunity.
2. **People must make decisions quickly**—Time is of the essence and people simply do not have time to sift through all the information manually.
3. **People must apply sophisticated analysis techniques, such as modelling and forecasting, to make good decisions**—Information systems substantially reduce the time required to perform these sophisticated analysis techniques.
4. **People must protect the corporate asset of organizational information**—Information systems offer the security required to ensure organizational information remains safe.

FIGURE 3.2

Primary Reasons for Growth of Decision-Making Information Systems

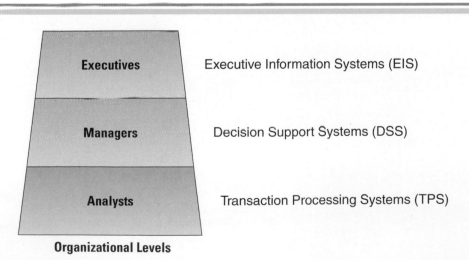

FIGURE 3.3

IT Systems in an Enterprise

Executives — Executive Information Systems (EIS)

Managers — Decision Support Systems (DSS)

Analysts — Transaction Processing Systems (TPS)

Organizational Levels

in order for proper and sound decision making to occur and that the underlying data found in transaction processing systems must be accurate and reliable in order for higher-level decision-making systems to be effective. The reason for this is that data stored in lower-level transaction processing systems are often used to source the information contained in higher-level decision-making systems. Thus, it is imperative that transactional data is accurate and reliable, and that the information in these systems is consistent across the enterprise. Otherwise, the information used from these systems by higher-end executive and decision-making systems will be in error, potentially leading to misguided decisions by management. This could steer the organization off-course in reaching its strategic goals and objectives—not a position any firm wants to be in.

TRANSACTION PROCESSING SYSTEMS

Transactional information encompasses all of the information contained within a single business process or unit of work, and its primary purpose is to support the performing of daily operational tasks. Examples of transactional information include purchasing stocks, making an airline reservation, or withdrawing cash from an ATM. Organizations use transactional information when performing operational tasks and repetitive decisions such as analyzing daily sales reports to determine how much inventory to carry.

Analytical information encompasses all organizational information, and its primary purpose is to support the performing of managerial analysis tasks. Analytical information includes transactional information along with other information such as market and industry information. Examples of analytical information include trends, sales, product statistics, and future growth projections. Managers use analytical information when making important ad hoc decisions such as whether the organization should build a new manufacturing plant or hire additional sales personnel.

The structure of a typical organization is similar to a pyramid. Organizational activities occur at different levels of the pyramid. People in the organization have unique information needs and thus require various sets of IT tools (see Figure 3.4). At the lower levels of the pyramid, people perform daily tasks such as processing transactions. ***Online transaction processing (OLTP)*** is the capturing of transaction and event information using technology to (1) process the information according to defined business rules, (2) store the information, and (3) update existing information to reflect the new information. During OLTP, the organization must capture every detail of transactions and events. A ***transaction processing system (TPS)*** is the basic business system that serves the operational level (analysts) in an organization. The most common example of a TPS is an operational accounting system such as a payroll system or an order-entry system.

FIGURE 3.4

Enterprise View of Information and Information Technology

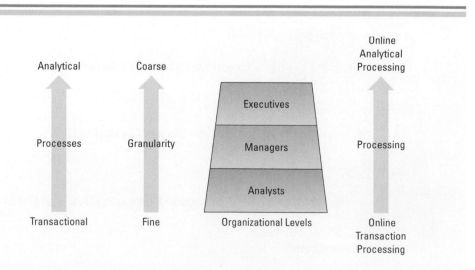

Moving up through the organizational pyramid, people (typically managers) deal less with the details ("finer" information) and more with meaningful aggregations of information ("coarser" information) that help them make broader decisions for the organization. (Granularity means fine and detailed or "coarse" and abstract information.) **Online analytical processing (OLAP)** is the manipulation of information to create business intelligence in support of strategic decision making. **Business intelligence** is a broad, general term describing information that people use to support their decision-making efforts.

DECISION SUPPORT SYSTEMS

At limousine and transportation company BostonCoach, managers must dispatch fleets of hundreds of vehicles as efficiently as possible. BostonCoach requires a real-time dispatching system that considers inventory, customer needs, and soft dimensions such as weather and traffic. Researchers at IBM's Thomas J. Watson Research Center built BostonCoach a mathematical algorithm for a custom dispatch system that combines information about weather, traffic conditions, driver locations, and customer pickup requests and determines which cars to assign to which customers. The system is so efficient that, after launching it, BostonCoach experienced a 20-percent increase in revenues.[8]

A **decision support system (DSS)**, such as BostonCoach's, models information to support managers and business professionals during the decision-making process. Three quantitative models often used by DSS include:

1. **Sensitivity analysis** is the study of the impact that changes in one (or more) parts of the model have on other parts of the model. Users change the value of one variable repeatedly and observe the resulting changes in other variables.

2. **What-if analysis** checks the impact of a change in an assumption on the proposed solution. For example, "What will happen to the supply chain if a blizzard in Alberta reduces holding inventory from 30 percent to 10 percent?" Users repeat this analysis until they understand all the effects of various situations. Figure 3.5

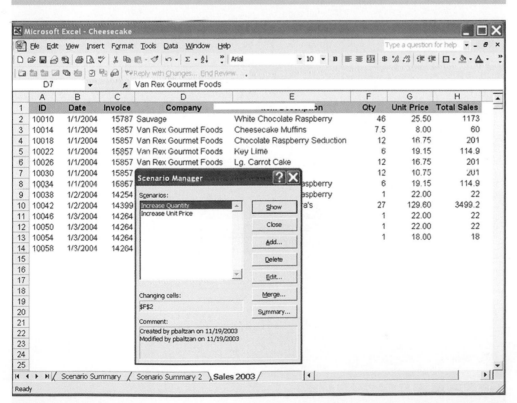

FIGURE 3.5

Example of What-If Analysis in Microsoft Excel

displays an example of what-if analysis using Microsoft Excel. The tool is calculating the net effect of a 20-percent increase in sales on the company's bottom line.

3. **Goal-seeking analysis** finds the inputs necessary to achieve a goal such as a desired level of output. Instead of observing how changes in a variable affect other variables as in what-if analysis, goal-seeking analysis sets a target value (a goal) for a variable and then repeatedly changes other variables until the target value is achieved. For example, "How many customers are required to purchase a new product to increase gross profits to $5 million?" Figure 3.6 displays a goal-seeking scenario using Microsoft Excel. The model is seeking the monthly mortgage payment needed to pay off the remaining balance in 130 months.

One national insurance company uses DSSs to analyze the amount of risk the company is undertaking when it insures drivers who have a history of driving under the influence of alcohol. The DSS discovered that only 3 percent of married male homeowners in their forties received more than one DUI. The company decided to lower rates for customers falling into this category, which increased its revenue while mitigating its risk.[9]

Figure 3.7 displays how a TPS is used within a DSS. The TPS supplies transaction-based data to the DSS. The DSS summarizes and aggregates the information from the many different TPS systems, which assists managers in making informed decisions. Canadian Pacific Railway uses a DSS to analyze the movement of all its railcars and to track shipments against delivery commitments. Without this tool, the job of integrating and analyzing transaction-based data would be a difficult task.[10]

EXECUTIVE INFORMATION SYSTEMS

An **executive information system (EIS)** is a specialized DSS that supports senior-level executives within the organization. An EIS differs from a DSS because an EIS typically contains data from external sources as well as data from internal sources (see Figure 3.8).

FIGURE 3.6

Example of Goal-Seeking
Analysis in Microsoft Excel

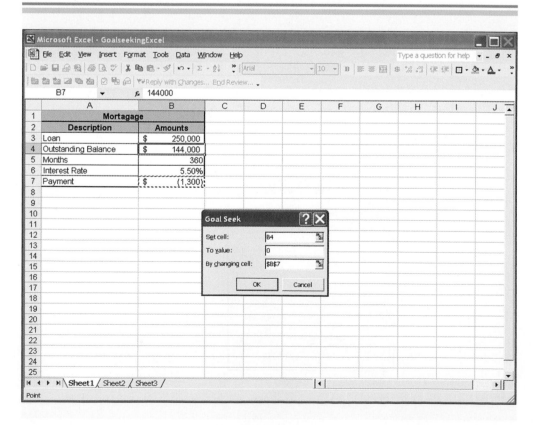

FIGURE 3.7

Interaction Between TPSs and DSSs

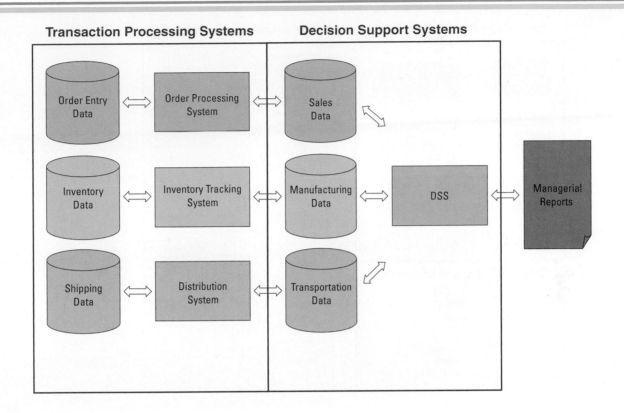

Consolidation, drill-down, and slice-and-dice are a few of the capabilities offered in most EISs.

■ **Consolidation** involves the aggregation of information and features simple roll-ups to complex groupings of interrelated information. Many organizations track financial information at a regional level and then consolidate the information at a single global level.

■ **Drill-down** enables users to view details, and details of details, of information. Viewing monthly, weekly, daily, or even hourly information represents drill-down capability.

■ **Slice-and-dice** is the ability to look at information from different perspectives. One slice of information could display all product sales during a given promotion. Another slice could display a single product's sales for all promotions.

Digital Dashboards

A common feature of an EIS is a digital dashboard. **Digital dashboards** integrate information from multiple components and tailor the information to individual preferences. Digital dashboards commonly use indicators to help executives quickly identify the status of key information or critical success factors. Following is a list of features included in a dashboard designed for a senior executive of an oil refinery:

■ A hot list of key performance indicators, refreshed every 15 minutes.

■ A running line graph of planned versus actual production for the past 24 hours.

■ A table showing actual versus forecasted product prices and inventories.

■ A list of outstanding alerts and their resolution status.

FIGURE 3.8

Interaction Between TPSs and EISs

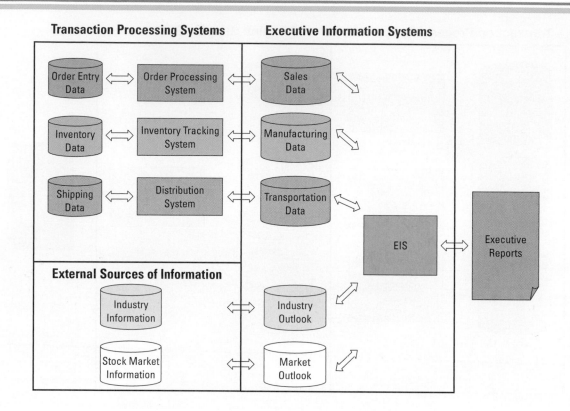

- A graph of crude-oil stock market prices.
- A scroll of headline news from Petroleum Company news, an industry news service.

Digital dashboards, whether basic or comprehensive, deliver results quickly. As digital dashboards become easier to use, more executives can perform their own analysis without inundating IT personnel with questions and requests for reports. According to an independent study by Nucleus Research, there is a direct correlation between use of digital dashboards and companies' return on investment (ROI). Figure 3.9 and Figure 3.10 display two different digital dashboards from Visual Mining.

EIS systems, such as digital dashboards, allow executives to move beyond reporting to using information to directly impact business performance. Digital dashboards help executives react to information as it becomes available and make decisions, solve problems, and change strategies daily instead of monthly.

Verizon Communications CIO Shaygan Kheradpir tracks 100-plus major IT systems on a single screen called "The Wall of Shaygan." Every 15 seconds, a new set of charts communicating Verizon's performance flashes onto a giant LCD screen in Kheradpir's office. The 44 screen shots cycle continuously, all day long, every day. The dashboard includes more than 300 measures of business performance that fall into one of three categories:

1. **Market pulse**—examples include daily sales numbers, market share, and subscriber turnover.
2. **Customer service**—examples include problems resolved on the first call, call center wait times, and on-time repair calls.
3. **Cost driver**—examples include number of repair trucks in the field, repair jobs completed per day, and call centre productivity.

FIGURE 3.9

Visual Mining NetCharts Corporate Financial Dashboard

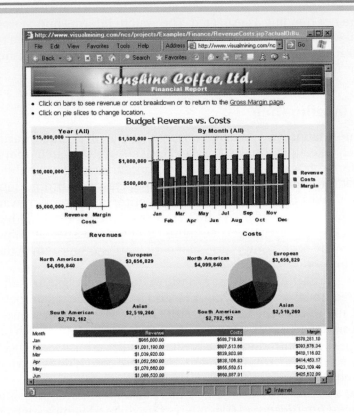

FIGURE 3.10

Visual Mining Sales Executive Dashboard

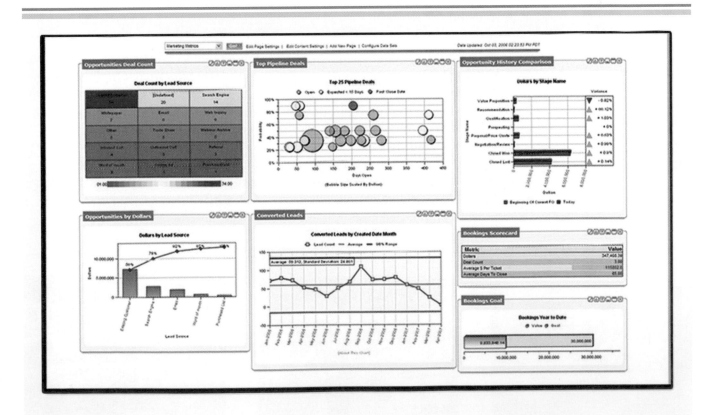

Kheradpir has memorized the screens and can tell at a glance when the lines on the charts are not trending as expected. The system informs him of events such as the percentage of customer calls resolved by voice systems, number of repair trucks in the field, and amount of time to resolve an IT system issue. The dashboard works the same way for 400 managers at every level of Verizon.[11]

Artificial Intelligence

Executive information systems are starting to take advantage of artificial intelligence to help executives make strategic decisions. RivalWatch offers a strategic business information service using artificial intelligence that enables organizations to track the product offerings, pricing policies, and promotions of online competitors. Clients can determine the competitors they want to watch and the specific information they wish to gather, ranging from products added, removed, or out of stock to price changes, coupons offered, and special shipping terms. Clients can check each competitor, category, and product either daily, weekly, monthly, or quarterly.

"Competing in the Internet arena is a whole different ballgame than doing business in the traditional brick-and-mortar world because you're competing with the whole world rather than the store down the block or a few miles away," said Phil Lumish, vice president of sales and marketing at RivalWatch.com. "With new products and campaigns being introduced at a breakneck pace, e-businesses need new tools to monitor the competitive environment, and our service is designed specifically to meet that need."[12]

Intelligent systems are various commercial applications of artificial intelligence. ***Artificial intelligence (AI)*** simulates human intelligence such as the ability to reason and learn. AI systems can learn or understand from experience, make sense of ambiguous or contradictory information, and even use reasoning to solve problems and make decisions effectively. AI systems can perform such tasks as boosting productivity in factories by monitoring equipment and signalling when preventive maintenance is required. The ultimate goal of AI is the ability to build a system that can mimic human intelligence. AI systems are beginning to show up everywhere:

- At Manchester Airport in England, the Hefner AI Robot Cleaner alerts passengers to security and nonsmoking rules while it scrubs up to 65,600 square feet of floor per day. Laser scanners and ultrasonic detectors keep it from colliding with passengers.

- Shell Oil's SmartPump keeps drivers in their cars on cold, wet winter days. It can service any automobile built after 1987 that has been fitted with a special gas cap and a windshield-mounted transponder that tells the robot where to insert the pump.

- Matsushita's courier robot navigates hospital hallways, delivering patient files, X-ray films, and medical supplies.

Examples of AI Systems

- The FireFighter AI Robot can extinguish flames at chemical plants and nuclear reactors with water, foam, powder, or inert gas. The robot puts distance between the human operator and the fire.[13]

AI systems dramatically increase the speed and consistency of decision making, solve problems with incomplete information, and resolve complicated issues that cannot be solved by conventional computing. There are many categories of AI systems; four of the most familiar are: (1) expert systems, (2) neural networks, (3) genetic algorithms, and (4) intelligent agents.

Expert Systems   *Expert systems* are computerized advisory programs that imitate the reasoning processes of experts in solving difficult problems. Human expertise is transferred to the expert system, and users can access the expert system for specific advice. Most expert systems reflect expertise from many humans and can therefore perform better analysis than any single expert. Typically, the system includes a knowledge base containing various accumulated experience and a set of rules for applying the knowledge base to each particular situation. The best-known expert systems play chess and assist in medical diagnosis. Expert systems are the most commonly used form of AI in the business arena because they fill the gap when human experts are difficult to find, retain, or too expensive.

Neural Networks   A *neural network*, also called an *artificial neural network*, is a category of AI that attempts to emulate the way the human brain works. The types of decisions for which neural networks are most useful are those that involve pattern or image recognition because a neural network can learn from the information it processes. Neural networks analyze large quantities of information to establish patterns and characteristics in situations where the logic or rules are unknown.

The finance industry is a veteran in neural network technology and has been relying on various forms of it for over two decades. The industry uses neural networks to review loan applications and create patterns or profiles of applications that fall into two categories: approved or denied. Other industries are following suit. For example, one neural network is being used by physicians at the Children's Hospital of Eastern Ontario to help keep watch over the progress of newborns. The hospital in collaboration with Carleton University has spent more than a decade developing a machine-intelligent system that can scour through reams of data looking for patterns. In this instance, vital signs and other medical information from babies are digitally recorded every few seconds and housed in one of the most complex medical databases in the country. Vital sign data from newborns with particular heart defects, body weights, and blood-pressures are analyzed by the neutral network to help predict valid patient outcomes in a reliable manner.[14]

Fuzzy logic is a mathematical method of handling imprecise or subjective information. The basic approach is to assign values between 0 and 1 to vague or ambiguous information. The higher the value, the closer it is to 1. The value zero is used to represent nonmembership, and the value one is used to represent membership. For example, fuzzy logic is used in washing machines that determine by themselves how much water to use or how long to wash (they continue washing until the water is clean). In accounting and finance, fuzzy logic allows people to analyze information with subjective financial values (intangibles such as goodwill) that are very important considerations in economic analysis. Fuzzy logic and neural networks are often combined to express complicated and subjective concepts in a form that makes it possible to simplify the problem and apply rules that are executed with a level of certainty.

Genetic Algorithms   A *genetic algorithm* is an artificial intelligence system that mimics the evolutionary, survival-of-the-fittest process to generate increasingly better solutions to a problem. A genetic algorithm is essentially an optimizing system: It finds the combination of inputs that gives the best outputs.

Genetic algorithms are best suited to decision-making environments in which thousands, or perhaps millions, of solutions are possible. Genetic algorithms can find and evaluate solutions with many more possibilities, faster and more thoroughly than a human. Organizations face decision-making environments for all types of problems that require optimization techniques such as the following:

■ Business executives use genetic algorithms to help them decide which combination of projects a firm should invest in, taking complicated tax considerations into account.

■ Investment companies use genetic algorithms to help in trading decisions.

■ Telecommunication companies use genetic algorithms to determine the optimal configuration of fibre-optic cable in a network that may include as many as 100,000 connection points. The genetic algorithm evaluates millions of cable configurations and selects the one that uses the least amount of cable.[15]

Intelligent Agents An *intelligent agent* is a special-purpose knowledge-based information system that accomplishes specific tasks on behalf of its users. Intelligent agents use their knowledge base to make decisions and accomplish tasks in a way that fulfills the intentions of a user. Intelligent agents usually have a graphical representation such as "Sherlock Holmes" for an information search agent.

One of the simplest examples of an intelligent agent is a shopping bot. A *shopping bot* is software that will search several retailer Web sites and provide a comparison of each retailer's offerings including price and availability. Increasingly, intelligent agents handle the majority of a company's Internet buying and selling and handle such processes as finding products, bargaining over prices, and executing transactions. Intelligent agents also have the capability to handle all supply chain buying and selling.

Another application for intelligent agents is in environmental scanning and competitive intelligence. For instance, an intelligent agent can learn the types of competitor information users want to track, continuously scan the Web for it, and alert users when a significant event occurs.

By 2010, some 4 million AI robots are expected to populate homes and businesses, performing everything from pumping gas to delivering mail. According to a new report by the United Nations and the International Federation of Robotics, more than half the AI robots will be toys and the other half will perform services. Bots will deactivate bombs, clean skyscraper windows, and vacuum homes.[16]

Data Mining

Wal-Mart consolidates point-of-sale details from its 3,000 stores and uses AI to transform the information into business intelligence. Data-mining systems sift instantly through the information to uncover patterns and relationships that would elude an army of human researchers. The results enable Wal-Mart to predict sales of every product at each store with uncanny accuracy, translating into huge savings in inventories and maximum payoff from promotional spending.

Data-mining software typically includes many forms of AI such as neural networks and expert systems. Data-mining tools apply algorithms to information sets to uncover inherent trends and patterns in the information, which analysts use to develop new business strategies. Analysts use the output from data-mining tools to build models that, when exposed to new information sets, perform a variety of data analysis functions. The analysts provide business solutions by putting together the analytical techniques and the business problem at hand, which often reveals important new correlations, patterns, and trends in information. A few of the more common forms of data-mining analysis capabilities include cluster analysis, association detection, and statistical analysis. Data mining is covered in detail in Chapter 7.

3.2 ENTERPRISE SYSTEMS

Trek, a leader in bicycle products and accessories, gained a 30-percent increase in market share by streamlining its information systems. The largest improvement realized from the new systems was the ability to obtain key management information to drive business decisions in line with the company's strategic goals. The system also included a highly successful Web site developed for the 1,400 Trek dealers where they could enter orders, check stock availability, view accounts receivable, and verify credit. Tonja Green, Trek channel manager for North America, stated, "We wanted to give our dealers an easier and quicker way to enter their orders and get information. Every week the number of Web orders increases by 25 to 30 percent due to the new system."[17]

The following sections in this chapter introduce supply chain management, customer relationship management, business process reengineering, and enterprise resource planning—enterprise systems organizations can use to make decisions and gain competitive advantages.

SUPPLY CHAIN MANAGEMENT

To understand a supply chain, consider a customer purchasing a Trek bike from a dealer. The supply chain begins when a customer places an order for a Trek bike with the dealer. The dealer purchases the bike from the manufacturer, Trek. Trek purchases the raw materials required to make the bike such as metal, packaging, and accessories from different suppliers. The supply chain for Trek encompasses every activity and party involved in the process of fulfilling the order from the customer for the new bike.

Supply chain management (SCM) involves the management of information flows between and among stages in a supply chain to maximize total supply chain effectiveness and profitability. The four basic components of supply chain management include:

1. **Supply chain strategy**—the strategy for managing all the resources required to meet customer demand for all products and services.

2. **Supply chain partners**—the partners chosen to deliver finished products, raw materials, and services including pricing, delivery, and payment processes along with partner relationship monitoring metrics.

3. **Supply chain operation**—the schedule for production activities including testing, packaging, and preparation for delivery. Measurements for this component include productivity and quality.

4. **Supply chain logistics**—the product delivery processes and elements including orders, warehouses, carriers, defective product returns, and invoicing.

Dozens of steps are required to achieve and carry out each of the above components. SCM software can enable an organization to generate efficiencies within these steps by automating and improving the information flows throughout and among the different supply chain components.

Wal-Mart and Procter & Gamble (P&G) implemented a successful SCM system, which linked Wal-Mart's distribution centres directly to P&G's manufacturing centres. Every time a Wal-Mart customer purchases a P&G product, the system sends a message directly to the factory alerting P&G to restock the product. The system also sends an automatic alert to P&G whenever a product is running low at one of Wal-Mart's distribution centres. This real-time information allows P&G to produce and deliver products to Wal-Mart without having to maintain large inventories in its warehouses. The SCM system saves time, reduces inventory, and decreases order-processing costs for P&G, which P&G passes on to Wal-Mart in the form of discounted prices.[18]

Figure 3.11 diagrams the stages of the SCM system for a customer purchasing a product from Wal-Mart. The diagram demonstrates how the supply chain is dynamic and involves the constant flow of information between the different parties. For example, a customer purchases a product from Wal-Mart and generates order information. Wal-Mart supplies the order information to its warehouse or distributor. The warehouse or distributor transfers the order information to the manufacturer, who provides pricing and availability information to the store and replenishes the product. Partners transfer all payments electronically.

Effective and efficient supply chain management systems can enable an organization to:

- Decrease the power of its buyers.
- Increase its own supplier power.
- Increase switching costs to reduce the threat of substitute products or services.
- Create entry barriers thereby reducing the threat of new entrants.
- Increase efficiencies while seeking a competitive advantage through cost leadership (see Figure 3.12).

FIGURE 3.11

Supply Chain for a Product Purchased from Wal-Mart

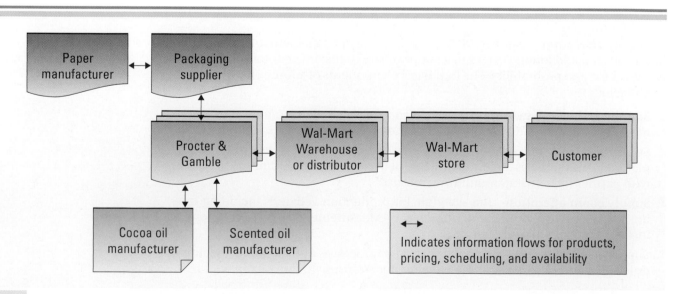

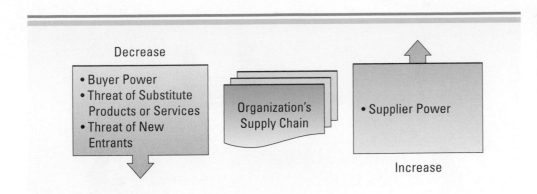

CUSTOMER RELATIONSHIP MANAGEMENT

Today, most competitors are simply a mouse-click away. The intense competition in today's marketplace forces organizations to switch from sales-focused strategies to customer-focused strategies.

Charles Schwab recouped the cost of a multimillion-dollar customer relationship management system in less than two years. The system, developed by Siebel, allows the brokerage firm to trace each interaction with a customer or prospective customer and then provide services (retirement planning, for instance) to each customer's needs and interests. The system provides Schwab with a complete view of its customers, which it uses to differentiate serious investors from nonserious investors. For example, automated deposits from paycheques are a sign of a serious investor, while stagnant balances signal a nonserious investor. Once Schwab is able to make this determination, the firm allocates its resources accordingly, saving money by not investing time or resources in subsidizing nonserious investors.[19]

Customer relationship management (CRM) involves managing all aspects of a customer's relationship with an organization to increase customer loyalty and retention and an organization's profitability. CRM allows an organization to gain insights into customers' shopping and buying behaviours. Kaiser Permanente, the United States' largest non-profit health plan provider, undertook a CRM strategy to improve and prolong the lives of diabetics. After compiling CRM information on 84,000 diabetic patients, Kaiser found that only 20 percent were getting their eyes checked routinely. (Diabetes is the leading cause of blindness.) As a result, Kaiser is now enforcing rigorous eye-screening programs for diabetics, along with creating support groups for obesity and stress (two more factors that make diabetes even worse). This CRM-based "preventive medicine" approach is saving Kaiser money and, more importantly, improving the health of diabetic patients.[20]

Figure 3.13 provides an overview of a typical CRM system. Customers contact an organization through various means including call centres, Web access, e-mail, faxes, and direct sales. A single customer may access an organization multiple times through many different channels. The CRM system tracks every communication between the customer and the organization and provides access to CRM information across different systems from accounting to order fulfillment. Understanding all customer communications allows the organization to communicate effectively with each customer. It gives the organization a detailed understanding of each customer's products and services regardless of the customer's preferred communication channel. A customer service representative can easily view detailed account information and history through a CRM system when providing information to a customer such as expected delivery dates, complementary product information, and customer payment and billing information.

CRM Strategy

Eddie Bauer ships 110 million catalogues a year, maintains two Web sites, and has more than 600 retail stores. The company collects information through customer transactions and analyzes the information to determine the best way to

FIGURE 3.13

Customer Relationship
Management Overview

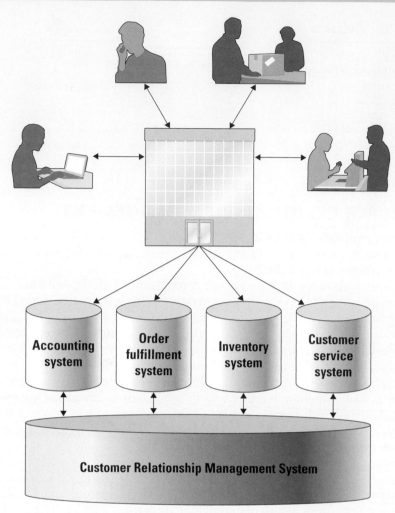

Customer Relationship Management System

↔ Customer information flows
are represented by arrows.

market to each individual customer. Eddie Bauer discovered that customers who shop across all three of its distribution channels—catalogues, Web sites, and stores—spend up to five times more than customers who shop through only one channel.

Michael Boyd, director of CRM at Eddie Bauer, stated, "Our experience tells us that CRM is in no way, shape, or form a software application. Fundamentally, it is a business strategy to try to optimize profitability, revenue, and satisfaction at an individual customer level. Everything in an organization, every single process, every single application, is a tool that can be used to serve the CRM goal."[21]

It is important to realize that CRM is not just a technology, but also a strategy that an organization must embrace on an enterprise level. Although there are many technical components of CRM, it is actually a process and business goal simply enhanced by technology. Implementing a CRM system can help an organization identify customers and design specific marketing campaigns tailored to each customer, thereby increasing customer spending. A CRM system also allows an organization to treat customers as individuals, gaining important insights into their buying preferences and behaviours and leading to increased sales, greater profitability, and higher rates of customer loyalty.

BUSINESS PROCESS REENGINEERING

A **business process** is a standardized set of activities that accomplish a specific task, such as processing a customer's order. **Business process reengineering (BPR)** is the analysis and redesign of workflow within and between enterprises. The concept of BPR traces its origins to management theories developed as early as the 19th century. The purpose of BPR is to make all business processes best-in-class. Frederick Taylor suggested in the 1880s that managers could discover the best processes for performing work and reengineer the process to optimize productivity. BPR echoes the classical belief that there is one best way to conduct tasks. In Taylor's time, technology did not allow large companies to design processes in a cross-functional or cross-departmental manner. Specialization was the state-of-the-art method to improve efficiency given the technology of the time.[22]

BPR reached its heyday in the early 1990s when Michael Hammer and James Champy published their best-selling book, *Reengineering the Corporation*. The authors promoted the idea that radical redesign and reorganization of an enterprise (wiping the slate clean) sometimes was necessary to lower costs and increase quality of service and that information technology was the key enabler for that radical change. Hammer and Champy believed that workflow design in most large corporations was based on invalid assumptions about technology, people, and organizational goals. They suggested seven principles of reengineering to streamline the work process and thereby achieve significant improvement in quality, time management, and cost (see Figure 3.14).[23]

Finding Opportunity Using BPR

Companies frequently strive to improve their business processes by performing tasks faster, cheaper, and better. Figure 3.15 displays different ways to travel the same road. A company could improve the way that it travels the road by moving from foot to horse and then from horse to car. However, true BPR would look at taking a different path. A company could forget about travelling on the same old road and use an airplane to get to its final destination. Companies often follow the same indirect path for doing business, not realizing there might be a different, faster, and more direct way of doing business.

Creating value for the customer is the leading factor for instituting BPR, and information technology often plays an important enabling role. Radical and fundamentally new business processes enabled Progressive Insurance to slash the claims settlement from 31 days to four hours. Typically, car insurance companies follow this standard claims resolution process: The customer gets into an accident, has the car towed, and finds a ride home. The customer then calls the insurance company to begin the claims process, which usually takes over a month (see Figure 3.16).[24]

Seven Principles of Business Process Reengineering
1. Organize around outcomes, not tasks.
2. Identify all the organization's processes and prioritize them in order of redesign urgency.
3. Integrate information processing work into the real work that produces the information.
4. Treat geographically dispersed resources as though they were centralized.
5. Link parallel activities in the workflow instead of just integrating their results.
6. Put the decision point where the work is performed, and build control into the process.
7. Capture information once and at the source.

FIGURE 3.14

Seven Principles of Business Process Reengineering

FIGURE 3.15

Better, Faster, Cheaper,
or BPR

FIGURE 3.16

Auto Insurance Claims Processes

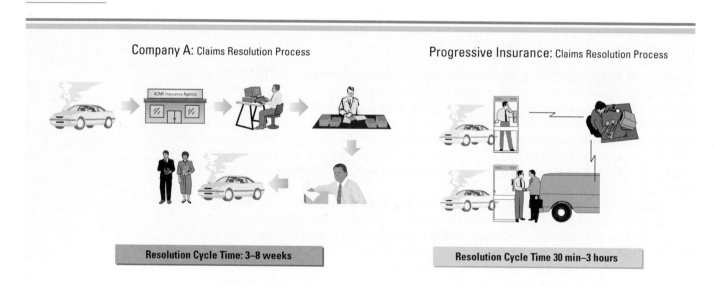

Progressive Insurance improved service to its customers by offering a mobile claims process. When a customer has a car accident, he or she calls in the claim on the spot. The Progressive claims adjuster comes to the accident and performs a mobile claims process, surveying the scene and taking digital photographs. The adjuster then offers the customer on-site payment, towing services, and a ride home. (see Figure 3.16).[25]

A true BPR effort does more for a company than simply improve it by performing a process better, faster, and cheaper. Progressive Insurance's BPR effort redefined best practices for its entire industry. Figure 3.17 displays the different types of change an organization can achieve, along with the magnitude of change and the potential business benefit.

Pitfalls of BPR

One hazard of BPR is that the company becomes so wrapped up in fighting its own demons that it fails to keep up with its competitors in offering new products or services. While American Express tackled a comprehensive reengineering of its credit card business, MasterCard and Visa introduced a new product—the corporate

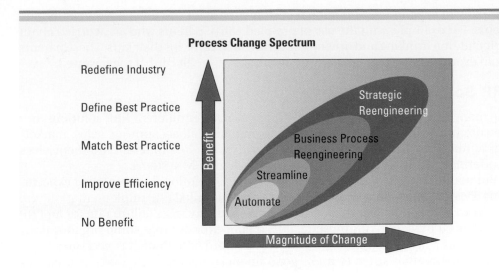

FIGURE 3.17

Process Change Spectrum

procurement card. American Express lagged a full year behind before offering its customers the same service.[26]

ENTERPRISE RESOURCE PLANNING

Many organizations fail to maintain consistency across business operations. If a single department, such as sales, decides to implement a new system without considering the other departments, inconsistencies can occur throughout the company. Not all applications are built to talk to each other, and if the sales function suddenly implements a new system that marketing and production cannot use or is inconsistent in the way it handles information, the company's operations become isolated.

Enterprise resource planning systems provide organizations with consistency. **Enterprise resource planning (ERP)** integrates all departments and functions throughout an organization into a single IT system (or integrated set of IT systems) so that employees can make decisions by viewing enterprisewide information on all business operations. An ERP system provides a method for effective planning and controlling of all the resources required to take, make, ship, and account for customer orders in a manufacturing, distribution, or service organization. The key word in enterprise resource planning is *enterprise*.

Coventry Connections, an Ottawa-based taxi cab company, operates a data-dispatch call centre for seven taxi fleets in the Ottawa, Gloucester, Oshawa, Kanata, and Nepean areas. To use the data-dispatch system, cab drivers pay Coventry a fee for maintenance, insurance, and equipment rentals; in turn, Conventry pays the drivers for the taxi chits they collect. A "taxi chit" is a slip of paper or small card issued by an employer to employees that taxi drivers would take as payment. Companies issue taxi chits in cases where employees need to get home safely having worked late into the evening or after celebrating at a company party or event. Conventry needs to collect these taxi chits in order to bill its corporate clients for the cost of the taxi chits.

Conventry uses SIA's Common Sense ERP system to facilitate its financial management processes, particularly around taxi chit processing. The system is built on IBM's WebSphere technology and utilizes an IBM iSeries server to support a GUI version of Common Sense. A cashiering application resides on the ERP system and is integrated with the ERP system's financial management tools. With the implementation of the ERP system, Conventry is in a position to introduce credit and debit account cards, as well as prepaid cards, to its corporate clients, thus eliminating the need for paper taxi chits. Bear in mind that processing paper taxi chits is a very manual process that can take as long as 45 days to collect money from clients. As chits come in they need to be sorted by customer, invoices need to be prepared and sent out, and payments need to be received. The ERP system not only allows Conventry to automate their system, and streamline their cash flow, the system allows the company to expand their traditional customer base for taxi chits beyond corporate clients. For example, with the use of pre-paid cards, parents who are worried about their children drinking and driving could buy such cards for their kids. These parents could even recharge these cards over the phone by credit card, if they wanted.[27]

ERP Software

The many ERP vendors on the market today each offer different ERP solutions, but the core functions are the same, focusing on financial, accounting, sales, marketing, human resources, operations, and logistics. Vendors differentiate themselves by offering distinct functionality such as CRM and SCM systems.

But many customers find that their chosen ERP solution does not meet expectations. Despite many improvements in the software, failed ERP implementations are still far too common. According to Gartner Inc., the average failure rate for an ERP project is 66 percent. With those results, it is no wonder that some organizations view ERP as a necessary, strategic evil. The key word here though is *necessary*.

Many companies strive to make good financial decisions by making smart investments. The best way to ensure a good investment in ERP is to understand why failure occurs and how to avoid it. The first challenge is that ERP comes in many flavours. Its main purpose is to provide support and automation to a business process. The business world has many different business models with many ERP products available that serve them.

Finding the Right ERP Solution

A good ERP system will be highly reflective of the business process in place at the company. This means the software must perform many different tasks and that makes it complex. Most companies do not carry a high degree of ERP software expertise on their staff, making it easy to choose the wrong package. The key to making an effective purchase is to have solid business processes. Successful ERP projects share three basic attributes:

1. Overall fit
2. Proper business analysis
3. Solid implementation plans[28]

Overall Fit   This refers to the degree of gaps that exist between the system and the business process. A well-fitting ERP has no major process gaps and very few minor ones. Think of a new ERP system as a suit. Typically, a customer buys a suit three ways: off the rack, off the rack and tailored to fit, or custom-made.

The way the solution fits the business process will normally determine the client's satisfaction level. Buying ERP off the rack is the equivalent of buying a canned software package. It fits some well, but not all. The customer can tailor the software so that its processes better line up with company processes. This is a good strategy provided the chosen package supports this. The downside is that it can get very expensive. Choosing a custom system can provide a great fit, but the company must thoroughly understand what it is doing and be able to support the associated financial burden.

Proper Business Analysis   The best way to determine which fit strategy is right is to conduct a thorough business analysis. Successful companies normally spend up to 10 percent of the project budget on a business analysis. A proper analysis must result in a documented list of the business processes at work within the company. This will provide a basic tool that can measure vendor capability.

Solid Implementation Plans   As with the installation of any successful process or machinery, a plan is needed to monitor the quality objectives and timelines. The plan will also employ processes such as workflow analysis and job combination to harvest savings.

A thorough implementation will transfer knowledge to system users. When the project is complete, employees must be capable of using the tools the new system provides. The users must also know what to do in cases when the process fluctuates. Most failed systems result from low-quality implementation. ERP is simply a tool. Tools that people do not know how to use can be as useless as having no tools at all.

INTEGRATING BUSINESS INFORMATION SYSTEMS

The above descriptions in this chapter have introduced you to various types of business information systems that exist across the enterprise such as supply chain management, customer relationship management, and enterprise resource planning. These are described in more detail in Chapters 4, 5, and 6. Though each is treated separately in different chapters, you should realize that these systems need to be tightly integrated in order to achieve maximum benefits in helping an organization achieve its goals and objectives. However, this is not always easy to do.

The challenge of integrating business information systems is that historically information systems were developed in organizations in a haphazard manner. Sadly, it was quite common for different departments in the same organization to deploy different hardware and software technologies that were not compatible or did not allow easy sharing of data between systems. Even when hardware and software components did match, often the description of basic data elements used in a company, such as customer name and address information, were defined differently in different systems thus preventing easy sharing of basic transactional data across the firm. Sometimes, the same transactional information would have to be re-entered manually across various systems to facilitate data exchange. All these incompatibilities resulted in long time delays and the introduction of erroneous data into business information systems creating reconciliation nightmares for people trying to fix things later on. (More details about the importance of integrating data across the enterprise and how to deploy and foster integrated business information systems through sound systems development and project management techniques are discussed in Chapter 10.)

Given this history, organizations have been working hard to deliver business information systems that work together smoothly and efficiently as possible. One reason for this is that organizations now recognize that tightly integrated business information systems lead to improved organizational decision making. Without this tight integration, wrong or contradictory information is fed into higher-level decision-making systems by various transaction-based systems, leading to potentially poor decision making.

So, though it is easier to build a business information system as a stand-alone entity, in the long run it is counter-productive. Smart organizations recognize the need to tightly integrate their business information systems as a means to facilitate proper decision making, as well as to achieve efficiency gains and competitive advantage.

The purpose of this chapter was to:

- provide a description of decision-making information systems,

- give an overview of the various business information systems used across the enterprise,

- explain the concept of decision making,

- showcase the differences between TPS, DSS, and EIS, and

- introduce the specific business information systems of SCM, CRM, BPR, and ERP.

The goal of providing you with this information was to provide you, the business student, with knowledge of the types of information systems that exist in an organization. By doing so, you should now have a better understanding of:

- how these systems can improve organizational performance and decision making, and

- the importance of integrating these various systems together.

KEY TERMS

Analytical information   76
Artificial intelligence   82
Business intelligence   77
Business process   89
Business process reengineering (BPR)   89
Consolidation   79
Customer relationship management (CRM)   87
Decision support system (DSS)   77
Digital dashboard   79
Drill-down   79

Enterprise resource planning (ERP)   91
Executive information system (EIS)   78
Expert system   83
Fuzzy logic   83
Genetic algorithm   83
Goal-seeking analysis   78
Intelligent agent   84
Intelligent system   82
Model   75
Neural network (artificial neural network)   83

Online analytical processing (OLAP)   77
Online transaction processing (OLTP)   76
Sensitivity analysis   77
Shopping bot   84
Slice-and-dice   79
Supply chain management (SCM)   85
Transaction processing system (TPS)   76
Transactional information   76
What-if analysis   77

CLOSING CASE ONE

Consolidating Touchpoints for Saab

This case illustrates the use of a CRM system in an organization.

Saab Cars USA imports more than 37,000 Saab sedans, convertibles, and wagons annually and distributes the cars to 220 U.S. dealerships. Saab competes in the premium automotive market, and its primary rivals attract customers through aggressive marketing campaigns, reduced prices, and inexpensive financing. Saab decided that the answer to beating its competition was not to spend capital on additional advertising, but to invest in Siebel Automotive, a customer relationship management system.

Until recently, the company communicated with its customers through three primary channels: (1) dealer network, (2) customer assistance centre, (3) lead management centre. Traditionally, each channel maintained its own customer database, and this splintered approach to managing customer information caused numerous problems for the company. For example, a prospective customer might receive a direct-mail piece from Saab one week, then an e-mail with an unrelated offer from a third-party marketing vendor the next week. The local dealer might not know of either activity, and therefore might deliver an ineffective pitch when the customer visited the showroom that weekend. Al Fontova, direct marketing manager with Saab Cars USA, stated he had over 3 million customer records and 55 files at three different vendors. Analyzing this information in aggregate was complicated, inefficient, and costly.

Saab required a solution that would provide a consolidated customer view from all three touchpoints. In 2003, Saab implemented the Siebel CRM solution, which provides Saab's call centre employees with a 360-degree view of each customer, including prior service-related questions and all the marketing communications they have received. Known internally as "TouchPoint," the Siebel application provides Saab's dealers with a powerful Web-based solution for coordinating sales and marketing activities. These tracking capabilities enable Saab to measure the sales results of specific leads, recommend more efficient selling techniques, and target its leads more precisely in the future. Using Siebel Automotive, Saab received the following benefits:

- Direct marketing costs decreased by 5 percent.
- Lead follow-up increased from 38 percent to 50 percent.
- Customer satisfaction increased from 69 percent to 75 percent.
- Saab gained a single view of its customers across multiple channels.29

Questions

1. How has implementing a CRM system enabled Saab to gain a competitive advantage?
2. Estimate the potential impact to Saab's business if it had not implemented a CRM system.
3. What additional benefits could Saab receive from implementing a supply chain management system?
4. Model Saab's supply chain.
5. How is Saab's CRM implementation going to influence its SCM practices?

CLOSING CASE TWO

Made-to-Order Businesses

This case illustrates the powerful impact enterprise systems have in helping organizations implement business strategies like mass customization.

In the past, customers had two choices for purchasing products: (1) purchase a mass-produced product like a pair of jeans or a candy bar or (2) commission a custom-made item that was perfect but cost a small fortune. Mass customization is a new trend in the retail business. Mass customization hits that sweet spot between harnessing the cost efficiencies of mass production and offering so many options that customers feel the product has been designed just for them. Today, many companies are using strategic information systems to implement mass customization business strategies.

Lands' End

Lands' End built a decision support system that could pinpoint a person's body size by taking just a few measurements and running a series of algorithms. The process begins when the customer answers questions on Lands' End's Web site about everything from waist size to inseam. Lands' End saves the data in its customer relationship management system, which is used for reorders, promotions, and marketing campaigns. The order is then sent to San Francisco where supply chain management software determines which one of five contracted manufacturers should receive the order. The chosen manufacturer then cuts and sews the material and ships the finished garment directly to the customer.

Over 40 percent of Lands' End shoppers prefer a customized garment to the standard-sized equivalent, even though each customized garment costs at least $23 more and takes four weeks to deliver. Customized clothes account for a growing percentage of Lands' End's $593 million online business. Reorder rates for Lands' End custom-clothing buyers are 34 percent higher than for buyers of its standard-sized clothing.

Nike

The original business model for Nike iD concentrated on connecting with consumers and creating customer loyalty. Nike iD's Web site allows customers to build their own running shoes. The process begins when customers choose from one of seven different styles and orders from numerous colour combinations. Dark-pink bottoms, red mesh, bright yellowing lining, purple laces, blue swoosh, and a eucalyptus green accent. Customers can even place eight-character personalized messages on the side. The cost averages about $35 more than buying the regular shoes in a store.

Once Nike receives the custom order, its supply chain management system sends it to one of 15 plants depending on production availability. Customers receive their shoes within four weeks. The program experienced triple-digit growth in just two years.

Stamps.com

Stamps.com made an agreement with the U.S. Postal Service to sell customized stamps. Customers could put pictures of their choice on an actual U.S. postage stamp. Pictures ranged from dogs to fiancées. The response was phenomenal: Within seven weeks Stamps.com processed and sold more than 2 million PhotoStamps at US$1 for a first-class stamp.

Thinking about mass customization as a goal changes the way businesses think about their customers. Using supply chain management and customer relationship management to implement mass customization can have a direct impact on a business's bottom line.[30]

Questions

1. What role does supply chain management and customer relationship management play in a mass customization business strategy?
2. How can Lands' End use its CRM system to improve its business?
3. How can Nike use a CRM system to improve its customer relations?
4. Why is Nike's supply chain management system critical to its Nike iD order fulfillment process?
5. Choose one of the examples above and explain how an ERP system could help facilitate the mass customization effort.
6. Choose one of the examples above and explain how the company is attempting to gain a competitive advantage with mass customization.
7. Identify one other business that could benefit from the use of mass customization. Explain why this business would need customer relationship management and supply chain management systems to implement a mass customization business strategy.

CLOSING CASE THREE

Information Systems Are Critical For Take-Off in Canada's Airline Industry

This case highlights the critical role information systems play in running the enterprise.

When asked about the Canadian airline industry's reliance on information systems, Stephen Smith sits up tall. As a seasoned airline executive with over 25 years experience working for airlines such as Air Canada, Zip Air, WestJet, Air Ontario, and Air Toronto, Stephen knows that the airline industry has long been an intensive user of information technology—a direct result of airlines like Air Canada who carry over 20 million passengers every year, on 200,000 flights. "In the old days, the inventory system to maintain passenger records and numbers booked on a flight, were done on paper, and hung on nails. While this system worked, it certainly wouldn't work in a day and age like today. Computerized information systems are essential."

Think about it. From a process perspective, each flight must be allocated an aircraft, with 'x' number of economy seats and 'y' number of executive class seats. Then, against that inventory, names, record locators and payment information must be matched to generate a ticket. That ticket must be then turned over to a gate agent, who then forwards it to the revenue accounting office, who then takes the money into revenue, as at this point, the revenue is earned.

When questioned about how airlines go about maximizing the revenue generated on every flight, Stephen explains how airlines rely heavily on the use of revenue management information systems. "Airlines, including Air Canada, invest heavily in revenue management systems. These systems forecast the demand for a flight at various fare levels based on historical demand. Without computers, this task would be next to impossible."

The reason for this is simply the proliferation of data involved. For a large airline carrier having hundreds of routes and multiple fare classes, the mathematical modelling required is beyond that of a human being. As a result, airlines invest millions of dollars into building and maintaining their revenue management systems in order to handle the vast amounts of data that must be processed. With hundreds or thousands of departures per day, the need for quick and accurate revenue management systems is critical for airlines in terms of helping them figure out what inventory to sell given the demand for flights and forecasts.

In fact, the need to manage revenue has become critical ever since deregulation of the airline industry in Canada has occurred. Since deregulation, carriers have been free to set their own airfares, and rather than trying to fill planes, airlines now try to maximize their revenue. Thus the emphasis for airlines these days is to fill planes with enough high-paying customers to cover costs and make a profit, as opposed to ensuring that all flights are simply full.[31]

What are revenue management systems? These are information systems used by airlines to calculate how many seats in each fare class are offered on particular legs of a flight at a given time taking into account current demand, historical data, and special one-time events that influence demands for travel. According to Mr. Smith, "the process of revenue management is a very, very sophisticated form of revenue control, which, based on historical booking trends, attempts to forecast the passenger demand for a flight, and what they might be willing to pay. The ideal scenario is that a passenger shows up at the last minute, there is one open seat on the flight, and they are willing to pay the amount the airline is asking for that last seat."

With the advent of the Web, airlines are well aware that customers are increasingly able to compare fares from all competitors with a few mouse clicks. An airline's fares have become almost totally visible and thus airlines are forced to implement competitive fares in their revenue management systems. If a fare is too high, a potential customer will buy from the competition; if a fare is too low, the airline loses out on potential revenue earned.[32]

These revenue management systems also need to set overbooking levels. Stephen Smith explains, "some people simply do not show up for their designated flights. Approximately 10% of passengers do not show up. These no-shows force airlines to overbook their flights, otherwise, 10% of an airline's revenue would not be realized— which means that for most airlines, they would become very unprofitable, very quickly."

Further, when taking into account cancelled flights, people changing bookings, delays, and re-bookings, the logic built into revenue management systems becomes very complicated, very fast. This complexity is exacerbated when one considers the fact that revenue systems must also deal with different fare structures for different types of passengers. In general, there are two types of passengers: those who must fly on that flight, on that day; and those who are willing to move flights, days, and even destinations. An example of the former are business travellers or those with medical appointments. An example of the latter are those on vacation, or going to meet friends and relatives. Obviously, those in the first group are far more willing to pay more for their flight, as the convenience of a flight on that day to their destination at that time is far more important than the cost of the flight. The second group are far more likely to gravitate to the cheapest flight, regardless of when it leaves (within reason) either by day or time; in fact, vacation travellers will even change countries based upon which flight is the cheapest. In addition, the first group (business travellers and those with medical appointments) normally books their flights much closer to flight time, as planning travel a month ahead for most businesses is not normal; this group rarely stays over weekends and wants to be able to change flights if plans change (which they frequently do). The second group, is completely different, planning much further ahead, staying over weekends, and rarely changing their plans.

As a result, airlines came up with various fare levels, and various requirements to obtain those fares. And revenue management must handle these requirements. The first fare was the "full fare economy fare," which was the most one could pay for an economy seat, but could be bought up to the last minute, and allowed the traveller to change flights without a penalty. Then there were 3-day advance fares, 7-day advance fares, and 14-day advance fares, each with a number of fares in each, allowing the traveller to change/not change/pay for a change as well as the requirement to stay over a Saturday night, or not. You can imagine doing this inventory for each flight, for 660 flights per day, for 365 days (most airlines only keep inventory of flights up to one year in advance) would be impossible without the help of computerized information systems.

To handle these different fare scenarios, the airlines set up fare "buckets" and "nest" them within broad groups, so that it allowed, for instance, a 3-day fare (normally more than a 7-day fare) to outsell its bucket, if there were 7-day fares still remaining. Once a flight booking goes above the expected higher booking rate, the lower fare inventory is shut down, as the flight is booking up faster than expected. Conversely, if the booking levels go below and expected lower booking rate, then the lower fares are opened up, as the flight is booking slower than expected. This analysis is done on every flight for every day for the entire year, every hour, as otherwise airlines could be caught flat footed, and oversell, or undersell a large number of flights for the entire year.

This sophistication is now being taken to the next level, as passengers who are the airlines' most loyal (for example, in Air Canada, Elite or Super Elite passengers) now have the ability to book a flight, even if it has been overbooked, or a certain fare group is sold out. This allows the airline to repay its most loyal customers with something not available to all customers.

In the future, airlines hope to be able to set up a fare schedule for each customer, depending on their buying habits, and loyalty to the airline. This is just another attempt, in a fixed cost industry, to buy loyalty, as almost every dollar of revenue drops to the bottom line of the airline, and the more a customer flies the airline, the more revenue they generate. A case in point is Air Canada's decision to implement a data warehouse to enhance Air Canada's yield marketing intelligence and provide the company with a scalable platform that facilitates future growth in CRM and finance analytics applications.[33]

In addition to revenue management, revenue accounting for an airline is also critical, as revenue cannot be taken into account until the customer has flown. This is another area where, since the demise of paper tickets (the vast majority of travel is now ticketless), computer systems must be able to match the customer with the fare that has been paid, to ensure they have followed the appropriate rules, and to take that fare into revenue.

Stephen Smith relaxes back in his chair and summarizes his thoughts on the airline industry's reliance on information systems, "As you can imagine, the ability to forecast passenger demand for a flight, at all different fare levels, is a very sophisticated process which was never considered back in the days that people counted tags for their flight inventory. For this reason, I can ensure you that information systems have become fundamentally critical to the daily operations of an airline. There's no turning back to paper now."

Questions

1. What advantages are there for an airline to use a revenue management system?
2. Are revenue management systems a competitive advantage or simply a new necessity for doing business in the airline industry today?

3. What other industries could benefit from the use of a revenue management system?
4. How could an airline use customer information to gain competitive advantage?
5. What types of metrics would airline executive want to see in a digital dashboard?
6. How would an airline's revenue management system be used for decision support?

MAKING BUSINESS DECISIONS

1. Making decisions

You are the vice president of human resources for a large consulting company. You are compiling a list of questions that you want each interviewee to answer. The first question on your list is, "How can information technology enhance your ability to make decisions at our organization?" Prepare a one-page report to answer this difficult question.

2. DSS and EIS

Dr. Rosen runs a large dental conglomerate—Teeth Doctors—that staffs more than 700 dentists in four provinces. Dr. Rosen is interested in purchasing a competitor called Dentix that has 150 dentists in three additional provinces. Before deciding whether to purchase Dentix, Dr. Rosen must consider several issues:

- The cost of purchasing Dentix.
- The location of the Dentix offices.
- The current number of customers per dentist, per office, and per province.
- The merger between the two companies.
- The professional reputation of Dentix.
- Other competitors.

Explain how Dr. Rosen and Teeth Doctors can benefit from the use of information systems to make an accurate business decision in regard to the potential purchase of Dentix.

3. SCM, CRM, and ERP

Jamie Ash is interested in applying for a job at a large software vendor. One of the criteria for the job is a detailed understanding of strategic initiatives such as SCM, CRM, and ERP. Jamie has no knowledge of any of these initiatives and cannot even explain what the acronyms mean. Jamie has come to you for help. She would like you to compile a summary of the three initiatives, including an analysis of how the three are similar and how they are different. Jamie would also like to perform some self-training via the Web so be sure to provide her with several additional links to key Web sites that offer detailed overviews on SCM, CRM, and ERP.

4. Finding information on decision support systems

You are working on the sales team for a small catering company that maintains 75 employees and generates $1 million in revenues per year. The owner, Pam Hetz, wants to understand how she can use decision support systems to help grow her business. Pam has an initial understanding of DSS systems and is interested in learning more about what types are available, how they can be used in a small business, and the cost associated with different DSS systems. In a group, research the Web site www.dssresources.com and compile a presentation that discusses DSS systems in detail. Be sure to answer all Pam's questions on DSS systems in the presentation.

5. Gaining business intelligence from strategic initiatives

You are a new employee in the customer service department at Premier One, a large pet food distributor. The company, founded by several veterinarians, has been in business for three years and focuses on providing nutritious pet food at a low cost. The company currently has 90 employees and operates in seven provinces. Sales over the past three years have tripled, and the manual systems currently in place are no longer sufficient to run the business. Your first task is to meet with your new team and create a presentation for the president and CEO describing supply chain management, customer relationship management, and enterprise resource planning systems. The presentation should highlight the main benefits Premier One can receive from these strategic initiatives along with any additional added business value that can be gained from the systems.

Supply Chain Management

4 CHAPTER

LEARNING OUTCOMES

4.1. List and describe the five components of a typical supply chain.

4.2. Define the relationship between information technology and the supply chain.

4.3. Identify the factors driving supply chain management.

4.4. Summarize the best practices for implementing a successful supply chain management system.

4.5. List and describe the four drivers of supply chain management.

4.6. Explain supply chain management strategies focused on efficiency.

4.7. Explain supply chain management strategies focused on effectiveness.

Why Do I Need To Know This ?

This chapter introduces the concept of supply chain management and how information technology can be used to ameliorate and improve supply chain management processes. In this sense, information systems enable companies to better manage the flow of information, materials, and financial payments that occurs between and among stages in a supply chain to maximize total supply chain effectiveness and profitability.

As a business student, you need to know the significance of a supply chain to organizational success and the critical role information technology plays in ensuring smooth operation of a supply chain. A supply chain consists of all direct and indirect parties involved in the procurement of a product or raw material. These parties can be internal groups or departments within an organization or external partner companies and end-customers. This chapter will emphasize the important role information technology plays in providing an underlying infrastructure and coordination mechanisms needed for a supply chain to function effectively and efficiently as possible. You need to know this in order to appreciate and understand the capabilities and limitations that information technology can afford, the benefits and challenges of employing information technology in a supply chain, as well as future supply chain trends where information systems will play a critical part.

Dell's Famous Supply Chain

Speed is at the core of everything Dell does. Dell assembles nearly 80,000 computers every 24 hours. The computer manufacturer has done more than any other company when it comes to tweaking its supply chain. About 10 years ago, Dell carried 20 to 25 days of inventory in a sprawling network of warehouses. Today, Dell does not have a single warehouse and carries only two hours of inventory in its factories and a maximum of just 72 hours across its entire operation. Dell's vast, global supply chain is in constant overdrive, making the company one of the fastest, most hyperefficient organizations on the planet.

Disaster Occurs

In 2002, a 10-day labour lockout shut down 29 West Coast ports in the United States extending from Los Angeles to Seattle, idled 10,000 union dockworkers, and blocked hundreds of cargo ships from unloading raw materials and finished goods. The port closings paralyzed global supply chains and ultimately cost U.S. consumers and businesses billions of dollars.

Analysts expected Dell, with its just-in-time manufacturing model, would be especially hard hit when parts failed to reach its two U.S.-based factories. Without warehouses filled with motherboards and hard drives the world's largest PC maker would simply find itself with nothing to sell within a matter of days. Dell knew all too well that its ultra-lean, high-speed business model left it vulnerable to just such a situation. "When a labour problem or an earthquake or a SARS epidemic breaks out, we've got to react quicker than anyone else," said Dick Hunter, the company's supply chain expert. "There's no other choice. We know these things are going to happen; we must move fast to fix them. We just can't tolerate any kind of delay."

Fortunately, the same culture of speed and flexibility that seems to put Dell at the mercy of disruptions also helps it deal with them. Dell was in constant, round-the-clock communication with its parts makers in Taiwan, China, and Malaysia and its U.S.-based shipping partners. Hunter dispatched a "tiger team" of 10 logistics specialists to Long Beach, California, and other ports; they worked with Dell's carrying and freight-forwarding networks to assemble a contingency plan.

When the tiger team confirmed that the closings were all but certain, Dell moved into high gear. It chartered 18 airplanes (747s) from UPS, Northwest Airlines, and China Airlines. A 747 holds the equivalent of 10 tractor-trailers—enough parts to manufacture 10,000 PCs. The bidding for the planes grew fierce, running as high as

US$1 million for a one-way flight from Asia to the United States. Dell got in the bidding early and kept costs around US$500,000 per plane. Dell also worked with its Asia-based suppliers to ensure that its parts were always at the Shanghai and Taipei airports in time for its returning charters to land, reload, refuel, and take off. The company was consistently able to get its planes to the United States and back within 33 hours, which kept its costs down and its supply chain moving.

Meanwhile, Dell had people on the ground in every major harbour. In Asia, the freight specialists saw to it that Dell's parts were the last to be loaded onto each cargo ship so they would be unloaded first when the ship hit the United States. The biggest test came when the ports reopened and companies scrambled to sort through the backed-up mess of thousands of containers. Hunter's tiger team had anticipated this logistical nightmare. Even though Dell had PC components in hundreds of containers on 50 ships, it knew the exact moment when each component cycled through the harbour, and it was among the first to unload its parts and speed them to its factories in Austin, Texas, and Nashville, Tennessee. In the end, Dell did the impossible: It survived a 10-day supply chain blackout with roughly 72 hours of inventory without delaying a single customer order.

The aftershocks of the port closings reverberated for weeks. Many companies began to question the wisdom of running so lean in an uncertain world, and demand for warehouse space soared as they piled up buffer inventory to insure against labour unrest, natural disasters, and terrorist attacks.

Building a "Dell-like" Supply Chain

Dell's ultimate competitive weapon is speed, which gives the technical giant's bottom line a real boost. Figure 4.1 displays a five-point plan for building a fast supply chain—direct from Dell.[1]

Dell-Like Supply Chain Plan
1. **The supply chain starts with the customer.** By cutting out retailers and selling directly to its customers, Dell is in a far better position to forecast real customer demand.
2. **Replace inventory with information.** To operate with close to zero inventory, Dell communicates constantly with its suppliers. It sends out status updates three times a day from its assembly plants; every week it updates its quarterly demand forecasts. By making communication its highest priority, Dell ensures the lowest possible inventory.
3. **If you cannot measure it, you cannot manage it.** Dell knows what works because it measures everything from days in inventory to the time it takes to build a PC. As Dell slashed those numbers, it got more efficient.
4. **Complexity slows you down.** Dell cut the number of its core PC suppliers from several hundred to about 25. It standardized critical PC components, which streamlined its manufacturing. Dell got faster by making things simpler.
5. **Create a watershed mind-set.** Dell is not content with incremental improvement; it demands massive change. Each year, it wants its Austin-based PC-assembly plant—already very fast—to improve production by 30 percent. "You don't get a big result if you do not challenge people with big goals," Dell CEO Kevin Rollins said.

FIGURE 4.1

How to Build a Dell-Like Supply Chain

INTRODUCTION

Companies that excel in supply chain operations perform better in almost every financial measure of success, according to a report from AMR Research Inc. When supply chain excellence improves operations, companies experience a 5-percent higher profit margin, 15-percent less inventory, 17-percent stronger "perfect order" ratings, and 35-percent shorter cycle times than their competitors. "The basis of competition for winning companies in today's economy is supply chain superiority," said Kevin O'Marah, vice president of research at AMR Research. "These companies understand that value chain performance translates to productivity and market-share leadership. They also understand that supply chain leadership means more than just low costs and efficiency: It requires a superior ability to shape and respond to shifts in demand with innovative products and services."[2]

Collecting, analyzing, and distributing transactional information to all relevant parties, supply chain management (SCM) systems help all the different entities in the supply chain work together more effectively. SCM systems provide dynamic holistic views of organizations. Users can "drill down" into detailed analyses of supply chain activities to find valuable information on the organizational operations.

BASICS OF SUPPLY CHAIN

The average company spends nearly half of every dollar it earns on production needs—goods and services it needs from external suppliers to keep producing. A *supply chain* consists of all parties involved, directly or indirectly, in the procurement of a product or raw material. *Supply chain management (SCM)* involves the management of information flows between and among stages in a supply chain to maximize total supply chain effectiveness and profitability.

In the past, companies focused primarily on manufacturing and quality improvements within their four walls; now their efforts extend beyond those walls to influence the entire supply chain including customers, customers' customers, suppliers, and suppliers' suppliers. Today's supply chain is a complex web of suppliers, assemblers, logistic firms, sales/marketing channels, and other business partners linked primarily through information networks and contractual relationships. SCM systems enhance and manage the relationships. The supply chain has three main links (see Figure 4.2):

1. Materials flow from suppliers and their upstream suppliers at all levels.

2. Transformation of materials into semifinished and finished products—the organization's own production processes.

3. Distribution of products to customers and their downstream customers at all levels.

Organizations must embrace technologies that can effectively manage and oversee their supply chains. SCM is becoming increasingly important in creating organizational efficiencies and competitive advantages. Best Buy checks inventory levels at each of its 750 stores in North America as often as every half hour with its SCM system, taking much of the guesswork out of inventory replenishment. Supply chain management improves ways for companies to find the raw components they need to make a product or service, manufacture that product or service, and deliver it to customers. Figure 4.3 highlights the five basic components of supply chain management.[3]

Technology advances in the five SCM components have significantly improved companies' forecasting and business operations. Businesses today have access to modelling and simulation tools, algorithms, and applications that can combine information from multiple sources to build forecasts for days, weeks, and months in advance. Better forecasts for tomorrow result in better preparedness today.

FIGURE 4.2

A Typical Supply Chain

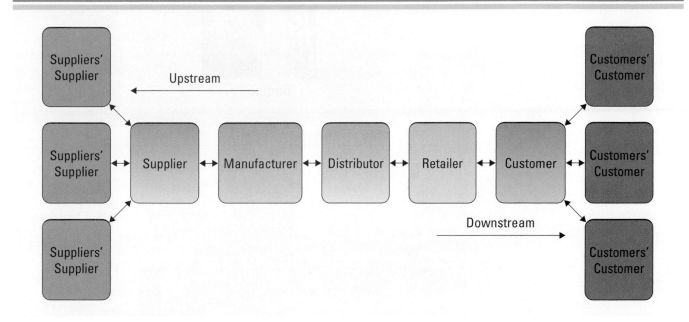

Mattel Inc. spent the past several years investing heavily in software and processes that simplify its supply chain, cut costs, and shorten cycle times. Using supply chain management strategies, the company cut weeks out of the time it takes to design, produce, and ship everything from Barbies to Hot Wheels. Mattel installed optimization software that measures, tweaks, and validates the operations of its seven distribution centres, seven manufacturing plants, and other facilities that make up its vast worldwide supply chain. Mattel improved forecasting from monthly to weekly. The company no longer produces more inventory than stores require and delivers inventory upon request. Mattel's supply chain moves quickly to make precise forecasts that help the company meet demand.[4]

INFORMATION TECHNOLOGY'S ROLE IN THE SUPPLY CHAIN

As companies evolve into extended organizations, the roles of supply chain participants are changing. It is now common for suppliers to be involved in product development and for distributors to act as consultants in brand marketing. The notion of virtually seamless information links within and between organizations is an essential element of integrated supply chains.

Information technology's primary role in SCM is creating the integrations or tight process and information linkages between functions within a firm—such as marketing, sales, finance, manufacturing, and distribution—and between firms, which allow the smooth, synchronized flow of both information and product between customers, suppliers, and transportation providers across the supply chain. Information technology integrates planning, decision-making processes, business operating processes, and information sharing for business performance management (see Figure 4.4). Considerable evidence shows that this type of supply chain integration results in superior supply chain capabilities and profits.[5]

For example, Canadian Tire, one of Canada's leading hard goods retailers, has successfully utilized information technology to support its Collaborative Planning,

FIGURE 4.3

The Five Basic Supply
Chain Management
Components

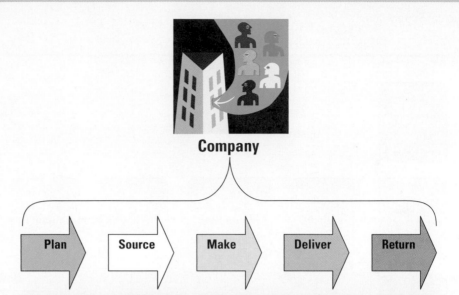

Company

| Plan | Source | Make | Deliver | Return |

THE FIVE BASIC SUPPLY CHAIN MANAGEMENT COMPONENTS
1. **Plan**—This is the strategic portion of supply chain management. A company must have a plan for managing all the resources that go toward meeting customer demand for products or services. A big piece of planning is developing a set of metrics to monitor the supply chain so that it is efficient, costs less, and delivers high quality and value to customers.
2. **Source**—Companies must carefully choose reliable suppliers that will deliver goods and services required for making products. Companies must also develop a set of pricing, delivery, and payment processes with suppliers and create metrics for monitoring and improving the relationships.
3. **Make**—This is the step where companies manufacture their products or services. This can include scheduling the activities necessary for production, testing, packaging, and preparing for delivery. This is by far the most metric-intensive portion of the supply chain, measuring quality levels, production output, and worker productivity.
4. **Deliver**—This step is commonly referred to as logistics. *Logistics* is the set of processes that plans for and controls the efficient and effective transportation and storage of supplies from suppliers to customers. During this step, companies must be able to receive orders from customers, fulfill the orders via a network of warehouses, pick transportation companies to deliver the products, and implement a billing and invoicing system to facilitate payments.
5. **Return**—This is typically the most problematic step in the supply chain. Companies must create a network for receiving defective and excess products and support customers who have problems with delivered products.

Forecasting, and Replenishment (CPFR) strategy that calls for increased and proactive collaboration with suppliers to improve forecast accuracy. The goal of this strategy is to enhance customer service, reduce inventory costs, and lower suppliers' costs; this is accomplished through heavy investments in information technology. The first step in the delivery of an information technology solution was implementation

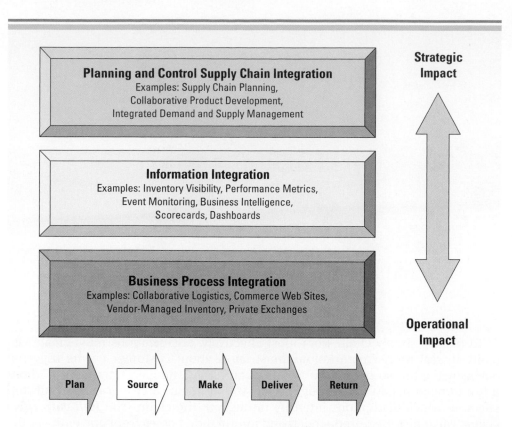

FIGURE 4.4

The Integrated Supply
Chain

The figure contains the following labels:

Planning and Control Supply Chain Integration
Examples: Supply Chain Planning,
Collaborative Product Development,
Integrated Demand and Supply Management

Information Integration
Examples: Inventory Visibility, Performance Metrics,
Event Monitoring, Business Intelligence,
Scorecards, Dashboards

Business Process Integration
Examples: Collaborative Logistics, Commerce Web Sites,
Vendor-Managed Inventory, Private Exchanges

Strategic Impact

Operational Impact

Plan → Source → Make → Deliver → Return

of a demand and fulfillment management system. This system allowed Canadian Tire to move from a reactive, purchase order-driven replenishment environment to a proactive time-phased forecasting process in which the company was able to consider consumer demand and generate a time-phased store demand forecast. Building upon the success of this system, the company has since created a Web-based environment that allows Canadian Tire to post and share information with its suppliers. As means of engaging suppliers and building supplier commitment to utilize this technology, suppliers must agree to a written "collaboration contract" prior to gaining access to the system. In return, Canadian Tire shares and discusses planning, forecasting, and replenishment information with these suppliers. For instance, Canadian Tire shares its aggregate demand forecast representing the demand for 440 stores for a 39-week time horizon, information on purchase orders outstanding, planned orders, and current and projected inventory levels at its distribution centres. Suppliers, through this Web-based environment, enter their own item forecast information. When items in the forecast comparison between Canadian Tire's projections and those of its suppliers fall outside acceptable tolerance ranges, the system automatically triggers an e-mail notification so that appropriate actions can be taken to prevent or mitigate future disruptions in the delivery and shipment of goods.[6]

Although people have been talking about the integrated supply chain for a long time, it has only been recently that advances in information technology have made it possible to bring the idea to life and truly integrate the supply chain. Visibility, consumer behaviour, competition, and speed are a few of the changes resulting from advances in information technology that are driving supply chains (see Figure 4.5).

Visibility

Supply chain visibility is the ability to view all areas up and down the supply chain. Making the change to supply chains requires a comprehensive strategy buoyed by information technology. Organizations can use technology tools that help them integrate upstream and downstream, with both customers and suppliers.

FIGURE 4.5

Factors Driving Supply
Chain Management

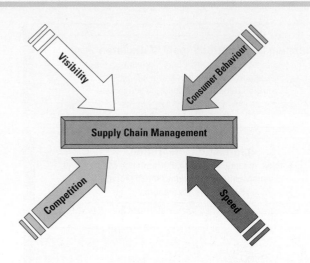

To make a supply chain work most effectively, organizations must create visibility in real time. Organizations must know about customer events triggered downstream, but so must their suppliers and their suppliers' suppliers. Without this information, partners throughout the supply chain can experience a bullwhip effect, in which disruptions intensify throughout the chain. The ***bullwhip effect*** occurs when distorted product demand information passes from one entity to the next throughout the supply chain. The misinformation regarding a slight rise in demand for a product could cause different members in the supply chain to stockpile inventory. These changes ripple throughout the supply chain, magnifying the issue and creating excess inventory and costs.

Today, information technology allows additional visibility in the supply chain. Electronic information flows allow managers to view their suppliers' and customers' supply chains. Some organizations have completely changed the dynamics of their industries because of the competitive advantage gained from high visibility in the supply chain. Dell is the obvious example. The company's ability to get product to the customer and the impact of the economics have clearly changed the nature of competition and caused others to emulate this model.

Consumer Behaviour

The behaviour of customers has changed the way businesses compete. Customers will leave if a company does not continually meet their expectations. They are more demanding because they have information readily available, they know exactly what they want, and they know when and how they want it. ***Demand planning software*** generates demand forecasts using statistical tools and forecasting techniques. Companies can respond faster and more effectively to consumer demands through supply chain enhancements such as demand planning software. Once an organization understands customer demand and its effect on the supply chain it can begin to estimate the impact that its supply chain will have on its customers and ultimately the organization's performance. The payoff for a successful demand planning strategy can be tremendous. One study found that companies have achieved impressive bottom-line results from managing demand in their supply chains, averaging a 50-percent reduction in inventory and a 40-percent increase in timely deliveries.[7]

Competition

Supply chain management software can be broken down into (1) supply chain planning software and (2) supply chain execution software. Both increase a company's ability to compete. ***Supply chain planning (SCP) software*** uses advanced mathematical algorithms to improve the flow and efficiency of the supply chain while reducing inventory. SCP depends entirely on information for its accuracy. An organization cannot expect the SCP output to be accurate unless correct and up-to-date information regarding customer orders, sales information, manufacturing capacity, and delivery capability is entered into the system.

An organization's supply chain encompasses the facilities where raw materials, intermediate products, and finished goods are acquired, transformed, stored, and sold. These facilities are connected by transportation links, where materials and products flow. Ideally, the supply chain consists of multiple organizations that function as efficiently and effectively as a single organization, with full information visibility. *Supply chain execution (SCE) software* automates the different steps and stages of the supply chain. This could be as simple as electronically routing orders from a manufacturer to a supplier. Figure 4.6 details how SCP and SCE software correlate to the supply chain.

General Motors, Ford, and DaimlerChrysler made history when the three automotive giants began working together to create a unified supply chain planning/execution system that all three companies and their suppliers could leverage. Gary Lapidus, Goldman Sachs Group's senior analyst, estimated that Newco, the name of the joint venture, will have a potential market capitalization of between $35 billion and $47 billion once it goes public, with annual revenues of around $3.5 billion.

The combined automotive giants' purchasing power is tremendous with GM spending $100 billion per year, Ford spending $94 billion, and DaimlerChrysler spending $86 billion. The ultimate goal of Newco is to process automotive production, from ordering materials and forecasting demand to making cars directly to consumer specifications through the Web. The automotive giants understand the impact strategic supply chain planning and execution can have on their competition.[8]

Speed

During the past decade, competition has focused on speed. New forms of servers, telecommunications, wireless applications, and software are enabling companies to perform activities that were once never thought possible. These systems raise the accuracy, frequency, and speed of communication between suppliers and customers,

FIGURE 4.6

Supply Chain Planning and Supply Chain Execution Software's Correlation to the Supply Chain

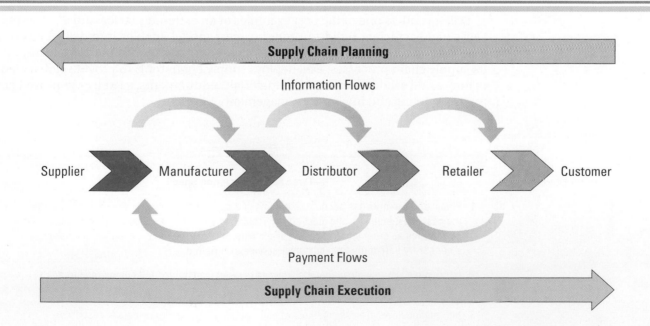

as well as between internal users. Another aspect of speed is the company's ability to satisfy continually changing customer requirements efficiently, accurately, and quickly. Timely and accurate information is more critical to businesses than ever before. Figure 4.7 displays the three factors fostering this change.

SUPPLY CHAIN MANAGEMENT SUCCESS FACTORS

To succeed in today's competitive markets, companies must align their supply chains with the demands of the markets they serve. Supply chain performance is now a distinct competitive advantage for companies proficient in the SCM area. GS1 Canada is well aware of this competitive advantage. GS1 Canada is a member organization of Global Standards One (GS1)—a global organization of over 100 members charged with developing standards and solutions to improve supply chain management. GS1 Canada developed the E-Commerce Community Network (ECCNet) Registry—Canada's online, standardized product registry for synchronized data exchange. With this registry, there is now a single point of access in Canada between suppliers and retailers, streamlining and supporting the day-to-day e-commerce requirements of the supply chain. Suppliers input information for each product just one time and the registry facilitates distribution to many customers. Additions and updates are always aligned. Such data synchronization ensures that the right amount of goods is available at the right place and at the right time. To date, more than 2,500 companies—representing over 300,000 products and more than 85 percent of the transactions in three areas (grocery, foodservice, and retail pharmacy)—have signed on as users of ECCnet Registry.[9]

To achieve success such as reducing operating costs, improving asset productivity, and compressing order cycle time, an organization should follow the seven principles of supply chain management outlined in Figure 4.8.

These seven principles run counter to previous built-in functional thinking of how companies organize, operate, and serve customers. Old concepts of supply chains are typified by discrete manufacturing, linear structure, and a focus on buy-sell transactions ("I buy from my suppliers, I sell to my customers"). Because the traditional supply chain is spread out linearly, some suppliers are removed from the end customer. Collaboration adds the value of visibility for these companies. They benefit by knowing immediately what is being transacted at the customer end of the supply chain (the end customer's activities are visible to them). Instead of waiting days or weeks (or months) for the information to flow upstream through the supply chain, with all the potential pitfalls of erroneous or missing information, suppliers can react in near real-time to fluctuations in end-customer demand.

Dell Inc. offers one of the best examples of an extremely successful SCM system. Dell's highly efficient build-to-order business model enables it to deliver customized computer systems quickly. As part of the company's continual effort to improve its supply chain processes, Dell deploys supply chain tools to provide global views of forecasted product demand and materials requirements, as well as improved factory scheduling and inventory management.

FIGURE 4.7

Factors Fostering Speed

Three Factors Fostering Speed
1. Pleasing customers has become something of a corporate obsession. Serving the customer in the best, most efficient, and most effective manner has become critical, and information about issues such as order status, product availability, delivery schedules, and invoices has become a necessary part of the total customer service experience.
2. Information is crucial to managers' abilities to reduce inventory and human resource requirements to a competitive level.
3. Information flows are essential to strategic planning for and deployment of resources.

FIGURE 4.8

Seven Principles
of Supply Chain
Management

Seven Principles of Supply Chain Management
1. Segment customers by service needs, regardless of industry, and then tailor services to those particular segments.
2. Customize the logistics network and focus intensively on the service requirements and on the profitability of the pre-identified customer segments.
3. Listen to signals of market demand and plan accordingly. Planning must span the entire chain to detect signals of changing demand.
4. Differentiate products closer to the customer, since companies can no longer afford to hold inventory to compensate for poor demand forecasting.
5. Strategically manage sources of supply, by working with key suppliers to reduce overall costs of owning materials and services.
6. Develop a supply chain information technology strategy that supports different levels of decision making and provides a clear view (visibility) of the flow of products, services, and information.
7. Adopt performance evaluation measures that apply to every link in the supply chain and measure true profitability at every stage.

Organizations should study industry best practices to improve their chances of successful implementation of SCM systems. The following are keys to SCM success.

Make the Sale to Suppliers

The hardest part of any SCM system is its complexity because a large part of the system extends beyond the company's walls. Not only will the people in the organization need to change the way they work, but also the people from each supplier that is added to the network must change. Be sure suppliers are on board with the benefits that the SCM system will provide.

Wean Employees Off Traditional Business Practices

Operations people typically deal with phone calls, faxes, and orders scrawled on paper and will most likely want to keep it that way. Unfortunately, an organization cannot disconnect the telephones and fax machines just because it is implementing a supply chain management system. If the organization cannot convince people that using the software will be worth their time, they will easily find ways to work around it, which will quickly decrease the chances of success for the SCM system.

Ensure the SCM System Supports the Organizational Goals

It is important to select SCM software that gives organizations an advantage in the areas most crucial to their business success. If the organizational goals support highly efficient strategies, be sure the supply chain design has the same goals.

Deploy in Incremental Phases and Measure and Communicate Success

Design the deployment of the SCM system in incremental phases. For instance, instead of installing a complete supply chain management system across the company and all suppliers at once, start by getting it working with a few key suppliers, and then move on to the other suppliers. Along the way, make sure each step is adding value through improvements in the supply chain's performance. While a big-picture perspective is vital to SCM success, the incremental approach means the SCM system should be implemented in digestible bites, and also measured for success one step at a time.

Be Future Oriented

The supply chain design must anticipate the future state of the business. Because the SCM system likely will last for many more years than originally planned, managers need to explore how flexible the systems will be when (not if) changes are required in the future. The key is to be certain that the software will meet future needs, not only current needs.[10]

SCM SUCCESS STORIES

Figure 4.9 depicts the top reasons more and more executives are turning to SCM to manage their extended enterprises. Figure 4.10 lists several companies using supply chain management to drive operations.

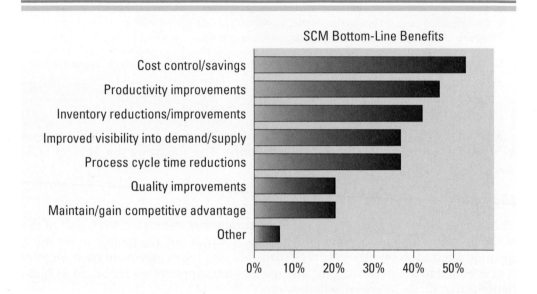

Companies Using Supply Chain To Drive Operations	
Dell	Business grows 17 percent per year with a $40 billion revenue base.
Nokia	Supply chain best practices are turning ideas into profitable businesses.
Procter & Gamble	Consumer-driven supply chain is the defining architecture for large consumer companies. Best practices in product innovation and supply chain effectiveness are tops.
IBM	Hardware supply chain product-development processes overhauled to the tune of 70 percent better, faster, and cheaper.
Wal-Mart Stores	Everyday low prices define the customer demand driving Wal-Mart's partner integrated supply chain.
Toyota Motor	Lean is one of the top three best practices associated with benchmarked supply chain excellence.
The Home Depot	Cutting-edge supply chain management improved logistics and innovative services.
Best Buy	SCM has radically thinned inventories and delivered enviable business positions.
Marks & Spencer	A pioneer in the use of radio frequency identification (RFID) in stores, Marks & Spencer manages to grow and stay lean.

Apple Computer initially distributed its business operations over 16 legacy applications. Apple quickly realized that it needed a new business model centred around an integrated supply chain to drive performance efficiencies. Apple devised an implementation strategy that focused on specific SCM functions—finance, sales, distribution, and manufacturing—that would most significantly help its business. The company decided to deploy leading-edge functionality with a new business model that provided:

- Build-to-order and configure-to-order manufacturing capabilities.
- Web-enabled configure-to-order order entry and order status for customers buying directly from Apple at Apple.com.
- Real-time credit card authorization.
- Available-to-promise and rules-based allocations.
- Integration to advanced planning systems.

Since its SCM system went live, Apple Computer has experienced substantial benefits in many areas including measurable improvements in its manufacturing processes, a decrease by 60 percent in its build-to-order and configure-to-order cycle times, and the ability to process more than 6,000 orders daily.[11]

OPENING CASE QUESTIONS

Dell's Famous Supply Chain

1. How might Dell use each of the five basic SCM components?
2. How has Dell influenced visibility, consumer behaviour, competition, and speed through the use of IT in its supply chain?
3. Explain the seven principles of SCM in reference to Dell's business model.

4.2 APPLYING A SUPPLY CHAIN DESIGN

USING INFORMATION TECHNOLOGY TO DRIVE THE SUPPLY CHAIN

This section takes a detailed look at how an organization can create a supply chain strategy focusing on efficiency and effectiveness. *Efficiency IT metrics* measure the performance of the IT system including throughput, speed, and availability. *Effectiveness IT metrics* measure the impact IT has on business processes and activities including customer satisfaction, conversion rates, and sell-through increases. An organization's goals and strategic objectives should determine its overall supply chain management strategy. The SCM strategy in turn determines how the supply chain will perform with respect to efficiency and effectiveness. The four primary drivers of supply chain management are:

1. Facilities
2. Inventory
3. Transportation
4. Information

An organization can use information technology to influence these four drivers in varying measure to push it toward either a supply chain strategy focusing on efficiency or a supply chain strategy focusing on effectiveness. The organization must decide on the trade-off it desires between efficiency and effectiveness for each driver. The selected combined impact of the various drivers then determines the efficiency and effectiveness of the entire supply chain. Figure 4.11 provides an overview of the four supply chain drivers in terms of their effect on overall efficiency and effectiveness.

FACILITIES DRIVER

A facility processes or transforms inventory into another product or it stores the inventory before shipping it to the next facility. Toyota is an example of a company that stresses *effectiveness* in its facilities. Toyota's goal is to open a facility in every major market where it does business. These local facilities protect the company from currency fluctuations and trade barriers and thus are more effective for Toyota's customers. An organization should consider three primary components when determining its facilities strategy:

1. Location
2. Capacity
3. Operational design

Location

An organization must determine where it will locate its facilities, an important decision that constitutes a large part of its supply chain strategy. Two primary options when determining facilities location are: (1) centralize the location to gain economies of scale, which increases efficiency, or (2) decentralize the locations to be closer to the customers, which increases effectiveness.

A company can gain economies of scale when it centralizes its facilities. However, this cost reduction decreases the company's effectiveness, since many of its customers may be located far away from the facility. The opposite is also true; having a number of different facilities located closer to customers reduces efficiency because of the increased costs associated with the additional facilities. Many other

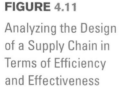

FIGURE 4.11

Analyzing the Design of a Supply Chain in Terms of Efficiency and Effectiveness

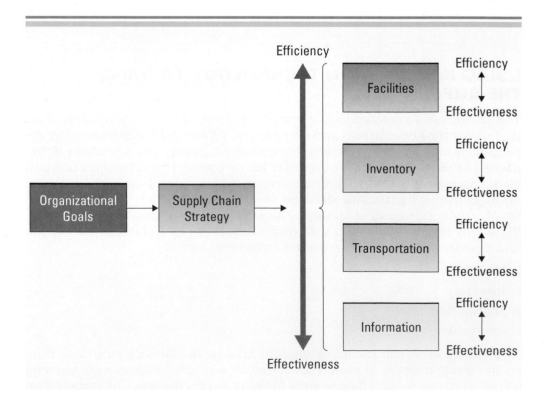

factors will influence location decisions including facility costs, employee expense, exchange rates, tax effects, and so on.

UPS uses package flow SCM systems at each of its locations. The custom-built software combines operations research and mapping technology to optimize the way boxes are loaded and delivered. The goal is to use the package flow software to cut the distance that delivery trucks travel by more than 160 million kilometres each year. The project will also help UPS streamline the profitability of each of its facility locations.

Capacity

Demand planning SCM software can help an organization determine capacity. An organization must determine the performance capacity level for each of its facilities. If it decides a facility will have a large amount of excess capacity, which provides the flexibility to respond to wide swings in demand, then it is choosing an effectiveness strategy. Excess capacity, however, costs money and can therefore decrease efficiency.

Operational Design

An organization must determine if it wants a product focus or a functional focus for its facilities operational design. If it chooses a product focus design, it is anticipating that the facility will produce only a certain type of product. All operations, including fabrication and assembly, will focus on developing a single type of product. This strategy allows the facility to become highly efficient in producing a single product.

If it chooses a functional design, the facility will perform a specific function (e.g., fabrication only or assembly only) on many different products. This strategy allows the facility to become more effective since it can use a single process on many different types of products (see Figure 4.12).

INVENTORY DRIVER

For most of business history, inventory has been a form of security. A warehouse bulging with components, or a distribution centre packed with finished products, meant that even when a customer forecast went wildly awry, there would still be enough supply on hand to meet demand. Ever since the 1980s, when General Motors began adopting Toyota's pioneering methods in lean manufacturing, fast companies have delayered, reengineered, and scrubbed the waste from their assembly lines and supply chains by slashing lead time and stripping inventory and spare capacity from their operations.

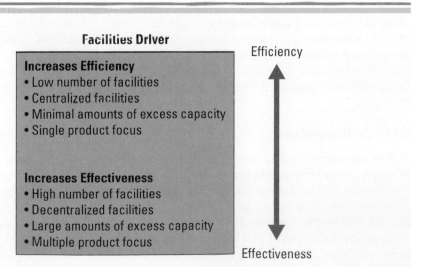

FIGURE 4.12

The Facilities Driver's Effect on Efficiency and Effectiveness

Companies require inventory to offset any discrepancies between supply and demand, but inventory is a major cost in any supply chain. Inventory's impact on a company's effectiveness versus efficiency can be enormous. Effectiveness results from more inventory, and efficiency results from less inventory. If a company's strategy requires a high level of customer effectiveness, then the company will locate large amounts of inventory in many facilities close to its customers. If a company's strategy requires a high level of efficiency, the strategy of a low-cost producer, for instance, then the company will maintain low levels of inventory in a single strategic location.

In order to help manage inventory levels, companies often turn to the use of information systems. For example, Howick Apparel Ltd.—a Canadian supplier and distributor of children's and young adult's garments that operates out of two manufacturing plants in Montreal, one in Saint-Sauveur, and three independent contracting plants located in Quebec—acquired a low-cost software system, Simtrak, to seamlessly connect to its top retailer, Sears, in order to monitor inventory levels and selling patterns. The Simtrak system, developed by a Montreal-based firm, helps Howick reduce inventory levels by downloading Sears' retail sales information and reproducing it in a manner that allows for rapid data analysis. With this information system, Howick is better able to forecast retail sales and control its inventory levels.[12]

Inventory management and control software provides control and visibility to the status of individual items maintained in inventory. The software maintains inventory record accuracy, generates material requirements for all purchased items, and analyzes inventory performance. Inventory management and control software provides the supply chain with information from a variety of sources including:

- Current inventory and order status.
- Cost accounting.
- Sales forecasts and customer orders.
- Manufacturing capacity.
- New-product introductions.

Inventory management and control software provides an organization with information when making decisions about two primary inventory strategies including:

1. Cycle inventory
2. Safety inventory

Cycle Inventory

Cycle inventory is the average amount of inventory held to satisfy customer demands between inventory deliveries. A company can follow either of two approaches regarding cycle inventory. The first approach is to hold a large amount of cycle inventory and receive inventory deliveries only once a month. The second approach is to hold a small amount of inventory and receive orders weekly or even daily. The trade-off is the cost comparison between holding larger lots of inventory for an effective supply chain and ordering products frequently for an efficient supply chain.

Safety Inventory

Safety inventory is extra inventory held in the event demand exceeds supply. For example, a toy store might hold safety inventory for the Christmas season. The risk a company faces when making a decision in favour of safety inventory is that in addition to the cost of holding it, if it holds too much, some of its products may go unsold and it may have to discount them—after the Christmas season, in the toy store example. However, if it holds too little inventory it may lose sales and risk losing customers. The company must decide if it wants to risk the expense of carrying too much inventory or to risk losing sales and customers (see Figure 4.13).

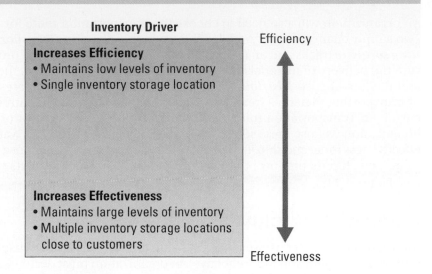

TRANSPORTATION DRIVER

Organizations use IT-enabled supply chain management systems that use quantitative analysis, decision support systems, and intelligent systems for configuring shipping plans. FedEx's entire business strategy focuses on its customers' need for highly effective transportation methods. Any company that uses FedEx to transport a package is focusing primarily on a safe and timely delivery and not on the cost of delivery. Many businesses even locate their facilities near FedEx hubs so that they can quickly transport inventory overnight to their customers.

An organization can use many different methods of transportation to move its inventories between the different stages in the supply chain. Like the other supply chain drivers, transportation cost has a large impact either way on effectiveness and efficiency. If an organization focuses on a highly effective supply chain, then it can use transportation to increase the price of its products by using faster, more costly transportation methods. If the focus is a highly efficient supply chain, the organization can use transportation to decrease the price of its products by using slower, less costly transportation methods. Two primary facets of transportation an organization should consider when determining its strategy are:

1. Method of transportation
2. Transportation route

Method of Transportation

An organization must decide how it wants to move its inventory through the supply chain. There are six basic methods of transportation: truck, rail, ship, air, pipeline, and electronic. The primary differences between these methods are the speed of delivery and price of delivery. An organization might choose an expensive method of transportation to ensure speedy delivery if it is focusing on a highly effective supply chain. On the other hand, it might choose an inexpensive method of transportation if it is focusing on a highly efficient supply chain. Some organizations will use a ***global inventory management system*** that provides the ability to locate, track, and predict the movement of every component or material anywhere upstream or downstream in the supply chain. So regardless of the chosen method of transportation, the organization can find its inventory anywhere in the supply chain.

Transportation Route

An organization will also need to choose the transportation route for its products. Two supply chain software modules can aid in this decision. *Transportation planning software* tracks and analyzes the movement of materials and products to ensure the delivery of materials and finished goods at the right time, the right place, and the lowest cost. *Distribution management software* coordinates the process of transporting materials from a manufacturer to distribution centres to the final customer. Transportation route directly affects the speed and cost of delivery. An organization will use these software modules to help it decide if it wants to use an effectiveness route and ship its products directly to its customers, or use an efficiency route and ship its products to a distributor that ships the products to customers (see Figure 4.14).

INFORMATION DRIVER

Information is a driver whose importance has grown as companies use it to become both more efficient and more effective. An organization must decide what information is most valuable in efficiently reducing costs or in improving effectiveness. This decision will vary depending on a company's strategy and the design and organization of the supply chain. Two things to consider about information in the supply chain are:

1. Information sharing.
2. Push verses pull information strategy.

Information Sharing

An organization must determine what information it wants to share with its partners throughout the stages of the supply chain. Information sharing is a difficult decision since most organizations do not want their partners to gain insight into strategic or competitive information. However, they do need to share information so they can coordinate supply chain activities such as providing suppliers with inventory order levels to meet production forecasts. Building trusting relationships is one way to begin to understand how much information supply chain partners require.

If an organization chooses an efficiency focus for information sharing, then it will freely share lots of information to increase the speed and decrease the costs of supply chain processing. If an organization chooses an effectiveness focus for information

FIGURE 4.14

The Transportation Driver's Effect on Efficiency and Effectiveness

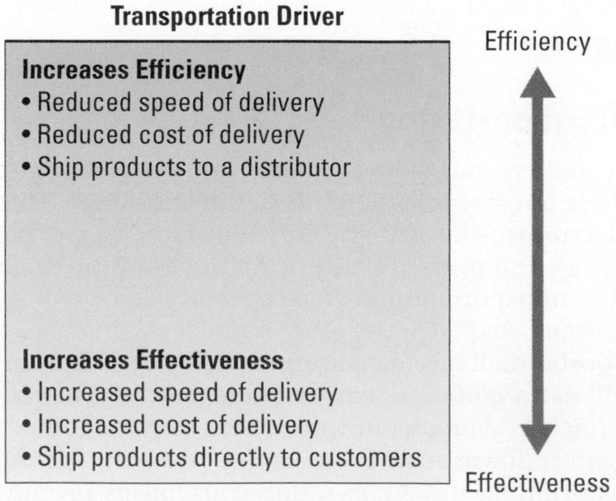

Transportation Driver

Increases Efficiency
- Reduced speed of delivery
- Reduced cost of delivery
- Ship products to a distributor

Increases Effectiveness
- Increased speed of delivery
- Increased cost of delivery
- Ship products directly to customers

Efficiency

Effectiveness

sharing, then it will share only selected information with certain individuals, which will decrease the speed and increase the costs of supply chain processing.

Push versus Pull Information Strategy

In a ***push technology*** environment, organizations send information. In a ***pull technology*** environment, organizations receive or request information. An organization must decide how it is going to share information with its partners. It might decide that it wants to push information out to partners by taking on the responsibility of sending information to them. On the other hand, it might decide that it wants its partners to take on the responsibility of getting information by having them directly access the information from the systems and pull the information they require.

Again, an organization must determine how much it trusts its partners when deciding on a push versus pull information-sharing strategy. Using a push information-sharing strategy is more effective because the organization has control over exactly what information is shared and when the information is shared. However, a push strategy is less efficient because there are costs associated with sending information such as computer equipment, applications, time, resources, and so forth.

Using a pull information-sharing strategy is more efficient since the organization does not have to undertake the costs associated with sending information. However, the pull strategy is less effective since the organization has no control over when the information is pulled. For example, if the company needs inventory there is no guarantee that the suppliers will pick up the information. Hence, an organization could find itself in trouble if its partners forget to obtain the information and fail to deliver the required products (see Figure 4.15).

APPLYING A SUPPLY CHAIN DESIGN

Figure 4.16 displays Wal-Mart's supply chain management design and how it correlates to its competitive strategy to be a reliable, low-cost retailer for a wide variety of mass consumption goods. Wal-Mart's supply chain emphasizes efficiency, but also maintains an adequate level of effectiveness.

- **Facilities focus**—efficiency: Wal-Mart maintains few warehouses and will build a new warehouse only when demand is high enough to justify one.
- **Inventory focus**—efficiency: Wal-Mart ships directly to its stores from the manufacturer. This significantly lowers inventory levels because stores maintain inventory, not stores and warehouses.

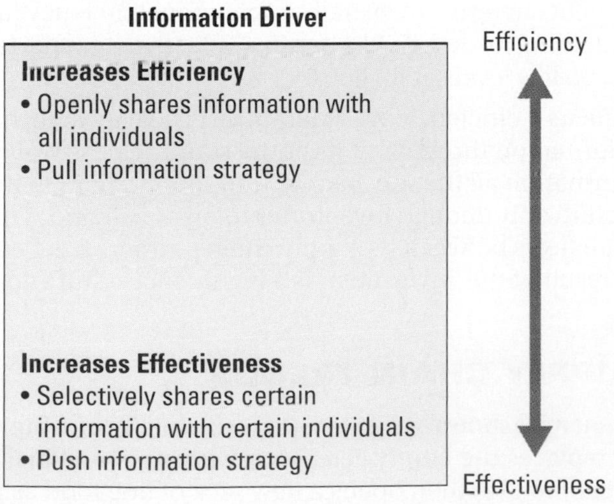

Information Driver

Increases Efficiency
• Openly shares information with all individuals
• Pull information strategy

Increases Effectiveness
• Selectively shares certain information with certain individuals
• Push information strategy

Efficiency

Effectiveness

FIGURE 4.15

The Information Driver's Effect on Efficiency and Effectiveness

FIGURE 4.16

Wal-Mart's Supply Chain Management Drivers

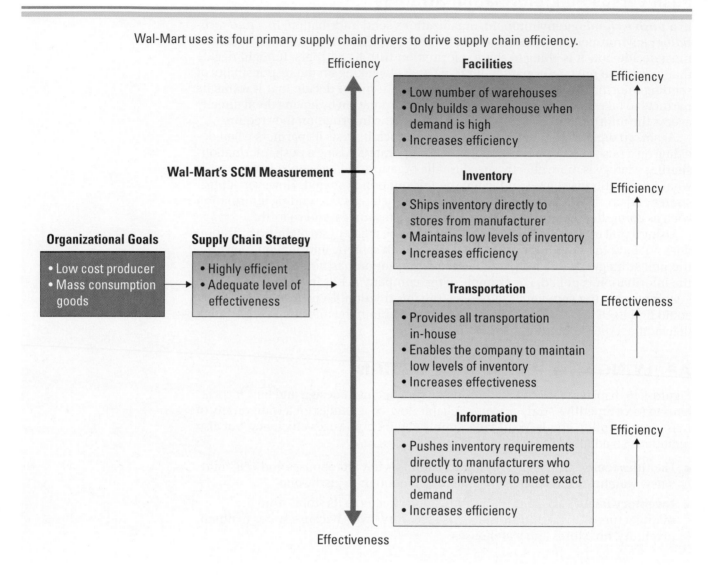

Wal-Mart uses its four primary supply chain drivers to drive supply chain efficiency.

■ **Transportation focus**—effectiveness: Wal-Mart maintains its own fleet of trucks. The benefits in terms of overall supply chain efficiency justify the expense of maintaining its own trucks because effective transportation allows Wal-Mart to keep low levels of inventory.

■ **Information focus**—efficiency: Wal-Mart invests heavily in technology and the flow of information throughout its entire supply chain. Wal-Mart pushes inventory information all the way back up the supply chain to its suppliers who then manufacture only enough inventories to meet demand. The cost to build the information flows between its supply chain partners has been tremendous. However, the result of this investment is a highly successful and efficient supply chain.[13]

FUTURE SUPPLY CHAIN TRENDS

A television commercial shows a man in a uniform quietly moving through a family home. The man replaces the empty cereal box with a full one just before a hungry child opens the cabinet. He then opens a new sack of dog food as the hungry bulldog eyes him warily, and finally hands a full bottle of shampoo to the man in the shower who had just run out. The next wave in supply chain management will be home-based supply chain fulfillment.

Walgreens, the largest retail pharmacy chain in the United States, is differentiating itself from other national chains by marketing itself as the family's just-in-time supplier. Consumers today are becoming incredibly comfortable with the idea of going online to purchase products when they want, how they want, and at the price they want. Walgreens is developing custom Web sites for each household that allow families to order electronically and then at their convenience go to the store to pick up their goods at a special self-service counter or the drive-through window. Walgreens is making a promise that goes beyond low prices and customer service and extends right into the home.[14]

The functionality in supply chain management systems is becoming more and more sophisticated as supply chain management matures. Now and in the future, the next stages of SCM will incorporate more functions such as marketing, customer service, and product development. This will be achieved through more advanced communication networks, adoption of more user-friendly decision support systems, and availability of shared information to all participants in the supply chain. SCM is an ongoing development as technology makes it possible to acquire information ever more accurately and frequently from all over the world, and introduces new tools to aid in the analytical processes that deal with the supply chain's growing complexity.

According to Forrester Research, Inc., American firms will spend US$35 billion over the next five years to improve business processes that monitor, manage, and optimize their extended supply chains. Figure 4.17 displays the fastest growing SCM components that can have the greatest potential impact on an organization's bottom line.[15]

New technologies are also going to improve the supply chain. Radio frequency identification (RFID) technologies use active or passive tags in the form of chips or smart labels that can store unique identifiers and relay this information to electronic readers. RFID will become an effective tool for tracking and monitoring inventory movement in a real-time SCM environment. The real-time information will provide managers with an instant and accurate view of inventories within the supply chain.

Using current SCM systems, the RFID will check the inventory status and then trigger the replenishment process. Organizations using RFIDs will be able to quickly and accurately provide current inventory levels (in real-time) at any point in the supply chain. Reducing inventory levels to their reorder points allows electronic regeneration of replenishment orders. With quick and accurate information about inventories, the use of safety stock levels guarding against uncertainty can also be reduced. Hence, the potential benefits of RFIDs include a reduction of human intervention (or required labour) and holding fewer inventories, which nets a reduction in operating costs.

Growing SCM Components	
Supply chain event management (SCEM)	Enables an organization to react more quickly to resolve supply chain issues. SCEM software increases real-time information sharing among supply chain partners and decreases their response time to unplanned events. SCEM demand will skyrocket as more and more organizations begin to discover the benefits of real-time supply chain monitoring.
Selling chain management	Applies technology to the activities in the order life cycle from inquiry to sale.
Collaborative engineering	Allows an organization to reduce the cost and time required during the design process of a product.
Collaborative demand planning	Helps organizations reduce their investment in inventory, while improving customer satisfaction through product availability.

FIGURE 4.17

Fast Growth SCM Components

An interesting project that involves the development and use of new technology for container tracking is the Canada–U.S. Cargo Security Project. This international/regional initiative has the support of Transport Canada and the ports of Halifax and Montreal, as well as U.S. federal and state agencies. The purpose of the project is to provide a rapidly assembled prototype test-bed for elements of cargo container supply chain security. The goal is to develop technology for international container shipping that maintains open borders and facilitates commerce, while improving security practices.[16]

Above all, the system validates and tracks the movement of containerized cargo by using technology to report a container's status and post it to a Web site in real time where it can be analyzed by authorized agencies. The technology involves use of a matchbook-sized "micro-impulse radar detector," which is so sensitive that it can sense if a person is moving in a container, or if an intruder has cut a hole in the side. A prototype has been developed and there are hopes to improve the system to create a small, lightweight integrated package that could be adopted by the container shipping industry en masse.[17]

OPENING CASE QUESTIONS

Dell's Famous Supply Chain

4. Identify the four primary drivers of SCM and explain how Dell uses each one to gain efficiency or effectiveness in its supply chain.

5. Choose one of the fast growth SCM components and explain how Dell can use it to increase business operations.

6. What is RFID and how could Dell use the technology to improve its supply chain?

The purpose of this chapter was:

■ to introduce the concept of supply chain management, and

■ to showcase how information technology can be used to improve supply chain processes.

As this chapter has illustrated, supply chains exist across a variety of sectors and industries. Various examples were given showcasing information technology's ability to help organizations improve their interactions with suppliers, manufacturers, distributors, warehouses, and customers. As a business student, you should understand this pivotal role that information technology plays in facilitating supply chain processes and in supporting the basic infrastructure and coordination needed for supply chains to function.

KEY TERMS

Bullwhip effect   108
Collaborative demand
     planning   121
Collaborative engineering   121
Cycle inventory   116
Demand planning
     software   108
Distribution management
     software   118
Effectiveness IT metrics   113
Efficiency IT metrics   113

Global inventory management
     system   117
Inventory management and
     control software   116
Logistics   106
Pull technology   119
Push technology   119
Safety inventory   116
Selling chain
     management   121
Supply chain   104

Supply chain event
     management (SCEM)   121
Supply chain execution (SCE)
     software   109
Supply chain management
     (SCM)   104
Supply chain planning (SCP)
     software   108
Supply chain visibility   107
Transportation planning
     software   118

CLOSING CASE ONE

Canada's CareNET Rescues the Health Care Supply Chain

This case illustrates the use of information technology in the health care sector to improve supply chain performance.

When compared to other organizations that rely on and order significant volumes of supplies and materials to run their businesses, hospitals are laggards in the deployment of information technology. Hospitals need a variety of materials, surgical instruments, and medical supplies on a daily basis. According to David Yundt, president and Chief Operation Officer at Hospital Logistics Inc., a for-profit hospital supply and logistics company launched by the University Health Network in Toronto, hospitals historically have focused their energy and capital on direct patient care as opposed to improving the supply chain. This problem is compounded when one considers the tight financial budgets that constrain hospital operations and the general inertia that exists in today's hospitals from moving away from labour-intensive, manual materials-management processes. With a highly fragmented hospital industry, there is no developed standard for naming, describing, ordering, and paying for the tens of thousands of products that hospitals use. Further, most hospitals lack integrated computer systems that handle ordering, tracking, and paying for supplies. This leads to poor buying habits by hospitals since supplies are purchased individually by physicians and clinicians rather than being contracted en masse at a greatly reduced contracted price.[18]

To the rescue comes CareNET Services Inc., an association of Canadian health care providers and suppliers established in 1990 that promotes, educates, facilitates, and supports the use of electronic commerce. CareNET's goal is to improve business processes and reduce costs throughout the health care supply chain. In 2007, CareNET membership consisted of 437 hospitals and long-term care facilities and 95 suppliers. CareNET Services Inc. is a federally incorporated Canadian company that offers all its member organizations an equal opportunity to communicate with one another.[19]

To facilitate this, CareNET utilizes an electronic data interchange system that simplifies the exchange of business documents between health care providers and suppliers. This information systems allows CareNET members and suppliers to transfer purchase orders, acknowledgements, invoices, and payments in a standard data format. This universally accessible format improves processes by allowing businesses to connect and transact with one another and by reducing costs throughout the health care supply chain. The result is more efficient procurement transactions: quotations, contracts, orders, order acknowledgements, advance ship notices, invoicing, and payment.

To ensure these transactions are delivered in a secure fashion and on time, CareNET relies on the expertise of BCE Emergis (www.emergis.ca), an information technology leader in Canada that focuses on the health and financial services sectors. The company develops and manages solutions that automate transactions and the secure exchange of information to increase the process efficiency and quality of service of its customers. Emergis has expertise in electronic health-related claims processing, health record systems, and pharmacy management solutions. In Canada, Emergis delivers its solutions to the main insurance companies, top financial institutions, government agencies, hospitals, large corporations, and 2,900 pharmacies. Its electronic health record solutions are also delivered in the U.S. and Australia.

According to Miriam Tuerk, president of BCE Emergis EBusiness Solutions, "there has never been a greater need for an efficient network in health care procurement . . . with CareNET, BCE Emergis can deliver supply chain efficiencies through a single process and a single point of integration between health care providers and their suppliers." This is good news for the health care sector.[20]

Questions

1. What problems plague the delivery of efficient supply chains in the Canadian health care sector?

2. How does CareNET help mitigate these problems? What aspects of CareNET help make the health care supply chain more effective and efficient?

3. SCM is experiencing explosive growth. Explain why this statement is true using CareNET as an example.

4. Evaluate CareNET's effect on each of the four factors that are driving SCM success.

CLOSING CASE TWO

Listerine's Journey

This case shows how information technology can enhance supply chain performance on a global scale.

When you use Listerine antiseptic mouthwash, you are experiencing the last step in a complex supply chain spanning several continents and requiring months of coordination by countless businesses and individuals. The resources involved in getting a single bottle of Listerine to a consumer are unbelievable. As raw material transforms into finished product, what will be Listerine travels around the globe and through multiple supply chains and information systems.

The Journey Begins

A farmer in Australia is harvesting a crop of eucalyptus for eucalyptol, the oil found in its leathery leaves. The farmer sells the crop to an Australian processing company, which spends about four weeks extracting the eucalyptol from the eucalyptus.

Meanwhile, in New Jersey, Warner-Lambert (WL) partners with a distributor to buy the oil from the Australian company and transport it to WL's Listerine manufacturing and distribution facility in Lititz, Pennsylvania. The load will arrive at Lititz about three months after the harvest.

At the same time, in Saudi Arabia, a government-owned operation is drilling deep under the desert for the natural gas that will yield the synthetic alcohol that gives Listerine its 43-proof punch. Union Carbide Corp. ships the gas via tanker to a refinery in Texas, which purifies it and converts it into ethanol. The ethanol is loaded onto another tanker, and then transported from Texas through the Gulf of Mexico to New Jersey, where it is transferred to storage tanks and transported via truck or rail to WL's plant. A single shipment of ethanol takes about six to eight weeks to get from Saudi Arabia to Lititz.

SPI Polyols Inc., a manufacturer of ingredients for the confectionery, pharmaceutical, and oral-care industries, buys corn syrup from farmers in the Midwest. SPI converts the corn syrup into sorbitol solution, which sweetens and adds bulk to the Cool Mint Listerine. The syrup is shipped to SPI's New Castle, Delaware, facility for processing and then delivered on a tank wagon to Lititz. The whole process, from the time the corn is harvested to when it is converted into sorbitol, takes about a month.

By now the ethanol, eucalyptol, and sorbitol have all arrived at WL's plant in Lititz, where employees test them, along with the menthol, citric acid, and other ingredients that make up Listerine, for quality assurance before authorizing storage in tanks. To mix the ingredients, flow meters turn on valves at each tank and measure out the right proportions, according to the Cool Mint formula developed by WL R&D in 1990. (The original amber mouthwash was developed in 1879.)

Next, the Listerine flows through a pipe to fillers along the packaging line. The fillers dispense the product into bottles delivered continuously from a nearby plastics company for just-in-time manufacturing. The bottles are capped, labelled, and fitted with tamper-resistant safety bands, then placed in shipping boxes that each hold one dozen 500-millilitre bottles. During this process, machines automatically check for skewed labels, missing safety bands, and other problems. The entire production cycle, from the delivery via pipe of the Listerine liquid to the point where bottles are boxed and ready to go, takes a matter of minutes. The line can produce about 300 bottles per minute—a far cry from the 80 to 100 bottles that the line produced per minute before 1994.

Each box travels on a conveyor belt to the palletizer, which organizes and shrink-wraps the boxes into 100-case pallets. Stickers with identifying bar codes are affixed to the pallets. Drivers forklift the pallets to the distribution centre, located in the same Lititz facility, from which the boxes are shipped around the world.

Finally, the journey is completed when a customer purchases a bottle of Listerine at a local drugstore or grocery store. In a few days, the store will place an order for a replacement bottle of Listerine. And so begins the cycle again.[21]

Questions

1. Summarize SCM and describe Warner-Lambert's supply chain strategy. Diagram the SCM components.
2. Detail Warner-Lambert's facilities strategy.
3. Detail Warner-Lambert's inventory strategy.
4. What would happen to Warner-Lambert's business if a natural disaster in Saudi Arabia depletes its natural gas resources?

5. Assess the impact to Warner-Lambert's business if the majority of the eucalyptus crop was destroyed in a natural disaster.
6. Detail Warner-Lambert's information strategy.

CLOSING CASE THREE

How Levi's Got Its Jeans into Wal-Mart

The case illustrates how information technology can improve supply chain performance between two companies.

People around the world recognize Levi's as an American icon, the cool jeans worn by movie stars James Dean and Marilyn Monroe. For one reason or another, however, the company failed to keep up with the fast-changing tastes of American teenagers. In particular, it missed the trend to baggy jeans that caught hold in the mid-1990s. Sales plummeted from $8.4 billion in 1996 to $4.8 billion in 2003, and Levi's U.S. market share dropped from 18.7 percent in 1997 to 12 percent in 2003, a huge decline of almost one-third in both dollars and market share.

Analyzing and Responding to What Happened

Competition hit Levi Strauss on both the high and low ends. Fashion-conscious buyers were drawn to high-priced brands like Blue Cult, Juicy, and Seven, which had more fashion cachet than Levi's. On the low end, parents were buying Wrangler and Lee jeans for their kids because on average they cost about $12 less than Levi's Red Tab brand. Wrangler and Lee were also the brands they found at discount retailers such as Wal-Mart, Target, and T. J. Maxx. David Bergen, Levi's chief information officer (CIO), described the company as "getting squeezed," and "caught in the jaws of death."

Levi Strauss's new CEO, Philip A. Marineau, came to the company from PepsiCo in 1999, a year after he helped PepsiCo surpass Coca-Cola in sales for the first time. Marineau recruited Bergen in 2000 from Carstation.com. Marineau quickly realized that turning Levi Strauss around would entail manufacturing, marketing, and distributing jeans that customers demanded, particularly customers at the low end where the mass market was located.

Bergen was eager to join Marineau's team because of his background in clothing, retailing, and manufacturing with companies such as The Gap and Esprit de Corps in the 1980s. He knew that Marineau's plan to anticipate customer wants would require up-to-date IT applications such as data warehousing, data mining, and customer relationship management (CRM) systems. He also knew that selling to mass market retailers would require upgrades to the supply chain management (SCM) systems, and he understood that globalization would necessitate standardized enterprise resource planning (ERP) systems. Overall, it was a challenge any ambitious CIO would covet. After all, designing and installing IT systems that drive and achieve key business initiatives is what it is all about.

Joining Wal-Mart

Wal-Mart was a pioneer in supply chain management systems, having learned early on that driving costs out of the supply chain would let it offer products to customers at the lowest possible prices, while at the same time assuring that products the customers demanded were always on the stores' shelves. Becoming one of Wal-Mart's 30,000 suppliers is not easy. Wal-Mart insists that its suppliers do business using up-to-date IT systems to manage the supply chain—not just the supply chain between Wal-Mart and its suppliers, but the supply chains between the suppliers and their suppliers as well. Wal-Mart has strict supply chain management system requirements that its business partners must meet.

Wal-Mart's requirements presented Levi Strauss with a serious hurdle to overcome because its supply chain management systems were in bad shape. Levi Strauss executives did not even have access to key information required to track where its products were moving in the supply chain. For example, they did not know how many pairs of jeans were in the factory awaiting shipment, how many were somewhere en route, or how many had just been unloaded at a customer's warehouse. According to Greg Hammann, Levi's U.S. chief customer officer, "Our supply chain could not deliver the services Wal-Mart expected."

Bergen created a cross-functional team of key managers from IT, finance, and sales to transform Levi Strauss's systems to meet Wal-Mart's requirements. Their recommendations included network upgrades, modifications to ordering and logistics applications, and data warehouse improvements, among others. Although Bergen realized that about half the changes required to current IT systems to accommodate the state-of-the-art demands of Wal-Mart would be a waste of resources since these systems were being replaced by a new SAP enterprise software system over the next five years, Levi Strauss could not wait for the SAP installation if it wanted Wal-Mart's business now, so it decided to move forward with the changes to the current systems.

The successful transformation of its supply chain management system allowed the company to collaborate with Wal-Mart. The company introduced its new signature line at Wal-Mart, which sells for around $27 and has fewer details in the finish than Levi's other lines, no trademark pocket stitching or red tab, for example. Wal-Mart wants big-name brands to lure more affluent customers into its stores, while still maintaining the low price points all Wal-Mart customers have come to expect. Wal-Mart Senior Vice President Lois Mikita noted that Wal-Mart "continues to tailor its selection to meet the needs of customers from a cross section of income levels and lifestyles." She also stated she is impressed with the level of detail Levi Strauss has put into its systems transformation efforts to "make the execution of this new launch 100 percent."

Achieving Business Success Through IT

Bergen's changes were a success and the percentage of products delivered on time quickly rose from 65 percent to 95 percent primarily because of the updated supply chain management system. Levi's total sales were also up in the third and fourth quarters of 2003, for the first time since 1996. NPD Group's Fashionworld is a research group that tracks apparel and footwear market trends. In 2003, Levi's appeared on NPD Fashionworld's top 10 list of brands preferred by young women, ending an absence of several years. Marshall Cohen, a senior industry analyst at NPD Fashionworld, noted that Levi's "hadn't been close to that for a while. Teens hadn't gravitated toward Levi's in years. That was incredible. A lot of that has to do with having the right style in the right place at the right time." The improved systems, Cohen noted, also helped the company get the right sizes to the right stores.

Another highly successful IT system implemented by Levi Strauss is a digital dashboard that executives can display on their PC screens. The dashboard lets an executive see the status of a product as it moves from the factory floor to distribution centres to retail stores. For example, the dashboard can display how Levi's 501 jeans are selling at an individual Kohl's store compared to forecasted sales. "When I first got here I didn't see anything," Hammann said. "Now I can drill down to the product level."

The digital dashboard alerts executives to trends that under the previous systems would have taken weeks to detect. For example, in 2003 Levi Strauss started to ship Dockers Stain Defender pants. Expected sales for the pants were around 2 million pairs. The digital dashboard quickly notified key executives that the trousers were selling around 2.5 million pairs. This information enabled them to adjust production upward in time to ship more pants, meet the increased demand, and avoid lost sales. Levi Strauss also uses the systems to control supply during key seasonal sales periods such as back-to-school and Christmas.

"If I look overconfident, I'm not," Bergen said. "I'm very nervous about this change. When we trip, we have to stand up real quick and get back on the horse, as they say." As if to reinforce Bergen's point, Gib Carey, a supply chain analyst at Bain, noted, "The place where companies do fail is when they aren't bringing anything new to Wal-Mart. Wal-Mart is constantly looking at 'How can I get the same product I am selling today at a lower price somewhere else?'"[22]

Questions

1. How did Levi Strauss achieve business success through the use of supply chain management?

2. What might have happened to Levi's if its top executives had not supported investments in SCM?

3. David Bergen, Levi's CIO, put together a cross-functional team of key managers from IT, finance, and sales to transform Levi's systems to meet Wal-Mart's requirements. Analyze the relationships between these three business areas and SCM systems. How can an SCM system help support these three critical business areas?

4. Describe the five basic SCM components in reference to Wal-Mart's business model.

5. Explain RFID and provide an example of how Levi's could use the technology to increase its business operations.

MAKING BUSINESS DECISIONS

1. Analyzing Dell's supply chain management system

Dell's supply chain strategy is legendary. Essentially, if you want to build a successful SCM system your best bet is to model your SCM system after Dell's. In a team, research Dell's supply chain management strategy on the Web and create a report discussing any new SCM updates and strategies the company is currently using that were not discussed in this text. Be sure to include a graphical presentation of Dell's current supply chain model.

2. Focusing on facilities

Focus is a large distributor of films and is owned and operated by Lauren O'Connell. The company has been in business for more than 50 years and distributes motion pictures to theatres all over the United States and Canada. Focus is in the middle of a supply chain overhaul and is currently deciding its supply chain strategy. Lauren has asked you to create a report discussing the company's options for its facilities including location, capacity, and operational design. The report should include two primary focuses: one on efficiency and one on effectiveness.

3. Investing in inventory

Poppa's Toy Store Inc. has more then 30 stores in six provinces. The chain has been owned and operated for the last 30 years by CEO Taylor Coombe. Taylor has been reading reports on supply chain management and is particularly interested in updating the company's current supply chain. It is the beginning of April and Taylor wants a new SCM system up and running before the Christmas season starts in November. Taylor is particularly interested in demand planning and forecasting for the entire company's inventory during its busiest season—Christmas. Taylor has asked you to create a report discussing the company's options for its inventory management strategy including cycle and safety inventory. The report should include two primary focuses: one on efficiency and one on effectiveness.

4. Increasing information

Galina's is a high-end auction house located in Vancouver. Galina's specializes in selling jewellery, art, and antique furniture primarily from estate sales. The owner, Galina Bucrya, would like to begin offering certain items for auction over the Internet. Galina is unfamiliar with the Internet and not quite sure how to pursue her new business strategy. You are working for Information Inc., a small business consulting company that specializes in e-business strategies. Galina has hired you to help her create her supply chain e-business strategy. Compile a report describing supply chain management, the potential benefits her company can receive from an SCM strategy, your recommendation for an efficient or effective SCM strategy, and your views on the future of SCM.

5. **Increasing revenues with SCM**

Cold Cream is one of the premier beauty supply stores in the metro Toronto area. People come from all over to sample the store's unique creams, lotions, makeup, and perfumes. The company receives its products from manufacturers around the globe. The company would like to implement an SCM system to help it better understand its customers and their purchasing habits. Create a report summarizing SCM systems and explain how an SCM system can directly influence Cold Cream's revenues.

Customer Relationship Management

CHAPTER 5

LEARNING OUTCOMES

5.1. Compare operational and analytical customer relationship management.

5.2. Explain the formula an organization can use to find its most valuable customers.

5.3. Describe and differentiate the CRM technologies used by marketing departments, sales departments, and customer service departments.

5.4. Identify the primary forces driving the explosive growth of customer relationship management.

5.5. Summarize the best practices for implementing a successful customer relationship management system.

5.6. Compare customer relationship management, supplier relationship management, partner relationship management, and employee relationship management.

Why Do I Need To Know This ?

This chapter elaborates upon the concept of customer relationship management (CRM), first introduced in Chapter 3, and discusses how information technology can be used to support firms in their interactions with customers. At the simplest level, organizations implement CRM to gain a better understanding of customer needs and behaviours, and information technology provides companies with a new channel to communicate with customers beyond those traditionally used by organizations such as face-to-face or paper-based methods.

The information technology channel is exciting in that it can be automated and personalized at the same time, conducted at significantly reduced costs, and available 24/7—at times most convenient to customers. Further, technology can be used to gather and assimilate information about customers regardless of the method of contact a customer chooses to interact with a company. Assimilating customer information obtained through various channels can help organizations know and better understand its customers and help improve customer relations.

Organizations recognize the importance of maintaining and fostering healthy relationships with customers. Doing so has a direct and positive effect on customer loyalty and retention. This adds to a company's profitability and provides an edge over competitors who fail to foster customer relationships. This is why customer relationship management is important and why you, the business student, need to know this.

As a business student, you should also be aware of and recognize the potential value of information technology in facilitating and improving customer relationships. Technology is at the heart of most customer relationship management strategies used by organizations today. You need to be knowledgeable of its benefits and the various ways it can be leveraged for organizational success.

Harnessing Customer Relationships at Fairmont Hotels & Resorts

Richard Wilson was impressed during his stay at Fairmont Vancouver Airport. He had just signed up for the hospitality chain's guest recognition program, "President's Club," and couldn't remember his loyalty program number when he checked in. He ended up not needing to know. The hotel employee simply asked Richard to supply his last name and the name of the company he worked for in order to pull up his file from the hotel's computer records. With his file displayed, the hotel employee quickly noticed that Richard's company information was out-of-date and that his credit card was going to expire within 30 days. So the employee asked Richard to leave his new business card at the desk so that his personal information could be updated in his records after he was checked in. Richard was thrilled with this personal care and attention, wishing other businesses could offer such a good level of service.[1]

Fairmont would be pleased with this story. It embarked on its guest recognition program as a means of offering special benefits and privileges to customers, as well as to reflect individual travel preferences and provide an enhanced level of service. The difficulty, however, in doing this well is a direct result of Fairmont's size and expanse. Fairmont Hotels & Resorts (FHR) is a leading owner/operator of luxury hotels and resorts around the world. Through its various holdings, FHR is North America's largest luxury hotel management company, with several distinctive city centre and resort hotels in Canada including The Fairmont Banff Springs in Alberta, Fairmont Le Château Frontenac in Quebec, and The Fairmont Algonquin in New Brunswick.

With such a large and expansive network of hotels and resorts, FHR realizes that information technology is critical to the success of a customer loyalty program like President's Club or any other customer relationship initiative.

Case in point is how the company consolidated guest information gathered across its hotel and resort locations. In 2001, when Canadian Pacific spun off Fairmont into its own independent company, FHR built a central repository of information about what its customers wanted. These included things like preferences for bed size, room proximity to elevators, local or national newspapers, and activities patrons might be interested in. The problem was that, at that time, each hotel maintained its own separate guest database and had no incentive or urgency to share this information with others. In response, Fairmont built one centralized database that gathered information from all its various property management systems. The result was the ability to have one, centralized and consistent view of each guest, regardless of which hotel a guest stayed in. According to Sean Taggart, Fairmont's Executive Director of Marketing Services, the project was all about capturing information about Fairmont's guests as a means of servicing them better and to deliver customized, personalized experiences for each guest at any Fairmont hotel. Moreover, according to Taggart, the guest database provided hotels with the ability to know and talk with guests, to service them based on their preferences and interests, regardless if they were high-repeat customers or if they were checking in at a Fairmont brand hotel they may have never been to before in their lives.[2]

Fairmont Hotels & Resorts is quite committed to providing its guests with leading technology solutions in its hotels to enhance the guest experience and foster customer relations. In 2006, the hotel conglomerate chose Superclick, through its wholly-owned Montreal-based subsidiary Superclick Networks, to provide dedicated 24/7 customer support to its guests using Superclick's state-of-the-art high-speed Internet services at various Fairmont hotel and resort locations worldwide. Fairmont's relationship with Superclick allows guests staying at Fairmont hotels or resorts to receive the same online experience with their laptops they would receive at home or in the office.[3]

Another example of FHR's use of information technology to improve guest relations and the customer experience is its consideration of self-service check-in kiosks. In 2005, Fairmont pioneered the idea in Toronto where people could use a kiosk to check in, pick up hotel keys, and even choose a room. Once guests swipe their credit card at the kiosk, a person doesn't need to enter any extra personal details. On leaving, guests can settle their accounts at the kiosk, drop off keys and even obtain a boarding pass for any Air Canada flight before heading to the airport.[4]

Fairmont seems to be ahead of the game when it comes to customer relationship management. A 2005 study conducted by the Manton Group in Toronto suggests that Canadian companies are faring poorly with respect to customer-intelligence. The study's report details how organizations in Canada are simply not doing a very good job at leveraging the customer data they collect, turning that data into knowledge, and coming up with solutions to provide the services customers want and need. The report outlines how a dozen Canadian companies in a variety of industries go about transforming the customer information they collect into customer-intelligence. The report grades these businesses on how well they manage their core customer-intelligence. These categories include strategy and objectives, customer-experience delivery, customer-intelligence practices, and intelligent customer-interaction channels. The report also evaluates companies on their ability to handle customers through various relationship phases: attraction, service, growth, and nurturing. In the report, the companies were given an overall average score of only 40 out of 100. Despite this low rating, there is some good news. The top four companies in the report that scored best embarked on customer relationship management initiatives that worked. These included things like loyalty programs, printing the savings a customer receives on the bottom of a receipt, using targeted promotion based on a customer's past history, or invitation-only product previews and gifts.[5]

So what can be taken from this? Basically that Canadian companies need to start improving on how they capitalize on the customer information they collect. According to Toronto-based Manton Group, this means harnessing customer-intelligence. To do this, organizations must understand that customer information is not customer-intelligence, and that customer information must be analyzed and interpreted to gain insight on customer needs, expectations, interests, and motivations. These insights can be gained from four customer data sources: 1) those that are stated ("what customers tell you"); 2) those that are observed ("how customers behave"); 3) those that are transacted ("what customers buy and how"); and 4) those that are inferred ("what customers are likely to do").[6]

As shown above, Fairmont Hotels & Resorts seems to be taking these lessons to heart. Through its strategic uses of information technology, such as its centralized guest repository, the company has demonstrated how information technology can be effectively employed to capture customer information and how this information can later be used to improve customer relationships and experiences. This has turned into real profits for the company. For example, Fairmont uses its customer-intelligence database to predict when it needs to set up promotions. For example, the company used the database one winter to advertise a third-night-free promotion communicated through direct mail and e-mail to selected guests who had stayed with the hotel chain before; this action generated about 20,000 room nights during a traditionally slow period.[7]

INTRODUCTION

ustomer relationship management (CRM) involves managing all aspects of a customer's relationship with an organization to increase customer loyalty and retention and an organization's profitability. As organizations begin to migrate from the traditional product-focused organization toward customer-driven organizations, they are recognizing their customers as experts, not just revenue generators. Organizations are quickly realizing that without customers, they simply would not exist and it is critical they do everything they can to ensure their customers' satisfaction. In an age when product differentiation is difficult, CRM is one of the most valuable assets a company can acquire. The sooner a company embraces CRM the better off it will be and the harder it will be for competitors to steal loyal and devoted customers.

BUSINESS BENEFITS OF CRM

1-800-Flowers.com achieved operational excellence by building customer intimacy to continue to improve profits and business growth. The company turned brand loyalty into brand relationships by using the vast amounts of information it collected to understand customers' needs and expectations. The floral delivery company adopted SAS Enterprise Miner to analyze the information in its CRM systems. Enterprise Miner sifts through information to reveal trends, explain outcomes, and predict results so that businesses can increase response rates and quickly identify their profitable customers. With the help of Enterprise Miner, 1-800-Flowers.com is continuing to thrive with revenues averaging 17-percent annual increases.[8]

CRM is a business philosophy based on the premise that those organizations that understand the needs of individual customers are best positioned to achieve sustainable competitive advantage in the future. Many aspects of CRM are not new to organizations; CRM is simply performing current business better. Placing customers at the forefront of all thinking and decision making requires significant operational and technology changes.

A customer strategy starts with understanding who the company's customers are and how the company can meet strategic goals. Alterna Savings, a Canadian credit union with branches in Ottawa, Toronto, Kingston, Pembroke, and North Bay, understands this and, in response, has rolled out a Web-based system called Summit iSpectrum developed by Summit Information Systems for the Canadian financial services industry. The Summit iSpectrum solution allows Alterna to pull all its client data into one central repository so that Alterna can deliver much faster customer service and improve the customer experience. As opposed to traditional mainframe systems that forced Alterna customer service representatives to utilize several different applications each with their own passwords and screens, the Summit iSpectrum solutions empowers front-line staff with easy and quick access to all the information they need to know about a customer in order to help that customer better.[9]

As the business world increasingly shifts from product focus to customer focus, most organizations recognize that treating existing customers well is the best source of profitable and sustainable revenue growth. In the age of e-business, however, an organization is challenged more than ever before to satisfy its customers. Figure 5.1 displays the benefits derived by an organization from a CRM strategy.

CCL Industries, a world leader in the development of specialty packaging and labelling solutions for the consumer products and health care industries, recognizes the importance of adopting a CRM strategy. CCL Industries was founded in Toronto in 1951, initially under the name of Connecticut Chemicals Limited, with a single production line and three people packaging aerosol products, which was

FIGURE 5.1

CRM Benefits

CRM Benefits
Provide better customer service
Improve call centre efficiency
Cross-sell products more effectively
Help sales staff close deals faster
Simplify marketing and sales processes
Discover new customers
Increase customer revenues

then a new product. The company has grown substantially since then. Its major customers include companies such as Clorox, Dow, Gillette, Nabisco, Pfizer, Procter & Gamble, and Unilever. Part of CCL's success is its adoption of a long-term view towards building customer relationships and managing them fairly and effectively. Relationships are seen as a vital corporate asset. As part of its CRM strategy, the company created an e-commerce portal to increase the firm's ability to interact with customers more effectively, and also to differentiate CCL from its competitors. Of importance though, CCL does not view technology as a substitute for its ability to bond with customers. Rather, the company views technology as something that can add value and should be used to complement and strengthen more traditional forms of CRM—not replace them.[10]

CRM BASICS

An organization can find its most valuable customers by using a formula that industry insiders call RFM—**R**ecency, **F**requency, and **M**onetary value. In other words, an organization must track:

- How recently a customer purchased items (recency).
- How frequently a customer purchases items (frequency).
- How much a customer spends on each purchase (monetary value).

Once a company has gathered this initial CRM information, it can compile it to identify patterns and create marketing campaigns, sales promotions, and services to increase business. For example, if Ms. Smith buys only at the height of the season, then the company should send her a special offer during the off-season. If Mr. Jones always buys software but never computers, then the company should offer him free software with the purchase of a new computer.

The CRM technologies discussed in this chapter can help organizations find answers to RFM and other tough questions, such as who are their best customers and which of their products are the most profitable.

The Evolution of CRM

Knowing the customer, especially knowing the profitability of individual customers, is highly lucrative in the financial services industry. Its high transactional nature has always afforded the financial services industry more access to customer information than other industries have, but it has embraced CRM technologies only recently.

Barclays Bank is a leading financial services company operating in more than 70 countries. In the United Kingdom, Barclays has over 10 million personal customers and about 9.3 million credit cards in circulation, and it serves 500,000 small business customers. Barclays decided to invest in CRM technologies to help it gain valuable insights into its business and customers.

FIGURE 5.2

Evolution of CRM

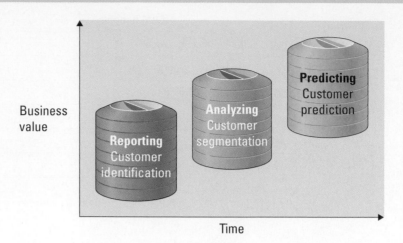

With the new CRM system, Barclays' managers are better able to predict the financial behaviour of individual customers and assess whether a customer is likely to pay back a loan in full and within the agreed-upon time period. This helps Barclays manage its profitability with greater precision because it can charge its customers a more appropriate rate of interest based on the results of the customer's risk assessment. Barclays also uses a sophisticated customer segmentation system to identify groups of profitable customers, both on a corporate and personal level, which it can then target for new financial products. One of the most valuable pieces of information Barclays discovered was that about 50 percent of its customers are nonprofitable and that less than 30 percent of its customers provide 90 percent of its profits.[11]

There are three phases in the evolution of CRM: (1) reporting, (2) analyzing, and (3) predicting. **_CRM reporting technologies_** help organizations identify their customers across other applications. **_CRM analysis technologies_** help organizations segment their customers into categories such as best and worst customers. **_CRM predicting technologies_** help organizations make predictions regarding customer behaviour such as which customers are at risk of leaving (see Figure 5.2 above).

Both operational and analytical CRM technologies can assist in customer reporting (identification), customer analysis (segmentation), and customer prediction. Figure 5.3 highlights a few of the important questions an organization can answer using CRM technologies.

FIGURE 5.3

Reporting, Analyzing, and Predicting Examples

REPORTING "Asking What Happened"	ANALYZING "Asking Why It Happened"	PREDICTING "Asking What Will Happen"
What is the total revenue by customer?	Why did sales not meet forecasts?	What customers are at risk of leaving?
How many units did we manufacture?	Why was production so low?	What products will the customer buy?
Where did we sell the most products?	Why did we not sell as many units as last year?	Who are the best candidates for a mailing?
What were total sales by product?	Who are our customers?	What is the best way to reach the customer?
How many customers did we serve?	Why was customer revenue so high?	What is the lifetime profitability of a customer?
What are our inventory levels?	Why are inventory levels so low?	What transactions might be fradulent?

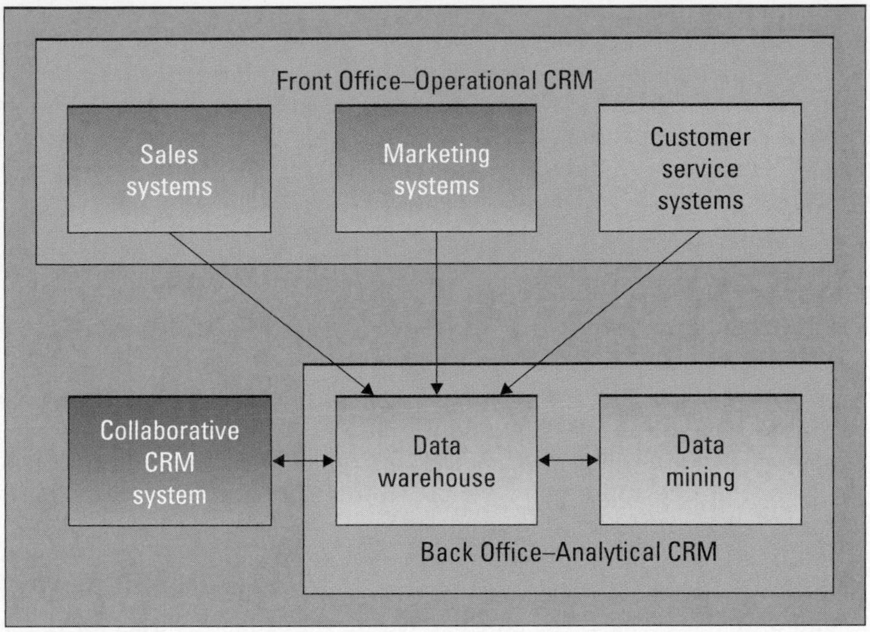

FIGURE 5.4
Operational CRM and Analytical CRM

Operational and Analytical CRM

Joe Guyaux knows the best way to win customers is to improve service. Under his leadership and with the help of Siebel CRM, the PNC retail banking team increased new consumer chequing customers by 19 percent in one year. Over the past year, PNC retained 21 percent more of its consumer chequing households as well as improved customer satisfaction by 9 percent.[12]

The two primary components of a CRM strategy are operational CRM and analytical CRM. ***Operational CRM*** supports traditional transactional processing for day-to-day front-office operations or systems that deal directly with the customers. ***Analytical CRM*** supports back-office operations and strategic analysis and includes all systems that do not deal directly with the customers. The primary difference between operational CRM and analytical CRM is the direct interaction between the organization and its customers. Figure 5.4 above provides an overview of operational CRM and analytical CRM.

USING INFORMATION TECHNOLOGY TO DRIVE OPERATIONAL CRM

Figure 5.5 displays the different technologies marketing, sales, and customer service departments can use to perform operational CRM.

Operational CRM Technologies		
Marketing	**Sales**	**Customer Service**
1. List generator	1. Sales management	1. Contact centre
2. Campaign management	2. Contact management	2. Web-based self-service
3. Cross-selling and up-selling	3. Opportunity management	3. Call scripting

FIGURE 5.5
Operational CRM Technologies for Sales, Marketing, and Customer Service Departments

Marketing and Operational CRM

Companies are no longer trying to sell one product to as many customers as possible; instead, they are trying to sell one customer as many products as possible. Marketing departments are able to transform to this new way of doing business by using CRM technologies that allow them to gather and analyze customer information to deploy successful marketing campaigns. In fact, a marketing campaign's success is directly proportional to the organization's ability to gather and analyze the right information. The three primary operational CRM technologies a marketing department can implement to increase customer satisfaction are:

1. List generator.
2. Campaign management.
3. Cross-selling and up-selling.

List Generator *List generators* compile customer information from a variety of sources and segment the information for different marketing campaigns. Information sources include Web site visits, Web site questionnaires, online and off-line surveys, flyers, toll-free numbers, current customer lists, and so on. After compiling the customer list, an organization can use criteria to filter and sort the list for potential customers. Filter and sort criteria can include such things as household income, education level, and age. List generators provide the marketing department with a solid understanding of the type of customer it needs to target for marketing campaigns.

Campaign Management *Campaign management systems* guide users through marketing campaigns performing such tasks as campaign definition, planning, scheduling, segmentation, and success analysis. These advanced systems can even calculate quantifiable results for return on investment (ROI) for each campaign and track the results in order to analyze and understand how the company can fine-tune future campaigns.

Cross-Selling and Up-Selling Two key sales strategies a marketing campaign can deploy are cross-selling and up-selling. *Cross-selling* is selling additional products or services to a customer. *Up-selling* is increasing the value of the sale. For example, McDonald's performs cross-selling by asking customers if they would like an apple pie with their meal. McDonald's performs up-selling by asking customers if they would like to super-size their meals. CRM systems offer marketing departments all kinds of information about their customers and their products, which can help them identify cross-selling and up-selling marketing campaigns.

The California State Automobile Association (CSAA) had to take advantage of its ability to promote and cross-sell CSAA automotive, insurance, and travel services to beat its competition. Accomplishing this task was easy once the company implemented E.piphany's CRM system. The system integrated information from all of CSAA's separate databases, making it immediately available to all employees through a Web-based browser. Employees could quickly glance at a customer's profile and determine which services the customer currently had and which services the customer might want to purchase based on her or his needs as projected by the software.[13]

Sales and Operational CRM

Siebel, one of the largest providers of CRM software, had 33,000 subscribers in January 2005. Salesforce.com, provider of on-demand Web-based customer relationship management software, added 40,000 subscribers during the first three months of 2005, more than all of Siebel's subscribers. Salesforce.com's total number of subscribers is over 300,000. Merrill Lynch, one of the biggest customers in the sales force market, signed on for 5,000 subscriptions for its global private client division, making the brokerage firm Salesforce.com's largest customer. Salesforce.com's new product, Customforce, includes tools for adding data analysis capabilities, spreadsheet-style mathematical formulas, business processes, and forecasting models.[14]

Sales departments were the first to begin developing CRM systems. Sales departments had two primary reasons to track customer sales information electronically. First, sales representatives were struggling with the overwhelming amount of customer account information they were required to maintain and track. Second, companies were struggling with the issue that much of their vital customer and sales information remained in the heads of their sales representatives. One of the first CRM components built to help address these issues was the sales force automation component. *Sales force automation (SFA)* is a system that automatically tracks all of the steps in the sales process. SFA products focus on increasing customer satisfaction, building customer relationships, and improving product sales by tracking all sales information.

Playground Real Estate, an Intrawest company headquartered in Vancouver, manages the sales and marketing campaigns for luxury ownership opportunities in major resorts worldwide, including Whistler Blackcomb and Mt. Tremblant. Playground took advantage of a customer relationship management solution developed by Maximizer Software to support Playground's sales activities. Playground uses Maximizer's CRM technology to monitor the results of marketing plans, track prospects, build relationships, manage customers, complete sales, and gauge the accuracy and activity of the sales pipeline. The tool also is used to control logistics of Playground's sales and marketing offices that are set up at each resort site. Playground employees like the CRM system since it is easy to learn and easy to tailor to the way Playground does its business. This frees Playground employees from having to fiddle and manipulate the CRM system and allows them to concentrate on the business of selling.[15]

The three primary operational CRM technologies a sales department can implement to increase customer satisfaction are:

1. Sales management CRM systems.
2. Contact management CRM systems.
3. Opportunity management CRM systems.

Sales Management CRM Systems   Figure 5.6 depicts the typical sales process, which begins with an opportunity and ends with billing the customer for the sale. Leads and potential customers are the lifeblood of all sales organizations, whether the products they are peddling are computers, clothing, or cars. How the leads are handled can make the difference between revenue growth or decline. *Sales management CRM systems* automate each phase of the sales process, helping individual sales representatives coordinate and organize all of their accounts. Features include calendars to help plan customer meetings, alarm reminders signalling important tasks, customizable multimedia presentations, and document generation. These systems even have the ability to provide an analysis of the sales cycle and calculate how each individual sales representative is performing during the sales process.

Contact Management CRM Systems   A *contact management CRM system* maintains customer contact information and identifies prospective customers for future sales. Contact management systems include such features as maintaining organizational charts, detailed customer notes, and supplemental sales information. For example, a contact management system can take an incoming telephone number and display the caller's name along with notes detailing previous conversations. This allows the sales representative to answer the telephone and say, "Hi Sue, how is your new laptop working? How was your vacation to the Yukon?" without receiving any reminders of such details first from the customer. The customer feels valued since the sales associate knows her name and even remembers details of their last conversation!

FIGURE 5.6

Overview of the Sales Process

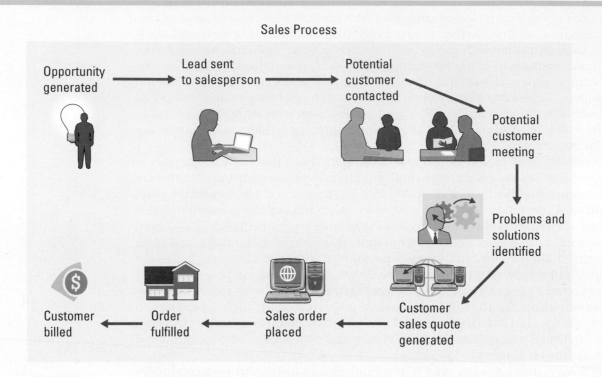

Sales Process

An $18.5-billion technology company, 3M is a leader in health care, safety, electronics, telecommunications, office, and consumer markets. The company began to focus on streamlining and unifying its sales processes with the primary goals of better customer segmentation and more reliable lead generation and qualification. To achieve these goals the company implemented a CRM system and soon found itself receiving the following benefits:

- Cutting the time it takes to familiarize sales professionals with new territories by 33 percent.

- Increasing management's visibility of the sales process.

- Decreasing the time it takes to qualify leads and assign sales opportunities by 40 percent.

One of the more successful campaigns driven by the CRM system allowed 3M to deliver direct mail to targeted government agencies and emergency services in response to the anthrax attacks in 2002. All inquiries to the mail campaign were automatically assigned to a sales representative who followed up with a quote. In little more than a week, the company had received orders for 35,000 respirator masks.[16]

Opportunity Management CRM Systems *Opportunity management CRM systems* target sales opportunities by finding new customers or companies for future sales. Opportunity management systems determine potential customers and competitors and define selling efforts including budgets and schedules. Advanced opportunity management systems can even calculate the probability of a sale, which can save sales representatives significant time and money when attempting to find new customers. The primary difference between contact management and opportunity management is that contact management deals with existing customers and opportunity management deals with new customers. Figure 5.7 displays six CRM pointers a sales representative can use to increase prospective customers.

Customer Service and Operational CRM

Andy Taylor became president of Enterprise, his father's $88 million rental-car company, in 1980. Today, it is the largest in North America, with $7 billion in revenue. How has he kept customer service a priority? By quantifying it. Enterprise surveys 1.7 million customers a year. If a branch's satisfaction scores are low, employees, even vice presidents, cannot be promoted. The result is self-propagating. Seeking better scores, managers make better hires. And because Enterprise promotes almost solely from within, nearly every executive—including Taylor, who started out washing cars—has a frontline understanding of what it takes to keep customers happy. "The company would never have gotten that 100-fold growth without Andy's knack for putting systems and processes in place so you can deliver consistent service," said Sandy Rogers, senior vice president of corporate strategy.[17]

Sales and marketing are the primary departments that interact directly with customers before a sale. Most companies recognize the importance of building strong relationships during the marketing and sales efforts; however, many fail to realize the importance of continuing to build these relationships after the sale is complete. It is actually more important to build postsale relationships if the company wants to ensure customer loyalty and satisfaction. The best way to implement postsale CRM strategies is through the customer service department.

One of the primary reasons a company loses customers is bad customer service experiences. Providing outstanding customer service is a difficult task, and many CRM technologies are available to assist organizations with this important activity. For example, by rolling out Lotus Instant Messaging to its customers, Avnet Computer Marketing has established an efficient, direct route to push valuable

CRM Pointers for Gaining Prospective Customers	
1. Get their attention	If you have a good prospect, chances are that he or she receives dozens of offers from similar companies. Be sure your first contact is professional and gets your customer's attention.
2. Value their time	When you ask for a meeting, you are asking for the most valuable thing a busy person has—time. Many companies have had great success by offering high-value gifts in exchange for a meeting with a representative. Just be careful because some organizations frown on expensive gifts. Instead, offer these prospective customers a report that can help them perform their jobs more effectively.
3. Overdeliver	If your letter offered a free DVD in exchange for a meeting, bring a box of microwave popcorn along with the movie. Little gestures like these tell customers that you not only keep your word, but also can be counted on to overdeliver.
4. Contact frequently	Find new and creative ways to contact your prospective customers frequently. Starting a newsletter and sending out a series of industry updates are excellent ways to keep in contact and provide value.
5. Generate a trustworthy mailing list	If you are buying a mailing list from a third party be sure that the contacts are genuine prospects, especially if you are offering an expensive gift. Be sure that the people you are meeting have the power to authorize a sale.
6. Follow up	One of the most powerful prospecting tools is a simple thank-you note. Letting people know that their time was appreciated may even lead to additional referrals.

FIGURE 5.7

CRM Pointers for Gaining Prospective Customers

information and updates out to its customers. The company uses Lotus Instant Messaging to provide real-time answers to customer questions by listing its support specialists' status by different colours on its Web site: green if they are available, red if they are not, or blue if they are out of the office. The customer simply clicks on a name to begin instant messaging or a chat session to get quick answers to questions.[18]

Before access to Lotus Instant Messaging, customers had to wait in "1-800" call queues or for e-mail responses for answers. The new system has increased customer satisfaction along with tremendous savings from fewer long-distance phone charges. Avnet also estimates that Lotus Instant Messaging saves each of its 650 employees 5 to 10 minutes a day.

The three primary operational CRM technologies a customer service department can implement to increase customer satisfaction are:

1. Contact centre.
2. Web-based self-service.
3. Call scripting.

Contact Centre Knowledge-management software, which helps call centres put consistent answers at customer-service representative's fingertips, is often long on promise and short on delivery. The problem? Representatives have to take time out from answering calls to input things they have learned—putting the "knowledge" in knowledge management.

Brad Cleveland, who heads the Incoming Calls Management Institute, said, "Software is just a tool. It doesn't do any good unless people across the organization are using it to its potential." Sharp Electronics is making it happen. Sharp's frontline representatives built the system from scratch. And as Sharp rolled out its network over the past four years, representatives' compensation and promotions were tied directly to the system's use. As a result, the customer call experience at Sharp has improved dramatically: The proportion of problems resolved by a single call has soared from 76 percent to 94 percent since 2000.[19]

A *contact centre* (or *call centre*) is where customer service representatives (CSRs) answer customer inquiries and respond to problems through a number of different customer touchpoints. A contact centre is one of the best assets a customer-driven organization can have because maintaining a high level of customer support is critical to obtaining and retaining customers. Numerous systems are available to help an organization automate its contact centres. Figure 5.8 highlights a few of the features available in contact centre systems.

Contact centres also track customer call history along with problem resolutions—information critical for providing a comprehensive customer view to the CSR. CSRs who can quickly comprehend and understand all of a customer's products and issues provide tremendous value to the customer and the organization. Nothing makes frustrated customers happier than not having to explain their problems to yet another CSR.

New emotion-detection software called Perform, created by Nice Systems, is designed to help companies improve customer service by identifying callers who are upset. When an elderly man distressed over high medical premiums hung up

FIGURE 5.8

Common Features Included in Contact Centres

Common Features Included in Contact Centres	
Automatic call distribution	A phone switch routes inbound calls to available agents.
Interactive voice response (IVR)	Directs customers to use touch-tone phones or keywords to navigate or provide information.
Predictive dialling	Automatically dials outbound calls and when someone answers, the call is forwarded to an available agent.

during his phone call to an insurance company's call centre, an IT system detected the customer's exasperation and automatically e-mailed a supervisor. The supervisor listened to a digital recording of the conversation, called the customer, and suggested ways to lower the premium. The system uses algorithms to determine a baseline of emotion during the first 5 to 10 seconds of a call, any deviation from the baseline triggers an alert.[20]

Web-Based Self-Service *Web-based self-service systems* allow customers to use the Web to find answers to their questions or solutions to their problems. FedEx uses Web-based self-service systems to allow customers to track their own packages without having to talk to a CSR. FedEx customers can simply log on to FedEx's Web site and enter their tracking number. The Web site quickly displays the exact location of the package and the estimated delivery time.

Another great feature of Web-based self-service is click-to-talk buttons. Click-to-talk buttons allow customers to click on a button and talk with a CSR via the Internet. Powerful customer-driven features like these add tremendous value to any organization by providing customers with real-time information without having to contact company representatives.[21]

Call Scripting Being a CSR is not an easy task, especially when the CSR is dealing with detailed technical products or services. *Call scripting systems* access organizational databases that track similar issues or questions and automatically generate the details for the CSR who can then relay them to the customer. The system can even provide a list of questions that the CSR can ask the customer to determine the potential problem and resolution. This feature helps CSRs answer difficult questions quickly while also presenting a uniform image so two different customers do not receive two different answers.

Documedics is a health care consulting company that provides reimbursement information about pharmaceutical products to patients and health care professionals. The company currently supports inquiries for 12 pharmaceutical companies and receives over 30,000 customer calls per month. Originally, the company had a data file for each patient and for each pharmaceutical company. This inefficient process resulted in the potential for a single patient to have up to 12 different information files if the patient was a client of all 12 pharmaceutical companies. To answer customer questions, a CSR had to download each customer file, causing tremendous inefficiencies and confusion. The company implemented a CRM system with a call scripting feature to alleviate the problem and provide its CSRs with a comprehensive view of every customer, regardless of the pharmaceutical company. The company anticipated 20-percent annual growth primarily because of the successful implementation of its new system.[22]

USING INFORMATION TECHNOLOGY TO DRIVE ANALYTICAL CRM

Maturing analytical CRM and behavioral modelling technologies are helping numerous organizations move beyond legacy benefits such as enhanced customer service and retention to systems that can truly improve business profitability. Unlike operational CRM that automates call centres and sales forces with the aim of enhancing customer transactions, analytical CRM solutions are designed to dig deep into a company's historical customer information and expose patterns of behaviour on which a company can capitalize. Analytical CRM is primarily used to enhance and support decision making and works by identifying patterns in customer information collected from the various operational CRM systems.

For many organizations, the power of analytical CRM solutions provides tremendous managerial opportunities. Depending on the specific solution, analytical CRM tools can slice-and-dice customer information to create made-to-order views of customer value, spending, product affinities, percentile profiles, and segmentations. Modelling tools can identify opportunities for cross-selling, up-selling, and expanding customer relationships.

Personalization occurs when a Web site can know enough about a person's likes and dislikes that it can fashion offers that are more likely to appeal to that person. Many organizations are now utilizing CRM to create customer rules and templates that marketers can use to personalize customer messages.

The information produced by analytical CRM solutions can help companies make decisions about how to handle customers based on the value of each and every one. Analytical CRM can help reveal information about which customers are worth investing in, which should be serviced at an average level, and which should not be invested in at all. For example, at the Bank of Montreal (BMO), a customer knowledge database was used by a statistical modelling group to calculate monthly customer economic profit. When the group ran their analysis to determine the relationship between "customer loyalty" and "customer spending potential" to identify potential new customers, BMO discovered there were strategic benefits in growing existing customer relationships for new business rather than trying to find brand new customers. David Moxley, the vice president overseeing BMO's customer knowledge management operation, commented, "We were pleased at how many additional wallet opportunities existed within our existing customer lists. In most cases, we found that we needed to acquire our own customers."[23]

Data gained from customers can also reveal information about employees. Wachovia Bank in the U.S. surveys customers—25,000 every month—for feedback on their service experience. It asks about individual employees and uses those answers in one-on-one staff coaching. A recent 20-minute coaching session at one branch made clear how this feedback—each customer surveyed rates 33 employee behaviours—can improve service. The branch manager urged an employee to focus on sincerity rather than on mere friendliness, to "sharpen her antenna" so she would listen to customers more intuitively, and to slow down rather than hurry up. That focus on careful, sincere, intuitive service has paid off: Wachovia has held the top score among banks in the American Customer Satisfaction Index since 2001.[24]

Analytical CRM relies heavily on data warehousing technologies and business intelligence to glean insights into customer behaviour. These systems quickly aggregate, analyze, and disseminate customer information throughout an organization. Figure 5.9 displays a few examples of the kind of information insights analytical CRM can help an organization gain.

UPS's data-intensive environment is supported by the largest IBM DB2 database in the world, consisting of 236 terabytes of data related to its analytical CRM tool. The shipping company's goal is to create one-to-one customer relationships, and it is using Quantum View tools that allow it to let customers tailor views of such things as shipment history and receive notices when a package arrives or is delayed. UPS has built more than 500 customer relationship management applications that run off of its data warehouse.[25]

Data warehouses are providing businesses with information about their customers and products that was previously impossible to locate, and the resulting payback can be tremendous. Organizations are now relying on business intelligence to provide them with hard facts that can determine everything from which type of marketing and sales campaign to launch, to which customers to target, at what time. Using CRM along with business intelligence allows organizations to make better, more informed decisions and to reap amazing unforeseen rewards.

Loyalty Management Group Canada, a Toronto-based company, runs the Air Miles rewards program used by over half of Canadian households. With their plastic Air Miles cards in hand, consumers can get their cards scanned at cash registers of participating retailers to gain reward points that later can be redeemed for "free" travel and other reward offerings. The key to the rewards program is the use of analytical CRM to research use of the Air Miles cards in terms of consumer preferences and spending habits. One key source of data is the initial sign-up form where members quite freely identify their private information, including age, address, family size, and total household income. This information is a treasure trove for Air Miles corporate sponsors, like Shell, Holt Renfrew, Blockbuster, Bank of Montreal, and provincial liquor boards, most of whom never had access to such personal data. Another key source of information occurs every time a customer makes a purchase. Merging these

FIGURE 5.9

Analytical CRM Information
Examples

Analytical CRM Information Examples	
1. Give customers more of what they want	Analytical CRM can help an organization go beyond the typical "Dear Mr. Smith" salutation. An organization can use its analytical CRM information to make its communications more personable. For example, if it knows a customer's shoe size and preferred brand it can notify the customer that there is a pair of size 12 shoes set aside to try on the next time the customer visits the store.
2. Find new customers similar to the best customers	Analytical CRM might determine that an organization does a lot of business with women 35 to 45 years old who drive SUVs and live within 50 kilometres of a certain location. The company can then find a mailing list that highlights this type of customer for potential new sales.
3. Find out what the organization does best	Analytical CRM can determine what an organization does better than its competitors. For example, if a restaurant caters more breakfasts to midsized companies than its competition does, it can purchase a specialized mailing list of midsized companies in the area and send them a mailing that features the breakfast catering specials.
4. Beat competitors to the punch	Analytical CRM can determine sales trends allowing an organization to offer the best customers deals before the competition has a chance to. For example, a clothing store might determine its best customers for outdoor apparel and send them an offer to attend a private sale right before the competition runs its outdoor apparel sale.
5. Reactivate inactive customers	Analytical CRM can highlight customers who have not done any business with the organization in a while. The organization can then send them a personalized letter along with a discount coupon. It will remind them of the company and may help spark a renewed relationship.
6. Let customers know they matter	Analytical CRM can determine what customers want and need, so an organization can contact them with this information. Anything from a private sale to a reminder that the car is due for a tune-up is excellent customer service.

two sources of customer information together, the data can help corporate sponsors make business decisions, like decide where to locate new stores and how to maximize sales to each customer. It also provides a means for sponsors to peek at one another's data and share customer information. As such, Loyalty Management is in essence in the customer data mining business. The company operates on the principle that the more you know about a customer, the better you can service that customer.[26]

OPENING CASE QUESTIONS

Harnessing Customer Relationships at Fairmont Hotels & Resorts

1. Summarize the evolution of CRM and provide an example of a reporting, analyzing, and predicting question Fairmont Hotel & Resorts (FHR) might ask its customers.

2. How has FHR effectively used CRM technology to improve its operations? What other CRM technologies could FHR employ to improve its operations?

3. Define analytical CRM. How has FHR effectively used analytical CRM? How important is analytical CRM to companies like FHR?

4. What is the difference between customer information and customer-intelligence, as described in the Opening Case Study? In your opinion, is there a difference between customer-intelligence and analytical CRM. If so, how?

CUSTOMER RELATIONSHIP MANAGEMENT'S EXPLOSIVE GROWTH

Brother International Corporation experienced skyrocketing growth in its sales of multifunction centres, fax machines, printers, and labelling systems in the late 1990s. Along with skyrocketing sales growth came a tremendous increase in customer service calls. When Brother failed to answer the phone fast enough, product returns started to increase. The company responded by increasing call centre capacity, and the rate of returns began to drop. However, Dennis Upton, CIO of Brother International, observed that all the company was doing was answering the phone. He quickly realized that the company was losing a world of valuable market intelligence (business intelligence) about existing customers from all those telephone calls. The company decided to deploy SAP's CRM solution. The 1.8 million calls Brother handled dropped to 1.57 million, which reduced call centre staff from 180 agents to 160 agents. Since customer demographic information is now stored and displayed on the agent's screen based on the incoming telephone number, the company has reduced call duration by an average of one minute, saving the company $700,000 per year.[27]

In the context of increasing business competition and mature markets, it is easier than ever for informed and demanding customers to defect since they are just a click away from migrating to an alternative. When customers buy on the Internet, they see, and they steer, entire value chains. The Internet is a "looking glass," a two-way mirror, and its field of vision is the entire value chain. While the Internet cannot totally replace the phone and face-to-face communication with customers, it can strengthen these interactions at all customer touchpoints. Customer Web interactions become conversations, interactive dialogs with shared knowledge, not just business transactions. Web-based customer care can actually become the focal point of customer relationship management and provide breakthrough benefits for both the enterprise and its customers, substantially reducing costs while improving service.

According to an AMR Research survey of more than 500 businesses in 14 key vertical markets, half of all current CRM spending is by manufacturers. Current users are allocating 20 percent of their IT budgets to CRM solutions. Those who have not invested in CRM may soon come on board: Of the respondents in the study who are not currently using CRM, roughly one-third plan to implement these types of technology solutions within the next year. Figure 5.10 shows the top CRM business drivers, and Figure 5.11 displays CRM spending over the last few years.

FIGURE 5.10

CRM Business Drivers

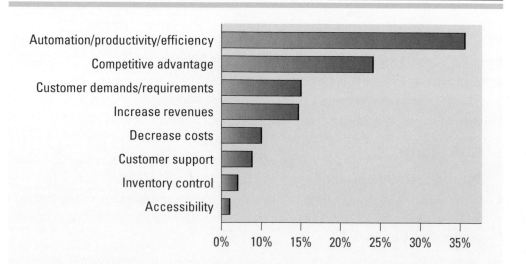

FIGURE 5.11

CRM Spending (US$ billions)

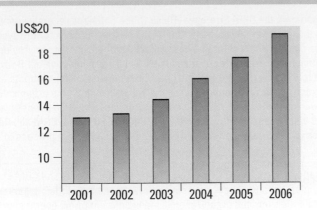

When you are dealing with sick customers, flexibility is key. That is why Walgreens in the United States has made healthy investments in customer service over the past 30 years, originating the drive-through pharmacy and pioneering a network for refilling prescriptions at any location. It should come as no surprise that Walgreens credited much of its growth to an increased investment in customer service. The company has developed new software that can print prescription labels in 14 languages and large-type labels for older patrons. Besides investing in customer-friendly technology, the 103-year-old chain is not forgetting the human touch. Walgreens spends more on payroll on stores where performance is below average, increasing the clerk-to-customer ratio; and it recently launched an online training program for all employees. With 19 straight quarters of double-digit earnings growth, the prescription appears to be working.[28]

CUSTOMER RELATIONSHIP MANAGEMENT SUCCESS FACTORS

Harrah's Entertainment in the U.S. is the world's largest provider of casino entertainment and hotel accommodations, such as that found in Las Vegas and Atlantic City. When a "lucky ambassador" greets a Harrah's guest at a video-poker machine by name, wishes her a happy birthday, and offers free tickets to a show, luck has nothing to do with it. The moment customers insert their loyalty card into a slot machine, the casino giant's $35 million-plus CRM system reveals every move they have ever made at any of its 28 properties. "If you start to have a really unfortunate visit, you start to think, 'Man, that place is really just bad luck,'" said Gary Loveman, Harrah's president and CEO. "If we see that coming, we can intervene" with perks to soothe the pain of gambling losses. While many companies struggle to employ CRM successfully, gathering massive amounts of data without using it to benefit customers, Harrah's is building on its mastery. In the future, its slot machines will spout real-time monetary credits and dinner coupons using new customer-recognition software and hardware, leaving even its losing customers feeling a little luckier.

CRM solutions make organizational business processes more intelligent. Organizations achieve this by understanding customer behaviour and preferences, then realigning product and service offerings and related communications to make sure they are synchronized with customer needs and preferences. If an organization is implementing a CRM system, it should study the industry best practices to help ensure a successful implementation (see Figure 5.12).

CRM is critical to business success. CRM is the key competitive strategy to stay focused on customer needs and to integrate a customer-centric approach throughout an organization. CRM can acquire enterprisewide knowledge about customers and improve the business processes that deliver value to an organization's customers, suppliers, and employees. Using the analytical capabilities of CRM can help a

FIGURE 5.12

CRM Industry Best
Practices

1. **Clearly Communicate the CRM Strategy**—Boise Office Solutions recently spent $29 million implementing a successful CRM system. One of the primary reasons for the system's success was that Boise started with a clear business objective for the system: to provide customers with greater economic value. Only after establishing the business objective did Boise Office Solutions invest in CRM technology to help meet the goal. Ensuring that all departments and employees understand exactly what CRM means and how it will add value to the organization is critical. Research by Gartner Dataquest indicates that enterprises that attain success with CRM have interested and committed senior executives who set goals for what CRM should achieve, match CRM strategies with corporate objectives, and tie the measurement process to both goals and strategies.

2. **Define Information Needs and Flows**—People who perform successful CRM implementations have a clear understanding of how information flows in and out of their organization. Chances are information comes into the organization in many different forms over many different touch points.

3. **Build an Integrated View of the Customer**—Essential to a CRM strategy is choosing the correct CRM system that can support organizational requirements. The system must have the corresponding functional breadth and depth to support strategic goals. Do not forget to take into account the system's infrastructure including ease of integration to current systems, discussed in greater detail later in this unit.

4. **Implement in Iterations**—Implement the CRM system in manageable pieces—in other words avoid the "big bang" implementation approach. It is easier to manage, measure, and track the design, building, and deployment of the CRM system when it is delivered in pieces. Most important, this allows the organization to find out early if the implementation is headed for failure and thus either kill the project and save wasted resources or change direction to a more successful path.

5. **Scalability for Organizational Growth**—Make certain that the CRM system meets the organization's future needs as well as its current needs. Estimating future needs is by far one of the hardest parts of any project. Understanding how the organization is going to grow, predicting how technology is going to change, and anticipating how customers are going to evolve are very difficult challenges. Taking the time to answer some tough questions up front will ensure the organization grows into, instead of out of, its CRM system.

company anticipate customer needs and proactively serve customers in ways that build relationships, create loyalty, and enhance bottom lines.

CURRENT TRENDS: SRM, PRM, AND ERM

Organizations are discovering a wave of other key business areas where it is beneficial to take advantage of building strong relationships. These emerging areas include supplier relationship management (SRM), partner relationship management (PRM), and employee relationship management (ERM).

Supplier Relationship Management

Supplier relationship management (SRM) focuses on keeping suppliers satisfied by evaluating and categorizing suppliers for different projects, which optimizes supplier selection. SRM applications help companies analyze vendors based on a number of key variables including strategy, business goals, prices, and markets. The company can then determine the best supplier to collaborate with and can work on developing strong relationships with that supplier. The partners can then work together to streamline processes, outsource services, and provide products that they could not provide individually.

With the merger of the Bank of Halifax and Bank of Scotland, the new company, HBOS, implemented an SRM system to provide consistent information to its suppliers. The system integrates procurement information from the separate Bank of Halifax and Bank of Scotland operational systems, generating a single repository of management information for consistent reporting and analysis. Other benefits HBOS derived from the SRM solution include:

- A single consolidated view of all suppliers.
- Consistent, detailed management information allowing multiple views for every executive.
- Elimination of duplicate suppliers.[29]

Partner Relationship Management

Organizations have begun to realize the importance of building relationships with partners, dealers, and resellers. *Partner relationship management (PRM)* focuses on keeping vendors satisfied by managing alliance partner and reseller relationships that provide customers with the optimal sales channel. PRM's business strategy is to select and manage partners to optimize their long-term value to an organization. In effect, it means picking the right partners, working with them to help them be successful in dealing with mutual customers, and ensuring that partners and the ultimate end customers are satisfied and successful. Many of the features of a PRM application include real-time product information on availability, marketing materials, contracts, order details, and pricing, inventory, and shipping information.

PRM is one of the smaller segments of CRM that has superb potential. PRM grew from a $580-million business to a $1.2-billion business in under four years. This is a direct reflection of the growing interdependency of organizations in the new economy. The primary benefits of PRM include:

- Expanded market coverage.
- Offerings of specialized products and services.
- Broadened range of offerings and a more complete solution.

Employee Relationship Management

Employee relationship management (ERM) provides employees with a subset of CRM applications available through a Web browser. Many of the ERM applications assist the employee in dealing with customers by providing detailed information on company products, services, and customer orders.

At Rackspace, a Web-hosting company, customer focus borders on the obsessive. Joey Parsons, 24, won the Straightjacket Award, the most coveted employee distinction at Rackspace. The award recognizes the employee who best lives up to the Rackspace motto of delivering "fanatical support," a dedication to customers that is so intense it borders on the loony. Rackspace motivates its staff by treating each team as a separate business, which is responsible for its own profits and losses and has its own ERM Web site. Each month, employees can earn bonuses of up to 20 percent of their monthly base salaries depending on the performance of their units by both financial and customer-centric measurements such as customer turnover, customer expansion, and customer referrals. Daily reports are available through the team's ERM Web site.[30]

FUTURE CRM TRENDS

In the future, CRM applications will continue to change from employee-only tools to tools used by suppliers, partners, and even customers. Providing a consistent view of customers and delivering timely and accurate customer information to all departments across an organization will continue to be the major goal of CRM initiatives.

As technology advances (intranet, Internet, extranet, wireless), CRM will remain a major strategic focus for companies, particularly in industries whose product is difficult to differentiate. Some companies approach this problem by moving to a low-cost producer strategy. CRM will be an alternative way to pursue a differentiation strategy with a nondifferentiable product.

CRM applications will continue to adapt wireless capabilities supporting mobile sales and mobile customers. Sales professionals will be able to access e-mail, order details, corporate information, inventory status, and opportunity information all from a PDA in their car or on a plane. Real-time interaction with human CSRs over the Internet will continue to increase.

CRM suites will also incorporate PRM and SRM modules as enterprises seek to take advantage of these initiatives. Automating interactions with distributors, resellers, and suppliers will enhance the corporation's ability to deliver a quality experience to its customers.

OPENING CASE QUESTIONS

Harnessing Customer Relationships at Fairmont Hotels & Resorts

5. How might Fairmont Hotels & Resort's (FHR) business model change if it decreased its investments in CRM technologies?

6. Describe the CRM industry best practices and explain how FHR is using each.

7. Explain SRM and how FHR could use it to improve its business.

8. Explain ERM and how FHR could use it to improve its business.

SUMMARY OF KEY THEMES

The purpose of this chapter was two-fold:

1. To elaborate upon the concept of customer relationship management. Specifically, two specific types of CRM were described: operational CRM and analytical CRM.

2. To illustrate how information technology can help companies implement operational and analytical CRM in practice. Through various examples and case studies presented in this chapter, information technology was shown to be a key enabler of CRM. That is, information technology was shown to provide organizations with the ability to launch and run successful CRM programs.

As a business student, you should understand this instrumental role that information technology plays in facilitating customer relationship management. However, it is important to keep in mind that CRM, first and foremost, is a business phenomenon, and not a technological one. As such, technology—though useful, and some would say even necessary—helps support CRM. Information technology itself is not CRM.

This is an important distinction. For example, all the benefits CRM technology can easily be undone by a thoughtless customer support representative who may in some action or word demonstrate that the organization does not care or understand its customers. Thus, technology can help organizations implement better and effective CRM, but at the end of the day, how a company's employees interact with a customer face-to-face is the real test of a company's ability to foster and promote healthy customer relations.

KEY TERMS

Analytical CRM 137
Automatic call distribution 142
Call scripting system 143
Campaign management
   system 138
Contact centre
   (call centre) 142
Contact management CRM
   system 139
CRM analysis
   technology 136
CRM predicting
   technology 136

CRM reporting
   technology 136
Cross-selling 138
Customer relationship
   management (CRM) 134
Employee relationship
   management (ERM) 149
Interactive voice response
   (IVR) 142
List generator 138
Operational CRM 137
Opportunity management
   CRM system 140

Partner relationship
   management (PRM) 149
Personalization 144
Predictive dialling 142
Sales force automation
   (SFA) 139
Sales management CRM
   system 139
Supplier relationship
   management (SRM) 148
Up-selling 138
Web-based self-service
   system 143

CLOSING CASE ONE

Fighting Cancer with Information

This case shows how one organization used a CRM solution to solve information issues.

"The mission of the American Cancer Society (ACS) is to cure cancer and relieve the pain and suffering caused by this insidious disease," said Zachary Patterson, chief information officer, ACS.

The ACS is a nationwide voluntary health organization in the United States dedicated to eliminating cancer as a major health problem by supporting research, education, advocacy, and volunteer service. Headquartered in Atlanta, Georgia, with 17 divisions and more than 3,400 local offices throughout the United States, the ACS represents the largest source of private nonprofit cancer research funds in the United States.

To support its mission, the ACS must perform exceptionally well in three key areas. First, it must be able to provide its constituents—more than 2 million volunteers, patients, and donors—with the best information available regarding the prevention, detection, and treatment of cancer. Second, ACS must be able to demonstrate that it acts responsibly with the funds entrusted to it by the public. "Among other things, that means being able to provide exceptional service when someone calls our call centre with a question about mammography screening or our latest antismoking campaign," said Terry Music, national vice president for Information Delivery at the ACS. Third, ACS must be able to secure donations of time and money from its constituent base. Its success in this area is directly related to providing excellent information and service, as well as having an integrated view of its relationship with constituents. "To succeed, we need to understand the full extent of each constituent's relationship with us so we can determine where there might be opportunities to expand that relationship," Music said.

The ACS was experiencing many challenges with its current information. "Our call centre agents did not know, for example, if a caller was both a donor and a volunteer, or if a caller was volunteering for the society in multiple ways," he said. "This splintered view made it challenging for American Cancer Society representatives to deliver personalized service and make informed recommendations regarding other opportunities within the society that might interest a caller."

The ACS chose to implement a customer relationship management solution to solve its information issues. Critical to the CRM system's success was consolidating information from various databases across the organization to provide a single view of constituents and all information required to serve them. After an evaluation process that included participation from individuals across the organization, the ACS chose Siebel Systems as its CRM solution provider. The society wanted to work with a company that could address both its immediate needs with a best-in-class e-business solution and its future requirements.

The Siebel Call Centre is specifically designed for the next generation of contact centres, enabling organizations to provide world-class customer service, generate increased revenue, and create a closed-loop information flow seamlessly over multichannel sales, marketing, and customer service operations. Siebel Call Centre empowers agents at every level by providing up-to-the-minute information and in-depth customer and product knowledge. This approach enables quick and accurate problem resolution and generates greater relationship opportunities. The ACS has received numerous benefits from the system including:

- Increased constituent satisfaction and loyalty by supporting personalized interactions between constituents and cancer information specialists.
- Improved productivity of cancer information specialists by consolidating all information required to serve constituents into a single view.
- Increased donations of time and money by helping call centre agents identify callers who are likely to be interested in expanding their relationship with the ACS.[31]

Questions

1. How could the ACS's marketing department use operational CRM to strengthen its relationships with its customers?
2. How could the ACS's customer service department use operational CRM to strengthen its relationships with its customers?
3. Review all of the operational CRM technologies and determine which one would add the greatest value to ACS's business.
4. Describe the benefits ACS could gain from using analytical CRM.
5. Summarize SRM and describe how ACS could use it to increase efficiency in its business.

Calling All Canadians

This case shows how other factors, beyond strictly information technology ones, affect CRM success.

With multiple communication channels available and so many CRM failures, many companies are concluding that the best method for providing customer service is good old-fashioned customer service provided by a real live person. At the same time that companies consider outsourcing their customer service departments to other countries in order to save money, many worry about foreign accents as well as time-zone issues related to offshore outsourcing.

For American companies, the obvious solution to these worries is Canada—its next door neighbour and friend. Due to several factors (such as an exchange rate that allows American companies to operate at substantially lower costs, cultural similarities, language affinities, access to a highly educated work force, and a technological infrastructure that is state-of-the art), Canada offers the U.S. a first-rate location to open customer service departments or call centres. According to Todd Evans, the director of Economic Analysis and Forecasting at Export Development Corporation, Canada is basically exporting its knowledge as a service to Americans, and between 2005 and 2010, service exports are expected to grow by 30 percent. This growth will support more than one million jobs and account for $65 billion of GDP for Canada; a significant chunk of that growth will be attributed to call centres services.[32]

Additional factors that make Canada attractive to American firms include Canada's multilingual workforce, political and economic stability, lower payroll taxes, and ability to service all aspects of the call centre industry including basic inbound and outbound calls, high-end multimedia voice, online financial services, and technical support. This is evidenced by several prominent call centres exporting their services to Americans today, for example: ACI in Quebec; Dell, Ford Credit, and Neiman Marcus in Alberta; Convergys and eBay in British Columbia; and AmeriCredit, EDS, IBM, and Sitel in Ontario.[33]

Canada has been a leader in the call centre industry for over a decade now. Since the early 1990s, "the Canadian call centre industry has grown at an annual rate of 20 percent," according to Steve Demmings, president of Site Selection Canada—a company that promotes and assists site selection for American and Canadian firms. "It all started back in 1994 when Manitoba and New Brunswick made a concerted effort to develop a local call centre industry in their provinces as a means to deal with these areas's high unemployment rates," Demmings said. Other provinces soon followed. Then the call centre industry "made a big move" to bring educational institutions on board. "Many colleges have set up call centre training programs," Demmings reported. The result has been an established industry with an excellent skilled labour pool. "American companies come up here to go shopping and we need to have the tableware on the table," Demmings explained.

What is important to U.S. outsourcing buyers is that many Canadian call centre customer service representatives (CSR) have made call centres their careers. Consequently, there is a much lower call centre employee turnover rate in Canada than in the United States. In the U.S., call centre staffing can be a problem. Christopher Fletcher, vice president and Research Director of CRM for the Aberdeen Group, stated, "It is tough to find people to staff a call centre [in America]. Turnover ranges from 25 percent to 50 percent annually or above. The skill sets of the people you have available are often equivalent to McDonald's."[34]

Perhaps Canada's biggest advantage is its sheer close physical proximity to the United States. The challenge of setting up call centres in other parts of the world can tip the scale in Canada's favour for American firms thinking of establishing offshore call centres. These challenges include more work to cover the basics such as site selection and hiring people; coping with different cultures, laws, standards, and languages, dealing with inferior infrastructures and greater bureaucracy and political instability, and enduring long flights and travel issues.

However, Canadians should not rest on their laurels. Several forces threaten to undermine Canada's ability to compete in the call centre industry, namely: a rising Canadian dollar that makes the domestic industry less competitive; increased competition from countries like India that have a large, educated workforce; and a general lack of unified leadership in Canada to guide future development in the call centre industry.[35]

Questions

1. What advantages are there for American companies looking to establish call centres in Canada?

2. Given the forces threatening Canada's ability to attract American companies to set up call centres in Canada, how secure do you think Canada is in its future in the call centre industry? What extent do you think future CRM technologies will erode Canada's advantages in attracting American business for call centres?

3. Explain how a contact centre (or call centre) can help an organization achieve its CRM goals.

4. What are the two different types of CRM and how can they be used to help a contact centre (or call centre) gain competitive advantage?

CLOSING CASE THREE

Revving Up Customer Relationships at Harley-Davidson

This case showcases how information technology can be used to improve customer relations.

There is a mystique associated with a Harley-Davidson motorcycle. No other motorcycle in the world has the look, feel, and sound of a Harley-Davidson. Demand for Harley-Davidson motorcycles outweighs supply even though the company produces 300,000 motorcycles per year, which generates over $4.6 billion in revenues. Some models have a two-year waiting list.

The company has won a number of awards including being rated:

- Second in *ComputerWorld's* Top 100 Best Places to Work in IT.
- Fifty-first in *Fortune's* 100 Best Companies to Work For.
- First in *Fortune's* 5 Most Admired Companies in the motor vehicles industry.
- First in the Top 10 Sincerest Corporations by the *Harris Interactive Report.*
- Second in the Top 10 Overall Corporations by the *Harris Interactive Report.*

The reason for such success is based, in part, on Harley-Davidson's strategic concern over the maintenance and growth of its customer relationships. Harley-Davidson realizes that each time a customer reaches out to them, Harley-Davidson has an opportunity to build a trusting relationship with that particular customer. As such, Harley-Davidson realizes that it takes more than just building and selling motorcycles to fulfill the dreams of its customers. For this reason, the company strives to deliver unforgettable experiences along with high-quality products.

One strategy to do this was the development of a customer-centric online store, www. Harley-Davidson.com. Bear in mind, the enormity of such a task. Harley-Davidson sells more than $580 million worth of parts and accessories to its loyal followers. Ken Ostermann, Harley-Davidson's manager of Electronic Commerce and Communications, recognized the company could increase parts and accessories sales if it could offer the products online.

However, the dilemma facing Ostermann's online strategy was that selling jackets, saddlebags, and T-shirts directly to consumers over the Web would bypass Harley-Davidson's

650 dealers, who depend on selling these high-margin accessories to fuel profits. Oster-mann's solution was to build an online store that prompted customers to select a participating Harley-Davidson dealership before placing any online orders. The selected dealership is then responsible for fulfilling the order. This strategy ensured dealers remained the focal point of customers' buying experiences.

To date, the company receives over one million visitors a month to its online store. To guarantee that every customer has a highly satisfying online buying experience, Harley-Davidson asks the dealers to agree to a number of standards including:

- Checking online orders twice daily.
- Shipping online orders within 24 hours.
- Responding to customer inquiries within 24 hours.

Another of Harley-Davidson's customer-centric strategies is its Harley's Owners Group (HOG), which offers an array of events, rides, and benefits to its members. HOG is the largest factory-sponsored motorcycle club in the world with more than 600,000 members and is one of the key drivers helping to build a strong sense of community among Harley-Davidson owners. Harley-Davidson has built a customer following that is extremely loyal, a difficult task to accomplish in any industry.[36]

Questions

1. What are the two different types of CRM and how has Harley-Davidson used them to become a customer-centric business?
2. Which of Harley-Davidson's customer-centric strategies is the most important for its business? Why?
3. Evaluate the Harley's Owners Group's CRM strategy and recommend an additional benefit Harley-Davidson could provide to its HOG members to increase customer satisfaction.
4. Describe three ways Harley-Davidson can extend its customer reach even further by performing CRM functions over the Internet.
5. What benefits could Harley-Davidson gain from using analytical CRM?
6. Explain ERM and describe how Harley-Davidson could use it to increase efficiency in its business.

MAKING BUSINESS DECISIONS

1. Customer relationship management strategies

On average, it costs an organization six times more to sell to a new customer than to sell to an existing customer. As the co-owner of a medium-sized luggage distributor, you have recently been notified that sales for the past three months have decreased by an average of 17 percent. The reasons for the decline in sales are numerous, including a poor economy, people's aversion to travel because of the threat of terrorist attacks, and some negative publicity your company received regarding a defective product line. In a group, explain how implementing a CRM system can help you understand and combat the decline in sales. Be sure to justify why a CRM system is important to your business and its future growth.

2. Comparing CRM vendors

As a team, search the Internet for at least one recent and authoritative article that compares or ranks customer relationship management systems. Select two packages from the list and compare their functions and features as described in the article(s) you found as well as on each company's Web site. Find references in the literature where companies that are using each package have reported their experiences, both good and bad. Draw on any other comparisons you can find. Prepare a presentation for delivery in class on the strengths and weaknesses of each package, which one you favour, and why.

3. Searching for employee loyalty

You are the CEO of Razz, a start-up Web-based search company, which is planning to compete directly with Google. The company had an exceptional first year and is currently receiving over 500,000 hits a day from customers all over the world. You have hired 250 people in the last four months, doubling the size of your organization. With so many new employees starting so quickly you are concerned about how your company's culture will evolve and whether your employees are receiving enough attention. You are already familiar with customer relationship management and how CRM systems can help an organization create strong customer relationships. However, you are unfamiliar with employee relationship management and you are wondering what ERM systems might be able to offer your employees and your company. Research the Web, create a report detailing features and functions of ERM systems, and determine what value will be added to your organization if you decide to implement an ERM solution.

4. Employee relationship management

All new employees at the Shinaberry Inn & Spa wear bathing suits during orientation to experience the spa's exfoliating showers and hot mineral baths. At the Shinaberry Saskatoon, new employees get the same penthouse champagne toast the hotel uses to woo meeting planners. And at many properties, employees arriving for their first day have their cars parked by the valet or get vouchers for a free night's stay. This innovative orientation program, which lets employees experience what guests experience began two years ago after focus groups pointed to empathy as a service differentiator. As a result, the company added empathy to the attributes for which it screens and a training program that involves listening to recorded guest phone calls. Even its discounted employee travel program gives employees yet another way to understand the guest experience. Design an ERM system that would help Shinaberry further its employee-centred culture. The ERM system must consider all employee needs.

5. Increasing revenues with CRM

Cold Cream is one of the premier beauty supply stores in the metro Toronto area. People come from all over to sample the store's unique creams, lotions, makeup, and perfumes. The store is four stories high with each department located on a separate floor. The company would like to implement a CRM system to help it better understand its customers and their purchasing habits. Create a report summarizing CRM systems and detail how such a system can directly influence Cold Cream's revenues.

6. Driving Up Profits with Successful Campaigns (or Driving Down?)

The Butterfly Café is a local hotspot located in downtown Calgary and offers specialty coffee, teas, and organic fruits and vegetables. The café holds a number of events to attract customers such as live music venues, poetry readings, book clubs, charity events, and local artist's night. A listing of all participants attending each event is tracked in the café's database. The café uses the information for marketing campaigns and offers customers who attend multiple events additional discounts. A marketing database company, InTheKnow.com, has offered to pay The Butterfly Café a substantial amount of money for access to its customer database, which it will then sell to other local businesses. The owner of the Butterfly Café, Mary Conzachi, has come to you for advice. Mary is not sure if her customers would appreciate her selling their personal information and how it might affect her business. However, the amount of money InTheKnow.com is offering is enough to finance her much needed new patio for the back of the café. InTheKnow.com has promised Mary that the sale will be completely confidential. What should Mary do?

7. Supporting Customers

Creative.com is an e-business that sells craft materials and supplies over the Internet. You have just started as the vice president of customer service, and you have a team of 45 customer service representatives. Currently, the only form of customer service is the 1-800 number and the company is receiving a tremendous number of calls regarding products, orders, and shipping information. The average wait time for a customer to speak to a customer service representative is 35 minutes. Orders are being cancelled and Creative.com is losing business due to its lack of customer service. Create a strategy to revamp the customer service centre at Creative.com and get the company back on track.

6

Enterprise Resource Planning

LEARNING OUTCOMES

6.1. Compare core enterprise resource planning components and extended enterprise resource planning components.

6.2. Describe the three primary components found in core enterprise resource planning systems.

6.3. Describe the four primary components found in extended enterprise resource planning systems.

6.4. Explain the business value of integrating supply chain management, customer relationship management, and enterprise resource planning systems.

Why Do I Need To Know This ?

This chapter introduces the concept of enterprise resource planning or ERP. This involves the integration of all internal daily operational processes conducted by a company, such as distribution, accounting, human resources, and manufacturing, into a single IT system or integrated set of IT systems.

The ERP concept emerged in the 1990s in response to the massive fortunes, time, and energy spent by organizations trying to support their back-office operations. Prior to this, departmental systems were built in isolation from one another and IT specialists and other organizational workers had to struggle to link together these incompatible systems. Companies literally spent hundreds of millions of dollars trying to integrate their internal departmental systems together, such as building highly customized interfaces between application systems and their stand-alone database structures.

ERP systems were the answer to this dilemma. They combined all the diverse needs of an organization's various departments and agencies into a single, integrated software program that operated on a single database. The idea was that, by doing so, departments could better share information and communicate with one another more easily. This could potentially yield huge cost savings and competitive advantages.

As a business student, you need to know this since ERP systems are the backbone of many business operations today. ERP systems are constantly evolving and it is important you understand why they exist, what they do, and the real benefits they potentially offer a company. You should also recognize the complexity and difficulty in trying to build one of these beasts, as you will likely find yourself involved in some aspects of an ERP installation or redesign. It is not for the faint of heart!

Shell Canada Fuels Productivity with ERP

Shell Canada is one of the nation's largest integrated petroleum companies and is a leading manufacturer, distributor, and marketer of refined petroleum products. The company, headquartered in Calgary, produces natural gas, natural gas liquids, and bitumen. Shell Canada is also the country's largest producer of sulphur. There is a Canada-wide network of 1,809 Shell-branded retail gasoline stations and convenience food stores from coast-to-coast.

In order to run such a complex and vast business operation successfully, the company relies heavily on the use of a mission-critical enterprise resource planning (ERP) system. The use of such a system is a necessity in helping the company integrate and manage its daily operations—operations that span from wells and mines, to processing plants, to oil trucks and gas pumps.

For example, the ERP system has helped the company immensely in terms of reducing and streamlining the highly manual process of third-party contractors submitting repair information and invoices. On average, there are between 2,500 and 4,000 service orders handled by these contractors per month on a nationwide basis.

Prior to the implementation of the ERP system, contractors had to send Shell Canada monthly, summarized invoices that listed maintenance calls the contractors made at various Shell gasoline stations. Each one of these invoices would take a contractor between eight and 20 hours to prepare. Collectively, the contractors would submit somewhere between 50 and 100 invoices every month to Shell Canada. This involved each invoice being reviewed by the appropriate territory manager and then forwarded to head office for payment processing. This alone consumed another 16 to 30 hours of labour per month. At head office, another 200 hours of work was performed by data entry clerks who had to manually enter batch invoice data into the payment system.

And this would be the amount of time needed if things went smoothly! More hours of labour were required to decipher and correct errors if any mistakes were introduced from all the manual invoice generation and data re-entry involved. Often errors concerning one line-item on an invoice would deter payment of the whole invoice. This irritated the contractors and did not help foster healthy contractor relationships.

To make matters worse, despite the hours involved and the amount of human data-handling required, detailed information about the service repairs that contractors did was often not entered into the payment system. And if it were entered, the information was not timely—it was often weeks or even months old by the time it made it into the payment processing system. As a result, Shell was not collecting sufficient information about what repairs were being done, what had caused the problem, and how it had been resolved.

Fortunately, the ERP solution solved these inadequacies by providing an integrated Web-based service order, invoicing, and payment submission system. With this tool, third-party contractors can enter service orders directly into Shell's ERP system via the Web. When this is done, the contractors can also enter detailed information about the work that was performed—sometimes even attaching photos and drawings to help describe the work that was done. With the ERP system, it only takes a few minutes for a contractor to enter details about a service order. Further, this information can be transmitted through a wireless PDA to the appropriate Shell manager for immediate approval—shaving extra time off in unnecessary delays.

Another bonus of the ERP system is that the contractors' monthly, summarized invoices can now be generated automatically and fed directly into the ERP's system's account payables application for processing. No re-keying of data required! Even better, if there is an issue or concern with one invoice item, the other items on the invoice can still be processed for payment.

Shell Canada's ERP system also handles other operational tasks. For example, the system can help speed up maintenance and repair operations at the company's refineries. With the ERP system in place, rather than trying to utilize a variety of disparate internal systems to access blueprints, schematic, spare parts lists, and other tools and information, workers at the refineries can now use the ERP system to access these things directly from a centralized database.

An added benefit of the ERP system is its ease-of-use. Past systems used by refinery workers were complex and difficult to search for information. The ERP system in place now has a portal-like interface that allows refinery workers to access the functions and information they need to keep operations running. The Web interface allows workers access to this information with one or two clicks of a mouse.

An important part of any successful ERP implementation is training end-users to learn how to utilize the system and to teach them about the functions and abilities of the ERP system. Recognizing this, Shell Canada offered its personnel both formal and informal ERP training. These proved to be invaluable in teaching end-users the mechanics of the system and raising awareness of the benefits of the system and the efficiencies that the ERP system could offer Shell Canada. This not only helped promote end-user acceptance of the ERP system, but also greatly increased employees' intentions to use the system in their daily work.

Shell Canada executives are pleased and optimistic about the advantages of the ERP system. With this new system, employees across the company have gained fast and easy access to the tools and information they need to conduct their daily operations.[1]

INTRODUCTION

*E*nterprise resource planning (ERP) integrates all departments and functions throughout an organization into a single IT system (or integrated set of IT systems) so that employees can make decisions by viewing enterprisewide information on all business operations.

SAP, the leading ERP vendor, boasts 20,000 installations and 10 million users worldwide. These figures represent only 30 percent of the overall ERP market. Figure 6.1 highlights a few reasons ERP solutions have proven to be such a powerful force.

ERP as a business concept resounds as a powerful internal information management nirvana: Everyone involved in sourcing, producing, and delivering the company's product works with the same information, which eliminates redundancies, reduces wasted time, and removes misinformation.

ENTERPRISE RESOURCE PLANNING

Turner Industries grew from $300 million in sales to $800 million in sales in less than 10 years thanks to the implementation of an ERP system. Ranked number 369 on the Forbes 500 list of privately held companies, Turner Industries is a leading industrial services firm. Turner Industries develops and deploys advanced software applications designed to maximize the productivity of its 25,000 employees and construction equipment valued at more than $115 million.

The company considers the biggest challenges in the industrial services industry to be completing projects on time, within budget, while fulfilling customers' expectations. To meet these challenges the company invested in an ERP system and named the project Interplan. Interplan won Constructech's Vision award for software innovation in the heavy construction industry. Interplan runs all of Turner's construction, turnaround, shutdown, and maintenance projects and is so adept at estimating and planning jobs that Turner Industries typically achieves higher profit margins on projects that use Interplan. As the ERP solution makes the company more profitable, the company can pass on the cost savings to its customers, giving the company an incredible competitive advantage.[2]

A common problem facing organizations is maintaining consistency across its business operations. If a single department, such as sales, decides to implement a new system without considering the other departments, it can cause inconsistencies throughout the company. A common problem occurs when one system saves (or fails to save) information that is not in other company systems. For example, a new sales system does not have a field to save e-mail addresses and the rest of the company's systems save e-mail addresses. Not all applications are built to talk to each other and if sales suddenly implements a new system that marketing and production cannot use or is inconsistent in the way it handles information, the company becomes siloed in its operations.

Enterprise resource planning systems provide organizations with consistency. An ERP system provides a method for the effective planning and controlling of all

FIGURE 6.1

Reasons ERP Systems Are Powerful Organizational Tools

Reasons ERP Systems Are Powerful Organizational Tools
ERP is a logical solution to the mess of incompatible applications that had sprung up in most businesses.
ERP addresses the need for global information sharing and reporting.
ERP is used to avoid the pain and expense of fixing legacy systems.

the resources required to take, make, ship, and account for customer orders in a manufacturing, distribution, or service organization. The key word in enterprise resource planning is *enterprise*.

The City of Winnipeg, in its quest to become one of Canada's most efficient municipalities, used ERP to streamline and integrate more than 100 diverse systems scattered across the city's various departments. According to Rodger Guinn, project director for the City of Winnipeg, the results have been remarkable, "Winnipeg went from being the last major Canadian city without ERP to being seen as the leader with world-class software and full integration." Prior to the ERP implementation, the city faced numerous challenges with its hodge-podge of incompatible and disconnected applications: a) inconsistent information and poor communication across departments; b) wasted purchasing power due to non-integrated procurement; c) lack of coordination of common activities such as human resources and payroll; d) limited analytical capability; and e) silos of functional organizational cultures and business practices with minimal touch points. The ERP system overcame these challenges by its ability to integrate the city's systems across all of its 14 departments, including police, transit, public works, water, and waste. Major components of the ERP were human resources and finance. With the ERP system, the City of Winnipeg is well positioned for future growth. According to Deloitte & Touche, the professional services firmed hired by the city to implement the ERP system, the "new system provides alignment between finance, human resources and information technology across all departments—along with real-time information management and employee self-service. The system also provides a stable and flexible platform for standardizing practices, policies, and procedures across departments, and for developing new applications such as competency management and career planning."[3]

CORE AND EXTENDED ERP COMPONENTS

Figure 6.2 provides an example of an ERP system with its core and extended components. ***Core ERP components*** are the traditional components included in most ERP systems and they primarily focus on internal operations. ***Extended ERP components*** are the extra components that meet the organizational needs not covered by the core components and primarily focus on external operations.

CORE ERP COMPONENTS

The three most common core ERP components focusing on internal operations are:

1. Accounting and finance.
2. Production and materials management.
3. Human resources.

Accounting and Finance ERP Components

Deeley Harley-Davidson Canada, the exclusive Canadian distributor of Harley-Davidson motorcycles, has improved inventory, turnaround time, margins, and customer satisfaction—all with the implementation of a financial ERP system. The system has opened up the power of information to the company and is helping it make strategic decisions when it still has the time to change things. The ERP system provides the company with ways to manage inventory, turnaround time, and utilize warehouse space more effectively.[4]

Accounting and finance ERP components manage accounting data and financial processes within the enterprise with functions such as general ledger, accounts payable, accounts receivable, budgeting, and asset management. One of the most useful features included in an ERP accounting/finance component is its credit-management feature. Most organizations manage their relationships with customers by setting credit limits, or a limit on how much a customer can

FIGURE 6.2

Core ERP Components and Extended ERP Components

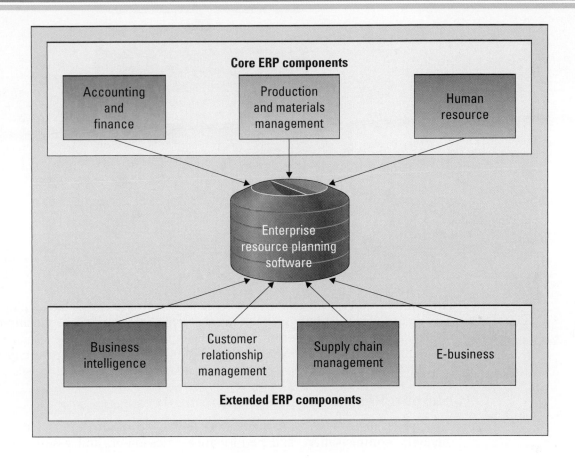

owe at any one time. The company then monitors the credit limit whenever the customer places a new order or sends in a payment. ERP financial systems help to correlate customer orders with customer account balances determining credit availability. Another great feature is the ability to perform product profitability analysis. ERP financial components are the backbone behind product profitability analysis and allow companies to perform all types of advanced profitability modelling techniques.

Production and Materials Management ERP Components

One of the main functions of an ERP system is streamlining the production planning process. ***Production and materials management ERP components*** handle the various aspects of production planning and execution such as demand forecasting, production scheduling, job cost accounting, and quality control. Companies typically produce multiple products, each of which has many different parts. Production lines, consisting of machines and employees, build the different types of products. The company must then define sales forecasting for each product to determine production schedules and materials purchasing. Figure 6.3 displays the typical ERP production planning process. The process begins with forecasting sales in order to plan operations. A detailed production schedule is developed if the product is produced, and a materials requirement plan is completed if the product is purchased.

Grupo Farmanova Intermed, located in Costa Rica, is a pharmaceutical marketing and distribution company that markets nearly 2,500 products to about 500 customers in Central and South America. The company identified a need for software that could

FIGURE 6.3

The Production Planning Process

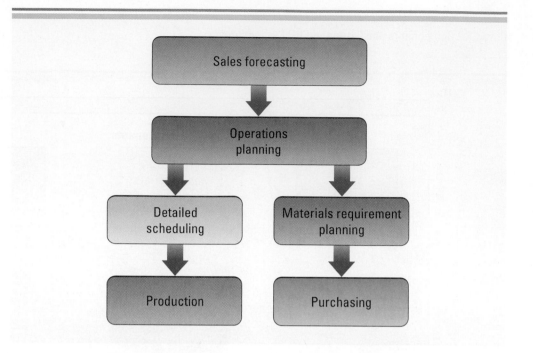

unify product logistics management in a single country. It decided to deploy People-Soft financial and distribution ERP components allowing the company to improve customer data management, increase confidence among internal and external users, and coordinate the logistics of inventory. With the new software the company enhanced its capabilities for handling, distributing, and marketing its pharmaceuticals.[5]

Human Resources ERP Components

Human resources ERP components track employee information including payroll, benefits, compensation, and performance assessment, and assure compliance with the legal requirements of multiple jurisdictions and tax authorities. Human resources components even offer features that allow the organization to perform detailed analysis on its employees to determine such things as the identification of individuals who are likely to leave the company unless additional compensation or benefits are provided. These components can also identify which employees are using which resources, such as online training and long-distance telephone services. They can also help determine whether the most talented people are working for those business units with the highest priority—or where they would have the greatest impact on profit.

EXTENDED ERP COMPONENTS

Extended ERP components are the extra components that meet the organizational needs not covered by the core components and primarily focus on external operations. Many of the numerous extended ERP components are Internet-enabled and require interaction with customers, suppliers, and business partners outside the organization. The four most common extended ERP components are:

1. Business intelligence.
2. Customer relationship management.
3. Supply chain management.
4. E-business.

Business Intelligence Components

ERP systems offer powerful tools that measure and control organizational operations. Many organizations have found that these valuable tools can be enhanced to provide even greater value through the addition of powerful business intelligence systems. **Business intelligence** describes information that people use to support their decision-making efforts. The business intelligence components of ERP systems typically collect information used throughout the organization (including data used in many other ERP components), organize it, and apply analytical tools to assist managers with decisions. Data warehouses are one of the most popular extensions to ERP systems, with over two-thirds of U.S. manufacturers adopting or planning such systems.[6]

Customer Relationship Management Components

ERP vendors are expanding their functionality to provide services formerly supplied by customer relationship management (CRM) vendors such as PeopleSoft and Siebel. **Customer relationship management (CRM)** involves managing all aspects of a customer's relationship with an organization to increase customer loyalty and retention and an organization's profitability. CRM components provide an integrated view of customer data and interactions allowing organizations to work more effectively with customers and be more responsive to their needs. CRM components typically include contact centres, sales force automation, and marketing functions. These improve the customer experience while identifying a company's most (and least) valuable customers for better allocation of resources.

Supply Chain Management Components

ERP vendors are expanding their functionality to provide services formerly supplied by supply chain management vendors such as i2 Technologies and Manugistics. **Supply chain management (SCM)** involves the management of information flows between and among stages in a supply chain to maximize total supply chain effectiveness and profitability. SCM components help an organization plan, schedule, control, and optimize the supply chain from its acquisition of raw materials to the receipt of finished goods by customers.

E-Business Components

The original focus of ERP systems was the internal organization. In other words, ERP systems are not fundamentally ready for the external world of e-business. The newest and most exciting extended ERP components are the e-business components. **E-business** means conducting business on the Internet, not only buying and selling, but also serving customers and collaborating with business partners. Two of the primary features of e-business components are e-logistics and e-procurement. **E-logistics** manages the transportation and storage of goods. **E-procurement** is the business-to-business (B2B) purchase and sale of supplies and services over the Internet.

E-business and ERP complement each other by allowing companies to establish a Web presence and fulfill orders expeditiously. A common mistake made by many businesses is deploying a Web presence before the integration of back-office systems or an ERP system. For example, one large toy manufacturer announced less than a week before Christmas that it would be unable to fulfill any of its Web orders. The company had all the toys in the warehouse, but it could not organize the basic order processing function to get the toys delivered to the consumers on time.

Customers and suppliers are now demanding access to ERP information including order status, inventory levels, and invoice reconciliation. Plus, the customers and partners want all this information in a simplified format available through a Web site. This is a difficult task to accomplish because most ERP systems are full of technical jargon, which is why employee training is one of the hidden costs associated with ERP implementations. Removing the jargon to accommodate untrained customers and partners is one of the more difficult tasks when Web-enabling an ERP system. To accommodate the growing needs of the e-business world, ERP vendors need to build two new channels of access into the ERP system information— one channel for customers (B2C) and one channel for businesses, suppliers, and partners (B2B).[7]

6.2 ERP VENDORS, SOFTWARE, INTEGRATION, AND FUTURE TRENDS

ERP VENDOR OVERVIEW

Companies that are successful in the digital economy understand that current business designs and models are insufficient to meet the challenges of doing business in the e-business era. A close look at such leading companies as Amazon.com, Dell, and Cisco will provide insight into a new kind of business model that focuses on having a finely tuned integration of business, technology, and process. These companies frequently use technology to streamline supply chain operations, improve customer loyalty, gain visibility into enterprisewide information, and ultimately drive profit growth. To thrive in the e-business world, organizations must structurally transform their internal architectures. They must integrate their disparate systems into a potent e-business infrastructure.

Applications such as SCM, CRM, and ERP are the backbone of e-business. Integration of these applications is the key to success for many companies. Integration allows the unlocking of information to make it available to any user, anywhere, anytime. Figure 6.4 displays the top three ERP vendors until December 2004 when Oracle bought PeopleSoft for $11.6 billion, after a takeover battle that lasted for 18 months. Figure 6.5 displays the new vendor overview.

The vendors highlighted in Figure 6.5 offer CRM and SCM modules. However, these modules are not as functional or flexible as the modules offered by industry leaders of SCM and CRM such as Siebel and i2 technologies, as depicted in Figure 6.6 and Figure 6.7. As a result, organizations face the challenge of integrating their new e-business systems with their preexisting applications and other vendor products.

ERP Software

There are many different ERP vendors on the market today, each offering different ERP solutions. The core ERP functions for each vendor are the same and focus on financial, accounting, sales, marketing, human resource, operations, and logistics. ERP vendors differentiate themselves by offering unique functionality such as CRM and SCM systems.

Many customers find that their chosen ERP solution does not meet their expectations. Despite many improvements in the software, the industry itself is well aware that failed ERP implementations are still far too common. According to Gartner Research, the average failure rate for an ERP project is 66 percent. It is no wonder that some manufacturers view ERP as a necessary, strategic evil. The key word here though is *necessary*.

Many companies strive to make good financial decisions by making smart investments. The best way to ensure a good investment in ERP is to understand why failure occurs and how to avoid it. The first challenge is that ERP is a product that comes in many flavours. Its main purpose is to provide support and automation to a business process. The business world has many different business models, and there are just as many ERP products available that serve them.

FIGURE 6.4

ERP Vendor Overview
(before December 31, 2004)

	Vendor		
Component	**PeopleSoft**	**Oracle**	**SAP**
Customer relationship management	X		X
Supply chain management	X	X	X
Financial management	X	X	X
Human resource management	X	X	X
Service automation	X		
Supplier relationship management	X		X
Enterprise performance management	X		
Business intelligence		X	
Learning management		X	
Order management		X	
Manufacturing		X	
Marketing		X	
Sales		X	

FIGURE 6.5

ERP Vendor Overview
(after December 31, 2004)

	Vendor	
Component	**Oracle**	**SAP**
Customer relationship management	X	X
Supply chain management	X	X
Financial management	X	X
Human resource management	X	X
Service automation	X	
Supplier relationship management	X	X
Enterprise performance management	X	
Business intelligence	X	
Learning management	X	
Order management	X	
Manufacturing	X	
Marketing	X	
Sales	X	

Finding the Right ERP Solution

A good ERP system will be highly reflective of the business process in place at the company. This means that the software must perform many different tasks and that makes it complex. Most companies do not carry a high degree of ERP software expertise on their staff and do not understand ERP to the degree they should, and this makes it easy

FIGURE 6.6

SCM Market Overview

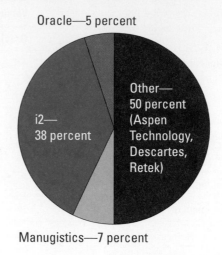

FIGURE 6.7

CRM Market Overview

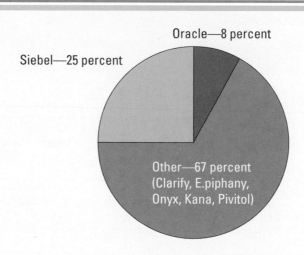

to choose the wrong package. The key to making an effective purchase is to have solid business processes. Successful ERP projects share three basic attributes:

1. Overall fit.
2. Proper business analysis.
3. Solid implementation plans.[8]

Overall Fit   This refers to the degree of gaps that exist between the system and the business process. A well-fitting ERP has no major process gaps and very few minor ones. Think of a new ERP system as a suit. Typically, a customer buys a suit three ways:

1. Off the rack.
2. Off the rack and tailor it to fit.
3. Custom made.

The way the solution fits the business process will normally determine the satisfaction level of the client. Buying ERP off the rack is the equivalent of buying a canned software package. It fits some well, but some not at all. That is why a customer can tailor a suit so that it fits better. Modifications can be made to the software so that its processes line up better with the company processes. This is a good strategy, provided the chosen package supports this. The downside is that it can get very expensive. Finally, the custom system can provide a great fit, but the company must thoroughly understand what it is doing and be able to support the heavy financial burden associated with a custom-build.

Proper Business Analysis   The best way to determine which fit strategy is right is to conduct a thorough business analysis. Successful companies normally spend up to 10 percent of the project budget on a business analysis. A proper analysis must result in a documented list of the business processes at work within the company. This will provide a basic tool that can measure vendor capability.

Solid Implementation Plans   Like the installation of any successful process or piece of machinery, a plan is needed to monitor the quality objectives and timelines. It will also employ processes like workflow analysis and job combination to harvest savings.

A thorough implementation will transfer knowledge to the system users. When the project is complete the users of the new system must be capable of using the tools it provides. The users must also know what to do in cases when the process fluctuates. The majority of failed systems are the result of poor-quality implementation. It is important to remember that ERP is simply a tool. Tools that people do not know how to use can be as useless as having no tools at all.

ERP BENEFITS AND RISKS (COST)

There is no guarantee of success for an ERP system. ERPs focus on how a corporation operates internally, and optimizing these operations takes significant time and energy. According to Meta Group, it takes the average company 8 to 18 months to see any benefits from an ERP system. The good news is that the average savings from new ERP systems are $1.9 million per year. Figure 6.8 displays a list of the five most common benefits an organization can expect to achieve from a successful ERP implementation.[9]

Along with understanding the benefits an organization can gain from an ERP system, it is just as important to understand the primary risk associated with an ERP implementation—cost. ERP systems do not come cheap. Meta Group studied total cost of ownership (TCO) for an ERP system. The study included hardware, software, professional services, and internal staff costs. Sixty-three companies were surveyed ranging in size from small to large over a variety of industries. The average TCO was $17 million (highest $348 million and lowest $460,000). The price tag for an ERP system can easily start in the multiple millions of dollars and implementation can take an average of 23 months. Figure 6.9 displays a few of the costs associated with an ERP system.

FIGURE 6.8

Common Benefits Received from ERP Systems

Common ERP Benefits
1. **Integrate financial information:** To understand an organization's overall performance, managers must have a single financial view.
2. **Integrate customer order information:** With all customer order information in a single system it is easier to coordinate manufacturing, inventory, and shipping to send a common message to customers regarding order status.
3. **Standardize and speed up manufacturing processes:** ERP systems provide standard methods for manufacturing companies to use when automating steps in the manufacturing process. Standardizing manufacturing processes across an organization saves time, increases production, and reduces head count.
4. **Reduce inventory:** With improved visibility in the order fulfillment process, an organization can reduce inventories and streamline deliveries to its customers.
5. **Standardize human resource information:** ERPs provide a unified method for tracking employees' time, as well as communicating HR benefits and services.

FIGURE 6.9

Associated ERP Risk (Cost)

Associated ERP Risk (Cost)
Software cost: Purchasing the software.
Consulting fees: Hiring external experts to help implement the system correctly.
Process rework: Redefining processes in order to ensure the company is using the most efficient and effective processes.
Customization: If the software package does not meet all of the company's needs, it may be required to customize the software.
Integration and testing: Ensuring all software products, including disparate systems not part of the ERP system, are working together or are integrated. Testing the ERP system includes testing all integrations.
Training: Training all new users.
Data warehouse integration and data conversion: Moving data from an old system into the new ERP system.

THE CONNECTED CORPORATION—INTEGRATING SCM, CRM, AND ERP

Most organizations today have no choice but to piece their applications together since no one vendor can respond to every organizational need; hence, customers purchase applications from multiple vendors. As a result, large companies usually have multiple applications that are not designed to work together, and find themselves having to integrate business solutions. For example, a single organization might choose its CRM components from Siebel, SCM components from i2, financial components and human resources components from Oracle. Figure 6.10

FIGURE 6.10

Primary Users and Business Benefits of Strategic Initiatives

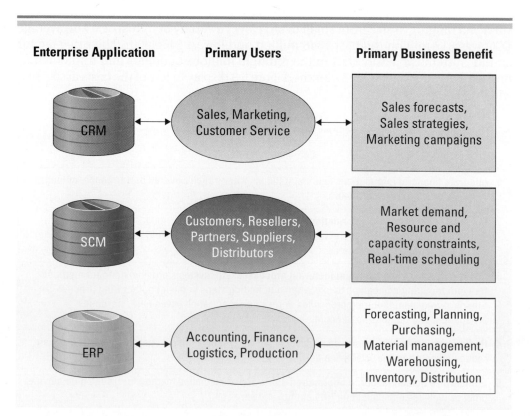

displays the general audience and purpose for each of the applications that have to be integrated.

Effectively managing the transformation to an integrated enterprise will be critical to the success of the 21st century organization. The key to an integrated enterprise is the integration of the disparate IT applications. An integrated enterprise infuses support areas, such as finance and human resources, with a strong customer orientation. Integrations are achieved using *middleware*—several different types of software that sit in the middle of and provide connectivity between two or more software applications. Middleware translates information between disparate systems. *Enterprise application integration (EAI) middleware* represents a new approach to middleware by packaging together commonly used functionality, such as providing prebuilt links to popular enterprise applications, which reduces the time necessary to develop solutions that integrate applications from multiple vendors. A few leading vendors of EAI middleware include Active Software, Vitria Technology, and Extricity.

Figure 6.11 displays the data points where these applications integrate and illustrates the underlying premise of e-business architecture infrastructure design: companies run on interdependent applications. If one application of the company does not function well, the entire customer value delivery system is affected. The world-class enterprises of tomorrow must be built on the foundation of world-class applications implemented today.

The heart of an ERP system is a central database that collects information from and feeds information into all the ERP system's individual application components (called modules), supporting diverse business functions such as accounting, manufacturing, marketing, and human resources. When a user enters or updates information in one module, it is immediately and automatically updated throughout the entire system, as illustrated in Figure 6.12.

ERP automates business processes such as order fulfillment—taking an order from a customer, shipping the purchase, and then billing for it. With an ERP system, when a customer service representative takes an order from a customer, he or she has all the information necessary to complete the order (the customer's credit rating and order history, the company's inventory levels, and the delivery schedule). Everyone else in the company sees the same information and has access to the database that holds the customer's new order. When one department finishes with the order, it is automatically routed via the ERP system to the next department. To find out where the order is at any point, a user need only log

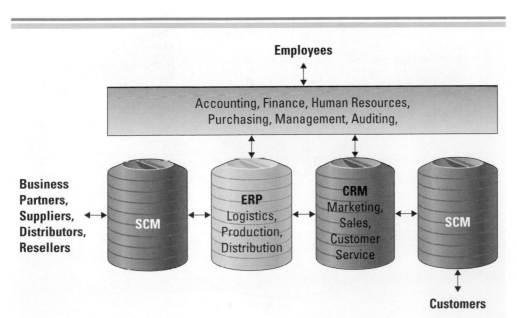

FIGURE 6.11

Integration between SCM, CRM, and ERP Applications

FIGURE 6.12

ERP Integration Flow

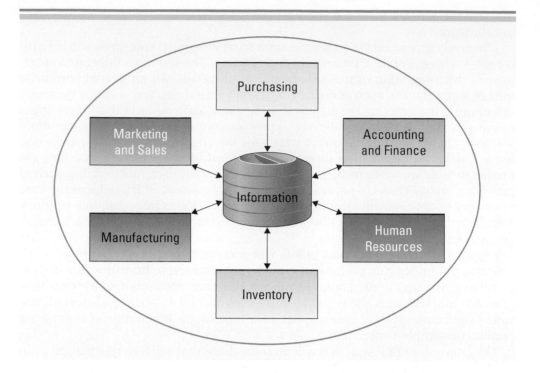

in to the ERP system and track it down, as illustrated in Figure 6.13. The order process moves like a bolt of lightning through the organization, and customers get their orders faster and with fewer errors than ever before. ERP can apply that same magic to the other major business processes, such as employee benefits or financial reporting.

To qualify as a true ERP solution, the system not only must integrate various organization processes, but also must be:

- **Flexible**—An ERP system should be flexible in order to respond to the changing needs of an enterprise.

FIGURE 6.13

ERP Process Flow

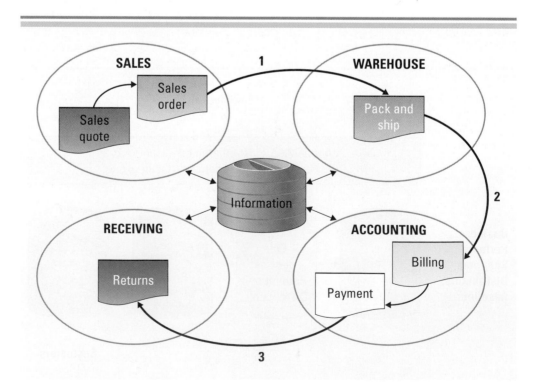

- **Modular and open**—An ERP system has to have an open system architecture, meaning that any module can be interfaced with or detached whenever required without affecting the other modules. The system should support multiple hardware platforms for organizations that have a heterogeneous collection of systems. It must also support third-party add-on components.
- **Comprehensive**—An ERP system should be able to support a variety of organizational functions and must be suitable for a wide range of business organizations.
- **Beyond the company**—An ERP system must not be confined to organizational boundaries but rather support online connectivity to business partners or customers.

Companies are expecting e-business to increase profitability, create competitive differentiation, and support innovative business practices. To achieve these goals, companies must evolve through distinct stages, from integrated processes to truly synchronized inter-enterprise communities. Getting e-business applications based on different technologies and with differing business models and data models to work together is a key issue for 21st century organizations.

THE FUTURE OF ERP

ERP places new demands not only on support and delivery information technology, but also on the way business processes have to be designed, implemented, monitored, and maintained. For example, several persons in different locations and with different hardware and software resources may simultaneously initiate a purchase process for the same product but with different selection criteria. Reliability, efficiency, and scalability are among the features that have to be embedded in e-business processes in ERP systems. Despite the rapid growth in the number of ERP installations, conducting ERP operations is still challenging.

Understanding the many different types of core and extended ERP components can help an organization determine which components will add the most value. The two biggest vendors in the ERP market are Oracle (which purchased PeopleSoft in 2004) and SAP. Figure 6.14 is an overview of a few of the components offered by each ERP vendor.

In the future, the line between ERP, SCM, and CRM will continue to blur as ERP vendors broaden the functionality of their product suites and redefine the packaging of their products. ERP vendors with comprehensive but modular components will dominate the next high-growth phase of the enterprise applications market. Since core functionality is virtually the same for all vendors, a vendor's success will primarily depend upon how quickly it incorporates other kinds of functionality such as the Internet, interface, and wireless technology.

Internet

The adoption of the Internet is one of the single most important forces reshaping the architecture and functionality of ERP systems and is responsible for the most important new developments in ERP. The Internet serves as a basis for extending ERP's traditional vision of integrating data and processes across an organization's functional departments to include sharing data and processes among multiple enterprises.

Interface

Most ERP suites offer a customizable browser that allows each employee to configure his or her own view of the system. A manager can also customize each employee's views of the system. This feature allows managers to control access to highly sensitive information such as payroll and performance appraisals. The same customizable browser will be used in the future to allow customers and partners to see only select ERP information via the Internet.

FIGURE 6.14

ERP Vendor Components

PeopleSoft (Purchased by Oracle)	
Component	**Description**
Application Integration	Integrate PeopleSoft and non-PeopleSoft applications at all levels with Portal Solutions, AppConnect, and Data Warehousing and Analytic Solutions.
Customer Relationship Management	Get immediate, seamless integration among customer, financial, supply chain, and employee management systems.
Enterprise Performance Management	Enable customers, suppliers, and employees to connect to set goals, develop plans, and measure progress with our integrated, scalable applications.
Financial Management	Get the power to compete in the business world with a comprehensive suite of pure Internet financial applications.
Human Capital Management (including Human Resources Management Solutions)	Manage and mobilize a unified, global workforce, and align workforce contribution with business objectives.
Service Automation	Optimize project investments, reduce project delivery costs, and maximize resources to increase utilization and value to your organization.
Supplier Relationship Management	Manage all aspects of supplier relationships including indirect and direct goods, as well as services procurement.
Supply Chain Management	Take advantage of solutions that promote business-to-business interaction throughout the supply chain, from customer to supplier.

Oracle	
Component	**Description**
Oracle Financials	Financial applications manage the flow of cash and assets into, out of, and within your enterprise: tracking thousands of transactions, setting fiscal goals for various departments, and allowing you to project future financial health as you record today's profits.
Oracle Human Resources Management	Oracle Human Resources Management System (HRMS) empowers businesses with the tools to find, extract, and analyze data related to human capital. This intelligence readies a company to rapidly deploy the best resources for maximum employee productivity, satisfaction, and retention.
Oracle Intelligence	Oracle Daily Business Intelligence accesses and shares unified information and analysis across the enterprise with a single definition of customers, suppliers, employees, and products.
Oracle Learning Management	Oracle Learning Management (Oracle iLearning, Oracle Training Management, and Oracle Human Resources Management System) provides a complete infrastructure that lets organizations manage, deliver, and track training, in both online and classroom environments.
Oracle Supply Chain Management	Oracle Supply Chain Management lets organizations gain global visibility, automate internal processes, and readily collaborate with suppliers, customers, and partners.
Oracle Manufacturing	Oracle Manufacturing optimizes production capacity beginning with raw materials through final products.
Oracle Order Management	Oracle's support of the complete fulfillment process from order to cash.
Oracle Marketing	Oracle Marketing drives profit by intelligently marketing to the most profitable customers. By leveraging a single repository of customer information, marketing professionals can better target and personalize their campaigns, and refine them in real time with powerful analytical tools.
Oracle Projects	To consistently deliver on time and on budget, an organization must fine-tune execution, align global organization with projects, and assign the right resources to the most important initiatives at the right time.
Oracle Sales	Oracle Sales allows an organization to learn more about its entire business to identify and target profitable opportunities.

FIGURE 6.14

(Continued)

SAP	
Component	**Description**
mySAP™ Customer Relationship Management	The fully integrated CRM solution that facilitates world-class service across all customer touchpoints.
mySAP™ Financials	The leading solution for operational, analytical, and collaborative financial management.
mySAP™ Human Resources (mySAP HR)	The HR resource that helps more than 7,800 organizations worldwide maximize their return on capital.
mySAP™ Marketplace	An online marketplace solution that allows your company to buy, sell, and conduct business around the clock and around the world.
mySAP™ Product Lifecycle Management	The collaborative solution that helps designers, engineers, and suppliers achieve new levels of innovation.
mySAP™ Supplier Relationship Management	Covers the full supply cycle—from strategic sourcing for lower costs to faster process cycles.
mySAP™ Supply Chain Management	Gives an organization the power to dramatically improve its planning, responsiveness, and execution. suppliers, customers, and partners.

Wireless Technology

Wireless technologies provide a means for users with handheld devices, such as PDAs and Web-enabled telephones, to connect to and interact with ERP systems. Most large ERP vendors will acquire smaller companies that specialize in wireless access. If they fail to do so, they will need to develop their own expertise in this area to build wireless access packages.

Wireless technologies will enable users to carry out the same transactions from their mobile devices as they used to do from any fixed device. Being able to buy and sell goods and services over mobile devices is an important step toward achieving the anywhere–anytime paradigm. In the future, location and time will no longer constrain organizations from completing their operations.

OPENING CASE QUESTIONS

Shell Canada Fuels Productivity with ERP

4. What advice would you give Shell Canada if it decided to choose a different ERP software solution?

5. How can integrating SCM, CRM, and ERP help improve business operations at Shell Canada?

6. Review the different components in Figure 6.14. Which components would you recommend as necessary for Shell Canada? As "nice-to-have" but not necessary? As "strategic"?

The purpose of the chapter was to describe and explain the concept of enterprise resource planning:

- The chapter illustrated how the integration of all internal daily operational processes conducted by a company into a single IT system or integrated set of IT systems could help improve operational efficiencies and reduce costs.

- Having these systems tightly integrated allows for smoother work flow.

As a business student, you need to know this since:

- An ERP system is often considered to be the core business system that drives a company's daily operations.

The deployment of ERP systems by organizations provides you, the business student, with an excellent example of how information technology can support business processes and requirements:

- The use of ERP solutions illustrates how business needs can (and should) drive the choice and implementation of information systems within a firm.

- Information technology is not used simply because it "is there" but rather because it enables an organization to operate more efficiently and effectively than it otherwise could.

Accounting and finance ERP
    component   162
Business intelligence   165
Core ERP component   162
Customer relationship
    management (CRM)   165
E-business   165
E-logistics   165

Enterprise application
    integration (EAI)
    middleware   171
Enterprise resource planning
    (ERP)   161
E-procurement   165
Extended ERP
    component   162

Human resources ERP
    component   164
Middleware   171
Production and materials
    management ERP
    component   163
Supply chain management
    (SCM)   165

Campus ERP

This case illustrates the challenges in implementing an ERP system.

When Stefanie Fillers returned to university she needed to log in to the school's new online registration system to make certain that the courses she was taking would allow her to graduate. She also wanted to waive her participation in her school's dental insurance plan. When the system crashed the day before classes began, Fillers, a second-year undergraduate student, was annoyed. But at least she knew where her classes were—unlike most first-year students.

Several schools around the country have experienced problems with nonfunctioning Web portals that prevented students from finding out where their classes were. At one university, financial aid was denied to 3,000 students by a buggy new ERP system, even though they had already received loan commitments. The school provided short-term loans for the cash-strapped students while the IT department and financial aid administrators scrambled to fix the complex system.

Disastrous ERP implementations have given more than a few post-secondary institutions black eyes. These recent campus meltdowns illustrate how the growing reliance on expensive ERP systems has created nightmare scenarios for some schools. In every case, the new systems were designed to centralize business processes in what historically has been a hodge-podge of discrete legacy systems. College and university administrators are drawn to ERP systems offering integrated views of finance, HR, student records, financial aid, and more.

ERP implementations are difficult, even in very top-down corporate environments. Getting them to work in academic settings, which are essentially a conglomeration of decentralized fiefdoms, has been nearly impossible. Staff members in the largely autonomous departments do not like the one-size-fits-all strategy of an ERP implementation. Plus, these nonprofit organizations generally lack the talent and financial resources to create and manage a robust enterprise system. Representatives from Oracle, which dominates the higher education market for ERP, say that much of the problem results from the inexperience of college and university IT departments and their tendency to rush implementations and inadequately test the new systems.

Standardizing at Stanford

These same problems confront colleges and universities around the world. For example, Stanford University bought into the late 1990s enterprise software pitch and never slowed down its implementation engine. "In hindsight, we tried to do too much in too little time," said Randy Livingston, Stanford's vice president of business affairs and CFO.

Starting in 2001, Stanford implemented student administration systems, PeopleSoft HR, Oracle financials, and several other ancillary applications. Years later, users still complain that they have lower productivity with the new systems than with the previous ones, which were supported by a highly customized mainframe. Users also have had difficulty accessing critical information on a timely basis. Livingston said many transactions, such as initiating a purchase requisition or requesting a reimbursement, now take longer for users than with the prior legacy system.

Stanford has also not realized any of the projected savings the vendors promised. "We are finding that the new ERP applications cost considerably more to support than our legacy applications," Livingston said. He does not know how much it will cost to get the enterprise systems working at acceptable user levels.

Stanford's IT department is still trying to get campuswide buy-in for the enterprise applications, which have necessitated new ways of doing business, which leads to nonuse of the new systems and costly customizations to keep all users satisfied. For example, Stanford's law school operates on a semester schedule, while the other six schools operate on a trimester schedule. "This means that every aspect of the student administration system needs to be configured differently for the law school," Livingston said. Within the schools, some faculty members are paid a 12-month salary; other schools pay by 9 months, 10 months, or 11 months. "The standard HR payroll system is not designed to handle all these unusual pay schedules," Livingston said.

To resolve the issues, Livingston has reorganized the IT department, which he hopes will be better able to manage the enterprise projects going forward. He also created a separate administrative systems group that reports directly to him, with responsibility for development, integration, and support of the major ERP systems.

The hurdles Stanford and other colleges and universities face with ERP systems are largely cultural ones. For instance, lean staffs and tight budgets at most campuses usually lead to a lack of proper training and systems testing. At Stanford, plenty of training was offered, but many users did not take it, Livingston said. He has set up new training programs, including a group of trainers who sit side by side with users to help them learn how to do complex tasks; periodic user group meetings; Web site and e-mail lists that offer more help; and expert users embedded in the various departments who aid their colleagues.

Stanford's IT was still struggling with integrating the enterprise systems when the newly launched PeopleSoft Web portal (called Axess) crashed in 2004. Axess could not handle the load of all the returning students trying to log in to the untested Web-based system at the same time, Livingston said. Stanford was able to fix those problems relatively quickly, but Livingston and his staff continue to struggle with the enterprise projects. The university's departments remain "highly suspicious and resistant" of his efforts to standardize and centralize business processes, Livingston said.[10]

Questions

1. How could core ERP components help improve business operations at your school?
2. How could extended ERP components help improve business operations at your school?
3. How can integrating SCM, CRM, and ERP help improve business operations at your school?
4. Review the different components in Figure 6.14. Which component would you recommend your school implement if it decided to purchase an ERP component?

CLOSING CASE TWO

ERP Expands into the SME Market

This case illustrates the challenges and benefits of implementing ERP systems in small and medium enterprises.

Enterprise Resource Planning is no longer the purview of large organizations. Many of the large-scale ERP vendors, such as SAP and Oracle, are attempting to enter the small to medium enterprise (SME) market in the hopes of expanding their client-base. However, despite some clever packaging and dumbing-down of the features offered, large-scale ERP vendors are finding it difficult to make significant headway with SMEs.

It's not that SMEs don't want ERP tools. On the contrary, ERP solutions will enable SMEs to streamline operational processes and provide fully integrated financial and sales management capabilities. This is very attractive to small/medium business. Many SMEs still operate with manual processes where automation would be of clear benefit. However, what many ERP vendors are finding is that SMEs constitute a different marketplace than what these large-scale ERP vendors are traditionally accustomed.

First, SMEs demand affordability and ease of use, more so than their large organizational cousins. Further, this must be achieved in an SME environment where software solutions abound, spending is frugal, IT departments are rare, and "out-of-the-box" solutions are preferred.

Second, large-scale ERP vendors are relatively unknown to most SME organizations. These vendors must start at square one in making this market space aware of whom they are and what their track records have been in this domain.

Third, in Canada, several large-scale ERP vendors have missed the mark when attempting to market their ERP solutions to SME companies. These vendors have geared their products and prices towards an American mid-market firm rather than a Canadian mid-market one. In Canada, an SME organization would compare in revenue and size with a small U.S. company, while an American mid-sized company would be comparable to some large Canadian organizations.

Fourth, and most importantly, the SME market space demands the use of partners (resellers) to sell software solutions. And this is new territory for large-scale ERP vendors who traditionally have relied on the use of a direct sales force to market its ERP solutions to companies.

In this regard, large-scale ERP vendors have little, if any, experience working with channel partners.

Paul Edwards, director—Strategic Partnering and Alliances for IDC Canada, agrees. According to Edwards, "In order to get any kind of traction in the mid-market space, or gain market share, you need partners. . . . [the large ERP vendors are] going to have to start developing partnerships [and] SAP, as an example, doesn't have a real strong partner base."[11]

One company that seems to have made great headway in this regard is Sage Software whose Sage Accpac ERP solution, formerly known as ACCPAC Advantage, has leveraged upon the success and infiltration of Accpac International's accounting applications among small and medium-sized companies. This is particularly true in Canada where about 50 percent of Accpac International's business has been in Canada and where the software has dominated the mid-market. Accpac International was acquired by Sage Software in March 2004. There are approximately 600 Sage Accpac dealers in North America certified to sell and implement the software.[12]

Two examples of successful use of Sage Accpac ERP are Body 'n Scents and System Sensor Canada. Canadian-based Body 'n Scents has been manufacturing fragrances and a popular hair care product for more than 50 years. Tired of its costly, industrial-strength ERP solution to manage manufacturing and financial processes, it chose to utilize Sage Accpac ERP along with a third-party manufacturing information systems product called MISys as a replacement solution. The new ERP system provides Body 'n Scents with a comprehensive, integrated system that is easy to use and affordable. The ERP system handles Body 'n Scents's multi-SKU business requirements and provides tools for managing the company's purchasing, planning, and production cycle. On the accounting side, the ERP system helped to streamline the entire sales process from initial quote to final invoice, to produce financial statements, track cash flow, and collect receivables. According to Paul Pit, director of Operations at Body 'n Scents, the ERP system allows the company to produce all of the month-end reports the company needs and know the profitability within two days after the close of each month.[13]

System Sensor Canada is one of the largest manufacturers of fire detection and notification products in the world. The Canadian branch of the company located in Mississauga, Ontario, served as a sales and distribution centre. The goal was to expand its focus to include manufacturing and e-commerce. As such, it turned to Sage Accpac ERP and the MI Sys Manufacturing System along with an online ordering solution written in the Microsoft .NET platform as a solution by which to integrate its accounting and online ordering systems. Prior to this new system, the company relied on a paper-intensive shipping system that had no connection or communication with System Sensor Canada's accounting software. Since the company was expanding, this paper-based system was inadequate and unwieldy, highly subject to human error, and costly—the company even had to hire additional staff to keep the process running. According to Peter Collier, managing director of System Sensor Canada, the new ERP solution has improved things dramatically, "Every application throughout the entire system is integrated via Sage AccPac and has contributed to our bottom line . . . Our Web-based ordering system has elevated our level of customer service and it now accounts for 40 percent of our business." Further, the new software has helped to reduce staff (despite the company's 30-percent growth each year) and inventory levels—adding to the overall profitability of the company.[14]

Questions

1. Why are large-scale ERP vendors having difficulty breaking into the SME market in Canada?

2. Why has the adoption of the Sage Accpac ERP by Canadian SME companies been so successful?

3. What future trends do you forsee in the deployment and use of ERP solutions in SMEs?

Intuitive ERP

This case highlights one specific ERP solution and its use by two separate Canadian manufacturers.

Intuitive Manufacturing Systems, headquartered in Kirkland, Washington, in the United States, is an international company that offers an ERP software application called Intuitive ERP for mid-sized manufacturers. The software helps mid-sized manufacturing companies achieve higher operational efficiency and profitability via seamless integration of business processes on an enterprise-wide level.

Since 1994, Intuitive has been dedicated to providing manufacturers with software solutions that truly add value to their business. The Intuitive ERP enterprise system, built with 100 percent Microsoft technology, has been designed with the future in mind: Intuitive ERP has a pure .NET managed code framework; and over 80 percent of the standard product features have been rewritten in pure .NET.

Intuitive ERP consists of both core and extended ERP components. These include:

- Enterprise Resource Planning (ERP). Handles all the front and back-office operations required by a discrete manufacturing company including planning, materials management and procurement, and financial business processes.
- Customer Relationship Management (CRM). Manages contact and account information for prospects, customers, vendors, and other business partners. Handles the complete sales cycle from prospect to customer. Creates and deploys targeted marketing campaigns to potential and current customers. Automate customer support with complete incident management.
- Business Intelligence. Tracks and analyzes over 50 key performance indicators, including inventory turns, average days to pay, etc. Analyzes and reports on transactional data using advanced On Line Analytical Processing (OLAP) and data warehousing technology. Monitors a company's financial status.
- E-Commerce. Allows customers to view product catalogue information, and to place and track orders, all securely over the Internet.

Companies from around the world have taken advantage of Intuitive ERP to improve their organization's daily operations, including these two Canadian manufacturers:

1. Fibre Connections

This global company manufactures and markets a wide variety of fibre optic cable assemblies, components, enclosures, and cabling connections. The company develops polishing procedures for numerous fibre optic connectors and components. Headquartered in Schomberg, Ontario, near Toronto, Fibre Connections has other key Canadian locations in Ottawa, Calgary, and Prince Edward Island.

With Intuitive ERP, the company reaped improved efficiencies in several areas, including:

- a reduction in administration staff from five to two people while increasing production levels;
- a 50-percent increase in their ability to generate quotes for custom products; an improvement in on-time deliveries from 85 percent to 97 percent;
- an increase in customer satisfaction since customers now have the ability to track shipment orders in real-time themselves over the Web; and,
- improvements in being able to purchase components needed for custom products at the right time and in the right quantities.

2. Westwinn Group Corp.—Harbercraft

This manufacturing company got its start making car-top boats for Sears-Canada in the 1950s. Today, the company supplies premium aluminum boats across the globe. Westwinn Group employs 90 people in its manufacturing plants in Vernon, British Columbia, and Sylven Lake, Alberta. Customers can select a variety of options and layouts for their boats and the boats are configured and manufactured to order at these plants.

Prior to the implementation of Intuitive ERP, the company faced several challenges with the DOS-based system that was used to support production and administration. For example, the DOS-based system was difficult to use and it did not have perpetual inventory tracking, MRP, or integrated accounting functionality. In fact, each sales invoice generated from this DOS-based system had to be manually re-entered into the accounting package.

With the implementation of Intuitive ERP, these problems went away. Within the first six months of using this new system, the company started seeing significant improvements to their bottom line in having a single, fully integrated system:

- they saved over 250 hours per month of employee time by eliminating duplicate data entry;
- they saw an instant increase in order and inventory accuracy; they managed to reduce inventory stockouts to almost zero;
- they were able to know exactly what to purchase and when;
- they saw improved accuracy in their bills of materials and shop picklists;
- they were able to cross-train staff more easily since everyone used the same system; and
- they doubled production without adding more administrative staff to handle the volume.

According to Brad Armstrong, vice president of Finance at Westwinn Group Corp., one of the most important benefits of Intuitive ERP is the ability to have instant access to information—something that only was a pipedream prior to the implementation of this system.[15]

Questions

1. How well do the components of the Intuitive ERP software product align with the ERP components described in this chapter?

2. What advantages did Fibre Connections and Westwinn Group Corp. realize with the introduction of Intuitive ERP? How well do these advantages resonate with the benefits of ERP described in this chapter?

3. The successful implementation of Intuitive ERP described above does not speak of any negative outcomes or drawbacks of introducing a new enterprise-wide information system in an organization. What challenges do you envision would occur in a company that decides to introduce such large-scale change? What drawbacks, if any, are there in adopting a software solution from a single vendor that serves such a critical and important role in an organization? How could one mitigate or lessen these drawbacks?

MAKING BUSINESS DECISIONS

1. Implementing an ERP system

Blue Dog Inc. is a leading manufacturer in the high-end sunglasses industry, reaching record revenue levels of over $250 million last year. Blue Dog is currently deciding on the possibility of implementing an ERP system to help decrease production costs and increase inventory control. Many of the executives are nervous about making such a large investment in an ERP system due to its low success rates. As a senior manager at Blue Dog Inc. you have been asked to compile a list of the potential benefits and risks associated with implementing an ERP system along with your recommendations for the steps the company can take to ensure a successful implementation.

2. **Most popular ERP component**

   Mackenzie Coombe is currently thinking about implementing an ERP solution in her online music company, The Burford Beat. The company is generating over $12 million in revenues and is growing by 150 percent a year. Create a one-page document explaining the advantages and disadvantages of ERP systems, why ERP systems include CRM and SCM components, and why the most popular ERP component in today's marketplace is the accounting and finance core component.

3. **Value-added ERP**

   Pirate's Pizza is a large pizza chain that operates 700 franchises in five provinces. The company is currently contemplating implementing a new ERP system, which is expected to cost $7 million and take 18 months to implement. Once the system is completed, it is expected to generate $12 million a year in decreased costs and increased revenues. You are working in the finance department for the company and your boss has asked you to compile a report detailing the different financial metrics you can use to assess the business value of the new ERP system. Once your report is completed, the company will make a decision about purchasing the ERP system.

4. **Collaboration on intranets**

   MyIntranet.com is a worldwide leader providing online intranet solutions. The MyIntranet.com online collaboration tool is a solution for small businesses and groups inside larger organizations that need to organize information, share files and documents, coordinate calendars, and enable efficient collaboration, all in a secure, browser-based environment. MyIntranet.com has just added conferencing and group scheduling features to its suite of hosted collaboration software. Explain why infrastructure integration is critical to the suite of applications to function within this environment.

5. **Gaining efficiency with collaboration**

   During the past year, you have been working for a manufacturing firm to help improve its supply chain management by implementing enterprise resource planning and supply chain management systems. For efficiency gains, you are recommending that the manufacturing firm should be turning toward collaborative systems. The firm has a need to share intelligent plans and forecasts with supply chain partners, reduce inventory levels, improve working capital, and reduce manufacturing changeovers. Given the technologies presented to you in this unit, what type of system(s) would you recommend to facilitate your firm's future needs?

6. **Increasing revenues with ERP**

   Cold Cream is one of the premier beauty supply stores in the metro Toronto area. People come from all over to sample the store's unique creams, lotions, makeup, and perfumes. The company receives its products from manufacturers around the globe. The company would like to implement an ERP system to help it better understand its customers and their purchasing habits. Create a report summarizing ERP systems and explain how an ERP system can directly influence Cold Cream's revenues.

Information Matters

3

SECTION

This section of the textbook concentrates on the information component of information technology. Most people view IT strictly from a technological paradigm, but in fact, IT's power and influence is not so much a factor of its technical nature, but rather on what that technical infrastructure carries, houses, and supports: information.

The purpose of this section is to highlight this point and raise awareness of the importance of information to organizational success. Understanding the significance of information is a fundamental learning of this section. Companies that properly manage information as a key organizational resource have a definite advantage over competitors that don't. Treating information as a corporate asset yields success in the marketplace.

To communicate this message, this section approaches the concept of information management from three distinct vantage points.

First, in Chapter 7, the distinction between data and information is made. The chapter illustrates how organizations must properly manage data stored in transactional databases and how that data can be transformed into information through the implementation of enterprise-wide data warehouses.

Second, in Chapter 8, how organizations go about accessing, sharing, and using information is discussed. This chapter describes how organizations can ensure employees have access to the information they need, can share that information with each other, and can utilize that information best by turning information into knowledge. When employees are armed with knowledge, they become empowered to deliver innovations, forge best practices, and develop new products and services for the company.

Third, in Chapter 9, the treatment of information is highlighted. As a key organizational resource, information must be protected from misuse and harm. This involves addressing ethical concerns around the collection, storage, and usage of information, protecting information privacy, and ensuring that information is secure against unauthorized access and attack.

In short, this section of the textbook deals with the concept of information and underscores the point that information does matter to organizational success.

7

Databases and Data Warehouses

LEARNING OUTCOMES

7.1. List, describe, and provide an example of each of the five characteristics of high quality information.

7.2. Define the relationship between a database and a database management system.

7.3. Describe the advantages an organization can gain by using databases.

7.4. Define the fundamental concepts of the relational database model.

7.5. Describe the role and purpose of a database management system and list the four components of a database management system.

7.6. Describe the two primary methods for integrating information across multiple databases.

7.7. Describe the roles and purposes of data warehouses and data marts in an organization.

7.8. Compare the multidimensional nature of data warehouses (and data marts) with two-dimensional nature of databases.

7.9. Identify the importance of ensuring cleanliness of information throughout an organization.

7.10. Explain the relationship between business intelligence and a data warehouse.

Why Do I Need To Know This **?**

This chapter introduces the concept of information and its relative importance to organizations. It distinguishes between data stored in transactional databases and information housed in enterprise-wide data warehouse systems. The chapter also provides an overview of database fundamentals and the steps required to integrate various bits of data stored across multiple, operational data stores into a comprehensive and centralized repository of summarized information.

As a business student, you need to know this, since you must understand the difference between transactional data and summarized information and the different types of questions you would use a transactional database or enterprise data warehouse to answer. You need to be aware of the complexity of storing data in databases and the level of effort required to transform operational data into meaningful, summarized information. You need to realize the power of information and the competitive advantage a data warehouse brings an organization in terms of facilitating business intelligence. Understanding and knowing these things will prepare you in becoming a functional and informed employee in today's modern corporation.

Searching for Revenue—Google

Google founders Sergey Brin and Larry Page recently made *Forbes* magazine's list of world billionaires. Google, famous for its highly successful search engine, experienced a 850-percent revenue growth in 2005.

How Google Works

Figure 7.1 displays the life of an average Google query. The Web server sends the query to the index servers. The content inside the index server is similar to the index at the back of a book; it tells which pages contain the words that match any particular query term. Then the query travels to the document servers, which actually retrieve the stored documents and generate snippets to describe each search result. Finally, the search engine returns the results to the user. All these activities occur within a fraction of a second.

Google consists of three distinct parts:

1. The Web crawler, known as Googlebot, finds and retrieves Web pages and passes them to the Google indexer. Googlebot functions much like a Web browser. It

FIGURE 7.1

Sample Google Architecture

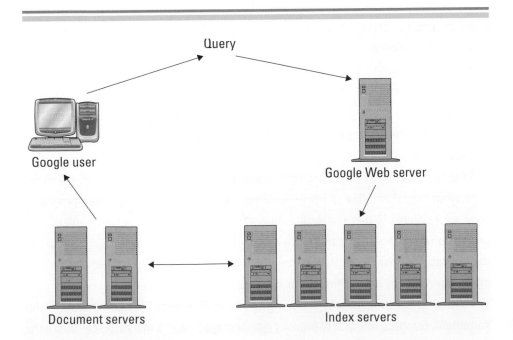

sends a request for a Web page to a Web server, downloads the entire page, and then hands it off to Google's indexer. Googlebot can request thousands of different Web pages simultaneously.

2. The indexer indexes every word on each page and stores the resulting index of words in a huge database. This index is sorted alphabetically by search term, with each index entry storing a list of documents in which the term appears and the location within the text where it occurs. Indexing the full text of Web pages allows Google to go beyond simply matching single search terms. Google gives more priority to pages that have search terms near each other and in the same order as the query. Google can also match multi-word phrases and sentences.

3. The query processor compares the search query to the index and recommends the documents that it considers most relevant. Google considers more than a hundred factors in determining which documents are most relevant to a query, including the popularity of the page, the position and size of the search terms within the page, and the proximity of the search terms to one another. The query processor has several parts, including the user interface (search box), the "engine" that evaluates queries and matches them to relevant documents, and the results formatter.

Selling Words

Google's primary line of business is its search engine; however, the company does not generate revenue from people using its site to search the Internet. It generates revenue from the marketers and advertisers that are paying to place their ads on the site.

Around 200 million times each day, people from all over the world access Google to perform searches. AdWords, a part of the Google site, allows advertisers to bid on common search terms. The advertisers simply enter in the keywords they want to bid on and the maximum amounts they want to pay per click, per day. Google then determines a price and a search ranking for those keywords based on how much other advertisers are willing to pay for the same terms. Pricing for keywords can range from 6 cents to $3.50 a click. A general search term like *tropical vacation* costs less than a more specific term like *Hawaiian vacation*. Whoever bids the most for a term appears in a sponsored advertisement link either at the top or along the side of the search-results page.

Paid search is the ultimate in targeted advertising because consumers type in exactly what they want. One of the primary advantages of paid search Web programs such as AdWords is that customers do not find it annoying, as is the problem with some forms of Web advertising such as banner ads and pop-up ads. According to the Interactive Advertising Bureau, overall industry revenues from paid search surpassed banner ads in the third quarter of 2003.

"A big percentage of queries we get are commercial in nature," said Salar Kamangar, Google's director of product management. "It is a marketplace where the advertisers tell us about themselves by telling us how much each lead is worth. They have an incentive to bid how much they really want to pay, because if they underbid, their competitors will get more traffic." Kamangar came up with the AdWords concept and oversees that part of the business. AdWords accounts for the vast majority of Google's annual revenue, and the company has over 150,000 advertisers in its paid-search program, up from zero in 2002.

Expanding Google

Google has a secret weapon working for its research and development department—hackers. Hackers actually develop many of the new and unique ways to expand Google. The company elicits hacker ideas through its application program interface (API), a large piece of the Google code. The API enables developers to build applications around the Google search engine. By making the API freely available, Google has inspired a community of programmers that are extending Google's capabilities. "It's working," said Nelson Minar, who runs the API effort. "We get clever hacks, educational uses, and wacky stuff. We love to see people do creative things with our product." A few of the successful developed applications include:

Banana Slug, www.bananaslug.com. For customers who hit a dead end with Google search, the site adds a random word to search text that generates surprising results.

Cookin' with Google, www.researchbuzz.org. Enter in the ingredients that are in the fridge and the site returns potential recipes for those ingredients.

Google Alert, www.googlealert.com. Google Alert automatically searches the Web for information on a topic and returns the results by e-mail.

RateMyProfessors.com, www.ratemyprofessors.com. The goal of this site was to create a place where students could rank their teachers. However, too many jokesters typing in false professor names such as "Professor Harry Leg" and "Professor Ima Dog" left the information on the site questionable. The developers turned to the Google API to create an automatic verification tool. If Google finds enough mentions in conjunction with a professor or university then it considers the information valid and posts it to the Web site.

Froogle, www.froogle.com. Google launched a beta version of a new shopping search tool called "Froogle" that the company claims is the most comprehensive product search engine available. Froogle has 15 product categories in its directory. Similar to the Google Directory, customers can view products either by using a keyword search or by drilling down through a particular category and its subcategories.

Stopping Google

As part of its Google Print Library Project, the company is working to scan all or parts of the book collections of the University of Michigan, Harvard University, Stanford University, the New York Public Library, and Oxford University. It intends to make those texts searchable on Google and to sell advertisements on the Web pages.

The Authors Guild filed a lawsuit against search engine Google, alleging that its scanning and digitizing of library books constitutes a "massive" copyright infringement. "This is a plain and brazen violation of copyright law," Nick Taylor, president of the New York-based Authors Guild, said in a statement about the lawsuit, which is seeking class action status. "It's not up to Google or anyone other than the authors, the rightful owners of these copyrights, to decide whether and how their works will be copied."

In response, Google defended the program in a company blog posting. "We regret that this group chose to sue us over a program that will make millions of books more discoverable to the world—especially since any copyright holder can exclude their books from the program," wrote Susan Wojcicki, vice president of product management. "Google respects copyright. The use we make of all the books we scan through the Library Project is fully consistent with both the fair use doctrine under U.S. copyright law and the principles underlying copyright law itself, which allow everything from parodies to excerpts in book reviews."[1]

INTRODUCTION

Information is powerful. Information is useful in telling an organization how its current operations are performing and estimating and strategizing how future operations might perform. New perspectives open up when people have the right information and know how to use it. The ability to understand, digest, analyze, and filter information is key to success for any professional in any industry.

However, it is important to distinguish between data and information. **Data** are raw facts that describe the characteristics of an event. Characteristics for a sales event could include the date, item number, item description, quantity ordered, customer name, and shipping details. **Information** is data converted into a meaningful and useful context. Information from sales events could include best-selling item, worst-selling item, best customer, and worst customer.

UNDERSTANDING INFORMATION

Google recently reported a 200-percent increase in sales of its new Enterprise Search Appliance tool. Companies use the tool to search corporate information for answers to customer questions and to fulfill sales orders. Hundreds of Google's customers, including Xerox, Nextel Communications, Procter & Gamble, and Boeing, are using the tool. The ability to search, analyze, and comprehend information is vital for any organization's success. The incredible growth in sales of the Enterprise Search Appliance tool is a strong indicator that businesses desire technologies that help organize and provide access to information.[2]

When addressing a significant business issue, employees must be able to obtain and analyze all the relevant information so they can make the best decision possible. Organizational information comes at different levels, formats, and "granularities." **Information granularity** refers to the extent of detail within the information (fine and detailed or coarse and abstract information). On one end of the spectrum is coarse granularity, or highly summarized information. At the other end is fine granularity, or information that contains a great amount of detail. If employees are using a supply chain management (SCM) system to make decisions, they might find their suppliers send information in different formats and granularities, and at different levels. One supplier might send detailed information in a spreadsheet, another supplier might send summary information in a Word document, and still another might send aggregate information from a database. Employees must be able to correlate the different levels, formats, and granularities of information when making decisions.

Successfully collecting, compiling, sorting, and finally analyzing information from multiple levels, in varied formats, exhibiting different granularities can provide tremendous insight into how an organization is performing. Taking a hard look at organizational information can yield exciting and unexpected results such as potential new markets, new ways of reaching customers, and even new ways of doing business. Figure 7.2 displays the different types of information found in organizations.

Samsung Electronics took a detailed look at over 10,000 reports from its resellers to identify "lost deals" or orders lost to competitors. The analysis yielded the enlightening result that 80 percent of lost sales occurred in a single business unit, the health care industry. Furthermore, Samsung was able to identify that 40 percent of its lost sales in the health care industry were going to one particular competitor. Before performing the analysis, Samsung was heading into its market blind. Armed with this valuable information, Samsung is changing its selling strategy in the health care industry by implementing a new strategy to work more closely with hardware vendors to win back lost sales.[3]

Information Types	Range	Examples
Information Levels	Individual	Individual knowledge, goals, and strategies
	Department	Departmental goals, revenues, expenses, processes, and strategies
	Enterprise	Enterprisewide revenues, expenses, processes, and strategies
Information Formats	Document	Letters, memos, faxes, e-mails, reports, marketing materials, and training materials
	Presentation	Product, strategy, process, financial, customer, and competitor presentations
	Spreadsheet	Sales, marketing, industry, financial, competitor, customer, and order spreadsheets
	Database	Customer, employee, sales, order, supplier, and manufacturer databases
Information Granularities	Detail (Fine)	Reports for each salesperson, product, and part
	Summary	Reports for all sales personnel, all products, and all parts
	Aggregate (Coarse)	Reports across departments, organizations, and companies

Not all companies are successful at managing information. Staples, the office-supplies superstore, opened its first store in 1986 with state-of-the-art technology. The company experienced rapid growth and soon found itself overwhelmed with the resulting volumes of information. The state-of-the-art technology quickly became obsolete and the company was unable to obtain any insight into its massive volumes of information. A simple query such as identifying the customers who purchased a computer, but not software or peripherals, took hours. Some of the queries required several days to complete and by the time the managers received answers to their queries it was too late.[4]

Information Quality

Westpac Financial Services (WFS), one of the four major banks in Australia, serves millions of customers from its many core systems, each with its own database. The databases maintain information and provide users with easy access to the stored information. Unfortunately, the company failed to develop information-capturing standards; one system had a field to capture e-mail addresses while another system did not, which led to inconsistent organizational information. Duplicate customer information among the different systems was another major issue, and the company continually found itself sending conflicting or competing messages to customers from different operations of the bank. A customer could also have multiple accounts within the company, one representing a life insurance policy and one representing a credit card. WFS had no way to identify that the two different customer accounts were for the same customer.

WFS had to solve its information quality problems immediately if it was to remain competitive. The company purchased NADIS (Name & Address Information Integrity Software), a software solution that filters customer information and highlights

Characteristics of High-Quality Information	
Accuracy	Are all the values correct? For example, is the name spelled correctly? Is the dollar amount recorded properly?
Completeness	Are any of the values missing? For example, is the address complete including street, city, province, and postal code?
Consistency	Is aggregate or summary information in agreement with detailed information? For example, do all total fields equal the true total of the individual fields?
Uniqueness	Is each transaction, entity, and event represented only once in the information? For example, are there any duplicate customers?
Timeliness	Is the information current with respect to the business requirements? For example, is information updated weekly, daily, or hourly?

FIGURE 7.3

Characteristics of
High-Quality Information

missing, inaccurate, and redundant information. Customer service ratings are on the rise for WFS now that the company can operate its business with a single and comprehensive view of each of its customers.[5]

Business decisions are only as good as the quality of the information used to make the decisions. Figure 7.3 reviews five characteristics common to high-quality information: accuracy, completeness, consistency, uniqueness, and timeliness. Figure 7.4 displays these issues in a sample information set.

Figure 7.4 highlights several issues with low-quality information including:

1. The first issue is *missing* information. The customer's first name is missing. (See item 1 in Figure 7.4.)

2. The second issue is *incomplete* information since the street address contains only a number and not a street name.

3. The third issue is definitely an example of *inaccurate* information since a phone number is located in the e-mail address field.

4. The fourth issue is a probable *duplication* of information since the only slight difference between the two customers is the spelling of the last name. Similar street addresses and phone numbers make this likely.

5. The fifth issue is potential *wrong* information because the customer's phone and fax numbers are the same. Some customers might have the same number for

FIGURE 7.4

Examples of Low-Quality Information

1 *Missing* information (no first name)   2. *Incomplete* information (no street)   3. *Inaccurate* information (invalid e-mail)

ID	Last Name	First Name	Street	City	Province	Postal Code	Phone	Fax	E-mail
113	Smith		434 Euclid	Toronto	ON	M5S 2S9	(416) 777-1258	(416) 777-5544	ssmith@yahoo.ca
114	Jones	Jeff	12A	Toronto	ON	M5S 2T2	(416) 666-6868	(416) 666-6868	(416) 666-6868
115	Roberts	Jenny	66 Portland	Toronto	ON	M5S 3S7	527-1122	759-5654	jr@msn.ca
116	Robert	Jenny	66 Portland	Toronto	ON	M5S 3S7	527-1122	759-5654	jr@msn.ca

4. Probable *duplicate* information (similar names, same address, phone number)   5. Potential *wrong* information (are the phone and fax numbers the same or is this an error?)   6. *Incomplete* information (missing area codes)

phone and fax line, but the fact that the customer also has this number in the e-mail address field is suspicious.

6. The sixth issue is *incomplete* information since there is not a valid area code for the phone and fax numbers.

Recognizing how quality issues occur will allow organizations to begin to correct them. The four primary sources of low-quality information are:

1. Online customers intentionally enter inaccurate information to protect their privacy.

2. Information from different systems have different information entry standards and formats.

3. Call centre operators enter abbreviated or erroneous information by accident or to save time.

4. Third party and external information contain inconsistencies, inaccuracies, and errors.[6]

Addressing the above sources of information inaccuracies will significantly improve the quality of organizational information and the value extracted from the information.

Understanding the Costs of Poor Information   Using the wrong information can lead to making the wrong decision. Making the wrong decision can cost time, money, and even reputations. Every business decision is only as good as the information used to make the decision. Bad information can cause serious business ramifications such as:

- Inability to accurately track customers, which directly affects strategic initiatives such as customer relationship management and supply chain management.

- Difficulty identifying the organization's most valuable customers.

- Inability to identify selling opportunities and wasted revenue from marketing to nonexistent customers and nondeliverable mail.

- Difficulty tracking revenue because of inaccurate invoices.

- Inability to build strong relationships with customers, which increases their buyer power.

Understanding the Benefits of Good Information   High-quality information can significantly improve the chances of making a good decision and directly increase an organization's bottom line. Lillian Vernon Corp., a catalogue company, used Web analytics to discover that men preferred to shop at Lillian Vernon's Web site instead of looking through its paper catalogue. Based on this information, the company began placing male products more prominently on its Web site and soon realized a 15-percent growth in sales to men.[7]

EMCO Corporation—founded in London, Ontario in 1906 as the Empire Brass Manufacturing Company Limited—is one of Canada's largest integrated distributors of products for the construction industry. The company utilizes visualization software developed by Vancouver-based Antarctica Systems to display all the company's data at a glance. The software allows top management to view company-critical information, like inventory levels and profit margins, on an interactive map instead of a spreadsheet. Further, once a trouble spot is identified, management can click and zoom to drill down to lower-level information to investigate and understand the underlying data better. Such software tools allow companies like EMCO to quickly make sense of the transactional information they collect, identify problem areas, and make better informed decisions about how to react to trouble spots.[8]

There are numerous examples of companies that have used their high-quality information to make solid strategic business decisions. Quality information does not automatically guarantee that every decision made is going to be a good one, since people ultimately make decisions. But such information ensures that the basis of the decisions is accurate. The success of the organization depends on appreciating and leveraging the true value of timely and quality information.

DATABASE FUNDAMENTALS

Like any resource, an organization must manage information properly. That is, an organization must:

1. Determine what information it requires.
2. Acquire that information.
3. Organize the information in a meaningful fashion.
4. Assure the information's quality.
5. Provide software tools so that employees throughout the organization can access the information they require.

At the very heart of most—if not all—management information systems is a database and a database management system. A *database* maintains information about various types of objects (inventory), events (transactions), people (employees), and places (warehouses). A *database management system (DBMS)* is software through which users and application programs interact with a database. Think of it this way: A DBMS is to a database as word processing software is to a document or as spreadsheet software is to a spreadsheet. One is the information and the other is the software people use to manipulate the information.

The primary task of a database is to store and organize every piece of information related to transactions (for instance, the sale of a product) and business events (such as the hiring of a new employee). As such, databases store a tremendous amount of detailed information. The primary task of a DBMS then is to allow users to create, access, and use information stored in a database.

All kinds of information, from e-mails and contact information to financial information and sales records, are stored in databases. There are many different models for organizing information in a database, including the hierarchical database, network database, and the most prevalent—the relational database model. In a *hierarchical database model*, information is organized into a tree-like structure that allows repeating information using parent/child relationships, in such a way that it cannot have too many relationships. Hierarchical structures were widely used in the first mainframe database management systems. However, owing to their restrictions, hierarchical structures often cannot be used to relate to structures that exist in the real world. The *network database model* is a flexible way of representing objects and their relationships. Where the hierarchical model structures information as a tree of records, with each record having one parent record and many children, the network model allows each record to have multiple parent and child records, forming a lattice structure. The *relational database model* is a type of database that stores information in the form of logically related two-dimensional tables. This text focuses on the relational database model.

DATABASE ADVANTAGES

From a business perspective, databases offer many advantages, including:

- Increased flexibility.
- Increased scalability and performance.
- Reduced redundancy.
- Increased integrity (quality).
- Increased security.

Increased Flexibility

Databases tend to mirror business structures, and a good database can handle changes quickly and easily, just as any good business needs to be able to handle changes quickly and easily. Equally important, databases provide flexibility in allowing each user to access the information in whatever way best suits his or her needs.

The distinction between logical and physical views is important in understanding flexible database user views. The *physical view* of information deals with the physical storage of information on a storage device such as a hard disk. The *logical view* of information focuses on how users logically access information to meet their particular business needs. This separation of logical and physical views is what allows each user to access database information differently. That is, while a database has only one physical view, it can easily support multiple logical views. One user might want a customer report presented in alphabetical format, in which case last name should appear before first name. Another user might want customer names appearing as first name and then last name. Both are easily achievable, but different logical views of the same physical information.

Increased Scalability and Performance

Unlike other provinces that piggyback income tax calculation and collection on federal government tax returns, Quebec directly levies and collects its own personal income tax. This autonomy gives Quebec greater leeway in applying taxation as a tool of public policy, but it also burdens the province with the task of storing and protecting swelling, terabyte-sized amounts of taxpayer information managed in separate Oracle databases deployed across a multitude of servers and desktops. In the late 1990s, Quebec's Revenue Ministry recognized this problem and selected VERITAS NetBackup DataCentre software to implement a single, scalable solution that would satisfy the province's database needs.[9]

Only a database could "scale" to handle the massive volumes of information involved in Quebec's collection of personal income tax data. *Scalability* refers to how well a system can adapt to increased demands. *Performance* measures how quickly a system performs a certain process or transaction. Some organizations, such as eBay, must be able to support hundreds or thousands of online users including employees, partners, customers, and suppliers, who all want to access and share information. Databases today scale to exceptional levels, allowing all types of users and programs to perform information processing and information-searching tasks.

Reduced Redundancy

Redundancy is the duplication of information, or storing the same information in multiple places. Redundant information occurs because organizations frequently capture and store the same information in multiple locations. The primary problem with redundant information is it is often inconsistent, which makes it difficult to determine which values are the most current or most accurate. Not having correct information is confusing and frustrating for employees and disruptive to an organization. One primary goal of a database is to eliminate information redundancy by recording each piece of information in only one place in the database. Eliminating information redundancy saves space, makes performing updates easier, and improves quality.

Increased Integrity (Quality)

Information integrity is a measure of the quality of information. Within a database environment, *integrity constraints* are rules that help ensure the quality of information. Integrity constraints are defined and built into the database. The database (more appropriately, the database management system) ensures that users can never violate these constraints. There are two types of integrity constraints: (1) relational integrity constraints and (2) business-critical integrity constraints.

Relational integrity constraints are rules that enforce basic and fundamental information constraints. For example, a referential integrity constraint would not allow someone to create an order for a nonexistent customer, provide a markup percentage that was negative, or order zero pounds of raw materials from a supplier.

Business-critical integrity constraints enforce business rules vital to an organization's success and often require more insight and knowledge than relational integrity constraints. Consider a supplier of fresh produce to large grocery chains such as Safeway. The supplier might implement a business-critical integrity constraint stating that no produce returns are accepted after 15 days past delivery. That would make sense because of the chance of spoilage of the produce. These types of integrity constraints tend to mirror the very rules by which an organization achieves success.

The specification and enforcement of integrity constraints produce higher-quality information that will provide better support for business decisions. Organizations that establish specific procedures for developing integrity constraints typically see a decline in information error rates and an increase in the use of organizational information.

Increased Security

Information is an organizational asset. Like any asset, an organization must protect its information from unauthorized users or misuse. As systems become increasingly complex and more available over the Internet, security becomes an even bigger issue. Databases offer many security features including passwords, access levels, and access controls.

Passwords provide authentication of the user who is gaining access to the system. Access levels determine who has access to the different types of information, and access controls determine what type of access they have to the information. Customer service representatives might need read-only access to customer order information so they can answer customer order inquiries; they might not have or need the authority to change or delete order information. Managers might require access to employee files, but they should have access only to their own employees' files, not the employee files for the entire company. Various security features of databases ensure that individuals have only certain types of access to certain types of information.

As well as information security, databases can increase personal security too. For example, the Royal Canadian Mounted Police is leading the way by building a National Integrated Interagency Information (N-III) system that will allow police and law enforcement agencies from coast-to-coast to produce consolidated database search results across multiple police databases from a single seamless query. In this way, N-III will help ensure Canadian homes and communities remain safe by delivering complete and accurate information to Canadian law enforcement agencies.[10]

RELATIONAL DATABASE FUNDAMENTALS

The relational database model is a type of database that stores information in the form of logically related two-dimensional tables. Consider how the Coca-Cola Bottling Company of Egypt (TCCBCE) implemented an inventory-tracking database to improve order accuracy by 27 percent, decrease order response time by 66 percent, and increase sales by 20 percent. With over 7,400 employees, TCCBCE owns and operates 11 bottling plants and 29 sales and distribution centres, making it one of the largest companies in Egypt.

Traditionally, the company sent distribution trucks to each customer's premises to take orders and deliver stock. Many problems were associated with this process including numerous information entry errors, which caused order-fulfillment time to take an average of three days. To remedy the situation, Coca-Cola decided to create presales teams equipped with handheld devices to visit customers and take orders electronically. On returning to the office, the teams synchronized orders with the company's inventory-tracking database to ensure automated processing and rapid dispatch of accurate orders to customers.[11]

Entities, Entity Classes, and Attributes

Figure 7.5 illustrates the primary concepts of the relational database model—entities, entity classes, attributes, keys, and relationships. An *entity* is a person, place, thing, transaction, or event about which information is stored. An *entity class*

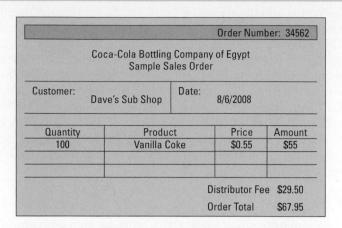

Order Number: 34562

Coca-Cola Bottling Company of Egypt
Sample Sales Order

Customer: Dave's Sub Shop	Date: 8/6/2008

Quantity	Product	Price	Amount
100	Vanilla Coke	$0.55	$55

Distributor Fee $29.50
Order Total $67.95

P K   CUSTOMER

Customer ID	Customer Name	Contact Name	Phone
23	Dave's Sub Shop	David Logan	(204)333-4545
43	Pizza Palace	Debbie Fernandez	(604)345-5432
765	T's Fun Zone	Tom Repicci	(902)565-6655

PK   FK   ORDER   FK

Order ID	Order Date	Customer ID	Distributor ID	Distributor Fee	Total Due
34561	7/4/2008	23	MB8001	$22.00	$145.75
34562	8/6/2008	23	MB8001	$12.95	$67.95
34563	6/5/2008	765	NS9001	$29.50	$249.50

PK PK ORDER LINE FK   FK

Order ID	Line Item	Product ID	Quantity
34561	1	12345AA	75
34561	2	12346BB	50
34561	3	12347CC	100
34562	1	12349EE	300
34563	1	12345AA	100
34563	2	12346BB	100
34563	3	12347CC	50
34563	4	12348DD	50
34563	5	12349EE	100

PK   DISTRIBUTOR

Distributor ID	Distributor Name
MB8001	Manitoba Shipping
ON3001	Ontario Trucking
NS9001	Nova Scotia Distributors

PK   PRODUCT

Product ID	Product Description	Price
12345AA	Coca-Cola	$0.55
12346BB	Diet Coke	$0.55
12347CC	Sprite	$0.55
12348DD	Diet Sprite	$0.55
12349EE	Vanilla Coke	$0.55

(often called a table) is a collection of similar entities. The entity classes of interest in Figure 7.5 are CUSTOMER, ORDER, ORDER LINE, PRODUCT, and DISTRIBUTOR. Notice that each entity class (the collection of similar entities) is stored in a different two-dimensional table. *Attributes*, also called fields or columns, are characteristics or properties of an entity class. In Figure 7.5, the attributes for CUSTOMER include *Customer ID, Customer Name, Contact Name,* and *Phone*. Attributes for PRODUCT include *Product ID, Product Description,* and Price. Each specific entity in an entity class (e.g., Dave's Sub Shop in the CUSTOMER table) occupies one row in its respective table. The columns in the table contain the attributes.

Keys and Relationships

To manage and organize various entity classes within the relational database model, developers must identify primary keys and foreign keys and use them to create logical relationships. A ***primary key*** is a field (or group of fields) that uniquely identifies a given entity in a table. In CUSTOMER, the *Customer ID* uniquely identifies each entity (customer) in the table and is the primary key. Primary keys are important because they provide a way of distinguishing each entity in a table.

A ***foreign key*** in the relational database model is a primary key of one table that appears as an attribute in another table and acts to provide a logical relationship between the two tables. Consider Manitoba Shipping, one of the distributors appearing in the DISTRIBUTOR table. Its primary key, *Distributor ID,* is MB8001. Notice that *Distributor ID* also appears as an attribute in the ORDER table. This establishes the fact that Manitoba Shipping (*Distributor ID* MB8001) was responsible for delivering orders 34561 and 34562 to the appropriate customer(s). Therefore, *Distributor ID* in the ORDER table creates a logical relationship (who shipped what order) between ORDER and DISTRIBUTOR.

DATABASE MANAGEMENT SYSTEMS

Ford's European plant manufactures more than 5,000 vehicles a day and sells them in over 100 countries. Every component of every model must conform to complex European standards, including passenger safety standards and pedestrian and environmental protection standards. These standards govern each stage of Ford's manufacturing process from design to final production. The company needs to obtain many thousands of different approvals each year to comply with the standards. Overlooking just one means the company cannot sell the finished vehicle, which brings the production line to a standstill and could potentially cost Ford up to 1 million euros per day. Ford built the Homologation Timing System (HTS), based on a relational database, to help it track and analyze these standards. The reliability and high performance of the HTS have helped Ford substantially reduce its compliance risk.[12]

As displayed in Figure 7.6, a user can directly interact with a database using different types of technology tools such as views and report generators. Users can also interact with a database by using application programs such as accounting, marketing, and manufacturing applications.

Austrian Federal Railways maintains its entire railway system—which includes over 5,849 kilometres of track, 5,993 bridges and viaducts, 240 tunnels, and 6,768 crossings—with an Oracle database. Multiple applications run on the database including accounting, order processing, and geographic applications that pinpoint railway equipment locations. The database contains over 80 billion characters and supports more than 1,200 users. Many organizations use databases similar to Austrian Federal Railways' to manage large amounts of information.[13]

A DBMS is composed of four primary components—data definition, data manipulation, application generation, and data administration (see Figure 7.7).

Data Definition Component

The ***data definition component*** of a DBMS helps create and maintain the data dictionary and the structure of the database. The ***data dictionary*** is a file that stores

FIGURE 7.6

User Interaction with a Database and DBMS

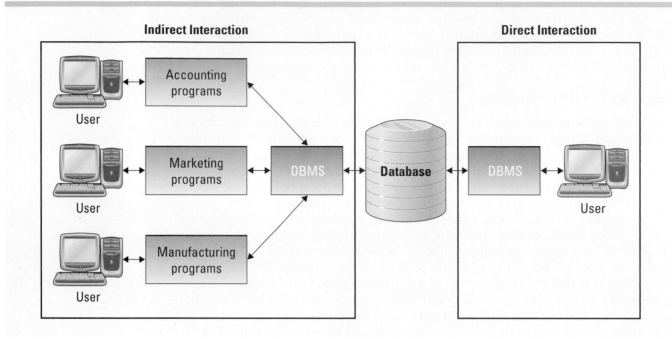

definitions of data types, identifies the primary and foreign keys, and maintains the relationships among the tables. The data dictionary essentially defines the logical properties of the data that the database contains. Figure 7.8 displays typical logical properties of data.

All the logical properties shown in Figure 7.8 are important, and they vary depending on the type of data. A typical address field might have a *Type* logical property of alphanumeric, meaning that the field can accept numbers, letters, and special characters. This would be an example of a relational integrity constraint. The validation rule requiring that a discount cannot exceed 100 percent is an example of a business-critical integrity constraint.

The data dictionary is an important part of the DBMS because users can consult the dictionary to determine the different types of data. The data dictionary also supplies users with vital information when creating reports such as column names and data formats.

FIGURE 7.7

Four Components of a
Database Management
System

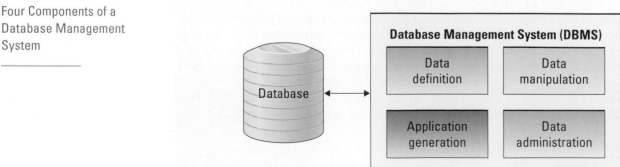

FIGURE 7.8

Logical Field Properties
in a Database

Logical Property	Example
Field name	Name of field such as *Customer ID* or *Product ID*
Type	Alphanumeric, numeric, date, time, currency, etc.
Form	Each phone number must have the area code (XXX) XXX-XXXX
Default value	The default value for area code is (303)
Validation rule	A discount cannot exceed 100 percent
Entry rule	The field must have a valid entry—no blanks are allowed
Duplicate rule	Duplicate data is not allowed

Data Manipulation Component

Of the four DBMS components, users probably spend the most time working with data manipulation. The ***data manipulation component*** allows users to create, read, update, and delete data in a database. A DBMS contains a variety of data manipulation tools including views, report generators, query-by-example tools, and structured query language.

A ***view*** allows users to see the contents of a database, make any required changes, perform simple sorting, and query the database to find the location of specific information. ***Report generators*** allow users to define formats for reports along with what data they want to see in the report (see Figure 7.9).

FIGURE 7.9

Sample Report Using
Microsoft Access

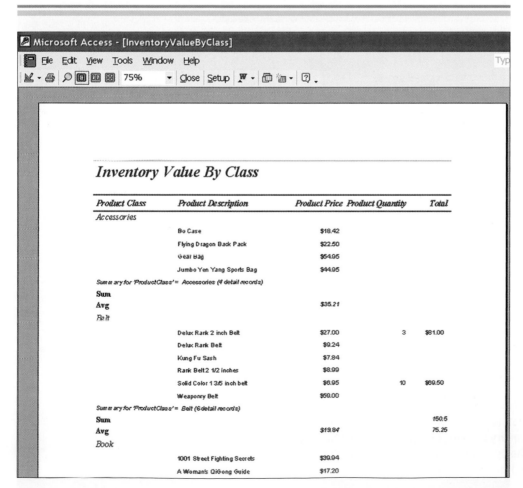

Most often, users will create queries to access information in a database. A query is simply a question, such as "How many customers live in California?" **Query-by-example (QBE) tools** allow users to graphically design the answers to specific questions. Figure 7.10 displays Microsoft's Access QBE tool with a query asking which customers have ordered which products. Using a QBE, a user can design this query by asking the DBMS to pull all of the product descriptions for each order for every customer. Figure 7.11 displays the results to this query.

Structured query language (SQL) is a standardized fourth-generation query language found in most DBMSs. SQL performs the same function as QBE, except that the user must type statements instead of pointing, clicking, and dragging in a graphical environment. The basic form of an SQL statement is SELECT......FROM ......WHERE. Figure 7.12 displays the corresponding SQL statement required to perform the query from Figure 7.10. To write queries in SQL, users typically need some formal training and a solid technical background. Fortunately, QBE tools and their drag-and-drop design features allow nonprogrammers to quickly and easily design complex queries without knowing SQL.

Application Generation and Data Administration Components

For the most part, users will be focusing on data manipulation tools to build views, reports, and queries. IT specialists primarily use the application generation and

FIGURE 7.10

Sample QBE Using Microsoft Access

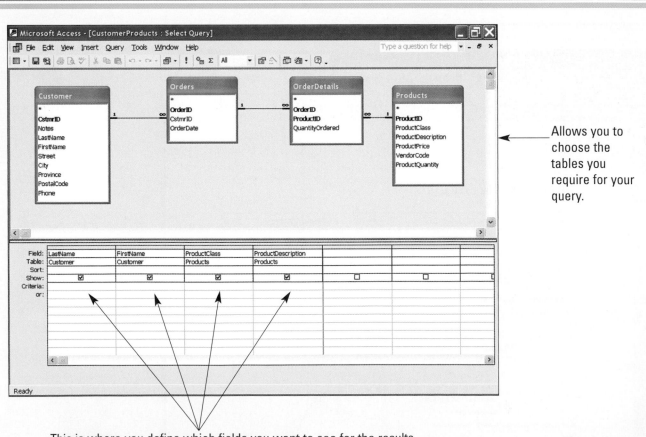

Allows you to choose the tables you require for your query.

This is where you define which fields you want to see for the results of your query. This query asks for the customer's last name and first name, along with the customer's corresponding product class and product description from the customer's orders.

FIGURE 7.11

Results to the QBE
in Figure 7.10

LastName	FirstName	ProductClass	ProductDescription
Meadows	Sara	Clothing	Practice slippers
Calahan	Casey	Weapon	3-sword set with stand
Calahan	Casey	Clothing	Patience in Chineese letters t-shirt
Calahan	Casey	Weapon	Black oak 3-section staff
Calahan	Casey	Clothing	Practice slippers
Lewis	Ronnie	Weapon	3-sword set with stand
Lewis	Ronnie	Clothing	Bruce Lee t-shirt
Chinn	Bridgett	Weapon	Samari Warrior Sword with stand.
Chinn	Bridgett	Clothing	Bruce Lee t-shirt
Chinn	Bridgett	Weapon	3-sword set with stand
Chinn	Bridgett	Clothing	Patience in Chineese letters t-shirt
Rivers	Ramona	Weapon	Samari Warrior Sword with stand.
Amstont	Sandy	Weapon	Samari Warrior Sword with stand.
Amstont	Sandy	Clothing	Bruce Lee t-shirt
Hill	James	Weapon	Samari Warrior Sword with stand.
Hill	James	Clothing	Bruce Lee t-shirt
Hill	James	Weapon	3-sword set with stand
Hill	James	Weapon	Samari Warrior Sword with stand.
Hill	James	Weapon	Samari Warrior Sword with stand.
Florentine	Haven	Weapon	3-sword set with stand
Calahan	Thomas	Clothing	Bruce Lee t-shirt
Calahan	Thomas	Weapon	Samari Warrior Sword with stand.
Calahan	Thomas	Weapon	3-sword set with stand
Benton	Cleo	Weapon	3-sword set with stand
Bernstein	Benon	Weapon	Samari Warrior Sword with stand.
Bernstein	Benon	Weapon	3-sword set with stand
Guo	Amy	Weapon	3-sword set with stand
Wagoner	Sam	Clothing	Patience in Chineese letters t-shirt

Record: 41 of 72

Datasheet View

data administration components. Even though most users will probably not be using these components, it is still important they understand what they are and the functions they support.

The **application generation component** includes tools for creating visually appealing and easy-to-use applications. IT specialists use application generation components to build programs for users to enter and manipulate information with an interface specific to their application needs. Consider a manager involved in the management of an organization's supply chain. Using the application generation component, an IT specialist could build a supply chain management application

FIGURE 7.12

SQL Version of the QBE Query in Figure 7.10

```
SELECT  Customer.LastName, Customer.FirstName,
        Products.ProductClass, Products.ProductDescription
FROM    Products
        INNER JOIN ((Customer INNER JOIN Orders ON
        (Customer.CstmrID = Orders.CstmrID) AND (Customer.CstmrID
        = Orders.CstmrID))
        INNER JOIN OrderDetails ON Orders.OrderID =
        OrderDetails.OrderID) ON Products.Product ID =
        OrderDetails.ProductID;
```

software tool for the manager that would contain various menu options including add a supplier, order from a supplier, check the status of an order, and so on. This application would be easier and more intuitive for the manager to use on a consistent basis than requiring the manager to use views, report generators, and QBE tools.

The **data administration component** provides tools for managing the overall database environment by providing facilities for backup, recovery, security, and performance. Again, IT specialists directly interact with the data administration component.

Most organizations have several strategic-level IT positions—CIO (chief information officer), CTO (chief technology officer), CSO (chief security officer), CPO (chief privacy officer), and CKO (chief knowledge officer). People in these positions oversee the use of the data administration component. The CPO is responsible for ensuring the ethical and legal use of information. Therefore, he or she would direct the use of the security features of the data administration component, implement policies and procedures concerning who has access to different types of information, and control what functions they can perform on that information (read-only, update, delete). The CTO is responsible for ensuring the efficiency of IT systems and would direct the use of the backup, recovery, and performance features of the data administration component.

INTEGRATING DATA AMONG MULTIPLE DATABASES

Until the 1990s, each department in the United Kingdom's Ministry of Defence (MOD) and army headquarters had its own systems, each system had its own database, and sharing information among the departments was difficult. Manually inputting the same information multiple times into the different systems was also time-consuming and inefficient. In many cases, management could not even compile the information it required to answer questions and make decisions.

The army solved the problem by integrating its systems, or building connections between its many databases. These integrations allow the army's multiple systems to automatically communicate by passing information between the databases, eliminating the need for manual information entry into multiple systems because after entering the information once, the integrations sent the information immediately to all other databases. The integrations not only enable the different departments to share information, but have also dramatically increased the quality of the information. The army can now generate reports detailing its state of readiness and other vital issues, nearly impossible tasks before building the integrations among the separate systems.[14]

An **integration** allows separate systems to communicate directly with each other. Similar to the UK's army, an organization will maintain multiple systems, with each system having its own database. Without integrations, an organization will (1) spend considerable time entering the same information in multiple systems and (2) suffer from the low quality and inconsistency typically embedded in redundant information. While most integrations do not eliminate all redundant information, they can ensure the consistency of it across multiple systems.

An organization can choose from two integration methods. The first is to create forward and backward integrations that link processes (and their underlying databases) in the value chain. A **forward integration** takes information entered into a given system and sends it automatically to all downstream systems and processes. A **backward integration** takes information entered into a given system and sends it automatically to all upstream systems and processes.

Figure 7.13 demonstrates how this method works across the systems or processes of sales, order entry, order fulfillment, and billing. In the order entry system, for example, an employee can update the information for a customer. That information, via the integrations, would be sent upstream to the sales system and downstream to the order fulfillment and billing systems.

Ideally, an organization wants to build both forward and backward integrations, which provide the flexibility to create, update, and delete information in

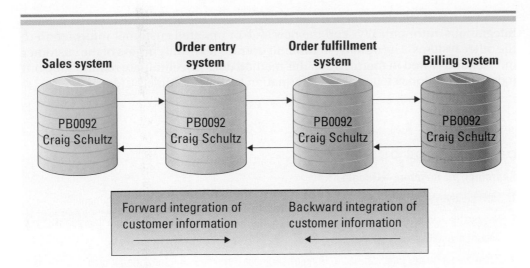

Forward integration of customer information

Backward integration of customer information

any of the systems. However, integrations are expensive and difficult to build and maintain and most organizations build only forward integrations (sales through billing in Figure 7.13). Building only forward integrations implies that a change in the initial system (sales) will result in changes occurring in all the other systems. Integration of information is not possible for any changes occurring outside the initial system, which again can result in inconsistent organizational information. To address this issue, organizations can enforce business rules that all systems, other than the initial system, have read-only access to the integrated information. This will require users to change information in the initial system only, which will always trigger the integration and ensure that organizational information does not get out of sync.

The second integration method builds a central repository for a particular type of information. Figure 7.14 provides an example of customer information integrated using this method across four different systems in an organization. Users can create, update, and delete customer information only in the central

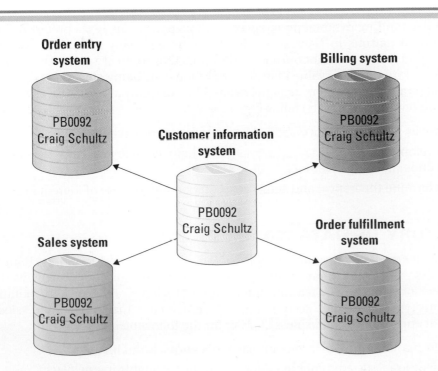

FIGURE 7.14

Integrating Customer
Information among
Databases

customer database. As users perform these tasks on the central customer database, integrations automatically send the new and/or updated customer information to the other systems. The other systems limit users to read-only access of the customer information stored in them. Again, this method does not eliminate redundancy, but it does ensure consistency of the information among multiple systems.

OPENING CASE QUESTIONS

Searching for Revenue—Google

1. How did the Web site RateMyProfessors.com solve its problem of low-quality information?

2. Review the five common characteristics of high-quality information and rank them in order of importance to Google's business.

3. What would be the ramifications to Google's business if the search information it presented to its customers was of low quality?

4. Describe the different types of database. Why should Google use a relational database?

5. Identify the different types of entities, entity classes, attributes, keys, and relationships that might be stored in Google's AdWords relational database.

7.2 DATA WAREHOUSING

ACCESSING ORGANIZATIONAL INFORMATION

Applebee's Neighborhood Grill & Bar in the United States posts annual sales in excess of $3.7 billion and is actively using information from its data warehouse to increase sales and cut costs. The company gathers daily information for the previous day's sales into its data warehouse from 1,500 restaurants located in 49 states and seven countries.

Understanding regional preferences, such as patrons in Texas preferring steaks more than patrons in New England, allows the company to meet its corporate strategy of being a neighbourhood grill appealing to local tastes. The company has found tremendous value in its data warehouse by being able to make business decisions about customers' regional needs. The company also uses data warehouse information to perform the following:

- Base its labour budgets on actual number of guests served per hour.
- Develop promotional sale item analysis to help avoid losses from overstocking or understocking inventory.
- Determine theoretical and actual costs of food and the use of ingredients.[15]

HISTORY OF DATA WAREHOUSING

In the 1990s as organizations began to need more timely information about their business, they found that traditional operational information systems were too cumbersome to provide relevant information efficiently and quickly. Operational systems typically include accounting, order entry, customer service, and sales and are not appropriate for business analysis for the following reasons:

- Information from other operational applications is not included.
- Operational systems are not integrated, or not available in one place.

- Operational information is mainly current—does not include the history that is required to make good decisions.

- Operational information frequently has quality issues (errors)— the information needs to be cleansed.

- Without information history, it is difficult to tell how and why things change over time.

- Operational systems are not designed for analysis and decision support.

During the latter half of the 20th century, the numbers and types of databases increased. Many large businesses found themselves with information scattered across multiple platforms and variations of technology, making it almost impossible for any one individual to use information from multiple sources. Completing reporting requests across operational systems could take days or weeks using antiquated reporting tools that were designed more or less to execute the business rather than run the business. From this idea, the data warehouse was born as a place where relevant information could be held for completing strategic reports for management. The key here is the word *strategic* as most executives were less concerned with the day-to-day operations than they were with a more overall look at the model and business functions.

A key idea within data warehousing is to take information from multiple platforms/technologies (as varied as spreadsheets, databases, and word files) and place them in a common location that uses a common querying tool. In this way operational databases could be held on whatever system was most efficient for the operational business, while the reporting/strategic information could be held in a common location using a common language. Data warehouses take this a step further by giving the information itself commonality by defining what each term means and keeping it standard. An example of this would be gender, which can be referred to in many ways (Male, Female, M/F, 1/0), but should be standardized on a data warehouse with one common way of referring to each sex (M/F).

This design makes decision support more readily available without affecting day-to-day operations. One aspect of a data warehouse that should be stressed is that it is *not* a location for *all* a business's information, but rather a location for information that is interesting, or information that will assist decision makers in making strategic decisions relative to the organization's overall mission.

Data warehousing is about extending the transformation of data into information. Data warehouses offer strategic level, external, integrated, and historical information so businesses can make projections, identify trends, and decide key business issues. The data warehouse collects and stores integrated sets of historical information from multiple operational systems and feeds them to one or more data marts. It may also provide end-user access to support enterprisewide views of information.

DATA WAREHOUSE FUNDAMENTALS

A **data warehouse** is a logical collection of summarized information—gathered from many different operational databases—that supports business analysis activities and decision-making tasks. The term data warehouse was coined in 1990 by Bill Inmon, who is known as the "Father of Data Warehousing." He describes a data warehouse as a subject-oriented, integrated, time-variant, and non-volatile collection of data used to support organizational decision making, where:

- *Subject-oriented* means that data is organized around major subject areas of the company (like customer, vendor, product) instead of around a company's on-going business operations or business applications found in transactional processing systems.

- *Integrated* means that data is gathered into a data warehouse from a variety of operational data sources and merged into a coherent and consistent whole.

- *Time-variant* means that all data in a data warehouse is time-stamped with a particular time period, such as weekly, monthly, quarterly, or yearly.
- *Non-volatile* means that data in a data warehouse is stable and once loaded never changes. That is, as new data is added, data is never removed or modified.[16]

The primary purpose of a data warehouse is to aggregate information throughout an organization into a single repository in such a way that employees can make decisions and undertake business analysis activities. Therefore, while databases store the details of all transactions (for instance, the sale of a product) and events (hiring a new employee), data warehouses store that same information but in an aggregated form more suited to supporting decision-making tasks. Aggregation, in this instance, can include totals, counts, averages, and the like.

The data warehouse modelled in Figure 7.15 compiles information from internal databases or transactional/operational databases and external databases through ***extraction, transformation, and loading (ETL),*** which is a process that extracts information from internal and external databases, transforms the information using a common set of enterprise definitions, and loads the information into a data warehouse. The data warehouse then sends subsets of the information to data marts. A ***data mart*** contains a subset of data warehouse information. To distinguish between data warehouses and data marts, think of data warehouses as having a more organizational focus and data marts having focused information subsets particular to the needs of a given business unit such as finance or production and operations.

Lands' End created an organizationwide data warehouse so all its employees could access organizational information. Lands' End soon discovered that there could be "too much of a good thing." Many of its employees would not use the data

FIGURE 7.15

Model of a Typical Data Warehouse

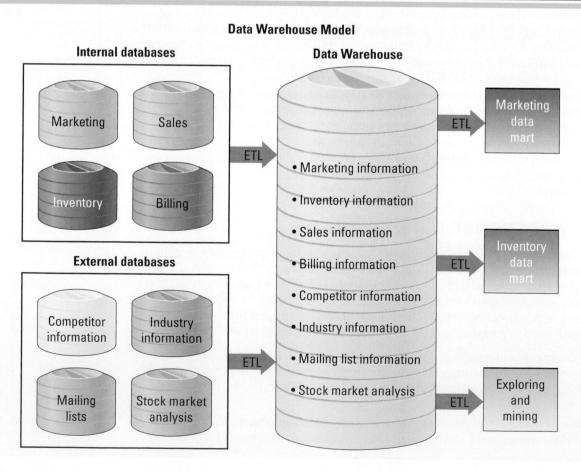

warehouse because it was simply too big, too complicated, and had too much irrelevant information. Lands' End knew there was valuable information in its data warehouse, and it had to find a way for its employees to easily access the information. Data marts were the perfect solution to the company's information overload problem. Once the employees began using the data marts, they were ecstatic at the wealth of information. Data marts were a huge success for Lands' End.[17]

Multidimensional Analysis

A relational database contains information in a series of two-dimensional tables. In a data warehouse and data mart, information is multidimensional, meaning it contains layers of columns and rows. For this reason, most data warehouses and data marts are *multidimensional databases*. A *dimension* is a particular attribute of information. Each layer in a data warehouse or data mart represents information according to an additional dimension. A **cube** is the common term for the representation of multidimensional information. Figure 7.16 displays a cube (*Cube a*) that represents store information (the layers), product information (the rows), and promotion information (the columns).

Once a cube of information is created, users can begin to slice-and-dice the cube to drill down into the information. The second cube (*Cube b*) in Figure 7.16 displays a slice representing promotion II information for all products at all stores. The third cube (*Cube c*) in Figure 7.16 displays only information for promotion III, product B, at store 2. By using multidimensional analysis, users can analyze information in a number of ways and with any number of dimensions. Users might want to add dimensions of information to a current analysis including product category, region, and even forecasted versus actual weather. The true value of a data warehouse is its ability to provide multidimensional analysis that allows users to gain insights into their information.

Data warehouses and data marts are ideal for off-loading some of the querying against a database. For example, querying a database to obtain an average of sales for product B at store 2 while promotion III is under way might create a considerable processing burden for a database, essentially slowing down the time it takes another person to enter a new sale into the same database. If an organization performs numerous queries against a database (or multiple databases), aggregating that information into a data warehouse will be beneficial.

FIGURE 7.16

A Cube of Information for Performing a Multidimensional Analysis on Three Stores for Five Products and Four Promotions

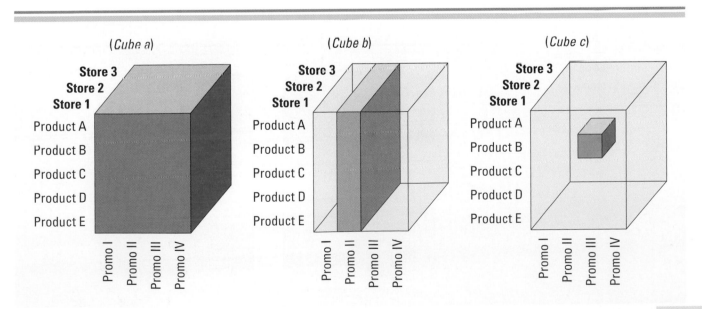

Information Cleansing or Scrubbing

Maintaining quality information in a data warehouse or data mart is extremely important. The Data Warehousing Institute estimates that low-quality information costs businesses hundreds of billions of dollars annually. That number may seem high, but it is not. If an organization is using a data warehouse or data mart to allocate dollars across advertising strategies, low-quality information will definitely have a negative impact on its ability to make the right decision.[18]

To increase the quality of organizational information and thus the effectiveness of decision making, businesses must formulate a strategy to keep information clean. This is the concept of *information cleansing or scrubbing*, a process that weeds out and fixes or discards inconsistent, incorrect, or incomplete information.

Specialized software tools exist that use sophisticated algorithms to parse, standardize, correct, match, and consolidate data warehouse information. This is vitally important because data warehouses often contain information from several different databases, some of which can be external to the organization. In a data warehouse, information cleansing occurs first during the ETL process and second on the information once it is in the data warehouse. Companies can choose information cleansing software from several different vendors including Oracle, SAS, Ascential Software, and Group 1 Software. Ideally, scrubbed information is error-free and consistent.

Dr Pepper/Seven Up, Inc., was able to integrate its myriad databases in a data warehouse (and subsequently data marts) in less than two months, giving the company access to consolidated, clean information. Approximately 600 people in the company regularly use the data marts to analyze and track beverage sales across multiple dimensions, including various distribution routes such as bottle/can sales, fountain food-service sales, premier distributor sales, and chain and national accounts. The company is now performing in-depth analysis of up-to-date sales information that is clean and error-free.[19]

Looking at customer information highlights why information cleansing is necessary. Customer information exists in several operational systems. In each system all details of this customer information could change from the customer ID to contact information (see Figure 7.17). Determining which contact information is accurate and correct for this customer depends on the business process that is being executed.

Figure 7.18 displays a customer name entered differently in multiple operational systems. Information cleansing allows an organization to fix these types of inconsistencies and cleans the information in the data warehouse. Figure 7.19 displays the typical events that occur during information cleansing.

Achieving perfect information is almost impossible. The more complete and accurate an organization wants its information to be, the more it costs (see Figure 7.20). The trade-off for perfect information lies in accuracy versus completeness. Accurate information means it is correct, while complete information

FIGURE 7.17

Contact Information in Operational Systems

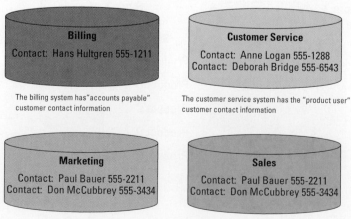

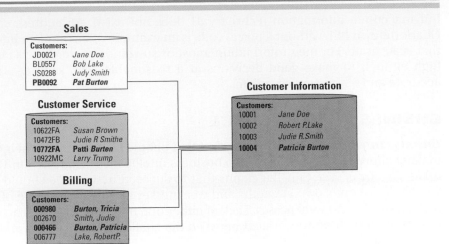

FIGURE 7.18

Standardizing Customer
Name from Operational
Systems

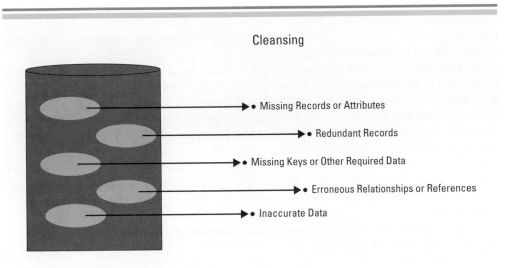

FIGURE 7.19

Information Cleansing
Activities

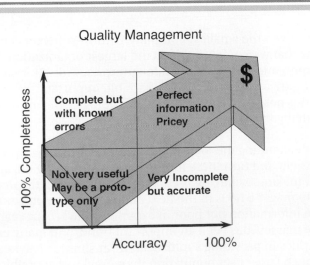

FIGURE 7.20

Accurate and Complete
Information

means there are no blanks. A birth date of 31/02/1991 is an example of complete but inaccurate information (February 31 does not exist). An address containing Charlottetown PEI, without a postal code is an example of incomplete information that is accurate. For their information, most organizations determine a percentage high enough to make good decisions at a reasonable cost, such as 85-percent accurate and 65-percent complete.

BUSINESS INTELLIGENCE

Business intelligence (BI) is information that people use to support their decision-making efforts. An early reference to business intelligence occurs in Sun Tzu's book titled *The Art of War*. Sun Tzu claims that to succeed in war, one should have full knowledge of one's own strengths and weaknesses and full knowledge of the enemy's strengths and weaknesses. Lack of either one might result in defeat. A certain school of thought draws parallels between the challenges in business and those of war, specifically:

- Collecting information.
- Discerning patterns and meaning in the information.
- Responding to the resultant information.

Before the start of the information age in the late 20th century, businesses sometimes collected information from nonautomated sources. Businesses then lacked the computing resources to properly analyze the information and often made commercial decisions based primarily on intuition.

As businesses started automating more and more systems, more and more information became available. However, collection remained a challenge due to a lack of infrastructure for information exchange or to incompatibilities between systems. Reports sometimes took months to generate. Such reports allowed informed long-term strategic decision making. However, short-term tactical decision making continued to rely on intuition.

In modern businesses, increasing standards, automation, and technologies have led to vast amounts of available information. Data warehouse technologies have set up repositories to store this information. Improved ETL have increased the speedy collecting of information. Business intelligence has now become the art of sifting through large amounts of data, extracting information, and turning that information into actionable knowledge.

Enabling Business Intelligence

Competitive organizations accumulate business intelligence to gain sustainable competitive advantage, and they may regard such intelligence as a valuable core competence in some instances. The principal BI enablers are technology, people, and corporate culture.

Technology   Even the smallest company with BI software can do sophisticated analyses today that were unavailable to the largest organizations a generation ago. The largest companies today can create enterprisewide BI systems that compute and monitor metrics on virtually every variable important for managing the company. How is this possible? The answer is technology—the most significant enabler of business intelligence.

People   Understanding the role of people in BI allows organizations to systematically create insight and turn these insights into actions. Organizations can improve their decision making by having the right people making the decisions. This usually means a manager who is in the field and close to the customer rather than an analyst rich in information but poor in experience. In recent years "business intelligence for the masses" has been an important trend, and many organizations have made great strides in providing sophisticated yet simple analytical tools and information to a much larger user population than previously possible.

Culture A key responsibility of executives is to shape and manage corporate culture. The extent to which the BI attitude flourishes in an organization depends in large part on the organization's culture. Perhaps the most important step an organization can take to encourage BI is to measure the performance of the organization against a set of key indicators. The actions of publishing what the organization thinks are the most important indicators, measuring these indicators, and analyzing the results to guide improvement display a strong commitment to BI throughout the organization.

DATA MINING

Ruf Strategic Solutions helps organizations employ statistical approaches within a large data warehouse to identify customer segments that display common traits. Marketers can then target these segments with specially designed products and promotions. **Data mining** is the process of analyzing data to extract information not offered by the raw data alone. Data mining can also begin at a summary information level (coarse granularity) and progress through increasing levels of detail (drilling down), or the reverse (drilling up).[20]

To perform data mining, users need data-mining tools. **Data-mining tools** use a variety of techniques to find patterns and relationships in large volumes of information and infer rules from them that predict future behaviour and guide decision making. Data-mining tools for data warehouses and data marts include query tools, reporting tools, multidimensional analysis tools, statistical tools, and intelligent agents.

Sega of America, one of the largest publishers of video games, uses a data warehouse and statistical tools to distribute its advertising budget of more than US$50 million a year. With its data warehouse, product line specialists and marketing strategists "drill" into trends of each retail store chain. Their goal is to find buying trends that help them determine which advertising strategies are working best and how to reallocate advertising resources by media, territory, and time. Figure 7.21 displays the average organizational spending on data-mining tools over the next few years.[21]

Data-mining tools apply algorithms to information sets to uncover inherent trends and patterns in the information, which analysts use to develop new business strategies. Analysts use the output from data-mining tools to build models that, when exposed to new information sets, perform a variety of information analysis functions. The analysts provide business solutions by putting together the analytical techniques and the business problem at hand, which often reveals important new correlations, patterns, and trends. The more common forms of data-mining analysis capabilities include cluster analysis, association detection, and statistical analysis.

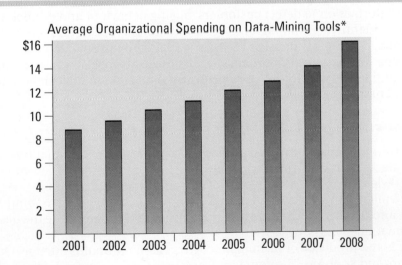

Average Organizational Spending on Data-Mining Tools*

FIGURE 7.21

Data-Mining Tools Investment Forecast

*In millions of US dollars

Cluster Analysis

Cluster analysis is a technique used to divide an information set into mutually exclusive groups such that the members of each group are as close together as possible to one another and the different groups are as far apart as possible. Cluster analysis is frequently used to segment customer information for customer relationship management systems to help organizations identify customers with similar behavioural traits, such as clusters of best customers or one-time customers. Cluster analysis also has the ability to uncover naturally occurring patterns in information.

Such data-mining tools that "understand" human language are finding unexpected applications in medicine. IBM and the Mayo Clinic unearthed hidden patterns in medical records, discovering that infant leukemia has three distinct clusters, each of which probably benefits from tailored treatments. Caroline A. Kovac, general manager of IBM Life Sciences, expects that mining the records of cancer patients for clustering patterns will turn up clues pointing the way to "tremendous strides in curing cancer."[22]

Association Detection

Maytag Corporation, a well-known home and commercial appliance manufacturer, employs hundreds of R&D engineers, data analysts, quality assurance specialists, and customer service personnel who all work together to ensure that each generation of appliances is better than the previous generation. Maytag is an example of an organization that is gaining business intelligence with association detection data-mining tools.

Association detection reveals the degree to which variables are related and the nature and frequency of these relationships in the information. Maytag's warranty analysis tool, for instance, uses statistical analysis to automatically detect potential issues, provide quick and easy access to reports, and perform multidimensional analysis on all warranty information. This association detection data-mining tool enables Maytag's managers to take proactive measures to control product defects even before most of its customers are aware of the defect. The tool also allows Maytag personnel to devote more time to value-added tasks such as ensuring high quality on all products rather than waiting for or manually analyzing monthly reports.[23]

Many people refer to association detection algorithms as *association rule generators* because they create rules to determine the likelihood of events occurring together at a particular time or following each other in a logical progression. Percentages usually reflect the patterns of these events, for example, "55 percent of the time, events A and B occurred together," or "80 percent of the time that items A and B occurred together, they were followed by item C within three days."

One of the most common forms of association detection analysis is market basket analysis. **Market basket analysis** analyzes such items as Web sites and checkout scanner information to detect customers' buying behaviour and predict future behaviour by identifying affinities among customers' choices of products and services (see Figure 7.22). Market basket analysis is frequently used to develop marketing campaigns for cross-selling products and services (especially in banking, insurance, and finance) and for inventory control, shelf-product placement, and other retail and marketing applications.

Statistical Analysis

Statistical analysis performs such functions as information correlations, distributions, calculations, and variance analysis, just to name a few. Data-mining tools offer knowledge workers a wide range of powerful statistical capabilities so they can quickly build a variety of statistical models, examine the models' assumptions and validity, and compare and contrast the various models to determine the best one for a particular business issue.

Kraft is the producer of instantly recognizable food brands such as Oreo, Ritz, DiGiorno, and Kool-Aid. The company implemented two data-mining applications

FIGURE 7.22

Market Basket Analysis

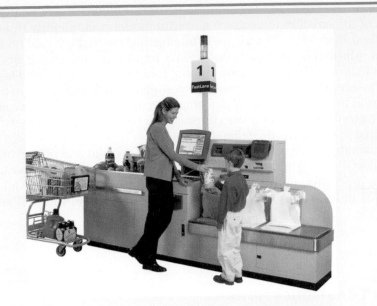

to assure consistent flavour, colour, aroma, texture, and appearance for all of its food lines. One application analyzed product consistency and the other analyzed process variation reduction (PVR).

The product consistency tool SENECA (Sensory and Experimental Collection Application) gathers and analyzes information by assigning precise definitions and numerical scales to such qualities as chewy, sweet, crunchy, and creamy. SENECA then builds models, histories, forecasts, and trends based on consumer testing and evaluates potential product improvements and changes.

The PVR tool ensures consistent flavour, colour, aroma, texture, and appearance for every Kraft product since even small changes in the baking process can result in huge disparities in taste. Evaluating every manufacturing procedure, from recipe instructions to cookie dough shapes and sizes, the PVR tool has the potential to generate significant cost savings for each product. Using these types of data-mining techniques for quality control and cluster analysis makes sure that the billions of Kraft products that reach consumers annually will continue to taste great with every bite.[24]

Forecasting is a common form of statistical analysis. Formally defined, ***forecasts*** are predictions made on the basis of time-series information. ***Time-series information*** is time-stamped information collected at a particular frequency. Examples of time-series information include Web visits per hour, sales per month, and calls per day. Forecasting data-mining tools allow users to manipulate the time series for forecasting activities. When discovering trends and seasonal variations in transactional information, use a time-series forecast to change the transactional information by units of time, such as transforming weekly information into monthly or seasonal information or hourly information into daily information. Companies base production, investment, and staffing decisions on a host of economic and market indicators in this manner. Forecasting models allow organizations to take into account all sorts of variables when making decisions.

Nestlé Italiana is part of the multinational giant Nestlé Group and currently dominates Italy's food industry. The company improved sales forecasting by 25 percent with its data-mining forecasting solution that enables the company's managers to make objective decisions based on facts instead of subjective decisions based on intuition. Determining sales forecasts for seasonal confectionery products is a crucial and challenging task. During Easter, Nestlé Italiana has only four weeks to market, deliver, and sell its seasonal products. The Christmas time frame is a little longer, lasting from six to eight weeks, while other holidays such as Valentine's Day and Mother's Day have shorter time frames of about one week.

The company's data-mining solution gathers, organizes, and analyzes massive volumes of information to produce powerful models that identify trends and predict confectionery sales. The business intelligence created is based on five years of historical information and identifies what is important and what is not important. Nestlé Italiana's sophisticated data-mining tool predicted Mother's Day sales forecasts that were 90-percent accurate. The company has benefited from a 40-percent reduction in inventory and a 50-percent reduction in order changes, all due to its forecasting tool. Determining sales forecasts for seasonal confectionery products is now an area in which Nestlé Italiana excels.[25]

Today, vendors such as Business Objects, Cognos, and SAS offer complete data-mining decision-making solutions. Moving forward, these companies plan to add more predictive analytical capabilities to their products. Their goal is to give companies more "what-if" scenario capabilities based on internal and external information.

OPENING CASE QUESTIONS

Searching for Revenue—Google

6. How could Google use a data warehouse to improve its business operations?

7. Why would Google need to scrub and cleanse the information in its data warehouse?

8. Identify a data mart that Google's marketing and sales department might use to track and analyze its AdWords revenue.

SUMMARY OF KEY THEMES

The purpose of this chapter was to provide you, the business student, with a detailed discussion concerning the distinction between:

- data and information, and

- operational transaction databases and summarized enterprise-wide data warehouses.

The chapter provided you with a robust description of:

- database fundamentals,

- how data in various operational data stores are extracted, transferred, and loaded into central data warehouses and data marts,

- the strategic and competitive advantages of transforming operational transactional data into summarized information that is subject-oriented, integrated, time-variant, and non-volatile, and

- the need to treat data and information as key organizational resources that must be managed with care and due diligence.

Treating data and information as key organizational resources offers companies several advantages, namely the ability:

- to make sound decisions based on accurate and reliable information, and

- to achieve business intelligence.

KEY TERMS

CLOSING CASE ONE

Scouting for Quality

This case illustrates how one organization improved information quality through centralization and standardization of its databases.

Scouts Canada, the country's leading youth organization for youth aged 5 to 26, has been part of the national landscape for over 100 years. There are approximately 3,600 boy scout groups scattered across most cities and towns in Canada. Over 78,000 young people enjoy Scouts Canada's programs today.[26]

A scout's motto is to "be prepared" and Scouts Canada's national office located in Ottawa did just that in their recent endeavour to integrate Scouts Canada's fragmented membership systems.

This project produced a single, integrated membership system for the whole country. Prior to its existence, each of Scouts Canada's 27 separate councils had its own membership systems that fed information to national headquarters. This data feed was not automatic. Rather, information was sent to national office by fax. Not only was national office receiving an overwhelming amount of paper, national office was also burdened with the task of manually re-entering this data into their own database system. This consumed a high amount of labour and time. According to Tom Obright, Director of Information Management for Scouts Canada, "it was one full week [spent] grabbing all these sheets and throwing them together into some kind of presentable format."

The problem was exacerbated when Scouts Canada decided to reduce staff. So, back in September 2001, a pilot membership management system was developed and tested with four participating councils. By January 2002, the other 23 councils started using the new membership management system. By doing so, Scouts Canada had standardized its registration for new members across all 27 councils.

Prior to this, each of the 27 councils had subtly different formats. One problem was the way each council went about entering insurance coverage information for new members. As a result, when there were 27 different membership systems, it took as much as six months to straighten out the data. Until then, it was dangerously open to interpretation when a new registrant was actually being covered by insurance.

The new centralized system has improved things dramatically. Duplicated data-entry efforts are now eliminated. The registration process is much quicker. And the new system has resolved the insurance coverage issue by properly coding when insurance coverage becomes in effect for each new member.

The 27 separate councils like the system very much. It has actually empowered them to do more with the data they are collecting. With the new centralized membership management system, each council can extract and download a copy of the system's baseline data and use that data on their own computers to generate whatever reports they wish.

By conducting this integration project, Scouts Canada has successfully turned 27 separate databases into one quality unifying database that has improved business performance and reporting. Having access to information that is accurate, current, and standardized across all areas of the company allows Scouts Canada to make better informed decisions.[27]

Questions

1. Explain the importance of high-quality information for Scouts Canada.
2. Review the five common characteristics of quality information and rank them in order of importance for Scouts Canada.
3. How could data warehouses and data marts be used to help Scouts Canada improve the efficiency and effectiveness of its operations?
4. What kind of data marts might Scouts Canada might want to build to help the association analyze its operational performance?
5. Do the managers at Scouts Canada actually have all the information they require to make an accurate decision? Explain the statement "it is never possible to have all of the information required to make the best decision possible."

CLOSING CASE TWO

Mining the Data Warehouse

This case provides several examples of how organizations use a data warehouse for improved information reporting and business decision-making.

According to a Merrill Lynch survey in 2006, business intelligence software and data-mining tools were at the top of CIOs' technology spending list. Following are a few examples of how companies are using data warehousing and data-mining tools to gain valuable business intelligence.

Ben & Jerry's

These days, when we all scream for ice cream, Ben & Jerry's cuts through the din by using integrated query, reporting, and online analytical processing technology from BI software vendor Business Objects. Through an Oracle database and with BI from Business Objects, Ben & Jerry's tracks the ingredients and life of each pint. If a consumer calls in with a complaint, the consumer affairs staff matches the pint with which supplier's milk, eggs, cherries, or whatever did not meet the organization's near-obsession with quality.

The BI tools let Ben & Jerry's officials access, analyze, and act on customer information collected by the sales, finance, purchasing, and quality-assurance departments. The company can determine what milk customers prefer in the making of the ice cream. The technology helped Ben & Jerry's track more than 12,500 consumer contacts in 2005. The information ranged from comments about the ingredients used in ice cream to queries about social causes supported by the company.[28]

ALTANA Pharma Inc. Canada

ALTANA Pharma Inc., a Nycomed company, is one of Canada's fastest growing pharmaceutical companies. Headquartered in Oakville, Ontario, with more than 265 employees across the country, ALTANA Pharma is active in the research and development of products in the key areas of gastroenterology and respirology. The company strives to produce safe, effective, and useful medicines to help Canadians and their physicians manage a variety of health problems.[29]

To improve its marketing initiatives, ALTANA Pharma implemented a Business Intelligence (BI) solution. This data warehouse system imports transactional pharmaceutical prescription and sales data from pharmacies and hospitals across Canada. This raw data is collected by IMS Health—an organization with 350 employees working out of Montreal and Toronto—and purchased by ALTANA Pharma for import into the data warehouse. ALTANA Pharma believes that there is strategic advantage in analyzing this purchased data in order to identify and better understand drug treatment and utilization trends. According to Dave Slaney, manager—Information Technology at ALTANA Pharma, it is extremely important for a pharmaceutical company to understand the prescribing habits of physicians from both a drug adoption and drug loyalty perspective. And loading transactional prescription and sales data into a data warehouse solution allows the company to do just that.

To ensure that ALTANA Pharma analyzes the collected data correctly, the marketing intelligence team at the company collaborated with internal and external experts to understand what the prescription and sales data meant. Only by doing so could they ensure that they were making sense of the data and interpreting results correctly. This was crucial in allowing them to make accurate business decisions based on their data analysis. It appears to be working. For instance, the marketing intelligence team finds the data warehouse to be helpful in establishing strategies. Likewise, sales analysts use information from the data warehouse to create reports for sales personnel that allow them to stay ahead of the competition.[30]

Noodles & Company

Noodles & Company has more than 70 restaurants throughout Colorado, Illinois, Maryland, Michigan, Minnesota, Texas, Utah, Virginia, and Wisconsin. The company recently purchased Cognos BI tools to help implement reporting standards and communicate real-time operational information to field management throughout the United States.

Before implementing the first phase of the Cognos solution, IT and finance professionals spent days compiling report requests from numerous departments including sales and marketing, human resources, and real estate. Since completing phase one, operational Cognos reports are being accessed on a daily basis through the Noodles & Company Web site. This provides users with a single, 360-degree view of the business and consistent reporting throughout the enterprise.

Noodles & Company users benefit from the flexible query and reporting capabilities, allowing them to see patterns in the information to leverage new business opportunities. Cognos tools can pull information directly from a broad array of relational, operational, and other systems.[31]

Questions

1. How is Ben & Jerry's using BI tools to remain successful and competitive in a saturated market?

2. Why is understanding transactional prescription and sales data critical to ALTANA Pharma's use of its BI tool?

3. Why is 100-percent accurate and complete information impossible for Noodles & Company to obtain?

4. Describe how each of the companies above is using BI from its data warehouse to gain a competitive advantage.

CLOSING CASE THREE

Harrah's—Gambling Big on Technology

This case illustrates how database technologies can support an organization's business strategy.

The large investment made by Harrah's Entertainment Inc. in its information technology strategy has been tremendously successful. The results of Harrah's investment include:

- 10-percent annual increase in customer visits.
- 33-percent increase in gross market revenue.
- Yearly profits of over $239 million.
- Highest three-year ROI (return on investment) in the industry.
- A network that links over 42,000 gaming machines in 26 casinos across 12 states.
- Rated number six of the 100 best places to work in IT for 2003 by *ComputerWorld* magazine.
- Recipient of 2000 Leadership in Data Warehousing Award from the Data Warehousing Institute (TDWI), the premier association for data warehousing.

The casino industry is highly competitive (rivalry among existing competitors is fierce). Bill Harrah was a man ahead of his time when he opened his first bingo parlor in 1937 with the commitment of getting to know each one of his customers. In 1984, Phil Satre, president and CEO of Harrah's, continued that commitment to customers. In search of its competitive advantage, Harrah's invested in an enterprisewide technology infrastructure to maintain Bill Harrah's original conviction: "Serve your customers well and they will be loyal."

Harrah's Commitment to Customers

Harrah's recently implemented its patented Total Rewards™ program to help build strong relationships with its customers. The program rewards customers for their loyalty by tracking their gaming habits across its 26 properties and currently maintains information on over 19 million customers, information the company uses to analyze, predict, and maximize each customer's value.

One major reason for the company's success is Harrah's implementation of a service-oriented strategy. Total Rewards allows Harrah's to give every customer the appropriate amount of personal attention, whether it's leaving sweets in the hotel room or offering free meals. Total Rewards works by providing each customer with an account and a corresponding card that the player swipes each time he or she plays a casino game. The program collects information on the amount of time the customers gamble, their total winnings and losses, and their betting strategies. Customers earn points based on the amount of time they spend gambling, which they can then exchange for comps such as free dinners, hotel rooms, tickets to shows, and even cash.

Total Rewards helps employees determine which level of service to provide each customer. When a customer makes a reservation at Harrah's, the service representative taking the call can view the customer's detailed information including the customer's loyalty level, games typically played, past winnings and losses, and potential net worth. If the service representative notices that the customer has a Diamond loyalty level, the service representative knows that customer should never have to wait in line and always receive free upgrades to the most expensive rooms.

"Almost everything we do in marketing and decision making is influenced by technology," says Gary Loveman, Harrah's chief operating officer. "The prevailing wisdom in this business is that the attractiveness of property drives customers. Our approach is different. We stimulate demand by knowing our customers. For example, if one of our customers always vacations at Harrah's in April, they will receive a promotion in February redeemable for a free weekend in April."

Gaining Business Intelligence with a Data Warehouse

Over 90 million customers visit Harrah's each year, and tracking a customer base larger than the population of Germany is a challenge. To tackle this challenge Harrah's began developing a system called WINet (Winner's Data Network). WINet links all Harrah's properties, allowing the company to collect and share customer information on an enterprisewide basis. WINet collects customer information from all the company transactions, game machines, and hotel management and reservations systems and places the information in a central data warehouse. Information in the data warehouse includes both customer and gaming information recorded in hourly increments. The marketing department uses the data warehouse to analyze customer information for patterns and insights, which allows it to create individualized marketing programs for each customer based on spending habits. Most important, the data warehouse allows the company to make business decisions based on information, not intuition.

Casinos traditionally treat customers as though they belong to a single property, typically the place the customer most frequently visits. Harrah's was the first casino to realize the potential of rewarding customers for visiting more than one property. Today, Harrah's has found that customers who visit more than one of its properties represent the fastest growing revenue segment. In the first two years of the Total Rewards program, the company received a $115-million increase in revenue from customers who gambled at more than one casino.

Harrah's also uses business intelligence to determine gaming machine performance. Using the data warehouse, Harrah's examines the performance and cost structure of each individual gaming machine. The company can quickly identify games that do not deliver optimal operational performance and can make a decision to move or replace the games. The capability to assess the performance of each individual slot machine has provided Harrah's with savings in the tens of millions of dollars. CIO Tim Stanley stated, "As we leverage more data from our data warehouse and increase the use and sophistication of our decision science analytical tools, we expect to have many new ways to improve customer loyalty and satisfaction, drive greater revenues, and decrease our costs as part of our ongoing focus on achieving sustainable profitability and success."

Security and Privacy

Some customers have concerns about Harrah's information collection strategy since they want to keep their gambling information private. The good news for these customers is that casinos are actually required to be more mindful of privacy concerns than most companies. For example, casinos cannot send marketing material to any underage persons. To adhere to strict government regulations, casinos must ensure that the correct information security and restrictions are in place. Many other companies actually make a great deal of money by selling customer information. Harrah's will not be joining in this trend since its customer information is one of its primary competitive advantages.

The Future of Harrah's

Harrah's current systems support approximately $160,000 in revenue per hour (that's almost $29 million weekly). In the future, Harrah's hopes to become device-independent by allowing employees to access the company's data warehouse via PDAs, handheld computers, and even cell phones. "Managing relationships with customers is incredibly important to the health of our business," Stanley says. "We will apply whatever technology we can to do that."[32]

Questions

1. Identify the effects poor information might have on Harrah's service-oriented business strategy.
2. How does Harrah's use database technologies to implement its service-oriented strategy?

3. Harrah's was one of the first casino companies to find value in offering rewards to customers who visit multiple Harrah's locations. Describe the effects on the company if it did not build any integrations among the databases located at each of its casinos. How could Harrah's use distributed databases or a data warehouse to synchronize customer information?

4. Estimate the potential impact to Harrah's business if there is a security breach in its customer information.

5. Identify three different types of data marts Harrah's might want to build to help it analyze its operational performance.

6. What might occur if Harrah's fails to clean or scrub its information before loading it into its data warehouse?

7. Describe cluster analysis, association detection, and statistical analysis and explain how Harrah's could use each one to gain insights into its business.

MAKING BUSINESS DECISIONS

1. Explaining relational databases

You have been hired by Vision, a start-up recreational equipment company in British Columbia. Your manager, Holly Henningson, is unfamiliar with databases and their associated business value. Holly has asked you to create a report detailing the basics of databases. Holly would also like you to provide a detailed explanation of relational databases along with their associated business advantages.

2. Entities and attributes

Martex Inc. is a Canadian manufacturer of athletic equipment, and its primary lines of business include running, tennis, golf, swimming, basketball, and aerobics equipment. Martex currently supplies four primary vendors including Sam's Sports, Total Effort, The Underline, and Maximum Workout. Martex wants to build a database to help it organize its products. In a group, identify the different types of entities, entity classes, attributes, keys and relationships Martex will want to consider when designing its database.

3. Integrating information

You are currently working for the Public Transportation Department of Chatfield. The department controls all forms of public transportation including buses, subways, and trains. Each department has about 300 employees and maintains its own accounting, inventory, purchasing, and human resource systems. Generating reports across departments is a difficult task and usually involves gathering and correlating the information from the many different systems. It typically takes about two weeks to generate the quarterly balance sheets and profit and loss statements. Your team has been asked to compile a report recommending what the Public Transportation Department of Chatfield can do to alleviate its information and system issues. Be sure that your report addresses the various reasons departmental reports are presently difficult to obtain as well as how you plan to solve this problem.

4. Information timeliness

Information timeliness is a major consideration for all organizations. Organizations need to decide the frequency of backups and the frequency of updates to a data warehouse. In a team, describe the timeliness requirements for backups and updates to a data warehouse for each of the following:

- Weather tracking systems.
- Car dealership inventories.

- Vehicle tire sales forecasts.
- Interest rates.
- Restaurant inventories.
- Grocery store inventories.

5. Improving information quality

HangUps Corporation designs and distributes closet organization structures. The company operates five systems—order entry, sales, inventory management, shipping, and billing. The company has severe information quality issues including missing, inaccurate, redundant, and incomplete information. The company wants to implement a data warehouse containing information from the five different systems to help maintain a single customer view, drive business decisions, and perform multidimensional analysis. Identify how the organization can improve its information quality when it begins designing and building its data warehouse.

6. Determining information quality issues

Real People is a magazine geared toward working individuals that provides articles and advice on everything from car maintenance to family planning. Real People is currently experiencing problems with its magazine distribution list. Over 30 percent of the magazines mailed are returned because of incorrect address information, and each month it receives numerous calls from angry customers complaining that they have not yet received their magazines. Below is a sample of Real People's customer information. Create a report detailing all of the issues with the information, potential causes of the information issues, and solutions the company can follow to correct the situation.

ID	First Name	Middle Initial	Last Name	Street	City	Prov.	Postal Code
433	M	J	Jones	13 Hamilton	Hamilton	ON	L8P 1X9
434	Margaret	J	Jones	13 First Ave.	Hamilton	ON	L8P 1X9
434	Brian	F	Hoover	Lake Ave.	Winnipeg	MB	L8P 1X9
435	Nick	H	Schweitzer	65 Apple Lane	Vancouver	AB	T2J 0P5
436	Richard	A		567 55th St.	Moose Jaw	SK	S6J 1N2
437	Alana	B	Smith	121 Tenny Dr.	Fredericton	NB	E3B55A3
438	Trevor	D	Darrian	90 FFDXRTH	Sydney	NS	B1P 6K6

7. Mining the data warehouse

Alana Smith is a senior buyer for a large wholesaler that sells different types of arts and crafts to greeting card stores such as Hallmark. Alana's latest marketing strategy is to send all of her customers a new line of handmade picture frames from Russia. All of Alana's information supports her decision for the new line. Her analysis predicts that the frames should sell an average of 10 to 15 per store, per day. Alana is excited about the new line and is positive it will be a success.

One month later Alana learns that the frames are selling 50 percent below expectations and averaging between five to eight frames sold daily in each store. Alana decides to access the company's data warehouse information to determine why sales are below expectations. Identify several different dimensions of information that Alana will want to analyze to help her decide what is causing the problems with the picture frame sales.

8. Cleansing information

You are working for BI, a start-up business intelligence consulting company. You have a new client that is interested in hiring BI to clean up its information. To determine how good your work is, the client would like your analysis of the following spreadsheet.

CUST ID	First Name	Last Name	Address	City	Province	Postal Code	Phone	Last Order Date
233620	Christopher	Lee	12421 W Olympic Blvd	Montreal	QC	H2A 1QP	(403)680-7848	18/04/2007
233621	Bruce	Brandwen	268 W 44th St	Toronto	AB	MS9 2X3	(416)471-6077	03/05/2007
233622	Glr	Johnson	4100 E Dry Creek Rd	Whitehorse	YT	Y0A 4D3	(867)712-5461	06/06/2007
233623	Dave	Owens	466 Commerce Rd	Bathurst	NB	24401-4432	(506)851-0362	19/03/2007
233624	John	Colbourne	124 Action St	Corner Brook	NL	A2H	(709)987-0100	24/04/2007
233629	Dan	Gagliardo	2875 Union Rd	Dartmouth	NS	B3A 5T2	(902)558-8191	04/13/2007
23362	Damanceee	Allen	1633 Broadway	Selkirk	MB	R1A 4L4	(204)708-1576	
233630	Michael	Peretz	235 E 45th St	London	ON	N6C 3H7	(519)210-1340	30/04/2007
233631	Jody	Veeder	440 Cardinal Dr	Niagara Falls	ON	L7P 1X7	(905)238-9690 X227	27/31/2007
233632	Michael	Kehrer	3015 SSE Loop 323	Abbotsford	BC	V3G 222	(250)579-3229	28/04/
233633	Erin	Yoon	3500 Carillon Pt	Edmunston	NB	L8R 6B2	(506)897-7221	25/03/2007
233634	Madeline	Shefferly	4100 Bloor St W	Toronto	ON	M5T 7N3	(416)486-3949	33/03/2007
233635	Steven	Conduit	1332 Enterprise Dr	Vancouver	BC	V6E 3L5	(604)692-5900	27/04/2007
233635	Joseph	Kovach	1332 Enterprise Dr	Vancouver	BC	V6E 3L5	(604)692-5900	28/04/2007
233637	Richard	Jordan	1700 N	Calgary	AB	T3B 5S5	(403)581-6770	19/03/2007
233638	Scott	M	1655 Crofton Blvd	Calgary	AB	T3B 7P9	(514)729-8155	28/04/2007
233639	Susan	Shragg	1875 Century Park	Halifax	NS	B3K 8T5	(902)785-0511	29/04/2027
233640	Rob	Ponto	29777 Telegraph Rd	Winnipeg	MB	4Z4-R3B	(204)204-4724	05/05/2007

Helping Organizations Access, Share, and Use Information

8

CHAPTER

LEARNING OUTCOMES

8.1. Explain how collaboration can help companies turn information into knowledge.

8.2. Identify the different ways in which companies can collaborate using technology.

8.3. Compare the different categories of collaboration technologies.

8.4. Understand the difference between knowledge management and knowledge management systems.

8.5. Explain how enterprise portals can help organizations access, share, and utilize information better.

8.6. Provide an example of a content management system along with its business purpose.

8.7. Evaluate the advantages of a workflow management system.

8.8. Explain how groupware can benefit a business.

Why Do I Need To Know This ?

As described in the last chapter, information is a powerful asset. It is a key organizational resource that enables companies to carry out business initiatives and plans. Those companies that are able to manage this key resource well are primed for competitive advantage and success.

In response, many organizations are striving to find ways to help employees, customers, and business partners access the information they need, share this information with others, and use and incorporate this information in their daily work. Doing so allows companies to not only get work done, but also encourages the sharing and generation of new ideas that lead to the development of innovations, improved work habits, and best practices.

Information technology is a key tool that allows all this to happen. Information technology can improve the access and flow of information in a company. As such, information technology can help facilitate business processes and growth.

This is the focus of this chapter—to showcase how information technology can help organizations capitalize upon the power of information by providing mechanisms for improved information access, sharing, and use. This includes access and use of structured information found in transactional databases and data warehouses, unstructured information found in textual documents and e-mail messages, and information that organizational employees possess.

As a business student, you need to be aware of how information technologies, especially newer ones such as knowledge management systems and enterprise portals, can help a company's bottom-line by leveraging the power of information. By being conscious of the usefulness of information access and sharing tools, you will appreciate the opportunities for success they afford and will see the need to champion their usage in companies in order to help organizations better succeed in the marketplace.

Leveraging Knowledge at Bell Canada

Bell Canada Enterprises (BCE) is Canada's largest communications company. Its main subsidiary, Bell Canada, provides local telephone, long distance, wireless communications, Internet access, satellite television, and other services through some 27 million customer connections. The telecommunications giant operates in a fast-paced and highly competitive environment. New competitors and innovative technologies constantly threaten to capture Bell Canada's stronghold on the Canadian marketplace. To stay ahead of the pack, Bell Canada recognizes the importance of providing its employees with easy access to the most current information.

In response, Bell Canada has built the Market Knowledge Centre (MKC) portal—a one-stop, self-directed learning tool—to help employees attain high levels of competency and enable knowledge sharing at Bell Canada and within the BCE family of companies.

The objectives of the MKC portal are to:

- enable Bell Canada to meet competitive challenges in the marketplace,
- enrich the company's hiring and training programs,
- increase technological literacy among employees, and
- provide resources to employees that can help them develop their knowledge and competencies.[1]

In short, the MKC portal is an electronic library on Bell Canada's intranet that gives employees access to authoritative and recent information on topics pertaining to their interests and work-related tasks. Employees visit the MKC portal to read the latest publications from in-house experts and outside consultants. The documentation available on the portal varies widely covering telecommunications, technologies, business, marketing, and management. Information is not constrained just to text-based documents; other forms include audio-conferences and invitations to live briefings or seminars.

The beauty of this tool is that it provides information access from each employee's desktop. Employees are not constrained by physical geography, unavailable copies, or hours of operation—typical problems voiced in the past by employees trying to access paper-based collections housed in traditional corporate libraries.

Further, the MKC portal can be customized to individual needs. Employees can personalize the portal so they have access to the subjects of interest to them. They do this by creating personal folders on the portal. When users find documents of interest on the portal, they can tag or bookmark these documents, save them in their personal folders, and create annotations or comments to organize their reading choices. To promote even greater simplicity for organizing and accessing relevant documents, the latest version of the portal contains a "MyFolder" function that allows end-users to tag any item and save it in personal folders.

The portal facilitates both search and browse functions. Employees can locate documents of interest through keyword search. End-users can browse the library collection by broad subject categories, author, and date; such a facility helps employees get an overview of what is contained in the collection—kind of like what happens when someone strolls through the stacks of a traditional library getting a sense of things and randomly finding material of interest.

Through these features, the MKC portal helps employees do their jobs better. The portal provides key strategic and tactical information needed by employees to support their projects. A large chunk of this information is research-related. Working in a fast-changing environment, Bell Canada recognizes the need to provide current research results to employees. As a result, the portal is updated daily in content providing the latest research results to employees as soon as they are available. If desired, employees can sign up for weekly alerts sent by e-mail to keep them informed about the latest additions to the electronic library. In fact, this form of "push" technology—where the portal informs end-users about new material rather than the end-users having to "pull" the information out themselves by constantly checking for updates—can be targeted so that only new material matching a user's profile of interest is reported.

There are savings for the company in delivering the MKC portal. The portal eliminates duplicate spending on consultant reports, trade magazines, and industry documents across the enterprise by centralizing subscriptions to online databases and electronic journals and negotiating corporate-wide distribution licences with suppliers. The portal has also replaced the need to maintain and staff physical library locations within Bell Canada at its Montreal, Toronto, and Ottawa locations.

A dedicated staff of trained information specialists maintain the MKC portal to keep it fresh, current, and robust. This entails major updates of the portal in the release of a new versions (occurs about once every three years) and smaller updates that offer incremental enhancements to the portal interface and its collection. This staff is also charged with providing end-user customer support to employees. Typically this involves fielding more demanding in-depth research questions from employees than answering quick reference questions that employees can easily address themselves. With respect to the research queries posed to information specialists supporting the portal, the support staff are expected to not only deliver the requested information but also to analyze, synthesize, and present this information back to end-users in usable formats that are "ready-to-use" in presentations, spreadsheets, or documents.

To ensure the MKC portal is responsive to the needs of the company, performance measures of client satisfaction are conducted regularly. Employee feedback is critical for evaluating the utility of this tool and figuring out what enhancements are needed. This can be done by polling end-users through client surveys and interviews and/or analyzing portal server logs to understand employee usage behaviour concerning various portal functions and visits to portal pages. Both information support staff and the portal tool itself need to be measured.

Information specialists supporting the portal, who provide value-added research services to employees, can be measured according to their:

- responsiveness,
- relevancy of information provided,
- value of information provided,
- impact of information provided on business decisions,
- timeliness of response,
- proactiveness,
- likelihood to use the service again,
- likelihood to recommend the service to another employee, and
- overall satisfaction with the research service.

The portal itself can be measured by asking clients about their experiences regarding:

- usability,
- information content,
- features, and
- satisfaction with search results.[2]

To promote the portal, Bell Canada schedules regular "lunch and learn" session for employees.

Overall, the MKC portal offers many benefits to Bell Canada. The tool ensures more informed decision-making, increased distribution of research and corporate materials, higher employee satisfaction through provision of continual online learning, savings in duplicate spending on publication dissemination and maintaining multiple physical library locations, and improved collaboration between departments and work teams.[3]

INTRODUCTION

Chapter 7 described the difference between data and information. Data was described as "raw facts" that portray the characteristics of an event, such as a date, item number, or quantity ordered. Information was described as data converted into a meaningful and useful context. In this sense, information can be thought of as "meaningful data," such as the identification of the best-selling item or worst-selling item from sales data collected by a company.

In this chapter, we continue this train of thought and position knowledge along the data–information–knowledge continuum. Knowledge is described as "actionable information." Simply put, information becomes knowledge when information can be acted upon.

For example, consider carpenters. They are knowledgeable individuals who know a lot about woodworking. That is, they are able to pull together all the information they have gathered over the years about woodworking and put that information into action by actually knowing how to build something. However, if we wrote down all the information about woodworking in a book and gave it to a non-woodworking expert, that person would not necessarily be any more knowledgeable about woodworking and able to build something. That person would definitely be more informed, but would not be considered knowledgeable unless that person were able to understand the information in the book and put that information into action.

The point of this example is to showcase that having information about a topic does not make a person knowledgeable. Rather, to be considered knowledgeable, a person needs to understand or comprehend that information, be able to make inferences between various tidbits of information presented, and most importantly be able to apply that information into action.

In this light, information can be viewed as the building block or stimuli for knowledge. Knowledge is created when information is understood, when disparate facts are connected together, and when insights are gleaned. As such, information is truly a foundation for the generation of new knowledge.

It is important to understand the distinction between information and knowledge as it raises important questions for organizations as they try to capitalize on the information they collect. For example, where does knowledge reside? Is it stored in databases and data warehouses? Inside textual documents, reports, and e-mail messages? Or, is it stored in the heads of organizational workers?

There are two trains of thoughts on the answer. A computer scientist would argue that knowledge is contained within formalized data structures and that technologies exist today, such as artificial intelligence and intelligent agents, which are capable of understanding the meaning of the information stored in formalized data structures and taking actions based on this understanding. A humanist or information studies scholar would argue the opposite saying that knowledge is resident in human beings and that though information technologies can store and process data and information quite well, it is up to users to interpret and make sense of the information these technologies provide.

Both viewpoints are valid and it will be interesting to see how this will play out as more advances in computing are made over the decades. However, information technologies today are limited in their capacity to turn information into knowledge, and most organizations have realized this. In response, organizations are grappling with ways to extract information out of their massive data and information repositories, document collections, customer communications, and consultant reports and turn that information into knowledge.

What most organizations have found is that helping employees access, share, and utilize information is perhaps the best way to convert information into knowledge. Organizations are realizing that having information sit in a database, document, or e-mail archive does little for knowledge creation. Companies are beginning to understand that to be knowledgeable and act knowingly they must find ways to help their employees get at information as quickly and efficiently as possible, easily share that information with others, and use that information in their work.

Thus many companies are turning to new information technologies, such as collaboration systems and enterprise portals, to give people the tools to access, share, and use information better. These new technologies add business-value and are helping companies leverage their know-how.

The first section of this chapter illustrates the power of collaboration and knowledge management to organizational success. It does this by starting off with a description of how information is accessed, shared, and utilized by teams, partnerships, and alliances, and then going into a discussion about collaboration and knowledge management in general. The second section of this chapter describes a relatively new type of information system—the enterprise portal—and provides commentary on how companies are leveraging the power of enterprise portals to foster collaboration and improve information access, sharing, and use across the organization.

TEAMS, PARTNERSHIPS, AND ALLIANCES

To be successful—and avoid being eliminated by the competition—an organization must constantly undertake new initiatives, address both minor and major problems, and capitalize on significant opportunities. To support these activities, an organization often will create and utilize teams, partnerships, and alliances because the expertise needed is beyond the scope of a single individual or organization. These teams, partnerships, and alliances can be formed internally among a company's employees or externally with other organizations (see Figure 8.1).

Businesses of all sizes and in all markets have witnessed the benefits of leveraging their IT assets to create competitive advantage. Whereas information technology efforts in the past were aimed at increasing operational efficiency, the advent and proliferation of network-based computing (the Internet being the most visible, but not only, example) has enabled organizations to build systems with which all sorts of communities can interact. The ultimate result will allow organizations to do business with customers, business partners, suppliers, governments and regulatory agencies, and any other community relevant to their particular operation or activity.

In the same way that organizations use internal teams, they are increasingly forming alliances and partnerships with other organizations. The ***core competency***

FIGURE 8.1

Teams, Partnerships, and Alliances Within and External to an Organization

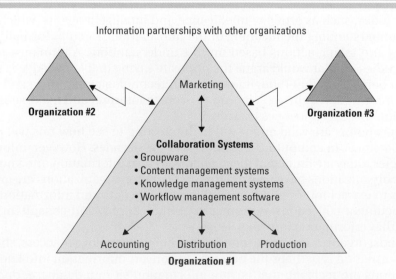

of an organization is its key strength, a business function that it does better than any of its competitors. Apple Computer is highly regarded for its strength in product design, while Accenture's core competency is the design and installation of information systems. A *core competency strategy* is one in which an organization chooses to focus specifically on what it does best (its core competency) and forms partnerships and alliances with other specialist organizations to handle nonstrategic business processes. Strategic alliances enable businesses to gain competitive advantages through access to a partner's resources, including markets, technologies, and people. Teaming up with another business adds complementary resources and capabilities, enabling participants to grow and expand more quickly and efficiently, especially fast-growing companies that rely heavily on outsourcing many areas of their business to extend their technical and operational resources. In the outsourcing process, they save time and boost productivity by not having to develop their own systems from scratch. They are then free to concentrate on innovation and their core business.

Information technology makes such business partnerships and alliances easier to establish and manage. An *information partnership* occurs when two or more organizations cooperate by integrating their IT systems, thereby providing customers with the best of what each can offer. The advent of the Internet has greatly increased the opportunity for IT-enabled business partnerships and alliances.

For example, an information partnership between the federal government (Industry Canada), provinces and territories (Ontario, British Columbia, and Yukon), and local governments (City of Kamloops, Regional Municipality of Halton and its two municipalities Milton and Halton Hills, and City of Whitehorse) has simplified the task of obtaining permits for large and small Canadian enterprises. These partners worked together to develop the BizPal (Business Permits and Licences) solution to provide a single point for businesses to obtain the necessary information when applying for permits and licences across all levels of government. Prior to this one-stop shopping solution, businesses were forced to enter the same information several times and make multiple payments. By collaborating together and allowing information to be shared, these government partners have successfully deployed an integrated information technology solution that benefits Canadian companies wishing to start up a business.[4]

COLLABORATION

Heineken has shortened its inventory cycle time for beer production and distribution from three months to four weeks. By using its collaborative system to forecast demand and expedite shipping, the company has dramatically cut inventory levels and shipping costs while increasing sales.

Over the past few years most business processes have changed on various dimensions (e.g., flexibility, interconnectivity, coordination style, autonomy) because of market conditions and organizational models. Frequently, information is located within physically separated systems as more and more organizations spread their reach globally. This creates a need for a software infrastructure that enables collaboration systems.

A *collaboration system* is an IT-based set of tools that supports the work of teams by facilitating the sharing and flow of information. Collaboration solves specific business tasks such as telecommuting, online meetings, deploying applications, and remote project and sales management (see Figure 8.2).

Collaboration systems allow people, teams, and organizations to leverage and build upon the ideas and talents of staff, suppliers, customers, and business partners. It involves a unique set of business challenges that:

- Include complex interactions between people who may be in different locations and desire to work across function and discipline areas.

- Require flexibility in work process and the ability to involve others quickly and easily.

- Call for creating and sharing information rapidly and effortlessly within a team.

FIGURE 8.2

Collaborative Business
Areas

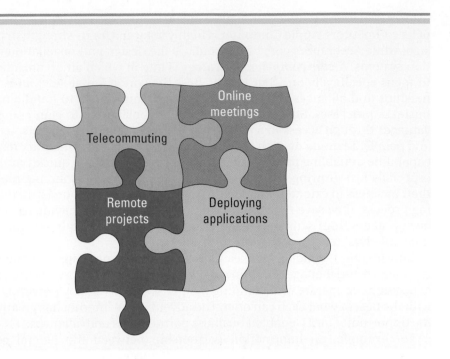

Most organizations collaborate with other companies in some capacity. Consider the supplier–customer relationship, which can be thought of in terms of a continuous life cycle of engagement, transaction, fulfillment, and service activities. Rarely do companies excel in all four life cycle areas, either from a business process or from a technology-enabled aspect. Successful organizations identify and invest in their core competencies, and outsource or collaborate for those competencies that are not core to them. Collaboration systems fall into one of two categories:

1. **Unstructured collaboration** (sometimes referred to as **information collaboration**) includes document exchange, shared whiteboards, discussion forums, and e-mail. These functions can improve personal productivity, reducing the time spent searching for information or chasing answers.

2. **Structured collaboration** (or **process collaboration**) involves shared participation in business processes, such as workflow, in which knowledge is hard-coded as rules. This is beneficial in terms of improving automation and the routing of information.

Regardless of location or format—be it unstructured or structured—relevant accurate information must be readily and consistently available to those who need it anytime, anywhere, and on any device. The integration of IT systems enables an organization to provide employees, partners, customers, and suppliers with the ability to access, find, analyze, manage, and collaborate on content. The collaboration can be done across a wide variety of formats, languages, and platforms. Figure 8.3 illustrates many of the typical collaborative functions within most organizations.

Lockheed Martin Aeronautics Company's ability to share complex project information across an extended supply chain in real time was key in its successful bid of a $21.5-billion contract with the U.S. Department of Defense (DoD) to build 21 supersonic stealth fighters. New American government procurement rules require defence contractors to communicate effectively to ensure that deadlines are met, costs are controlled, and projects are managed throughout the life cycle of the contract.[5]

In anticipation of the contract, the Fort Worth, Texas, unit of Lockheed Martin Corporation developed a real-time collaboration system that can tie together its partners, suppliers, and DoD customers via the Internet. The platform lets participants collectively work on product design and engineering tasks as well as supply

FIGURE 8.3

Typical Collaborative
Business Functions

Function	Collaborator(s)	Business Function(s)
Planning and forecasting	Supplier, Customer	Real-time information sharing (forecast information and sales information)
Product design	Supplier, Customer	Document exchange, computer-aided design (CAD)
Strategic sourcing	Supplier	Negotiation, supplier performance management
Component compatibility testing	Supplier	Component compatibility
Pricing	Supplier, Customer	Pricing in supply chain
Marketing	Supplier, Customer	Joint/coop marketing campaigns, branding
Sales	Customer	Shared leads, presentations, configuration and quotes
Make-to-order	Customer	Requirements, capabilities, contract terms
Order processing	Supplier, Customer	Order solution
Fulfillment: Logistics and service	Supplier, Customer	Coordination of distribution
International trade logistics	Customer	Document exchange, import/export documents
Payment	Customer	Order receipt, invoicing
Customer service/support	Supplier, Customer	Shared/split customer support

chain and life cycle management issues. Lockheed will host all transactions and own the project information. The platform will let DoD and Lockheed project managers track the daily progress of the project in real time. This is the first major DoD project with such a requirement. The contract, awarded to the Lockheed unit and partners Northrop Grumman Corp. and BAE Systems, is the first instalment in what could amount to a $225-billion program for 3,000 jet fighters over 40 years. The strengths of the collaboration process lie with the integration of many 15 systems.

KNOWLEDGE MANAGEMENT

Knowledge management (KM) involves capturing, classifying, evaluating, retrieving, and sharing information assets in a way that provides context for effective decisions and actions. KM is the systematic, effective management and utilization of an organization's information resources that contain or embody knowledge. These sources include people (human experts); paper documents; electronic word documents; presentations and spreadsheets; and data warehouse solutions.

It is best to think of KM in the broadest context. Succinctly put, KM is the process through which organizations generate value from their intellectual and knowledge-based assets. Most often, generating value from such assets involves codifying what employees, partners, and customers know, and sharing that information among employees, departments, and even with other companies to devise best practices. However, codification is not always the goal of KM—often organizational knowledge resides within human experts and it is best to cultivate and utilize that expertise in that form rather than trying to explicitly document or codify that know-how in some formal manner.

It is important to note that the above description of KM is not all about technology; while KM is often facilitated by IT, technology by itself is not KM. Knowledge management is about how companies cultivate and promote practices (behaviours) and the use of tools (such as information technologies) that help capture, store, organize, and make the best use of information within and across the enterprise to increase and leverage organizational knowledge and know-how.

Think of a golf caddie as a simplified example of a knowledge worker. Good caddies do more than carry clubs and track down wayward balls. When asked, a good caddie will give advice to golfers, such as, "The wind makes the ninth hole play 15 yards longer." Accurate advice may lead to a bigger tip at the end of the day. The golfer, having derived a benefit from the caddie's advice, may be more likely to play that course again. If a good caddie is willing to share what he knows with other caddies, then they all may eventually earn bigger tips. How would KM work to make this happen? The caddie master may decide to reward caddies for sharing their knowledge by offering them credits for pro shop merchandise. Once the best advice is collected, the course manager would publish the information in notebooks (or make it available on PDAs) and distribute them to all the caddies. The end result of a well-designed KM program is that everyone wins. In this case, caddies get bigger tips and deals on merchandise, golfers play better because they benefit from the collective experience of caddies, and the course owners win because better scores lead to repeat business.

KM in Business

KM has assumed greater urgency in Canadian business over the past few years as millions of baby boomers prepare to retire. When they punch out for the last time, the knowledge they gleaned about their jobs, companies, and industries during their long careers will walk out with them—unless companies take measures to retain their insights. In addition, CIOs who have entered into outsourcing agreements must address the thorny issue of transferring the knowledge of their full-time staff members, who are losing their jobs because of an outsourcing deal, to the outsourcer's employees.

Knowledge can be a real competitive advantage for an organization. Information technology can distribute an organization's knowledge base by interconnecting people and digitally gathering their expertise. The primary objective of knowledge management is to be sure that a company's knowledge of facts, sources of information, and solutions are readily available to all employees whenever it is needed.

Such knowledge management requires that organizations go well beyond providing information contained in spreadsheets, databases, and documents. It must include expert information that typically resides in people's heads. A *knowledge management system (KMS)* supports the capturing, organization, and dissemination of knowledge (i.e., know-how) throughout an organization. It is up to the organization to determine what information qualifies as knowledge.

Explicit and Tacit Knowledge

Not all information is valuable. Individual companies must determine what information qualifies as intellectual and knowledge-based assets. In general, intellectual and knowledge-based assets fall into one of two categories: explicit or tacit. As a rule, *explicit knowledge* consists of anything that can be documented, archived, and codified, often with the help of IT. Examples of explicit knowledge are assets such as patents, trademarks, business plans, marketing research, and customer lists.

Tacit knowledge is the knowledge contained in people's heads. The challenge inherent in tacit knowledge is figuring out how to recognize, generate, share, and manage knowledge that resides in people's heads. While information technology in the form of e-mail, instant messaging, and related technologies can help facilitate the dissemination of tacit knowledge, identifying it in the first place can be a major obstacle. Shadowing and joint problem solving are two best practices for transferring or re-creating tacit knowledge inside an organization.

Shadowing With *shadowing*, less experienced staff observe more experienced staff to learn how their more experienced counterparts approach their work. Dorothy Leonard and Walter Swap, two knowledge management experts, stress the importance of having the protégé discuss his or her observations with the expert to deepen the dialogue and crystallize the knowledge transfer.

Joint Problem Solving Another sound approach is *joint problem solving* by expert and novice. Because people are often unaware of how they approach problems or do their work and therefore cannot automatically generate step-by-step instructions for doing whatever they do, having a novice and expert work together on a project will bring the expert's approach to light. The difference between shadowing and joint problem solving is that shadowing is more passive. With joint problem solving, the expert and the novice work hand in hand on a task.[6]

Information is of little use unless it is analyzed and made available to the right people, at the right place, and at the right time. To get the most value from intellectual assets, knowledge must be shared. An effective KMS system should help do one or more of the following:

- Foster innovation by encouraging the free flow of ideas.
- Improve customer service by streamlining response time.
- Boost revenues by getting products and services to market faster.
- Enhance employee retention rates by recognizing the value of employees' knowledge.
- Streamline operations and reduce costs by eliminating redundant or unnecessary processes.

A creative approach to knowledge management can result in improved efficiency, higher productivity, and increased revenues in practically any business function. Figure 8.4 indicates the reasons organizations launch KMS.

In the United States, software is helping ChevronTexaco Corporation improve how it manages the assets in oil fields by enabling employees in multiple

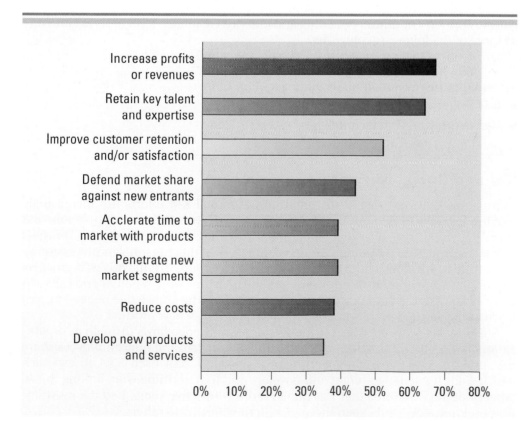

FIGURE 8.4

Key Reasons Organizations Launch Knowledge Management Systems

disciplines to easily access and share the information they need to make decisions. ChevronTexaco teams of 10 to 30 people are responsible for managing the assets, such as the drilling equipment, pipelines, and facilities, for a particular oil field. Within each team, earth scientists and various engineers with expertise in production, reservoir, and facilities work together to keep the oil field up and running. Each member of the asset team needs to communicate with other members to make decisions based on the collection and analysis of huge amounts of information from various departments. Individual team members can look at information from the perspective of their own department.

This has helped ChevronTexaco achieve a 30-percent productivity gain, a 50-percent improvement in safety performance, and more than $2.3 billion in operating cost reductions. Through KMSs, ChevronTexaco has restructured its gasoline retailing business and now drills oil and gas wells faster and cheaper.[7]

Not every organization matches ChevronTexaco's success with KM. Numerous KM projects have failed over the past few years, generating an unwillingness to undertake—or even address—KM issues among many organizations. However, KM is an effective tool if it is tied directly to discrete business needs and opportunities. Beginning with targeted projects that deliver value quickly, companies can achieve the success that has proved elusive with many big-bang approaches. Successful KM projects typically focus on creating value in a specific process area, or even just for a certain type of transaction. Companies should start with one job at a time—preferably the most knowledge-oriented one—and build KM into a job function in a way that actually helps employees do their work better and faster, then expand to the next most knowledge-intensive job, and so on. Celebrating even small success with KM will help build a base of credibility and support for future KM projects.

KM Technologies

KM is not a purely technology-based concept. Organizations that implement a centralized database system, electronic message board, Web portal, or any other collaborative tool in the hope that they have established a KMS are wasting both their time and money.

Although tools don't make a KMS, such a system does need tools, from standard, off-the-shelf e-mail packages to sophisticated collaboration tools designed specifically to support community building and identity. Generally, KMS tools fall into one or more of the following categories:

- Knowledge repositories (databases).
- Expertise tools.
- E-learning applications.
- Discussion and chat technologies.
- Search and data mining tools.

KM and Social Networking

Companies that have been frustrated by traditional KM efforts are increasingly looking for ways to find out how knowledge flows through their organization, and social networking analysis can show them just that. *Social networking analysis (SNA)* is a process of mapping a group's contacts (whether personal or professional) to identify who knows whom and who works with whom. In enterprises, it provides a clear picture of how far-flung employees and divisions work together and can help identify key experts in the organization who possess the knowledge needed to, say, solve a complicated programming problem or launch a new product.

M&M maker Mars used SNA to identify how knowledge flows through its organizations, who holds influence, who gives the best advice, and how employees share information. The Canadian government's central IT unit used SNA to establish which skills it needed to retain and develop, and to determine who, among the 40 percent of the workforce that was due to retire within five years, had the most important knowledge and experience to begin transferring to others.[8]

SNA is not a replacement for traditional KM tools such as knowledge databases or portals, but it can provide companies with a starting point for how best to proceed with KM initiatives. As a component to a larger KM strategy, SNA can help companies identify key leaders and then set up a mechanism, such as communities of practice, so that those leaders can pass on their knowledge to colleagues. To identify experts in their organizations, companies can use software programs that track e-mail and other kinds of electronic communication.[9]

OPENING CASE QUESTIONS

Leveraging Knowledge at Bell Canada

1. What type of information does the MKC portal collect and distribute as a means of promoting knowledge sharing and learning? How is this type of information different than that found in transactional databases and data warehouses containing summarized information?

2. Give examples of decision-making scenarios where information obtained from the MKC portal would be used. How would these decision-making scenarios differ from those where employees use transactional information obtained from databases? From summarized information obtained from data warehouses and data marts?

3. How has a centralized MKC portal improved knowledge sharing and information partnerships within Bell Canada and across the BCE family of companies? What is the ROI of centralizing the MKC portal solution?

4. What enhancements could be made to the MKC portal to further promote collaboration among project teams at Bell Canada and across BCE?

5. What enhancements could be made to the MKC portal to further promote employees understanding the information obtained from the portal and their ability to potentially put that information into action? That is, what features or functions added to the portal would help employees glean insights, make deductions, and forge new insights?

8.2 ENTERPRISE PORTALS

WHAT ARE ENTERPRISE PORTALS?

As a means to improve information access, sharing, and use, many organizations have implemented *enterprise portals*. These are single-point Web browser interfaces used within an organization to promote the gathering, sharing, and dissemination of information throughout an enterprise.[10]

Other synonymous terms, less frequently utilized to represent enterprise portals, are *corporate portals* and *business portals*.

These information systems provide employees with a path to all-encompassing content, services, and applications through one access point. Unlike departmental-based Web sites hosted on a company's intranet or internal Web-based network, an enterprise portal's primary purpose is to provide a transparent directory of information located throughout an organization, not act as a separate source of information itself. In this sense, the primary purpose of an enterprise portal is to function as an information gateway or launch pad for employees to various sorts of information. In recent years, such gateways have become organizational necessities due to the proliferation of departmental-based Web sites throughout the firm and the desire to provide employees with both internal and external company-related information.

Enterprise portals are popular Web-based knowledge management solutions. Coined in a Merrill Lynch report, enterprise portals are described as applications that enable companies to unlock internally and externally stored information, and provide users a single gateway to personalized information needed to make informed business decisions."[11]

To promote an enterprise portal's utilization, organizations typically hard-wire the portal to be the default homepage that appears on an employee's personal Web browser when launched.

The primary purpose of a portal is to navigate people; its secondary purpose is to provide unique content. This is in contrast to other types of Internet sites, such as external or departmental Web sites, where the primary purpose is to disseminate information and keep people at that specific site.

The excitement over enterprise portals by major corporations in recent years is due in large part to the success *Yahoo!* had with its 1996 launch of a personalized portal service called *MyYahoo!*, which allowed users to customize their own Web interfaces to filter and provide information that was relevant and meaningful to them. Corporations were quick to notice the success of this product in terms of its adoption and use by the general public and started to investigate ways to develop a similar view of corporate information.

Yahoo! is a portal exemplar. The site contains subject categories to facilitate browsing information by category, a robust search engine, and hyperlinks to information items. In this way, the site functions as a transparent source of information to other resources rather than a supplier of information itself. In this respect, *Yahoo!* functions as a launch pad or gateway to information contained elsewhere. In addition, *Yahoo!* incorporates productivity tools such as e-mail, online chat, address books, maps etc. These more advanced productivity tools provide incentives for users to visit the site.

Overall, enterprise portals are following a similar trajectory as consumer portals, such as *Yahoo!*, though over much shorter time frames. First version portals containing referential links to information plus a search engine are quickly evolving into more complex, interactive gateways that embed applications to enhance personal and work group productivity, all within time periods as short as 12 months.

Common elements contained within enterprise portal designs include:

- an *enterprise taxonomy* or classification of information categories that help organize information for easy retrieval,
- a *search engine* to facilitate more specific and exact information requests, and
- *hypertext links* to both internal and external Web sites and information sources.

More advanced enterprise portal features include access to work group productivity tools such as e-mail, calendars, work flow and project management software, expense reporting and travel reservation applications, as well as more specialized functions for transaction-based information processing where users can read, write, and update corporate data directly through the portal interface.

In addition to the above, enterprise portals can possess a variety of other features that help support information access, sharing, and use. These include:

1. Some sort of *publishing facility* that enables users to post and index information directly into the portal themselves.

2. Some sort of *automatic indexing facility* that classifies information items posted on the portal using an algorithm. These algorithms typically count the frequency of words in a document and select the best terms from that document to serve as index terms that are unique enough to identify that document from those in the rest of the document collection. Indexing documents with the best descriptive

terms will increase the chances of that document being retrieved when a user searches for information using those terms.

3. *Subscription facilities* that notify and distribute relevant information on a regular basis to a specific user or a group of users. These can occur on demand or can be automatically routed according to user profiles contained in the enterprise portal and/or stored requests for information previously specified by users.

4. *Intelligent agents* that understand a user's preferences and roles and assists that user in finding information of relevance and tailoring the presentation of information on the Web interface in a way that is most helpful for the user.

THE POTENTIAL OF ENTERPRISE PORTALS

There is much evidence indicating the potential role of enterprise portals to facilitate knowledge creation, distribution, and use, as well as to promote collaboration throughout the organization. Case study analysis has shown that to leverage enterprise portals for knowledge work and to promote collaboration, these systems must comprise three distinct areas, as illustrated in Figure 8.5:

1. An information ***content space*** to facilitate information access and retrieval.

2. A ***communication space*** to support discussion among employees, especially with respect to the negotiation of collective interpretations and shared meanings about the information accessed and retrieved.

3. A work ***coordination space*** to support cooperative work action between employees, facilitate workflow processes, and the accomplishment of work tasks.[12]

As an information content space, enterprise portals can help organizations with improved information storage and retrieval. Access to information is not just restricted to textual documents, but also includes access to data stored in transactional databases and summarized information stored in data warehouses. Further, information can be retrieved in a variety of ways on the portal. That is, the information is pulled (requested) by users themselves or pushed (filtered) to them directly.

As a communication space, enterprise portals can help organizational users make better sense of the information they receive by providing users with channels and connections to other human experts. This can be accomplished through the provision of rich information channels, such as instant messaging environments or online discussion rooms, to help organizational workers engage in conversations with others in the firm. In this way, new perspectives and innovation can result, and perhaps be stored back in the portal's knowledge base for later re-use. In this regard, the portal can help facilitate the creation of new knowledge in an organization and its use across the firm.

As a coordination space, enterprise portals can give employees the ability to coordinate work processes, gain access to work application software, and manage

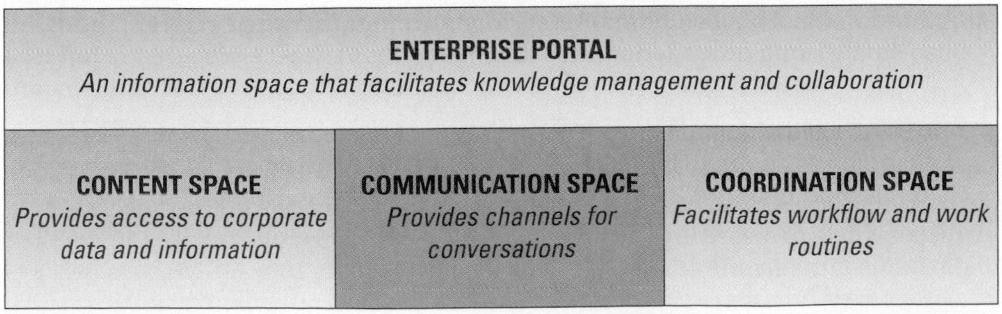

FIGURE 8.5

An Enterprise Portal as an Information Space for Knowledge Management and Collaboration the flow of information necessary for cooperation between various organizational units. This necessitates the need for portals to have functionality in their designs to automate work flows, coordinate routines, and manage projects, as well as signal the expertise of others in the organization and their availability for cooperative action.

Enterprise portals typically incorporate the integration of many systems, including:

- Content management systems
- Workflow management systems
- Groupware systems

CONTENT MANAGEMENT SYSTEMS

A *content management system* provides tools to manage the creation, storage, editing, and publication of information in a collaborative environment. As a Web site grows in size and complexity, the business must establish procedures to ensure that things run smoothly. At a certain point, it makes sense to automate this process and use a content management system to manage this effectively. The content management system marketplace is complex, incorporating document management, digital asset management, and Web content management. Figure 8.6 highlights the three primary types of content management systems. Figure 8.7 lists the major content management system vendors.

Content management software is helping BMW Group Switzerland accelerate personalized, real-time information about products, services, prices, and events to its dealers countrywide. BMW uses a process that allows dealers to specify what information is seen by which employee, as well as to deliver marketing materials solely to members of the sales department, and technical specifications and support documents only to mechanics. That enhanced personalization eliminates the chance that information is sent to the wrong dealership or to the wrong individual, which provides higher quality customer service. The content management software also enables nontechnical employees to create pages using predefined layout templates, simplifying the Web publishing process. More than 500 people use the solution daily, and all employees are able to publish information without calling on IT specialists, while maintaining the look and feel of the BMW brand.[13]

FIGURE 8.6

Common Types of Content Management Systems

Common Types of Content Management Systems	
Document management system (DMS)	DMS—Supports the electronic capturing, storage, distribution, archiving, and accessing of documents. A DMS optimizes the use of documents within an organization independent of any publishing medium (for example, the Web). A DMS provides a document repository with information about other information. The system tracks the editorial history of each document and its relationships with other documents. A variety of search and navigation methods are available to make document retrieval easy. A DMS manages highly structured and regulated content, such as pharmaceutical documentation.
Digital asset management system (DAM)	DAM—Though similar to document management, DAM generally works with binary rather than text files, such as multimedia file types. DAM places emphasis on allowing file manipulation and conversion, for example, converting GIF files to JPEG.
Web content management system (WCM)	WCM—Adds an additional layer to document and digital asset management that enables publishing content both to intranets and to public Web sites. In addition to maintaining the content itself, WCM systems often integrate content with online processes like e-business systems.

FIGURE 8.7

Major Content Management
Systems Vendors

Vendors	Strengths	Weaknesses
Documentum www.documentum.com	Document and digital asset management	Personalization features not as strong as competitors
FatWire www.fatwire.com	Web content management	May not scale to support thousands of users
InterWoven www.interwoven.com	Collaboration, enterprise content management	Requires significant customization
Percussion www.percussion.com	Web content management	May not scale to support thousands of users
Stellent www.stellent.com	Document conversion to Web-ready formats	Engineering for very large implementations with thousands of users
Vignette www.vignette.com	Personalization	Document management and library services are not as robust as others

WORKFLOW MANAGEMENT SYSTEMS

A *workflow* defines all the steps or business rules, from beginning to end, required for a business process. Therefore, *workflow management systems* facilitate the automation and management of business processes and control the movement of work through the business process. Work activities can be performed in series or in parallel and involve people and automated computer systems. In addition, many workflow management systems allow the opportunity to measure and analyze the execution of the process because workflow systems allow the flow of work between individuals and/or departments to be defined and tracked. Workflow software helps automate a range of business tasks and electronically route the right information to the right people at the right time. Users are notified of pending work, and managers can observe status and route approvals through the system quickly.

There are two primary types of workflow systems: messaging-based and database-based. *Messaging-based workflow systems* send work assignments through an e-mail system. The workflow system automatically tracks the order for the work to be assigned and, each time a step is completed, the system automatically sends the work to the next individual in line. For example, each time a team member completes a piece of the project, the system would automatically send the document to the next team member.

Database-based workflow systems store documents in a central location and automatically ask the team members to access the document when it is their turn to edit the document. Project documentation is stored in a central location and team members are notified by the system when it is their turn to log in and work on their portion of the project.

Either type of workflow system helps to present information in a unified format, improves teamwork by providing automated process support, and allows team members to communicate and collaborate within a unified environment. Figure 8.8 lists some typical features associated with workflow management systems.

New York City was experiencing a record number of claims, ranging from injuries resulting from slips on sidewalks to medical malpractice at city hospitals. The city processes over 30,000 claims and incurs $280 million in claim costs annually. Claims are generally filed with the Comptroller's Office, which investigates them and offers to settle meritorious claims. The New York City Comptroller's Office,

FIGURE 8.8

Workflow Management
Systems Features

Workflow Feature	Description
Process definition tool	A graphical or textual tool for defining a business process. Each activity within the process is associated with a person or a computer application. Rules are created to determine how the activities progress across the workflow and which controls are in place to govern each activity.
Simulation, prototyping, and piloting	Some systems allow workflow simulation or create prototype and/or pilot versions of a particular workflow to test systems on a limited basis before going into production.
Task initiation and control	The business process defined above is initiated and the appropriate resources (either human and/or IT related) are scheduled and/or engaged to complete each activity as the process progresses.
Rules-based decision making	Rules are created for each step to determine how workflow-related information is to be processed, routed, tracked, and controlled. As an example, one rule might generate e-mail notifications when a condition has been met. Another rule might implement conditional routing of documents and tasks based on the content of fields.
Document routing	In simple systems, this is accomplished by passing a file or folder from one recipient to another (e.g., an e-mail attachment). In sophisticated systems, document routing is completed by checking the documents in and out of a central repository. Both systems might allow for "redlining" of the documents so that each person in the process can add their own comments without affecting the original document.
Applications to view and manipulate information	Word-processors, spreadsheets, and production systems are used to allow workers to create, update, and view information.
Work list	Current tasks are quickly identified along with such things as a due date, goal date, and priority by using work lists. In some systems, an anticipated workload is displayed as well. These systems analyze where jobs are in the workflow and how long each step should take, and then estimate when various tasks will reach a worker's desk.
Task automation	Computerized tasks are automatically invoked. These might include such things as letter writing, e-mail notices, or execution of production systems. Task automation often requires customization of the basic workflow product.
Event notification	Employees can be notified when certain milestones occur or when workload increases.
Process monitoring	The workflow system can provide an organization with valuable information on current workload, future workload, bottlenecks (current or potential), turn-around time, or missed deadlines.
Tracking and logging of activities	Information about each step can be logged. This might include such things as start and completion times, worker(s) assigned to the task, and key status fields. Later, this information can be used to analyze the process or to provide evidence that certain tasks were in fact completed.

with the assistance of its consultants Xerox and Universal Systems Inc., utilized a workflow management system to enhance revenues and decrease operating costs. With the implementation of the Omnibus Automated Image Storage Information System (OAISIS) for processing contracts and claims, New York City will save over $22 million.

Numerous city organizations were involved in the workflow management system, including Bureau of Law and Adjustment, Office of Contracts/Administration, Management and Accounting Systems, and Bureau of Information Systems.

In supporting all these New York City organizations, the system performs many functions that were previously labour-intensive and detracted from the quality and efficiency of investigations. The workflow management system screens claims to determine accordance with statutory requirements. Acknowledgment letters are generated automatically, with little or no resource allocation involved in assignment of claims or routing of claims to specific work locations. Status letters are automatically generated by the system for certain claim types, thus allowing the Comptroller's Office to keep claimants informed two months, five months, and one year from the date of their filing. All this is done automatically by the workflow management system.

Workflow management systems allow management to schedule individual systematic claim reviews without disrupting the investigation. Management can also see the entire claim process graphically and determine bottlenecks. Deployment of additional resources to needed areas occurs without a management analysis of a particular process problem.

GROUPWARE SYSTEMS

Groupware is software that supports team interaction and dynamics including calendaring, scheduling, and videoconferencing. Organizations can use this technology to communicate, cooperate, coordinate, solve problems, compete, or negotiate. While traditional technologies like the telephone qualify as groupware, the term refers to a specific class of technologies relying on modern computer networks, such as e-mail, newsgroups, videophones, and chat rooms. Groupware systems fall along two primary categories (see Figure 8.9):

1. Users of the groupware are working together at the same time (real-time or synchronous groupware) or different times (asynchronous groupware).

2. Users are working together in the same place (co-located or face-to-face) or in different places (non-co-located or distance).

The groupware concept integrates various systems and functionalities into a common set of services or a single (client) application. In addition, groupware can represent a wide range of systems and methods of integration. Figure 8.10 displays the advantages groupware systems offer an organization over single-user systems.

Lotus Notes is one of the world's leading software solutions for collaboration that combines messaging, groupware, and the Internet. The structure of Notes allows it to track, route, and manage documents. Systems that lend themselves to Notes involve tracking, routing, approval, document management, and organization.

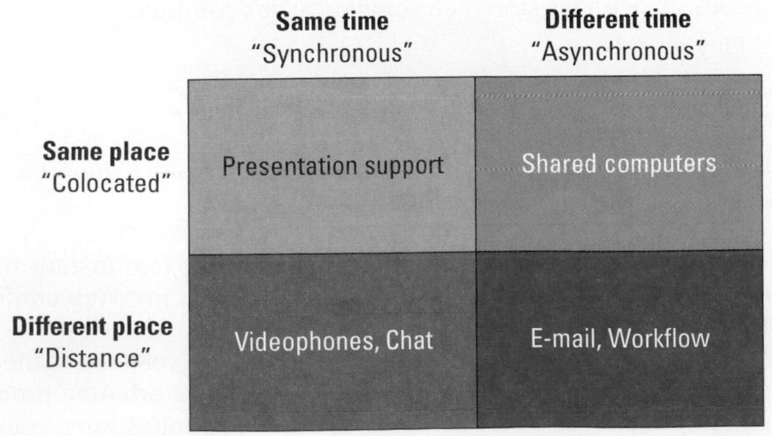

FIGURE 8.9

Groupware Systems

	Same time "Synchronous"	Different time "Asynchronous"
Same place "Colocated"	Presentation support	Shared computers
Different place "Distance"	Videophones, Chat	E-mail, Workflow

FIGURE 8.10

Groupware Advantages

Groupware System Advantages
Facilitating communication (faster, easier, clearer, more persuasive)
Enabling telecommuting
Reducing travel costs
Sharing expertise
Forming groups with common interests where it would not be possible to gather a sufficient number of people face-to-face
Saving time and cost in coordinating group work
Facilitating group problem solving

Toyota developed an intranet system to promote information sharing within the company and to raise productivity. Unfortunately, the company's conventional e-mail system became overloaded, generating problems. Users did not receive incoming messages and were not able to send messages. Individual departments had introduced their own e-mail systems, which were not always compatible. Messages to other mail systems, including those outside the company, experienced delays. To deal with these difficulties, Toyota's information systems department reviewed the e-mail system and restructured it so that e-mail, now recognized as an important communication tool, is utilized more effectively in business transactions.[14]

OTHER ENTERPRISE PORTAL TOOLS

A variety of other tools are embedded in enterprise portals to help improve collaboration among groups as well as individual organizational workers. E-mail is by far the dominant collaboration application, but real-time collaboration tools like instant messaging are creating a new communication dynamic within organizations. *Instant messaging* (sometimes called *IM* or *IMing*) is a type of communications service that enables someone to create a kind of private chat room with another individual in order to communicate in real-time over the Internet. In 1992, AOL deployed IM to the consumer market, allowing users to communicate with other IMers through a buddy list. Most of the popular instant messaging programs provide a variety of features, such as:

- Web links: Share links to favourite Web sites.
- Images: Look at an image stored on someone else's computer.
- Sounds: Play sounds.
- Files: Share files by sending them directly to another IMer.
- Talk: Use the Internet instead of a phone to talk.
- Streaming content: Receive real-time or near-real-time stock quotes and news.
- Instant messages: Receive immediate text messages.

Commercial vendors such as AOL and Microsoft offer free instant messaging tools. Real-time collaboration, such as instant messaging, live Web conferencing, and screen or document sharing, creates an environment for decision making. AOL, Microsoft's MSN, and Yahoo! have begun to sell enterprise versions of their instant messaging services that match the capabilities of business-oriented products like IBM's Lotus Sametime. Figure 8.11 demonstrates the IM application presence within IT systems.

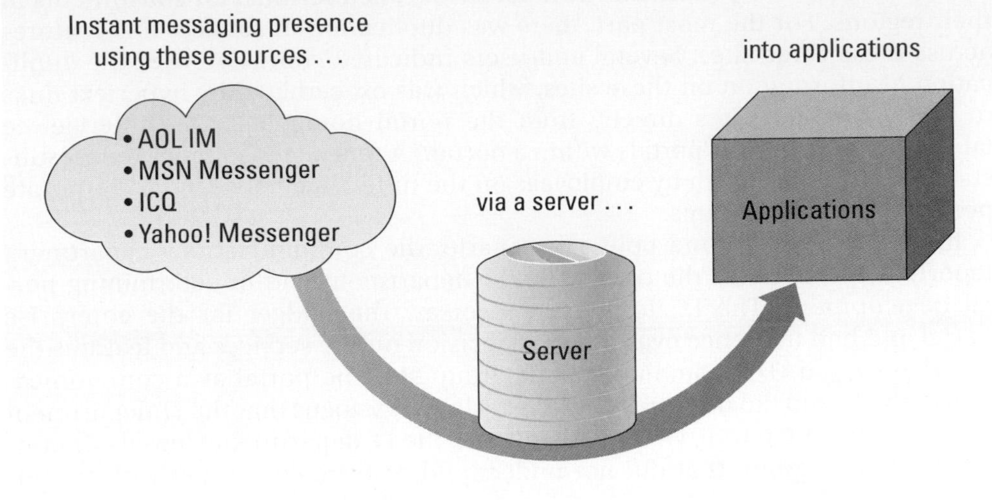

FIGURE 8.11

Instant Messaging
Application

Instant messaging presence
using these sources . . .

into applications

- AOL IM
- MSN Messenger
- ICQ
- Yahoo! Messenger

via a server . . .

Applications

Server

IBM Lotus software has released new versions of its real-time collaboration platform, IBM Lotus Instant Messaging and IBM Lotus Web Conferencing, plus its mobile counterpart, IBM Lotus Instant Messaging Everyplace. These built-for-business products let an organization offer presence awareness, secure instant messaging, and Web conferencing. The products give employees instant access to colleagues and company information regardless of time, place, or device.

The bigger issue in collaboration for organizations is cultural. Collaboration brings teams of people together from different regions, departments, and even companies—people who bring different skills, perceptions, and capabilities. A formal collaboration strategy helps create the right environment as well as the right systems for team members.

FACTORS AFFECTING ENTERPRISE PORTAL ADOPTION AND USE

Though enterprise portals offer organizations the potential for improved knowledge work and collaboration, in one case study of the adoption and use of an enterprise portal at a large Canadian company, several broad factors were identified that impact the degree to which an enterprise portal would be potentially used. Surprisingly, none of the major factors were technical in nature. The major factors were:

1. The *information politics* surrounding the design and development of the portal.
2. The *system development process* by which the portal was maintained.
3. The *information culture* of the organization.[15]

With respect to **information politics**, there were two broad political struggles over ownership of the information posted and available on the enterprise portal. The first was among three internal communications groups within the company over management of information content on the portal. The second was between communications and the IT division, which controlled the financial purse strings of the portal's development.

In terms of the first political scenario, the three internal groups comprised two regional communications groups (Ontario and Quebec) each responsible for product-oriented communications within their respective regions, and one enterprise-wide group (Ottawa), which primarily concerned itself with the communication of corporate strategies to company shareholders and stakeholders. Of the three groups, Ontario was responsible for administering the information content on the company portal. However, since the portal serviced communications across the enterprise, the other two groups had an interest in the management of the portal content as well. In addition, both Ontario and Quebec serviced separate departmental intranet sites (called forums) for constituents in their regions. For the most part, there was duplication of services and features across these three sites. Several end-users indicated confusion over the duplication of information on these sites, which was exacerbated by hypertext links to the two forum sites directly from the portal homepage. One interviewee labelled the forums as "portals within a portal." A recent consultant's report substantiated the confusion by employees on the difference between the corporate portal and the two forums.

In terms of the second political scenario, the communications department reported concern over the control the IT department had in determining portal development. The IT department oversaw the budget for the enterprise portal and had influence over the final decision on the services and features the portal provided. The communications group saw the portal as a communications vehicle and did not agree with the technology-focus that the IT department promoted for the portal. On the other hand, the IT department viewed communications as a group that did not understand or were concerned with technical constraints and limitations, such as bandwidth and system response time, in designing a corporate portal. According to one informant from IT, communications envisioned "everything being on the portal" without thinking through the technical feasibility of providing such a solution. Admittedly, this informant agreed that IT was the real owner of the portal since the group controlled the portal's purse-strings and discussed the influence IT had over the portal design as a result.

With respect to the *systems development process*, there were various procedures for making portal enhancements. For minor content changes, the communications department accessed a content management system that allowed them to publish news items, post pictures, and conduct surveys through this tool. However, for content that could not be modified directly by the tool, Communications called the customer service help desk, filed a trouble ticket, and waited for the appropriate people from a third-party systems solution provider to make the content change. This sometimes took an extraordinary amount of time.

Suggestions for enhancements to the portal's features and functions were gathered and prioritized by the communications department on a continuous basis. Employees could send their suggestions through a feedback option at the bottom of every portal Web page. Deemed changes were costed out by a third-party systems solution provider and brokered by IT. In this capacity, IT functioned as an intermediary between the organization and the solution provider. However, not all employee suggestions were addressed, causing dissatisfaction among users who took the time to submit ideas for portal enhancements. To make matters worse, a policy existed that promised new versions of the portal were to be released every 60 days. This put artificial time pressure on system designers and caused the release of new versions of the portal that had little modification—only a few new features were added in the end and much of it was a re-packaging of the old portal.

Other system development process factors influenced the design of the portal. Three identified in the case study were time, cost, and available personnel. For example, the portal content team in communications consisted of only three full-time equivalents, making this a constraint towards addressing changes to the portal requested by employees in a timely fashion.

With respect to *information culture*, five sub-factors were identified as being significant in impacting the adoption and use of the enterprise portal:

1. Information sharing.
2. Information overload.
3. Information access.
4. Information control.
5. Attitudes towards using the portal.

In terms of *information sharing*, most users indicated a general ease of sharing documents, plans, and reports between colleagues and project team members with whom they worked. Trust seemed to be a predominant factor in determining whether information was shared or not.

Less sharing occurred among employees when it involved people with whom they were unfamiliar or when there was a fear of protecting one's domain or job security. In terms of the impact on the portal, most people who were willing to share documents and ideas via this type of medium were more likely to do so if there was a facility that restricted access to shared documents to pre-defined individuals only. Some users indicated an unwillingness to contribute documents and ideas to a public space for fear that there may be unexpected disciplinary actions. Users commented on the need for the environment to support sharing in terms of both a physical means to do so and a context free of repercussions and critical judgments.

With respect to *information overload*, many users voiced their frustration in trying to search for information within the portal. Typically, employees indicated that the portal search engine returned hit list items that were not relevant, or the list of items was too long to peruse in an efficient and timely manner.

In terms of *information access*, the corporation had a strong desire to make the enterprise portal the primary vehicle for information distribution and function as a gateway to the thousands of departmental Web sites. In fact, the stated goal of the portal was "to provide [the] internal employee population with a centralized online source for news information and applications that help them do their jobs." Though this was the planned goal, in reality not everyone in the organization had access to the portal. For example, many field workers had no access to a computer at all; those that did often utilized older technology that restricted them from accessing the current version of the enterprise portal.

With respect to *information control*, standardization of information seemed to be a predominant theme. Both the IT and communications groups indicated that they wanted to rationalize the enterprise portal, though from different perspectives. For instance, IT wanted to standardize the portal's technological design (e.g., the use of standard-approved Web page development tools, the inclusion of standard buttons on departmental Web sites back to the portal home page). Communications, with its emphasis on creating an internal company presence within the company, wanted to standardize the portal's look and feel (e.g., the use of corporate colours, standard fonts, and the placement of the company logo at the top of departmental Web sites' main pages) as well as the content posted on the portal (i.e., the group currently edits and standardizes the wording of content written by others in the organization before it is posted on the portal). Both groups indicated a need to standardize the company's "undernets"—ad hoc departmental Web sites developed by employees that were not formally registered with the portal and did not usually follow standard Web development guidelines. There was mixed reaction from users on the control over Web site design. Some employees saw the necessity of setting standards; however, several users were vocal in their opposition to the company's control over Web design.

In terms of *attitudes towards using the portal*, analysis of the case study data hinted at the changing nature and perception of the use of the portal among employees. One end-user noticed the oscillation of acceptance and use of portal-based information and commented on its back and forward nature. She also commented that employees with longer experience in the company were less accepting of Web-based information sources. Many employees were unaware of the features and functions available in the portal and hence had a poor image of how the portal could help them in their work and were less likely to utilize the portal in their day-to-day work.

Figure 8.12 summarizes the lessons learned from this case study of the factors affecting the adoption and use of a company's enterprise portal.

Insights into the challenges facing the implementation of enterprise portals in organizations can be derived from the field of *Computer Supported Cooperative Work (CSCW)*. CSCW refers to a field of research concerned with the development

FIGURE 8.12

Lessons from a Case Study
on the Adoption and Use of
an Enterprise Portal

Lesson	Description
Lesson #1	In terms of **information politics**, the human struggle over an enterprise portal's content and functionality can lead to resultant designs that favour certain stakeholder groups rather than address end-user needs.
Lesson #2	In terms of the **system development process**, a perceived slowness in changes to an enterprise portal's design or information content can lead to user dissatisfaction.
	In terms of **information culture**, there are several lessons to be learned:
Lesson #3A	■ With respect to **information sharing**, the provision of protected, secure areas in an enterprise portal to pre-defined individuals or groups can lead to greater exchange of documents and ideas.
Lesson #3B	■ With respect to **information overload**, the filtering of information within an enterprise portal can lead to greater user acceptance of the system.
Lesson #3C	■ With respect to **information access**, providing quick and universal access to an enterprise portal can lead to heightened usage.
Lesson #3D	■ With respect to **information control**, offering a means to tailor the display and presentation of information on an enterprise portal can increase user satisfaction with the system.
Lesson #3E	■ With respect to **attitude towards using an enterprise portal**, a positive perception towards and awareness of an enterprise portal's functionality can lead to greater user adoption.

and use of software to help groups increase their competency in working together. Since the mid-1980s, CSCW researchers have explored various ways in which organizational structure and culture affect the adoption and use of groupware, and how groupware, in turn, influences the organizational context itself.

According to CSCW researchers, some of the more pertinent reasons why groupware fails are that:

- they require some people to do additional work who often are not the ones who perceive a direct benefit from use of the groupware application,
- they call for a critical mass of users to adopt the system,
- they lead to activity that may disrupt social processes, and
- they are hampered by poor developer intuition on multi-user needs.

With any enterprise-wide information system that supports collaboration and communication across groups, there is difficulty in getting people to trust the system, share information with others, and be held accountable in their electronic communications to a larger community. Several CSCW researchers caution that social and cultural factors may inhibit the adoption and use of groupware in organizations more so than technological factors.

Figure 8.13 provides insights from the CSCW field on how to minimize the challenges facing the implementation of enterprise portal applications in organizations.[16]

Insight	Description
Ensure that everyone benefits	Groupware that only satisfies the information needs of a subset of employees is detrimental to the overall adoption and use of the system. To be successful, groupware requires a critical mass of users. Enterprise portals should follow suit and provide sufficient information resources and functions that address the needs and uses of a broad cross-section of employees.
Create incentives for use	Though it would be nice, users will not flock to an enterprise portal simply because they should, or because it is there to use. Employees need encouragement. First, they need to be educated on the benefits of utilizing an enterprise portal and trained on how to use it. Ideally, this should be done on a continual basis, and not just once during portal launch. In addition, employees need rewards to encourage use of the system. Incentives are key to promoting groupware adoption and use. Collaboration and information sharing are not natural ways for people to work, especially in competitive organizational cultures that emphasize and reward individual contributions through job advancements, cash incentives, and other such perks. People have a tendency to hoard information and keep knowledge to themselves. Posting one's ideas for posterity on an enterprise portal and risking potential criticism by everyone in the firm is a deterrent to sharing one's knowledge. To combat this natural tendency takes some effort. Employee incentives can help in this regard.
Promote multiple perspectives	Much of the CSCW literature reports on the demise of groupware system use when management curtails open discourse and dialogue. Organizations can benefit from groupware technology when the company is accepting of the ideas of collaboration and group sharing. This means not only tolerating, but rather promoting, electronic interactions in groupware that induce people to talk more frankly and equally. Management should not adopt a critical and punitive attitude towards open dialogue.
Understand current work practice	Any new form of groupware will change the way work gets done. For instance, the introduction of an enterprise portal could significantly change patterns of information sharing through the increased exchange of formal and informal information across the enterprise. In the past, such communication was often restricted by physical proximity and social acquaintance. To handle such change, organizations need to anticipate how an enterprise portal, or new functionality available in the portal, will be received in the workplace prior to implementation. This can be done by understanding current work practice and social interaction, and using these insights to build features and functions in portal design that minimize disruption in social processes, such as violations of social taboos, threats against existing political structures, or de-motivations to crucial users.

OPENING CASE QUESTIONS

Leveraging Knowledge at Bell Canada

6. Is the MKC portal an enterprise portal? Explain why or why not.

7. What features or functions could be added to the MKC portal to improve its potential as an enterprise portal?

8. Assume Bell Canada has an enterprise portal (let's call it Bellnet) that is independent of the MKC portal. In this sense, the MKC portal would be a sub-portal of Bellnet. What are the advantages of setting things up this way? The disadvantages?

9. Using the lessons and insights listed in Figures 8.12 and 8.13 as a guide, what advice would you give Bell Canada to promote the avid use of the MKC portal?

SUMMARY OF KEY THEMES

This chapter discussed various ways that information technology can help organizations access, share, and use information. The chapter described how organizations can leverage information technology to give employees:

- better access to the information they need,

- improved ways of sharing that information with each other, and

- a heightened means of turning information into knowledge.

This chapter also stressed that information comes in many different shapes and sizes:

- It can be structured information found in databases.

- It can be unstructured information found in documents and memos—in paper or electronic form.

- It can be thoughts and ideas that employees possess.

Though trying to leverage such a wide range of complex information sources can be challenging and difficult, there is a real pay-off for organizations that do:

- When employees are armed with the right information at the right time, they become empowered to turn that information into "action" by delivering innovations, forging best practices, and developing new products and services for the company.

  As a business student, you need to know this, since you will soon be working in organizations yourself. If you recognize the importance of facilitating information access, promoting information sharing, and encouraging information use in a company (especially with the help of information technologies), you will be better prepared to help your organization work collaboratively together and promote knowledge generation, sharing, and use across the enterprise.

KEY TERMS

Attitudes towards using
  the portal 245
Business portals 235
Collaboration
  system 229
Communication
  space 237
Computer supported
  cooperative work
  (CSCW) 245
Content management
  system 238
Content space 237
Coordination space 237
Core competency 228
Core competency
  strategy 229
Corporate portals 235
Database-based
  workflow system 239

Digital asset management
  system (DAM) 238
Document management
  system (DMS) 238
Enterprise portal 235
Explicit knowledge 232
Groupware 241
Information access 245
Information control 245
Information culture 244
Information overload 245
Information
  partnership 229
Information politics 243
Information sharing 245
Instant messaging
  (IM, IMing) 242
Knowledge management
  (KM) 231

Knowledge management
  system (KMS) 232
Messaging-based workflow
  system 239
Social networking analysis
  (SNA) 234
Structured collaboration
  (process collaboration) 230
Systems development
  process 244
Tacit knowledge 232
Unstructured
  collaboration (information
  collaboration) 230
Web content management
  system (WCM) 238
Workflow 239
Workflow management
  system 239

DreamWorks Animation Collaboration

This case showcases the use of collaboration software in an organization.

Hewlett-Packard (HP) and DreamWorks Animation SKG were the first to introduce a collaboration studio for simulating face-to-face business meetings across long distances. Vyomesh Joshi, executive vice president at HP, and Jeffrey Katzenberg, CEO of DreamWorks, officially unveiled the HP Halo Collaboration Studio in New York City in 2005. Halo enables people in different locations to communicate in a vivid, face-to-face environment in real time. Whether across a country or across the ocean, users can see and hear one another's physical and emotional reactions to conversation and information.

By giving participants the remarkable sense that they are in the same room, the Halo Collaboration Studio is already transforming the way businesses such as PepsiCo, Advanced Micro Devices, and DreamWorks communicate across the globe. Halo significantly increases team effectiveness, provides faster decision-making capabilities, and decreases the need for travel.

"The HP Halo Collaboration Studio enables remote teams to work together in a setting so lifelike that participants feel as though they are in the same room," Joshi said. "To create this experience, HP is harnessing its expertise in colour science, imaging, and networking in this new category of innovation. It is something we believe will not only disrupt the traditional videoconferencing market, but will also change the way people work in a global market."

Early in the production of the animated film *Shrek 2,* DreamWorks realized a significant return on investment using the Halo technology. By connecting its California teams in Glendale and Redwood City, DreamWorks was able to speed up many aspects of the production.

"In 2002, while we were producing *Shrek 2*, we realized that DreamWorks needed face-to-face collaboration between key creative talent in different locations," Katzenberg said. "We weren't satisfied with the available videoconferencing systems, so we designed a collaboration solution that would fulfill our needs. HP took the system and turned it into Halo, which is now the only solution on the market that allows this kind of effective communication."

Halo Connection

To connect via Halo, organizations purchase at least two Halo rooms set up for six people each. Three plasma displays in each room enable participants to see those they are collaborating with in life-size images. The rooms come equipped with studio-quality audio and lighting, and participants use a simple on-screen user interface to begin collaborating with just a few mouse clicks.

An intricate software control system ensures Halo rooms work easily and seamlessly together. The control system also provides precise image and colour calibration, so participants see each other as they appear in real life. A dedicated HP Halo Video Exchange Network provides a high-bandwidth experience with imperceptible delays between Halo studios worldwide.

To ensure a 24/7 connection and eliminate the need for enterprises to manage the operation and maintenance of a Halo room, services offered include network operations and management, remote diagnostics and calibration, concierge, equipment warranty, and ongoing service and repair.

Participants can easily share documents and data directly from their notebook PCs with individuals in other rooms using a collaboration screen mounted above the plasma displays. The rooms also contain a high-magnification camera that enables individuals to zoom in on objects on a table, revealing the finest of details and colour shading, and a phone that opens a conference call line to those not in one of the Halo rooms.

"We believe there is a personal connection that comes with Halo that just clearly doesn't come from any other kind of technology we've used in the past," said Steve Reinemund, CEO of PepsiCo. "Halo is one of the best investments we've made to improve the effectiveness of our business and work/life balance for our people."[17]

Questions

1. How can companies use Halo to increase their business efficiency?
2. Explain how a company like PepsiCo can use Halo to gain a competitive advantage in its industry.
3. How can knowledge management be increased by using a product such as Halo?
4. Why would a company like DreamWorks, that is not IT focused, be interested in collaboration technology?
5. What are a few of the security issues surrounding this type of technology?

CLOSING CASE TWO

Enterprise Content Management at Statoil

This case illustrates the use and benefits of utilizing a content management system in an organization.

Statoil is the world's third largest exporter of crude oil and a substantial supplier of natural gas to the European market. The company has approximately 25,500 employees in locations scattered over 34 countries. Based in Norway, Statoil is the leading operator on the Norwegian continental shelf and experiencing strong growth in international production.[18]

Since 2002, the company has adopted an e-collaboration strategy. The goal of the strategy is to create a corporate "knowledge reservoir" that provides global access to a common pool of digital assets and is used to support work processes and share information between Statoil and its customers, employees, and business partners.

Access to this knowledge reservoir is provided through an information portal and controlled through the assignment of end-user roles. For instance, a customer would have much more limited access to information housed in the knowledge reservoir than a Statoil employee would.

The need for this strategy arose from the information overload that burdened the company. Typical for many decentralized organizations, Statoil's information was scattered across a number of different storage media and applications. The total number of databases in 2002 exceeded 5,500.

The core foundation of the knowledge reservoir is content management. This involves the ability to support a content lifecycle in the company that effectively deals with the capture, transformation, storage, security, distribution, retrieval, and eventual destruction of documents. Though Statoil is making great gains in facilitating such content management practices, it is also facing some challenges in getting there.

The largest problem is how content is currently maintained throughout the company. There are literally thousands of heterogeneous content databases involving stand-alone intranet and extranet applications and over 800 databases containing archived documents. Though technically all these are accessible across the enterprise, logically people are unaware of the availability of documents residing in those shared content areas, and hence, much of the material never gets loaded into a centralized, shared content management system. Having so much content resident outside of a shared, centralized content management system has negative implications on archiving, version management, publication, and workflow.

Another difficulty is that people still tend to use personal e-mail folders to manage document attachments, rather than post documents once in a central location for others to use. E-mailing attachments causes network congestion and chews up precious file storage space. If stored centrally, a document is stored just once and people can simply reference the document there if needed.

Another challenge is that the storage of files in their original production format makes retrieval of these items difficult after a few years. This is because content management system technologies change and the format of these production files do not. On the flip-side, updating the format to be compatible with content management system technologies may make these files unusable for retrieval by the original application that produced them. The best solution would be to store content in application-independent formats.

Difficulties also stem from the lack of embedded routines that could potentially delete unwanted information stored across production or archiving systems. This results in the redundant storage of information and the over-accumulation of content. To clean up content, Statoil has to issue "campaigns" to encourage employees to delete unnecessary information.

Another challenge pertains to search. There is no single integrated search facility that can retrieve documents across the thousands of other heterogeneous content-based systems. This largely is a result of different business units utilizing different taxonomies to classify their content and storing their content in different physical structures. Hence, information retrieval across business units is problematic, despite best intentions of the company.

Though these challenges are obstacles to the effective management of corporate content, Statoil is making great strides in overcoming them. To date, the e-collaboration strategy has yielded several successes for the company, including:

- a basic content management solution,
- automatic archiving,
- long-term storage of content with separate data indices,
- automatic security levels of information based on metadata,
- integration of existing standard office tools,
- a corporate yellow pages,
- one common portal framework,
- training services for the content management solution,
- implementation of content management guidelines for use by third-party solution providers (i.e., for working on projects with partners), and
- the establishment of required e-learning modules for employees.

In this sense, Statoil is doing well in creating and managing information content, regardless of whether it is sourced internally within the organization or externally from information suppliers, and in automating the content lifecycle, from creation to archival, with information delivered to the recipient independent of time, place, or media.[19]

Questions

1. Why do you think content management is such a critical part of Statoil's strategy?
2. Comment on the utility and importance of Statoil's use of an information portal to promote enterprise-wide content management?
3. To what extent do you think Statoil's predicament of information overload is typical for organizations in Canada?
4. What lessons learned and insights from the chapter's discussion on the factors affecting the adoption and use of enterprise portal could help promote Statoil's adoption and use of its content management initiative?

Saving Costs at Costco

This case showcases the benefits of utilizing a document management system.

For Costco Wholesale to provide quality, brand-name merchandise at substantially lower prices, it must communicate quickly and effectively with thousands of vendors. The company cannot afford slow response times when accessing purchase orders, debit memos, or invoices; unsatisfactory image quality; or indirect access to transaction documents. Costco began the search for a technology that could handle its growing volume of paper, microfilm, and microfiche. The company processes 30,000 documents per day and has more than 75 million documents scanned in total.

Costco chose Stellent Imaging and Business Process Management because of its open architecture, competitive price, and multiple features, which provided a rapid return on investment. Costco worked with ImageSource, Inc., a Stellent solution provider, on design and implementation.

With Stellent, Costco processes about 6.7 million documents per year. Imaged documents can be accessed in seconds. Costco also gained easy storage and quick retrieval of information and integration of workflow processes with computer data. Faster payment processing and easier transaction storage and retrieval improved service to warehouse, depot, and vendor customers. Faster document retrieval times and quicker problem resolution led to increased vendor satisfaction. Costco recouped the cost of the Stellent solution in just 11 months of operation and saved $8 million in labour and payment term discounts. Today, 750 of Costco's 2,000 corporate office employees use the Stellent system including:

- The accounts payable group accesses invoices related to expense and merchandise functions.
- The accounting department scans and stores capital expenditure and fixed asset documents, which can be accessed by the facilities department.
- Costco's legal department uses Stellent to process and store vendor maintenance and setup agreements and other documents.
- The tax department improved its audit process now that it can randomly review a sampling of historical transaction documents.
- Regional offices can also quickly access vendor invoices and rebate documents via a Web browser.[20]

Questions

1. Identify content management and document management and explain how Costco is using them to improve business operations.
2. Provide an example of a few of the documents that Costco must maintain electronically.
3. How might other Costco departments benefit from a document management system?
4. The Stellent Imaging and Business Process Management solution allowed Costco to grow as a company without increasing expenses. Identify another business that could benefit from the Stellent Imaging and Business Process Management solution.

MAKING BUSINESS DECISIONS

1. Collaboration on intranets

MyIntranet.com is a worldwide leader providing online intranet solutions. The MyIntranet.com online collaboration tool is a solution for small businesses and groups inside larger organizations that need to organize information, share files and documents, coordinate calendars, and enable efficient collaboration, all in a secure, browser-based environment. MyIntranet.com has just added conferencing and group scheduling features to its suite of hosted collaboration software. Explain why infrastructure integration is critical to the suite of applications to function within this environment.

2. Gaining efficiency with collaboration

During the past year, you have been working for a manufacturing firm to help improve its supply chain management by implementing enterprise resource planning and supply chain management systems. For efficiency gains, you are recommending that the manufacturing firm should be turning toward collaborative systems. The firm has a need to share intelligent plans and forecasts with supply chain partners, reduce inventory levels, improve working capital, and reduce manufacturing changeovers. Given the technologies presented to you in this unit, what type of system(s) would you recommend to facilitate your firm's future needs?

9

CHAPTER

Information Ethics, Information Privacy, and Information Security

LEARNING OUTCOMES

9.1. Summarize the guidelines for creating an information privacy policy.

9.2. Identify the differences between an ethical computer use policy and an acceptable use policy.

9.3. Describe the relationship between an e-mail privacy policy and an Internet use policy.

9.4. Explain the effects of spam on an organization.

9.5. Summarize the different monitoring technologies.

9.6. Explain the importance of an employee monitoring policy.

9.7. Describe the relationship between information security policies and an information security plan.

9.8. Summarize the five steps to creating an information security plan.

9.9. Provide an example of each of the three primary information security areas: (1) authentication and authorization, (2) prevention and resistance, and (3) detection and response.

9.10. Describe the relationships and differences between hackers and viruses.

Why Do I Need To Know This **?**

This chapter concerns itself with protecting information from potential misuse. Organizations must ensure they collect, capture, store, and use information in an ethical manner. This could be any sort of information they collect and utilize, including information about customers, partners, and employees. Steps must be taken by companies to ensure that personal information collected about someone remains private. This is not just a nice thing to do. Canadian law requires it. And perhaps most importantly, information must be physically kept secure to prevent access and possible dissemination and use by unauthorized sources.

As a business student, you need to know this since privacy and security issues are the top concerns voiced by customers and consumers today. These concerns directly influence a consumer's likelihood to embrace electronic technologies and conduct business over the Web. In this sense, these concerns affect a company's bottom line. You don't have to look too far to find evidence in recent news reports about how the stock price of organizations dramatically falls when information privacy and security breaches are made known. Further, organizations face potential litigation if they fail to meet their ethical, privacy, and security obligations concerning the handling of information in their companies.

How information is accessed, protected, and utilized within organizations has become priority one today. As such, it is important that you, the business student, become cognizant of the issues surrounding the protection of information in organizations and an advocate of the proper treatment of information across the enterprise from ethical, privacy, and security perspectives.

Embracing Privacy at the City of Hamilton

Recognizing the real concerns of Canadians over how well governments handle and protect the personal information they collect, the City of Hamilton has taken the lead in ensuring that any risks to the inadvertent release and misuse of personal information are minimized. The goal is to limit the exposure of personal information collected by the City about individual constituents. The City recognizes that doing so is not only in the best interests of citizens, but also in the best interests of the City. For example, as a municipal corporation, Hamilton operates under the authority of the Ontario Municipal Act 2001, and as a municipal government, the City of Hamilton is subject to the Municipal Freedom of Information and Protection of Privacy Act (MFIPPA). By complying with such legislation, the City of Hamilton is able to meet its statutory obligations as a municipal organization.

The City of Hamilton has found that protecting citizen information is a challenging task. At no time was this more evident than in early 2006—less than five months after the launch of the myhamilton.ca portal—when an incident with the portal served to bring to the forefront new and ever emerging threats and risks in the areas of privacy and the protection of personal information. The myhamilton portal is an on-line gateway to community resources, general information, and government services that brings together numerous and diverse community organizations in the City of Hamilton. The incident concerned the accidental access to private information. A citizen, attempting to renew his/her dog licence using the new online service, exposed a serious unknown technology vulnerability in the application. By entering an incorrect file number, the user was able to return personal information (name and address) for a different dog owner in the community. Upon learning of the issue, municipal staff reacted swiftly in removing the problem functionality. In the following months, staff from both the municipal Freedom of Information (FOI) Office and the City's Information Technology Services (ITS) division worked with the Office of the Privacy Commissioner of Canada (OPC) to make public the breach and to redesign, and ultimately reinstate, new functionality with safeguards to prevent unauthorized access of personal information.

The greatest lesson learned from the dog-licence incident—and a message the City of Hamilton continues to deliver today—is that technology is just a tool. It is human behaviour (i.e., hacking, purposeful misuse, an inability to take proper measures or mistakes in design and implementation) that ultimately results in the realization of privacy breaches.

According to Shannon McKay, e-Government Coordinator for the City of Hamilton, this is why education and awareness is the key to getting it right and ensuring organizations minimize the risks associated with privacy threats and potential breaches. "Like any threat or risk, the better you plan for and anticipate risks, the more prepared you'll be. This means determining upfront and early on, if and how personal information will be collected, used, and/or disclosed in delivering a program or service."

Which is why, a little later that same year, the City of Hamilton commissioned its first ever Privacy Impact Assessment (PIA) to identify any potential privacy risks, before proceeding with a User Adoption and Uptake Research project being conducted by McMaster University researchers. The project investigated end-user adoption of the myhamilton.ca portal and involved the data collection of Web tracking information and personal demographic information from Hamiltonians who agreed to participate in the study. The PIA process was invaluable. In this case, the City needed to eliminate any and all risk related to the possibility of an individual's identity being discerned through unauthorized access to the research data. Ensuring a technical means to effectively separate participant data from any exposure to unwanted identification was something all agreed was not up for discussion nor debate. Adequately protecting participants and their personal information was non-negotiable.

In going through its first Privacy Impact Assessment, McKay worked closely with staff in the Freedom of Information Office, Legal Services and ITS, as well as the McMaster researchers, to undertake substantial measures to prevent the possibility of a privacy breach, while at the same time ensuring the purpose of the research project and the needs of the researchers could be met without putting the corporation at risk. These measures included hiring a consultant to re-program how the Web tracking data and questionnaire data were stored and coded in the project's databases. The data table structures had to be redesigned so that any identifiable personal information was not stored nor associated with any Web tracking or questionnaire data. This prevented any inadvertent linking of a participant's identity to his or her data. Other measures included setting up user privileges on the database tables to restrict access to the research data by City personnel.

According to McKay, "We've learned invaluable lessons having experienced what we did with the dog licence application and the research project PIA. As a result, we regularly share our experiences with others, internal to the City, as well as with fellow municipal colleagues. We work with staff in the corporation to not only make them aware of the risk and threats, but also to stress the importance of planning effectively. This includes assessing risk, ensuring safeguards, assigning accountability, taking action, and making due diligence provisions. Now, if even a simple Web form or online survey is requested, we have measures in place to ensure that the owner of this service has connected with the appropriate staff in our FOI office to make certain the fundamental principles of a PIA and potential privacy issues are understood and that the appropriate risk mitigation strategies have been adhered to."

The City of Hamilton's lessons learned and firsthand experience from both the dog-licence incident and the User Adoption and Uptake Study has served to heighten awareness of potential privacy issues in other areas of the portal, as well as in those areas of the corporation where there exists processes related to the provision of personal information that do no involve technology.

Today, as a result of regular and more effective communications, staff in ITS acknowledge that privacy protection is fast becoming a core consideration in all of its project planning and implementation. The next step is to work closely with senior management and staff in the various business units to develop the appropriate policies and processes, along with training and communication strategies.

The City of Hamilton is embracing privacy, not only as part of its mandate, but as a reality of everyday e-life. As such, the City serves as a good example for other governments to follow. Governments must be vigilant with respect to protecting citizen privacy. They need to be aware of the legal issues they face with respect to any potential privacy breach. They must also be proactive in their privacy planning, especially when designing and rolling out any new e-Government solution or making enhancements to existing ones.

INTRODUCTION

The ethical issues surrounding copyright infringement and intellectual property rights are consuming the e-business world. Advances in technology make it easier for people to copy everything from music to pictures. Technology poses new challenges for our *ethics*—the principles and standards that guide our behaviour toward other people. Review Figure 9.1 for an overview of concepts, terms, and ethical issues stemming from advances in technology.

Privacy is one of the largest issues facing organizations. **Privacy** is the right to be left alone when you want to be, to have control over your own personal possessions, and not to be observed without your consent. Privacy is related to **confidentiality**, which is the assurance that messages and information are available only to those who are authorized to view them. Some of the most problematic decisions facing organizations lie in the murky and turbulent waters of privacy. The burden comes from the knowledge that each time employees make a decision regarding issues of privacy, the outcome could potentially sink the company.

Trust between companies, customers, partners, and suppliers is the support structure of e-business. One of the main ingredients in trust is privacy. Privacy continues to be one of the primary barriers to the growth of e-business. People are concerned their privacy will be violated because of interactions on the Web. Unless an organization can effectively address this issue of privacy, its customers, partners, and suppliers might lose trust in the organization, which would hurt its business. Figure 9.2 displays the results from a *CIO* survey as to how privacy issues reduce trust for e-businesses.

FIGURE 9.1

Technology-Related
Ethical Issues

Intellectual property	Intangible creative work that is embodied in physical form.
Copyright	The legal protection afforded an expression of an idea, such as a song, video game, and some types of proprietary documents.
Fair use doctrine	In certain situations, it is legal to use copyrighted material.
Pirated software	The unauthorized use, duplication, distribution, or sale of copyrighted software.
Counterfeit software	Software that is manufactured to look like the real thing and sold as such.

FIGURE 9.2

How Privacy Can Reduce
Trust for E-Business

Primary Reasons Privacy Issues Reduce Trust for E-Business
1. Loss of personal privacy
2. 37 percent of Internet users are "a lot" more inclined to purchase a product on a Web site that has a privacy policy
3. Effective privacy would convert more Internet users to Internet buyers

INFORMATION ETHICS

Information ethics concerns the ethical and moral issues arising from the development and use of information technologies, as well as the creation, collection, duplication, distribution, and processing of information itself (with or without the aid of computer technologies).

Individuals determine how to use information and how information affects them. How individuals behave toward each other, how they handle information and technology, are largely influenced by their ethics. Ethical dilemmas usually arise not in simple, clear-cut situations but out of a clash between competing goals, responsibilities, and loyalties. Inevitably, the decision process has more than one socially acceptable "correct" decision. Figure 9.3 contains examples of ethically questionable or unacceptable uses of information technology.

People make arguments for or against—justify or condemn—the behaviours in Figure 9.3. Unfortunately, there are few hard and fast rules for always determining what is and is not ethical. Knowing the law will not always help because what is legal might not always be ethical, and what might be ethical is not always legal. Because technology is so new and pervasive in unexpected ways, the ethics surrounding information are still being defined. Figure 9.4 displays the four quadrants of ethical and legal behaviour. The ideal goal for organizations is to make decisions within quadrant I that are both legal and ethical.

Information Has No Ethics

Jerry Rode, CIO of Saab Cars USA, realized he had a public relations fiasco on his hands when he received an e-mail from an irate customer. Saab had hired four Internet marketing companies to distribute electronic information about Saab's new models to its customers. Saab specified that the marketing campaign be

Examples of Questionable Information Technology Use
Individuals copy, use, and distribute software.
Employees search organizational databases for sensitive corporate and personal information.
Organizations collect, buy, and use information without checking the validity or accuracy of the information.
Individuals create and spread viruses that cause trouble for those using and maintaining IT systems.
Individuals hack into computer systems to steal proprietary information.
Employees destroy or steal proprietary organization information such as schematics, sketches, customer lists, and reports.

FIGURE 9.3

Ethically Questionable or Unacceptable Information Technology Use

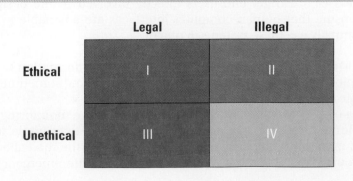

FIGURE 9.4

Acting Ethically and Legally Are Not Always the Same

opt-in, implying that it would contact only the people who had agreed to receive promotions and marketing material via e-mail. Unfortunately, one of the marketing companies apparently had a different definition of opt-in and was e-mailing all customers regardless of their opt-in decision.

Rode fired the errant marketing company and immediately developed a formal policy for the use of customer information. "The customer doesn't see ad agencies and contracted marketing firms. They see Saab USA spamming them," Rode said. "Finger-pointing after the fact won't make your customers feel better."[1]

Information has no ethics. Information does not care how it is used. It will not stop itself from spamming customers, sharing itself if it is sensitive or personal, or revealing details to third parties. Information cannot delete or preserve itself. Therefore, it falls on the shoulders of those who own the information to develop ethical guidelines on how to manage the information.

Information Ethics In The Workplace

The rampant introduction and use of information technology in the workplace has led to many ethical concerns for employers. For instance, information technology has reduced or eliminated some types of jobs; not everyone gets retrained when an information technology changes job roles. Though technology has eliminated numerous monotonous tasks and jobs in organizations, technology has also introduced brand new monotonous tasks too. You only have to visit any large organization's Account Receivables and Payables department to see row upon row of employees working in cubicles doing manual data entry into computer information systems, day in, day out, everyday. Not fun.

Systems That Don't Respect Human Dignity   Another ethical issue concerns the dehumanization of workers through the introduction of new technology. Sometimes, in the "wisdom" of information technology designers to build systems that maximize profit and reduce costs, new systems that are introduced into organizations make tasks too easy. Users are not challenged or they are forced not to think, causing workers to feel dehumanized. For example, "pickers' at a Canadian Tire Distribution Centre in Brampton, Ontario were given hand-held devices that instructed workers to pick up certain items in a certain order and to place those items into totes for loading onto trucks. The hand-held technology was so specific, it even told workers when to "turn right" or "turn left" in order to make optimal use of their time. Workers were annoyed and rejected the new technology as they found it depersonalizing and took away from them the elements of the job that made their work interesting.

Sometimes, information systems deployed in organizations are overly regimented and inflexible, causing employees to endure painful screen navigations or wait for long response times between transactions. Building information systems with poor interface designs creates an ethical issue for employers if they allow and condone the development of such systems on a regular basis.

Several things can be done to circumvent or mitigate these information technology-related ethical concerns. For example, systems designers can build information systems that respect worker intelligence and dignity. The systems design process can also get end-users directly involved in the design of these systems to ensure that human-computer interfaces are amenable to the people who will eventually use these systems in practice.

Employee Monitoring   Today, many employers use information technology to monitor employees. Sometimes this can be a good thing. And sometimes it can lead to severe ethical concerns.

Good uses of employee monitoring would be when the monitoring is required to get work done or to boost organizational productivity. For example, in the trucking industry, monitoring the location of truck drivers on the road allows dispatch officers to route deliveries more effectively, or to provide emergency road-side assistance to truck drivers when needed. In all types of organizations, managers need to track down the location of key personnel at certain times, so having monitoring technologies to identify the location of such employees would be beneficial to the organization. Monitoring technologies can also be used to keep unauthorized personnel out of restricted areas.

Ethical concerns over employee monitoring occurs when the monitoring is unprecedented or overly intrusive. In such circumstances, employee monitoring can be seen as violating workers' privacy and personal freedom. In the worst scenario, employees may not even know they are being monitored or how the information collected about them is being used. For example, is it being collected to build or support a case of employee termination? There are several ways companies can monitor employee behaviour. This can be done by monitoring employee e-mail and Web usage, or even through the use of Web-based security cameras deployed in the buildings where people work.

All this unethical monitoring has implications. Workers' stress levels rise dramatically. Many in the organization feel the inappropriate use of monitoring robs them of their dignity in the workplace.

So what can be done to prevent the unethical use of information technology to monitor employees? If the monitoring is not really necessary, then organizations should simply not monitor their employees. However, if it is, then let employees have some control over the monitoring activity. Perhaps they can disable it, or opt out all together. Perhaps give them the means to review the monitoring information collected about them to check its validity and correctness, and to correct any potential mistakes. For sure, employers need to communicate to employees what monitoring is happening in the organization and why it is needed. If employees understand why employee monitoring is required (e.g., for performance measurement purposes; for the detection of illegal activity), how long the monitoring records will be kept, who has access to these records, then it will be more likely that employees will accept and tolerate the monitoring.

Legal precedents that hold businesses financially responsible for their employees' actions drives the decision of whether to monitor what employees do on company time with corporate resources. Increasingly, employee monitoring is not a choice; it is a risk-management obligation. Michael Soden, CEO of the Bank of Ireland, issued a mandate stating that company employees could not surf illicit Web sites with company equipment. Next, he hired Hewlett-Packard to run the IT department. A Hewlett-Packard employee soon discovered illicit Web sites on Soden's computer. Soden resigned.[2]

A survey of workplace monitoring and surveillance practices in the United States by the American Management Association (AMA) and the ePolicy Institute showed the degree to which companies are turning to monitoring:

- 82 percent of the study's 1,627 respondents acknowledged conducting some form of electronic monitoring or physical surveillance.
- 63 percent of the companies stated that they monitor Internet connections.
- 47 percent acknowledged storing and reviewing employee e-mail messages.[3]

Many employees use their company's high-speed Internet access to shop, browse, and surf the Web. Fifty-nine percent of all 2004 Web purchases in the United States were made from the workplace, according to ComScore Networks. Vault.com determined that 47 percent of employees spend at least half an hour a day surfing the Web.[4]

This research indicates that managers should monitor what their employees are doing with their Web access. Most managers do not want their employees conducting personal business during working hours. For these reasons many organizations have increasingly taken the Big Brother approach to Web monitoring with software that tracks Internet usage and even allows the boss to read employees' e-mail. Figure 9.5 highlights a few reasons the effects of employee monitoring are worse than the lost productivity from employee Web surfing.

FIGURE 9.5

Employee Monitoring
Effects

Employee Monitoring Effects
1. Employee absenteeism is on the rise, almost doubling in 2004 to 21 percent. The lesson here might be that more employees are missing work to take care of personal business. Perhaps losing a few minutes here or there—or even a couple of hours—is cheaper than losing entire days.
2. Studies indicate that electronic monitoring results in lower job satisfaction, in part because people begin to believe the quantity of their work is more important than the quality.
3. Electronic monitoring also induces what psychologists call "psychological reactance": the tendency to rebel against constraints. If you tell your employees they cannot shop, they cannot use corporate networks for personal business, and they cannot make personal phone calls, then their desire to do all these things will likely increase.

This is the thinking at SAS Institute, a private software company consistently ranked in the top 10 on many "Best Places to Work" surveys. SAS does not monitor its employees' Web usage. The company asks its employees to use company resources responsibly, but does not mind if they occasionally check sports scores or use the Web for shopping.

Many management gurus advocate that organizations whose corporate cultures are based on trust are more successful than those whose corporate cultures are based on distrust. Before an organization implements monitoring technology it should ask itself, "What does this say about how the organization feels about its employees?" If the organization really does not trust its employees, then perhaps it should find new ones. If an organization does trust its employees, then it might want to treat them accordingly. An organization that follows its employees' every keystroke is unwittingly undermining the relationships with its employees.[5]

Information technology monitoring is tracking people's activities by such measures as number of keystrokes, error rate, and number of transactions processed. Figure 9.6 displays different types of monitoring technologies currently available.

FIGURE 9.6

Monitoring Technologies

Common Monitoring Technologies	
Key logger, or key trapper, software	A program that, when installed on a computer, records every keystroke and mouse click.
Hardware key logger	A hardware device that captures keystrokes on their journey from the keyboard to the motherboard.
Cookie	A small file deposited on a hard drive by a Web site containing information about customers and their Web activities. Cookies allow Web sites to record the comings and goings of customers, usually without their knowledge or consent.
Adware	Software that generates ads that install themselves on a computer when a person downloads some other program from the Internet.
Spyware (sneakware or stealthware)	Software that comes hidden in free downloadable software and tracks online movements, mines the information stored on a computer, or uses a computer's CPU and storage for some task the user knows nothing about.
Web log	Consists of one line of information for every visitor to a Web site and is usually stored on a Web server.
Clickstream	Records information about a customer during a Web surfing session such as what Web sites were visited, how long the visit was, what ads were viewed, and what was purchased.

INFORMATION PRIVACY

The concern over the protection of personal information has become a real concern for everyday Canadians. For example, a recent study that surveyed 1,000 Canadians discovered that 50 percent of respondents had a "fairly low level" to a "very low level" of trust that organizations such as banks, credit cards companies, and retail shops would be able to protect personal data.[6]

In the electronic government domain, a similar concern over the protection of personal information can be found. For instance, evidence from a national survey about citizen satisfaction with Canadian government online services speaks to the importance of paying attention to privacy concerns. This very well regarded and highly-publicized survey, known as *Citizens First,* was administered by the Institute for Citizen-Centred Service (ICCS) and the Institute for Public Administration in Canada (IPAC). Results from the survey indicate that although other factors help promote citizen satisfaction with the Internet, such as outcome, ease of finding information, sufficient information, site navigation, and visual appeal, the key driver that directly impacts whether or not citizens will transact online are their concerns over information security and information privacy. For security, there are high levels of concerns over information storage, transmission, and access and identity verification. However, for privacy and the protection of personal information, there are even stronger concerns about consolidation of information, unauthorized access, and sharing without permission.[7]

Information privacy concerns the legal right or general expectation of individuals, groups, or institutions to determine for themselves when, and to what extent, information about them is communicated to others. In essence, information privacy is about how personal information is collected and shared.

Issues or concerns about the collection and sharing of personal information occur in companies whenever uniquely identifiable data or information relating to a person is collected and stored. These concerns exist regardless of the format in which personal information is stored. That is, information privacy breaches pertain to personal data and information stored electronically or otherwise.

Breaches in information privacy occur when improper disclosure of personal information are made. This often stems from a lack of proper controls in organizations that protect how personal information is collected, stored, accessed, and distributed. Most often, information privacy pertains to personally sensitive information pertaining to individuals, such as health information, police records, financial information (income, purchases, spending habits), genetic information, and demographic information (e.g., name, age, weight, height, religion, ethnic origin, place of birth, number of dependants).

Information privacy is not about the prevention of collecting and sharing personal information. Often personal information must be collected to complete a business transaction. For example, if a customer orders a product off the Web, it is necessary for a company to collect and share personal information, such as an address and credit card number, internally or with business partners to facilitate delivery of the ordered product. Rather, information privacy is about recognizing the sensitivity of personal information and protecting that information from inappropriate disclosure or unauthorized access.

To facilitate information privacy, many countries have established legislation to protect the collection and sharing of personal information. However, there are great variations in this legislation around the world.

Europe

On one end of the spectrum lies European nations with their strong information privacy laws. Most notably, all member countries of the European Union adhere to a Directive on the protection of personal data. A directive is a legislative act of the European Union that requires member states to achieve a particular result without dictating the means of how to achieve that result.

The Directive on the protection of personal data grants European Union members the following rights:

- the right to know the source of personal data processing and the purposes of such processing,
- the right to access and/or rectify inaccuracies in one's own personal data,
- the right to disallow the use of personal data.

These rights are based on eight key principles pertaining to the collection or storage of personal data. The Directive defines personal data to cover both facts and opinions about an individual. Any organization processing personal data of a person living in the European Union must comply with these eight key principles as outlined in the Directive; these state that the data must be:

- fairly and lawfully processed,
- processed for limited purposes,
- adequate, relevant, and not excessive,
- accurate,
- not kept longer than necessary,
- processed in accordance with the data subject's rights,
- secure, and
- not transferred to countries without adequate protection.

This last right restricts the flow of personal information outside the European Union by permitting its transfer to only countries that provide an "adequate" level of privacy protection—adequate in the sense that these other countries have to offer a level of privacy protection equivalent to that of the European Union. When first implemented, this part of the Directive caused some concerns since other countries outside the European Union had much weaker privacy protection laws. Greatly concerned were organizations in the United States. Such organizations were at a legal risk if the personal data of European citizens were transferred to computer servers in the U.S.—a likely scenario in today's global world of electronic business. This led to extensive negotiations. The result was the establishment of a "safe harbour" program in the United States. This program provides a framework for organizations in the U.S. to show evidence of compliance with the European Union Directive. In this way, American companies can self-declare their compliance with the key principles of the Directive and do business with European Union nations without worrying about European citizens suing them.

All European member states adopted legislation pursuant to the Directive or adapted their existing laws to comply with the Directive. Each country also has its own supervisory authority to monitor levels of protection afforded by the legislation.

The United States

On the other end of the spectrum lies the United States. In that country, information privacy is not highly legislated nor regulated. There is no all-encompassing law that regulates the use of personal data or information. In many cases, access to public information is considered culturally acceptable, such as obtaining credit reports for employment or housing purposes. The reason for this may be historical. In the United States, the first amendment protects free speech and in many instances the protection of privacy conflicts with this amendment.

There are some exceptions. Though very few states recognize an individual's right to privacy, California has enshrined an inalienable right to privacy in California's constitution. The California legislature has enacted several pieces of legislation aimed at protecting citizen information privacy. For example, California's Online Privacy Protection Act, established in 2003, requires commercial Web sites or online services that collect personal information of California residents to clearly post a privacy policy on the Web site or online service and to comply with this policy.

Other exceptions include the Children's Online Privacy Protection Act (COPPA) and the Health Insurance Portability and Accountability Act (HIPAA).

COPPA is a federal law established in 1998 that applies to the collection of personal information from American children who are under 13 years of age. The Act outlines what a Web site should include in its privacy policy, how to go about seeking consent from a parent or guardian, and the responsibilities an operator of a Web site has to protect children's online safety and privacy. This law applies to any Web site that is perceived to be targeting American children. So if a toy company established in Canada wants to sells its toys in the United States, the company's Web site would have to comply with the collection and use of information as outlined in COPPA. To show compliance requires a substantial amount of paperwork. As a result, many Web sites completely disallow underage users to join online communities and Web sites. As such, one of COPPA's largest impacts has been the complete shutdown of Web sites that cater to children and a large number of general audience Web sites deciding not to offer services to children at all. Not complying to COPPA can be costly. For example, in September 2006, the Web site Xanga was fined US$1 million for violating COPPA legislation.

HIPAA was enacted by the United States Congress in 1996. There are provisions in HIPPA that establish national standards for the electronic data interchange of health care related transactions between health care providers, insurance plans, and employers. Embellished in these standards are rules for the handling and protection of personal health care information.

Canada

Canada's privacy laws follow very closely to the European model. Canada as a nation is quite concerned about protecting the personal information of its citizens. Its primary privacy law is the Personal Information Protection and Electronic Documents Act (PIPEDA).

Its pre-cursor was the Privacy Act established in 1983 that imposed restrictions on the handling of personal information within federal government departments and agencies only. This information concerned such things as:

- pension and employment insurance files,
- medical records,
- tax records,
- security clearances,
- student loan applications, and
- military records.

PIPEDA came into effect in January 2001 and, like the Privacy Act, applied only to federally regulated organizations. By January 2004, PIPEDA's reach extended beyond government borders and applied to all other types of organizations, including commercial businesses. By doing so, Canada's PIPEDA law brought Canada into compliance with the European Union's Directive on the protection of personal data. Hence, since January 2004, Canada no longer needed to implement safe harbour provisions, like those found in the United States, for organizations wishing to collect and store personal information on European Union citizens.

The purpose of PIPEDA is to provide Canadians with a right of privacy with respect to how their personal information is collected, used, or disclosed by an organization. This is most important today, especially in the private sector, when information technology increasingly facilitates the collection and free flow of information.

The privacy provisions encapsulated within PIPEDA are based on the Canadian Standards Association's Model Code for the Protection of Personal Information, recognized as a national standard in 1996. The Standard addresses ways in which organizations can collect, use, and disclose personal information. It also addresses the rights of individuals to have access to their personal information and to have it corrected if necessary.

Figure 9.7 outlines the 10 guiding principles of PIPEDA as they apply to organizations. The gist of these 10 guiding principles can be easily remembered as the "3Cs": the notion of informed Consent; the notion of Choice; and the notion of Control.

Sometimes there are circumstances when information privacy concerns are over-ruled. For example, law enforcement agencies and journalists need to collect, use, and disclose personal information without obtaining the consent of the individuals in question. PIPEDA allows such exceptions. These exceptions include:

- personal information collected, used, or disclosed solely for journalistic, artistic, or literary purposes,
- if the action clearly benefits the individual or if obtaining permission could infringe on the information's accuracy,
- where such data can contribute to a legal investigation or aid in an emergency where people's lives and safety could be at stake, and
- if disclosure aids, in times of emergency, matters of legal investigation, or facilitates the conservation of historically important records.[8]

What does PIPEDA mean for you, a citizen of Canada? Several things.

FIGURE 9.7

10 Guiding Principles of PIPEDA for Organizations

	Guiding Principle	Description
1.	Accountability	An organization is responsible for personal information under its control and shall designate an individual or individuals who are accountable for the organization's compliance with the following principles.
2.	Identifying Purposes	The purposes for which personal information is collected shall be identified by the organization at or before the time the information is collected.
3.	Consent	The knowledge and consent of the individual are required for the collection, use, or disclosure of personal information, except when inappropriate.
4.	Limiting Collection	The collection of personal information shall be limited to that which is necessary for the purposes identified by the organization. Information shall be collected by fair and lawful means.
5.	Limiting Use, Disclosure, and Retention	Personal information shall not be used or disclosed for purposes other than those for which it was collected, except with the consent of the individual or as required by the law. Personal information shall be retained only as long as necessary for fulfillment of those purposes.
6.	Accuracy	Personal information shall be as accurate, complete, and up-to-date as is necessary for the purposes for which it is to be used.
7.	Safeguards	Personal information shall be protected by security safeguards appropriate to the sensitivity of the information.
8.	Openness	An organization shall make readily available to individuals specific information about its policies and practices relating to the management of personal information.
9.	Individual Access	Upon request, an individual shall be informed of the existence, use and disclosure of his or her personal information and shall be given access to that information. An individual shall be able to challenge the accuracy and completeness of the information and have it amended as appropriate.
10.	Challenging Compliance	An individual shall be able to address a challenge concerning compliance with the above principles to the designated individual or individuals for the organization's compliance.

Source: Privacy Provisions Highlights, Department of Justice, 2005. Reproduced with the permission of the Minister of Public Works and Government Services Canada, 2007.

First, it *requires* organizations to:

- obtain consent when they collect, use, or disclose your personal information,
- supply you with a product or service even if you refuse consent for the collection, use, or disclosure of your personal information unless the information is essential to the transaction,
- collect information by fair and lawful means, and
- provide personal information policies that are clear, understandable, and readily available.

Second, it *encourages* organizations to:

- destroy personal information that is no longer needed for the purposes for which it was collected.

Third, it *gives* you (the citizen) the right to:

- know why an organization collects, uses, or discloses your personal information,
- expect an organization to collect, use, or disclose your personal information reasonably and appropriately and not to use the information for any purposes other than that to which you have consented,
- know who in the organization is responsible for protecting your personal information,
- expect an organization to protect your personal information by taking appropriate security measures,
- expect the personal information about you to be accurate, complete, and up-to-date,
- obtain access to your personal information and ask for corrections, and
- complain about how an organization handles your personal information by first going to the Privacy Officer within the organization, and if not satisfied, to then seek intervention from either the Privacy Commissioner of Canada or the Provincial Privacy Commissioner.

DEVELOPING POLICIES FOR INFORMATION ETHICS AND INFORMATION PRIVACY

Treating sensitive corporate information as a valuable resource is good management. Building a corporate culture based on ethical principles that employees can understand and implement is responsible management. In an effort to provide guidelines for ethical information management, *CIO* magazine (along with over 100 CIOs) developed six principles for ethical information management displayed in Figure 9.8.

FIGURE 9.8

CIO Magazine's Six Principles for Ethical Information Management

Six Principles for Ethical Information Management
1. Information is a valuable corporate asset and should be managed as such, like cash, facilities, or any other corporate asset.
2. The CIO is steward of corporate information and is responsible for managing it over its life cycle—from its generation to its appropriate destruction.
3. The CIO is responsible for controlling access to and use of information, as determined by governmental regulation and corporate policy.
4. The CIO is responsible for preventing the inappropriate destruction of information.
5. The CIO is responsible for bringing technological knowledge to the development of information management practices and policies.
6. The CIO should partner with executive peers to develop and execute the organization's information management policies.

Organizations should develop written policies establishing employee guidelines, personnel procedures, and organizational rules for information. These policies set employee expectations about the organization's practices and standards and protect the organization from misuse of computer systems and IT resources. If an organization's employees use computers at work, the organization should, at a minimum, implement ePolicies. *ePolicies* are policies and procedures that address the ethical use of computers and Internet usage in the business environment. These policies typically embody the following:

- Ethical computer use policy.
- Information privacy policy.
- Acceptable use policy.
- E-mail privacy policy.
- Internet use policy.
- Anti-spam policy.
- Employee monitoring policy.

Ethical Computer Use Policy

One of the essential steps in creating an ethical corporate culture is establishing an ethical computer use policy. An *ethical computer use policy* contains general principles to guide computer user behaviour. For example, the ethical computer use policy might explicitly state that users should refrain from playing computer games during working hours. This policy ensures the users know how to behave at work and the organization has a published standard by which to deal with user infractions. For example, after appropriate warnings, the company may terminate an employee who spends significant amounts of time playing computer games at work.

There are variations in how organizations expect their employees to use computers, but in any approach, the overriding principle when seeking appropriate computer use should be informed consent. The users should be *informed* of the rules and, by agreeing to use the system on that basis, *consent* to abide by the rules.

An organization should make a conscientious effort to ensure all users are aware of the policy through formal training and other means. If an organization were to have only one ePolicy, it should be an ethical computer use policy since it is the starting point and the umbrella for any other policies the organization might establish.

Information Privacy Policy

Scott Thompson is the executive vice president of Inovant, the company Visa set up to handle its technology. Thompson errs on the side of caution in regard to Visa's information: He bans the use of Visa's customer information for anything outside its intended purpose—billing.

Visa's customer information details how people are spending their money, in which stores, on which days, and even at what time of day. Sales and marketing departments around the country no doubt are salivating at any prospect of gaining access to Visa's databases. "They would love to refine the information into loyalty programs, target markets, or even partnerships with Visa. There are lots of creative people coming up with these ideas. This whole area of information sharing is enormous and growing. For the marketers, the sky's the limit," Thompson said. Privacy specialists along with Thompson developed a strict credit card information policy, which the company follows.

The question now is can Thompson guarantee that unethical use of his information will not occur? Many experts do not believe that he can. In a large majority of cases, the unethical use of information happens not through the malicious scheming of a rogue marketer, but rather unintentionally. For instance, information is collected and stored for some purpose, such as record keeping or billing. Then, a sales or marketing professional figures out another way to use it internally, share it with partners, or sell it to a trusted third party. The information is "unintentionally" used for new purposes. The classic example in the United States of this type of unintentional information reuse is the Social Security number, which started simply as a way to identify government retirement benefits and is now used as a sort of universal personal ID, found on everything from drivers' licences to savings accounts.

An organization that wants to protect its information should develop an information privacy policy. An *information privacy policy* contains general principles regarding information privacy. Figure 9.9 highlights a few guidelines an organization can follow when creating an information privacy policy.

Acceptable Use Policy

An *acceptable use policy (AUP)* is a policy that a user must agree to follow in order to be provided access to a network or to the Internet. *Nonrepudiation* is a contractual stipulation to ensure that e-business participants do not deny (repudiate) their online actions. A nonrepudiation clause is typically contained in an AUP.

Many businesses and educational facilities require employees or students to sign an acceptable use policy before gaining network access. When signing up with an Internet service provider (ISP), each customer is typically presented with an AUP, which states that they agree to adhere to certain stipulations (see Figure 9.10).

FIGURE 9.9

Organizational Guidelines for Creating an Information Privacy Policy

Creating an Information Privacy Policy
1. **Adoption and implementation of a privacy policy.** An organization engaged in online activities or e-business has a responsibility to adopt and implement a policy for protecting the privacy of personal information. Organizations should also take steps that foster the adoption and implementation of effective online privacy policies by the organizations with which they interact, for instance, by sharing best practices with business partners.
2. **Notice and disclosure.** An organization's privacy policy must be easy to find, read, and understand. The policy must clearly state: ■ What information is being collected? ■ The use of information being collected. ■ Possible third-party distribution of that information. ■ The choices available to an individual regarding collection, use, and distribution of the collected information. ■ A statement of the organization's commitment to information security. ■ What steps the organization takes to ensure information quality and access.
3. **Choice and consent.** Individuals must be given the opportunity to exercise choice regarding how personal information collected from them online may be used when such use is unrelated to the purpose for which the information was collected. At a minimum, individuals should be given the opportunity to opt out of such use.
4. **Information security.** Organizations creating, maintaining, using, or disseminating personal information should take appropriate measures to assure its reliability and should take reasonable precautions to protect it from loss, misuse, or alteration.
5. **Information quality and access.** Organizations should establish appropriate processes or mechanisms so that inaccuracies in material personal information, such as account or contact information, may be corrected. Other procedures to assure information quality may include use of reliable sources, collection methods, appropriate consumer access, and protection against accidental or unauthorized alteration.

FIGURE 9.10

Acceptable Use Policy
Stipulations

Acceptable Use Policy Stipulations
1. Not using the service as part of violating any law.
2. Not attempting to break the security of any computer network or user.
3. Not posting commercial messages to groups without prior permission.
4. Not performing any nonrepudiation.
5. Not attempting to send junk e-mail or spam to anyone who does not want to receive it.
6. Not attempting to mail bomb a site. A *mail bomb* is sending a massive amount of e-mail to a specific person or system resulting in filling up the recipient's disk space, which, in some cases, may be too much for the server to handle and may cause the server to stop functioning.

E-Mail Privacy Policy

E-mail is so pervasive in organizations that it requires its own specific policy. In a recent survey, 80 percent of professional workers identified e-mail as their preferred means of corporate communications. Trends also show a dramatic increase in the adoption rate of instant messaging (IM) in the workplace. While e-mail and IM are common business communication tools, there are risks associated with using them. For instance, a sent e-mail is stored on at least three or four different computers (see Figure 9.11). Simply deleting an e-mail from one computer does not delete it off the other computers. Companies can mitigate many of the risks of using electronic messaging systems by implementing and adhering to an e-mail privacy policy.[9]

One of the major problems with e-mail is the user's expectations of privacy. To a large extent, this exception is based on the false assumption that e-mail privacy protection exists somehow analogous to that of Canada Post standard mail. This is simply not true.

Generally, the organization that owns the e-mail system can operate the system as openly or as privately as it wishes. That means that if the organization wants to read everyone's e-mail, it can do so. If it chooses not to read any, that is allowable too. Hence, it is up to the organization to decide how much, if any, e-mail it is going to read. Then, when it decides, it must inform the users, so that they can consent to

FIGURE 9.11

E-Mail Is Stored on Multiple
Computers

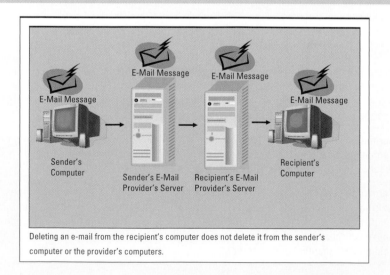

Deleting an e-mail from the recipient's computer does not delete it from the sender's computer or the provider's computers.

this level of intrusion. In other words, an ***e-mail privacy policy*** details the extent to which e-mail messages may be read by others.

Organizations must create an e-mail privacy policy. Figure 9.12 displays a few of the key stipulations generally contained in an e-mail privacy policy.

Internet Use Policy

Similar to e-mail, the Internet has some unique aspects that make it a good candidate for its own policy. These include the large amounts of computing resources that Internet users can expend, thus making it essential that such use be legitimate. In addition, the Internet contains numerous materials that some believe are offensive and, hence, some regulation is required. An ***Internet use policy*** contains general principles to guide the proper use of the Internet. Figure 9.13 lists a few important stipulations that might be included in an Internet use policy.

Anti-Spam Policy

Chief technology officer (CTO) of the law firm Fenwick and West, Matt Kesner reduced incoming spam by 99 percent and found himself a corporate hero. Before the spam reduction, the law firm's partners (whose time is worth $400 to $675 an hour) found themselves spending hours each day sifting through 300 to 500 spam messages. The spam blocking engineered by Kesner traps between 5,000 and 7,000 messages a day.[10]

FIGURE 9.12

E-Mail Privacy Policy Stipulations

E-Mail Privacy Policy Stipulations
1. The policy should be complementary to the ethical computer use policy.
2. It defines who legitimate e-mail users are.
3. It explains the backup procedure so users will know that at some point, even if a message is deleted from their computer, it will still be on the backup tapes.
4. It describes the legitimate grounds for reading someone's e-mail and the process required before such action can be taken.
5. It informs that the organization has no control of e-mail once it is transmitted outside the organization.
6. It explains what will happen if the user severs his or her connection with the organization.
7. It asks employees to be careful when making organizational files and documents available to others.

FIGURE 9.13

Internet Use Policy Stipulations

Internet Use Policy Stipulations
1. The policy should describe available Internet services because not all Internet sites allow users to access all services.
2. The policy should define the organization's position on the purpose of Internet access and what restrictions, if any, are placed on that access.
3. The policy should complement the ethical computer use policy.
4. The policy should describe user responsibility for citing sources, properly handling offensive material, and protecting the organization's good name.
5. The policy should clearly state the ramifications if the policy is violated.

Spam is unsolicited e-mail. An ***anti-spam policy*** simply states that e-mail users will not send unsolicited e-mails (or spam). Spam plagues all levels of employees within an organization from receptionists to CEOs. Estimates indicate that spam accounts for 40 percent to 60 percent of most organizations' e-mail traffic. Spam clogs e-mail systems and siphons IT resources away from legitimate business projects.[11]

It is difficult to write anti-spam policies, laws, or software because there is no such thing as a universal litmus test for spam. One person's spam is another person's newsletter. End users have to be involved in deciding what spam is because what is unwanted can vary widely not just from one company to the next, but from one person to the next. What looks like spam to the rest of the world could be essential business communications for certain employees.

John Zarb, CIO of Libbey, a manufacturer of glassware, china, and flatware, tested Guenivere (a virus and subject-line filter) and SpamAssassin (an open source spam filter). He had to shut them off after 10 days because they were rejecting important legitimate e-mails. As Zarb quickly discovered, once an organization starts filtering e-mail, it runs the risk of blocking legitimate e-mails that look like spam. Avoiding an unacceptable level of "false positives" requires a delicate balancing act. The IT team tweaked the spam filters and today, the filters block about 70 percent of Libbey's spam, and Zarb said the "false positive" rate is far lower, but still not zero. Figure 9.14 highlights a few methods an organization can follow to prevent spam.

Employee Monitoring Policy

The best path for an organization planning to engage in employee monitoring is open communication surrounding the issue. A recent survey discovered that communication about monitoring issues is weak for most organizations. One in five companies did not even have an acceptable use policy and one in four companies did not have an Internet use policy. Companies that did have policies usually tucked them into the rarely probed recesses of the employee handbook, and then the policies tended to be of the vague and legal jargon variety: "XYZ company reserves the right to monitor or review any information stored or transmitted on its equipment." Reserving the right to monitor is materially different from clearly stating that the company does monitor, listing what is tracked, describing what is looked for, and detailing the consequences for violations.

An organization must formulate the right monitoring policies and put them into practice. Employee monitoring policies explicitly state how, when, and where the company monitors its employees. CSOs that are explicit about what the company does in the way of monitoring and the reasons for it, along with actively educating their employees about what unacceptable behaviour looks like, will find that employees not only acclimate quickly to a policy, but also reduce the CSO's burden by policing themselves. Figure 9.15 displays several common stipulations an organization can follow when creating an employee monitoring policy.

FIGURE 9.14

Spam Prevention Tips

Spam Prevention Tips
■ **Disguise e-mail addresses posted in a public electronic place.** When posting an e-mail address in a public place, disguise the address through simple means such as replacing "jsmith@domain.com" with "jsmith at domain dot com." This prevents spam from recognizing the e-mail address.
■ **Opt out of member directories that may place an e-mail address online.** Choose not to participate in any activities that place e-mail addresses online. If an e-mail address is placed online be sure it is disguised in some way.
■ **Use a filter.** Many ISPs and free e-mail services now provide spam filtering. While filters are not perfect, they can cut down tremendously on the amount of spam a user receives.

FIGURE 9.15

Employee Monitoring Policy
Stipulations

Employee Monitoring Policy Stipulations
1. Be as specific as possible.
2. Always enforce the policy.
3. Enforce the policy in the same way for everyone.
4. Expressly communicate that the company reserves the right to monitor all employees.
5. Specifically state when monitoring will be performed.
6. Specifically state what will be monitored (e-mail, IM, Internet, network activity, etc.).
7. Describe the types of information that will be collected.
8. State the consequences for violating the policy.
9. State all provisions that allow for updates to the policy.
10. Specify the scope and manner of monitoring for any information system.
11. When appropriate, obtain a written receipt acknowledging that each party has received, read, and understood the monitoring policies.

OPENING CASE QUESTIONS

Embracing Privacy at the City of Hamilton

1. Why is protecting information privacy in the best interests of both Hamiltonians and the City of Hamilton?
2. What steps did the City of Hamilton take to address privacy concerns in the McMaster University research project?
3. What policies could the City of Hamilton implement internally to protect citizen information privacy?
4. What lessons can be learned from the opening case study that will help other organizations better protect the personal information they collect?

9.2 INFORMATION SECURITY

PROTECTING INFORMATION

Organizational information is a key resource. Just as organizations protect their assets—keeping their money in an insured bank or providing a safe working environment for employees—they must also protect their information. With security breaches on the rise and computer hackers everywhere, an organization must put in place strong information security measures to survive.

For example, millions of credit card accounts were compromised after hackers stole customer information in 2006 from the computer systems of TJX Cos. TJX is the United States parent firm of Canadian retailers Winners and HomeSense. As of 2007, there are 184 Winners and 68 HomeSense stores in Canada. The stolen information covered customer purchases transacted between 2003 and 2006. Two million Visa credit card accounts and 20 million Visa cards globally were affected.[12]

In 2007, the Privacy Commissioner of Canada, Jennifer Stoddart, launched an investigation into a CIBC personal information breach involving nearly half a million people. The issue was the loss of a backup computer file containing personal information on approximately 470,000 clients of a subsidiary of the bank, Talvest Mutual Funds. The missing personal data was in a file that disappeared "while in transit" between offices. The information may have included client names, addresses, signatures, dates of birth, bank account numbers, beneficiary information, and Social Insurance Numbers.[13]

Also in 2007, hundreds of Rogers' cable and Internet customer orders, containing personal information such as driver's licence numbers and Social Insurance Numbers, were found abandoned in a downtown Toronto parking lot near Ryerson University. In its defence, Rogers blamed an employee of the company it hired to sell its cable TV and Internet services.[14]

Though these breaches made national news, what is discerning is that Canada really does not know the extent of privacy and security breaches. This is because PIPEDA legislation does not make it mandatory for organizations to notify people of data breaches involving personal information. However, as of April 2007, Stoddart has called for amendments to PIPEDA to make public notification of security breaches mandatory by companies. This suggested change would give consumers advanced notice to take action (such as verifying their credit card history and possibly cancelling credit cards). The amendment would also encourage business to take privacy matters more seriously and take measures to better protect sensitive customer information. There is some apathy among Canadian private sector companies in complying with Canadian data and information protection laws. A study produced in 2006 indicates a general failure on behalf of Canadian retailers to adequately understand or deal with accountability, openness, access, and consent; the capacity of retailers to safeguard personal information, or even know if a security breach has occurred, is also suspect.[15]

Interestingly, though the United States has weaker privacy legislation than Canada, about 30 American states have already introduced mandatory notification laws. This is in large part due to a major privacy and security breach in 2005 involving a data company that sold personal information on thousands of United States residents inadvertently to a criminal organization.[16]

The message here is that all businesses must understand the importance of information security, whether it is enforceable by law or not. ***Information security*** is a broad term encompassing the protection of information from accidental or intentional misuse by persons inside or outside an organization. Figure 9.16 displays the typical size of an organization's information security budget relative to the

FIGURE 9.16

Organization's Security Budget

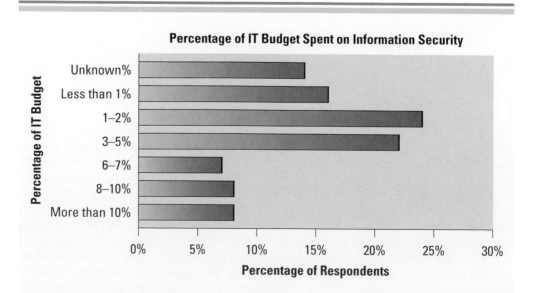

organization's overall IT budget from the CSI/FBI 2004 Computer Crime and Security Survey conducted in the U.S. Forty-six percent of respondents indicated that their organization spent between 1 and 5 percent of the total IT budget on security. Only 16 percent indicated that their organization spent less than 1 percent of the IT budget on security.

Figure 9.17 displays the spending per employee on computer security broken down by both public and private industries in the United States. The highest average computer security investment per employee was found in the transportation industry.[17]

Security is perhaps the most fundamental and critical of all the technologies/disciplines an organization must have squarely in place to execute its business strategy. Without solid security processes and procedures, none of the other technologies can develop business advantages.

THE FIRST LINE OF DEFENCE—PEOPLE

With current advances in technologies and business strategies such as CRM, organizations are able to determine valuable information such as who are the top 20 percent of the customers that produce 80 percent of all revenues. Most organizations view this type of information as critical, and they are implementing security measures to prevent the information from walking out the door or falling into the wrong hands. Enterprises can implement information security lines of defence through people first and through technology second.

Adding to the complexity of information security is the fact that organizations must enable employees, customers, and partners to access information electronically to be successful in this electronic world. Doing business electronically automatically creates tremendous information security risks for organizations. Surprisingly, the biggest issue surrounding information security is not a technical issue, but a people issue.

FIGURE 9.17

Security Spending per Employee

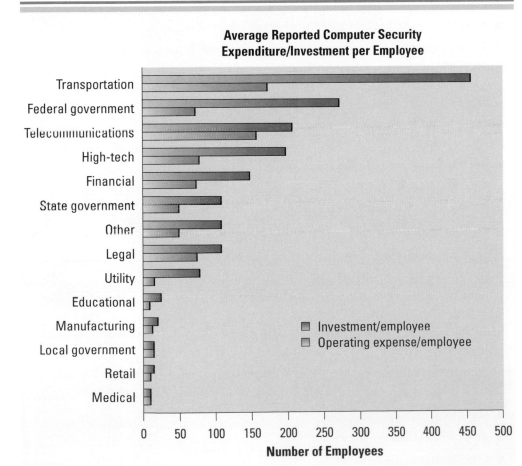

The CSI/FBI Computer Crime and Security Survey reported that 38 percent of respondents indicated security incidents originated within the enterprise. ***Insiders*** are legitimate users who purposely or accidentally misuse their access to the environment and cause some kind of business-affecting incident. Most information security breaches result from people misusing an organization's information either advertently or inadvertently. For example, many individuals freely give up their passwords or write them on sticky notes next to their computers, leaving the door wide open to intruders.[18]

The director of information security at a large health care company discovered how easy it was to create an information security breach when she hired outside auditors to test her company's security awareness. In one instance, auditors found that staff members testing a new system had accidentally exposed the network to outside hackers. In another, auditors were able to obtain the passwords of 16 employees when the auditors posed as support staff; hackers frequently use such "social engineering" to obtain passwords. ***Social engineering*** is using one's social skills to trick people into revealing access credentials or other information valuable to the attacker. Dumpster diving, or looking through people's trash, is another way social engineering hackers obtain information.[19]

Information security policies identify the rules required to maintain information security. An ***information security plan*** details how an organization will implement the information security policies. Figure 9.18 is an example of an Information Security Plan adopted by the University of Denver in the United States.

FIGURE 9.18

Sample Information Security Plan

Interim Information Security Plan

This Information Security Plan ("Plan") describes the University of Denver's safeguards to protect information and data in compliance ("Protected Information") with the Financial Services Modernization Act of 1999, also known as the Gramm Leach Bliley Act, 15 U.S.C. Section 6801. These safeguards are provided to:

- Ensure the security and confidentiality of Protected Information;
- Protect against anticipated threats or hazards to the security or integrity of such information; and
- Protect against unauthorized access to or use of Protected Information that could result in substantial harm or inconvenience to any customer.

This Information Security Plan also provides for mechanisms to:

- Identify and assess the risks that may threaten Protected Information maintained by the University of Denver;
- Develop written policies and procedures to manage and control these risks;
- Implement and review the plan; and
- Adjust the plan to reflect changes in technology, the sensitivity of covered data and information and internal or external threats to information security.

Identification and Assessment of Risks to Customer Information

The University of Denver recognizes that it has both internal and external risks. These risks include, but are not limited to:

- Unauthorized access of Protected Information by someone other than the owner of the covered data and information
- Compromised system security as a result of system access by an unauthorized person
- Interception of data during transmission
- Loss of data integrity
- Physical loss of data in a disaster
- Errors introduced into the system

FIGURE 9.18

(*continued*)

Interim Information Security Plan *(continued)*

- Corruption of data or systems
- Unauthorized access of covered data and information by employees
- Unauthorized requests for covered data and information
- Unauthorized access through hardcopy files or reports
- Unauthorized transfer of covered data and information through third parties

The University of Denver recognizes that this may not be a complete list of the risks associated with the protection of Protected Information. Since technology growth is not static, new risks are created regularly. Accordingly, the Information Technology Department and the Office of Student Affairs will actively participate with and seek advice from an advisory committee made up of university representatives for identification of new risks. The University of Denver believes current safeguards used by the Information Technology Department are reasonable and, in light of current risk assessments are sufficient to provide security and confidentiality to Protected Information maintained by the University.

Information Security Plan Coordinators

The University CIO and the Vice President for Student Affairs, in consultation with an advisory committee, have been appointed as the coordinators of this Plan. They are responsible for assessing the risks associated with unauthorized transfers of covered data and information and implementing procedures to minimize those risks to the University of Denver.

Design and Implementation of Safeguards Program

Employee Management and Training

During employee orientation, each new employee in departments that handle Protected Information will receive proper training on the importance of confidentiality of Protected Information.

Physical Security

The University of Denver has addressed the physical security of Protected Information by limiting access to only those employees who have a business reason to know such information.

Information Systems

The University of Denver has policies governing the use of electronic resources and firewall and wireless policies. The University of Denver will take reasonable and appropriate steps consistent with current technological developments to make sure that all Protected Information is secure and to safeguard the integrity of records in storage and transmission. The University of Denver will develop a plan to ensure that all electronic Protected Information is encrypted in transit.

Selection of Appropriate Service Providers

Due to the specialized expertise needed to design, implement, and service new technologies, vendors may be needed to provide resources that the University of Denver determines not to provide on its own. In the process of choosing a service provider that will maintain or regularly access Protected Information, the evaluation process shall include the ability of the service provider to safeguard Protected Information. Contracts with service providers may include the following provisions:

- A stipulation that the Protected Information will be held in strict confidence and accessed only for the explicit business purpose of the contract;
- An assurance from the contract partner that the partner will protect the Protected Information it receives.

Continuing Evaluation and Adjustment

This Information Security Plan will be subject to periodic review and adjustment, especially when due to the constantly changing technology and evolving risks. The Coordinators, in consultation with the Office of General Counsel, will review the standards set forth in this policy and recommend updates and revisions as necessary. It may be necessary to adjust the plan to reflect changes in technology, the sensitivity of student/customer data and internal or external threats to information security.

The first line of defence an organization should follow is to create an information security plan detailing the various information security policies. A detailed information security plan can alleviate people-based information security issues. Figure 9.19 displays the five steps for creating an information security plan.

Figure 9.20 provides the top 10 questions from Ernst & Young that managers should ask to ensure their information is secure.

FIGURE 9.19

Creating an Information
Security Plan

Five Steps for Creating an Information Security Plan	
1. **Develop the information security policies**	Identify who is responsible and accountable for designing and implementing the organization's information security policies. Simple, yet highly effective types of information security policies include requiring users to log off of their systems before leaving for lunches or meetings, never sharing passwords with anyone, and changing personal passwords every 60 days. The chief security officer (CSO) will typically be responsible for designing these information security policies.
2. **Communicate the information security policies**	Train all employees on the policies and establish clear expectations for following the policies. For example, let all employees know that they will receive a formal reprimand for leaving a computer unsecured.
3. **Identify critical information assets and risks**	Require the use of user IDs, passwords, and antivirus software on all systems. Ensure any systems that contain links to external networks have the appropriate technical protections such as firewalls or intrusion detection software. A *firewall* is hardware and/or software that guards a private network by analyzing the information leaving and entering the network. *Intrusion detection software (IDS)* searches out patterns in information and network traffic to indicate attacks and quickly responds to prevent any harm.
4. **Test and reevaluate risks**	Continually perform security reviews, audits, background checks, and security assessments.
5. **Obtain stakeholder support**	Gain the approval and support of the information security polices from the board of directors and all stakeholders.

FIGURE 9.20

Top 10 Questions Managers
Should Ask Regarding
Information Security

Top 10 Questions Managers Should Ask Regarding Information Security
1. Does our board of directors recognize information security is a board level issue that cannot be left to the IT department alone?
2. Is there clear accountability for information security in our organization?
3. Do our board members articulate an agreed-upon set of threats and critical assets? How often do we review and update these?
4. How much is spent on information security and what is it being spent on?
5. What is the impact on the organization of a serious security incident?
6. Does our organization view information security as an enabler? (For example, by implementing effective security, could we enable our organization to increase business over the Internet?)
7. What is the risk to our business of getting a reputation for low information security?
8. What steps have we taken to ensure that third parties will not compromise the security of our organization?
9. How do we obtain independent assurance that information security is managed effectively in our organization?
10. How do we measure the effectiveness of our information security activities?

THE SECOND LINE OF DEFENCE—TECHNOLOGY

Arkansas State University (ASU), in the United States, recently completed a major network upgrade that brought gigabit-speed network capacity to every dorm room and office on its campus. The university was concerned that the new network would be a tempting playground for hackers. To reduce its fear, the university installed intrusion detection software (IDS) from Cisco Systems to stay on top of security and potential network abuses. Whenever the IDS spots a potential security threat, such as a virus or a hacker, it alerts the central management system. The system automatically pages the IT staff, who deal with the attack by shutting off access to the system, identifying the hacker's location, and calling campus security.[20]

Once an organization has protected its intellectual capital by arming its people with a detailed information security plan, it can begin to focus its efforts on deploying the right types of information security technologies such as the IDS installed at Arkansas State.

International Data Corp. estimated worldwide spending on IT security software, hardware, and services would top $35 billion in 2004. Organizations can deploy numerous technologies to prevent information security breaches. When determining which types of technologies to invest in, it helps to understand the three primary information security areas:

1. Authentication and authorization.
2. Prevention and resistance.
3. Detection and response.[21]

Authentication and Authorization

Authentication is a method for confirming users' identities. Once a system determines the authentication of a user, it can then determine the access privileges (or authorization) for that user. *Authorization* is the process of giving someone permission to do or have something. In multiple-user computer systems, user access or authorization determines such things as file access, hours of access, and amount of allocated storage space. Authentication and authorization techniques are broken down into three categories, and the most secure type involves a combination of all three:

1. Something the user knows such as a user ID and password.
2. Something the user has such as a smart card or token.
3. Something that is part of the user such as a fingerprint or voice signature.

Something the User Knows Such As a User ID and Password The first type of authentication, using something the user knows, is the most common way to identify individual users and typically consists of a unique user ID and password. However, this is actually one of the most *ineffective* ways for determining authentication because passwords are not secure. All it typically takes to crack a password is enough time. More than 50 percent of help-desk calls are password related, which can cost an organization significant money, and passwords are vulnerable to being coaxed out of somebody by a social engineer.

Identity theft is the forging of someone's identity for the purpose of fraud. The fraud is often financial fraud, to apply for and use credit cards in the victim's name or to apply for a loan. Figure 9.21 displays several examples of identity theft.

Phishing is a common way to steal identities online. *Phishing* is a technique to gain personal information for the purpose of identity theft, usually by means of fraudulent e-mail. One way to accomplish phishing is to send out e-mail messages that look as though they came from legitimate businesses such as the Royal Bank of Canada or Desjardins Financial Security. The messages appear to be genuine with official-looking formats and logos. These e-mails typically ask for verification of important information like passwords and account numbers. The reason given is often that this personal information is required for accounting or auditing purposes. Since

FIGURE 9.21

Examples of Identity Theft

Identity Theft Examples
In March 2006, a man and a woman were arrested for redirecting people's mail using a change of address form from Canada Post. Redirecting mail provides thieves with an abundant source of personal information about people and gives thieves more time to engage in fraudulent activity before victims are even suspicious. To entice people to provide enough personal information so that a change of address form could be filled out, the man and woman posted a fake online job offer and just waited for people to send them their personal information.[22]
Personal information can be stolen from a magnetic strip on the back of debit and credit cards through the use of small electronic devices called "skimmers" or "wedges." Thieves typically swipe cards through a skimmer at gas stations, restaurants, and ATM machines. In 2006, thieves in Auckland, New Zealand, skimmed the debit cards of 60 ATM users at the Auckland Bank of New Zealand; that information was used in Toronto by the fraudsters to steal $40,000.[23]
The security of information is often only as good as the integrity of employees working in organizations who have access to personal information of customers and fellow employees. In April 2006, an instance of such insider theft occurred at the Bank of Canada where two people employed by EDS Canada—a third-party systems outsourcer that provided back-office administration and support for the Bank of Canada's Canada Savings Bond (CSB) program—were arrested. These two individuals victimized eight account holders of the CSB Payroll Savings Program for a total of about $100,000.[24]
An 82-year-old woman in Fort Worth, Texas, discovered that her identity had been stolen when the woman using her name was involved in a four-car collision. For 18 months, she kept getting notices of lawsuits and overdue medical bills that were really meant for someone else. It took seven years for her to get her financial good name restored after the identity thief charged over $100,000 on her 12 fraudulently acquired credit cards.
A 42-year-old retired Army captain in Rocky Hill, Connecticut, found that an identity thief had spent $260,000 buying goods and services that included two trucks, a Harley-Davidson motorcycle, and a time-share vacation home in South Carolina. The victim discovered his problem only when his retirement pay was garnisheed to pay the outstanding bills.

the e-mails look authentic, up to one in five recipients respond with the information, and subsequently becomes a victim of identity theft and other fraud.

Something the User Has Such As a Smart Card or Token The second type of authentication, using something that the user has, offers a much more effective way to identify individuals than a user ID and password. Tokens and smart cards are two of the primary forms of this type of authentication. *Tokens* are small electronic devices that change user passwords automatically. The user enters his or her user ID and token-displayed password to gain access to the network. A *smart card* is a device that is around the same size as a credit card, containing embedded technologies that can store information and small amounts of software to perform some limited processing. Smart cards can act as identification instruments, a form of digital cash, or a data storage device with the ability to store an entire medical record.

Something That Is Part of the User Such As a Fingerprint or Voice Signature The third kind of authentication, using something that is part of the user, is by far the best and most effective way to manage authentication. *Biometrics* (narrowly defined) is the identification of a user based on a physical characteristic, such as a fingerprint, iris, face, voice, or handwriting. Unfortunately, biometric authentication can be costly and intrusive. For example, iris scans are expensive and considered intrusive by most people. Fingerprint authentication is less intrusive and inexpensive but is also not 100-percent accurate.

Prevention and Resistance

Prevention and resistance technologies stop intruders from accessing intellectual capital. A division of Sony Inc., Sony Pictures Entertainment (SPE), defends itself from attacks by using an intrusion detection system to detect new attacks as they occur. SPE develops and distributes a wide variety of products including movies, television, videos, and DVDs. A compromise to SPE security could result in costing the company valuable intellectual capital as well as millions of dollars and months of time. The company needed an advanced threat management solution that would take fewer resources to maintain and require limited resources to track and respond to suspicious network activity. The company installed an advanced intrusion detection system allowing it to monitor all of its network activity including any potential security breaches.[25]

The cost of downtime or network operation failures can be devastating to any business. For example, eBay experienced a 22-hour outage in June 2000 that caused the company's market cap to plunge an incredible $6.4 billion. Downtime costs for businesses can vary from $100 to $1 million per hour. An organization must prepare for and anticipate these types of outages resulting most commonly from hackers and viruses. Technologies available to help prevent and build resistance to attacks include content filtering, encryption, and firewalls. [26]

Content Filtering

Content filtering occurs when organizations use software that filters content to prevent the transmission of unauthorized information. Organizations can use content filtering technologies to filter e-mail and prevent e-mails containing sensitive information from transmitting, whether the transmission was malicious or accidental. It can also filter e-mails and prevent any suspicious files from transmitting such as potential virus-infected files. E-mail content filtering can also filter for spam, a form of unsolicited e-mail.

Encryption

Encryption scrambles information into an alternative form that requires a key or password to decrypt the information. If there is an information security breach and the information was encrypted, the person stealing the information will be unable to read it. Encryption can switch the order of characters, replace characters with other characters, insert or remove characters, or use a mathematical formula to convert the information into some sort of code. Companies that transmit sensitive customer information over the Internet, such as credit card numbers, frequently use encryption.

Some encryption technologies use multiple keys like public key encryption. *Public key encryption (PKE)* is an encryption system that uses two keys: a public key that everyone can have and a private key for only the recipient (see Figure 9.22). When

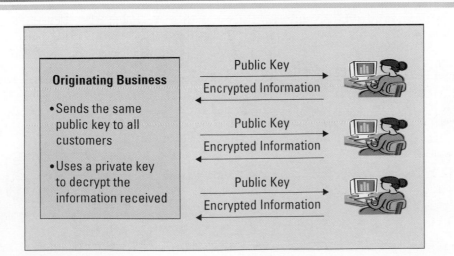

FIGURE 9.22

Public Key Encryption (PKE) System

implementing security using multiple keys, the organization provides the public key to all of its customers (end consumers and other businesses). The customers use the public key to encrypt their information and send it along the Internet. When it arrives at its destination, the organization would use the private key to unscramble the encrypted information.

Firewalls

One of the most common defences for preventing a security breach is a firewall. A firewall is hardware and/or software that guards a private network by analyzing the information leaving and entering the network. Firewalls examine each message that wants entrance to the network. Unless the message has the correct markings, the firewall prevents it from entering the network. Firewalls can even detect computers communicating with the Internet without approval. As Figure 9.23 illustrates, organizations typically place a firewall between a server and the Internet.

Detection and Response

The final area where organizations can allocate resources is in detection and response technologies. If prevention and resistance strategies fail and there is a security breach, an organization can use detection and response technologies to mitigate the damage. The most common type of defence within detection and response technologies is antivirus software.

A single worm can cause massive damage. In August 2003, the "Blaster worm" infected over 50,000 computers worldwide and was one of the worst outbreaks of the year. Jeffrey Lee Parson, 18, was arrested by U.S. cyber investigators for unleashing the damaging worm on the Internet. The worm replicated itself repeatedly, eating up computer capacity, but did not damage information or programs. The worm generated so much traffic that it brought entire networks down.

The FBI used the latest technologies and code analysis to find the source of the worm. Prosecutors said that Microsoft suffered financial losses that significantly exceeded $5,000, the statutory threshold in most hacker cases. Parson, charged with

FIGURE 9.23

Sample Firewall Architecture Connecting Systems Located in Toronto, New York, and Munich

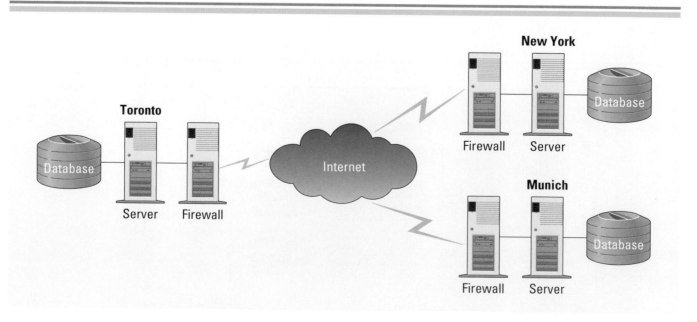

intentionally causing or attempting to cause damage to a computer, was sentenced to 18 months in prison, three years of supervised release, and 100 hours of community service. "What you've done is a terrible thing. Aside from injuring people and their computers, you shook the foundation of technology," U.S. District Judge Marsha Pechman told Parson.

"With this arrest, we want to deliver a message to cyber-hackers here and around the world," said U.S. Attorney John McKay in Seattle. "Let there be no mistake about it, cyber-hacking is a crime. We will investigate, arrest, and prosecute cyber-hackers."[27]

Typically, people equate viruses (the malicious software) with hackers (the people). While not all types of hackers create viruses, many do. Figure 9.24 provides an overview of the most common types of hackers and viruses.

Some of the most damaging forms of security threats to e-business sites include malicious code, hoaxes, spoofing, and sniffers (see Figure 9.25).

Implementing information security lines of defence through people first and through technology second is the best way for an organization to protect its vital information. The first line of defence is securing information by creating an information security plan detailing the various information security policies. The second line of defence is investing in technology to help secure information through authentication and authorization, prevention and resistance, and detection and response.

FIGURE 9.24

Hackers and Viruses

Hackers—people very knowledgeable about computers who use their knowledge to invade other people's computers.

- *White-hat hackers*—work at the request of the system owners to find system vulnerabilities and plug the holes.

- *Black-hat hackers*—break into other people's computer systems and may just look around or may steal and destroy information.

- *Hactivists*—have philosophical and political reasons for breaking into systems and will often deface the Web site as a protest.

- *Script kiddies* or *script bunnies*—find hacking code on the Internet and click-and-point their way into systems to cause damage or spread viruses.

- *Cracker*—a hacker with criminal intent.

- *Cyberterrorists*—seek to cause harm to people or to destroy critical systems or information and use the Internet as a weapon of mass destruction.

Viruses—software written with malicious intent to cause annoyance or damage.

- *Worm*—a type of virus that spreads itself, not only from file to file, but also from computer to computer. The primary difference between a virus and a worm is that a virus must attach to something, such as an executable file, in order to spread. Worms do not need to attach to anything to spread and can tunnel themselves into computers.

- *Denial-of-service attack (DoS)*—floods a Web site with so many requests for service that it slows down or crashes the site.

- *Distributed denial-of-service attack (DDoS)*—attacks from multiple computers that flood a Web site with so many requests for service that it slows down or crashes. A common type is the Ping of Death, in which thousands of computers try to access a Web site at the same time, overloading it and shutting it down.

- *Trojan-horse virus*—hides inside other software, usually as an attachment or a downloadable file.

- *Backdoor programs*—viruses that open a way into the network for future attacks.

- *Polymorphic viruses and worms*—change their form as they propagate.

FIGURE 9.25

Security Threats to
E-Business

Security Threats to E-Business
Elevation of privilege is a process by which a user misleads a system into granting unauthorized rights, usually for the purpose of compromising or destroying the system. For example, an attacker might log onto a network by using a guest account, and then exploit a weakness in the software that lets the attacker change the guest privileges to administrative privileges.
Hoaxes attack computer systems by transmitting a virus hoax, with a real virus attached. By masking the attack in a seemingly legitimate message, unsuspecting users more readily distribute the message and send the attack on to their co-workers and friends, infecting many users along the way.
Malicious code includes a variety of threats such as viruses, worms, and Trojan horses.
Spoofing is the forging of the return address on an e-mail so that the e-mail message appears to come from someone other than the actual sender. This is not a virus but rather a way by which virus authors conceal their identities as they send out viruses.
Spyware is software that comes hidden in free downloadable software and tracks online movements, mines the information stored on a computer, or uses a computer's CPU and storage for some task the user knows nothing about. According to the National Cyber Security Alliance, 91 percent of the study had spyware on their computers that can cause extremely slow performance, excessive pop-up ads, or hijacked home pages.
A ***sniffer*** is a program or device that can monitor data travelling over a network. Sniffers can show all the data being transmitted over a network, including passwords and sensitive information. Sniffers tend to be a favourite weapon in the hacker's arsenal.
Packet tampering consists of altering the contents of packets as they travel over the Internet or altering data on computer disks after penetrating a network. For example, an attacker might place a tap on a network line to intercept packets as they leave the computer. The attacker could eavesdrop or alter the information as it leaves the network.

OPENING CASE QUESTIONS

Embracing Privacy at the City of Hamilton

5. In the City of Hamilton example, how can the City's embracement of privacy mitigate future information security problems?

6. What is the biggest information security roadblock facing organizations, like the City of Hamilton, attempting to achieve compliance with privacy legislation?

7. Can technology alone at the City of Hamilton guarantee information is kept secure? Why or why not?

8. Privacy and security breaches, like the City of Hamilton's dog-licence incident, are unfortunately a common occurrence in organizations today. What recent privacy and security breaches have been in the media lately? Do you think things will get worse before getting better? How can organizations better prepare themselves against future privacy and security breaches?

The purpose of the chapter was to highlight the need for organizations to protect information from misuse:

- Discussion first centred on the concept of information ethics—how organizations need to be aware of the moral issues surrounding the development and use of information and information technology.

- From there, information privacy was examined. Here, emphasis was placed on understanding the legal obligations and general expectations on organizations in terms of how personal information is collected, shared, and stored.

- Last, discussion focused on information security and the two levels of defence that organizations have to protect their information resources: people and technology.

As a business student, you need to know this since ethical, privacy, and security concerns over the treatment of information and information technology are of paramount importance in organizations today.

- Nowhere is this more true than in Canada where PIPEDA privacy legislation puts legal pressure on companies to guarantee that the personal information they collect remains private and secure.

- Companies that fail to do so not only face legal repercussions, but also the wrath of consumers who have high expectations on how their personal information is handled by companies.

KEY TERMS

Acceptable use policy (AUP) 269
Adware 262
Anti-spam policy 272
Authentication 279
Authorization 279
Backdoor program 283
Biometrics 280
Black-hat hacker 283
Clickstream 262
Confidentiality 258
Content filtering 281
Cookie 262
Copyright 258
Counterfeit software 258
Cracker 283
Cyberterrorist 283
Denial-of-service attack (DoS) 283
Distributed denial-of-service attack (DDoS) 283
Elevation of privilege 284
E-mail privacy policy 271
Encryption 281
ePolicies 268
Ethical computer use policy 268

Ethics 258
Fair use doctrine 258
Firewall 278
Hacker 283
Hactivist 283
Hardware key logger 262
Hoaxes 284
Identity theft 279
Information ethics 259
Information privacy 263
Information privacy policy 269
Information security 274
Information security plan 276
Information security policies 276
Information technology monitoring 262
Insider 276
Intellectual property 258
Internet use policy 271
Intrusion detection software (IDS) 278
Key logger software (key trapper) 262

Mail bomb 270
Malicious code 284
Nonrepudiation 269
Packet tampering 284
Phishing 279
Pirated software 258
Polymorphic virus and worm 283
Privacy 258
Public key encryption (PKE) 281
Script kiddies or script bunnies 283
Smart card 280
Sniffer 284
Social engineering 276
Spam 272
Spoofing 284
Spyware (sneakware or stealthware) 262
Token 280
Trojan-horse virus 283
Virus 283
Web log 262
White-hat hacker 283
Worm 283

WestJet Accepts Blame About Spying On Air Canada Rival

This case illustrates the ethics and ramifications of breaching private information.

In May 2006, a resolution was reached in a corporate espionage case between WestJet and Air Canada. WestJet admitted culpability in accessing confidential information via an Air Canada Web site.

Accessing this information, Air Canada claimed, allowed WestJet to identify Air Canada's most profitable routes and plan their expansion accordingly. Being privy to this information, Air Canada claimed, allowed WestJet to unfairly adjust its own scheduling and pricing information and to gain a valuable springboard in starting new routes and terminating others. In addition, Air Canada claimed, it allowed WestJet to identify booking trends, information tremendously valuable to any airline.

In a press release jointly issued with Air Canada, WestJet accepted "full responsibility" stating that "the conduct was both unethical and unacceptable." In the press release, WestJet admitted that certain members of its management team had "engaged in an extensive practice of covertly accessing a password-protected proprietary employee Web site maintained by Air Canada to download detailed and commercially sensitive information without authorization or consent from Air Canada."[28]

What was truly alarming about this incident was that this corporate spying occurred with the knowledge and direction of the highest management levels at WestJet. It did not stop until the breach was discovered by Air Canada.

Here are the series of events, according to the Calgary Herald:

- In 2002, Jeffrey Lafond, joined WestJet as a financial analyst. Lafond formerly worked at Canadian Airlines for five years; that employment ended when Canadian Airlines was bought by Air Canada.

- As part of Lafond's severance package, he could receive two free trips per year, which could be booked through an Air Canada employee Web site.

- Realizing the importance of Air Canada's bookings, Lafond showed the Web site to Scott Butler, WestJet's director of Strategic Planning. Butler told Mark Hill, a vice president and WestJet founder.

- Hill and Butler asked for Lafond's Air Canada employee number and personal code; Lafond asked them for indemnity against potential legal liability.

- From his home computer in Victoria, B.C., Hill started using Lafond's code to access the Web site. Each night, he spent about 90 minutes checking Air Canada's load factors on different routes. However, this proved too time-consuming. In response, another West-Jet employee created an automated "screen scraper" program to collect and parse Air Canada's information. Sometimes this program hit Air Canada's Web site over 1,000 times a day. Hill would scan the material, sometimes passing it on to other WestJet employees.

- In the summer of 2003, Air Canada was beginning to get suspicious of WestJet's access to Air Canada passenger load information.

- In December 2003, a whistle-blower from WestJet informed Air Canada management about the situation. Air Canada corporate security began investigating unauthorized access to Air Canada's reservation system.

- In early February 2004, investigators reported an unusually high number of accesses—243,630 times—to the system over a 10-month period via Lafond's employee number.

- On April 6, 2004, Air Canada launched a $5-million lawsuit against WestJet and its two employees, Mark Hill and Jerffrey Lafond, alleging unauthorized access to private information from its company Web site.

- On July 14, 2004, Hill resigned from WestJet.
- On July 22, 2004, Air Canada upped the lawsuit to $220 million.
- In 2006, two years after the original lawsuit was filed, an out-of-court settlement was reached with all legal proceedings dropped. The settlement had WestJet agreeing to pay settlement costs of $15.5 million. This amount included a $10-million donation made in Air Canada's name to children's charities across the nation and payment of Air Canada's litigation costs of $5.5 million.[29]

Mr. Clive Beddoe, co-founder of Calgary-based WestJet in 1996 and former president of WestJet Airlines, admits that WestJet has learned painful lessons. In direct response to the fall-out from Air Canada's lawsuit, WestJet quickly introduced a whistle-blower policy and beefed-up its "code of business conduct."[30]

Questions

1. Was WestJet's access to Air Canada's Web site information ethical? Legal? Explain.
2. To what extent do you think unauthorized access to private competitor information is commonplace in organizations?
3. Does Air Canada have any responsibility in WestJet's ability to access Air Canada's private information? Explain.
4. What people-measures could Air Canada implement to prevent future unauthorized access to private information?
5. What technology-measures could Air Canada implement to prevent future unauthorized access to private information?

CLOSING CASE TWO

Hacker Hunters

This case offers several examples of breaches in information security.

Hacker hunters are the new breed of crime fighter. They employ the same methodology used to fight organized crime in the 1980s—informants and the cyberworld equivalent of wiretaps. Daniel Larking, a 20-year veteran who runs the FBI's Internet Crime Complaint Center, taps online service providers to help track down criminal hackers. Leads supplied by the FBI and eBay helped Romanian police round up 11 members of a gang that set up fake eBay accounts and auctioned off cell phones, laptops, and cameras they never intended to deliver.

On October 26, 2004, the FBI unleashed Operation Firewall, targeting the ShadowCrew, a gang whose members were schooled in identity theft, bank account pillage, and selling illegal goods on the Internet. ShadowCrew's 4,000 gang members lived in a dozen countries and across the United States. For months, agents had been watching their every move through a clandestine gateway into their Web site, shadowcrew.com. One member turned informant and called a group meeting, ensuring the members would be at home on their computers during a certain time, when the Secret Service issued orders to move in on the gang. The move was synchronized around the globe to prevent gang members from warning each other via instant messages. Twenty-eight gang members in eight states and six countries were arrested, most still at their computers. Authorities seized dozens of computers and found 1.7 million credit card numbers and more than 18 million e-mail accounts.

ShadowCrew's Operations

The alleged ringleaders of ShadowCrew included Andres Mantovani, 23, a part-time community college student in Arizona, and David Appleyard, 45, a former New Jersey mortgage broker. Mantovani and Appleyard allegedly were administrators in charge of running the Web site and recruiting members. The site created a marketplace for over 4,000 gang members who bought and sold hot information and merchandise. The Web site was open for business 24 hours a day, but since most of the members held jobs, the busiest time was from 10 p.m. to 2 a.m. on Sundays. Hundreds of gang members would meet online to trade credit card information, passports, and even equipment to make fake identity documents. Platinum credit cards cost more than gold ones and discounts were offered for package deals. One member known as "Scarface" sold 115,695 stolen credit card numbers in a single trade. Overall, the gang made more than US$4 million in credit card purchases over two years. ShadowCrew was equivalent to an eBay for the underworld. The site even posted crime tips on how to use stolen credit cards and fake IDs at big retailers.

The gang stole credit card numbers and other valuable information through clever tricks. One of the favourites was sending millions of phishing e-mails—messages that appeared to be from legitimate companies such as Yahoo!— designed to steal passwords and credit card numbers. The gang also hacked into corporate databases to steal account data. According to sources familiar with the investigation, the gang cracked the networks of 12 unidentified companies that were not even aware their systems had been breached.

Police Operations

Brian Nagel, an assistant director at the Secret Service, coordinated the effort to track the ShadowCrew. Allies included Britain's national high-tech crimes unit, the Royal Canadian Mounted Police, and the Bulgarian Interior Ministry. Authorities turned one of the high-ranking members of the gang into a snitch and had the man help the Secret Service set up a new electronic doorway for ShadowCrew members to enter their Web site. The snitch spread the word that the new gateway was a more secure way to the Web site. It was the first-ever tap of a private computer network. "We became shadowcrew.com," Nagel said. Mantovani and Appleyard were slated for trail in late 2005. Authorities anticipated using case evidence to make additional arrests.[31]

Questions

1. What types of technology could big retailers use to prevent identity thieves from purchasing merchandise?
2. What can organizations do to protect themselves from hackers looking to steal account data?
3. Authorities frequently tap online service providers to track down hackers. Do you think it is ethical for authorities to tap an online service provider and read people's e-mail? Why or why not?
4. Do you think it was ethical for authorities to use one of the high-ranking officials to trap other gang members? Why or why not?
5. In a team, research the Internet and find the best ways to protect yourself from identity theft.

CLOSING CASE THREE

Thinking Like the Enemy

This case illustrates how some organizations are preparing themselves against hacking threats.

David and Barry Kaufman, the founders of the Intense School, recently added several security courses, including the five-day "Professional Hacking Boot Camp" and "Social Engineering in Two Days."

Information technology departments must know how to protect organizational information. Therefore, organizations must teach their IT personnel how to protect their systems, especially in light of the many privacy and security regulations that demand secure systems. The concept of sending IT professionals to a hacking school seems counterintuitive; it is somewhat similar to sending accountants to an Embezzling 101 course. The Intense School does not strive to breed the next generation of hackers, however, but to teach its students how to be "ethical" hackers: to use their skills to build better locks, and to understand the minds of those who would attempt to crack them.

The main philosophy of the security courses at the Intense School is simply "To know thy enemy." In fact, one of the teachers at the Intense School is none other than Kevin Mitnick, the famous hacker who was imprisoned from 1995 to 2000. Teaching security from the hacker's perspective, as Mitnick does, is more difficult than teaching hacking itself. A hacker just needs to know one way into a system, David Kaufman noted, but a security professional needs to know all of the system's vulnerabilities. The two courses analyze those vulnerabilities from different perspectives.

The hacking course teaches ways to protect against the mischief typically associated with hackers: worming through computer systems through vulnerabilities that are susceptible to technical, or computer-based, attacks. Mitnick's social engineering course, by contrast, teaches the more frightening art of worming through the vulnerabilities of the people using and maintaining systems—getting passwords and access through duplicity, not technology. People that take this class, or read Mitnick's book, *The Art of Deception*, never again think of passwords or the trash bin the same way.

So how does the Intense School teach hacking? With sessions on dumpster diving (the unsavory practice of looking for passwords and other bits of information on discarded papers), with field trips to case target systems, and with practice runs at the company's in-house "target range," a network of computers set up to thwart and educate students.

One feature of the Intense School that raises a few questions is that the school does not check on morals at the door: Anyone paying the tuition can attend the school. Given the potential danger that an unchecked graduate of a hacking school could represent, it is surprising that the police do not collect the names of the graduates. But perhaps it gets them anyhow—several governmental agencies have sent students to the school.[32]

Questions

1. How could an organization benefit from attending one of the courses offered at the Intense School?

2. What are the two primary lines of security defence and how can organizational employees use the information taught by the Intense School when drafting an information security plan?

3. Determine the differences between the two primary courses offered at the Intense School, "Professional Hacking Boot Camp" and "Social Engineering in Two Days." Which course is more important for organizational employees to attend?

4. If your employer sent you to take a course at the Intense School, which one would you choose and why?

5. What are the ethical dilemmas involved with having such a course offered by a private company?

MAKING BUSINESS DECISIONS

1. Firewall decisions

You are the CEO of Inverness Investments, a medium-sized venture capital firm that specializes in investing in high-tech companies. The company receives over 30,000 e-mail messages per year. On average, there are two viruses and three successful hackings against the company each year, which result in losses to the company of about $250,000 per year. Currently, the company has antivirus software installed but does not have any firewalls.

Your CIO is suggesting implementing 10 firewalls for a total cost of $80,000. The estimated life of each firewall is about three years. The chances of hackers breaking into the system with the firewalls installed are about 3 percent. Annual maintenance costs on the firewalls is estimated around $15,000. Create an argument for or against supporting your CIO's recommendation to purchase the firewalls. Are there any considerations in addition to finances?

2. Preventing identity theft

Identity theft is one of the fastest-growing crimes. If you are a victim of identity theft, your financial reputation can be ruined, making it impossible for you to cash a cheque or receive a bank loan. Learning how to avoid identity theft can be a valuable activity. Research the following Web sites and draft a document stating the best ways to prevent identity theft.

- www.safecanada.ca/identitytheft_e.asp—The Government of Canada's Web site providing information and services on public safety.
- www.privcom.gc.ca/fs-fi/02_05_d_10_e.asp—The Office of the Privacy Commissioner of Canada's fact sheet on identity theft.
- cmcweb.ca/epic/site/cmc-cmc.nsf/en/fe00084e.html—Canada's Consumer Measures Committee's Web site pertaining to identity theft.
- www.canadapost.ca/corporate/about/security/id_theft-e.asp—Canada Post's information about identity theft.
- www.cippic.ca/en/faqs-resources/identity-theft—The Canadian Internet Policy and Public Interest Clinic's information about identity theft.

3. Discussing the three areas of information security

Great Granola Inc. is a small business operating out of Saskatchewan. The company specializes in selling homemade granola, and its primary sales vehicle is through its Web site. The company is growing exponentially and expects its revenues to triple this year to $15 million. The company also expects to hire 60 additional employees to support its growing number of customers. Sally Smith, the CEO, is aware that if her competitors discover the recipe for her granola, or who her primary customers are, it could easily ruin her business. Sally has hired you to draft a document discussing the different areas of information security, along with your recommendations for providing a secure e-business environment.

4. Information privacy

A study by the Annenberg Public Policy Center at the University of Pennsylvania shows that 95 percent of people who use the Internet at home think they should have a legal right to know everything about the information that Web sites collect from them. Research also shows that 57 percent of home Internet users incorrectly believe that when a Web site has an information privacy policy it will not share personal information with other Web sites or companies. In fact, the research found that after showing the users how companies track, extract, and share Web site information to make money, 85 percent found the methods unacceptable, even for a highly valued site. Write a short paper arguing for or against an organization's right to use and distribute personal information gathered from its Web site.

5. Spying on e-mail

Technology advances now allow individuals to monitor computers that they do not even have physical access. New types of software can capture an individual's incoming and outgoing e-mail and then immediately forward that e-mail to another person. For example, if you are at work and your child is home from school and she receives an e-mail from John at 3:00 pm, at 3:01 pm you will receive a copy of that e-mail sent to your e-mail address. A few minutes later, if she replies to John's e-mail, within seconds you will again receive a copy of what she sent to John. Describe two scenarios (other than the above) for the use of this type of software: (1) where the use would be ethical, (2) where the use would be unethical, and (3) where the use isn't clear if it is ethical or unethical (grey area).

6. **Stealing software**

The software industry fights against pirated software on a daily basis. The major centres of software piracy are in places like Russia and China where salaries and disposable income are comparatively low. People in developing and economically depressed countries will fall behind the industrialized world technologically if they cannot afford access to new generations of software. Considering this, is it reasonable to blame someone for using pirated software when it could potentially cost him or her two months' salary to purchase a legal copy? Create an argument for or against the following statement: "Individuals who are economically less fortunate should be allowed access to software free of charge in order to ensure that they are provided with an equal technological advantage."

Building Information Systems

This section of the textbook explains how organizations go about building information systems. It's a complex task requiring an understanding of user needs, computing infrastructures, and the ability to translate user requirements into a technical design that works for people. It also is a task that requires extensive planning and people skills to make it all happen. Easier said than done! Too often, information systems development projects are criticized for going over budget, being delayed, or lacking in desired functionality.

The purpose of this section of the textbook is to describe the various ways information systems can be built in organizations, the challenges that come along with the process, and the beauty of how well things turn out if systems are built according to good design principles and sound management practices.

To communicate this message, this section comprises three separate chapters. Chapter 10 provides an overview of how enterprise applications are developed in companies and the traditional systems development life cycle that is used to build information systems. Chapter 11 examines networks, telecommunications, and wireless computing fundamentals—the core communications technologies that information systems developers typically incorporate into their enterprise-wide application designs. Chapter 12 provides an overview of hardware/software basics and enterprise architecture—things that comprise an organization's underlying information infrastructure and must be understood and managed correctly in order to build and maintain information systems.

10 Systems Development

CHAPTER

Why Do I Need To Know This ?

This chapter provides an overview of how organizations go about developing information systems. As a business student, you need to know this, since information systems are the underlying foundation of how companies operate. Having a basic understanding of the principles of building information systems will make you a more valuable employee. You will be able to identify trouble spots early on and make suggestions during the design process that will result in a better delivered information systems project—one that you and your organization will be happier and more satisfied with.

It is analogous to getting a house constructed from a housing developer or builder. You could sit back and let the developers do all the design work and construction on their own and take your chances that the finished house will meet all your needs (yeah, right). Or, you could watch and participate in the design process and physical construction where your input would be used to steer the development of the finished product.

The same is true for building information systems applications in organizations. Your knowledge of the systems development process will allow you to participate and add input into the final design of the developed product.

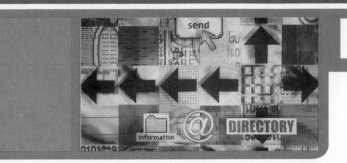

Canadian Youth Design Their Own Youth Portal

What is Youth.gc.ca? It's a Government of Canada portal dedicated to helping young Canadian citizens find information of relevance and interest. The portal provides a launch pad or gateway to a wide variety of information of specific interest to Canadian youth regarding employment, careers, education, justice, culture, health etc.—all from national, regional, and local perspectives. The idea behind Youth.gc.ca is to create one place that Canadian youth can find everything of interest without having to visit umpteen different Web sites hosted by various federal departments and agencies.

Launched in 2002 as "YouthPath," Youth.gc.ca was one of many innovative Web projects created as part of the "Government On-Line" initiative. The Government of Canada knew it would probably miss the mark if government bureaucrats were left to design a Web site that would attract and retain interest among young Canadians. Youth are savvy Internet users and are accustomed to utilizing Web sites that are fun, cool, engaging, and interactive. The answer was to follow a Participatory Design (PD) approach to design where representative end-users would play an active and meaningful role in the design of the Web site. They would become designers themselves by developing and organizing information categories and links for the site, and suggesting ideas that would be taken seriously by design consultants. Using these suggestions, the design consultants developed prototypes for "representative end-users" to comment upon. Representative end-users then voted for their favourite prototypes, which in turn, became the resulting system design used in practice.

Over 400 youths between the ages of 15 and 24 from across Canada participated in the initial development of the Youth portal via a secure online workspace.

It was important to the federal government to ensure that youth involved in the design project fairly represented the Canadian youth population. As such, broad calls for participation across the country were made over various print, Web-based, and face-to-face mediums. This included recruitment through a network of local youth-serving agencies, career and information fairs at community colleges and universities, and a call for participants via a Web site dedicated to the project.

Two types of calls were made: one for a Core Team and one for a Virtual Team. The Core Team comprised 19 individuals situated in the National Capital region of Ottawa. The role of this team was to act as team leaders to Virtual Team members. Each Core Team member was responsible for leading a specific subset of the Virtual Team composed of roughly 20 youth citizens who were geographically scattered across the country. It was felt that having Core Team members, who were youths themselves, would be better than seasoned Government of Canada employees at relaying assignments and tasks to a distributed Virtual Team of youths.

A restriction on the call for participants was the need to constrain recruitment of Core Team members to the National Capital region of Ottawa; however this was primarily for logistical reasons. Of relevance to the call was the purposeful recruitment of a diverse group of participants:

■ those with and without technical interests in the Web,
■ those reflecting the multicultural nature of Canada,
■ those from both French and English parts of Canada, and
■ those representative of marginalized groups.

To ensure all youth citizens involved in the project could avidly and equally participate in design, regardless of their economic background or availability of a computer at home, the Government of Canada loaned computers to those Youth Team members who did not have the available means to participate themselves.

One strength of the design process was that youth's participation was meaningful. Youth participants segmented into Core and Virtual Teams had very clear roles. Moreover, these roles were purposeful and added value to the final design. The activities directed to youth participants clearly translated into the layout and functionality of the portal interface, such as developing a logo for the site, deciding on the type of information to post, or figuring out how to organize the information on the portal that made sense to youth.

To increase youth engagement and participation in the project, the design process was set up in a way to ensure an element of fun. For example,

■ The online workspace that participants utilized to complete their activities and tasks was innovative and offered a creative workspace through which to design. The environment facilitated social interaction, both project and non-project related.
■ There was also tolerance in allowing flexibility in youth participation. No ramifications resulted for those who participated in bursts of activity.
■ There were ample reward items for participants contributing the best design ideas and suggestions (e.g., webcams, cordless mice, cordless keyboards, and a free trip to Ottawa to attend the portal launch!).
■ There were offerings of praise and recognition to youth participants.

Good effort was also expended in fostering a respectful and cooperative relationship between the youth involved in design and civil service project team members. For instance, federal employees would regularly provide youth citizens involved in the project with information updates in the online workspace on the status of the project and how their ideas and suggestions were translated into design. Government of Canada employees also regularly met face-to-face with members of the youth Core Team who lived in close proximity to the National Capital area.

To help Virtual Team members with their use of the online workspace, a Virtual Moderator was assigned to the tool to answer questions posted online by youth participants and to provide technical assistance on a continuous basis. To gain trust and acceptance of this person—an Ottawa civil servant—the Virtual Moderator was a youth himself (under the age of 24). By assigning a youthful employee to play this role, the Canadian government thought that such a person could more easily relate to youth team members in that this person could "speak their language."[1]

The concept of leveraging the avid participation of youth citizens has been a big part of the Web site since its launch in 2002. A major component of the site continues to be the Canadian Youth Connection (CYC) Forum, a mechanism for Canadian youth to give feedback about youth services provided by the Government of Canada. This online space is a secure online environment for young Canadians where they can:

- meet and interact with other youth from across the nation,
- participate in surveys and online testing of various government services for youth,
- express their opinions and engage in discussions on various issues,
- gain volunteer experience,
- develop their critical thinking skills, and
- have fun![2]

INTRODUCTION

Organizations must learn how to build and implement systems to remain competitive. Software that is built correctly can support agile organizations and can transform as the organization and its business transforms. Software that effectively meets employee needs will help an organization become more productive and enhance decision making. Software that does not meet employee needs may have a damaging effect on productivity and can even cause a business to fail. Employee involvement along with using the right implementation methodology when developing software is critical to the success of an organization.

DEVELOPING SOFTWARE

Nike's SCM system failure, which spun out of control to the tune of US$400 million, is legendary. Nike blamed the system failure on its SCM vendor, i2 Technologies. Nike states that i2 Technologies' demand and supply planning module created serious inventory problems. The i2 deployment, part of a multimillion-dollar e-business upgrade, caused Nike CEO Philip Knight to famously say, "This is what we get for our $400 million?" The SCM vendor saw its stock plummet with the Nike disaster, along with its reputation. Katrina Roche, i2's chief marketing officer, asserted that Nike failed to use the vendor's implementation methodology and templates, which contributed to the problem.[3]

Software development problems often lead to high-profile disasters. Hershey's glitch in its ERP implementation made front page news and cost the company millions. Hershey said computer problems with its SAP software system created a backlog of orders, causing slower deliveries, and resulting in lower earnings. Statistics released in 2006 show that U.S. companies spent $250 billion in 2005 to repair damage caused by software defects.[4]

If software does not work, the organization will not work. Traditional business risk models typically ignored software development, largely because most organizations considered the impact from software and software development on the business to be minor. In the digital age, however, software success, or failure, can lead directly to business success, or failure. Almost every large organization in the world relies on software, either to drive its business operations or to make its products work. As organizations' reliance on software grows, so do the business-related consequences of software successes and failures as displayed in Figure 10.1.

FIGURE 10.1

Business-Related Consequences of Software Success and Failure

Business-Related Consequences of Software Success and Failure
Increase or decrease revenues—Organizations have the ability to directly increase profits by implementing successful IT systems. Organizations can also lose millions when software fails or key information is stolen or compromised.
Repair or damage to brand reputation—Technologies such as CRM can directly enhance a company's brand reputation. Software can also severely damage a company's reputation if it fails to work as advertised or has security vulnerabilities that affect its customers' trust.
Prevent or incur liabilities—Technology such as CAT scans, MRIs, and mammograms can save lives. Faulty technology used in airplanes, automobiles, pacemakers, or nuclear reactors can cause massive damage, injury, or death.
Increase or decrease productivity—CRM and SCM software can directly increase a company's productivity. Large losses in productivity can also occur when software malfunctions or crashes.

The lucrative advantages of successful software implementations provide significant incentives to manage software development risks. However, more than half of software development projects come in late or over budget and the majority of successful projects maintain fewer features and functions than originally specified. Organizations also cancel around 33 percent of these projects during development. Understanding the basics of software development methodologies will help organizations avoid potential software development pitfalls and ensure that software development efforts are successful.[5]

SOFTWARE DEVELOPMENT METHODOLOGIES

Today, systems are so large and complex that teams of architects, analysts, developers, testers, and users must work together to create the millions of lines of custom-written code that drive enterprises. For this reason, developers have created a number of different systems development life cycle methodologies including *waterfall, rapid application development (RAD), extreme programming, agile,* and *participatory design.* The oldest of these, and the best known, is the waterfall methodology: a sequence of phases in which the output of each phase becomes the input for the next (see Figure 10.2).

Waterfall Methodology

The traditional **waterfall methodology** is a sequential, activity-based process in which each phase in the systems development life cycle is performed sequentially from planning through implementation and maintenance. The waterfall methodology is one of the oldest software development methods and has been around for more than 30 years. The success rate for software development projects that follow this approach is only about 1 in 10. One primary reason for such a low success rate is that the waterfall methodology does not sufficiently consider the level of uncertainty in new projects and the creativity required to complete software development projects in several aspects (see Figure 10.3).

Unfortunately, business requirements change as the business changes, which calls for considerable feedback and iterative consultation for all business requirements. Essentially, software is "soft" and it must be easily changed and manipulated

FIGURE 10.2

The Traditional Waterfall Methodology

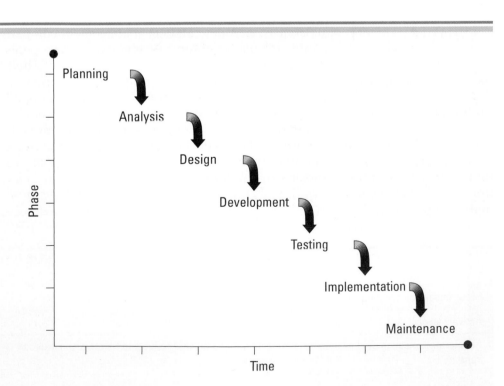

FIGURE 10.3

Issues Related to the
Waterfall Methodology

Issues Related to the Waterfall Methodology	
The business problem	Any flaws in accurately defining and articulating the business problem in terms of what the business users actually require flow onward to the next phase.
The plan	Managing costs, resources, and time constraints is difficult in the waterfall sequence. What happens to the schedule if a programmer quits? How will a schedule delay in a specific phase impact the total cost of the project? Unexpected contingencies may sabotage the plan.
The solution	The waterfall methodology is problematic in that it assumes users can specify all business requirements in advance. Defining the appropriate IT infrastructure that is flexible, scalable, and reliable is a challenge. The final IT infrastructure solution must meet not only current but also future needs in terms of time, cost, feasibility, and flexibility. Vision is inevitably limited at the head of the waterfall.

to meet the changing dynamics of an organization. As people's understanding of the business problems evolve, so must the software. For this reason, it is counterproductive to define all requirements precisely upfront since, by the time the software goes into production, which can be several months or even years after completing the initial analysis phase, chances are the business problems have changed as well as the business.

Rapid Application Development Methodology (RAD)

In response to the faster pace of business, rapid application development has become a popular route for accelerating systems development. *Rapid application development (RAD)* (also called *rapid prototyping*) *methodology* emphasizes extensive user involvement in the rapid and evolutionary construction of working prototypes of a system to accelerate the systems development process. Figure 10.4 displays the fundamentals of RAD.

A *prototype* is a smaller-scale representation or working model of the users' requirements or a proposed design for an information system. The prototype is an essential part of the analysis phase when using the RAD methodology.

PHH Vehicle Management Services, an American fleet-management company with over 750,000 vehicles, wanted to build an enterprise application that opened the entire vehicle information database to customers over the Internet. To build the application quickly, the company abandoned the traditional waterfall approach. Instead, a team of 30 developers began prototyping the Internet application, and the company's customers evaluated each prototype for immediate feedback. The development team released new prototypes that incorporated the customers' feedback every six weeks. The PHH Interactive Vehicle application went into production seven months after the initial work began. Over 20,000 customers, using a common browser, can now access the PHH Interactive site at any time from anywhere in the world to review their accounts, analyze billing information, and order vehicles.[6]

FIGURE 10.4

Fundamentals of RAD

Fundamentals of RAD
Focus initially on creating a prototype that looks and acts like the desired system.
Actively involve system users in the analysis, design, and development phases.
Accelerate collecting the business requirements through an interactive and iterative construction approach.

Extreme Programming Methodology

Extreme programming (XP) methodology breaks a project into tiny phases, and developers cannot continue on to the next phase until the first phase is complete. The primary difference between the waterfall and XP methodologies is that XP divides its phases into iterations with user feedback. The waterfall approach develops the entire system, whereas XP develops the system in iterations (see Figure 10.5). XP is a lot like a jigsaw puzzle; there are many small pieces. Individually the pieces make no sense, but when they are combined (again and again) an organization can gain visibility into the entire new system.

Microsoft Corporation developed Internet Explorer and Netscape Communications Corporation developed Communicator using extreme programming. Both companies did a nightly compilation (called a build) of the entire project, bringing together all the current components. They established release dates and expended considerable effort to involve customers in each release. The extreme programming approach allowed both Microsoft and Netscape to manage millions of lines of code as specifications changed and evolved over time. Most important, both companies frequently held user design reviews and strategy sessions to solicit and incorporate user feedback.[7]

XP is a significant departure from traditional software development methodologies, and many organizations in different industries have developed successful software using it. One reason for XP's success is its stress on customer satisfaction. XP empowers developers to respond to changing customer and business requirements, even late in the systems development life cycle, and XP emphasizes teamwork. Managers, customers, and developers are all part of a team dedicated to delivering quality software. XP implements a simple, yet effective way to enable groupware-style development. The XP methodology promotes quickly being able to respond to changing requirements and technology.

FIGURE 10.5

The Iterative Approach

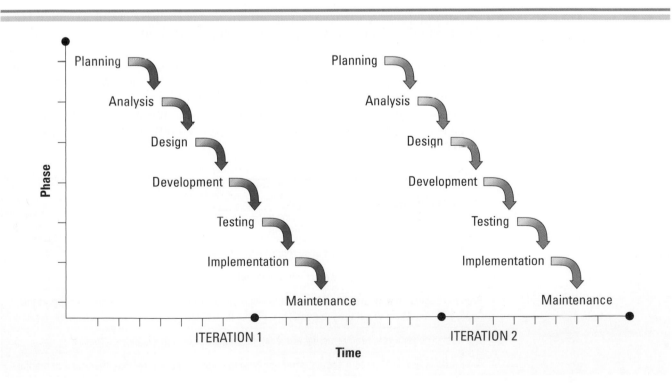

Agile Methodology

The **agile methodology**, a form of XP, aims for customer satisfaction through early and continuous delivery of useful software components. Agile is similar to XP but with less focus on team coding and more on limiting project scope. An agile project sets a minimum number of requirements and turns them into a deliverable product. Agile means what it sounds like: fast and efficient; small and nimble; lower cost; fewer features; shorter projects.

The Agile Alliance is a group of software developers whose mission is to improve software development processes and whose manifesto is displayed in Figure 10.6.

The Gartner Research estimates that 65 percent of agile projects are successful. This success rate is extraordinary compared to the 10 percent success rate of waterfall projects. The following are the primary principles an organization should follow for successful agile software development.[8]

Slash the Budget   Small budgets force developers and users to focus on the essentials. Small budgets also make it easier to kill a failing project. For example, imagine that a project that has already cost $20 million is going down the tubes. With that much invested, it is tempting to invest another $5 million to rescue it rather than take a huge loss. All too often, the system fails and the company ends up with an even bigger loss.

Jim Johnson, chairman of the Standish Group, says he forced the CIO of one Fortune 500 company to set a US$100,000 ceiling on all software development projects. There were no exceptions to this business rule without approval from the CIO and CEO. Johnson claims the company's project success rate went from 0 percent to 50 percent.[9]

If It Doesn't Work, Kill It   Bring all key stakeholders together at the beginning of a project and as it progresses bring them together again to evaluate the software. Is it doing what the business wants and, more important, requires? Eliminate any software that is not meeting business expectations. This is called triage, and it's "the perfect place to kill a software project," said Pat Morgan, senior program manager at Compaq's Enterprise Storage Group. He holds monthly triage sessions and says they can be brutal. "At one [meeting], engineering talked about a cool process they were working on to transfer information between GUIs. No one in the room needed it. We killed it right there. In our environment, you can burn a couple of million dollars in a month only to realize what you're doing isn't useful."[10]

Keep Requirements to a Minimum   Start each project with what the software must absolutely do. Do not start with a list of everything the software should do. Every software project traditionally starts with a requirements document that will often have hundreds or thousands of business requirements. The Standish Group estimates that only 7 percent of the business requirements are needed for any given

FIGURE 10.6

The Agile Alliance Manifesto

The Agile Alliance Manifesto
Early and continuous delivery of valuable software will satisfy the customer.
Changing requirements, even late in development, are welcome.
Businesspeople and developers must work together daily throughout the project.
Projects should be built around motivated individuals. Give them the environment and support they need, and trust them to get the job done.
The best architectures, requirements, and designs emerge from self-organizing teams.
At regular intervals, the team should reflect on how to become more effective, then tune and adjust its behaviour accordingly.

application. Keeping requirements to a minimum also means that scope creep and feature creep must be closely monitored. *Scope creep* occurs when the scope of the project increases. *Feature creep* occurs when developers add extra features that were not part of the initial requirements. Both scope creep and feature creep are major reasons software development fails.[11]

Test and Deliver Frequently   As often as once a week, and not less than once a month, complete a part of the project or a piece of software. The part must be working and it must be bug-free. Then have the customers test and approve it. This is the agile methodology's most radical departure from traditional development. In some traditional software projects, the customers did not see any working parts or pieces for years.

Assign Non-IT Executives to Software Projects   Non-IT executives should coordinate with the technical project manager, test iterations to make sure they are meeting user needs, and act as liaisons between executives and IT. Having the business side involved full-time will bring project ownership and a desire to succeed to all parties involved. SpreeRide, a market research outfit, used the agile methodology to set up its company's Web site. The project required several business executives designated full-time. The company believes this is one of the primary reasons that the project was successfully deployed in less than three months.[12]

Participatory Design

The *participatory design (PD) methodology* promotes the active involvement of users in the information systems development process. It is an approach towards systems design originating in Scandinavia where there is a history of direct and effective participation of workers in design activities and decision making. With PD, "the people destined to *use* the system play a critical role in *designing* it."[13]

Here, the traditional designer/user relationship is reversed: users are viewed as the experts—the ones with the most knowledge about what they do and what they need—and the designers as technical consultants or coaches.

Two often cited benefits of PD are the development of systems that better match user needs, and heightened user trust and acceptance of the system.

The PD approach is based on several tenets:

- The design process makes a difference for participants.
- Implementation of the results from the design process are likely.
- It is fun to participate.[14]

The first two points refer to the political side of having users participate in design. The project must make a difference for participants. If they perceive the system as having little benefit or relevance to their daily lives, the likelihood of engaging users actively in the project is remote at best. Further, if participants perceive their inclusion in the process as only a gesture of goodwill or a half-hearted attempt at understanding user needs, participants will not "buy-in." Participants need to feel their contributions are meaningful and will be put into action, not just recorded and put aside.

The last point concentrates on the design process itself; it must be fun for users to participate. To secure the active engagement of users in design, steps must be taken to overcome obstacles of hard work and boredom that is inherently part of any systems project.

To encourage healthy cooperation between user and designer, PD advocates suggest:

1. creating opportunities for mutual learning between users and traditional systems designers (e.g., each has knowledge that the other can benefit from),
2. utilizing design tools that are familiar to users (e.g., using pens, papers, flipcharts instead of entity-relationship or data-flow diagrams),
3. employing language that end-users know (no computer techno-babble allowed!),

4. starting the design process with the current practice of users, that is, understand how users currently conduct activities that the future system will help users perform, and use that knowledge as a springboard for determining ways to make improvements,

5. facilitating other design activities in a way that encourages users to envision future situations of working with the final system—this will allow users to experience and contemplate how the emerging design may affect their lives in practice.[15]

PROJECT MANAGEMENT

The above description of various software development methodologies highlights the complexity and difficulty in designing information system solutions. It is a challenging task. Organizations have been grappling over how to improve the development of information systems for years. Many have found success in treating the design and roll-out of information systems applications as formal projects that must be managed accordingly. Hence, many companies are treating application systems development initiatives as projects in the hopes of delivering systems that are on time, within budget, and satisfy user needs and expectations.

What is a project? A *project* is a temporary endeavour undertaken to create a unique product or service. According to the Project Management Institute, *project management* is the application of knowledge, skills, tools, and techniques to project activities in order to meet or exceed stakeholder needs and expectations from a project. *Project management software* specifically supports the long-term and day-to-day management and execution of the steps in a project (such as building a new warehouse or designing and implementing a new IT system).

Horizon Blue Cross Blue Shield of New Jersey, a US\$6-billion-plus health insurance provider, allocated several hundred million dollars to IT over a five-year period to tackle tasks such as consolidating five enterprise software platforms, managing compliance with regulatory offices, and simplifying new product development. These IT initiatives involved hundreds of skilled people working on hundreds of concurrently developing projects. Horizon's executives needed to gain visibility into all projects, subsets of projects, and existing and planned projects collectively. The company considered a rigorous and formalized project management strategy fundamental to the project's success. Horizon decided to implement IT project management software from Business Engine Inc. to manage its projects. The software collects information through standardized templates created for Microsoft Project, which are stored in an enterprise database, and then fed into Business Engine's analytical tool, called Ben. Each user can then view and manipulate spreadsheets and graphs, share documents, track revisions, and run what-if scenarios in their personalized digital dashboard view. With the help from Business Engine, Horizon is managing IT projects and assets as if they were investments, tracking their performance against business goals, assessing their individual return and value to the company, and helping sort out which projects require greater attention and resources and which require reduced attention and resources. Horizon found itself ahead of schedule on over 70 percent of its IT projects.[16]

Figure 10.7 displays the relationships between the three primary variables in any project—(1) time, (2) cost, and (3) scope. These three variables are interdependent. For example, decreasing a project's timeframe means either increasing the cost of the project or decreasing the scope of the project to meet the new deadline. Increasing a project's scope means either increasing the project's timeframe or increasing the project's cost—or both—to meet the increased scope changes. Project management is the science of making intelligent trade-offs between time, cost, and scope. All three of the factors combined determine a project's quality.

Studies show that the failure rate of IT projects is much higher in organizations that do not exercise disciplined project management. Figure 10.8 displays the top six reasons why IT projects fail according to *Information Week's* research survey of 150 IT managers.

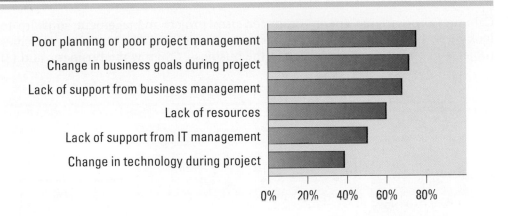

FIGURE 10.7

Project Management
Interdependent
Variables

FIGURE 10.8

Why IT Projects Fall
Behind Schedule
or Fail

A successful project is typically on time, within budget, meets the business's requirements, and fulfills the customer's needs. The Hackett Group analyzed its client database (which includes 2,000 companies, including 81 Fortune 100 companies) and discovered:

■ Three in 10 major IT projects fail.

■ 21 percent of the companies state that they cannot adjust rapidly to market changes.

■ One in four validate a business case for IT projects after completion.[17]

Nicolas Dubuc, collaborative project manager at Rhodia Inc., a $6.6-billion worldwide manufacturer of specialty chemicals, uses Microsoft's software to develop project management templates and methodologies for its 18 divisions. "We're designing a platform for rapid application development that will enhance opportunities for innovation," Dubuc said.

Today, the leaders in the project management software market include Microsoft, Primavera, Oracle, and SAP. Microsoft Project is the core project management tool for many organizations and dominates with more than 8 million users and over 80 percent of the market share. If an organization wants to deliver successful, high-quality software on time and under budget, it must take advantage of project management software.

Project Management Fundamentals

Project deliverables are any measurable, tangible, verifiable outcome, result, or item that is produced to complete a project or part of a project. Examples of project deliverables include design documents, testing scripts, and requirements documents.

Project milestones represent key dates when a certain group of activities must be performed. For example, completing the planning phase might be a project milestone. If a project milestone is missed, then chances are the project is experiencing problems.

A *project manager* is an individual who is an expert in project planning and management, defines and develops the project plan, and tracks the plan to ensure all key project milestones are completed on time.

The art and science of project management must coordinate numerous activities as displayed in Figure 10.9. Project managers perform numerous activities, and three of these primary activities are:

1. Choosing strategic projects.
2. Setting the project scope.
3. Managing resources and maintaining the project plan.

Choosing Strategic Projects

Calpine Corp., a large energy producer, uses project management software to look at its IT investments from a business perspective. The company classifies projects in one of three ways: (1) run the business, (2) grow the business, and (3)

FIGURE 10.9

Project Management Roles

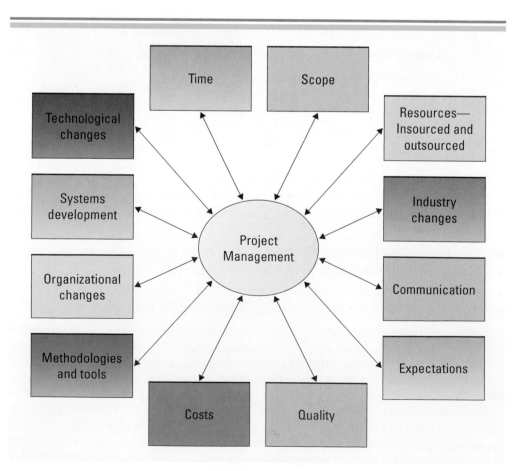

transform the business. Calpine splits its $110 million in assets accordingly: 60 percent for running the business, 20 percent for growing the business, and 20 percent for transforming the business. Calpine evaluates each of its 30 to 35 active projects for perceived business value against project costs. For the company to pursue a project it must pass a return on investment (ROI) hurdle. A business project must minimally provide two times ROI, and a transformation project must provide five times ROI.[18]

One of the most difficult decisions organizations make is determining the projects in which to invest time, energy, and resources. An organization must identify what it wants to do and how it is going to do it. The "what" part of this question focuses on issues such as justification for the project, definition of the project, and expected results of the project. The "how" part of the question deals with issues such as project approach, project schedule, and analysis of project risks. Determining which projects to focus corporate efforts on is as necessary to projects as each project is to an organization. Figure 10.10 displays the three common techniques an organization can use to select projects.

Before its merger with Hewlett-Packard, Compaq decided to analyze and prioritize its system development projects. Knowing that the CIO wanted to be able to view every project, project management leaders quickly identified and removed non-strategic projects. At the end of the review process, the company cancelled 39 projects, saving the organization $16.6 million. Most Fortune 100 companies are receiving bottom-line benefits similar to Compaq's from implementing a project management solution.[19]

Organizations also need to choose and prioritize projects in such a way that they can make responsible decisions as to which projects to eliminate. Jim Johnson, chairman of the Standish Group, has identified project management as the process that can make the difference in project success. According to Johnson, "Companies need a process for taking a regular look at their projects and deciding, again and again, if the investment is going to pay off. As it stands now, for most companies, projects can take on a life of their own."[20]

An organization must build in continuous self-assessment, which allows earlier termination decisions on failing projects, with the associated cost savings. This frees capital and personnel for dedication to projects that are worth pursuing. The elimination of a project should be viewed as successful resource management, not as an admission of failure.

Setting the Project Scope

Once an organization defines the projects it wants to pursue, it must set the project scope. *Project scope* defines the work that must be completed to deliver a product

FIGURE 10.10

Techniques for Choosing Strategic Projects

Techniques for Choosing Strategic Projects
1. **Focus on organizational goals**—Managers are finding tremendous value in choosing projects that align with the organization's goals. Projects that address organizational goals tend to have a higher success rate since they are important to the entire organization.
2. **Categorize projects**—There are various categories that an organization can group projects into to determine a project's priority. One type of categorization includes problem, opportunity, and directives. Problems are undesirable situations that prevent an organization from achieving its goals. Opportunities are chances to improve the organization. Directives are new requirements imposed by management, government, or some other external influence. It is often easier to obtain approval for projects that address problems or directives because the organization must respond to these categories to avoid financial losses.
3. **Perform a financial analysis**—A number of different financial analysis techniques can be performed to help determine a project's priority. A few of these include net present value, return on investment, and payback analysis. These financial analysis techniques help determine the organization's financial expectations for the project.

with the specified features and functions. The project scope statement is important because it specifies clear project boundaries. The project scope typically includes the following:

- **Project product**—a description of the characteristics the product or service has undertaken.
- **Project objectives**—quantifiable criteria that must be met for the project to be considered a success.
- **Project deliverables**—any measurable, tangible, verifiable outcome, result, or item that is produced to complete a project or part of a project.
- **Project exclusions**—products, services, or processes that are not specifically a part of the project.

The project objectives are one of the most important areas to define because they are essentially the major elements of the project. When an organization achieves the project objectives, it has accomplished the major goals of the project and the project scope is satisfied. Project objectives must include metrics so that the project's success can be measured. The metrics can include cost, schedule, and quality metrics along with a number of other metrics. Figure 10.11 displays the SMART criteria—useful reminders on how to ensure that the project has created understandable and measurable objectives.

Managing Resources and Maintaining the Project Plan

Managing people is one of the hardest and most critical efforts a project manager undertakes. How to resolve conflicts within the team and how to balance the needs of the project with the personal/professional needs of the team are a few of the challenges facing project managers. More and more project managers are the main (and sometimes sole) interface with the client during the project. As such, communication, negotiation, marketing, and salesmanship are just as important to the project manager as financial and analytical acumen. There are many times when the people management side of project management made the difference in pulling off a successful project.

A **project plan** is a formal, approved document that manages and controls project execution. Figure 10.12 displays the characteristics of a well-defined project plan. The most important part of the plan is communication. The project manager must communicate the plan to every member of the project team and to any key stakeholders and executives. The project plan must also include any project assumptions and be detailed enough to guide the execution of the project. A key to achieving project success is earning consensus and buy-in from all key stakeholders. By including key stakeholders in project plan development, the project manager allows them to have ownership of the plan. This often translates to greater commitment, which in turn results in enhanced motivation and productivity.

The two primary diagrams most frequently used in project planning are PERT and Gantt charts.

A **PERT (Program Evaluation and Review Technique) chart** is a graphical network model that depicts a project's tasks and the relationships between those

FIGURE 10.11

SMART Criteria for Successful Objective Creation

- Specific
- Measurable
- Agreed upon
- Realistic
- Time framed

FIGURE 10.12

Project Plan
Characteristics

Characteristics of a Well-Defined Project Plan
Easy to understand
Easy to read
Communicated to all key participants (key stakeholders)
Appropriate to the project's size, complexity, and criticality
Prepared by the team, rather than by the individual project manager

tasks. A **dependency** is a logical relationship that exists between the project tasks, or between a project task and a milestone. PERT charts define dependency between project tasks before those tasks are scheduled (see Figure 10.13). The boxes in Figure 10.13 represent project tasks, and the project manager can adjust the contents of the boxes to display various project attributes such as schedule and actual start and finish times. The arrows indicate that one task is dependent on the start or completion of another task. The **critical path** is a path from the start to the finish that passes through all the tasks that are critical to completing the project in the shortest amount of time. PERT charts frequently display a project's critical path.

A **Gantt chart** is a simple bar chart that depicts project tasks against a calendar. In a Gantt chart, tasks are listed vertically and the project's time frame is listed horizontally. A Gantt chart works well for representing the project schedule. It also shows actual progress of tasks against the planned duration. Figure 10.14 displays a software development project using a Gantt chart.

FIGURE 10.13

PERT Chart Expert,
a PERT Chart Example

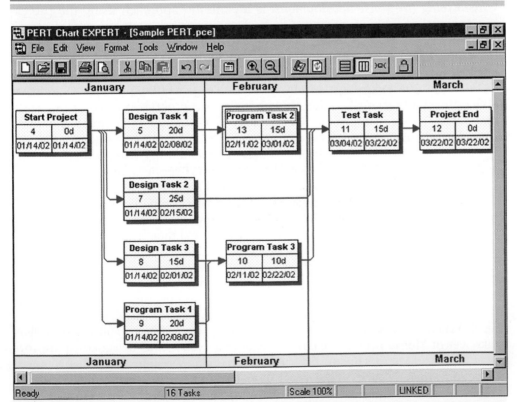

FIGURE 10.14

Microsoft Project, a
Gantt Chart Example

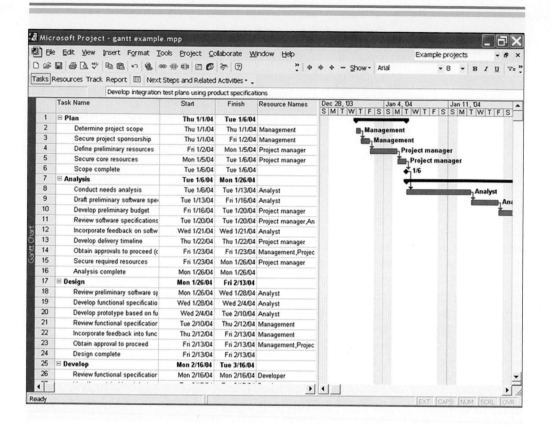

OUTSOURCING

There are basically two options available to organizations wishing to develop their own information systems applications. They can develop the information systems in-house or they can outsource the development elsewhere.

Insourcing (in-house development) is a common approach using the professional expertise within an organization to develop and maintain the organization's information technology systems. Insourcing has been instrumental in creating a viable supply of IT professionals and in creating a better quality workforce combining both technical and business skills.

Outsourcing is an arrangement by which one organization provides a service or services for another organization that chooses not to perform them in-house. In some cases, the entire information technology department is outsourced, including planning and business analysis as well as the installation, management, and servicing of the network and workstations. Outsourcing can range from a large contract under which an organization such as IBM manages IT services for a company such as Xerox, to the practice of hiring contractors and temporary office workers on an individual basis. Figure 10.15 compares the functions companies have outsourced, and Figure 10.16 displays the primary reasons companies outsource.

Sometimes organizations who previously developed their own in-house systems solutions on a regular basis have switched gears and now adopt an outsourcing philosophy. For example, Merrill Lynch recently signed a contract that outsourced much of the responsibility for its new wealth management systems platform to Thomson Financial (a large market data vendor). More than 400 people from Merrill Lynch, Thomson Financial, and a number of other vendors worked feverishly on this project—Merrill Lynch's biggest outsourcing initiative ever. This highly complex US$1-billion makeover of Merrill Lynch's wealth management system was designed to improve the efficiency of Merrill's financial advisers. With the new system, Merrill Lynch advisers can now manage more of the assets of their high net-worth customers. However, this new system development approach represents a major shift in the way Merrill Lynch conducted IT initiatives in the past. In the 1990s, Merrill Lynch developed its

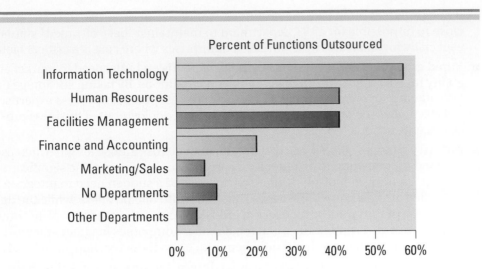

FIGURE 10.15

Common Departments
Outsourced by
Organizations

Percent of Functions Outsourced

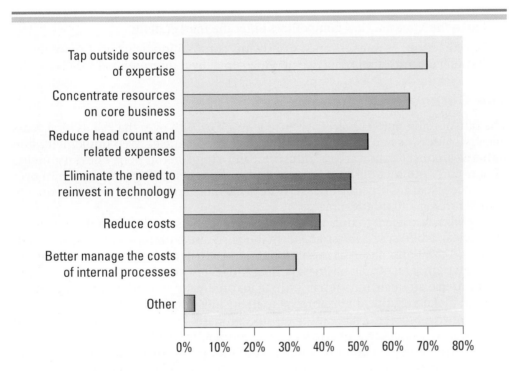

FIGURE 10.16

Reasons Companies
Outsource

previous system, Trusted Global Advisor (TGA), as it did any other major system—all in-house. Back then, the thought of outsourcing a critical business system to a vendor was viewed as highly unfavourable by most financial services organizations.[21]

Ever since Eastman Kodak announced that it was outsourcing its information systems function in 1988 to IBM, DEC, and Businessland, large organizations have found it acceptable to transfer their IT assets, leases, and staff to outsourcers. In view of the changes in sourcing, the key question now is not "should we outsource IT?" but rather "where and how can we take advantage of the rapidly developing market of IT services providers?" Some of the influential drivers affecting the growth of the outsourcing market include:

- **Core competencies.** Many companies have recently begun to consider outsourcing as a means to fuel revenue growth rather than just a cost-cutting measure. Outsourcing enables an organization to maintain an up-to-date technology infrastructure while freeing it to focus on revenue growth goals by reinvesting cash and human capital in areas offering the greatest return on investment.

- **Financial savings.** It is typically cheaper to hire workers in China and India than similar workers in Canada. Technology is advancing at such an accelerated rate that companies often lack the resources, workforce, or expertise to keep up. It is close to impossible for an IT department to maintain a "best-of-breed" status, especially for small and medium-sized enterprises where cost is a critical factor.

- **Rapid growth.** A company's sustainability depends on both speed to market and ability to react quickly to changes in market conditions. By taking advantage of outsourcing, an organization is able to acquire best practices process expertise. This facilitates the design, building, training, and deployment of business processes or functions.

- **Industry changes.** High levels of reorganization across industries have increased demand for outsourcing to better focus on core competencies. The significant increase in merger and acquisition activity created a sudden need to integrate multiple core and non-core business functions into one business, while the deregulation of the utilities and telecom industries created a need to ensure compliance with government rules and regulations. Companies in either situation turned to outsourcing so they could better focus on industry changes at hand.

- **The Internet.** The pervasive nature of the Internet as an effective sales channel has allowed clients to become more comfortable with outsourcing. Barriers to entry, such as lack of capital, are dramatically reduced in the world of e-business due to the Internet. New competitors enter the market daily.

- **Globalization.** As markets open worldwide, competition heats up. Companies may engage outsourcing service providers to deliver international services.

The Outsourcing Phenomenon

The outsourcing market has experienced strong growth over the last several years because of businesses' need to focus on core competencies, Web implementation initiatives, consolidation across industries, and a tight labour pool. The outsourcing of non-core, transaction-based processes has gained significant momentum over the last few years as organizations have become more comfortable with the concept of outsourcing and its advantages.

Organizations elect to outsource for a variety of reasons. Some of these reasons are tactical, while others are strategic. In the past, outsourcing was often used tactically, as a quick-fix, short-term solution to a particular need or problem, that did not form part of an overall business strategy. In recent years, many companies have begun to use strategic outsourcing where an organization works with suppliers in order to make a significant improvement in business performance.

No one would seriously expect an oil company to outsource its exploration and refining functions; pharmaceutical companies probably would not outsource their research and development; and few, if any, major automakers would consider outsourcing their production planning or marketing campaigns. These activities are core to their businesses and often the means for differentiation in the marketplace and a source of competitive advantage. Businesses outsource their non-core functions, such as payroll and IT. By outsourcing IT, most organizations can cut costs, improve service, and focus on their core business. According to research firm IDC, the worldwide IT outsourcing market will reach US$230 billion by 2009.[22]

Best Buy Co. Inc. is a leading specialty retailer for consumer electronics, personal computers, entertainment software, and appliances. Best Buy needed to find a strategic IT partner that could help the company leverage its IT functions in order to meet its business objectives. Best Buy further wanted to integrate its disparate enterprise systems and minimize its operating expenses. Best Buy outsourced these functions to Accenture, a global management consulting, technology services, and outsourcing company. The comprehensive outsourcing relationship that drove Best Buy's transformation produced spectacular results that were measurable in every key area of its business, such as a 20-percent increase in key category revenue that translated into a US$25-million profit improvement.[23]

According to PricewaterhouseCoopers' survey of CEOs from 452 of the fastest growing U.S. companies, "Businesses that outsource are growing faster, larger, and more profitably than those that do not. In addition, most of those involved in outsourcing say

they are saving money and are highly satisfied with their outsourcing service providers."
Figure 10.17 lists common areas for outsourcing opportunities across industries.

Outsourcing Benefits

The many benefits associated with outsourcing include:

- Increased quality and efficiency of a process, service, or function.
- Reduced operating expenses.
- Focusing resources on core profit-generating competencies.
- Reduced exposure to risks involved with large capital investments.
- Access to outsourcing service provider's economies of scale.
- Access to outsourcing services provider's expertise and best-in-class practices.
- Access to advanced technologies.
- Increased flexibility with the ability to respond quickly to changing market demands.
- Avoiding costly outlay of capital funds.
- Reduced head count and associated overhead expense.
- Reduced frustration and expense related to hiring and retaining employees in an exceptionally tight job market.
- Reduced time to market for products or services.

Outsourcing Options

In the early 1990s, British Petroleum (BP) began looking at IT outsourcing as a way to radically reduce costs and gain more flexible and higher-quality IT resources that directly improve the overall business. Over the past decade, all companies within the global BP Group have incorporated outsourcing initiatives in their business plans. BP's information technology costs were reduced by 40 percent globally over the first three years of the outsourcing engagement and have continued at a 10-percent reduction year after year, leading to hundreds of millions of dollars in savings to BP.[24]

Information technology outsourcing enables organizations to keep up with market and technology advances—with less strain on human and financial resources and more assurance that the IT infrastructure will keep pace with evolving business priorities (see Figure 10.18). Planning, deploying, and managing IT environments is both a tactical and a strategic challenge that must take into account a company's organizational, industrial, and technological concerns.

The three different forms of outsourcing options are:

1. **Onshore outsourcing** is the process of engaging another company within the same country for services.

FIGURE 10.17

Outsourcing
Opportunities

Industry	Outsourcing Opportunities
Banking and finance	Cheque and electronic payment processing, credit report issuance, delinquency management, securities, and trades processing
Insurance	Claims reporting and investigation, policy administration, cheque processing, risk assessment
Telecommunications	Invoice and bill production, transaction processing
Health care	Electronic data interchange, database management, accounting
Transportation	Ticket and order processing
Government	Loan processing, fine payment processing
Retail	Electronic payment processing

FIGURE 10.18

Outsourcing Models
and Cost Savings

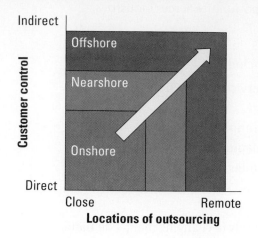

2. **Nearshore outsourcing** refers to contracting an outsourcing arrangement with a company in a nearby country. Often this country will share a border with the native country.

3. **Offshore outsourcing** is using organizations from developing countries to write code and develop systems. In offshore outsourcing the country is geographically far away.

The Challenges of Outsourcing

Outsourcing comes with several challenges. These arguments are valid and should be considered when a company is thinking about outsourcing. Many challenges can be avoided with proper research on the outsourcing service provider. The challenges include:

- **Contract length.** Most of the outsourced IT contracts are for a relatively long period (several years). This is because of the high cost of transferring assets and employees as well as maintaining technological investment. The long period of the contract causes three particular problems:

  1. Difficulties in getting out of a contract if the outsourcing service provider turns out to be unsuitable.

  2. Problems in foreseeing what the business will need over the next five or 10 years (typical contract lengths), hence creating difficulties in establishing an appropriate contract.

  3. Problems in reforming an internal IT department after the contract period is finished.

- **Competitive edge.** Effective and innovative use of IT can give an organization a competitive edge over its rivals. A competitive business advantage provided by an internal IT department that understands the organization and is committed to its goals can be lost in an outsourced arrangement. In an outsourced arrangement, IT staff are striving to achieve the goals and objectives of the outsourcing service provider, which may conflict with those of the organization.

- **Confidentiality.** In some organizations, the information stored in the computer systems is central to the enterprise's success or survival, such as information about pricing policies, product mixing formulas, or sales analysis. Some companies decide against outsourcing for fear of placing confidential information in the hands of the provider, particularly if the outsourcing service provider offers services to companies competing in the same marketplace. Although the organization usually dismisses this threat, claiming it is covered by confidentiality clauses in a contract, the organization must assess the potential risk and costs of a confidentiality breach in determining the net benefits of an outsourcing agreement.

- **Scope definition.** Most IT projects suffer from problems associated with defining the scope of the system. The same problem afflicts outsourcing arrangements. Many difficulties result from contractual misunderstandings between the organization and the outsourcing service provider. In such circumstances, the organization believes that the service required is within the contract scope while the service provider is sure it is outside the scope and so is subject to extra fees.

OPENING CASE QUESTIONS

Canadian Youth Design Their Own Youth Portal

1. In what ways did the development and design of Youth.gc.ca follow participatory design principles?

2. What challenges do you think an organization would face if they followed a PD approach to information systems design?

3. The Youth.gc.ca example illustrated the various steps and energy taken to ensure that a wide and representative set of end-users were involved in the design process. Should the same philosophy be followed by all organizations in general? Why or why not?

4. To what extent could PD design projects, like Youth.gc.ca, benefit from project management principles and techniques? To what extent could all software development methodologies benefit from project management principles and techniques?

5. To what extent would outsourcing be useful or appropriate in PD design projects like Youth.gc.ca? Would outsourcing be more suitable to another software development methodology? If so, which one(s)?

10.2 THE SYSTEMS DEVELOPMENT LIFE CYCLE

The *systems development life cycle (SDLC)*, also known as the "software life cycle" or the "application life cycle," is the overall process for developing information systems from planning and analysis through implementation and maintenance (see Figure 10.19).

The systems development life cycle is the foundation for all systems development methodologies, and there are literally hundreds of different activities associated with each phase in the SDLC. Typical activities include determining budgets, gathering systems requirements, and writing detailed user documentation. The activities performed during each systems development project vary (see Figure 10.20).

PHASE 1: PLANNING

1. Planning: The *planning phase* involves establishing a high-level plan of the intended project and determining project goals. Planning is the first and most critical phase of any systems development effort an organization undertakes, regardless of whether the effort is to develop a system that allows customers to order products over the Internet, determine the best logistical structure for warehouses around the world, or develop a strategic information alliance with another organization. Organizations must carefully plan the activities (and determine why they are necessary) to be successful.

The three primary activities involved in the planning phase are:

1. Identify and select the system for development.
2. Assess project feasibility.
3. Develop the project plan.

FIGURE 10.19

The Systems
Development
Life Cycle

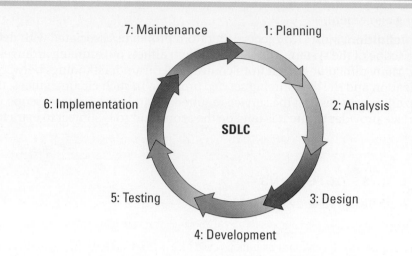

FIGURE 10.20

Common Activities
Performed During
Systems
Development

SDLC Phase	Activities
1. Planning	■ Identify and select the system for development ■ Assess project feasibility ■ Develop the project plan
2. Analysis	■ Gather business requirements ■ Create process diagrams ■ Perform a buy versus build analysis
3. Design	■ Design the IT infrastructure ■ Design system models
4. Development	■ Develop the IT infrastructure ■ Develop the database and programs
5. Testing	■ Write the test conditions ■ Perform the system testing
6. Implementation	■ Determine implementation method ■ Provide training for the system users ■ Write detailed user documentation
7. Maintenance	■ Build a help desk to support the system users ■ Perform system maintenance ■ Provide an environment to support system changes

Identify and Select the System for Development

Systems are successful only when they solve the right problem or take advantage of the right opportunity. Systems development focuses on either solving a problem or taking advantage of an opportunity. Determining which systems are required to support the strategic goals of an organization is one of the primary activities performed during the planning phase. Typically, employees generate proposals to build new information systems when they are having a difficult time performing their jobs. Unfortunately, most organizations have limited resources and cannot afford to develop all proposed information systems. Therefore, they look to critical success factors to help determine which systems to build.

A ***critical success factor (CSF)*** is a factor that is critical to an organization's success. To determine which system to develop, an organization tracks all the proposed systems and prioritizes them by business impact or critical success factors. This allows the business to prioritize which problems require immediate attention and which problems can wait. Figure 10.21 displays possible evaluation criteria for determining which projects to develop.

Assess Project Feasibility

A *feasibility study* determines if the proposed solution is feasible and achievable from a financial, technical, and organizational standpoint. Typically, an organization will define several alternative solutions that it can pursue to solve a given problem. A feasibility study is used to determine if the proposed solution is achievable, given the organization's resources and constraints in regard to technology, economics, organizational factors, and legal and ethical considerations. Figure 10.22 displays the different types of feasibility studies an organization can perform.

Develop the Project Plan

Developing a project plan is one of the final activities performed during the planning phase and it is one of the hardest and most important activities. The project plan is the guiding force behind on-time delivery of a complete and successful system. It logs and tracks every single activity performed during the project. If an activity is missed, or takes longer than expected to complete, the project plan must be updated to reflect these changes. Updating the project plan must be performed in every subsequent phase during the systems development effort.

FIGURE 10.21

Evaluation Criteria for Determining Software Development Projects

Evaluation Criteria	Description
Value chain analysis	The value chain determines the extent to which the new system will add value to the organization. Systems with greater value are given priority over systems with less value.
Strategic alignment	Projects that are in line with the organization's strategic goals and objectives are given priority over projects not in line with the organization's strategic goals and objectives.
Cost/benefit analysis	A cost/benefit analysis determines which projects offer the organization the greatest benefits with the least amount of cost.
Resource availability	Determine the amount and type of resources required to complete the project and determine if the organization has these resources available.
Project size, duration, and difficulty	Determine the number of individuals, amount of time, and technical difficulty of the project.

FIGURE 10.22

Different Types of Feasibility Studies

Types of Feasibility Studies	
Economic feasibility study (often called a cost-benefit analysis)	Identifies the financial benefits and costs associated with the systems development project.
Legal and contractual feasibility study	Examines all potential legal and contractual ramifications of the proposed system.
Operational feasibility study	Examines the likelihood that the project will attain its desired objectives.
Schedule feasibility study	Assesses the likelihood that all potential time frames and completion dates will be met.
Technical feasibility study	Determines the organization's ability to build and integrate the proposed system.

PHASE 2: ANALYSIS

The *analysis phase* involves analyzing end-user business requirements and refining project goals into defined functions and operations of the intended system. The analysis phase is critical. A good start is essential and the organization must spend as much time, energy, and resources as necessary to perform a detailed, accurate analysis. The three primary activities involved in the analysis phase are:

1. Gather business requirements.
2. Create process diagrams.
3. Perform a buy versus build analysis.

Gather Business Requirements

Business requirements are the detailed set of business requests that the system must meet to be successful. At this point, there is little or no concern with any implementation or reference to technical details. For example, the types of technology used to build the system, such as an Oracle database or the Java programming language, are not yet defined. The only focus is on gathering the true business requirements for the system. A sample business requirement might state, "The system must track all customer sales by product, region, and sales representative." This requirement states what the system must do from the business perspective, giving no details or information on how the system is going to meet this requirement.

Gathering business requirements is basically conducting an investigation in which users identify all the organization's business needs and take measurements of these needs. Figure 10.23 displays different methods organizations use to gather business requirements.

The *requirements definition document* contains the final set of business requirements, prioritized in order of business importance. The system users review the requirements definition document and determine if they will sign off on the business requirements. *Sign-off* is the system users' actual signatures indicating they approve all of the business requirements. One of the first major milestones on the project plan is usually the users' sign-off on business requirements.

A large data storage company implemented a project called Python whose purpose was to control all the company's information systems. Seven years, tens of millions of dollars, and 35 programmers later, Python was cancelled. At the end of the project, Python had over 1,800 business requirements of which 900 came from engineering and were written in order to make the other 900 customer requirements work. By the time the project was cancelled, it was unclear what the primary goals, objectives, and needs of the project were. Management should have realized Python's issues when the project's requirements phase dragged on, bulged, and took years to complete. The sheer number of requirements should have raised a red flag.[25]

FIGURE 10.23

Methods for Gathering Business Requirements

Methods for Gathering Business Requirements
Perform a *joint application development (JAD)* session where employees meet, sometimes for several days, to define or review the business requirements for the system.
Interview individuals to determine current operations and current issues.
Compile questionnaires to survey employees to discover issues.
Make observations to determine how current operations are performed.
Review business documents to discover reports, policies, and how information is used throughout the organization.

Create Process Diagrams

Once a business analyst takes a detailed look at how an organization performs its work and its processes, the analyst can recommend ways to improve these processes to make them more efficient and effective. *Process modelling* involves graphically representing the processes that capture, manipulate, store, and distribute information between a system and its environment. One of the most common diagrams used in process modelling is the data flow diagram. A *data flow diagram (DFD)* illustrates the movement of information between external entities and the processes and data stores within the system (see Figure 10.24). Process models and data flow diagrams establish the specifications of the system. *Computer-aided software engineering (CASE)* tools are software suites that automate systems analysis, design, and development. Process models and data flow diagrams can provide the basis for the automatic generation of the system if they are developed using a CASE tool.

Perform a Buy versus Build Analysis

An organization faces two primary choices when deciding to develop an information system: (1) it can buy the information system from a vendor or (2) it can build the system itself. *Commercial off-the-shelf (COTS)* software is a software package or solution that is purchased to support one or more business functions and information systems. Most customer relationship management, supply chain management, and enterprise resource planning solutions are COTS. Typically, a cost-benefit analysis forms the basis of the buy versus build decision. Figure 10.25 displays a few questions an organization must consider when contemplating the buy versus build decision.

Three key factors an organization should also consider when contemplating the buy versus build decision are: (1) time to market, (2) corporate resources, and (3) core competencies (see Figure 10.26). Weighing the complex relationship between each of these three variables will help an organization make the right choice.

When making the all-important buy versus build decision consider when the product must be available, how many resources are available, and how the

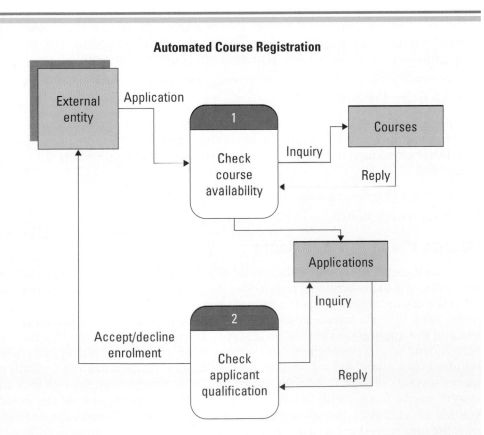

FIGURE 10.24

Sample Data Flow Diagram

FIGURE 10.25

Buy versus Build
Decision Questions

Buy versus Build Decision Questions
Do any currently available products fit the organization's needs?
Are unavailable features important enough to warrant the expense of in-house development?
Can the organization customize or modify an existing COTS to fit its needs?
Is there a justification to purchase or develop based on the cost of acquisition?

FIGURE 10.26

Key Factors
in Buy versus
Build Decisions

Three Key Factors in Buy versus Build Decisions	
1. Time to market	If time to market is a priority, then purchasing a good base technology and potentially building on to it will likely yield results faster than starting from scratch.
2. Availability of corporate resources	The buy versus build decision is a bit more complex to make when considering the availability of corporate resources. Typically, the costs to an organization to buy systems such as SCM, CRM, and ERP are extremely high. These costs can be so high—in the multiple millions of dollars—that acquiring these technologies might make the entire concept economically unfeasible. Building these systems, however, can also be extremely expensive, take indefinite amounts of time, and constrain resources.
3. Corporate core competencies	The more an organization wants to build a technical core competency, the less likely it will want to buy.

organization's core competencies affect the product. If these questions can be definitely answered either yes or no, then the answer is easy. However, most organizations cannot answer these questions with a solid yes or no. Most organizations need to make a trade-off between the lower cost of buying a system and the need for a system that meets all of their requirements. Finding a system to buy that meets all an organization's unique business requirements is next to impossible.

PHASE 3: DESIGN

The *design phase* involves describing the desired features and operations of the system including screen layouts, business rules, process diagrams, pseudo code, and other documentation. The two primary activities involved in the design phase are:

1. Design the IT infrastructure.
2. Design system models.

Design the IT Infrastructure

The system must be supported by a solid IT infrastructure or chances are the system will crash, malfunction, or not perform as expected. The IT infrastructure must meet the organization's needs in terms of time, cost, technical feasibility, and flexibility. Most systems run on a computer network with each employee having a client and the application running on a server. During this phase, the IT specialists recommend what types of clients and servers to buy including memory and storage requirements, along with software recommendations. An organization typically explores several different IT infrastructures that must meet current as well as future system needs. For example, databases must be large enough to hold the current volume of customers plus all new customers that the organization expects to gain over the next several years (see Figure 10.27).

FIGURE 10.27

Sample IT Infrastructure

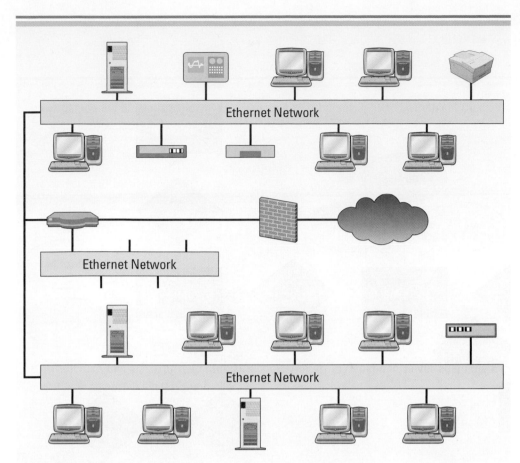

Design System Models

Modelling is the activity of drawing a graphical representation of a design. An organization should model everything it builds including reports, programs, and databases. Many different types of modelling activities are performed during the design phase including:

- The ***graphical user interface (GUI)*** is the interface to an information system. GUI screen design is the ability to model the information system screens for an entire system using icons, buttons, menus, and submenus.
- ***Data models*** represent a formal way to express data relationships to a database management system (DBMS).
- ***Entity relationship diagram (ERD)*** is a technique for documenting the relationships between entities in a database environment (see Figure 10.28).

PHASE 4: DEVELOPMENT

The ***development phase*** involves taking all of the detailed design documents from the design phase and transforming them into the actual system. In this phase, the project transitions from preliminary designs to the actual physical implementation. The two primary activities involved in the development phase are:

1. Develop the IT infrastructure.
2. Develop the database and programs.

Develop the IT Infrastructure

The platform upon which the system will operate must be built before building the actual system. In the design phase, an organization creates a blueprint of the

FIGURE 10.28

Sample Entity Relationship Diagram

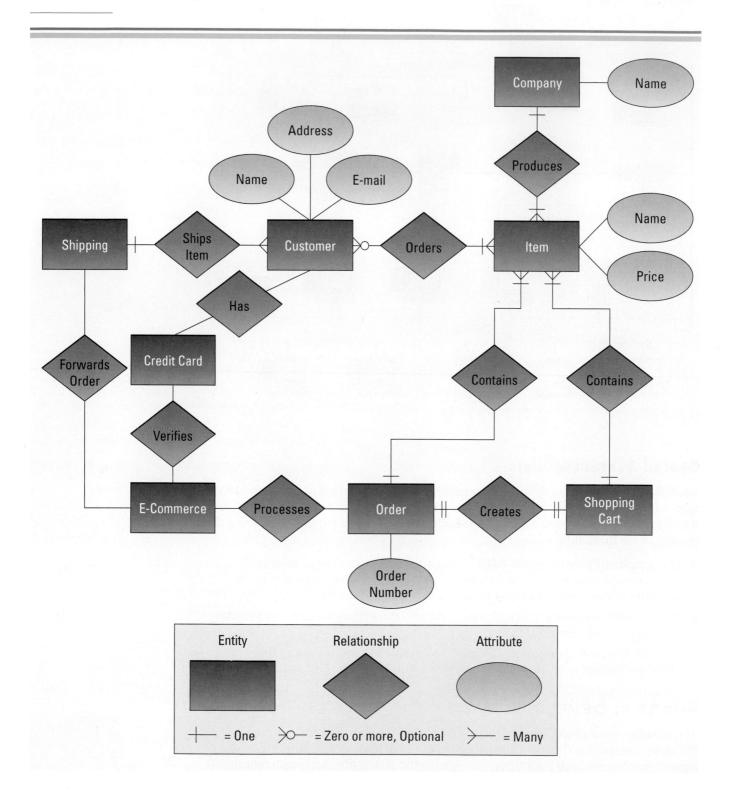

proposed IT infrastructure displaying the design of the software, hardware, and telecommunication equipment. In the development phase, the organization purchases and implements the required equipment to support the IT infrastructure.

Most new systems require new hardware and software. It may be as simple as adding memory to a client or as complex as setting up a wide area network across several provinces.

Develop the Database and Programs

Once the IT infrastructure is built, the organization can begin to create the database and write the programs required for the system. IT specialists perform these functions and it may take months or even years to design and create all the needed elements to complete the system.

PHASE 5: TESTING

The *testing phase* involves bringing all the project pieces together into a special testing environment to test for errors, bugs, and interoperability, in order to verify that the system meets all the business requirements defined in the analysis phase. The two primary activities involved in the testing phase are:

1. Write the test conditions.
2. Perform the system testing.

Write the Test Conditions

Testing is critical. An organization must have excellent test conditions to perform an exhaustive test. *Test conditions* are the detailed steps the system must perform along with the expected results of each step. Figure 10.29 displays several test conditions for testing user log-on functionality in a system. The tester will execute each test condition and compare the expected results with the actual results in order to verify that the system functions correctly. Notice in Figure 10.29 how each test condition is extremely detailed and states the expected results that should occur when executing each test condition. Each time the actual result is different from the expected result, a "bug" is generated and the system goes back to development for a bug fix.

Test condition 6 in Figure 10.29 displays a different actual result than the expected result because the system failed to allow the user to log on. After this test

FIGURE 10.29

Sample Test Conditions

Test Condition Number	Date Tested	Tester	Test Condition	Expected Result	Actual Result	Pass/ Fail
1	1/1/05	Emily Hickman	Click on System Start Button	Main Menu appears	Same as expected result	Pass
2	1/1/05	Emily Hickman	Click on Logon Button in Main Menu	Logon Screen appears asking for Username and Password	Same as expected result	Pass
3	1/1/05	Emily Hickman	Type Emily Hickman in the User Name Field	Emily Hickman appears in the User Name Field	Same as expected result	Pass
4	1/1/05	Emily Hickman	Type Zahara 123 in the password field	XXXXXXXXX appears in the password field	Same as expected result	Pass
5	1/1/05	Emily Hickman	Click on O.K. button	User logon request is sent to database and user name and password are verified	Same as expected result	Pass
6	1/1/05	Emily Hickman	Click on Start	User name and password are accepted and the system main menu appears	Screen appeared stating logon failed and username and password were incorrect	Fail

condition fails, it is obvious that the system is not functioning correctly and it must be sent back to development for a bug fix.

A typical system development effort has hundreds or thousands of test conditions. Every single test condition must be executed to verify that the system performs as expected. Writing all the test conditions and performing the actual testing of the software takes a tremendous amount of time and energy. Testing is critical to the successful development of any system.

Perform the System Testing

System developers must perform many different types of testing to ensure that the system works as expected. Figure 10.30 displays the more common types of tests performed during the testing phase.

PHASE 6: IMPLEMENTATION

The *implementation phase* involves placing the system into production so users can begin to perform actual business operations with the system. The three primary activities involved in the implementation phase are:

1. Write detailed user documentation.

2. Determine implementation method.

3. Provide training for the system users.

Write Detailed User Documentation

System users require *user documentation* that highlights how to use the system. This is the type of documentation that is typically provided along with the new system. System users find it extremely frustrating to have a new system without documentation.

Determine Implementation Method

An organization must choose the right implementation method to ensure a successful system implementation. There are four primary implementation methods an organization can use (see Figure 10.31).

Provide Training for the System Users

An organization must provide training for the system users. The two most popular types of training are online training and workshop training. *Online training* runs

FIGURE 10.30

Types of Tests
Performed During
the Testing Phase

Types of Tests Performed During the Testing Phase	
Application (or system) testing	Verifies that all units of code work together and the total system satisfies all of its functional and operational requirements.
Backup and recovery testing	Tests the ability of an application to be restarted after failure.
Documentation testing	Verifies that the instruction guides are helpful and accurate.
Integration testing	Exposes faults in the integration of software components or software units.
Regression testing	Determines if a functional improvement or repair to the system has affected the other functional aspects of the software.
Unit testing	Tests each unit of code as soon as the unit is complete to expose faults in the unit regardless of its interaction with other units.
User acceptance testing (UAT)	Determines whether a system satisfies its acceptance criteria, enabling the customer to decide whether or not to accept a system.

FIGURE 10.31

Primary
Implementation
Methods

Primary Implementation Methods	
1. Parallel implementation	Using both the old and new systems until it is evident that the new system performs correctly.
2. Phased implementation	Implementing the new system in phases (e.g., accounts receivables then accounts payable) until it is evident that the new system performs correctly and then implementing the remaining phases of the new system.
3. Pilot implementation	Having only a small group of people use the new system until it is evident that the new system performs correctly and then adding the remaining people to the new system.
4. Plunge implementation	Discarding the old system completely and immediately using the new system.

over the Internet or off a CD-ROM. System users perform the training at any time, on their own computers, at their own pace. This type of training is convenient for system users because they can set their own schedule for the training. ***Workshop training*** is set in a classroom-type environment and led by an instructor. Workshop training is recommended for difficult systems where the system users require one-on-one time with an individual instructor.

PHASE 7: MAINTENANCE

The ***maintenance phase*** involves performing changes, corrections, additions, and upgrades to ensure the system continues to meet the business goals. Maintaining the system is the final sequential phase of any systems development effort. The three primary activities involved in the maintenance phase are:

1. Build a help desk to support the system users.
2. Perform system maintenance.
3. Provide an environment to support system changes.

Build a Help Desk to Support the System Users

A ***help desk*** is a group of people who respond to internal system user questions. Typically, internal system users have a phone number for the help desk they call whenever they have issues or questions about the system. Staffing a help desk that answers internal user questions is an excellent way to provide comprehensive support for new systems.

Perform System Maintenance

Maintenance is fixing or enhancing an information system. Many different types of maintenance must be performed on the system to ensure it continues to operate as expected. These include:

- **Adaptive maintenance**—making changes to increase system functionality to meet new business requirements.
- **Corrective maintenance**—making changes to repair system defects.
- **Perfective maintenance**—making changes to enhance the system and improve such things as processing performance and usability.
- **Preventive maintenance**—making changes to reduce the chance of future system failures.

Provide an Environment to Support System Changes

As changes arise in the business environment, an organization must react to those changes by assessing the impact on the system. It might well be that the system needs to adjust to meet the ever-changing needs of the business environment. If so, an organization must modify its systems to support the business environment.

A ***change management system*** includes a collection of procedures to document a change request and define the steps necessary to consider the change based on the expected impact of the change. Most change management systems require that a change request form be initiated by one or more project stakeholders (users, customers, analysts, developers). Ideally, these change requests are reviewed by a ***change control board (CCB)*** responsible for approving or rejecting all change requests. The CCB's composition typically includes a representative for each business area that has a stake in the project. The CCB's decision to accept or reject each change is based on an impact analysis of the change. For example, if one department wants to implement a change to the software that will increase both deployment time and cost, then the other business owners need to agree that the change is valid and that it warrants the extended time frame and increased budget.

SOFTWARE PROBLEMS ARE BUSINESS PROBLEMS

Only 28 percent of projects are developed within budget and delivered on time and as promised. The primary reasons for project failure are:

- Unclear or missing business requirements.
- Skipping SDLC phases.
- Failure to manage project scope.
- Failure to manage project plan.
- Changing technology.[26]

Unclear or Missing Business Requirements

The most common reason systems fail is because the business requirements are either missing or incorrectly gathered during the analysis phase. The business requirements drive the entire system. If they are not accurate or complete, the system will not be successful.

It is important to discuss the relationship between the SDLC and the cost for the organization to fix errors. An error found during the analysis and design phase is relatively inexpensive to fix. All that is typically required is a change to a Word document. However, exactly the same error found during the testing or implementation phase is going to cost the organization an enormous amount to fix because it has to change the actual system. Figure 10.32 displays how the cost to fix an error grows exponentially the later the error is found in the SDLC.

Skipping SDLC Phases

The first thing individuals tend to do when a project falls behind schedule is to start skipping phases in the SDLC. For example, if a project is three weeks behind in the development phase, the project manager might decide to cut testing down from six weeks to three weeks. Obviously, it is impossible to perform all the testing in half the time. Failing to test the system will lead to unfound errors, and chances are high that the system will fail. It is critical that an organization perform all phases in the SDLC during every project. Skipping any of the phases is sure to lead to system failure.

Failure to Manage Project Scope

As the project progresses, the project manager must track the status of each activity and adjust the project plan if an activity is added or taking longer than expected. Scope creep occurs when the scope of the project increases. Feature creep occurs when developers add extra features that were not part of the initial requirements.

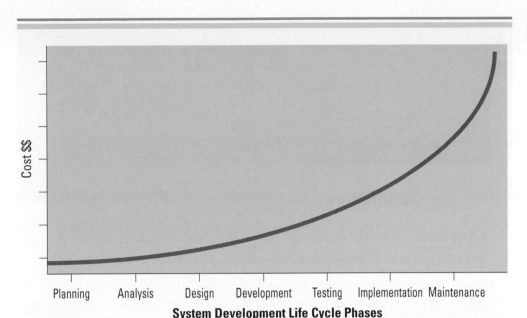

FIGURE 10.32

The Cost of Finding
Errors

Cost $$

Planning   Analysis   Design   Development   Testing   Implementation   Maintenance

System Development Life Cycle Phases

Scope creep and feature creep are difficult to manage and can easily cause a project to fall behind schedule.

Failure to Manage Project Plan

Managing the project plan is one of the biggest challenges during systems development. The project plan is the road map the organization follows during the development of the system. Developing the initial project plan is the easiest part of the project manager's job. Managing and revising the project plan is the hard part. The project plan is a living document since it changes almost daily on any project. Failing to monitor, revise, and update the project plan can lead to project failure.

Changing Technology

Many real-world projects have hundreds of business requirements, take years to complete, and cost millions of dollars. Gordon Moore, co-founder of Intel Corporation, observed in 1965 that chip density doubles every 18 months. This observation, known as Moore's law, simply means that memory sizes, processor power, and so on, all follow the same pattern and roughly double in capacity every 18 months. As Moore's law states, technology changes at an incredibly fast pace; therefore, it is possible to have to revise an entire project plan in the middle of a project as a result of a change in technology. Technology changes so fast that it is almost impossible to deliver an information system without feeling the pain of changing technology.

OPENING CASE QUESTIONS

Canadian Youth Design Their Own Youth Portal

6. Describe the different types of feasibility studies and explain how the Government of Canada could use a technical feasibility study to avoid software development failure.

7. Review the buy versus build decision and explain why the Government of Canada chose to build its Youth portal.

8. Why would software testing be critical to the development of Youth.gc.ca?

9. What are the primary reasons for software project failure? Explain how the Government of Canada's decision to follow a PD approach mitigated these concerns, if at all.

The purpose of this chapter was to provide you, the business student, with a detailed overview of the various ways in which organizations go about developing information systems. Major lessons raised in this chapter were as follows:

- Systems development encompasses a wide array of phases from initial planning right through to implementation and maintenance.

- Companies have a variety of software development methodologies and insourcing/outsourcing options at their disposal.

- Due to the complexity and problems in designing systems, many organizations are wisely choosing to follow good project management practices to better guarantee that the information systems they build are delivered on time, within budget, and meet user needs.

As such, the chapter provided you, the business student, with sufficient knowledge of the design process so that you will be better able to participate and contribute towards the successful development and implementation of information systems projects in organizations you will work in upon graduation.

KEY TERMS

Agile methodology   302
Analysis phase   318
Business requirement   318
Change control board
   (CCB)   326
Change management
   system   326
Commercial off-the shelf
   (COTS)   319
Computer-aided software
   engineering (CASE)   319
Critical path   309
Critical success factor
   (CSF)   316
Data flow diagram (DFD)   319
Data model   321
Dependency   309
Design phase   320
Development phase   321
Entity relationship diagram
   (ERD)   321
Extreme programming (XP)
   methodology   301
Feasibility study   317
Feature creep   303
Gantt chart   309

Graphical user interface
   (GUI)   321
Help desk   325
Implementation phase   324
Insourcing (in-house
   development)   310
Joint application development
   (JAD)   318
Maintenance   325
Maintenance phase   325
Modelling   321
Nearshore outsourcing   314
Offshore outsourcing   314
Online training   324
Onshore outsourcing   313
Outsourcing   310
Participatory design (PD)
   methodology   303
PERT (Program Evaluation and
   Review Technique) chart   308
Planning phase   315
Process modelling   319
Project   304
Project deliverable   306
Project exclusion   308
Project management   304

Project management
   software   304
Project manager   306
Project milestone   306
Project objective   308
Project plan   308
Project product   308
Project scope   307
Prototype   300
Rapid application development
   (RAD) (rapid prototyping)
   methodology   300
Requirements definition
   document   318
Scope creep   303
Sign-off   318
Systems development life cycle
   (SDLC)   315
Test condition   323
Testing phase   323
User documentation   324
Waterfall methodology   299
Workshop training   325

CLOSING CASE ONE

HP's Software Problems

This case showcases how easy it is for a systems development project to go awry and cause major problems for an organization.

With IT projects, pessimism—otherwise known as contingency planning—is the only way to keep small technology problems from becoming full-blown business disasters. Christina Hanger had little reason to be pessimistic in May 2004, when she was moving one of Hewlett-Packard's biggest North American divisions onto a centralized ERP system from SAP. As the leader of an IT consolidation project rooted in HP's acquisition of Compaq two years earlier, Hanger, HP senior vice president of Americas operations and IT, had an unbroken record of success migrating five product groups within the two former companies onto one of two SAP systems.

Hanger had every reason to believe that the sixth would go well too. Even so, she knew to be prepared for problems. At approximately US$7.5 billion in annual revenue, the division involved with this latest project, Industry Standard Servers (ISS), is much larger than any of the others that Hanger had migrated to SAP to that point. Hanger took the contingency plan that her team had developed for the other five migrations and adjusted it to accommodate the ISS division's larger sales volume. She planned for three weeks of IT snafus, mostly focused on what might happen as a result of tweaking a legacy order-entry system to work with the new SAP system. The contingency plan addressed business impacts too. HP banked three weeks' worth of extra servers and took over an empty portion of an HP factory in Omaha to stand by for any overflow of orders that needed special configurations (for example, an unusual component or software combination) and could not be stockpiled ahead of time.

"We had a series of small problems, none of which individually would have been too much to handle. But together they created the perfect storm," stated Gilles Bouchard, CIO and executive vice president of global operations. Starting when the system went live at the beginning of June and continuing throughout the rest of the month, as many as 20 percent of customer orders for servers stopped dead in their tracks between the legacy order-entry system and the SAP system. As IT problems go, this was not too big: Some data modelling issues between the legacy system and the SAP system prevented the SAP system from processing some orders for customized products. These programming errors were fixed within four or five weeks. However, Hanger and her business colleagues from the ISS division who were on the project steering committee never envisioned the degree to which these programming glitches would affect the business.

Orders began to backlog quickly, and HP did not have enough manual workarounds to keep servers flowing fast enough to meet customer demand. Angry customers picked up the phone and called HP—or worse, competitors Dell and IBM. In a commodity market such as servers, customer loyalty is built upon a company's ability to configure products to order and get them delivered on time. HP could do neither for much of the summer. In a third-quarter conference call on August 12, HP chairman and CEO Carly Fiorina pegged the financial impact at US$160 million: a US$120-million order backlog that resulted in US$40 million in lost revenue. That is more than the cost of the project itself, which AMR Research estimates to be $30 million. The headlines all claimed an IT disaster, but in fact, HP's disaster resulted from a few relatively small problems in IT that snowballed into a much bigger problem for the business: the inability to cope with the order backlog. This was a disaster that could have been prevented—not by trying to eliminate every possibility for error in a major IT system migration, which is virtually impossible, but by taking a much broader view of the impact that these projects can have on a company's supply chain.[27]

Questions

1. Which of the seven phases of the systems development life cycle is least important to HP? The most important? Why?

2. Which of the different software development methodologies should HP use to implement successful systems? Why?

3. Identify the primary reasons for software project failure and explain which ones HP experienced on its ERP build.

4. Describe the different types of feasibility studies and explain how HP could use a technical feasibility study to avoid software development failure.

5. Review the buy versus build decision and explain why HP chose to buy its ERP system.

6. Why is testing critical to HP's software development process?

Reducing Ambiguity in Business Requirements

This case illustrates the importance of properly identifying business requirements for a systems development project.

The number one reason projects fail is bad business requirements. Business requirements are considered "bad" because of ambiguity or insufficient involvement of end users during analysis and design.

A requirement is unambiguous if it has the same interpretation for all parties. Different interpretations by different participants will usually result in unmet expectations. Here is an example of an ambiguous requirement and an example of an unambiguous requirement:

■ Ambiguous requirement: The financial report must show profits in local and Canadian currencies.

■ Unambiguous requirement: The financial report must show profits in local and Canadian currencies using the exchange rate printed in *The Globe and Mail* for the last business day of the period being reported.

Ambiguity is impossible to prevent completely because it is introduced into requirements in natural ways. For example:

■ Requirements can contain technical implications that are obvious to the IT developers but not to the customers.

■ Requirements can contain business implications that are obvious to the customer but not to the IT developers.

■ Requirements may contain everyday words whose meanings are "obvious" to everyone, yet different for everyone.

■ Requirements are reflections of detailed explanations that may have included multiple events, multiple perspectives, verbal rephrasing, emotion, iterative refinement, selective emphasis, and body language—none of which are captured in the written statements.

Tips for Reviewing Business Requirements

When reviewing business requirements always look for the following words to help dramatically reduce ambiguity:

■ *And* and *or* have well-defined meanings and ought to be completely unambiguous, yet they are often understood only informally and interpreted inconsistently. For example, consider the statement "The alarm must ring if button T is pressed and if button F is pressed." This statement may be intended to mean that to ring the alarm, both buttons must be pressed or it may be intended to mean that either one can be pressed. A statement like this should never appear in a requirement because the potential for misinterpretation is too great. A preferable approach is to be very explicit, for example, "The alarm must ring if both buttons T and F are pressed simultaneously. The alarm should not ring in any other circumstance."

■ *Always* might really mean "most of the time," in which case it should be made more explicit. For example, the statement "We always run reports A and B together" could be challenged with "In other words, there is never any circumstance where you would run A without B and B without A?" If you build a system with an "always" requirement, then you are actually building the system to never run report A without report B. If a user suddenly wants report B without report A, you will need to make significant system changes.

- *Never* might mean rarely, in which case it should be made more explicit. For example, the statement "We never run reports A and B in the same month" could be challenged with, "So that means that if I see that A has been run, I can be absolutely certain that no one will want to run B." Again, if you build a system that supports a "never" requirement, then the system users can never perform that requirement. For example, the system would never allow a user to run reports A and B in the same month, no matter what the circumstances.

- Boundary conditions are statements about the line between true and false and do and do not. These statements may or may not be meant to include end points. For example, "We want to use method X when there are up to 10 pages, but method Y otherwise." If you were building this system, would you include page 10 in method X or in method Y? The answer to this question will vary causing an ambiguous business requirement.[28]

Questions

1. Why are ambiguous business requirements the leading cause of system development failures?
2. Why do the words and and or tend to lead to ambiguous requirements?
3. Research the Web and determine other reasons for "bad" business requirements.
4. What is wrong with the following business requirement: "The system must support employee birthdays since every employee always has a birthday every year."

CLOSING CASE THREE

Staying on Track—Toronto Transit

This case illustrates the benefits of utilizing project management software for project success.

Schedules are at the heart of the Toronto Transit Commission's (TTC) celebrated transit system, which services over 1 million customers daily. More than 50 large engineering and construction projects are underway to expand, upgrade, and maintain Toronto's transit systems and structures. One such project was the Sheppard project, which consisted of constructing a new six-kilometre line north of the city. The Sheppard took more than five years to complete with a total cost of $970 million.

The TTC's challenge is to keep its 50 individual projects, most of which fall within the $2 million to $110 million price range and span an average of five years, on schedule and under budget. Staying on top of so many multifaceted, multiyear, and often interdependent projects adds additional complexity for the company. The TTC uses Primavera Project Planner (P3) to create a single master schedule for all of its engineering and construction projects.

The TTC's 50 individual projects average 100 to 150 activities each, with some projects encompassing as many as 500 to 600 activities. "Seeing the big picture is important, not only for the 300 people who work in the Engineering and Construction branch of the TTC, but for the entire 9,000-person organization," said Vince Carroll, head scheduler for the Engineering and Construction branch. "Engineering managers need to see how other projects may impact their own. Materials and procurement managers need to track project progress. Senior managers need to be able to communicate with city government to secure funding. Marketing and public relations people need the latest information to set public expectations. And most important of all," Carroll said, "the operations group needs to stay informed of what is happening so that they can adjust the schedules that run the trains."

Carroll and his team of 25 people create, update, and publish a master schedule that summarizes the individual status of each project, shows the logical links between projects, and provides an integrated overview of all projects. The master schedule helps the team effectively and regularly communicate the status of all projects currently under way throughout the Toronto Transit system.

The master schedule organizes projects according to their location in the capital budget. For example, projects can be organized according to those that have been allotted funding for expansion, state of good repair, legislative reasons, or environmental reasons. Each project is organized by its logical flow—from planning, analysis, design, through the maintenance phase. The final report shows positive and negative balances for each project and a single overview of the status of all the engineering and construction projects. Carroll and his team use PERT charts to create time-scaled logic diagrams and then convert this information to bar charts for presentation purposes in the master schedule. The TTC is currently linking its master schedule directly to its payroll system, enabling it to track the number of hours actually worked versus hours planned.[29]

Questions

1. How is information technology being used by the TTC for project management?
2. Describe Gantt charts and explain how the TTC could use one to communicate project status.
3. Describe PERT charts and explain how the TTC could use one to communicate project status.
4. Using this case study of the TTC as a guide, under what circumstances should organizations utilize project management software to help manage projects?

MAKING BUSINESS DECISIONS

1. Selecting a systems development methodology

Exus Incorporated is an international billing outsourcing company. Exus currently has revenues of $5 billion, over 3,500 employees, and operations on every continent. You have recently been hired as the CIO. Your first task is to increase the software development project success rate, which is currently at 20 percent. To ensure that future software development projects are successful, you want to standardize the systems development methodology across the entire enterprise. Currently, each project determines which methodology it uses to develop software.

Create a report detailing three additional system development methodologies that were not covered in this text. Compare each of these methodologies to the traditional waterfall approach. Finally, recommend which methodology you want to implement as your organizational standard. Be sure to highlight any potential roadblocks you might encounter when implementing the new standard methodology.

2. Understanding project failure

You are the director of project management for Stello, a global manufacturer of high-end writing instruments. The company sells to primarily high-end customers, and the average price for one of its fine writing instruments is about $350. You are currently implementing a new customer relationship management system and you want to do everything you can to ensure a successful systems development effort. Create a document summarizing the five primary reasons why this project could fail, along with your strategy to eliminate the possibility of system development failure on your project.

3. Missing phases in the systems development life cycle

Hello Inc. is a large concierge service for executives operating in Vancouver, Montreal, and Toronto. The company performs all kinds of services from dog walking to airport transportation. Your manager, Dan Martello, wants to skip the testing phase during the company's financial ERP implementation. Dan feels that since the system came from a vendor it should work correctly. To meet the project's looming deadline he wants to skip the testing phase. Draft a memo explaining to Dan the importance of following the SDLC and the ramifications to the business if the financial system is not tested.

4. Refusing to sign off

You are the primary client on a large extranet development project. After carefully reviewing the requirements definition document, you are positive that there are missing, ambiguous, inaccurate, and unclear requirements. The project manager is pressuring you for your sign-off since he has already received sign-off from five of your co-workers. If you fail to sign off on the requirements, you are going to put the entire project at risk since the time frame is nonnegotiable. What would you do? Why?

5. Saving failing systems

Crik Candle Company manufactures low-end candles for restaurants. The company generates over $40 million in annual revenues and has more than 300 employees. You are in the middle of a large multimillion-dollar supply chain management implementation. Your project manager has just come to you with the information that the project might fail for the following reasons:

- Several business requirements were incorrect and the scope has to be doubled.
- Three developers recently quit.
- The deadline has been moved up a month.

Develop a list of options that your company can follow to ensure the project remains on schedule and within budget.

6. Feasibility studies

John Lancert is the new managing operations director for a large construction company, LMC. John is currently looking for an associate who can help him prioritize the 60 proposed company projects. You are interested in working with John and have decided to apply for the job. John has asked you to compile a report detailing why project prioritization is critical for LMC, along with the different types of feasibility studies you would recommend that LMC use when determining which projects to pursue.

11

CHAPTER

Networks, Telecommunications, and Wireless Computing

LEARNING OUTCOMES

11.1. Compare LANs, WANs, and MANs.

11.2. List and describe the four components that differentiate networks.

11.3. Compare the two types of network architectures.

11.4. Describe different network topologies.

11.5. Describe TCP/IP along with its primary purpose.

11.6. Identify the different media types found in networks.

11.7. Explain how a wireless device helps an organization conduct business anytime, anywhere, anyplace.

11.8. Describe RFID and how it can be used to help make a supply chain more effective.

11.9. List and discuss the key factors inspiring the growth of wireless technologies.

11.10. Describe the business benefits associated with enterprise mobility.

Why Do I Need To Know This **?**

This chapter provides an overview of networks, tele-communications, and wireless computing funda-mentals. These are the core communications technologies that information systems developers typically incorporate into their enterprise-wide application designs.

As a business student, you need to know this since these technologies form the backbone of an organization's com-munications infrastructure. The business of your organi-zation relies heavily upon this infrastructure to process transactions and share information among employees, customers, and partners.

Thus, understanding basic networking communications terminology and how communication technologies can support your organization's business will make you a more knowledgeable and informed employee. You will be more able to partake in discussions on how to leverage this technology in your organization and be cognizant of the benefits and limitations of this technology too.

The Digital Hospital

For years, health care has missed the huge benefits that information technology has bestowed upon the rest of the economy. During the 1990s, productivity in health care services declined, according to estimates from Economy.com Inc. That is a huge underachievement in a decade of strong gains from the overall economy. This is beginning to change as hospitals, along with insurers and the government, are stepping up their IT investments. Hospitals are finally discarding their clumsy, sluggish first-generation networks and are beginning to install laptops, software, and Internet technologies.

Hackensack University Medical Center in Hackensack, New Jersey, is one of the United States' most aggressive technology adopters, investing US$72 million in IT projects since 1998. The IT investments are paying off for the hospital with patient mortality rates decreasing—down 16 percent in four years—and quality of care and productivity increasing. The most important piece of Hackensack's digital initiatives is the networked software that acts as the hospital's central nervous system. Using wireless laptops, nurses log in to the system to record patient information and progress. Doctors tap into the network via wireless devices to order prescriptions and lab tests. Everything is linked, from the automated pharmacy to the X-ray lab, eliminating the need for faxes, phone calls, and other administrative hassles. Figure 11.1 displays the hospital's IT systems development projects.

Health care spending accounts for 15 percent of the U.S. economy, or US$1.7 trillion. It is so gargantuan that any efficiency gains will affect the overall economy. Dr. David Brailer, President George W. Bush's point man on health IT initiatives, predicts that IT investments will lead to US$140 billion a year in cost savings by 2014. More important than saving money is saving lives. Poor information kills some 7,000 Americans each year just by missing drug-interaction problems, according to the National Academy of Sciences Institute of Medicine. Hospital errors result in 100,000 deaths annually. Early evidence indicates that proper technology can reduce this amount. Hospitals using electronic prescription systems have seen 80 percent fewer prescription errors.[1]

FIGURE 11.1

Hospital IT Systems
Development Projects

Hackensack University Medical Center IT's Projects
■ Patients can use 37-inch plasma TVs in their rooms to surf the Internet for information about their medical conditions. They can also take interactive classes about their condition and find out how to take care of themselves after discharge.
■ From virtually anywhere in the world, physicians can make their hospital rounds with the help of a life-size robot, Mr. Rounder. Using laptops with joysticks and Web links, doctors drive the robot around the hospital to confer by remote video with patients and other doctors. When a blizzard prevented Dr. Garth Ballantynes from reaching the hospital, he used Mr. Rounder to make his rounds from his home 130 kilometres away.
■ Pocket-sized PCs that hook wirelessly into the hospital's network allow doctors the freedom to place pharmacy orders and pull up medical records from anywhere in the hospital.
■ Nurses use wireless laptops to record patients' vitals signs, symptoms, and medications. Doctors can sign into the same central system from the laptops to order prescriptions and lab tests and read their patient's progress.
■ The hospital's internal Web site stores all of its medical images. Doctors can view crystal-clear digital versions of their patients' X-rays, MRIs, and CT scans from any computer in or out of the hospital.
■ A giant robot named Robbie, equipped with arms, reads prescriptions entered into the hospital's computer system and then grabs medications stored on pegs on the wall. The pills are then dropped into containers that are marked for each patient.

INTRODUCTION

elecommunication systems enable the transmission of data over public or private networks. A *network* is a communications, data exchange, and resource-sharing system created by linking two or more computers and establishing standards, or protocols, so that they can work together. Telecommunication systems and networks are traditionally complicated and historically inefficient. However, businesses can benefit from today's modern network infrastructures that provide reliable global reach to employees and customers. Businesses around the world are moving to network infrastructure solutions that allow greater choice in how they go to market—solutions with global reach. These alternatives include wireless, voice-over internet protocol (VoIP), and radio-frequency identification (RFID). This chapter takes a detailed look at key telecommunication, network, and wireless technologies being integrated into businesses around the world.

NETWORK BASICS

Music is the hottest new product line at ubiquitous coffee retailer Starbucks. In Starbucks stores, customers can burn CDs while sipping coffee, thanks to the company's own online music library and increasingly sophisticated in-store network. Networks range from small two-computer networks to the biggest network of all, the Internet. A network provides two principle benefits: the ability to communicate and the ability to share. E-mail is the most popular form of network communication. Figure 11.2 highlights the three different types of networks, and Figure 11.3 graphically depicts each network type.

Networks are differentiated by the following:

- Architecture—peer-to-peer, client/server.
- Topology—bus, star, ring, hybrid, wireless.
- Protocols—Ethernet, Transmission Control Protocol/Internet Protocol (TCP/IP).
- Media—coaxial, twisted-pair, fibre-optic.

FIGURE 11.2

Network Types

Network Types	
Local area network (LAN)	A computer network that uses cables or radio signals to link two or more computers within a geographically limited area, generally one building or a group of buildings. A networked office building, school, or home usually contains a single LAN. The linked computers are called workstations.
Wide area network (WAN)	A computer network that provides data communication services for business in geographically dispersed areas (such as across a country or around the world). The Internet is a WAN that spans the world.
Metropolitan area network (MAN)	A computer network that provides connectivity in a geographic area or region larger than that covered by a local area network, but smaller than the area covered by a wide area network. A university or business may have a MAN that joins the different LANs across its campus.

FIGURE 11.3

LAN, WAN, and MAN

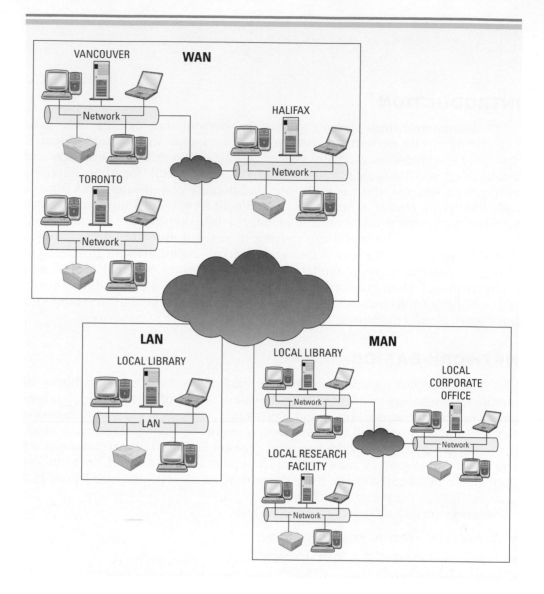

ARCHITECTURE

The two primary types of network architectures are: peer-to-peer networks and client/server networks.

Peer-to-Peer Networks

A *peer-to-peer (P2P) network* is any network without a central file server and in which all computers in the network have access to the public files located on all other workstations, as illustrated in Figure 11.4. Each networked computer can allow other computers to access its files and use connected printers while it is in use as a workstation without the aid of a server.

While Napster may be the most widely known example of a P2P implementation, it may also be one of the most narrowly focused since the Napster model takes advantage of only one of the many capabilities of P2P computing: file sharing. The technology has far broader capabilities, including the sharing of processing, memory, and storage, and the supporting of collaboration among vast numbers of distributed computers. Peer-to-peer computing enables immediate interaction among people and computer systems.

FIGURE 11.4

Peer-to-Peer (P2P) Networks

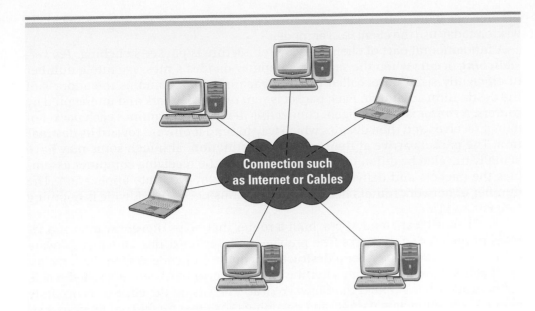

Client/Server Networks

A *client* is a computer that is designed to request information from a server. A *server* is a computer that is dedicated to providing information in response to external requests. A *client/server network* is a model for applications in which the bulk of the back-end processing, such as performing a physical search of a database, takes place on a server, while the front-end processing, which involves communicating with the users, is handled by the clients (see Figure 11.5). A *network operating system (NOS)* is the operating system that runs a network, steering information between computers and managing security and users. The client/server model has

FIGURE 11.5

Client/Server Network

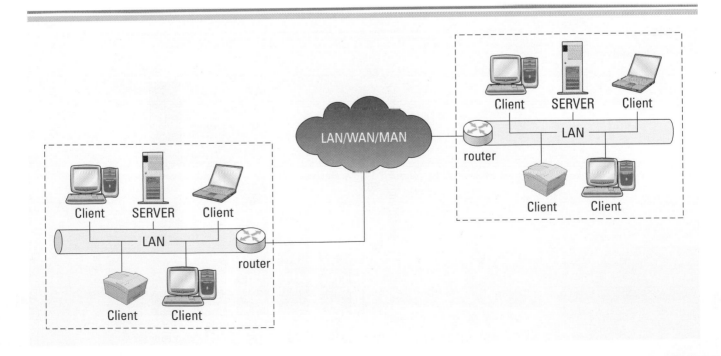

become one of the central ideas of network computing. Most business applications written today use the client/server model.

A fundamental part of client/server architecture is packet-switching. **Packet-switching** occurs when the sending computer divides a message into a number of efficiently sized units called packets, each of which contains the address of the destination computer. Each packet is sent on the network and intercepted by routers. A **router** is an intelligent connecting device that examines each packet of data it receives and then decides which way to send it onward toward its destination. The packets arrive at their intended destination, although some may have actually traveled by different physical paths, and the receiving computer assembles the packets and delivers the message to the appropriate application. The number of network routers being installed by businesses worldwide is booming (see Figure 11.6).

Eva Chen, CIO at Trend Micro, built a router that helps prevent worms and viruses from entering networks. The problem with most existing antivirus software is that it starts working after a destructive sequence of code is identified, meaning it starts doing its job only after the virus or worm has been unleashed inside the network. Chen's router, the Network VirusWall, sits on the edge of a corporate network, scanning data packets and detaining those that might contain viruses or worms. Any suspicious packets are compared with up-to-the-second information from Trend Micro's virus-tracking command centre. Viruses and worms are then deleted and refused entry to the network, allowing the company to perform a preemptive strike.[2]

TOPOLOGY

Networks are assembled according to certain rules. Cables, for example, have to be a certain length; each cable strand can support only a certain amount of network traffic. A **network topology** refers to the geometric arrangement of the actual physical organization of the computers (and other network devices) in a network. Topologies vary depending on cost and functionality. Figure 11.7 highlights the five common topologies used in networks, and Figure 11.8 displays each topology.

FIGURE 11.6

Worldwide Router Growth

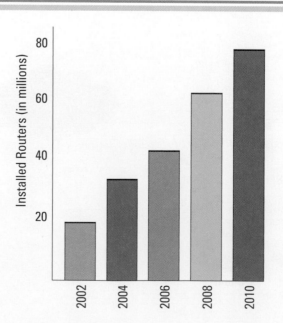

FIGURE 11.7

Five Network Topologies

Network Topologies	
Bus	All devices are connected to a central cable, called the bus or backbone. Bus networks are relatively inexpensive and easy to install for small networks.
Star	All devices are connected to a central device, called a hub. Star networks are relatively easy to install and manage, but bottlenecks can occur because all data must pass through the hub.
Ring	All devices are connected to one another in the shape of a closed loop, so that each device is connected directly to two other devices, one on either side of it. Ring topologies are relatively expensive and difficult to install, but they offer high bandwidth and can span large distances.
Hybrid	Groups of star-configured workstations are connected to a linear bus backbone cable, combining the characteristics of the bus and star topologies.
Wireless	Devices are connected by a receiver/transmitter to a special network interface card that transmits signals between a computer and a server, all within an acceptable transmission range.

FIGURE 11.8

Network Topologies

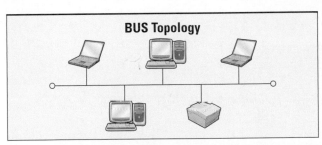

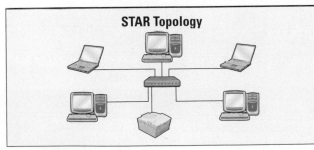

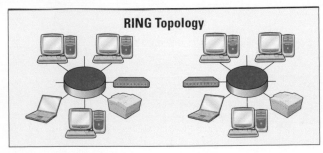

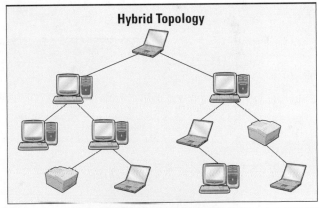

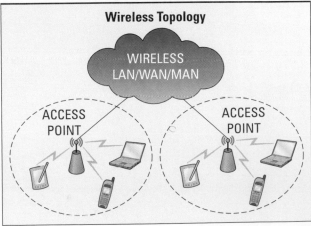

PROTOCOLS

A *protocol* is a standard that specifies the format of data as well as the rules to be followed during transmission. Simply put, for one computer (or computer program) to talk to another computer (or computer program) they must both be talking the same language, and this language is called a protocol.

A protocol is based on an agreed-upon and established standard, and this way all manufacturers of hardware and software that are using the protocol do so in a similar fashion to allow for interoperability. *Interoperability* is the capability of two or more computer systems to share data and resources, even though they are made by different manufacturers. The most popular network protocols used are Ethernet and Transmission Control Protocol/Internet Protocol (TCP/IP).

Ethernet

Ethernet is a physical and data layer technology for LAN networking (see Figure 11.9). Ethernet is the most widely installed LAN access method, originally developed by Xerox and then developed further by Xerox, Digital Equipment Corporation, and Intel. When it first began to be widely deployed in the 1980s, Ethernet supported a maximum theoretical data transfer rate of 10 megabits per second (Mbps). More recently, Fast Ethernet has extended traditional Ethernet technology to 100 Mbps peak, and Gigabit Ethernet technology extends performance up to 1,000 Mbps.

Ethernet has survived as the major LAN technology—it is currently used for approximately 85 percent of the world's LAN-connected PCs and workstations—because its protocol has the following characteristics:

- Is easy to understand, implement, manage, and maintain.
- Allows low-cost network implementations.

FIGURE 11.9

Ethernet Protocol

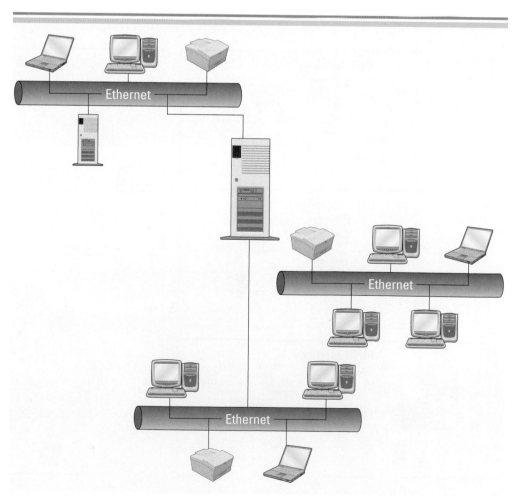

- Provides extensive flexibility for network installation.
- Guarantees successful interconnection and operation of standards-compliant products, regardless of manufacturer.

Transmission Control Protocol/Internet Protocol

The most common telecommunication protocol is Transmission Control Protocol/Internet Protocol (TCP/IP), which was originally developed by the Department of Defense to connect a system of computer networks that became known as the Internet. *Transmission Control Protocol/Internet Protocol (TCP/IP)* provides the technical foundation for the public Internet as well as for large numbers of private networks. The key achievement of TCP/IP is its flexibility with respect to lower-level protocols. TCP/IP uses a special transmission method that maximizes data transfer and automatically adjusts to slower devices and other delays encountered on a network. Although more than 100 protocols make up the entire TCP/IP protocol suite, the two most important of these are TCP and IP. **TCP** provides transport functions, ensuring, among other things, that the amount of data received is the same as the amount transmitted. **IP** provides the addressing and routing mechanism that acts as a postmaster. Figure 11.10 displays TCP/IP's four-layer reference model:

- Application layer—serves as the window for users and application processes to access network services.
- Transport layer—handles end-to-end packet transportation.
- Internet layer—formats the data into packets, adds a header containing the packet sequence and the address of the receiving device, and specifies the services required from the network.
- Network interface layer—places data packets on the network for transmission.

The TCP/IP suite of applications includes five protocols—file transfer, simple mail transfer, telnet, hypertext transfer, and simple network management (see Figure 11.11).

Another communication reference model is the seven-layer Open System Interconnection (OSI) reference model. Figure 11.12 show the OSI model's seven layers.

The lower layers (1 to 3) represent local communications, while the upper layers (4 to 7) represent end-to-end communications. Each layer contributes protocol functions that are necessary to establish and maintain the error-free exchange of information between network users.

For many years, users thought the OSI model would replace TCP/IP as the preferred technique for connecting multivendor networks. But the slow pace of OSI standards as well as the expense of implementing complex OSI software and having products certified for OSI interoperability will preclude this from happening.

FIGURE 11.10

TCP/IP Four-Layer Reference Model

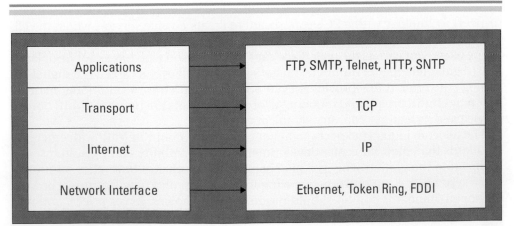

Applications	FTP, SMTP, Telnet, HTTP, SNTP
Transport	TCP
Internet	IP
Network Interface	Ethernet, Token Ring, FDDI

FIGURE 11.11

TCP/IP Applications

TCP/IP Applications	
File Transfer Protocol (FTP)	Allows files containing text, programs, graphics, numerical data, and so on to be downloaded off or uploaded onto a network.
Simple Mail Transfer Protocol (SMTP)	TCP/IP's own messaging system for e-mail.
Telnet Protocol	Provides terminal emulation that allows a personal computer or workstation to act as a terminal, or access device, for a server.
Hypertext Transfer Protocol (HTTP)	Allows Web browsers and servers to send and receive Web pages.
Simple Network Management Protocol (SNMP)	Allows the management of networked nodes to be managed from a single point.

FIGURE 11.12

Open System Interconnection Model

OSI Model
7. Application
6. Presentation
5. Session
4. Transport
3. Network
2. Data Link
1. Physical

Voice over IP (VoIP)   Originally, phone calls made over the Internet had a reputation of offering poor call quality, lame user interfaces, and low call-completion rates. With new and improved technology and IT infrastructures, Internet phone calls now offer similar quality to traditional telephone calls. Today, many consumers are making phone calls over the Internet by using voice over Internet protocol (VoIP). *Voice over IP (VoIP)* uses TCP/IP technology to transmit voice calls over long-distance telephone lines. In fact, VoIP transmits over 10 percent of all phone calls in the United States and this number is growing exponentially.

VoIP and e-mail work in similar ways. The user sends a call over the Internet in packets of audio data tagged with the same destination. VoIP reassembles the packets once they arrive at their final destination.

Numerous vendors offer VoIP services; however, the service works differently depending on the vendor's IT infrastructure. The start-up Skype pairs P2P (peer-to-peer) technology with a PC's sound card to create a voice service, which the client can use to call other Skype users. Unfortunately, the user can talk only to other Skype users. Vonage lets the user place calls to any person who has a mobile or landline (regular telephone) number. Vonage sends the call over a cable via a digital-to-analog converter. A few providers even offer an adapter for a traditional handset that plugs into a broadband modem. All of these vendors are providing VoIP, but the service and its features can vary significantly.

The telecom industry expects great benefits from combining VoIP with emerging standards that allow for easier development, interoperability among systems, and application integration. This is a big change for an industry that relies on proprietary systems to keep customers paying for upgrades and new features. The VoIP and open-standards combo should produce more choices, lower prices, and new applications.

Writing voice applications may never be as common as writing computer applications. But the spread of VoIP will make it easier to manage applications and add capabilities to the voice feature set. In a decade, the telecom network "will be like getting water out of the tap," predicts Stef van Aarle, vice president of marketing and strategy at Lucent Worldwide Services. "The only time you think of it will be when it doesn't work. And software is the glue that makes it all easy to use."

Upstarts like Vonage and Skype are bringing VoIP to the masses. But a bigger opportunity lurks in the $2-billion corporate phone market. New York-based start-up Popular Telephony is offering a new VoIP technology that dramatically cuts corporate phone costs while letting workers take their office phones anywhere. Its secret: peer-to-peer software called Peerio that is built right into handsets.

CEO Dmitry Goroshevsky founded the company to bring PC economics to the office telephone system. A traditional workplace setup requires a dedicated voice network and a private branch exchange, or PBX, to connect to the outside world and can cost up to $1 million (see Figure 11.13). Cisco has been selling an IP PBX, which uses a data network for voice calls. But Popular Telephony eliminates pricey hardware. Using an ordinary PC, network administrators assign an extension to each phone. Peerio-enabled handsets, which will be sold through discount retailers and office supply stores, plug directly into a company's data network, where calls are routed through a gateway and then out. Since Peerio is based on Internet protocol, office workers can use their phones wherever there is a broadband connection. And though companies pay the usual rates to call conventional landline and mobile phone numbers, ringing up other Peerio and VoIP users will not cost a dime. A handful of licensees are manufacturing the phones.[3]

MEDIA

Network transmission media refers to the various types of media used to carry the signal between computers. When information is sent across the network, it is converted into electrical signals. These signals are generated as electromagnetic waves (analogue signalling) or as a sequence of voltage pulses (digital signalling). To be sent from one location to another, a signal must travel along a physical path. The physical path that is used to carry a signal between a signal transmitter and a signal receiver is called the transmission media. The two types of transmission media are wire (guided) and wireless (unguided).

Wire Media

Wire media are transmission material manufactured so that signals will be confined to a narrow path and will behave predictably. The three most commonly used types of guided media are (see Figure 11.14):

- Twisted-pair wiring
- Coaxial cable
- Fibre-optic cable

FIGURE 11.13

Typical Telephone Start-up Costs for a 1,000-Person Office

Telephone System	Typical Telecom System	IP-Based System	Peerio
Requirements	■ Phones ■ Private branch exchange (PBX) ■ Voice switches ■ Dedicated voice network	■ Phones ■ IP PBX ■ Existing data network ■ Gateway	■ Phones ■ PC ■ Existing data network ■ Gateway
Total Cost	$1,000,000	$500,000	$100,000

FIGURE 11.14

Twisted-Pair, Coaxial Cable,
and Fibre-Optic

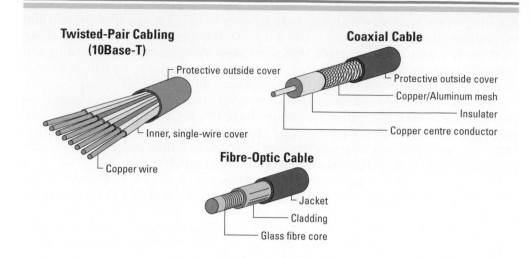

Twisted-Pair Wiring   *Twisted-pair wiring* refers to a type of cable composed of four (or more) copper wires twisted around each other within a plastic sheath. The wires are twisted to reduce outside electrical interference. Twisted-pair cables come in shielded and unshielded varieties. Shielded cables have a metal shield encasing the wires that acts as a ground for electromagnetic interference. Unshielded twisted-pair (UTP) is the most popular and is generally the best option for LAN networks. The quality of UTP may vary from telephone-grade wire to high-speed cable. The cable has four pairs of wires inside the jacket. Each pair is twisted with a different number of twists per inch to help eliminate interference from adjacent pairs and other electrical devices. The RJ-45 connectors on twisted-pair cables resemble large telephone connectors.

Coaxial Cable   *Coaxial cable* is cable that can carry a wide range of frequencies with low signal loss. It consists of a metallic shield with a single wire placed along the center of a shield and isolated from the shield by an insulator. This type of cable is referred to as coaxial because it contains one copper wire (or physical data channel) that carries the signal and is surrounded by another concentric physical channel consisting of a wire mesh. The outer channel serves as a ground for electrical interference. Because of this grounding feature, several coaxial cables can be placed within a single conduit or sheath without significant loss of data integrity.

Fibre-Optic Cable   *Fibre optic* (or *optical fibre*) refers to the technology associated with the transmission of information as light impulses along a glass wire or fibre. The 10Base-FL and 100Base-FX optical fibre cable are the same types of cable used by most telephone companies for long-distance service. Optical fibre cable can transmit data over long distances with little loss in data integrity. In addition, because data are transferred as a pulse of light, optical fibre is not subject to interference. The light pulses travel through a glass wire or fibre encased in an insulating sheath.

Optical fibre's increased maximum effective distance comes at a price. Optical fibre is more fragile than wire, difficult to split, and labour intensive to install. For these reasons, optical fibre is used primarily to transmit data over extended distances where the hardware required to relay the data signal on less expensive media would exceed the cost of optical fibre installation. It is also used where large amounts of data need to be transmitted on a regular basis.

Wireless Media

Wireless media are natural parts of the Earth's environment that can be used as physical paths to carry ~~electrical~~ *electromagnetic* signals. The atmosphere and outer space are examples of wireless media that are commonly used to carry signals. These media can carry such electromagnetic signals as microwave, infrared light waves, and radio waves.

Network signals are transmitted through all media as a type of waveform. When transmitted through wire and cable, the signal is an electrical waveform. When transmitted through fibre-optic cable, the signal is a light wave, either visible or infrared light. When transmitted through the Earth's atmosphere, the signal can take the form of waves in the radio spectrum, including microwaves, infrared, or visible light.

Recent advances in radio hardware technology have produced significant advancements in wireless networking devices: the cellular telephone, wireless modems, and wireless LANs. These devices use technology that in some cases has been around for decades but until recently was too impractical or expensive for widespread use.

E-BUSINESS NETWORKS

To set up an e-business even a decade ago would have required an individual organization to assume the burden of developing the entire network infrastructure. Today, industry-leading companies have developed Internet-based products and services to handle many aspects of customer and supplier interactions. "In today's retail market, you cannot be a credible national retailer without having a robust Web site," says Dennis Bowman, senior vice president and CIO of Circuit City, who adds that customers now expect seamless retailing just as they expect stores that are clean and well stocked. For this reason, retailers are working furiously to integrate their e-business sites with their inventory and point-of-sale (POS) systems so that they can accept in-store returns of merchandise bought online and allow customers to buy on the Web and pick up in the store.

Some companies, such as Best Buy, Circuit City, Office Depot, and Sears, already have their physical and online stores integrated. These companies have been the fast movers because they already had an area in their stores for merchandise pickup (usually for big, bulky items like TVs and appliances), and because long before the Web they had systems and processes in place that facilitated the transfer of a sale from one store to another. Other retailers are partially integrated. Bed Bath & Beyond, Eddie Bauer, Linens 'n' Things, The Gap, and others let customers return but not pick up online-ordered merchandise in stores. To take on the challenge of e-business integration, an organization needs a secure and reliable IT infrastructure for mission-critical systems (see Figure 11.15).

FIGURE 11.15

E-Business Network Characteristics

E-Business Network Characteristics
■ Provide for the transparent exchange of information with suppliers, trading partners, and customers.
■ Reliably and securely exchange information internally and externally via the Internet or other networks.
■ Allow end-to-end integration and provide message delivery across multiple systems, in particular, databases, clients, and servers.
■ Respond to high demands with scalable processing power and networking capacity.
■ Serve as the integrator and transaction framework for both digital businesses and traditional brick-and-mortar businesses that want to leverage the Internet for any type of business.

A *virtual private network (VPN)* is a way to use the public telecommunication infrastructure (e.g., Internet) to provide secure access to an organization's network (see Figure 11.16). A *value-added network (VAN)* is a private network, provided by a third party, for exchanging information through a high-capacity connection. To date, organizations engaging in e-business have relied largely on VPNs, VANs, and other dedicated links handling electronic data interchange transactions. These traditional solutions are still deployed in the market and for many companies will likely hold a strategic role for years to come. However, conventional technologies present significant challenges:

- By handling only limited kinds of business information, these contribute little to a reporting structure intended to provide a comprehensive view of business operations.

- They offer little support for the real-time business process integration that will be essential in the digital marketplace.

- Relatively expensive and complex to implement, conventional technologies make it difficult to expand or change networks in response to market shifts.

FIGURE 11.16

Virtual Private Network Example

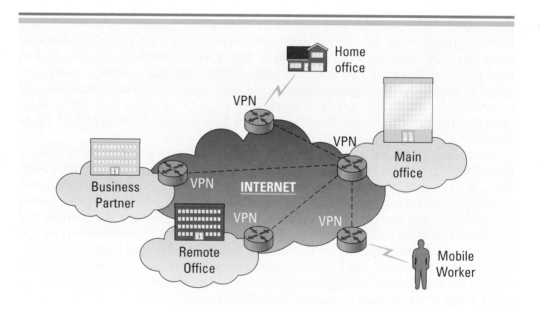

WIRELESS FIDELITY

In Waterloo, Ontario, sits a 120,000-square-foot building where Mike Lazaridis's 20-year dream is coming to life. Seven 36-metre-long assembly lines are stamping out wallet-size BlackBerrys—the wireless handhelds now in the hands of more than 1.3 million users worldwide—at a rate of about 230 an hour. Lazaridis, the co-CEO of Research in Motion (RIM), gave the go-ahead earlier this year to ratchet up plant production from five days a week to seven. Orders are surging, and so RIM's BlackBerry-making machine does not sleep.[4]

Wireless fidelity (wi-fi) is a means of linking computers using infrared or radio signals. Wi-fi is a type of Ethernet, which makes the wireless network a straightforward extension of the wired network. Wireless users can run the same network applications they use on an Ethernet LAN. Wireless communication can be installed using the existing network infrastructure with minimal retraining or system changes. Laptop users can roam throughout their locales while remaining in contact with the network via strategically placed access points that are plugged into the wired network. One of the biggest benefits of using wireless communications is its ability to deliver real-time information.

The Value of Timely Information

The need for timely information can change for each business decision. Some decisions require weekly or monthly information while other decisions require daily information. Timeliness is an aspect of information that depends on the situation. In some industries, information that is a few days or weeks old can be relevant, while in other industries information that is a few minutes old can be almost worthless. Some organizations, such as 911 centres, stock traders, and banks, require consolidated, up-to-the-second information, 24 hours a day, seven days a week. Other organizations, such as insurance and construction companies, require only daily or even weekly information.

Real-time information means immediate, up-to-date information. *Real-time systems* provide real-time information in response to query requests. Many organizations use real-time systems to exploit key corporate transactional information. In a survey of 700 IT executives by Evans Data Corp., 48 percent of respondents said they were already analyzing information in or near real-time, and another 25 percent reported plans to add real-time systems.[5]

Real-time systems provide valuable information for supporting corporate strategies such as customer relationship management. Bell Mobility Inc., Canada's largest wireless carrier, staffs over 550 customer service representatives and uses E.piphany Inc.'s Real-Time tool to make the right customer offers at the right time without having to rely on guesswork. The results from the first month after implementation of the Real-Time tool are displayed in Figure 11.17.[6]

The growing demand for real-time information stems from organizations' need to make faster and more effective decisions, keep smaller inventories, operate more efficiently, and track performance more carefully. Nevertheless, timeliness is relative. Organizations need fresh, timely information to make good decisions.

FIGURE 11.17

Results from Bell Mobility's Real-Time Tool

Bell Mobility's Real-Time Tool Results
■ 18 percent increase in sales per hour
■ 16 percent increase in total inbound marketing revenue
■ 75 percent decrease in total time to create and deploy a new marketing campaign

Information also needs to be timely in the sense that it meets employees' needs, but no more. If employees can absorb information only on an hourly or daily basis, there is no need to gather real-time information in smaller increments.

MBIA Insurance Corp. uses overnight updates to feed its real-time systems. Employees use this information to make daily risk decisions for mortgages, insurance policies, and other services. The company found that overnight updates were sufficient, as long as users could gain immediate access to the information they needed to make business decisions during the day.[7]

Most people request real-time information without understanding one of the biggest pitfalls associated with real-time information—continual change. Imagine the following scenario: Three managers meet at the end of the day to discuss a business problem. Each manager has gathered information at different times during the day to create a picture of the situation. Each manager's picture may be different because of this time discrepancy. Their views on the business problem may not match since the information they are basing their analysis on is continually changing. This approach may not speed up decision making, and may actually slow it down.

Organizations must evaluate the timeliness of the information required for each business decision. Organizations do not want to find themselves using real-time information to make a bad decision faster.

BUSINESS DRIVERS FOR WIRELESS TECHNOLOGIES

United Parcel Service and FedEx have been using wireless technologies for years, making it possible for information about dispatching and deliveries to travel between couriers and central stations. FedEx's famous tracking system, which can find a package's location from its tracking number, uses a wireless courier-management system.

The terms *mobile* and *wireless* are often used synonymously, but actually denote two different technologies. *Mobile technology* means the technology can travel with the user, but it is not necessarily in real-time; users can download software, e-mail messages, and Web pages onto their personal digital assistant (PDA), laptop, or other mobile device for portable reading or reference. Information collected while on the road can be synchronized with a PC or corporate server.

Wireless technology, on the other hand, gives users a live (Internet) connection via satellite or radio transmitters. International Data Corporation forecasts that by 2010 nearly two-thirds of handheld devices will include integrated wireless networking. For instance, newly announced PDAs integrate phones, text messaging, Web browsers, and organizers. Figure 11.18 displays the factors inspiring the growth of wireless technologies.[8]

State government agencies, such as transportation departments, use wireless devices to collect field information, tracking inventory, reporting times, monitoring logistics, and completing forms—all from a mobile environment. The transportation industry is using wireless devices to help determine current locations and alternate driving routes.

FIGURE 11.18

Wireless Drivers

Drivers of Wireless Technology Growth	
Universal access to information and applications	People are mobile and have more access to information than ever before, but they still need to get to the point where they can access all information anytime, anywhere, anyplace.
The automation of business processes	Wireless technologies have the ability to centralize critical information and eliminate redundant processes.
User convenience, timeliness, and ability to conduct business 24/7/365	People delayed in airports no longer have to feel cut off from the world or their office. Through wireless tools and wireless solutions such as a BlackBerry RIM device, they can access their information anytime, anywhere, anyplace.

Wireless technology is rapidly evolving and is playing an increasing role in the lives of people throughout the world. The final key factor driving the increased use of wireless devices is the sheer number of wireless device users. With such a large market, businesses simply must embrace wireless technologies or be left behind.

Wireless technologies are transforming how we live, work, and play. Hand-held devices continue to offer additional functionality, and cellular networks are advancing rapidly in their increased speed and throughput abilities. These enabling technologies fuel widespread adoption and creation of new and innovative ways to perform business. The big changes that will re-create workplaces, industries, and organizations are coming from wireless technologies. Figure 11.19 displays a few common examples of wireless technologies that are changing our world.

ADVANTAGES OF ENTERPRISE MOBILITY

Organizations have realized that while the value of electronic corporate information can be nearly limitless, it is worth nothing if employees cannot access it. Work does not always get done at an office desk, and the ability to connect remote workers to the information they require to perform their job provides benefits to an organization.

Wireless laptops facilitate emergency room registration so doctors can start working on the patients as soon as the medics wheel them into the hospital. High-end tractors equipped with wireless sensors help farmers monitor everything from the weather to the amount of seed released. Tractors that break down automatically e-mail the service department with the information for the repair. Roaming ticket sellers armed with wi-fi-enabled devices and belt-mounted printers shorten the wait at the front gate at theme parks such as Universal Studios in Orlando, Florida. Figure 11.20 lists the wireless technologies influencing business mobility, which are described in detail in the following section.

Wireless Devices Changing Business
■ **Wireless local area network (wLAN):** uses radio waves rather than wires to transmit information across a local area network.
■ **Cellular phones and pagers:** provide connectivity for portable and mobile applications, both personal and business.
■ **Cordless computer peripherals:** connect wirelessly to a computer, such as a cordless mouse, keyboard, and printer.
■ **Satellite television:** allows viewers in almost any location to select from hundreds of channels.
■ **WiMax wireless broadband:** enables wireless networks to extend as far as 48 kilometres and transfer information, voice, and video at faster speeds than cable. It is perfect for Internet service providers (ISPs) that want to expand into sparsely populated areas, where the cost of bringing in cable wiring or DSL is too high.
■ **Security sensor:** alerts customers to break-ins and errant pop flies. Its dual sensors record vibration and acoustic disturbances—a shattered window—to help avoid false alarms.

FIGURE 11.19

Wireless Technologies Changing Business

Wireless Technologies Influencing Business Mobility
■ **Bluetooth:** creating a niche market for traditionally cabled devices.
■ **Radio frequency identification tags (RFID):** possessing the potential to reinvent the supply chain. Wal-Mart's suppliers must now use the tags for pallets and cases of merchandise.
■ **Satellite:** changing the way television and radio stations operate. Plus, global positioning systems (GPS) allow drivers of cars and trucks, captains of boats and ships, backpackers, hikers, skiers, and pilots of aircraft to ascertain their location anywhere on Earth.

FIGURE 11.20

Wireless Technologies Influencing Business Mobility

Bluetooth

One challenge to wireless devices is their size. Everyone wants their mobile devices to be small, but many people also curse the tiny, cryptic keyboards that manufacturers squeeze into smart phones and PDAs. The laws of physics have proved a significant barrier to solving this problem, but VKB Inc.'s Bluetooth Virtual Keyboard offers a possible solution (see Figure 11.21). VKB's technology uses a red laser to illuminate a virtual keyboard outline on any surface. Despite its futuristic look, the laser is really just a visual guide to where users put their fingers. A separate illumination and sensor module invisibly tracks when and where each finger touches the surface, translating that into keystrokes or other commands.[9]

Bluetooth is an omnidirectional wireless technology that provides limited-range voice and data transmission over the unlicensed 2.4-GHz frequency band, allowing connections with a wide variety of fixed and portable devices that normally would have to be cabled together. Bluetooth headsets allow users to cut the cord and make calls even while their cell phones are tucked away in a briefcase. Wireless Bluetooth printing allows users of a Bluetooth-enabled PDA or laptop to connect to any printer via a Bluetooth adapter connected to the printer's parallel port.

Since Bluetooth's development in 1994 by the Swedish telecommunications company Ericsson, more than 1,800 companies worldwide have signed on to build products to the wireless specification and promote the new technology in the marketplace. The engineers at Ericsson code-named the new wireless technology Bluetooth to honour a 10th-century Viking King, Harald Bluetooth, who is credited with uniting Denmark and bringing order to the country.

Bluetooth capability is enabled in a device by means of an embedded Bluetooth chip and supporting software. Although Bluetooth is slower than competing wireless LAN technologies, the Bluetooth chip enables Bluetooth networking to be built into a wide range of devices—even small devices such as cellular phones and PDAs. Bluetooth's maximum range is 9 metres, limiting it to gadget-to-gadget communication. There are more than 1,000 Bluetooth products on the market, with 10 more introduced each week.

Radio Frequency Identification (RFID)

Radio frequency identification (RFID) technologies use active or passive tags in the form of chips or smart labels that can store unique identifiers and relay this information to electronic readers. At Starbucks, good service is nearly as important as

FIGURE 11.21

Bluetooth Virtual Keyboard

Beams of light, which detect the user's movements, make up this virtual keyboard. It can be integrated into mobile phones, laptops, tablet PCs, or even sterile medical environments.

good coffee to customer loyalty. But when a delivery person comes knocking on the back door to drop off muffins, it means employees may need to leave their countertop posts, jeopardizing customer service. To help solve the problem, Starbucks is considering using radio frequency identification technology as part of a proposed plan to let its 40,000 suppliers drop off pastries, milk, coffee beans, and other supplies at night, after stores have closed. This solution solves one problem while causing another: How does Starbucks ensure that delivery people do not walk out with as much stuff as they dropped off?

To solve the problem, the company will distribute to its suppliers cards with RFID chips that give delivery people access to stores at night, while recording who is coming and going. ***RFID tags*** contain a microchip and an antenna, and typically work by transmitting a serial number via radio waves to an electronic reader, which confirms the identity of a person or object bearing the tag.

RFID technology is finally coming into its own. Wal-Mart asked suppliers to attach RFID tags to product shipment pallets by the end of 2005 to automate tracking. However, drawbacks to RFID technology, including its high cost and concerns about consumer privacy, must be overcome before it finds widespread use. Figure 11.22 displays the three components of RFID, and Figure 11.23 shows how tracking with RFID tags is expected to work in the supply chain.

As many as 10,000 radio frequency identification tags are taking to the skies, affixed to everything from airline seats to brakes, as part of the Airbus A380, a 550-seat jet that began service in 2006. The tags contain serial numbers, codes, and maintenance history that makes it easier to track, fix, and replace parts. Not to be outdone, Boeing is using tags on many of the parts in its 787 Dreamliner, a mid-sized, twin engine jet airliner scheduled to enter service in May 2008.

These initiatives are not the first use of RFID in the airline industry, but they represent aggressive plans to further leverage the real-time and detail capabilities of RFID. In 2000, Boeing began equipping all its tools and toolboxes with RFID tags. Similarly, Airbus began tagging its ground equipment and tools soon after.[10]

FIGURE 11.22

Three RFID Components

The Three Components to an RFID System

Tag—A microchip holds data, in this case an EPC (electronic product code), a set of numbers unique to an item. The rest of the tag is an antenna that transmits data to a reader.
EPC example: 01-0000A77-000136BR5

Reader—A reader uses radio waves to read the tag and sends the EPC to computers in the supply chain.

Computer Network—Each computer in the supply chain recognizes the EPC and pulls up information related to the item, such as dates made and shipped, price, and directions for use, from a server maintained by the manufacturer. The computers track the item's location throughout the supply chain.

FIGURE 11.23

RFID in the Supply Chain

RFID in the Retail Supply Chain

RFID tags are added to every product and shipping box. At every step of an item's journey, a reader scans one of the tags and updates the information on the server.

The Manufacturer

A reader scans the tags as items leave the factory.

The Distribution Centre

Readers in the unloading area scan the tags on arriving boxes and update inventory, avoiding the need to open packages.

The Store

Tags are scanned upon arrival to update inventory. At the racks, readers scan tags as shirts are stocked. At the checkout counter, a cashier can scan individual items with a handheld reader. As items leave the store, inventory is updated. Manufacturers and retailers can observe sales patterns in real time and make swift decisions about production, ordering, and pricing.

The Home

The consumer can have the tag disabled at the store for privacy or place readers in closets to keep track of clothes. With customers' approval, stores can follow purchasing patterns and notify them of sales.

Integrating RFID and Software Integrating RFID with enterprise software is expected to change the way companies manage maintenance, combat theft, and even augment business processes. Oracle and SAP have begun adding RFID capability to their enterprise application suites. Oracle's RFID and Sensor-Based Services analyze and respond to data from RFID so the information can be integrated with Oracle's applications.

RFID tags are evolving, too, and the advances will provide more granular information to enterprise software. Today's tags can store an electronic product code. In time, tags could hold more information, making them portable mini-databases.

The possibilities of RFID are endless. Delta Air Lines recently completed a pilot project that used baggage tags incorporating RFID chips instead of the standard bar codes. With RFID readers installed at counters and key sorting locations, not a single duffel was misplaced. The system worked so well that Delta intends to roll it out across the United States in 2007.[11]

Satellite

Microwave transmitters, especially satellite systems, are commonly used to transmit network signals over great distances. A microwave transmitter uses the atmosphere (or outer space) as the transmission medium to send the signal to a microwave receiver. The microwave receiver then either relays the signal to another microwave transmitter or translates the signal to some other form, such as digital impulses, as illustrated in Figure 11.24. Originally, this technology was used almost exclusively for satellite and long-range communication. Recently, however, developments in cellular technology allow complete wireless access to networks, intranets, and the Internet via microwave transmission.

XM Satellite Radio made a tech-savvy decision when it decided to develop the chipsets for XM's radios in-house rather than outsourcing the job. The move allowed the XM service to launch faster and better, giving the company a lead over its archrival, Sirius Satellite Radio. Both companies are growing quickly. Satellite

FIGURE 11.24

Satellite Microwave Link

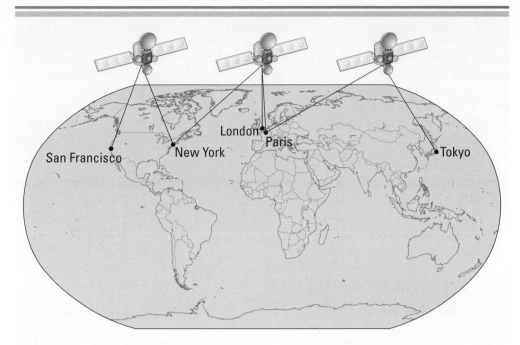

radio is big business, and Sirius recently signed a contract with Howard Stern for $500 million over five years.[12]

Global Positioning System (GPS)

The U.S. Department of Defense installed more than 30 satellites in space over the equator to help the military identify positions on Earth. In 1993, the Defense Department made this global positioning technology available for commercial use to anyone who has a GPS. A *global positioning system (GPS)* is a device that determines current latitude, longitude, speed, and direction of movement. GPS devices have special microprocessors that analyze satellite signals. Sirf Technology specializes in building GPS microprocessors and charges about US$13 per device to put its GPS chipset in phones, electronics, and car navigation systems. Since going public in 2004, Sirf Technology has seen revenue climb 60 percent to US$117 million with net profits of US$30.7 million. With new federal regulation forcing wireless operators to include GPS in their phones and networking equipment, chip demand is sure to explode.[13]

The market for GPS services has grown to over US$5 billion with expectations for demand to double over the next few years. Tracking, navigation, and hardware promise to be multibillion-dollar markets by 2010. UPS plans to outfit 75,000 drivers with GPS-enabled handhelds to help them reach destinations more efficiently. The handhelds will also trigger e-mail alerts if a company vehicle speeds or ventures into unauthorized areas. Steve Wozniak, Apple co-founder, started a company in 2002 named Wheels of Zeus that combines GPS data with local wireless networking. The technology helps parents keep tabs on their children or can alert IT managers when company-owned computers leave the premises. Zingo, in the United Kingdom, uses GPS-enabled cars and text messaging to help subscribers hail cabs.

A *geographic information system (GIS)* is designed to work with information that can be shown on a map. Companies that deal in transportation use GISs combined with database and GPS technology. Airlines and shipping companies can plot routes with up-to-the-second information on the location of all their transport vehicles. Hospitals can keep track of where personnel are located by using a GIS and sensors in the ceiling that pick up the transmission of badges worn by hospital staff.

Automobiles have GPSs linked to maps that display in a screen on the dashboard driving directions and exact location of the vehicle. GM offers the OnStar system, which sends a continuous stream of information to the OnStar centre about the car's exact location. The new OnStar Vehicle Diagnostics automatically performs hundreds of diagnostic checks on four key operating systems—the engine/transmission, antilock brakes, air bags, and OnStar systems—in GM vehicles. The vehicle is programmed to send the results via e-mail to the owner each month. The unique e-mail report also provides maintenance reminders based on the current odometer reading, remaining engine oil life, and other relevant ownership information.[14]

Some cell phone providers equip their phones with GPS chips that enable users to be located to within a geographical location about the size of a tennis court. This allows emergency services such as 911 to find a cell phone user. Marketers are monitoring cell phone GPS development, hoping to be able to call potential customers when they are walking past their store to let them know of a special sale.[15]

THE FUTURE OF WIRELESS

One of the strangest Internet innovations in recent history was Microsoft's toilet project. It was a widely reported weird-news item in the spring of 2003, later revealed to be a hoax, and even later to be confirmed by Microsoft as an actual project, albeit a defunct one. The gist of the story was that Microsoft U.K. wanted to create a portable toilet, the iLoo, with a built-in high-speed Internet connection, wireless keyboard, and height-adjustable plasma monitor—a contraption, so they said, that would appeal to the British market.

Now it seems that the restroom and the Internet are converging yet again. A *hotspot* consists of one or more access points positioned on a ceiling, wall, or other strategic spot in a public place to provide maximum wireless coverage for a specific area. Users in range of the hotspot can then access the Internet from their wireless device. The latest front in the wireless hotspot movement is the U.S. interstate rest area. "I know it sounds strange at first, but when you think about it, rest areas are a great fit for wi-fi," said Mark Wheeler, CEO of I Spot Networks, a wireless Internet service provider. Wheeler noted that highway travellers often actively seek out an Internet connection because the Internet has become so integral to 21st-century life.

Working in conjunction with U.S. state transportation departments, I Spot Networks is rolling out hotspots along interstates in Iowa, Missouri, and Nebraska. The company also targets more conventional hotspot locations, such as hotels and coffee shops, but it believes that heavily travelled interstate corridors are an overlooked hotspot opportunity.

Analysts predict there will be more than 1.4 billion wireless subscribers by the end of 2010, with about 500 million of those using wireless Internet access. The growth of the wireless market will drive the development of new wireless technology, which in turn will create a larger market for Bluetooth connectivity, which allows wireless handheld devices, personal computers, and laptops to work together. Analysts expect Bluetooth shipments to rise from fewer than 1 million in 2001 to 3 billion in 2010.[16]

Gartner Inc. predicts that the future will belong to "The Real-Time Enterprise," the organization that thrives in uncertain times because it can detect sooner and respond faster. Wireless technologies clearly play a major role in increasing an organization's agility.

Wireless access to corporate e-mail systems, often the primary catalyst to an organization's first significant venture into wireless technology, has become the focus of much attention. E-mail is the foremost communication system in most organizations, surpassing voice mail in importance and interest (see Figure 11.25).[17]

Organizations are fast approaching the point where they will have the technical wireless infrastructure to support an always-on connection that will let users roam seamlessly from Starbucks, to a customer site, to conference rooms, and even to a comfortable chair in front of the TV at home.

Application	Western Europe	Eastern Europe	United States
On 6-point interest scale, 6 = high interest, and 1 = low interest:			
E-mail	4.5	4.7	4.3
Payment authorization/enablement	3.4	3.8	3.0
Banking/trading online	3.5	3.4	3.2
Shopping/reservations	3.0	3.1	2.9
Interactive games	2.0	2.2	2.4

FIGURE 11.25

Current Mobile Phone Users' Applications Interest

OPENING CASE QUESTIONS

The Digital Hospital

5. Why is real-time information important to hospitals?

6. How is Hackensack University Medical Center using wireless technology to improve its operations?

7. Identify three wireless technologies that are changing the way businesses operate and explain how hospitals can use these technologies to improve their operations.

The purpose of this chapter was to provide you, the business student, with a detailed overview of the various telecommunications technologies employed by organizations today. This included discussion on:

- Network types (LAN, WAN, MAN),
- Network architectures (peer-to-peer, client/server),
- Network topologies (bus, star, ring, hybrid, wireless),
- Network protocols (Ethernet, TCP/IP, VoIP),
- Network media (coaxial, twisted-pair, fibre-optic),
- E-business networks (VPN, VAN),
- Wireless fidelity (wi-fi), and
- Business mobility technologies (Bluetooth; RFID; satellite; GPS, GIS).

Organizations are taking advantage of these technologies in the information systems applications they are building.

This chapter also discussed:

- Business drivers for wireless technologies, and
- The future of wireless.

It is important that you, the business student, understand what technologies are available and how businesses can leverage these technologies in their day-to-day operations.

KEY TERMS

Bluetooth 352
Client 339
Client/server network 339
Coaxial cable 346
Ethernet 342
Fibre optic (or optical fibre) 346
Geographic information system (GIS) 355
Global positioning system (GPS) 355
Interoperability 342
Local area network (LAN) 337
Metropolitan area network (MAN) 337
Microwave transmitter 354
Network 337

Network operating system (NOS) 339
Network topology 340
Network transmission media 345
Packet-switching 340
Peer-to-peer (P2P) network 338
Protocol 342
Radio frequency identification (RFID) 352
Real-time information 349
Real-time system 349
RFID tag 353
Router 340
Server 339

Telecommunication system 337
Transmission Control Protocol/Internet Protocol (TCP/IP) 343
Twisted-pair wiring 346
Value-added network (VAN) 348
Virtual private network (VPN) 348
Voice over IP (VoIP) 344
Wide area network (WAN) 337
Wireless fidelity (wi-fi) 349
Wireless media 346
Wire media 345

Free Trading with RFID

This case illustrates a novel use of RFID technologies to showcase the use and potential abuse of this technology by organizations.

In 2006, Vancouver multidisciplinary artist Nancy Nisbet went on a six-month road tour across Canada, the United States, and Mexico with a mission to exchange her personal belongings with others using RFID technologies. Coined "Exchange" (www.exchangeproject.ca), one of the main purposes of the project was to raise awareness of the use and potential abuse of RFID to others.

What Nancy did (quite creatively!) was pack every single one of her worldly possessions in a transport truck, travelled the continent, and freely traded her belongings with anyone that crossed her path. What possessions you ask? Things like crutches, furniture, old photographs, and clothing. All items were conspicuously tagged with a Radio Frequency Identification microchip in an effort to make RFID visible and provoke thoughtful and informed questioning of the limits and liabilities of this technology.

At each scheduled stop on her route, Nancy and her assistants would park the truck, lower the ramps, unload at least half the goods, and invite any bystanders to look through the belongings. If a particular item caught the eye of somebody, that person would take the good to the "mini house"—a temporary technical centre that operated on wireless technology—where the customer could check-out the item while checking-in some other item that the person owned. Since each item was tagged with RFID, things could be tracked in a database. Interestingly, part of the artistic-side of the project involved the customer relaying the story behind their giveaway object to the crew. This history was captured via audio files as a means to capture the context behind the exchange of goods.[18]

To ensure that the technology was in place and working correctly prior to the outset of her journey, Nancy engaged the services of Richmond B.C.-based NJE Consulting. NJE's hardware and software solution consisted of specially-programmed Personal Digital Assistants (PDAs) equipped with high-frequency RFID readers. Nisbet and her assistants used the PDAs on each trade to scan the RFID tags on incoming and outgoing items. It was also possible with these PDAs to record voice messages about the new incoming item (i.e., the personal background story) and to take digital camera images of these items. Touch-screen buttons on the PDA interface also allowed incoming items to be categorized according to a pre-defined classification scheme. All this information (RFID, voice, photo, and item category) was linked in the system database located on a server housed in Nisbet's truck.

According to Bartek Muszynski, president of NJE Consulting, the firm "managed to integrate data from multiple sources including RFID, voice, and image into a single, coherent database" and successfully overcome significant data-synchronization challenges. Though the system in its current form does not have commercial application, it is not difficult to imagine how a similar system might find a myriad of commercial uses, such as from auction houses that routinely deal with large numbers of physical items that all require careful description and tracking, justice departments and agencies that need to track court evidence, or other applications involving lab sample tracking, document tracking, rental goods tracking, and general asset tracking.[19]

Questions

1. Explain the fundamentals of RFID and how it is being used to track the exchange of goods on Nisbet's truck?

2. What concerns was Nisbet trying to raise awareness about in her cross-continent road trip? That is, what potential abuses of RFID technologies was Nisbet trying to showcase to others?

3. How could NJE's hardware/software solution be applied at your university or college?

UPS versus FedEx: Head-to-Head on Wireless

The case illustrates the different approaches organizations can take when utilizing wireless technologies.

Federal Express and United Parcel Service are always seeking a competitive edge over one another. And as the two companies are encroaching on each other's primary businesses (UPS on overnight delivery and FedEx on ground delivery), they are concurrently stepping up their wireless deployments as well. The reason: operational efficiency—a critical business requirement aimed at shaving costs, increasing reach, and doing more with the same resources.

Their approaches to deploying wireless technologies over the past 15 years have been markedly different; FedEx has led the way with cutting-edge applications, while UPS has been slower and more deliberate. FedEx deploys new technologies as soon as it can justify the cost and demonstrate improved efficiencies and customer benefit. UPS refreshes its technology base roughly every five to seven years, when it rolls out a unified system in stages that it synchronizes with the life span of the older system. But the goal is the same for both companies: to use next-generation wireless technologies to better manage the delivery of millions of packages that flow through dozens of sorting facilities every day.

The two companies are exploiting new wireless technologies in their differing attempts at aiding the two main components of their operations: pickup/delivery and packaging/sorting. Both are also looking ahead to potential applications of radio frequency identification and GPS wireless technologies.

	UPS	FedEx
Main hub:	Louisville, Kentucky	Memphis, Tennessee
Total packages handled each day:	13.6 million	5 million
Number of air deliveries daily:	2 million	3.1 million
Wireless devices in field:	90,000	80,000
Wireless devices in sorting facilities:	55,000	70,000
Wireless access points:	9,000	5,000

Seeking New Benefits from Wireless

In addition to their major package-scanning retooling efforts, FedEx and UPS continue to investigate what business benefits they might gain from other wireless technologies. Two have gained particular attention: RFID tags, which could replace bar code scanners, and GPS, which can precisely locate field units.

As UPS and FedEx are showing, wireless technology provides the medium through which dynamic exchange happens. Interconnectedness allows drivers to talk, computers to interact, and businesses to work together. Whether it is wireless routing or fueling of trucks, it is all happening dynamically. Although few companies have the scale of UPS and FedEx, they can adopt many of the wireless technologies scaled to their size, and use devices and network components that fit their operations.[20]

Questions

1. Explain the fundamentals of wireless fidelity.
2. Describe the differences between UPS and FedEx's use of wi-fi.
3. Identify two types of wireless business opportunities the companies could use to gain a competitive advantage.

4. How could RFID help the companies deal with potential security issues?

5. Develop a Bluetooth, GPS, or satellite product that the parcel delivery business could use to improve efficiencies.

Watching Where You Step—Prada

The case shows the importance of utilizing telecommunications technology only when it makes business sense.

Prada estimates its sales per year at $24 million. The luxury retailer recently spent millions on IT for its futuristic "epicentre" store, but the flashy technology turned into a high-priced hassle. The company will need to generate annual sales of $75 million to turn a profit on its new high-tech investment.

When Prada opened its $44-million Manhattan flagship in the United States, architect Rem Koolhaas promised a radically new shopping experience. He kept the promise—though not quite according to plan. Customers were soon enduring hordes of tourists, neglected technology, and the occasional thrill of being stuck in experimental dressing rooms. A few of the problems associated with the store:

- Fickle fitting rooms. Doors that turn from clear to opaque confuse shoppers and frequently fail to open on cue.

- Failed RFID. Touchscreens meant to spring to life when items are placed in the RFID "closets" are often just blank.

- Pointless personal digital assistants (PDA). Salesclerks let the handheld devices gather dust and instead check the stockroom for inventory.

- Neglected network. A lag between sales and inventory systems makes the wireless network nearly irrelevant.

This was not exactly the vision for the high end boutique when it debuted its new high-tech store. Instead, the 22,000-square-foot SoHo shop was to be the first of four "epicentre" stores around the world that would combine cutting-edge architecture and 21st-century technology to revolutionize the luxury shopping experience. Prada poured roughly 25 percent of the store's budget into IT, including a wireless network to link every item to an Oracle inventory database in real time using radio frequency identification (RFID) tags on the clothes. The staff would roam the floor armed with PDAs to check whether items were in stock, and customers could do the same through touchscreens in the dressing rooms.

However, most of the flashy technology today sits idle, abandoned by employees who never quite embraced the technology. On top of that, many gadgets, such as automated dressing-room doors and touchscreens, are either malfunctioning or ignored. Packed with experimental technology, the clear-glass dressing-room doors were designed to open and close automatically at the tap of a foot pedal, then turn opaque when a second pedal sent an electric current through the glass. Inside, an RFID-aware rack would recognize a customer's selections and display them on a touchscreen linked to the inventory system.

In practice, the process was hardly that smooth. Many shoppers never quite understood the pedals and disrobed in full view, thinking the door had turned opaque. That is no longer a problem, since the staff usually leaves the glass opaque, but often the doors are stuck. Some of the chambers are open only to VIP customers during peak traffic times.

With the smart closets and handhelds out of commission, the wireless network in the store is nearly irrelevant, despite its considerable expense. As Prada's debt reportedly climbed to around $1.1 billion in late 2001, the company shelved plans for the fourth epicentre store, in

San Francisco. A second store opened in Tokyo in 2003 to great acclaim, albeit with different architects in a different market. Though that store incorporates similar cutting-edge concepts, architect Jacques Herzog emphasized that avant-garde retail plays well only in Japan. "This building is clearly a building for Tokyo," he told *The New York Times*. "It couldn't be somewhere else."

The multimillion-dollar technology is starting to look more like technology for technology's sake than an enhancement of the shopping experience, and the store's failings have prompted Prada to reevaluate its epicentre strategy.[21]

Questions

1. Would you consider Prada's use of technology cutting-edge? Why or why not?
2. Prada's attempt to use RFID to check inventory in real time failed because of the staff's refusal to use the system. What could Prada have done to make the implementation of RFID successful?
3. Identify an additional strategic use of RFID for Prada's high-tech store.
4. What should Prada do differently when designing its next store to ensure its success?
5. Identify a new use of wireless technology for Prada's next store.

MAKING BUSINESS DECISIONS

1. **Wireless fitness**

   Sandifer's Fitness Club is located in beautiful British Columbia. Rosie Sandifer has owned and operated the club for 20 years. The club has three outdoor pools, two indoor pools, 10 racquetball courts, 10 tennis courts, an indoor and outdoor track, along with a four-story exercise equipment and massage therapy building. Rosie has hired you as a summer intern specializing in information technology. The extent of Rosie's current technology includes a few PCs in the accounting department and two PCs with Internet access for the rest of the staff. Your first assignment is to create a report detailing networks and wireless technologies. The report should explain how the club could gain a business advantage by implementing a wireless network. If Rosie likes your report, she will hire you as the full-time employee in charge of information technology. Be sure to include all of the different uses for wireless devices the club could implement to improve its operations.

2. **Secure access**

   Organizations that have traditionally maintained private, closed systems have begun to look at the potential of the Internet as a ready-made network resource. The Internet is inexpensive and globally pervasive: Every phone jack is a potential connection. However, the Internet lacks security. What obstacles must organizations overcome to allow secure network connections?

3. **Integrating wireless worlds**

   Tele-Messaging is a next-generation integrated Internet and wireless messaging service that offers services to ISPs, telecommunications carriers, and portal companies. According to Tele-Messaging's research, the primary reason that 90 percent of the people go online is for e-mail. However, the challenge for Tele-Messaging is how to successfully attract and retain these customers. Customers want more than free calls to sign up and are looking for a host of additional services with whiz-bang technology to give them the information they want, when they want it, anywhere, and in the method most convenient to them. List the infrastructures needed to deliver the technology with the necessary reliability, availability, and scalability demanded by Tele-Messaging's customers.

4. Communicating with instant messages

You are working for a new start-up magazine, *Jabber Inc.,* developed for information professionals that provides articles, product reviews, case studies, evaluation, and informed opinions. You need to collaborate on news items and projects, and exchange data with a variety of colleagues inside and outside the *Jabber Inc.* walls. You know that many companies are now embracing the instant messaging technology. Prepare a brief report for the CIO that will explain the reasons IM is not just a teenage fad, but also a valuable communications tool that is central to everyday business.

5. Rolling out with networks

As organizations begin to realize the benefits of adding a wireless component to their network, they must understand how to leverage this emerging technology. Wireless solutions have come to the forefront for many organizations with the rollout of more standard, cost-effective, and secure wireless protocols. With wireless networks, increased business agility may be realized by continuous data access and synchronization. However, with the increased flexibility come many challenges. Develop a report detailing the benefits an organization could obtain by implementing wireless technology. Also, include the challenges that a wireless network presents along with recommendations for any solutions.

12

CHAPTER

IT Architectures

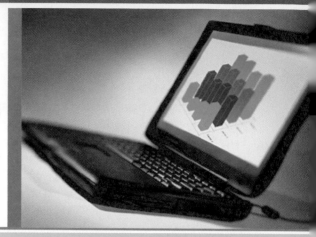

LEARNING OUTCOMES

12.1. Describe the six major categories of hardware and provide an example of each.

12.2. Identify the different computer categories and explain their potential business uses.

12.3. Explain the difference between primary and secondary storage, and what each is used for.

12.4. List the common input, output, storage, and communication devices.

12.5. Describe the eight categories of computers by size.

12.6. Define the relationship between operating system software and utility software.

12.7. Explain the three components of an enterprise architecture.

12.8. Describe how an organization can implement a solid information architecture.

12.9. List and describe the five primary characteristics of an infrastructure architecture.

12.10. Compare Web services and open systems.

Why Do I Need To Know This ?

This chapter provides an overview of hardware/software basics and enterprise architecture—the foundation of an enterprise's underlying information infrastructure. As a business student, you need to know this since this foundation is literally the base upon which all information systems are built in an organization.

Knowing the fundamentals of this core is paramount to understanding how information systems technically function and how they are maintained. This knowledge will serve you well in understanding your future organization's information infrastructure and the potential and limitations this infrastructure has on your firm's ability to build and support its information systems.

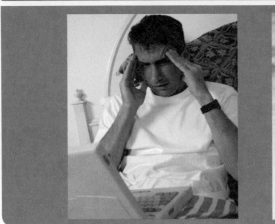

Electronic Breaking Points

What happens when someone accidentally spills a cup of hot coffee on a laptop, puts a USB memory key in a washing machine, or drops an iPod in the sand? How much abuse can electronic products take and keep on working? *PC World* tested several products to determine their breaking points.[1]

Laptop

A Gateway laptop was placed in a shoulder bag and smashed into several doors and walls. It was also dropped off a two-metre-high bookcase to simulate a drop from an airplane's overhead bin. Finally, it was knocked off a desk onto a carpeted floor without the bag. After all the abuse, the Gateway consistently rebooted and recognized the wireless network; however, the battery did become slightly dislodged and the optical drive opened.

Severe physical damage was caused when the laptop was dropped onto a hardwood floor. The laptop's screen cracked, and the black plastic moulding above the keyboard cracked. Plastic splinters littered the floor, and the optical drive refused to open.

Spilling coffee in a travel-size mug onto the keyboard caused a slight sizzle, after which the Gateway's blue light winked out. The machine was quickly turned off, the battery removed, the liquid drained, the keys mopped, and the unit set aside. Unfortunately, the laptop never recovered.

Smart Phone

The PalmOne Treo 600 smart phone was stepped on, buried in the sand, bounced around in a car, and dropped off a desk onto carpeted and hardwood floors. Even though the Treo 600 was not protected by a shock-absorbent case or plastic screen cover, there were no signs of failure. Repeatedly knocking it off the desk onto a carpeted floor also left it undamaged, although the unit did turn off on several occasions.

The desk-to-hardwood-floor test produced scratches but nothing else. If dropped when in phone mode, the Treo automatically turned off. If an application was running—the calculator, for example—the device stayed on and the data remained on the screen, though a mysterious extra numeral nine appeared every time it was dropped.

MP3 Player

A 6 GB silver iPod Mini went for a bouncy car ride, was dropped on wet grass and dry pavement, was knocked off a desk onto carpeted and hardwood floors, and was finally dropped in dry sand. Bouncing inside the car caused a couple of skips. Drops on soft wet grass and carpet had no ill effect. Dropping it from the car seat to the curb and off a desk onto a hardwood floor produced a few nicks and caused songs to skip and the device to shut down repeatedly. Still, all the unit's features continued to work after the abuse, and songs played.

However, the Mini did not like the beach. Without the benefit of a protective case or plastic display covering on the unit, sand became wedged under the scroll wheel, affecting all controls. Feature settings could be seen and highlighted, but the crunching sand prevented the Mini from launching them. The unit turned on but could not turn off until the iPod's automatic shutdown feature took over.

Memory Stick

Lexar claims that its JumpDrive Sport 256 MB USB 2.0 Flash Drive is "built for the rugged life." A rubber cap protects the device, absorbing shock from any drops. For these experiments, the device was used without its cap. It was dropped, stepped on, buried in the sand, and knocked off a desk onto a hardwood floor. It also took a spin through the washing machine and dryer and was even run over by a car.

There is truth in advertising. Neither water, heat, sand, nor car could keep the memory stick from its appointed storage rounds. The car did squeeze the metal USB connector tip a tad tighter, but the device was still able to make contact with the USB port, and it worked perfectly.

Memory Card

The SanDisk SD 64 MB memory card is easy to misplace, but not easy to break. It was swatted off a desk onto a hardwood floor, dropped, stepped on, and buried in the sand. It also underwent a two-rinse cycle in the wash in a jeans pocket and then tumbled in the dryer for an hour on a high-heat setting. The SanDisk memory card aced every torture test.

For tips on how to protect electronic products, review Figure 12.1.

FIGURE 12.1

How to Protect Electronic
Products

Protecting Electronic Products
Bag it. Place your products in a cushioned case or shock-absorbent travel bag. The secret is to make sure it has plenty of padding.
Get protection. Almost every technology manufacturer offers some type of warranty and equipment-replacement program. For example, Sprint in the U.S. provides the PCS Total Equipment Protection service, which costs $5.50 per month and covers loss, theft, and accidental damage to a cell phone.
Clean up spills. Try these tips to bring a laptop and data back from the dead after a spill. 1. **Disconnect the battery.** The faster the battery is disconnected the less likely components will burn out. 2. **Empty it.** Turn over the device and pour out as much liquid as possible. 3. **Open it up.** Remove the optical drive and keyboard. This can be tricky, so check the user manual for instructions. Once open, use a towel to soak up as much liquid as possible. According to Herman De Hoop, Hewlett-Packard's technical marketing manager, you can even use a hair dryer set on cool (not hot) to dry the liquid. 4. **Leave it alone.** Let the device sit for at least 12 to 24 hours. Robert Enochs, IBM's worldwide product manager for the ThinkPad Series, warns that you should not turn the device on until all the liquid is gone and it is completely dry. 5. **Plug and pray.** Reassemble the device, and if it powers up, copy off important data, and then call the manufacturer. Even if the unit works, a professional cleaning is recommended. 6. **Enter a recovery program.** For an average price of $1,000, enlist the help of data recovery services like DriveSavers to rescue data from drowned hard disks.

INTRODUCTION

Managers need to determine what types of hardware and software will satisfy their current and future business needs, the right time to buy the equipment, and how to protect their IT investments. This does not imply that managers need to be experts in all areas of technology; however, building a basic understanding of hardware and software can help them make the right IT investment choices.

Information technology (IT) is any computer-based tool that people use to work with information and support the information and information-processing needs of an organization. Information technology can be composed of the Internet, a personal computer, a cell phone that can access the Web, a personal digital assistant, or presentation software. All of these technologies help to perform specific information processing tasks. There are two basic categories of information technology: hardware and software. *Hardware* consists of the physical devices associated with a computer system. *Software* is the set of instructions that the hardware executes to carry out specific tasks. Software, such as Microsoft Excel, and various hardware devices, such as a keyboard and a monitor, interact to create a spreadsheet or a graph. This chapter covers the basics of computer hardware and software including terminology, characteristics, and the associated managerial responsibilities for building a solid enterprise architecture.

HARDWARE BASICS

In many industries, exploiting computer hardware is key to gaining a competitive advantage. Frito-Lay gained a competitive advantage by using handheld devices to track the strategic placement and sale of items in convenience stores. Sales representatives could track sale price, competitor information, the number of items sold, and item location in the store all from their handheld device.[2]

A *computer* is an electronic device operating under the control of instructions stored in its own memory that can accept, manipulate, and store data. A computer system consists of six hardware components (see Figure 12.2). Figure 12.3 displays how these components work together to form a computer system.

FIGURE 12.2

Hardware Components of a Computer System

Six Hardware Components	
Central processing unit (CPU)	The actual hardware that interprets and executes the program (software) instructions and coordinates how all the other hardware devices work together.
Primary storage	The computer's main memory, which consists of the random access memory (RAM), cache memory, and the read-only memory (ROM) that is directly accessible to the central processing unit (CPU).
Secondary storage	Equipment designed to store large volumes of data for long-term storage (e.g., diskette, hard drive, memory card, CD).
Input devices	Equipment used to capture information and commands (e.g., keyboard, scanner).
Output devices	Equipment used to see, hear, or otherwise accept the results of information processing requests (e.g., monitor, printer).
Communication devices	Equipment used to send information and receive it from one location to another (e.g., modem).

FIGURE 12.3
How the Hardware Components Work Together

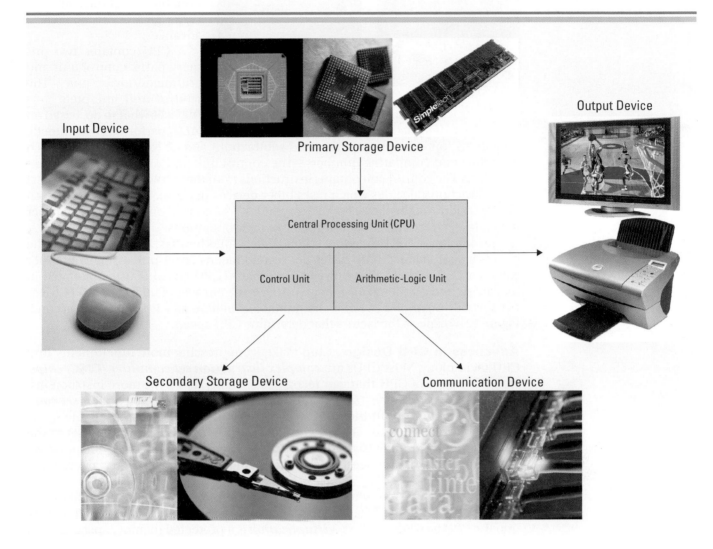

Central Processing Unit

The dominant manufacturers of CPUs today include Intel (with its Celeron and Pentium lines for personal computers) and Advanced Micro Devices (AMD) (with its Athlon series). AMD was initially dismissed as a company that simply cloned current chips, producing processors that mimic the features and capabilities of those from industry leader Intel. However, over the past few years, AMD has begun introducing innovative CPUs that are forcing Intel into the unfamiliar position of reacting to competition. AMD led the way in transforming the processor market by creating chips that handle 64 bits of data at a time, up from 32 bits. It also broke new territory when it became the first provider of dual-core processors for the server market. Hector Ruiz, chairman and CEO of AMD, stated, "In our position there is only one thing we can do: Stay close to our customers and end users, understand what they need and want, and then simply out-innovate the competition. Innovation is at the centre of our ability to succeed. We cannot win by just copying the competition."[3]

The *central processing unit (CPU)* (or *microprocessor*) is the actual hardware that interprets and executes the program (software) instructions and coordinates how all the other hardware devices work together. The CPU is built on a small flake

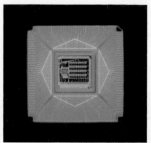

of silicon and can contain the equivalent of several million transistors. CPUs are unquestionably one of the 20th century's greatest technological advances.

A CPU contains two primary parts: control unit and arithmetic/logic unit. The **control unit** interprets software instructions and literally tells the other hardware devices what to do, based on the software instructions. The **arithmetic-logic unit (ALU)** performs all arithmetic operations (for example, addition and subtraction) and all logic operations (such as sorting and comparing numbers). The control unit and ALU perform different functions. The control unit obtains instructions from the software. It then interprets the instructions, decides which tasks other devices perform, and finally tells each device to perform the task. The ALU responds to the control unit and does whatever it dictates, performing either arithmetic or logic operations.

The number of CPU cycles per second determines how fast a CPU carries out the software instructions; more cycles per second means faster processing, and faster CPUs cost more than their slower counterparts. CPU speed is usually quoted in megahertz and gigahertz. **Megahertz (MHz)** is the number of millions of CPU cycles per second. **Gigahertz (GHz)** is the number of billions of CPU cycles per second. Figure 12.4 displays the factors that determine CPU speed.

Advances in CPU Design Chip makers are pressing more functionality into CPU technology. Most CPUs are **complex instruction set computer (CISC) chips**, which is a type of CPU that can recognize as many as 100 or more instructions, enough to carry out most computations directly. **Reduced instruction set computer (RISC) chips** limit the number of instructions the CPU can execute to increase processing speed. The idea of RISC is to reduce the instruction set to the bare minimum, emphasizing the instructions used most of the time and optimizing them for the fastest possible execution. An RISC processor runs faster than a CISC processor.

In the next few years, better performance, systems management capabilities, virtualization, security, and features to help track computer assets will be built directly into the CPU (see Figure 12.5). **Virtualization** is a protected memory space created by the CPU allowing the computer to create virtual machines. Each virtual machine can run its own programs isolated from other machines.

FIGURE 12.4

Factors That Determine CPU Speed

CPU Speed Factors
Clock speed—the speed of the internal clock of a CPU that sets the pace at which operations proceed within the computer's internal processing circuitry. Clock speed is measured in megahertz (MHz) and gigahertz (GHz). Faster clock speeds bring noticeable gains in microprocessor-intensive tasks, such as recalculating a spreadsheet.
Word length—number of bits (0s and 1s) that can be processed by the CPU at any one time. Computers work in terms of bits and bytes using electrical pulses that have two states: on and off. A **binary digit (bit)** is the smallest unit of information that a computer can process. A bit can be either a 1 (on) or a 0 (off). A group of eight bits represents one natural language character and is called a **byte**.
Bus width—the size of the internal electrical pathway along which signals are sent from one part of the computer to another. A wider bus can move more data, hence faster processing.
Chip line width—the distance between transistors on a chip. The shorter the chip line width the faster the chip since more transistors can be placed on a chip and the data and instructions travel short distances during processing.

FIGURE 12.5

Chip Advancements
by Manufacturer

Chip Advancements
AMD: Security, virtualization, and advanced power-management technology.
IBM: Cryptography for additional security and floating point capability for faster graphics processing.
Intel: Cryptography for additional security, hardware-assisted virtualization, and Active Management Technology for asset tracking, patching, and software updates.
Sun Microsystems: Cryptography for additional security, increased speed for data transmission and receipt, and the ability to run 32 computations simultaneously.

Primary Storage

Primary storage is the computer's main memory, which consists of the random access memory (RAM), cache memory, and the read-only memory (ROM) that is directly accessible to the CPU.

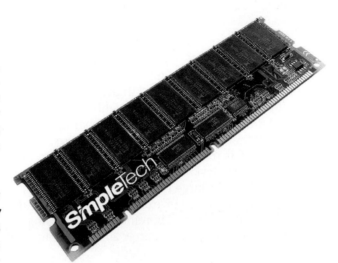

Random Access Memory

Random access memory (RAM) is the computer's primary working memory, in which program instructions and data are stored so that they can be accessed directly by the CPU via the processor's high-speed external data bus.

RAM is often called read/write memory. In RAM, the CPU can write and read data. Most programs set aside a portion of RAM as a temporary workspace for data so that one can modify (rewrite) as needed until the data is ready for printing or storage on secondary storage media, such as a hard drive or memory key. RAM does not retain its contents when the power to the computer is switched off, hence individuals should save their work frequently. When the computer is turned off, everything in RAM is wiped clean. *Volatility* refers to RAM's complete loss of stored information if power is interrupted. RAM is volatile and its contents are lost when the computer's electric supply fails.

Cache Memory   *Cache memory* is a small unit of ultra-fast memory that is used to store recently accessed or frequently accessed data so that the CPU does not have to retrieve this data from slower memory circuits such as RAM. Cache memory that is built directly into the CPU's circuits is called primary cache. Cache memory contained on an external circuit is called secondary cache.

Read-Only Memory (ROM)   *Read-only memory (ROM)* is the portion of a computer's primary storage that does not lose its contents when one switches off the power. ROM contains essential system programs that neither the user nor the computer can erase. Since the computer's internal memory is blank during start-up, the computer cannot perform any functions unless given start-up instructions. These instructions are stored in ROM.

Flash memory is a special type of rewriteable read-only memory (ROM) that is compact and portable. *Memory cards* contain high-capacity storage that holds data such as captured images, music, or text files. Memory cards are removable; when one is full the user can insert an additional card. Subsequently, the data can be downloaded from the card to a computer. The card can then be erased and used again. Memory cards are typically used in digital devices such as cameras, cellular phones, and personal digital assistants (PDA). **Memory sticks** provide nonvolatile memory for a range of portable devices including computers, digital cameras, MP3 players, and PDAs.

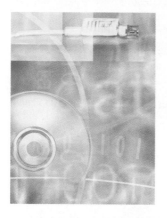

Secondary Storage

Storage is a hot area in the business arena as organizations struggle to make sense of exploding volumes of data. Storage sales grew more than 16 percent to nearly $9 billion in 2004, according to IDC market research. **Secondary storage** consists of equipment designed to store large volumes of data for long-term storage. Secondary storage devices are nonvolatile and do not lose their contents when the computer is turned off. Some storage devices, such as a hard disk, offer easy update capabilities and a large storage capacity. Others, such as CD-ROMs, offer limited update capabilities but possess large storage capacities.

Storage capacity is expressed in bytes, with megabytes being the most common. A **megabyte** (**MB** or **M** or **Meg**) is roughly 1 million bytes. Therefore, a computer with 256 MB of RAM translates into the RAM being able to hold roughly 256 million characters of data and software instructions. A **gigabyte (GB)** is roughly 1 billion bytes. A **terabyte (TB)** is roughly 1 trillion bytes (refer to Figure 12.6).

Most standard desktops have a hard drive with storage capacity in excess of 80 GB. Hard drives for large organizational computer systems can hold in excess of 100 TB of information. For example, a typical double-spaced page of pure text is roughly 2,000 characters. Therefore, a 40 GB (40 gigabyte or 40 billion characters) hard drive can hold approximately 20 million pages of text.

Common storage devices include:

- Magnetic medium
- Optical medium

Magnetic Medium   **Magnetic medium** is a secondary storage medium that uses magnetic techniques to store and retrieve data on disks or tapes coated with magnetically sensitive materials. Like iron filings on a sheet of waxed paper, these materials are reoriented when a magnetic field passes over them. During write operations, the read/write heads emit a magnetic field that orients the magnetic materials on the disk or tape to represent encoded data. During read operations, the read/write heads sense the encoded data on the medium.

FIGURE 12.6

Binary Terms

Term	Size
Kilobyte (KB)	1,024 Bytes
Megabyte (MB)	1,024 KB 1,048,576 Bytes
Gigabyte (GB)	1,024 MB (10^9 bytes)
Terabyte (TB)	1,024 GB (10^{12} bytes) 1 TB = Printing of 1 TB would require 50,000 trees to be made into paper and printed
Petabyte (PB)	1,024 TB (10^{15} bytes) 200 PB = All production of digital magnetic tape in 1995
Exabyte (EB)	1,024 PB (10^{18} bytes) 2 EB = total volume of information generated worldwide annually 5 EB = all words ever spoken by human beings

One of the first forms of magnetic medium developed was magnetic tape. ***Magnetic tape*** is an older secondary storage medium that uses a strip of thin plastic coated with a magnetically sensitive recording medium. The most popular type of magnetic medium is a hard drive. A ***hard drive*** is a secondary storage medium that uses several rigid disks coated with a magnetically sensitive material and housed together with the recording heads in a hermetically sealed mechanism. Hard drive performance is measured in terms of access time, seek time, rotational speed, and data transfer rate.

Optical Medium Optical medium is a secondary storage medium for computers on which information is stored at extremely high density in the form of tiny pits. The presence or absence of pits is read by a tightly focused laser beam. Optical medium types include:

- **Compact disk-read-only memory (CD-ROM) drive—** an optical drive designed to read the data encoded on CD-ROMs and to transfer this data to a computer.

- **Compact disk-read-write (CD-RW) drive—**an optical drive that enables users to erase existing data and to write new data repeatedly to a CD-RW.

- **Digital video disk (DVD)—**a CD-ROM format capable of storing up to a maximum of 17 GB of data; enough for a full-length feature movie.

- **DVD-ROM drive—**a read-only drive designed to read the data encoded on a DVD and transfer the data to a computer.

- **Digital video disk-read/write (DVD-RW)—**a standard for DVD discs and player/recorder mechanisms that enables users to record in the DVD format.

CD-ROMs and DVDs offer an increasingly economical medium for storing data and programs. The overall trend in secondary storage is toward more direct-access methods, higher capacity with lower costs, and increased portability.

Input Devices

An ***input device*** is equipment used to capture information and commands. A keyboard Is used to type in information, and a mouse is used to point and click on buttons and icons. Numerous input devices are available in many different environments, some of which have applications that are more suitable in a personal setting than a business setting. A keyboard, mouse, and scanner are the most common forms of input devices (see Figures 12.7 and 12.8).

New forms of input devices allow people to exercise and play video games at the same time. The Kilowatt Sport from Powergrid Fitness lets people combine strength training with their favourite video games. Players can choose any PlayStation or Xbox game that uses a joystick to run the elliptical trainer. After loading the game, participants stand on a platform while pushing and pulling a resistance rod in all directions to control what happens in the game. The varied movement targets muscle groups on the chest, arms, shoulders, abdomen, and back. The machine's display shows information such as pounds or kilograms lifted and current resistance level, and players can use one-touch adjustment to vary the degree of difficulty.[4]

Another new input device is a stationary bicycle. A computer design team of graduate and undergraduate students at MIT built the Cyclescore, an integrated video game and bicycle. The MIT students tested current games on the market but found users would stop pedalling to concentrate on the game. To engage users, the team is designing games that interact with the experience of exercise itself, for example, monitoring heart rate and adjusting the difficulty of the game according to the user's

FIGURE 12.7

Manual Input Devices

Manual Input Devices
Joystick—widely used as an alternative to the keyboard for computer games and some professional applications, such as computer-aided design.
Keyboard—provides a set of alphabetic, numeric, punctuation, symbol, and control keys.
Microphone—captures sounds such as a voice for voice-recognition software.
Mouse—one or more control buttons housed in a palm-sized case and designed so that one can move it about on the table next to the keyboard.
Pointing stick—causes the pointer to move on the screen by applying directional pressure (popular on notebooks and PDAs).
Touch screen—allows the use of a finger to point at and touch a particular function to perform.
Touchpad—a form of a stationary mouse on which the movement of a finger causes the pointer on the screen to move.

FIGURE 12.8

Automated Input Devices

Automated Input Devices
Bar code scanner—captures information that exists in the form of vertical bars whose width and distance apart determine a number.
Digital camera—captures still images or video as a series of 1s and 0s.
Magnetic ink character reader—reads magnetic ink numbers printed on cheques that identify the bank, chequing account, and cheque number.
Optical-character recognition—converts text into digital format for computer input.
Optical-mark recognition (OMR)—detects the presence or absence of a mark in a predetermined place (popular for multiple-choice exams).
Point-of-sale (POS)—captures information at the point of a transaction, typically in a retail environment.
Radio frequency identification (RFID)—uses active or passive tags in the form of chips or smart labels that can store unique identifiers and relay this information to electronic readers.

bicycling capabilities. In one game, the player must pedal to make a hot-air balloon float over mountains, while collecting coins and shooting at random targets.[5]

Output Devices

An *output device* is equipment used to see, hear, or otherwise accept the results of information processing requests. Among output devices, printers and monitors

are the most common; however, speakers and plotters (special printers that draw output on a page) are widely used (see Figure 12.9). In addition, output devices are responsible for converting computer-stored information into a form that can be understood.

A new output device based on sensor technology aims to translate American Sign Language (ASL) into speech, enabling the millions of people who use ASL to better communicate with those who do not know the rapid gesturing system. The AcceleGlove is a glove lined on the inside with sensors embedded in rings. The sensors, called accelerometers, measure acceleration and can categorize and translate finger and hand movements. Additional, interconnected attachments for the elbow and shoulder capture ASL signs that are made with full arm motion. When users wear the glove while signing ASL, algorithms in the glove's software translate the hand gestures into words. The translations can be relayed through speech synthesizers or read on a PDA-size computer screen. Inventor Jose L. Hernandez-Rebollar started with a single glove that could translate only the ASL alphabet. Now, the device employs two gloves that contain a 1,000-word vocabulary.[6]

Other new output devices are being developed every day. Needapresent.com, a British company, has developed a vibrating USB massage ball, which plugs into a computer's USB port to generate a warm massage for sore body parts during those long evenings spent coding software or writing papers. Needapresent.com also makes a coffee cup warmer that plugs into the USB port.[7]

Communication Devices

A *communication device* is equipment used to send information and receive it from one location to another. A telephone modem connects a computer to a phone line in order to access another computer. The computer works in terms of digital signals, while a standard telephone line works with analogue signals. Each digital signal represents a bit (either 0 or 1). The modem must convert the digital signals of a computer into analogue signals so they can be sent across the telephone line. At the other end, another modem translates the analogue signals into digital signals, which can then be used by the other computer. Figure 12.10 displays the different types of modems.

Output Devices
Cathode-ray tube (CRT)—a vacuum tube that uses an electron gun (cathode) to emit a beam of electrons that illuminates phosphors on a screen as the beam sweeps across the screen repeatedly. A monitor is often called a CRT.
Liquid crystal display (LCDs)—a low-powered display technology used in laptop computers where rod-shaped crystal molecules change their orientation when an electrical current flows through them.
Laser printer—a printer that forms images using an electrostatic process, the same way a photocopier works.
Ink-jet printer—a printer that makes images by forcing ink droplets through nozzles.
Plotter—a printer that uses computer-directed pens for creating high-quality images, blueprints, schematics, etc.

FIGURE 12.9

Output Devices

FIGURE 12.10

Comparing Modems

Carrier Technology	Description	Speed	Comments
Dial-up Access	On demand access using a modem and regular telephone line (POT).	2400 bps to 56 Kbps	■ Cheap but slow.
Cable	Special cable modem and cable line required.	512 Kbps to 20 Mbps	■ Must have existing cable access in area. ■ Bandwidth is shared.
DSL Digital Subscriber Line	This technology uses the unused digital portion of a regular copper telephone line to transmit and receive information. A special modem and adapter card are required.	128 Kbps to 8 Mbps	■ Doesn't interfere with normal telephone use. ■ Bandwidth is dedicated. ■ Must be within 5 km (3.1 miles) of telephone company switch.
Wireless (LMCS)	Access is gained by connection to a high speed cellular like local multipoint communications system (LMCS) network via wireless transmitter/receiver.	30 Mbps or more	■ Can be used for high speed data, broadcast TV and wireless telephone service.
Satellite	Newer versions have two-way satellite access, removing need for phone line.	6 Mbps or more	■ Bandwidth is not shared. ■ Some connections require an existing Internet service account. ■ Setup fees can range from $500–$1000.

COMPUTER CATEGORIES

Supercomputers today can hit processing capabilities of well over 200 teraflops—the equivalent of everyone on earth performing 35,000 calculations per second (see Figure 12.11). For the past 20 years, federally funded supercomputing research

FIGURE 12.11

Supercomputer

has given birth to some of the computer industry's most significant technology breakthroughs including:

- Clustering, which allows companies to chain together thousands of PCs to build mass-market systems.
- Parallel processing, which provides the ability to run two or more tasks simultaneously and is viewed as the chip industry's future.
- Mosaic browser, which morphed into Netscape and made the Web a household name.

Federally funded supercomputers have also advanced some of the country's most dynamic industries, including advanced manufacturing, gene research in the life sciences, and real-time financial-market modelling.[8]

Computers come in different shapes, sizes, and colours. Some are small enough to carry around, while others are the size of a telephone booth. Size does not always correlate to power, speed, and price (see Figure 12.12).

MIT's Media Lab is developing a laptop that it will sell for US$100 each to government agencies around the world for distribution to millions of underprivileged schoolchildren. Using a simplified sales model and reengineering the device helped MIT reach the $100 price point. Almost half the price of a current laptop comprises marketing, sales, distribution, and profit. Of the remaining costs, the display panel and backlight account for roughly half while the rest covers the operating system. The low-cost laptop will use a display system that costs less than US$25, a 500 MHz processor from AMD, a wireless LAN connection, 1 GB of storage, and the Linux operating system. The machine will automatically connect with others. China and Brazil have already ordered 3 million and 1 million laptops, respectively. MIT's goal is to produce around 150 million laptops per year.[9]

SOFTWARE BASICS

Hardware is only as good as the software that runs it. Over the years, the cost of hardware has decreased while the complexity and cost of software have increased. Some large software applications, such as customer relationship management systems, contain millions of lines of code, take years to develop, and cost millions of dollars. The two main types of software are system software and application software.

System Software

System software controls how the various technology tools work together along with the application software. System software includes both operating system software and utility software.

Operating System Software Linus Torvalds, a shy Finnish programmer, may seem an unlikely choice to be one of the world's top managers. However, Linux, the software project he created while a university student, is now one of the most powerful influences on the computer world. Linux is an operating system built by volunteers and distributed for free and has become one of the primary competitors to Microsoft. Torvalds coordinates Linux development with a few dozen volunteer assistants and more than 1,000 programmers scattered around the globe. They contribute code for the kernel—or core piece—of Linux. He also sets the rules for dozens of technology companies that have lined up behind Linux, including IBM, Dell, Hewlett-Packard, and Intel.

While basic versions of Linux are available for free, Linux is having a considerable financial impact. According to market researcher IDC, the total market for Linux devices and software will increase from US$11 billion in 2004 to US$35.7 billion by 2008.[10]

Operating system software controls the application software and manages how the hardware devices work together. When using Excel to create and print a graph, the operating system software controls the process, ensures that a printer is attached and has paper, and sends the graph to the printer along with instructions on how to print it.

Operating system software also supports a variety of useful features, one of which is multitasking. *Multitasking* allows more than one piece of software to be used at a

FIGURE 12.12

Computer Categories

Computer Category	Description	Size
Personal digital assistant (PDA)	A small handheld computer that performs simple tasks such as taking notes, scheduling appointments, and maintaining an address book and a calendar. The PDA screen is touch-sensitive, allowing a user to write directly on the screen, capturing what is written.	Fits in a person's hand
Laptop	A fully functional computer designed to be carried around and run on battery power. Laptops come equipped with all of the technology that a personal desktop computer has, yet weigh as little as two pounds.	Similar to a textbook
Tablet	A pen-based computer that provides the screen capabilities of a PDA with the functional capabilities of a laptop or desktop computer. Similar to PDAs, tablet PCs use a writing pen or stylus to write notes on the screen and touch the screen to perform functions such as clicking on a link while visiting a Web site.	Similar to a textbook
Desktop	Available with a horizontal system box (the box is where the CPU, RAM, and storage devices are held) with a monitor on top, or a vertical system box (called a tower) usually placed on the floor within a work area.	Fits on a desk
Workstation	Similar to a desktop but has more powerful mathematical and graphics processing capabilities and can perform more complicated tasks in less time. Typically used for software development, Web development, engineering, and e-business tools.	Fits on a desk
Minicomputer (midrange computer)	Designed to meet the computing needs of several people simultaneously in a small to medium-size business environment. A common type of minicomputer is a server and is used for managing internal company networks and Web sites. Minicomputers are more powerful than desktop computers but also cost more, ranging in price from $5,000 to several hundred thousand dollars.	Ranges from fitting on a desk to the size of a filing cabinet
Mainframe computer	Designed to meet the computing needs of hundreds of people in a large business environment. Mainframe computers are a step up in size, power, capability, and cost from minicomputers. Mainframes can cost in excess of $1 million. With processing speeds greater than 1 trillion instructions per second (compared to a typical desktop that can process about 2.5 billion instructions per second), mainframes can easily handle the processing requests of hundreds of people simultaneously.	Similar to a refrigerator
Supercomputer	The fastest, most powerful, and most expensive type of computer. Organizations such as NASA that are heavily involved in research and number crunching employ supercomputers because of the speed with which they can process information. Other large, customer-oriented businesses such as General Motors and AT&T employ supercomputers just to handle customer information and transaction processing.	Similar to a car

FIGURE 12.13

Operating System Software

Operating System Software	
Linux	An open source operating system that provides a rich environment for high-end workstations and network servers. Open source refers to any program whose source code is made available for use or modification as users or other developers see fit.
Mac OS X	The operating system of Macintosh computers.
Microsoft Windows	Generic name for the various operating systems in the Microsoft Windows family, including Microsoft Windows CE, Microsoft Windows 98, Microsoft Windows ME, Microsoft Windows 2000, Microsoft Windows XP, Microsoft Windows NT, and Microsoft Windows Server 2003.
MS-DOS	The standard, single-user operating system of IBM and IBM-compatible computers, introduced in 1981. MS-DOS is a command-line operating system that requires the user to enter commands, arguments, and syntax.
UNIX	A 32-bit multitasking and multiuser operating system that originated at AT&T's Bell Laboratories and is now used on a wide variety of computers, from mainframes to PDAs.

time. Multitasking is used when creating a graph in Excel and simultaneously printing a word processing document. With multitasking, both pieces of application software are operating at the same time. There are different types of operating system software for personal environments and for organizational environments (see Figure 12.13 above).

Utility Software   *Utility software* provides additional functionality to the operating system. Utility software includes antivirus software, screen savers, and anti-spam software. Figure 12.14 displays a few types of available utility software.

FIGURE 12.14

Utility Software

Types of Utility Software	
Crash-proof	Helps save information if a computer crashes.
Disk image for data recovery	Relieves the burden of reinstalling and tweaking scores of applications if a hard drive crashes or becomes irretrievably corrupted.
Disk optimization	Organizes information on a hard disk in the most efficient way.
Encrypt data	Protects confidential information from unauthorized eyes. Programs such as BestCrypt simply and effectively apply one of several powerful encryption schemes to hard drive information. Users unlock the information by entering a password in the BestCrypt control panel. The program can also secure information on rewritable optical disks or any other storage media assigned a drive letter.
File and data recovery	Retrieves accidental deletion of photos or documents in Windows XP by utilities such as Free Undelete, which searches designated hard drive deletion areas for recognizable data.
Text protect	In Microsoft Word, prevents users from typing over existing text after accidentally hitting the Insert key. Launch the Insert Toggle Key program, and the PC will beep whenever a user presses the Insert key.
Preventative security	Through programs such as Window Washer, erases file histories, browser cookies, cache contents, and other crumbs that applications and Windows leave on a hard drive.
Spyware	Removes any software that employs a user's Internet connection in the background without the user's knowledge or explicit permission.
Uninstaller	Can remove software that is no longer needed.

Application Software

Application software is used for specific information processing needs, including payroll, customer relationship management, project management, training, and many others. Application software is used to solve specific problems or perform specific tasks. From an organizational perspective, payroll software, collaborative software such as videoconferencing (within groupware), and inventory management software are all examples of application software (see Figure 12.15).

FIGURE 12.15

Application Software

Types of Application Software	
Browser	Enables the user to navigate the World Wide Web. The two leading browsers are Netscape Navigator and Microsoft Internet Explorer.
Communication	Turns a computer into a terminal for transmitting data to and receiving data from distant computers through the telephone system.
Data management	Provides the tools for data retrieval, modification, deletion, and insertion; for example, Access, MySQL, and Oracle.
Desktop publishing	Transforms a computer into a desktop publishing workstation. Leading packages include Adobe FrameMaker, Adobe PageMaker, and QuarkXpress.
E-mail	Provides e-mail services for computer users, including receiving mail, sending mail, and storing messages. Leading e-mail software includes Microsoft Outlook, Microsoft Outlook Express, and Eudora.
Groupware	Increases the cooperation and joint productivity of small groups of co-workers.
Presentation graphics	Creates and enhances charts and graphs so that they are visually appealing and easily understood by an audience. A full-features presentation graphics package such as Lotus Freelance Graphics or Microsoft PowerPoint includes facilities for making a wide variety of charts and graphs and for adding titles, legends, and explanatory text anywhere in the chart or graph.
Programming	Possesses an artificial language consisting of a fixed vocabulary and a set of rules (called syntax) that programmers use to write computer programs. Leading programming languages include Java, C ++, C#, and .NET.
Spreadsheet	Simulates an accountant's worksheet onscreen and lets users embed hidden formulas that perform calculations on the visible data. Many spreadsheet programs also include powerful graphics and presentation capabilities to create attractive products. The leading spreadsheet application is Microsoft Excel.
Word processing	Transforms a computer into a tool for creating, editing, proofreading, formatting, and printing documents. Leading word processing applications include Microsoft Word and WordPerfect.

OPENING CASE QUESTIONS

Electronic Breaking Points

1. Identify the six hardware categories and place each product listed in the case in its appropriate category.
2. Describe the CPU and identify which products would use a CPU.
3. Describe the relationship between memory sticks and laptops. How can a user employ one to help protect information loss from the other?
4. What different types of software might each of the products listed in the case use?

ENTERPRISE ARCHITECTURES

In the U.S., a 66-hour failure of an FBI database that performed background checks on gun buyers was long enough to allow criminals to buy guns. The database failed at 1:00 p.m. on a Thursday and was not restored until 7:30 a.m. Sunday. The FBI must complete a gun check within three days; if it fails to do so, a merchant is free to make the sale. During this outage, any gun checks that were in progress were not finished, allowing merchants to complete those gun sales at their own discretion.[11]

To support the volume and complexity of today's user and application requirements, information technology needs to take a fresh approach to enterprise architectures by constructing smarter, more flexible environments that protect from system failures and crashes. *Enterprise architectures* include the plans for how an organization will build, deploy, use, and share its data, processes, and IT assets. A unified enterprise architecture will standardize enterprisewide hardware and software systems, with tighter links to the business strategy. A solid enterprise architecture can decrease costs, increase standardization, promote reuse of IT assets, and speed development of new systems. The end result being that the right enterprise architecture can make IT cheaper, strategic, and more responsive. The primary business goals of enterprise architectures are displayed in Figure 12.16.

Enterprise architectures are never static; they continually change. Organizations use enterprise architects to help manage change. An *enterprise architect (EA)* is a person grounded in technology, fluent in business, a patient diplomat, and provides the important bridge between IT and the business. T-Mobile International's enterprise architects review projects to ensure they are soundly designed, meet the business objectives, and fit in with the overall enterprise architecture. One T-Mobile project was to create software that would let subscribers customize the ring sounds on their cell phones. The project group assumed it would have to create most of the software from scratch. However, T-Mobile's EAs found software already written elsewhere at T-Mobile that could be reused to create the new application. The reuse reduced the development cycle time by eight months, and the new application was available in less than six weeks.[12]

Companies that have created solid enterprise architectures, such as T-Mobile, are reaping huge rewards in savings, flexibility, and business alignment. Basic enterprise architectures contain three components (see Figure 12.17).

1. *Information architecture* identifies where and how important information, like customer records, is maintained and secured.
2. *Infrastructure architecture* includes the hardware, software, and telecommunications equipment that, when combined, provide the underlying foundation to support the organization's goals.
3. *Application architecture* determines how applications integrate and relate to each other.

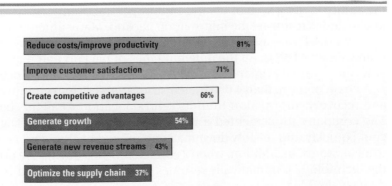

FIGURE 12.16

Primary Business Goals of Enterprise Architectures

FIGURE 12.17

Three Components of
Enterprise Architecture

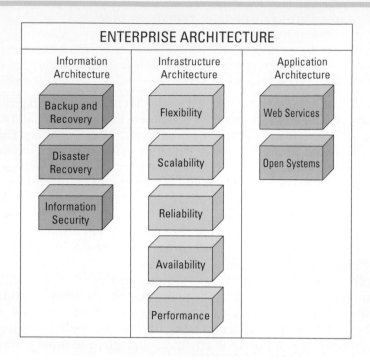

INFORMATION ARCHITECTURE

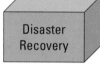 

Information architecture identifies where and how important information, like customer records, is maintained and secured. A single backup or restore failure can cost an organization more than time and money; some data cannot be recreated, and the business intelligence lost from that data can be tremendous. Chief information officers should have enough confidence that they could walk around and randomly pull out cables to prove that the systems are safe. The CIO should also be secure enough to perform this test during peak business hours. If the thought of this test makes the CIO cringe, then the organization's customers should be cringing also. Three primary areas an enterprise information architecture should focus on are:

1. Backup and recovery
2. Disaster recovery
3. Information security

Backup and Recovery

Each year businesses lose time and money because of system crashes and failures. One way to minimize the damage of a system crash is to have a backup and recovery strategy in place. A **backup** is an exact copy of a system's information. **Recovery** is the ability to get a system up and running in the event of a system crash or failure and includes restoring the information backup. Many different types of backup and recovery media are available, including redundant storage servers, tapes, disks, and even CDs and DVDs. All the different types of backup and recovery media are reliable; their primary differences are the speed and associated costs.

A chain of more than 4,000 franchise locations, 7-Eleven Taiwan uploads backup and recovery information from its central location to all its chain locations daily. The company implemented a new technology solution by Digital Fountain that could quickly and reliably download and upload backup and recovery information to all its stores. In addition, when a connection fails during the download or upload, the technology automatically resumes the download without having to start over, saving valuable time.[13]

Organizations should choose a backup and recovery strategy that is in line with its business goals. If the organization deals with large volumes of critical information, it will require daily backups, perhaps even hourly backups, to storage servers. If the organization deals with small amounts of noncritical information, then it might require only weekly backups to tapes, CDs, or DVDs. Deciding how often to back up information and what media to use is a critical business decision. If an organization decides to back up on a weekly basis, then it is taking the risk that, if a total system crash occurs, it could lose a week's worth of work. If this risk is acceptable, then a weekly backup strategy will work. If this risk is unacceptable, then the organization needs to move to a daily backup strategy. Some organizations find the risk of losing a day's worth of work too high and move to an hourly backup strategy.

Two techniques used to help in case of system failure are fault tolerance and failover. **Fault tolerance** is a computer system designed that in the event a component fails, a backup component or procedure can immediately take its place with no loss of service. Fault tolerance can be provided with software, or embedded in hardware, or provided by some combination. **Failover** is a backup operational mode in which the functions of a computer component (such as a processor, server, network, or database) are assumed by secondary system components when the primary component becomes unavailable through either failure or scheduled downtime. A failover procedure involves automatically offloading tasks to a standby system component so that the procedure is as seamless as possible to the end user. Used to make systems more fault tolerant, failover is typically an integral part of mission-critical systems that must be constantly available.

Disaster Recovery

In the U.S., a northern Ohio power company, FirstEnergy, missed signs that there were potential problems in its portion of North America's electrical grid. The events that followed left an estimated 50 million people in the U.S. and Canada in the dark. The failings are laid out in the widely reported findings of a joint U.S./Canada task force that investigated the causes of the blackout and recommended what to do to avoid big-scale outages in the future. The report detailed many procedures or best practices including:

- Mind the enterprise architectures.
- Monitor the quality of computer networks that provide data on power suppliers and demand.
- Make sure the networks can be restored quickly in the case of downtime.
- Set up disaster recovery plans.
- Provide adequate staff training, including verbal communication protocols "so that operators are aware of any IT-related problems that may be affecting their situational awareness of the power grid."[14]

Disasters such as power outages, floods, and even harmful hacking strike businesses every day. Organizations must develop a disaster recovery plan to prepare for such occurrences. A **disaster recovery plan** is a detailed process for recovering information or an IT system in the event of a catastrophic disaster such as a fire or flood. Spending on disaster recovery is rising worldwide among financial institutions (see Figure 12.18).

A comprehensive disaster recovery plan takes into consideration the location of the backup information. Many organizations store backup information in an off-site facility. StorageTek specializes in providing off-site information storage and disaster recovery solutions. A comprehensive disaster recovery plan also foresees the possibility that not only the computer equipment but also the building where employees work may be destroyed. A **hot site** is a separate and fully equipped facility where the company can move immediately after a disaster and resume business. A **cold site** is a separate facility that does not have any computer equipment, but is a place where employees can move after a disaster.

A **disaster recovery cost curve** charts (1) the cost to the organization of the unavailability of information and technology and (2) the cost to the organization of recovering from a disaster over time. Figure 12.19 displays a disaster recovery cost curve and shows that where the two lines intersect is the best recovery plan in terms of cost and time. Creating an organization's disaster recovery cost curve is no small task. It must consider the cost of losing information and technology within each department or functional area, and the cost of losing information and technology across the whole enterprise. During the first few hours of a disaster, those costs will be low but become increasingly higher over time. With those costs in hand, an organization must then determine the costs of recovery. Cost of recovery during the first few hours of a disaster is exceedingly high and diminishes over time.

Marshall & Swift, which provides property valuation services, may be located in sunny Los Angeles, but the company barely averted a major disaster when Hurricane Charley ripped through southwest Florida in 2004. Many of the nation's largest insurance companies rely on Marshall & Swift's 200-plus servers to process claims and calculate the costs of rebuilding commercial and residential properties. Within one month of the Florida hurricane, the number of claims jumped from 20,000 to a whopping 180,000. This sudden surge in server utilization could have spelled disaster.

Fortunately, Marshall & Swift used an application performance management solution called ProactiveNet that identifies when an application or system is operating outside of its normal parameters and pinpoints the most likely source of the problem. ProactiveNet alerted the company's IT department to an improper balance of application, Web, and database servers. Some servers were being underutilized while others were being overburdened, thereby causing degradations in overall system performance. Marshall & Swift quickly began monitoring the usage patterns of each server and moved certain servers to ensure that all requests were processed in a timely matter.[15]

FIGURE 12.18

Financial Institutions' Worldwide Spending on Disaster Recovery

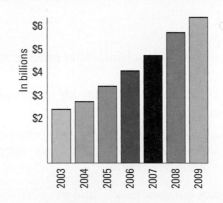

FIGURE 12.19

The Disaster Recovery Cost Curve

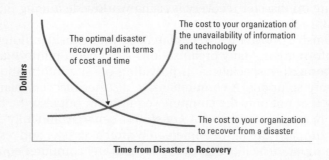

Information Security

Security professionals are under increasing pressure to do the job right and cost-effectively as networks extend beyond organizations to remote users, partners, and customers, and to cell phones, PDAs, and other mobile devices. Regulatory requirements to safeguard data have increased. Concerns about identity theft are at an all-time high. Hacking and other unauthorized access contribute to the approximately 10 million instances of identity theft each year, according to the U.S. Federal Trade Commission. A good information architecture includes a strong information security plan, along with managing user access and up-to-date antivirus software and patches.[16]

Managing User Access   Managing user access to information is a critical piece of the information architecture. Passwords may still be the weakest link in the security chain. At Vitas Healthcare Corporation, with a workforce of 6,000 and operations across 15 U.S. states, authorized employees enter as many as a half-dozen passwords a day to access multiple systems. While it is important to maintain password discipline to secure customers' health care data, maintaining and managing the situation creates a drag on the IT department. "Our help desk spends 30 percent of their time on password management and provisioning," said John Sandbrook, senior IT director.

The company began using Fischer International Corporation's Identity Management Suite to manage passwords and comply with data-access regulations. The ID-management product includes automated audit, reporting, and compliance capabilities, plus a common platform for password management, provisioning, and self-service. With the software, Vitas can enforce stronger passwords with seven, eight, or nine characters, numbers, and capital letters that frequently change. The company anticipates curbing help-desk password time by 50 percent.[17]

Up-to-Date Antivirus Software and Patches   There is little doubt that security is a top priority for business managers, regardless of the size of their company. Among Fortune 500 companies, more than 80 percent of those surveyed described updating security procedures, tools, and services as a key business priority. That desire holds true for small, midsize, or large companies and for IT managers and corporate managers.

The main focus for most managers is preventing hackers, spammers, and other malcontents from entering their networks, and nearly two-thirds are looking to enhance their network-security-management, intrusion-detection, content-filtering, and anti-spam software. More than half also plan to upgrade their encryption software.[18]

Microsoft issues patches for its software on the second Tuesday of every month. These patches must be downloaded and installed on all systems across the entire enterprise if the company wants to keep its systems protected. At OMD, a media buying and planning subsidiary of Omnicom Group Inc., the network administrator had to manually install critical patches on all 100 servers, taking more than a week to deploy the patch across the company. Now, OMD uses automated installation software for patches and upgrades. The company purchased Altiris Management Suite for Dell servers, which let it move ahead with applying patches without taking down entire systems and balancing patch-deployment timing among servers so that all departments were not down at once during a patch install. Given everything else that security professionals need to think about, automated installation software is a welcome relief.[19]

INFRASTRUCTURE ARCHITECTURE

Gartner Inc. estimates that the typical Web application goes down 170 hours per year. At Illinois-based online brokerage OptionsXpress, application performance problems can have a serious impact on livelihoods. Nearly 7,000 options traders visit the OptionsXpress Web site at any given time, completing nearly 20,000

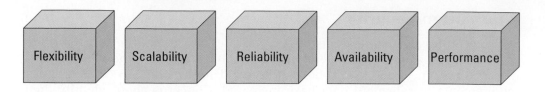

transactions a day. With all this online traffic, the brokerage's IT administrators were always up against the clock when recreating troublesome applications offline in the development environment. The company struggled to unlock the mystery behind a troublesome trading application that was forcing traders to resubmit orders. Some times the application would just die and then restart itself for no apparent reason.[20]

Infrastructure architecture includes the hardware, software, and telecommunications equipment that, when combined, provide the underlying foundation to support the organization's goals. As an organization changes, its systems must be able to change to support its operations. If an organization grows by 50 percent in a single year, its systems must be able to handle a 50-percent growth rate. Systems that cannot adapt to organizational changes can severely hinder the organization's ability to operate. The future of an organization depends on its ability to meet its partners and customers on their terms, at their pace, any time of the day, in any geographic location. The following are the five primary characteristics of a solid infrastructure architecture:

1. Flexibility
2. Scalability
3. Reliability
4. Availability
5. Performance

Flexibility

Organizations must watch today's business, as well as tomorrow's, when designing and building systems. Systems must be flexible enough to meet all types of business changes. For example, a system might be designed to include the ability to handle multiple currencies and languages, even though the company is not currently performing business in other countries. When the company starts growing and performing business in new countries, the system will already have the flexibility to handle multiple currencies and languages. If the company failed to recognize that its business would someday be global, it would need to redesign all its systems to handle multiple currencies and languages, not easy once systems are up and running.

Scalability

Estimating organizational growth is a challenging task. Growth can occur in a number of different forms including more customers and product lines and expansion into new markets. **Scalability** refers to how well a system can adapt to increased demands. A number of factors can create organizational growth including market, industry, and economy factors. If an organization grows faster than anticipated, it might experience all types of performance degradations, ranging from running out of disk space to a slowdown in transaction speeds. Anticipating expected—and unexpected—growth is key to building scalable systems that can support that growth.

MSNBC's Web site typically received moderate traffic. On September 11, 2001, the site was inundated with more than 91 million page views as its customers were trying to find out information about the terrorist attacks. Fortunately, MSNBC had anticipated this type of surging demand and built adaptable systems accordingly, allowing it to handle the increased page view requests.[21]

Capacity planning determines the future IT infrastructure requirements for new equipment and additional network capacity. Performing a capacity plan is one way to ensure the IT infrastructure is scalable. It is cheaper for an organization to implement an IT infrastructure that considers capacity growth at the beginning of a system launch than to try to upgrade equipment and networks after the system has been implemented. Not having enough capacity leads to performance issues and hinders the ability of knowledge workers to perform their jobs. If 100 workers are using the Internet to perform their jobs and the company purchases bandwidth that is too small and the network capacity is too small, the workers will spend a great deal of time just waiting to get information from the Internet. Waiting for an Internet site to return information is not very productive.

In the U.S., a computer glitch caused Delta Air Lines subsidiary Comair to cancel 1,100 flights Christmas Day 2004. The problem occurred when snowstorms caused the airline to ground flights, and the resulting quagmire overwhelmed its aging crew-scheduling system, causing further cancellations. Delta's crew-scheduling system is being replaced by one that can scale to handle more transaction.[22]

Reliability

Reliability ensures all systems are functioning correctly and providing accurate information. Reliability is another term for accuracy when discussing the correctness of systems within the context of efficiency IT metrics. Inaccurate information processing occurs for many reasons, from the incorrect entry of data to information corruption. Unreliable information puts the organization at risk when making decisions based on the information.

Availability

Availability (an efficiency IT metric) addresses when systems can be accessed by users. *High availability* refers to a system or component that is continuously operational for a desirably long length of time. Availability is typically measured relative to "100 percent operational" or "never failing." A widely held but difficult-to-achieve standard of availability for a system or product is known as "five 9s" (99.999 percent) availability.

Some companies have systems available 24/7 to support business operations and global customer and employee needs. With the emergence of the Web, companies expect systems to operate around the clock. A customer who finds that a Web site closes at 9:00 p.m. is not going to be a customer long.

Systems, however, must come down for maintenance, upgrades, and fixes. One challenge organizations face is determining when to schedule system downtime if the system is expected to operate continually. Exacerbating the negative impact of scheduled system downtime is the global nature of business. Scheduling maintenance during the evening might seem like a great idea, but the evening in one city is the morning somewhere else in the world, and global employees may not be able to perform their jobs if the system is down. Many organizations overcome this problem by having redundant systems, allowing the organization to take one system down by switching over to a redundant, or duplicate, system.

Performance

Performance measures how quickly a system performs a certain process or transaction (in terms of efficiency IT metrics of both speed and throughput). Not having enough performance capacity can have a devastating, negative impact on a business. A customer will wait only a few seconds for a Web site to return a request before giving up and moving on to another Web site. To ensure adaptable systems performance, capacity planning helps an organization determine future IT infrastructure requirements for new equipment and additional network capacity. It is cheaper for an organization to design and implement an IT infrastructure that envisions performance capacity growth than to update all the equipment after the system is already operational.

Abercrombie & Fitch (A&F) uses the Internet to market its distinctive image of being a fashion trendsetter to one of its largest customer segments, college students. The company designed its enterprise architecture with the help of IBM, which ensured www.abercrombie.com paralleled the same sleek but simple design of A&F

Quarterly, the company's flagship magazine. Abercrombie & Fitch knew that its Web site had to be accessible, available, reliable, and scalable to meet the demands of its young customers. Young customers tend to be Internet savvy, and their purchasing habits vary from customers who only shop for sale items at midnight to customers who know exactly what they want immediately. The highly successful Web site gives customers not only an opportunity to shop online, but also a taste of the Abercrombie & Fitch lifestyle through downloadable MP3s, calendars, and desktop accessories.[23]

APPLICATION ARCHITECTURE

Gartner Inc. research indicates that application problems are the single largest source of downtime, causing 40 percent of annual downtime hours and 32 percent of average downtime costs. Application architecture determines how applications integrate and relate to each other. Advances in integration technology—primarily

Web services and open systems—are providing new ways for designing more agile, more responsive enterprise architectures that provide the kind of value businesses need. With these new architectures, IT can build new business capabilities faster, cheaper, and in a vocabulary the business can understand.[24]

Web Services

Web services promise to be the next major frontier in computing. **Web services** contain a repertoire of Web-based data and procedural resources that use shared protocols and standards permitting different applications to share data and services. The major application of Web services is the integration among different applications. Before Web services, organizations had trouble with interoperability. **Interoperability** is the capability of two or more computer systems to share data and resources, even though they are made by different manufacturers. If a supply chain management (SCM) system can talk to (share information with) a customer relationship management (CRM) system, interoperability exists between the two systems. The traditional way that organizations achieved interoperability was to build integrations. Now, an organization can use Web services to perform the same task.

In the U.S., Verizon's massive enterprise architecture includes three different companies, GTE, Bell Atlantic, and Nynex, each with its own complex systems. To find a customer record in any of the three companies' systems, Verizon turns to its search engine, called Spider. Spider is Verizon's version of Google, and it's helping Verizon's business to thrive.

Spider contains a vital customer information Web service that encapsulates Verizon's business rules, which help it to access the correct data repository when looking for customer information. Whenever a new system is built that needs to link to customer information, all the developer has to do is reuse the Web service that will link to the customer records. Because Verizon has the Web service in place as part of its enterprise architecture, development teams can build new applications within a month, as opposed to six months.[25]

Web services encompass all the technologies that are used to transmit and process information on and across a network, most specifically the Internet. It is easiest to think of an individual Web service as software that performs a specific task, with that task being made available to any user who needs its service. For example, a "Deposit" Web service for a banking system might allow customers to perform the task of depositing money to their accounts. The Web service could be used by a bank teller, by the customer at an ATM, and/or by the customer performing an online transaction through a Web browser.

The "Deposit" Web service demonstrates one of the great advantages of using the Web service model to develop applications. Developers do not have to reinvent the wheel every time they need to incorporate new functionality. A Web service is really a piece of reusable software code. A software developer can quickly build a new application by using many of these pieces of reusable code. The two primary parts of Web services are events and services.

Events Events are the eyes and ears of the business expressed in technology—they detect threats and opportunities and alert those who can act on the information. Pioneered by telecommunication and financial services companies, this involves using IT systems to monitor a business process for events that matter—a stock-out in the warehouse or an especially large charge on a consumer's credit card—and automatically alert the people best equipped to handle the issue. For example, a credit monitoring system automatically alerts a credit supervisor and shuts down an account when the system processes a $7,000 charge on a credit card with a $6,000 limit.

Services Services are more like software products than they are coding projects. They must appeal to a broad audience, and they need to be reusable if they are going to have an impact on productivity. Early forms of services were defined at too low a level in the architecture to interest the business, such as simple "Print" and "Save" services. The new services are being defined at a higher level; they describe such things as "Credit Check," "Customer Information," and "Process Payment." These services describe a valuable business process. For example, "Credit Check" has value not just for programmers who want to use that code in another application, but also for businesspeople who want to use it across multiple products—say, auto loans and mortgages—or across multiple business.

The trick to building services is finding the right level of granularity. T-Mobile builds services starting at the highest level and then works its way down to lower levels, helping to ensure it does not build services that no one uses. The company first built a "Send Message" Web service and then built a "Send SMS Message" Web service that sends messages in special formats to different devices such as cell phones and pagers.

In the U.S., Lydian Trust's enterprise architects designed a Web service called "Get Credit" that is used by several different business units for loan applications. "Get Credit" seeks out credit ratings over the Internet from the major credit bureaus. One day, one of the credit bureaus' Web servers crashed, and Lydian Trust's "Get Credit" Web service could not make a connection. Since the connection to the server was loosely linked, the system did not know what to do. "Get Credit" was not built to make more than one call. So, while it waited for a response, hundreds of loan applications sat idle.

Lydian Trust's loan officers had to work overnight to ensure that all of the applications were completed within 24 hours as promised by the company. Fortunately, Lydian Trust's customers never felt the pain; however, its employees did. Systems must be designed to deal with the existence of certain events, or the lack of an event, in a way that does not interrupt the overall business. The "Get Credit" Web service has been modified to include an automatic e-mail alert to a supervisor whenever the Web service encounters a delay.[26]

Open Systems

Microsoft Internet Explorer's share of the Web browser market has dipped below 90 percent because of Mozilla's Firefox, an open source Web browser. According to WebSideStory, which has been tracking the Firefox versus Internet Explorer numbers, the Mozilla-made open source browser had captured 5 percent of the U.S. market in January 2005, an increase of almost a full percentage point in a month. Firefox claimed more than 25 million copies of the browser had been downloaded in its first 15 weeks of release.[27]

An *open system* is a broad, general term that describes nonproprietary IT hardware and software made available by the standards and procedures by which their products work, making it easier to integrate them. Amazon.com embraced open source technology converting from Sun's proprietary operating system to Linux. The switch to an open source operating system, such as Linux, is simplifying the process by which Amazon.com associates can build links to Amazon.com applications into their Web sites.[28]

The designs of open systems allow for information sharing. In the past, different systems were independent of each other and operated as individual islands of control. The sharing of information was accomplished through software drivers and devices that routed data allowing information to be translated and shared between systems. Although this method is still widely used, its limited capability and added cost are not an effective solution for most organizations. Another drawback to the stand-alone system is it can communicate only with components developed by a single manufacturer. The proprietary nature of these systems usually results in costly repair, maintenance, and expansion because of a lack of competitive forces. On the other hand, open system integration is designed to:

- Allow systems to seamlessly share information. The sharing of information reduces the total number of devices, resulting in an overall decrease in cost.
- Capitalize on enterprise architectures. This avoids installing several independent systems, which creates duplication of devices.
- Eliminate proprietary systems and promote competitive pricing. Often a sole-source vendor can demand its price and may even provide the customer with less than satisfactory service. Utilization of open systems allows users to purchase systems competitively.

OPENING CASE QUESTIONS

Electronic Breaking Points

5. How can an organization use an information architecture to protect its IT investment in electronic devices outlined in the case?

6. How can an organization use the devices mentioned in the case to protect information security?

7. Identify the five primary characteristics and rank them in order of importance for a laptop (1 highest, 5 lowest).

8. Describe how a "Customer Phone Number" Web service could be used by one of the products outlined in the case.

SUMMARY OF KEY THEMES

The purpose of this chapter was to provide you, the business student, with a detailed overview of:

- the various hardware and software components in an organization,

- the activities that surround the regular maintenance and up-keep of a firm's information architecture, and

- the primary characteristics that make up a solid information infrastructure.

Organizations pay special attention to these computing basics since they realize that these form the underlying foundation that support a firm's information systems:

- A solid underlying infrastructure is a necessity for ensuring the security, reliability, quality and responsiveness of a firm's information systems.

- This is important to understand as these systems are the tools that companies utilize and heavily rely upon to run their businesses and compete in today's competitive environment.

As such, it is important that you understand the components and activities surrounding an organization's computing infrastructure in order that you may be attuned to what is involved and take steps, when you work in organizations upon graduation, to ensure this infrastructure is kept up-to-date and running smoothly as possible.

KEY TERMS

Application architecture   381
Application software   380
Arithmetic-logic unit
   (ALU)   370
Availability   387
Backup   382
Binary digit (bit)   370
Byte   370
Cache memory   371
Capacity planning   386
Central processing unit (CPU)
   (or microprocessor)   369
Cold site   383
Communication
   device   375
Complex instruction set
   computer (CISC) chip   370
Computer   368
Control unit   370
Disaster recovery cost
   curve   384
Disaster recovery
   plan   383
Enterprise architect
   (EA)   381
Enterprise
   architecture   381

Failover   383
Fault tolerance   383
Flash memory   371
Gigabyte (GB)   372
Gigahertz (GHz)   370
Hard drive   373
Hardware   368
High availability   387
Hot site   383
Information
   architecture   381
Information technology
   (IT)   368
Infrastructure
   architecture   381
Input device   373
Interoperability   388
Magnetic medium   372
Magnetic tape   373
Megabyte (MB, M,
   or Meg)   372
Megahertz (MHz)   370
Memory card   371
Memory stick   372
Multitasking   377

Open system   389
Operating system
   software   377
Output device   374
Performance   387
Primary storage   371
Random access memory
   (RAM)   371
Read-only memory
   (ROM)   371
Recovery   382
Reduced instruction set
   computer (RISC)
   chip   370
Reliability   387
Scalability   386
Secondary storage   372
Software   368
System software   377
Terabyte (TB)   372
Utility software   379
Virtualization   370
Volatility   371
Web service   388

Chicago Tribune's Server Consolidation a Success

This case shows how a proper computing infrastructure can benefit the organization.

The *Chicago Tribune* is the seventh-largest newspaper in the United States. Overhauling its data centre and consolidating servers was a difficult task; however, the payoff was tremendous. The *Chicago Tribune* successfully moved its critical applications from a mishmash of mainframes and older Sun Microsystems servers to a new dual-site enterprise architecture, which has resulted in lower costs and increased reliability throughout the company.

The paper's new enterprise architecture clustered its servers over a 3-km distance, lighting up a 1 Gbps dark-fibre link—an optical fibre that is in place but not yet being used—between two data centres. This architecture lets the newspaper spread the processing load between the servers while improving redundancy and options for disaster recovery. The transfer to the new architecture was not smooth. A small piece of software written for the transition contained a coding error that caused the *Tribune*'s editorial applications to experience intermittent processing failures. As a result, the paper was forced to delay delivery to about 40 percent of its 680,000 readers and cut 24 pages from a Monday edition, costing the newspaper nearly US$1 million in advertising revenue.

After editorial applications were stabilized, the *Tribune* proceeded to migrate applications for operations—the physical production and printing of the newspaper—and circulation to the new enterprise architecture. "As we gradually took applications off the mainframe, we realized that we were incurring very high costs in maintaining underutilized mainframes at two different locations," said Darko Dejanovic, vice president and CTO of the Tribune Co., which owns the *Chicago Tribune*, the *Los Angeles Times*, Long Island's *Newsday*, and about a dozen other metropolitan newspapers. "By moving from two locations to one, we've achieved several million dollars in cost savings. There's no question that server consolidation was the right move for us.

"The Tribune Co. is excited about its new enterprise architecture and is now looking to consolidate software across its newspapers. Currently, each newspaper maintains its own applications for classified advertising and billing, which means the parent company must support about 10 billing packages and the same number of classified-ad programs. The Tribune Co. has found that most of the business processes can be standardized. So far, it has standardized about 95 percent of classified-ad processes and about 90 percent of advertising-sales processes. Over the next three years, the Tribune Co. will replace the disparate billing and ad applications across the company with a single package that will be used by all business units. The different newspapers will not necessarily share the same data, but they will have the same processes and the same systems for accessing them. Over time, that will allow some of the call centres to handle calls for multiple newspapers; East Coast centres will handle the early-morning calls and West Coast centres the late-day and evening calls.

The Tribune Co. is looking at a few additional projects including the implementation of hardware that will allow its individual applications to run on partial CPUs, freeing up processor power and making more efficient use of disk space.[29]

Questions

1. Review the five characteristics of infrastructure architecture and rank them in order of their potential impact on the Tribune Co.'s business.

2. What is the disaster recovery cost curve? Where should the Tribune Co. operate on the curve?

3. Define backups and recovery. What are the risks to the Tribune Co.'s business if it fails to implement an adequate backup plan?

4. Why is a scalable and highly available enterprise architecture critical to the Tribune Co.'s current operations and future growth?

5. Identify the need for information security at the Tribune Co.

6. How could the Tribune Co. use a "Classified Ad" Web service across its different businesses?

CLOSING CASE TWO

UPS in the Computer Repair Business

This case illustrates how an organization must manage its computing infrastructure—sometimes in novel ways.

When people think of UPS they usually think of brown delivery trucks and employees in shorts dropping off and picking up packages. This image is about to change. UPS has now entered the laptop repair business. Toshiba is handing over its entire laptop repair operation to UPS Supply Chain Solutions, the shipper's $27 billion logistics outsourcing division. Toshiba's decision to allow a shipping company to fix its laptops might appear odd to many individuals. However, when you understand that the primary challenge of computer repair is more logistical than technical—Toshiba's business decision seems brilliant. "Moving a unit around and getting replacement parts consumes most of the time," explains Mark Simons, general manager at Toshiba's digital products division. "The actual service only takes about an hour."

UPS will send broken Toshiba laptops to its facility in Louisville, Kentucky, where UPS engineers will diagnose and repair defects. Consumers will notice an immediate change: In the past, repairs could take weeks, depending on whether Toshiba needed components from Japan. Since the UPS repair site is adjacent to its air hub, customers should get their machines back, as good as new, in just a matter of days. UPS has been servicing Lexmark and Hewlett-Packard printers since 1996 and has been performing initial inspections on laptops being returned to Toshiba since 1999.

The expanded Toshiba relationship is another step in UPS's strategy to broaden its business beyond package delivery into commerce services. The company already works with clients to manage inventory, ordering, and custom processes. It recently introduced a service to dispose of unwanted electrical devices. To take on laptop repair, UPS put 50 technicians through a Toshiba-certified training course.[30]

Questions

1. Do you think UPS's entrance into the laptop repair business was a good business decision? Why or why not?

2. Identify the different types of hardware UPS technicians might be working on when fixing laptops.

3. Assume you are a technician working at UPS. Explain to a customer the different types of memory and why only certain types of data are lost during a computer failure. Also identify a potential backup strategy you can suggest to the customer.

4. Assume you are a technician working at UPS. Explain to a customer the different types of software found in a typical laptop.

Fear the Penguin

This case shows how changes and advances in computing software can affect an organization's choice of what software to use.

Linux has proved itself the most revolutionary software of the past decade. Linus Torvalds, who wrote the kernel (the core) of the Linux operating system at age 21, posted the operating system on the Internet and invited other programmers to improve his code and users to download his operating system for free. Since then, tens of thousands of people have, making Linux perhaps the single largest collaborative project in the planet's history.

Today, Linux, if not its penguin mascot, is everywhere. You can find Linux inside a boggling array of computers, machines, and devices. Linux is robust enough to run the world's most powerful supercomputers, yet sleek and versatile enough to run inside consumer items like TiVo, cell phones, and handheld portable devices. Even more impressive than Linux's increasing prevalence in living rooms and pockets is its growth in the market for corporate computers. According to a recent poll by CIO.com, 39 percent of IT managers agreed that Linux would dominate corporate systems.

Since its introduction in 1991, no other operating system in history has spread as quickly across such a broad range of systems as Linux, and it has finally achieved critical mass. According to studies by market research firm IDC, Linux is the fastest-growing server operating system, with shipments expected to grow by 34 percent per year over the next four years. With its innovative open source approach, strong security, reliability, and scalability, Linux can help companies achieve the agility they need to respond to changing consumer needs and stay ahead of the game.

Thanks to its unique open source development process, Linux is reliable and secure. A "meritocracy," a team specifically selected for their competence by the technical developer community, governs the entire development process. Each line of code that makes up the Linux kernel is extensively tested and maintained for a variety of different platforms and application scenarios.

This open collaborative approach means the Linux code base continually hardens and improves itself. If vulnerabilities appear, they get the immediate attention of experts from around the world, who quickly resolve the problems. According to Security Portal, which tracks vendor response times, it takes an average of 12 days to patch a Linux bug compared to an average of three months for some proprietary platforms. With the core resilience and reliability of Linux, businesses can minimize downtime, which directly increases their bottom line.

The Spread of Open Systems

Businesses and governments are opting for open source operating systems like Linux instead of Windows. One attendee at the Linux Desktop Consortium in 2004 was Dr. Martin Echt, a cardiologist from Albany, New York. Dr. Echt, chief operating officer of Capital Cardiology Associates, an eight-office practice, discussed his decision to shift his business from Microsoft's Windows to Linux. Dr. Echt is not your typical computer geek or Linux supporter, and he is not the only one switching to Linux.

The State Council in China has mandated that all ministries install the local flavour of Linux, dubbed Red Flag, on their PCs. In Spain, the government has installed a Linux operating system that incorporates the regional dialect. The city of Munich, despite a personal visit from Microsoft CEO Steve Ballmer, is converting its 14,000 PCs from Windows to Linux.

"It's open season for open source," declared Walter Raizner, general manager of IBM Germany. One of the biggest corporate backers of Linux, IBM has more than 75 government customers worldwide, including agencies in France, Spain, Britain, Australia, Mexico, the United States, and Japan.

The move toward Linux varies for each country or company. For Dr. Echt, it was a question of lower price and long-term flexibility. In China, the government claimed national security as a reason to move to open source code because it permitted engineers to make sure there were no security leaks and no spyware installed on its computers. In Munich, the move was largely political. Regardless of the reason, the market is shifting toward Linux.

Microsoft versus Linux

Bill Gates has openly stated that Linux is not a threat to Microsoft. According to IDC analysts, Microsoft's operating systems ship with 93.8 percent of all desktops worldwide. Ted Schadler, IDC research principal analyst, states that despite the push of lower cost Linux players into the market, Microsoft will maintain its desktop market share for the following three reasons:

1. Linux adds features to its applications that most computer users have already come to expect.
2. Linux applications might not be compatible with Microsoft applications such as Microsoft Word or Microsoft Excel.
3. Microsoft continues to innovate, and the latest version of Office is beginning to integrate word processing and spreadsheet software to corporate databases and other applications.

The Future of Linux

IDC analyst Al Gillen predicts that an open source operating system will not enjoy explosive growth on the desktop for at least six or eight years. Still, even Gillen cannot deny that Linux's penetration continues to rise, with an estimated 18 million users. Gartner Dataquest estimates Linux's server market share will grow seven times faster than Windows.[31]

Questions

1. How does Linux differ from traditional software?
2. Should Microsoft consider Linux a threat? Why or why not?
3. How is open source software a potential trend shaping organizations?
4. How can you use Linux as an emerging technology to gain a competitive advantage?
5. Research the Internet and discover potential ways that open source software might revolutionize business in the future.

MAKING BUSINESS DECISIONS

1. Purchasing a computer

Dell is considered the fastest company on earth and specializes in computer customization. Connect to Dell's Web site at www.dell.com. Go to the portion of Dell's site that allows you to customize either a laptop or a desktop computer. First, choose an already prepared system and note its price and capability in terms of CPU speed, RAM size, monitor quality, and storage capacity. Now, customize that system to increase CPU speed, add more RAM, increase monitor size and quality, and add more storage capacity. What is the difference in price between the two? Which system is more in your price range? Which system has the speed and capacity you need?

2. Web-enabled cell phones

When categorizing computers by size for personal needs, we focused on PDAs, laptops, and desktop computers. Other variations include Web-enabled cell phones that include instant text messaging and Web computers. For this project, you will need a group of four people, which you will then split into two groups of two. Have the first group research Web-enabled cell phones, their capabilities and costs. Have that group make a purchase recommendation based on price and capability. Have the second group do the same for

Web computers. What is your vision of the future? Will we ever get rid of clunky laptops and desktops in favour of more portable and cheaper devices such as Web-enabled cell phones and Web computers? Why or why not?

3. Small business computers

Many different types of computers are available for small businesses. Use the Internet to find three different vendors of laptops or notebooks that are good for small businesses. Find the most expensive and the least expensive that the vendor offers and create a table comparing the different computers based on the following:

- CPU
- Memory
- Hard drive
- Optical drive
- Operating system
- Utility software
- Application software
- Support plan

Determine which computer you would recommend for a small business looking for an inexpensive laptop. Determine which computer you would recommend for a small business looking for an expensive laptop.

4. Planning for disaster recovery

You are the new senior analyst in the IT department at Beltz, a large snack food manufacturing company. The company is located on the beautiful south shoreline in Halifax. The company's location is one of its best and also worst features. The weather and surroundings are beautiful, but the threat of severe storms is high. Compile a disaster recovery plan that will minimize any risks involved with a natural disaster.

5. Comparing backup and recovery systems

Research the Internet to find three different vendors of backup and recovery systems. Compare and contrast the three systems and determine which one you would recommend if you were installing a backup and recovery system for a medium-sized business with 3,500 employees that maintains information on the stock market. Compile your findings in a presentation that you can give to your class that details the three systems' strengths and weaknesses, along with your recommendation.

6. Ranking the primary characteristics

In a group, review the list of IT infrastructure qualities and rank them in order of their impact on an organization's success. Use a rating system of 1 to 7, where 1 indicates the biggest impact and 7 indicates the least impact.

IT Infrastructure Qualities	Business Impact
Availability	
Accessibility	
Reliability	
Scalability	
Flexibility	
Performance	
Capacity Planning	

7. Designing an enterprise architecture

Components of a solid enterprise architecture include everything from documentation to business concepts to software and hardware. Deciding which components to implement and how to implement them can be a challenge. New IT components are released daily, and business needs continually change. An enterprise architecture that meets your organization's needs today may not meet those needs tomorrow. Building an enterprise architecture that is scalable, flexible, available, accessible, and reliable is key to your organization's success.

You are the enterprise architect (EA) for a large clothing company called Xedous. You are responsible for developing the initial enterprise architecture. Create a list of questions you will need answered to develop your architecture. Below is an example of a few of the questions you might ask.

- What are the company's growth expectations?
- Will systems be able to handle additional users?
- How long will information be stored in the systems?
- How much customer history must be stored?
- What are the organization's business hours?
- What are the organization's backup requirements?

The overall goal of the plug-ins is to provide additional information not covered in the text such as personal productivity using information technology, business basics, and business process. The plug-ins also offer faculty who find themselves in the situation of having to purchase an extra book to support Microsoft Office an all-in-one text. The plug-ins presented here offer integration with the core chapters and provide critical knowledge using essential business applications, such as Microsoft Excel, Microsoft Access, and Microsoft FrontPage using hands-on tutorials for comprehension and mastery. Plug-Ins T1 – T12 are located on the Online Learning Centre that accompanies this text at www.mcgrawhill.ca/olc/baltzan.

Plug-In	Description
T1. Personal Productivity Using IT	Plug-In T1 covers a number of things to do to keep a personal computer running effectively and efficiently. There are 12 topic areas covered in this plug-in. ■ Creating strong passwords ■ Performing good file management ■ Implementing effective backup and recovery strategies ■ Using Zip files ■ Writing professional e-mails ■ Stopping spam ■ Preventing phishing ■ Detecting spyware ■ Restricting instant messaging ■ Increasing PC performance ■ Using anti-virus software ■ Installing a personal firewall
T2. Basic Skills Using Excel	Plug-In T2 provides an introduction to the basics of using Microsoft Excel, a spreadsheet program for data management. It is designed to show the basics, along with a few fancy features. There are six topic areas covered in this plug-in. ■ Workbooks and worksheets ■ Working with cells and cell data ■ Printing worksheets ■ Formatting worksheets ■ Formulas ■ Working with charts and graphics
T3. Problem Solving Using Excel	Plug-In T3 provides a comprehensive tutorial on how to use a variety of Microsoft Excel functions and features for problem solving. There are five areas covered in this plug-in. ■ Lists ■ Conditional Formatting ■ AutoFilter ■ Subtotals ■ PivotTables
T4. Decision Making Using Excel	Plug-In T4 examines a few of the advanced business analysis tools used in Microsoft Excel that have the capability to identify patterns, trends, rules, and create "what-if" models. There are four topic areas covered in this plug-in. ■ IF ■ Goal Seek ■ Solver ■ Scenario Manager
T5. Designing Database Applications	Plug-In T5 provides specific details on how to design relational database applications. One of the most efficient and powerful information management computer-based applications is the relational database. There are four topic areas covered in this plug-in. ■ Entities and data relationships ■ Documenting logical data relationships ■ The relational data model ■ Normalization

(continued)

T6. Basic Skills and Tools Using Access	Plug-In T6 focuses on creating a Microsoft Access database file. One of the most efficient information management, computer-based applications, is Microsoft Access. Access provides a powerful set of tools for creating and maintaining a relational database. There are two topic areas covered in this plug-in. ■ Create a new database file ■ Create and modify tables
T7. Problem Solving Using Access	Plug-In T7 provides a comprehensive tutorial on how to query a database in Microsoft Access. Queries are essential for problem solving; allowing a user to sort information, summarize data (display totals, averages, counts, and so on), display the results of calculations on data, and choose exactly which fields are shown. There are three topic areas covered in this plug-in. ■ Create simple queries using the Simple Query Wizard ■ Advanced queries using calculated fields ■ Format results displayed in calculated fields
T8. Creating Forms and Reports Using Access	Plug-In T8 provides a comprehensive tutorial on entering data in a well-designed form and creating functional reports using Microsoft Access. A form is essential to use for data entry and a report is an effective way to present data in a printed format. There are two topic areas covered in this plug-in. ■ Creating, modifying, and running forms ■ Creating, modifying, and running reports
T9. Designing Web Pages	Plug-In T9 provides a comprehensive assessment into the functional aspects of Web design. Web sites are beginning to look more alike and to employ the same metaphors and conventions. The Web has now become an everyday tool whose design should not make users think. There are six topic areas in this plug-in. ■ The World Wide Web ■ The unknown(s) ■ The process of Web Design ■ HTML basics ■ Web Fonts ■ Web Graphics
T10. Basic Skills Using FrontPage	Plug-In T10 provides a tour of using FrontPage to create Web pages. FrontPage allows anyone with limited Web page design experience to create, modify, and maintain full-featured, professional-looking pages without having to learn how to code all the functions and features from scratch. There are seven topic areas covered in this plug-in. ■ Web sites, Web pages, and HTML ■ Navigation in FrontPage ■ Building a Web site ■ Working with graphics ■ Including hyperlinks ■ Presenting information in lists and tables ■ Formatting pages
T11. Business Basics	Plug-In T11 offers an introduction to the basics of business. There are nine topic areas covered in this plug-in. ■ Types of businesses ■ Internal operations of a corporation ■ Accounting ■ Marketing ■ Finance ■ Human resources ■ Management information systems ■ Production/operations ■ Sales
T12. Business Process	Plug-In T12 shows how investment in continuous process improvement, business process reengineering, or business process management is the same as any other technology-related investment. There are five topic areas covered in this plug-in. ■ Examining business processes ■ Business process design ■ Business process improvement ■ Business process management ■ Business process modeling examples

Apply Your Knowledge Project Overview

Project Number	Project Name	Project Type	Focus Area	Skill Set	Page Number
1	Capitalizing on Your Career	Business	IT/MIS	Careers in IT	412
2	Achieving Alignment	Business	General Business	Business-IT Alignment	413
3	Market Dissection	Business	General Business	Porter's Three Generic Strategies	413
4	Grading Security	Business	Security	Information Security Plan/Policies	414
5	Eyes Everywhere	Business	Security	Biometrics	415
6	Setting Boundaries	Business	Ethics	Ethical Dilemmas	416
7	Contemplating Sharing	Business	Ethics	Peer-to-Peer	416
8	Dashboard Design	Business	EIS	Digital Dashboard	417
9	Great Stories	Business	CRM	Disgruntled Customers	417
10	Classic Car Problems	Business	CRM	Business Efficiency	418
11	Building Visibility	Business	SCM	Business Effectiveness	418
12	Bean Integration	Business	ERP/CRM	Information Integration	419
13	Working Together	Business	Collaboration	Workflow	420
14	Different Dimensions	Business	Business Intelligence	Data Warehouse	421
15	Connecting Components	Business	Enterprise Architecture	Developing Systems	422
16	Internet Groceries	Business	E-Business	Business Analysis	422
17	Getting Personal	Business	E-Business	Mass Customization	423
18	Express Yourself	Business	E-Business	Web Site Development	423
19	Creating a Presence	Business	E-Business	Web Site Development	424
20	GoGo Gadgets	Business	Wireless	Competitive Advantage	424
21	Back on Your Feet	Business	Enterprise Architecture	Backup and Disaster Recovery	425
22	GEM Athletic Center	Business	SDLC	Business Requirements	425
23	Confusing Coffee	Business	SDLC	Business Requirements	426
24	Picking Projects	Business	Project Management	Prioritizing Projects	426
25	Keeping Time	Business	Project Management	Project Plan	426

(*continued*)

Project Number	Project Name	Project Type	Focus Area	Skill Set	Page Number
26	Controlling Your Spending	Excel	Personal Budget	Introductory Development: Formulas	427
27	Gearing for Cash	Excel	Cash Flow	Introductory Development: Formulas	428
28	Book Boxes	Excel	Strategic Analysis	Intermediate Development: Formulas	428
29	SplashEm	Excel	Strategic Analysis	Intermediate Development: Formulas	429
30	Tally's Purchases	Excel	Hardware and Software	Introductory Development: Formulas	430
31	Tracking Donations	Excel	Employee Relationships	Introductory Development: Formulas	430
32	All Aboard	Excel	Global Commerce	Introductory Development: Formulas	430
33	In with the Out	Excel	Outsourcing	Advanced Development: Formulas	430
34	Woods You	Excel	SCM	Advanced Development: Formulas	432
35	Bill's Boots	Excel	Profit Maximization	Intermediate Development: Formulas	432
36	Adequate Acquisitions	Excel	Break-Even Analysis	Intermediate Development: Formulas	433
37	Formatting Grades	Excel	Streamlining Data	Advanced Development: If, LookUp	433
38	Moving Espressos	Excel	SCM	Advanced Development: Absolute vs. Relative Values	434
39	Reducing Transports	Excel	SCM	Advanced Development: Pivot Table	434
40	Better Business	Excel	CRM	Intermediate Development: Pivot Table	435
41	Too Much Information	Excel	CRM	Advanced Development: Pivot Table	435
42	Gizmo Turnover	Excel	Data Mining	Advanced Development: Pivot Table	436
43	Managing Martin	Excel	Data Mining	Advanced Development: Pivot Table	436
44	Mountain Cycle	Excel	Break Even Analysis	Advanced Development: Goal Seek	437
45	Lutz Motors	Excel	Sales Analysis	Advanced Development: Scenario Manager	437
46	Animal Relations	Access	Business Analysis	Introductory Development	438
47	On-The-Level	Access	Business Intelligence	Introductory Development	439
48	iToys Inventory	Access	SCM	Intermediate Development	440
49	Call Around	Access	CRM	Intermediate Development	441
50	MoveIt	Access	Business Intelligence	Advanced Development	443

NOTES

Chapter 1

1. "Apple Profit Surges 95 Percent on iPod Sales," Yahoo! News, http://news.yahoo.com/s/afp/20060118/bs_afp/uscompanyearningsit_060118225009, accessed January 18, 2005; "Apple's IPod Success Isn't Sweet Music for Record Company Sales," Bloomberg.com, http://quote.bloomberg.com/apps/news?pid=nifea&&sid=aHP5Ko1pozM0, accessed November 2, 2005; Peter Burrows, "How Apple Could Mess Up Again," BusinessWeek online, http://yahoo.businessweek.com/technology/content/jan2006/tc20060109_432937.htm, accessed January 9, 2006.

2. en.wikipedia.org/wiki/Organizational_culture, accessed July 2005.

3. Kim Nash and Todd Spangler, "CIO Stars: Bigger Paydays," *Baseline,* August 2006, Issue 62, pp. 17–18, 2 pp.; "CIO Compensation Keeps Climbing," *CIO Insight,* 2006 Research, p. 31.

4. "The State of the CIO Around the World," *CIO,* April 2005, Vol. 18, Issue 12, p. 48.

5. Nick Bontis, "The Rising Star of the Chief Knowledge Officer," *Ivey Business Journal,* March/April 2002, Vol. 66, Issue 4, p. 20.

6. "Siemen's CKO Translates KM into Local Business Language to Prove Value," *KM Review,* May/June 2003, Vol. 6, Issue 2, p. 5.

7. Dave Lindorff, "General Electric and Real Time," www.cioinsight.com/article2/0,3959,686147,00.asp, accessed March 1, 2004.

8. Cisco Press, www.ciscopress.com/index.asp?rl=1, accessed March 15, 2004 .

9. Ken Blanchard, "Effectiveness vs. Efficiency," Wachovia Small Business, www.wachovia.com, accessed October 14, 2003.

10. United Nations Division for Public Economics and Public Administration, www.un.com, accessed November 10, 2003.

11. Ibid.

12. eBay Financial News, Earnings and Dividend Release, January 15, 2002.

13. "Sun and eBay Celebrate Record Uptime," www.sun.com/service/about/features/ebay.html, accessed January 14, 2004.

14. Gabriel Kahn and Cris Prystay, "'Charge It' Your Cellphone Tells Your Bank," *The Wall Street Journal,* August 13, 2003.

15. Andrew Wahl, "The Next Best Managers," *Canadian Business,* October 9–October 22, 2006, Vol. 79, Issue 20, p. 66; Libby Znaimer, "Adventures Come With The Territory," *Financial Post:* Weekend, *National Post,* November 18, 2006, FW8.

16. "The Best Managers," *BusinessWeek,* January 10, 2005, Issue 3915.

17. Ibid.

18. Monica Gutschi, "TransForce Just Keeps on Trucking Across Canada," *Dow Jones Newswires,* November 15, 2006.

19. "Innovative Managers," *BusinessWeek,* April 24, 2005.

20. www.thomaslfriedman.com, accessed September 2005.

Chapter 2

1. Beth Bacheldor, "From Scratch: Amazon Keeps Moving," *Information Week,* March 5, 2004; Gary Wolf, "The Great Library of Amazonia," *Wired,* October 23, 2003; "Amazon Company Information," *Forbes,* www.forbes.com, September 2005; and Rob Hof, "Amazon's Newest Product: Storage," *BusinessWeek,* March 13, 2006.

2. Cisco Press, www.ciscopress.com/index.asp?rl=1, accessed March 1, 2005

3. Adam Lashinsky, "Kodak's Developing Situation," *Fortune,* January 20, 2003, p. 176.

4. www.wired.com, accessed November 15, 2003.

5. Adam Lashinsky, "Kodak's Developing Situation," *Fortune,* January 20, 2003, p. 176.

6. Clayton Christensen, *The Innovator's Dilemma* (Boston: Harvard Business School, 1997).

7. Internet World Statistics, www.internetworldstats.com, January 2005.

8. info.cern.ch, accessed March 1, 2005.

9. "Internet Pioneers," www.ibiblio.org/pioneers/andreesen.html, accessed March 1, 2005.

10. Gunjan Bagla, "Bringing IT to Rural India One Village at a Time," *CIO Magazine,* March 1, 2005.

11. André R. Robillard and Toby Ward, "Turning the Dream into Reality: Harnessing People Power to Create a High Productivity Intranet," Information Highways Conference, Toronto, Ontario, March 29, 2006.

12. "Bell Canada Manages Content For Its Call Centre," *Transform Magazine,* www.transformmag.com/techselections/showArticle.jhtml?articleID=16101051, accessed February 26, 2007.

13. Amy Johnson, "A New Supply Chain Forged," *Computerworld,* September 30, 2002.

14. "Pratt & Whitney," *BusinessWeek,* June 2004.

15. "Case Study: Indigo Books & Music Inc.," www.microsoft.com/canada/casestudies/indigo.mspx, accessed February 26, 2007.

16. Laura Rohde, "British Airways Takes Off with Cisco," *Network World,* May 11, 2005.

17. www.t-mobile.com, accessed June 2005.

18. www.idc.com, accessed June 2005.

19. "A Site Stickier Than a Barroom Floor," *Business 2.0*, June 2005, p. 74.

20. www.emarketer.com, accessed January 2006.

21. www.cyberflowers.ca/aboutwho.html, accessed February 28, 2007.

22. Mali Rolph, "Florists Bloom Online," *Canadian Florist Magazine*, March 2002, available at http://florist.hortport.com/Past_Issues.htm?ID=778.

23. www.mediabuyerplanner.com/2007/01/25/trans-lux-installs-digital-billboards-in-louisiana-canada/, accessed February 28, 2007.

24. www.mediabuyerplanner.com/2006/02/14/digital_billboards_the_wave/, accessed February 28, 2007.

25. Rachel Metz, "Changing at the Push of a Button," *Wired*, September 27, 2004.

26. www.hotel-gatti.com, accessed June 2003.

27. Frank Quinn, "The Payoff Potential in Supply Chain Management," www.ascet.com, accessed June 15, 2003.

28. www.oecd.org, accessed June 2005.

29. www.vanguard.com, accessed June 2005.

30. "Watch Your Spending," *BusinessWeek*, May 23, 2004.

31. www.BidNavigator.com, accessed March 1, 2007.

32. Jack Welch, "What's Right About Wal-Mart," *CIO Magazine*, www.cio.com, accessed May 2005.

33. www.yankeegroup.com, accessed May 2005.

34. www.ingenio.com, accessed July 2005.

35. "E-Commerce Taxation," www.icsc.org/srch/government/ECommerceFebruary2003.pdf, accessed June 8, 2004.

36. Robert Hof, "Pierre M. Omidyar: The Web for the People," *BusinessWeek*, December 6, 2004; Margaret Kane, "eBay picks up PayPal for 1.5 Billion," Cnet News, news.com.com, accessed July 8, 2002; John Blau, "Are eBay and Skype a Good Fit?" Infoworld, www.inforworld.com, accessed September 8, 2005; and "Better Ask: IRS May Consider eBay Sales as Income," *USA Today*, March 27, 2005.

37. http://map.hamilton.ca/maphamilton/GISServ/GISServices.aspx, accessed March 2, 2007.

38. A. Little, "Hamilton, Ontario, Canada, Uses A GIS-Enhanced Web Site," *Public Management*, March 2006, pp. 34–35.

39. U. Ruhi, P. Takala, B. Detlor, and M. Hupfer, "Building Government Portals That Work: Guiding Principles From Community Informatics," Proceedings of the 7th McMaster World Congress in Electronic Business, Halifax, Nova Scotia, Canada, July 2006, pp. 13–15.

40. John Heilmann, "What's Friendster Selling?" *Business 2.0*, March 2004, p. 34.

Chapter 3

1. www.grocerygateway.com/about/default.asp, accessed February 19, 2007.

2. "The Challenges Confronting a Successful e-Business Start-Up: The Grocery Gateway Story," presentation given by Scott Bryan, Executive Vice President, Grocery Gateway on September 22, 2003 at the DeGroote School of Business, McMaster University.

3. www.grocerygateway.com/about/default.asp, accessed February 19, 2007.

4. www.cuberoute.com/AboutUs/Press/p24.html, accessed February 19, 2007.

5. Nathalie Kilby and Tim Maton, "Grocers Fail To Deliver Online," *Marketing Week*, 2006, Vol. 29 Issue 19, pp. 38–39, 2 pp.

6. "1,000 Executives Best Skillset," *The Wall Street Journal*, July 15, 2003.

7. "The Visionary Elite," *Business 2.0*, December 2003, pp. S1–S5.

8. "Boston Coach Aligns Service with Customer Demand in Real Time," www-1.ibm.com/services/us/index.wss, November 4, 2003.

9. "Industry Facts and Statistics," Insurance Information Institute, www.iii.org, accessed December 2005.

10. "Canadian Pacific Railway Uses Business Objects to Improve Asset Utilization," *Reuters Significant Developments*, January 10, 2001.

11. Christopher Koch, "How Verizon Flies by Wire," *CIO Magazine*, November 1, 2004.

12. Beth Bacheldor, "Steady Supply," *InformationWeek*, November 24, 2003, www.informationweek.com, accessed June 6, 2003.

13. Neil McManus, "Robots at Your Service," *Wired*, January 2003, p. 059.

14. Marlene Orton, "Health-Care System Getting Wired," *The Ottawa Citizen*, October 19, 2005, F2.

15. S. Begley, "Software au Natural," *Newsweek*, May 8, 2005.

16. McManus, "Robots at Your Service."

17. "Trek Standardizes Worldwide Operations on J. D. Edwards," www.jdedwards.com, accessed November 15, 2003.

18. Christopher Koch, "The ABC's of Supply Chain Management," www.cio.com, accessed October 12, 2003.

19. "Customer Success Stories," www.siebel.com, accessed November 12, 2003.

20. "Kaiser's Diabetic Initiative," www.businessweek.com, accessed November 15, 2003.

21. "Integrated Solutions—The ABCs of CRM," www.integratedsolutionsmag.com, accessed November 12, 2003.

22. Maureen Weicher, "Business Process Reengineering: Analysis and Recommendation," www.netlib.com, accessed February 12, 2005.

23. Michael Hammer and James Champy, *Reengineering the Corporation* (New York: HarperCollins Publishers, 2001).

24. Ibid.

25. Bruce Caldwell, "Missteps, Miscues—Business Reengineering Failures," *InformationWeek*, June 20, 1994, p. 50.
26. Barbara Ettorre, "Reengineering Tales from the Front," *Management Review*, January 1995; p. 13.
27. Poonam Khanna, "Fleet Hits the Street with Automated Dispatch," *Computing Canada,* November 25, 2005, p. 18.
28. Saul Berman, "Strategic Direction: Don't Reengineer Without It; Scanning the Horizon for Turbulence," *Planning Review*, November 1994, p. 18.
29. "Customer Success Stories," www.siebel.com, accessed November 12, 2005.
30. Rachel Metz, "Changing at the Push of a Button," *Wired*, September 27, 2004.
31. Mark Frary, "Seat Science," *Business Travel World,* February 2004, pp. 26–27, 2 p.
32. Losef Loew, "Draining the Fare Swamp," *Journal of Revenue and Pricing Management,* 2004, Vol. 3, No. 1, pp. 18–25.
33. "Air Canada Selects Teradata Data Warehouse for Revenue Management Analytics Application," *Reuters Significant Developments,* September 28, 2006.

Chapter 4

1. Bill Breen, "Living in Dell Time," *Fast Company,* November 2004, p. 86.
2. John Hagerty, "How Best to Measure Our Supply Chain," www.amrresearch.com, accessed March 3, 2005.
3. Andrew Binstock, "Virtual Enterprise Comes of Age," *InformationWeek,* November 6, 2004.
4. Mitch Betts, "Kinks in the Chain," *Computerworld,* December 17, 2005.
5. Walid Mougayar, "Old Dogs Learn New Tricks," *Business 2.0,* October 2000, www.Business2.com, accessed June 14, 2003.
6. G.S. Frodsham, N.J. Miller, and L.A. Mooney, CPFR Implementation at Canadian Tire and GlobalNetXchange (GNX), in D. Seifert (ed.), *Collaborative Planning, Forecasting, and Replenishment* (New York: American Management Association (AMACOM), 2003), pp. 140–161.
7. Fred Hapgood, "Smart Decisions," *CIO Magazine,* www.cio.com, accessed August 15, 2001.
8. "Creating a Value Network," *Wired.*
9. www.gs1ca.org/home.asp, accessed March 10, 2007.
10. "Creating a Value Network," *Wired.*
11. "The e-Biz Surprise," *BusinessWeek,* May 12, 2003, pp. 60–65.
12. http://strategis.ic.gc.ca/epic/site/apparel-vetements.nsf/en/ap03283e.html, accessed March 10, 2007.
13. Frank Quinn, "The Payoff Potential in Supply Chain Management," www.ascet.com, accessed June 15, 2003.
14. Mougayar, "Old Dogs Learn New Tricks."

15. Quinn, "The Payoff Potential," and William Copacino, "How to Become a Supply Chain Master," *Supply Chain Management Review,* September 1, 2001, www.manufacturing.net, accessed June 12, 2003.
16. www.ni2cie.org/cuscsp/about.asp, accessed March 10, 2007.
17. R.G. Edmonson, "The U.S.–Canadian Connection," *The Journal of Commerce,* Volume 7, Issue 9, Feb 27, 2006, pp. 26–28, 2 p.
18. J. King, "Health Care's Major Illness," *Computerworld,* May 10, 2004.
19. www.carenet.ca/, accessed March 5, 2007.
20. CCNMatthews (Canada), "BCE Emergis Renews Five-Year Agreement for CareNET e-Commerce Services," July 21, 2003.
21. Jennifer Bresnahan, "The Incredible Journey," *CIO Enterprise Magazine*, August 15, 1998, www.cio.com, accessed March 12, 2004.
22. Kim Girard, "How Levi's Got Its Jeans into Wal-Mart," *CIO Magazine*, July 15, 2003.

Chapter 5

1. Andy Holloway, "The Customer is King," *Canadian Business,* July 18, 2005, Vol. 78, Issue 14/15, pp. 62–65, 3 pp.
2. Ibid.
3. "Fairmont Hotels & Resorts Selects Superclick to Further Enhance," *Market News Publishing,* February 2, 2006.
4. Jane Knight, "How To Avoid The Angry Man With The Big Bill Bar—A Modern Mystery Solved," *The Times,* August 13, 2005, Travel 2 section.
5. Andy Holloway, "The Customer is King," *Canadian Business,* July 18, 2005, Vol. 78, Issue 14/15, pp. 62–65, 3 pp.
6. Mark Ryhorski, Richard Wilson, Jody Fisher, Dilip Soman, "Harnessing Customer Intelligence: Executive Summary," April 2005, Manton Group.
7. Andy Holloway, "The Customer is King," *Canadian Business,* July 18, 2005, Vol. 78, Issue 14/15, pp. 62–65, 3 pp.
8. "1800 flowers.com," *Business 2.0,* February 2004.
9. Alex Anderson, "Credit Union Hopes Web Services Will Improve Customer Experience," *Computing Canada,* September 9, 2005, Vol. 31, Issue 12, p. 13.
10. Ian Gordon and Connie Wente, "Customer Relationship Management at CCL," *Ivey Business Journal, Best Practice,* November/December 2001, pp. 23–25.
11. "Barclays, Giving Voice to Customer-Centricity," crm.insightexec.com, accessed July 15, 2003.
12. "Customer Success—PNC Retail Bank," www.siebel.com, accessed May 5, 2003.
13. California State Automobile Association Case Study, www.epiphany.com/customers/detail_csaa.html, accessed July 4, 2003.
14. www.salesforce.com, accessed June 2005.
15. "Playground Real Estate Realizes Significant Returns From Successful CRM Stratey Using Maximizer," *Electronic News Publishing,* February 13, 2007.

16. "3M Accelerates Revenue Growth Using Siebel eBusiness Applications," www.siebel.com, July 30, 2002, accessed July 10, 2003.

17. Chuck Salter, "Customer-Centred Leader: Chick-Fil-A," *Fast Company,* www.fastcopany.com, accessed April 14, 2007.

18. "Avnet Brings IM to Corporate America with Lotus Instant Messaging," www.websphereadvisor.com/doc/12196, accessed July 11, 2003.

19. Jena McGregor, "High Tech Achiever: Mini USA," *Fast Company,* www.fastcopany.com, accessed April 14, 2007.

20. www.nicesystems.com, accessed June 2005.

21. www.FedEx.com, accessed July 13, 2003.

22. "Documedics," www.siebel.com, accessed July 10, 2003.

23. Bob Angel, "Relationship Results," *CA Magazine,* January–February 2002, www.camagazine.com/index.cfm?ci_id=6764&la_id=1, accessed March 23, 2007.

24. Bob Evans, "Business Technology: Sweet Home," *InformationWeek,* February 7, 2005.

25. "Customer Success—UPS," www.sap.com, accessed April 5, 2003.

26. Kimberly Noble, Ross Laver, Michael MacLean, and John Schofield, "The *Data* Game," *Maclean's,* August 17, 1998, Vol. 111, Issue 33, p. 14, 6 pp.

27. "Customer Success—Brother," www.sap.com, accessed January 12, 2004.

28. "Customer Success," www.siebel.com, accessed May 5, 2003.

29. "Customer Success—Cisco," www.sap.com, accessed April 5, 2003.

30. "Customer Success," www.rackspace.com, accessed June 2005.

31. "Partnering in the Fight against Cancer," www.siebel.com, accessed July 16, 2003.

32. Terri-Sue Buchanan, "Call Centres: Ringing in Profits," *Export Wise,* Winter 2005, pp. 11–16, 6 pp.

33. Ibid.

34. "The Expanding Territory of Outsourcing," www.outsourcing.com, accessed August 15, 2003.

35. Terri-Sue Buchanan, "Call Centres: Ringing in Profits," *Export Wise,* Winter 2005, pp. 11–16, 6 pp.

36. www.investor.harley-davidson.com, accessed October 10, 2003; Bruce Caldwell, "Harley-Davidson Revs Up IT Horsepower," Internetweek.com, December 7, 2000; "Computerworld 100 Best Places to Work in IT 2003," *Computerworld,* June 9, 2003, pp. 36–48; Leroy Zimdars, "Supply Chain Innovation at Harley-Davidson: An Interview with Leroy Zimdars," *Ascet 2,* April 15, 2000; "Customer Trust: Reviving Loyalty in a Challenging Economy," Pivotal Webcast, September 19, 2002; "Harley-Davidson Announces Go-Live: Continues to Expand Use of Manugistics Supplier Relationship Management Solutions," www.manugistics.com, May 7, 2002; and Roger Villareal, "Docent Enterprise Increases Technician and Dealer Knowledge and Skills to Maximize Sales Results and Customer Service," www.docent.com, August 13, 2002.

Chapter 6

1. "IBM Helps Shell Canada Fuel New Productivity with PeopleSoft EnterpriseOne," case study, published on August 8, 2005, validated on February 5, 2007, available at www-306.ibm.com/software/success/cssdb.nsf/CS/AMWR-6F3L8U?OpenDocument&Site=default, accessed March 27, 2007.

2. "Customer Success Story—Turner Industries," www.jdedwards.com, accessed October 15, 2003.

3. "City of Winnipeg: Taking the Lead," Deloitte & Touche LLP–Canada, www.deloitte.com/dtt/case_study/0,1005,sid%253D3630%2526cid%253D80674,00.html, accessed March 28, 2007.

4. "Harley-Davidson on the Path to Success," www.peoplesoft.com/media/success, accessed October 12, 2003.

5. "Customer Success Story—Grupo Farmanova Intermed," www.jdedwards.com, accessed October 15, 2003.

6. "Customer Success Stories," www.jdedwards.com, accessed October 15, 2003.

7. Michael Doane, "A Blueprint for ERP Implementation Readiness," www.metagroup.com, accessed October 17, 2003.

8. Ibid.

9. Ibid.

10. Thomas Wailgum, "Big Mess on Campus," CIO Magazine, May 1, 2005.

11. Sandra Bolan, "Keeping Everyone in the Loop: ERP Systems for the Lucrative SMB Market has been Nothing but Lip Service Until Now," *Computer Dealer News,* Vol. 19, Issue 7, May 2, 2003, p.16(2).

12. Alexandra DeFelice, "Sage Accpac: On The Grow," *Accounting Technology,* Vol. 22, Issue 10, November 2006, p. 50.

13. www.sageaccpac.com/products/success/BodyNScentsSS.pdf, accessed March 29, 2007.

14. www.sageaccpac.com/products/success/SystemSensorSS.pdf, accessed March 29, 2007.

15. www.automated-design.ca/erp/, accessed March 29, 2007.

Chapter 7

1. Michael S. Malone, "IPO Fever," *Wired*, March 2004; and Google Knows Where You Are," *BusinessWeek*, February 2, 2004.

2. "Google Reveals High-Profile Users of Data Search Machine," Reuters News Service, August 13, 2003, www.chron.com, accessed September 3, 2003.

3. Mitch Betts, "Unexpected Insights," *Computerworld,* April 14, 2003, www.computerworld.com, accessed September 4, 2003.

4. Ibid.

5. "Data Mining: What General Managers Need to Know," *Harvard Management Update,* October 1999.

6. Barbara DePompa Reimers,"Too Much of a Good Thing," *Computerworld,* April 14, 2003.

7. Ibid.

8. "More Insight, Better Decisions," *KMWorld,* April 2004, Vol. 13. Issue 4, p. 6.

9. "Success Stories in Government Using VERITAS Software," www.kanatek.com/downloads/case_studies/Case_Study-VERITAS.pdf, accessed April 9, 2007.

10. "National Integrated Interagency Information (N-III) System," www.rcmpgrc.gc.ca/niii/index_e.htm, accessed April 9, 2007.

11. Julia Kiling, "OLAP Gains Fans among Data-Hungry Firms," *Computerworld,* January 8, 2001, p. 54.

12. Ibid.

13. Customer Success Stories, www.oracle.com, accessed September 20, 2003.

14. Ibid., accessed September 22, 2003.

15. Kathleen Melymuka, "Premier 100: Turning the Tables at Applebee's," *Computerworld,* www.computerworld.com, accessed February 24, 2003.

16. W.H. Inmon and Richard D. Hackathorn, *Using the Data Warehouse* (Mississauga, ON: John Wiley & Sons Canada, 1994).

17. Alice LaPante, "Big Things Come in Smaller Packages," *Computerworld,* June 24, 1996, pp. DW/6–7.

18. Tommy Peterson, "Data Cleansing," *Computerworld,* February 10, 2003.

19. "Dr Pepper/Seven Up, Inc.," www.cognos.com, accessed September 10, 2003.

20. "What Every Executive Needs to Know," www.akamai.com, accessed September 10, 2003.

21. Nikhil Hutheesing, "Surfing with Sega," *Forbes,* November 4, 2002, p. 58.

22. "Privacy, Security, Personal Health Records and the Enterprise," *CIO Magazine,* www.cio.com, accessed November 10, 2003.

23. LaPante, "Big Things Come in Smaller Packages," *Computerworld.*

24. "What Every Executive Needs to Know," www.akamai.com.

25. Ibid.

26. www.scouts.ca, accessed April 11, 2007.

27. Joshua Weinberger, *Customer Relationship Management,* Vol. 9, Issue 1, January 2005, pp. 45–46.

28. Julie Schlosser, "Looking for Intelligence in Ice Cream," *Fortune,* March 17, 2003; Leslie Goff, "Summertime Heats Up IT at Ben & Jerry's," *Computerworld,* July 2001.

29. www.altanapharma.ca/app/index.cfm, accessed July 3, 2007.

30. www.apos.com/Case%20Studies/ALTANA.shtml, accessed July 3, 2007.

31. Customer Success Stories, www.cognos.com, accessed January 2005.

32. Meridith Levinson, "Harrah's Knows What You Did Last Night," *Darwin Magazine,* May 2001; "Harrah's Entertainment Wins TDWI's 2000 DW Award," www.hpcwire.com, accessed October 10, 2003; Gary Loveman, "Diamonds in the Data Mine," *Harvard Business Review*, May 2003, p. 109; "NCR—Harrah's Entertainment, Inc.," www.ncr.com, accessed October 12, 2003; "Cognos and Harrah's Entertainment Win Prestigous Data Warehousing Award," 2002 News Release, www.cognos.com, accessed October 14, 2003; Kim Nash, "Casinos Hit Jackpot with Customer Data," www.cnn.com, accessed October 14, 2003.

Chapter 8

1. www.conferenceboard.ca/education/best-practices/pdf/BellCanada.pdf, accessed April 19, 2007.

2. Stephanie Boyd, "What's Next for Corporate Virtual Libraries?" *Online,* 2004, Vol. 28, Issue 6, pp. 14–24, 7 pp.

3. www.conferenceboard.ca/education/best-practices/pdf/BellCanada.pdf, accessed April 19, 2007.

4. Andrea Di Malo, "Joining Up Government Across Tiers: Canada's BizPal," Gartner, Industry Research, February 2006.

5. "D-FW Defense Contractors Show Mixed Fortunes since September 11," www.bizjournals.com/dallas/stories/2002/09/09/focus2.htm, accessed June 8, 2004.

6. Steve Konicki, "Collaboration Is Cornerstone of $19B Defense Contract," www.business2.com/content/magazine/indepth/2000/07/11/17966, accessed June 8, 2004.

7. "Knowledge Management Research Center," *CIO Magazine,* www.cio.com/research/knowledge, accessed December 2005.

8. Megan Santosus, "In The Know," *CIO Magazine,* January 2006.

9. Ibid.

10. B. Detlor, *Towards Knowledge Portals: From Human Issues to Intelligent Agents* (Dordrecht, The Netherlands: Kluwer Academic Publishers, 2004).

11. C.C. Shilakes, and J. Tylman, *Enterprise Information Portals* (White Paper) (New York: Merrill Lynch, 1998).

12. B. Detlor, "The Corporate Portal as Information Infrastructure: Towards a Framework for Portal Design," *International Journal of Information Management,* 2000, Vol. 20, Issue 2, pp. 91–101.

13. "Speeding Information to BMW Dealers," www.kmworld.com/resources/featurearticles/index.cfm?action=readfeature&Feature_ID=337, accessed June 8, 2004.

14. "Toyota's One-Stop Information Shop," www.istart.co.nz/index/HM20/PC0/PV21873/EX236/CS25653, accessed June 8, 2004.

15. B. Detlor, "The Influence of Information Ecology on E-Commerce Initiatives," *Internet Research,* 2001, Vol. 11, Issue 4) pp. 286–295.

16. B. Detlor, "Lessons from Computer-Supported Cooperative Work," in C. Gordon and C. Terra (eds.), *Realizing the Promise of Corporate Portals* (pp. 79–81) (Toronto ON: Butterworth-Heinnemann, 2002a).

17. "HP Unveils Halo Collaboration Studio," www.hp.com, December 12, 2005.

18. www.statoil.com, accessed April 21, 2007.

19. Bjorn Erik Munkvold, Tero Paivarinta, Anne Kristine Hodne, and Elin Stangeland, "Contemporary Issues of Enterprise Content Management: The Case of Statoil," *Scandinavian Journal of Information Systems,* 2006, Vol. 18, Issue 2, pp. 69–100, accessible at www.cs.aau.dk/SJIS/journal/volumes/volume18/no2/munkvoldetal-18-2.pdf.

20. "Customer Success," www.costco.com, accessed June 2005.

Chapter 9

1 Scott Berianato, "Take the Pledge," *CIO Magazine,* www.cio.com, accessed November 17, 2003.

2. Andy McCue, "Bank Boss Quits after Porn Found on PC," www.businessweek.com, accessed June 2004.

3. AMA Research, "Workplace Monitoring and Surveillance," www.amanet.org, accessed March 1, 2004.

4. www.vault.com, accessed January 2006.

5. AMA Research, "Workplace Monitoring and Surveillance."

6. "The Lowdown on Privacy and Security Threats," Global Technology Forum, March 2007, www.ebusinessforum.com, accessed April 25, 2007.

7. Institute for Citizen-Centred Service, *Citizens First 4,* Report, November 2005.

8. "Privacy Provision Highlights," http://canada.justice.gc.ca/en/news/nr/1998/attback2.html, accessed April 26, 2007.

9. AMA Research, "Workplace Monitoring and Surveillance," www.amanet.org, accessed March 1, 2004.

10 Ibid.

11. Ibid.

12 www.cbc.ca/money/story/2007/01/18/winnersbreach.html, accessed April 27, 2007.

13. www.cbc.ca/money/story/2007/01/18/cibc.html, accessed April 27, 2007.

14. www.cbc.ca/cp/technology/070409/z040950A.html, accessed April 27, 2007.

15. "Compliance with Canadian Data Protection Laws: Are Retailers Measuring Up?" The Canadian Internet Policy and Public Interest Clinic (April 2006), www.cippic.ca.

16. www.cbc.ca/cp/technology/070409/z040950A.html, accessed April 27, 2007.

17. "2005 CSI/FBI Computer Crime and Security Survey,". www.gocsi.com, accessed February 20, 2006.

18. "2005 CSI/FBI Computer Crime and Security Survey," www.gocsi.com, accessed February 20, 2006.

19. www.ey.com, accessed November 25, 2003.

20. "The Security Revolution," *CIO Magazine,* www.cio.com, accessed June 6, 2003.

21. Alice Dragoon, "Eight (Not So) Simple Steps to the HIPAA Finish Line," *CIO Magazine,* www.cio.com, accessed July 7, 2003.

22. Gloria Galloway, "Canada Post Tip Leads to Arrests in Identity Scam," *The Globe and Mail,* (Breaking News), March 9, 2006.

23. Lesley Deverall, "Information from ATM Cards Skimmed in Auckland Used in Canada to Fleece Accounts of Thousands," *IRN News,* April 10, 2006.

24. Mari-Len De Guzman, "Bank Fraud Trail Leads to Former Outsourcing Help," *ComputerWorld Canada,* April 28, 2006, www.itworldcanada.com//Pages/Docbase/ViewArticle.aspx?ID=idgml-3185acb5-1b95-4019-8bf9-a146ecf8446f, accessed April 28, 2007.

25. "Losses from Identity Theft to Total $221 Billion Worldwide," www.cio.com, accessed May 23, 2003.

26. "Sony Fights Intrusion with 'Crystal Ball,'" *CIO Magazine,* www.cio.com, accessed August 9, 2003.

27. Spam Losses to Grow to $198 Billion," *CIO Magazine,* www.cio.com, accessed August 9, 2003.

28. Joaquim P. Menezews, "WestJet Accepts Blame, Settles with Air Canada in Espionage Case," *IT World Canada,* May 29, 2006.

29. Lisa Schmidt, "WestJet Admits Spying on Rival: How the Upstart Airline Ended Up Paying $15.5M over an Espionage Caper with Air Canada," *Calgary Herald,* May 30, 2006.

30. Brent Jagg, "WestJet Chief Talks Exit Strategy," *The Globe and Mail* (Update), June 1, 2006.

31. "Hacker Hunters," *BusinessWeek,* May 30, 2005.

32. Berinato and Scalet, "The ABCs of Information Security." *CIO Magazine,* www.cio.com, accessed July 7, 2003.

Chapter 10

1. K. Finn and B. Detlor, "Youth and Electronic Government: Towards a Model of Civic Participation," *Quarterly Journal of Electronic Commerce,* 2002, Vol. 3, Issue 3, pp. 191–209.

2. www.youth.gc.ca, accessed May 2, 2007.

3. www.businessweek.com, accessed November 1, 2005.

4. "Software Costs," *CIO Magazine,* www.cio.com, accessed December 5, 2003.

5. "Defective Software Costs," *National Institute of Standards and Technology (NIST),* June 2002.

6. "Customer Success Story—PHH," www.informatica.com, accessed December 12, 2003.

7. "Building Events," www.microsoft.com, accessed November 15, 2003.

8. Agile Alliance Manifesto, www.agile.com, accessed November 1, 2003.
9. "Software Metrics," *CIO Magazine,* www.cio.com, accessed December 2, 2003.
10. "Building Software That Works," www.compaq.com, accessed November 14, 2003.
11. "Software Metrics," *CIO Magazine.*
12. www.agile.com, accessed November 10, 2003.
13. D. Schuler and A. Namioka (eds.), *Participatory Design: Principles and Practices* (Hillsdale, New Jersey: Lawrence Erlbaum Associates, 1993).
14. P. Ehn and D. Sjogren, "From System Descriptions to Scripts for Action," in J. Greenbaum and M. Kyng (eds.), *Design at Work: Cooperative Design of Computer Systems* (Hillsdale, New Jersey: Lawrence Erlbaum Associates, 1991), pp. 241–268.
15. J. Greenbaum and M. Kyng (eds.), *Design at Work: Cooperative Design of Computer Systems* (Hillsdale, NJ: Lawrence Erlbaum Associates, 1991).
16. "Customer Success—Horizon," www.businessengine. com, accessed October 15, 2003.
17. "Top Reasons Why IT Projects Fail," *InformationWeek,* www.infoweek.com, accessed November 5, 2003.
18. www.calpine.com, accessed December 14, 2003.
19. "The Project Manager in the IT Industry," www.si2.com, accessed December 15, 2003.
20. www.standishgroup.com, accessed December 12, 2003.
21. "Merrill Lynch and Thomson Financial to Develop Wealth Management Workstation," www.advisorpage.com/ modules.php?name=News&file=print&sid=666, accessed June 8, 2004.
22. "IBM/Lotus Domino Server Hosting Service," www.macro.com.hk/solution_Outsourcing.htm, accessed June 8, 2004.
23. www.forrester.com/find?SortType=Date&No=350&N=32, accessed June 8, 2004.
24. "BP: WebLearn," www.accenture.com/xd/xd.asp?it= enweb&xd=industries%5Cresources%5Cenergy%5C case%5Cener_bpweblearn.xml, accessed June 8, 2004.
25. "Python Project Failure," www.systemsdev.com, accessed November 14, 2003.
26. www.standishgroup.com, accessed November 14, 2003.
27. "Overcoming Software Development Problems," www.samspublishing.com, accessed October 2005.
28. www.microsoft.com, accessed November 16, 2003.
29. "Staying on Track at the Toronto Transit Commission," www.primavera.com, accessed December 16, 2003.

Chapter 11

1. Timothy Mullaney and Arlene Weintraub, "The Digital Hospital," *BusinessWeek,* March 28, 2005, and Michelle Delio, "How Secure Is Digital Hospital," *Wired,* March 28, 2001.
2. Eva Chen, "Shop Talk," *CIO Magazine,* October 15, 2004.

3. www.perrio.com, accessed November 2005.
4. Chris Murphy, "RIM Settles BlackBerry Suit," *InformationWeek,* March 6, 2006.
5. "Data Mining: What General Managers Need to Know," *Harvard Management Update,* October 1999.
6. Barbara DePompa Reimers, "Too Much of a Good Thing," *Computerworld,* www.computerworld.com, April 14, 2003.
7. Ibid.
8. "Handheld 2006–2010 Forecast and Analysis," *IDC,* www.idc.com, March 2006.
9. "The I-Tech Virtual Keyboard," www.laser-keyboard. com, accessed September 2005.
10. "Airbus Working with LogicaCMG on Tracking," www.usingrfid.com, accessed August 16, 2004.
11. Ibid.
12. "Howard Stern Making Jump to Satellite Radio," www.msnbc.msn.com, October 6, 2004.
13. "SiRF Technology and NEC Electronics Partner," www.sirf.com, accessed February 2002.
14. "GM Owners Are Finding an Easy and Convenient Way to Manage Car Care Through E-Mail," www.cnnmoney.com, accessed April 10, 2006.
15. Joe Wilcox, "Sit and Surf," Cnet news, news.com.com, accessed May 2, 2003.
16. Tiffany Kary, "Palm Plugs and Premiers," Cnet news, news.com.com, accessed March 19, 2005.
17. Ibid.
18. Julia Dault, "Continental Supplied: On a North American Road Trip, Nancy Nisbet Redefines Free Trade," *National Post,* May 25, 2006.
19. www.nje.ca/Index_CaseStudy_Exchange2006.htm, accessed May 9, 2007.
20. Galen Gruman, "UPS vs. FedEx: Head-to-Head on Wireless," *BusinessWeek,* June 1, 2004.
21. "Overcoming Software Development Problems," www.samspublishing.com, October 7, 2002, accessed November 16, 2003.

Chapter 12

1. "Electronic Breaking Points," *PC World,* August 2005.
2. Tom Davenport, "Playing Catch-Up," *CIO Magazine,* May 1, 2001.
3. "Hector Ruiz, Advanced Micro Devices," *BusinessWeek,* January 10, 2005.
4. www.powergridfitness.com, accessed October 2005.
5. Denise Brehm, "Sloan Students Pedal Exercise," www.mit.edu, accessed May 5, 2003.
6. Margaret Locher, "Hands That Speak," *CIO Magazine,* June 1, 2005.
7. www.needapresent.com, accessed October 2005.
8. Aaron Ricadela, "Seismic Shift," *Information Week,* March 14, 2005.
9. www.mit.com, accessed October 2005.

10. "The Linux Counter," counter.li.org, accessed October 2005.
11. Christine McGeever, "FBI Database Problem Halts Gun Checks," www.computerworld.com, accessed May 22, 2000.
12. www.cio.com, accessed November 2005.
13. "Distribution of Software Updates of Thousands of Franchise Locations Was Slow and Unpredictable," www.fountain.com, accessed October 10, 2003.
14. Christopher Koch, "A New Blueprint for the Enterprise," *CIO Magazine,* March 1, 2005.
15. www.marshall&swift.com, accessed November 2005.
16. "What Every Executive Needs to Know," www.akamai.com, accessed September 10, 2003.
17. Martin Garvey, "Manage Passwords," *Information Week,* May 20, 2005.
18. Ibid.
19. Ibid.
20. Martin Garvey, "Security Action Plans," *Information Week,* May 30, 2005.
21. Ibid.
22. "Can American Keep Flying?" *CIO Magazine,* www.cio.com, accessed February 15, 2003.
23. www.abercrombie&fitch.com, accessed November 2005.
24. Erick Schonfeld, "Linux Takes Flight," *Business 2.0,* January 2003, pp. 103–5.
25. "Looking at the New," *Information Week,* May 2005.
26. John Fontana, "Lydian Revs up with Web Services," *Network World,* March 10, 2004.
27. www.websidestory.com, accessed November 2005.
28. Ibid.
29. Tim Wilson, "Server Consolidation Delivers," *Information Week,* May 30, 2005.
30. Geoffrey James, "The Next Delivery? Computer Repair," CNNMoney.com, accessed July 1, 2004.
31. Erick Schonfeld, "Linux Takes Flight," *Business 2.0,* January 2003, pp. 103–5. Otis Port, "Will the Feud Choke the Life Out of Linux?" *BusinessWeek,* July 7, 2003, p. 81.

GLOSSARY

A

acceptable use policy (AUP) A policy that a user must agree to follow in order to be provided access to a network or to the Internet.

accounting and finance ERP component Manages accounting data and financial processes within the enterprise with functions such as general ledger, accounts payable, accounts receivable, budgeting, and asset management.

adware Software that generates ads that install themselves on a computer when a person downloads some other program from the Internet.

agile methodology A form of XP, aims for customer satisfaction through early and continuous delivery of useful software components.

analysis phase Analyzing end-user business requirements and refining project goals into defined functions and operations of the intended system.

analytical CRM Supports back-office operations and strategic analysis and includes all systems that do not deal directly with the customers.

analytical information Encompasses all organizational information, and its primary purpose is to support the performing of managerial analysis tasks.

anti-spam policy States that e-mail users will not send unsolicited e-mails (or spam).

application architecture Determines how applications integrate and relate to each other.

application generation component Includes tools for creating visually appealing and easy-to-use applications.

application service provider (ASP) A company that offers an organization access over the Internet to systems and related services that would otherwise have to be located in personal or organizational computers.

application software Used for specific information processing needs, including payroll, customer relationship management, project management, training, and many others.

arithmetic-logic unit (ALU) Performs all arithmetic operations (for example, addition and subtraction) and all logic operations (such as sorting and comparing numbers).

artificial intelligence (AI) Simulates human intelligence such as the ability to reason and learn.

associate program (affiliate program) Businesses can generate commissions or royalties from an Internet site.

association detection Reveals the degree to which variables are related and the nature and frequency of these relationships in the information.

attitudes towards using the portal The values, perceptions, and beliefs that end-users have towards utilizing a portal.

attribute Characteristics or properties of an entity class.

authentication A method for confirming users' identities.

authorization The process of giving someone permission to do or have something.

automatic call distribution A phone switch routes inbound calls to available agents.

availability Addresses when systems can be accessed by users.

B

backdoor program Viruses that open a way into the network for future attacks.

backup An exact copy of a system's information.

backward integration Takes information entered into a given system and sends it automatically to all upstream systems and processes.

banner ad Small ad on one Web site that advertises the products and services of another business, usually another dot-com business.

benchmark Baseline values the system seeks to attain.

benchmarking The process of continuously measuring system results, comparing those results to optimal system performance (benchmark values), and identifying steps and procedures to improve system performance.

binary digit (bit) The smallest unit of information that a computer can process.

biometric The identification of a user based on a physical characteristic, such as a fingerprint, iris, face, voice, or handwriting.

black-hat hacker Breaks into other people's computer systems and may just look around or steal and destroy information.

blog Web site in which items are posted on a regular basis and displayed in reverse chronological order.

Bluetooth An omnidirectional wireless technology that provides limited-range voice and data transmission over the unlicensed 2.4-GHz frequency band, allowing connections with a wide variety of fixed and portable devices that normally would have to be cabled together.

brick-and-mortar business A business that operates in a physical store without an Internet presence.

bullwhip effect Occurs when distorted product demand information passes from one entity to the next throughout the supply chain.

business-critical integrity constraint Enforces business rules vital to an organization's success and often requires more insight and knowledge than relational integrity constraints.

business intelligence (BI) Information that people use to support their decision-making efforts.

business portals This term is synonymous with the terms **corporate portal** and **enterprise portal**. *See* **enterprise portal**.

business process A standardized set of activities that accomplish a specific task, such as processing a customer's order.

business process reengineering (BPR) The analysis and redesign of workflow within and between enterprises.

business requirement The detailed set of business requests that the system must meet in order to be successful.

business-to-business (B2B) Applies to businesses buying from and selling to each other over the Internet.

business-to-business (B2B) marketplace An Internet-based service that brings together many buyers and sellers.

business-to-consumer (B2C) Applies to any business that sells its products or services to consumers over the Internet.

buyer power High when buyers have many choices of whom to buy from and low when their choices are few.

byte Group of eight bits represents one natural language character.

C

cache memory A small unit of ultra-fast memory that is used to store recently accessed or frequently accessed data so that the CPU does not have to retrieve this data from slower memory circuits such as RAM.

call scripting system Accesses organizational databases that track similar issues or questions and automatically generate the details for the CSR who can then relay them to the customer.

campaign management system Guides users through marketing campaigns performing such tasks as campaign definition, planning, scheduling, segmentation, and success analysis.

capacity planning Determines the future IT infrastructure requirements for new equipment and additional network capacity.

central processing unit (CPU) (or microprocessor) The actual hardware that interprets and executes the program (software) instructions and coordinates how all the other hardware devices work together.

change control board (CCB) Responsible for approving or rejecting all change requests.

change management A set of techniques that aid in evolution, composition, and policy management of the design and implementation of a system.

change management system Includes a collection of procedures to document a change request and define the steps necessary to consider the change based on the expected impact of the change.

chief information officer (CIO) Responsible for (1) overseeing all uses of information technology and (2) ensuring the strategic alignment of IT with business goals and objectives.

chief knowledge officer (CKO) Responsible for collecting, maintaining, and distributing the organization's knowledge.

chief privacy officer (CPO) Responsible for ensuring the ethical and legal use of information within an organization.

chief security officer (CSO) Responsible for ensuring the security of IT systems and developing strategies and IT safeguards against attacks from hackers and viruses.

chief technology officer (CTO) Responsible for ensuring the throughput, speed, accuracy, availability, and reliability of an organization's information technology.

clickstream Records information about a customer during a Web surfing session such as what Web sites were visited, how long the visit was, what ads were viewed, and what was purchased.

clickstream data Exact pattern of a consumer's navigation through a site.

click-and-mortar business A business that operates in a physical store and on the Internet.

click-through A count of the number of people who visit one site and click on an advertisement that takes them to the site of the advertiser.

client Computer that is designed to request information from a server.

client/server network A model for applications in which the bulk of the back-end processing, such as performing a physical search of a database, takes place on a server, while the front-end processing, which involves communicating with the users, is handled by the clients.

cluster analysis A technique used to divide an information set into mutually exclusive groups such that the members of each group are as close together as possible to one another and the different groups are as far apart as possible.

coaxial cable Cable that can carry a wide range of frequencies with low signal loss.

cold site A separate facility that does not have any computer equipment, but is a place where employees can move after a disaster.

collaboration system An IT-based set of tools that supports the work of teams by facilitating the sharing and flow of information.

collaborative demand planning Helps organizations reduce their investment in inventory, while improving customer satisfaction through product availability.

collaborative engineering Allows an organization to reduce the cost and time required during the design process of a product.

commercial off-the-shelf (COTS) A software package or solution that is purchased to support one or more business functions and information systems.

communication device Equipment used to send information and receive it from one location to another.

communication space An environment where people can converse and share ideas with others. The communication space within an enterprise portal consists of the various channels and features that allow end-users to connect with one another.

competitive advantage   A product or service that an organization's customers place a greater value on than similar offerings from a competitor.

complex instruction set computer (CISC) chip   Type of CPU that can recognize as many as 100 or more instructions, enough to carry out most computations directly.

computer   Electronic device operating under the control of instructions stored in its own memory that can accept, manipulate, and store data.

computer-aided software engineering (CASE)   Software suites that automate systems analysis, design, and development.

computer supported cooperative work (CSCW)   A field of research concerned with the development and use of software to help groups increase their competency in working together.

confidentiality   The assurance that messages and information are available only to those who are authorized to view them.

consolidation   Involves the aggregation of information and features simple roll-ups to complex groupings of interrelated information.

consumer-to-business (C2B)   Applies to any consumer that sells a product or service to a business over the Internet.

consumer-to-consumer (C2C)   Applies to sites primarily offering goods and services to assist consumers interacting with each other over the Internet.

contact centre (call centre)   Customer service representatives (CSRs) answer customer inquiries and respond to problems through a number of different customer touchpoints.

contact management CRM system   Maintains customer contact information and identifies prospective customers for future sales.

content filtering   Occurs when organizations use software that filters content to prevent the transmission of unauthorized information.

content management system   Provides tools to manage the creation, storage, editing, and publication of information in a collaborative environment.

content space   An environment where people can add, find, and access information content. This content space within an enterprise portal consists of a variety of information including textual documents, transactional databases, and summarized information.

control unit   Interprets software instructions and literally tells the other hardware devices what to do, based on the software instructions.

cookie   A small file deposited on a hard drive by a Web site containing information about customers and their Web activities.

coordination space   An environment where work tasks can be organized and accomplished by groups of people. The coordination space within an enterprise portal allows organizational employees to coordinate work processes, gain access to work application software, and manage the flow of information to get work tasks done.

copyright   The legal protection afforded an expression of an idea, such as a song, video game, and some types of proprietary documents.

core competency   An organization's key strength or business function that it does better than any of its competitors.

core competency strategy   When an organization chooses to focus specifically on what it does best (its core competency) and forms partnerships and alliances with other specialist organizations to handle nonstrategic business processes.

core ERP component   Traditional components included in most ERP systems and they primarily focus on internal operations.

corporate portals   This term is synonymous with the terms **business portal** and **enterprise portal**. *See* **enterprise portal.**

counterfeit software   Software that is manufactured to look like the real thing and sold as such.

cracker   A hacker with criminal intent.

critical path   A path from the start to the finish that passes through all the tasks that are critical to completing the project in the shortest amount of time.

critical success factor (CSF)   A factor that is critical to an organization's success.

CRM analysis technologies   Help organizations segment their customers into categories such as best and worst customers.

CRM predicting technologies   Help organizations make predictions regarding customer behaviour such as which customers are at risk of leaving.

CRM reporting technologies   Help organizations identify their customers across other applications.

cross-selling   Selling additional products or services to a customer.

cube   The common term for the representation of multidimensional information.

customer relationship management (CRM)   Involves managing all aspects of a customer's relationship with an organization to increase customer loyalty and retention and an organization's profitability

cyberterrorist   Seeks to cause harm to people or to destroy critical systems or information and use the Internet as a weapon of mass destruction.

cycle inventory   The average amount of inventory held to satisfy customer demands between inventory deliveries.

D

data   Raw facts that describe the characteristics of an event.

data administration component   Provides tools for managing the overall database environment by providing facilities for backup, recovery, security, and performance.

database   Maintains information about various types of objects (inventory), events (transactions), people (employees), and places (warehouses).

database management system (DBMS) Software through which users and application programs interact with a database.

database-based workflow system Stores documents in a central location and automatically asks the team members to access the document when it is their turn to edit the document.

data definition component Helps create and maintain the data dictionary and the structure of the database.

data dictionary A file that stores definitions of information types, identifies the primary and foreign keys, and maintains the relationships among the tables.

data flow diagram (DFD) Illustrates the movement of information between external entities and the processes and data stores within the system.

data manipulation component Allows users to create, read, update, and delete information in a database.

data mart Contains a subset of data warehouse information.

data mining The process of analyzing data to extract information not offered by the raw data alone.

data-mining tool Uses a variety of techniques to find patterns and relationships in large volumes of information and infer rules from them that predict future behaviour and guide decision making.

data model A formal way to express data relationships to a database management system (DBMS).

data warehouse A logical collection of information—gathered from many different operational databases—that supports business analysis activities and decision-making tasks.

decision support system (DSS) Models information to support managers and business professionals during the decision-making process.

demand planning software Generates demand forecasts using statistical tools and forecasting techniques.

denial-of-service attack (DoS) Floods a Web site with so many requests for service that it slows down or crashes the site.

dependency A logical relationship that exists between the project tasks, or between a project task and a milestone.

design phase Involves describing the desired features and operations of the system including screen layouts, business rules, process diagrams, pseudo code, and other documentation.

development phase Involves taking all of the detailed design documents from the design phase and transforming them into the actual system.

digital asset management system (DAM) Though similar to document management, DAM generally works with binary rather than text files, such as multimedia file types.

digital Darwinism Organizations that cannot adapt to the new demands placed on them for surviving in the information age are doomed to extinction.

digital dashboard Integrates information from multiple components and tailors the information to individual preferences.

digital divide When those with access to technology have great advantages over those without access to technology.

digital wallet Both software and information—the software provides security for the transaction and the information includes payment and delivery information (for example, the credit card number and expiration date).

disaster recovery cost curve Charts (1) the cost to the organization of the unavailability of information and technology and (2) the cost to the organization of recovering from a disaster over time.

disaster recovery plan A detailed process for recovering information or an IT system in the event of a catastrophic disaster such as a fire or flood.

disruptive technology A new way of doing things that initially does not meet the needs of existing customers.

distributed denial-of-service attack (DDoS) Attacks from multiple computers that flood a Web site with so many requests for service that it slows down or crashes.

distribution management software Coordinates the process of transporting materials from a manufacturer to distribution centres to the final customer.

dividend A distribution of earnings to shareholders.

document management system (DMS) Supports the electronic capturing, storage, distribution, archival, and accessing of documents.

drill-down Enables users to get details, and details of details, of information.

E

e-business The conducting of business on the Internet, not only buying and selling, but also serving customers and collaborating with business partners.

e-business model An approach to conducting electronic business on the Internet.

e-commerce The buying and selling of goods and services over the Internet.

effectiveness IT metric Measures the impact IT has on business processes and activities including customer satisfaction, conversion rates, and sell-through increases.

efficiency IT metric Measures the performance of the IT system itself including throughput, speed, and availability.

e-government Involves the use of strategies and technologies to transform government(s) by improving the delivery of services and enhancing the quality of interaction between the citizen-consumer within all branches of government.

e-logistics Manages the transportation and storage of goods.

electronic bill presentment and payment (EBPP) System that sends bills over the Internet and provides an easy-to-use mechanism (such as clicking on a button) to pay the bill.

electronic catalogue Presents customers with information about goods and services offered for sale, bid, or auction on the Internet.

electronic cheque Mechanism for sending a payment from a chequing or savings account.

electronic data interchange (EDI)   A standard format for exchanging business data.

electronic marketplace, or e-marketplace   Interactive business communities providing a central market space where multiple buyers and suppliers can engage in e-business activities.

elevation of privilege   Process by which a user misleads a system into granting unauthorized rights, usually for the purpose of compromising or destroying the system.

e-mail privacy policy   Details the extent to which e-mail messages may be read by others.

e-mall   Consists of a number of e-shops; it serves as a gateway through which a visitor can access other e-shops.

employee relationship management (ERM)   Provides employees with a subset of CRM applications available through a Web browser.

encryption   Scrambles information into an alternative form that requires a key or password to decrypt the information.

enterprise application integration (EAI) middleware   Represents a new approach to middleware by packaging together commonly used functionality, such as providing prebuilt links to popular enterprise applications, which reduces the time necessary to develop solutions that integrate applications from multiple vendors.

enterprise architect (EA)   Person grounded in technology, fluent in business, a patient diplomat, and provides the important bridge between IT and the business.

enterprise architecture   Includes the plans for how an organization will build, deploy, use, and share its data, processes, and IT assets.

enterprise portal   Single-point Web browser interfaces used within an organization to promote the gathering, sharing, and dissemination of information throughout an enterprise. An enterprise portal provides end-users with one-stop shopping for any information they need inside or outside the enterprise.

enterprise resource planning (ERP)   Integrates all departments and functions throughout an organization into a single IT system (or integrated set of IT systems) so that employees can make decisions by viewing enterprisewide information on all business operations.

entity   In the relational database model is a person, place, thing, transaction, or event about which information is stored.

entity class   In the relational database model is a collection of similar entities.

Entity relationship diagram (ERD)   A technique for documenting the relationships between entities in a database environment.

environmental scanning   The acquisition and analysis of events and trends in the environment external to an organization.

ePolicies   Policies and procedures that address the ethical use of computers and Internet usage in the business environment.

e-procurement   The B2B purchase and sale of supplies and services over the Internet.

e-shop (e-store or e-tailer)   A version of a retail store where customers can shop at any hour of the day without leaving their home or office.

ethernet   A physical and data layer technology for LAN networking.

ethical computer use policy   Contains general principles to guide computer user behavior.

ethics   Principles and standards that guide our behaviour toward other people.

executive information system (EIS)   A specialized DSS that supports senior level executives within the organization.

expert system   Computerized advisory programs that imitate the reasoning processes of experts in solving difficult problems.

explicit knowledge   Consists of anything that can be documented, archived, and codified, often with the help of IT.

extended ERP component   The extra components that meet the organizational needs not covered by the core components and primarily focus on external operations.

extraction, transformation, and loading (ETL)   A process that extracts information from internal and external databases, transforms the information using a common set of enterprise definitions, and loads the information into a data warehouse.

extranet   An intranet that is available to strategic allies (such as customers, suppliers, and partners).

extreme programming (XP) methodology   Breaks a project into tiny phases, and developers cannot continue on to the next phase until the first phase is complete.

F

failover   Backup operational mode in which the functions of a computer component (such as a processor, server, network, or database) are assumed by secondary system components when the primary component becomes unavailable through either failure or scheduled down time.

fair use doctrine   In certain situations, it is legal to use copyrighted material.

fault tolerance   A computer system designed that in the event a component fails, a backup component or procedure can immediately take its place with no loss of service.

feasibility study   Determines if the proposed solution is feasible and achievable from a financial, technical, and organizational standpoint.

feature creep   Occurs when developers add extra features that were not part of the initial requirements.

fibre optic (optical fibre)   The technology associated with the transmission of information as light impulses along a glass wire or fibre.

financial cybermediary   Internet-based company that facilitates payments over the Internet.

financial EDI (financial electronic data interchange)   Standard electronic process for B2B market purchase payments.

firewall   Hardware and/or software that guards a private network by analyzing the information leaving and entering the network.

first-mover advantage   An organization can significantly impact its market share by being first to market with a competitive advantage.

Five Forces model   Helps determine the relative attractiveness of an industry.

flash memory   A special type of rewriteable read-only memory (ROM) that is compact and portable.

forecast   Predictions made on the basis of time-series information.

foreign key   A primary key of one table that appears as an attribute in another table and acts to provide a logical relationship between the two tables.

forward integration   Takes information entered into a given system and sends it automatically to all downstream systems and processes.

fuzzy logic   A mathematical method of handling imprecise or subjective information.

G

Gantt chart   A simple bar chart that depicts project tasks against a calendar.

genetic algorithm   An artificial intelligence system that mimics the evolutionary, survival-of-the-fittest process to generate increasingly better solutions to a problem.

geographic information system (GIS)   Designed to work with information that can be shown on a map.

gigabyte (GB)   Roughly 1 billion bytes.

gigahertz (GHz)   The number of billions of CPU cycles per second.

global inventory management system   Provides the ability to locate, track, and predict the movement of every component or material anywhere upstream or downstream in the supply chain.

global positioning system (GPS)   A device that determines current latitude, longitude, speed, and direction of movement.

goal-seeking analysis   Finds the inputs necessary to achieve a goal such as a desired level of output.

graphical user interface (GUI)   The interface to an information system.

groupware   Software that supports team interaction and dynamics including calendaring, scheduling, and video-conferencing.

H

hacker   People very knowledgeable about computers who use their knowledge to invade other people's computers.

hactivist   Person with philosophical and political reasons for breaking into systems and will often deface the Web site as a protest.

hard drive   Secondary storage medium that uses several rigid disks coated with a magnetically sensitive material

and housed together with the recording heads in a hermetically sealed mechanism.

hardware   Consists of the physical devices associated with a computer system.

hardware key logger   A hardware device that captures keystrokes on their journey from the keyboard to the motherboard.

help desk   A group of people who respond to internal system user questions.

hierarchical database model   Information is organized into a tree-like structure that allows repeating information using parent/child relationships, in such a way that it cannot have too many relationships.

high availability   Refers to a system or component that is continuously operational for a desirably long length of time.

hoaxes   Attack computer systems by transmitting a virus hoax, with a real virus attached.

hot site   A separate and fully equipped facility where the company can move immediately after a disaster and resume business.

human resources ERP component   Tracks employee information including payroll, benefits, compensation, and performance assessment, and assures compliance with the legal requirements of multiple jurisdictions and tax authorities.

hypertext transfer protocol (HTTP)   The Internet standard that supports the exchange of information on the WWW.

I

identity theft   The forging of someone's identity for the purpose of fraud.

implementation phase   Involves placing the system into production so users can begin to perform actual business operations with the system.

information   Data converted into a meaningful and useful context.

information access   The ability to find and retrieve information.

information accuracy   Extent to which a system generates the correct results when executing the same transaction numerous times.

information architecture   Identifies where and how important information, like customer records, is maintained and secured.

information cleansing or scrubbing   A process that weeds out and fixes or discards inconsistent, incorrect, or incomplete information.

information control   The degree to which an organization regulates how and what information is created, displayed, shared, and used within an enterprise. In terms of enterprise portals, information control concerns the degree to which a company enforces standardization of how information is displayed on the portal and what information can be posted.

information culture   The shared attitudes, beliefs, and values held within an organization concerning the creation, distribution, and use of information. This concerns how information is shared, the degree to which information overload is minimized, how information can be accessed, the degree to which information is controlled, and people's attitude towards using applications, such as enterprise portals, which promote the gathering, sharing, and dissemination of information throughout the company.

information ethics   The moral principles concerning the creation, collection, duplication, distribution, and processing of information, as well as the development and use of information technologies.

information granularity   Refers to the extent of detail within the information (fine and detailed or "coarse" and abstract information).

information integrity   A measure of the quality of information.

information overload   The degree to which too much information is available to make informed decisions or remain informed about a topic.

information partnership   Occurs when two or more organizations cooperate by integrating their IT systems, thereby providing customers with the best of what each can offer.

information politics   The human struggle over the governance and management of organizational information.

information privacy   The legal right or general expectation of individuals, groups, or institutions to determine for themselves, when, and to what extent, information about them is communicated to others.

information privacy policy   Contains general principles regarding information privacy.

information reach   Refers to the number of people a business can communicate with, on a global basis.

information richness   Refers to the depth and breadth of information transferred between customers and businesses.

information security   A broad term encompassing the protection of information from accidental or intentional misuse by persons inside or outside an organization.

information security plan   Details how an organization will implement the information security policies.

information security policy   Identifies the rules required to maintain information security.

information sharing   The sharing of information within an organization and the ease with which ideas and facts are transferred readily between workers in an organization.

information technology (IT)   Any computer-based tool that people use to work with information and support the information and information-processing needs of an organization.

information technology monitoring   Tracking people's activities by such measures as number of keystrokes, error rate, and number of transactions processed.

infrastructure architecture   Includes the hardware, software, and telecommunications equipment that, when combined, provide the underlying foundation to support the organization's goals.

input device   Equipment used to capture information and commands.

insider   Legitimate users who purposely or accidentally misuse their access to the environment and cause some kind of business-affecting incident.

insourcing (in-house development)   A common approach using the professional expertise within an organization to develop and maintain the organization's information technology systems.

instant messaging (IM or IMing)   A type of communications service that enables someone to create a kind of private chat room with another individual in order to communicate in real-time over the Internet.

integration   Allows separate systems to communicate directly with each other.

integrity constraint   The rules that help ensure the quality of information.

intellectual property   Intangible creative work that is embodied in physical form.

intelligent agent   A special-purpose knowledge-based information system that accomplishes specific tasks on behalf of its users.

intelligent system   Various commercial applications of artificial intelligence.

interactive voice response (IVR)   Directs customers to use touch-tone phones or keywords to navigate or provide information.

interactivity   Measures the visitor interactions with the target ad.

intermediary   Agents, software, or businesses that bring buyers and sellers together that provide a trading infrastructure to enhance e-business.

Internet   A global public network of computer networks that pass information from one to another using common computer protocols.

Internet service provider (ISP)   A company that provides individuals and other companies access to the Internet along with additional related services, such as Web site building.

Internet use policy   Contains general principles to guide the proper use of the Internet.

interoperability   Capability of two or more computer systems to share data and resources, even though they are made by different manufacturers.

intranet   An internalized portion of the Internet, protected from outside access, that allows an organization to provide access to information and application software to only its employees.

intrusion detection software (IDS)   Searches out patterns in information and network traffic to indicate attacks and quickly responds to prevent any harm.

inventory management and control software   Provides control and visibility to the status of individual items maintained in inventory.

J

joint application development (JAD)   A session where employees meet, sometimes for several days, to define or review the business requirements for the system.

K

key logger software (key trapper)   A program that, when installed on a computer, records every keystroke and mouse click.

key performance indicator (KPI)   Measures that are tied to business drivers.

kiosk   Publicly accessible computer system that has been set up to allow interactive information browsing.

knowledge   Actionable information.

knowledge management (KM)   Involves capturing, classifying, evaluating, retrieving, and sharing information assets in a way that provides context for effective decisions and actions.

knowledge management system (KMS)   Supports the capturing, organization, and dissemination of knowledge (i.e., know-how) throughout an organization.

L

list generator   Compiles customer information from a variety of sources and segments the information for different marketing campaigns.

local area network (LAN)   Computer network that uses cables or radio signals to link two or more computers within a geographically limited area, generally one building or a group of buildings.

logical view   Focuses on how users logically access information to meet their particular business needs.

logistics   The set of processes that plans for and controls the efficient and effective transportation and storage of supplies from suppliers to customers.

loyalty program   Rewards customers based on the amount of business they do with a particular organization.

M

magnetic medium   Secondary storage medium that uses magnetic techniques to store and retrieve data on disks or tapes coated with magnetically sensitive materials.

magnetic tape   Older secondary storage medium that uses a strip of thin plastic coated with a magnetically sensitive recording medium.

mail bomb   Sends a massive amount of e-mail to a specific person or system resulting in filling up the recipient's disk space, which, in some cases, may be too much for the server to handle and may cause the server to stop functioning.

maintenance   The fixing or enhancing of an information system.

maintenance phase   Involves performing changes, corrections, additions, and upgrades to ensure the system continues to meet the business goals.

maintenance, repair, and operations (MRO) materials (also called **indirect materials**)   Materials necessary for running an organization but do not relate to the company's primary business activities.

malicious code   Includes a variety of threats such as viruses, worms, and Trojan horses.

management information system (MIS)   The function that plans for, develops, implements, and maintains IT hardware, software, and applications that people use to support the goals of an organization.

market basket analysis   Analyzes such items as Web sites and checkout scanner information to detect customers' buying behavior and predict future behaviour by identifying affinities among customers' choices of products and services.

mass customization   Ability of an organization to give its customers the opportunity to tailor its products or services to the customers' specifications.

megabyte (MB or M or Meg)   Roughly 1 million bytes.

megahertz (MHz)   The number of millions of CPU cycles per second.

memory card   Contains high-capacity storage that holds data such as captured images, music, or text files.

memory stick   Provides nonvolatile memory for a range of portable devices including computers, digital cameras, MP3 players, and PDAs.

messaging-based workflow system   Sends work assignments through an e-mail system.

metropolitan area network (MAN)   A computer network that provides connectivity in a geographic area or region larger than that covered by a local area network, but smaller than the area covered by a wide area network.

microwave transmitter   Commonly used to transmit network signals over great distances.

middleware   Different types of software that sit in the middle of and provide connectivity between two or more software applications.

mobile commerce, or **m-commerce**   The ability to purchase goods and services through a wireless Internet-enabled device.

model   A simplified representation or abstraction of reality.

modelling   The activity of drawing a graphical representation of a design.

multitasking   Allows more than one piece of software to be used at a time.

N

nearshore outsourcing   Contracting an outsourcing agreement with a company in a nearby country.

network   A communications, data exchange, and resource-sharing system created by linking two or more computers and establishing standards, or protocols, so that they can work together.

network database model   A flexible way of representing objects and their relationships.

network operating system (NOS)   The operating system that runs a network, steering information between computers and managing security and users.

network topology   Refers to the geometric arrangement of the actual physical organization of the computers (and other network devices) in a network.

network transmission media   Various types of media used to carry the signal between computers.

neural network (an artificial neural network)   A category of AI that attempts to emulate the way the human brain works.

nonrepudiation   A contractual stipulation to ensure that e-business participants do not deny (repudiate) their online actions.

O

offshore outsourcing   Using organizations from developing countries to write code and develop systems.

online ad   Box running across a Web page that is often used to contain advertisements.

online analytical processing (OLAP)   The manipulation of information to create business intelligence in support of strategic decision making.

online service provider (OSP)   Offers an extensive array of unique services such as its own version of a Web browser.

online training   Runs over the Internet or off a CD-ROM.

online transaction processing (OLTP)   The capturing of transaction and event information using technology to (1) process the information according to defined business rules, (2) store the information, and (3) update existing information to reflect the new information.

onshore outsourcing   The process of engaging another company within the same country for services.

open system   A broad, general term that describes nonproprietary IT hardware and software made available by the standards and procedures by which their products work, making it easier to integrate them.

operating system software   Controls the application software and manages how the hardware devices work together.

operational CRM   Supports traditional transactional processing for day-to-day front-office operations or systems that deal directly with the customers.

opportunity management CRM system   Targets sales opportunities by finding new customers or companies for future sales.

output device   Equipment used to see, hear, or otherwise accept the results of information processing requests.

outsourcing   An arrangement by which one organization provides a service or services for another organization that chooses not to perform them in-house.

P

packet tampering   Altering the contents of packets as they travel over the Internet or altering data on computer disks after penetrating a network.

packet-switching   Occurs when the sending computer divides a message into a number of efficiently sized units called packets, each of which contains the address of the destination computer.

participatory design (PD) methodology   A systems design approach originating in Scandinavia that calls for the active involvement of users in design where users are the experts and systems development staff are coaches or facilitators.

partner relationship management (PRM)   Focuses on keeping vendors satisfied by managing alliance partner and reseller relationships that provide customers with the optimal sales channel.

peer-to-peer (P2P) network   Any network without a central file server and in which all computers in the network have access to the public files located on all other workstations.

performance   Measures how quickly a system performs a certain process or transaction (in terms of efficiency IT metrics of both speed and throughput).

personalization   Occurs when a Web site can know enough about a person's likes and dislikes that it can fashion offers that are more likely to appeal to that person.

PERT (Program Evaluation and Review Technique) chart   A graphical network model that depicts a project's tasks and the relationships between those tasks.

phishing   Technique to gain personal information for the purpose of identity theft, usually by means of fraudulent e-mail.

physical view   The physical storage of information on a storage device such as a hard disk.

pirated software   The unauthorized use, duplication, distribution, or sale of copyrighted software.

planning phase   Involves establishing a high-level plan of the intended project and determining project goals.

podcasting   Distribution of audio or video files, such as radio programs or music videos, over the Internet to play on mobile devices and personal computers.

polymorphic virus and worm   Change their form as they propagate.

pop-under ad   Form of a pop-up ad that users do not see until they close the current Web browser screen.

pop-up ad   Small Web page containing an advertisement that appears on the Web page outside of the current Web site loaded in the Web browser.

portal   A Web site that offers a broad array of resources and services, such as e-mail, online discussion groups, search engines, and online shopping malls.

predictive dialling   Automatically dials outbound calls and when someone answers, the call is forwarded to an available agent.

primary key   A field (or group of fields) that uniquely identifies a given entity in a table.

primary storage   Computer's main memory, which consists of the random access memory (RAM), cache memory, and the read-only memory (ROM) that is directly accessible to the CPU.

privacy   The right to be left alone when you want to be, to have control over your own personal possessions, and not to be observed without your consent.

private exchange   A B2B marketplace in which a single buyer posts its need and then opens the bidding to any supplier who would care to bid.

process modelling   Involves graphically representing the processes that capture, manipulate, store, and distribute information between a system and its environment.

production and materials management ERP component
Handles the various aspects of production planning and execution such as demand forecasting, production scheduling, job cost accounting, and quality control.

project   A temporary endeavour undertaken to create a unique product or service.

project deliverable   Any measurable, tangible, verifiable outcome, result, or item that is produced to complete a project or part of a project.

project exclusion   Products, services, or processes that are not specifically a part of the project.

project management   The application of knowledge, skills, tools, and techniques to project activities in order to meet or exceed stakeholder needs and expectations from a project.

project management software   Supports the long-term and day-to-day management and execution of the steps in a project.

project manager   An individual who is an expert in project planning and management, defines and develops the project plan, and tracks the plan to ensure all key project milestones are completed on time.

project milestone   Represents key dates when a certain group of activities must be performed.

project objective   Quantifiable criteria that must be met for the project to be considered a success.

project plan   A formal, approved document that manages and controls project execution.

project product   A description of the characteristics the product or service has undertaken.

project scope   Defines the work that must be completed to deliver a product with the specified features and functions.

protocol   A standard that specifies the format of data as well as the rules to be followed during transmission.

prototype   A smaller-scale representation or working model of the user's requirements or a proposed design for an information system.

public key encryption (PKE)   Encryption system that uses two keys: a public key that everyone can have and a private key for only the recipient.

pull technology   Organizations receive or request information.

pure-play (virtual) business   A business that operates on the Internet only without a physical store.

push technology   Organizations send information.

Q

query-by-example (QBE) tool   Allows users to graphically design the answers to specific questions.

R

radio frequency identification (RFID)   Technologies using active or passive tags in the form of chips or smart labels that can store unique identifiers and relay this information to electronic readers.

random access memory (RAM)   The computer's primary working memory, in which program instructions and data are stored so that they can be accessed directly by the CPU via the processor's high-speed external data bus.

rapid application development (RAD) (also called rapid prototyping) methodology   Emphasizes extensive user involvement in the rapid and evolutionary construction of working prototypes of a system to accelerate the systems development process.

read-only memory (ROM)   The portion of a computer's primary storage that does not lose its contents when one switches off the power.

real simple syndication (RSS)   Family of Web feed formats used for Web syndication of programs and content.

real-time information   Immediate, up-to-date information.

real-time system   Provides real-time information in response to query requests.

recovery   The ability to get a system up and running in the event of a system crash or failure and includes restoring the information backup.

reduced instruction set computer (RISC) chip   Limits the number of instructions the CPU can execute to increase processing speed.

redundancy   The duplication of information, or storing the same information in multiple places.

reintermediation   Using the Internet to reassemble buyers, sellers, and other partners in a traditional supply chain in new ways.

relational database model   A type of database that stores information in the form of logically related two-dimensional tables.

relational integrity constraint   The rules that enforce basic and fundamental information-based constraints.

reliability   Ensures all systems are functioning correctly and providing accurate information.

report generator   Allows users to define formats for reports along with what information they want to see in the report.

requirements definition document   Contains the final set of business requirements, prioritized in order of business importance.

response time   The time it takes to respond to user interactions such as a mouse click.

reverse auction   An auction format in which increasingly lower bids are solicited from organizations willing to supply the desired product or service at an increasingly lower price.

RFID tag   Contains a microchip and an antenna, and typically works by transmitting a serial number via radio waves to an electronic reader, which confirms the identity of a person or object bearing the tag.

rivalry among existing competitors   High when competition is fierce in a market and low when competition is more complacent.

router   An intelligent connecting device that examines each packet of data it receives and then decides which way to send it onward toward its destination.

S

safety inventory   Includes extra inventory held in the event demand exceeds supply.

sales force automation (SFA)   A system that automatically tracks all of the steps in the sales process.

sales management CRM system   Automates each phase of the sales process, helping individual sales representatives coordinate and organize all of their accounts.

scalability   Refers to how well a system can adapt to increased demands.

scope creep   Occurs when the scope of the project increases.

script kiddies or script bunnies   Find hacking code on the Internet and click-and-point their way into systems to cause damage or spread viruses.

search engine optimization (SEO)   Set of methods aimed at improving the ranking of a Web site in search engine listings.

secondary storage   Consists of equipment designed to store large volumes of data for long-term storage.

secure electronic transaction (SET)   Transmission security method that ensures transactions are secure and legitimate.

secure socket layer (SSL)   (1) Creates a secure and private connection between a client and server computer, (2) encrypts the information, and (3) sends the information over the Internet.

selling chain management   Applies technology to the activities in the order life cycle from inquiry to sale.

sensitivity analysis   The study of the impact that changes in one (or more) parts of the model have on other parts of the model.

server   Computer that is dedicated to providing information in response to external requests.

service level agreement (SLA)   Defines the specific responsibilities of the service provider and sets the customer expectations.

shopping bot   Software that will search several retailer Web sites and provide a comparison of each retailer's offerings including price and availability.

sign-off   The system users' actual signatures indicating they approve all of the business requirements.

slice-and-dice   The ability to look at information from different perspectives.

smart card   A device that is around the same size as a credit card, containing embedded technologies that can store information and small amounts of software to perform some limited processing.

sniffer   A program or device that can monitor data traveling over a network.

social engineering   Using one's social skills to trick people into revealing access credentials or other information valuable to the attacker.

social networking analysis (SNA)   A process of mapping a group's contacts (whether personal or professional) to identify who knows whom and who works with whom.

software   The set of instructions that the hardware executes to carry out specific tasks.

spam   Unsolicited e-mail.

spamdexing   Uses a variety of deceptive techniques in an attempt to manipulate search engine rankings, whereas legitimate search engine optimization focuses on building better sites and using honest methods of promotion.

spoofing   The forging of the return address on an e-mail so that the e-mail message appears to come from someone other than the actual sender.

spyware (sneakware or stealthware)   Software that comes hidden in free downloadable software and tracks online movements, mines the information stored on a computer, or uses a computer's CPU and storage for some task the user knows nothing about.

structured collaboration (or process collaboration)   Involves shared participation in business processes, such as workflow, in which knowledge is hard coded as rules.

structured query language (SQL)   A standardized fourth-generation query language found in most DBMSs.

supplier power   High when buyers have few choices of whom to buy from and low when their choices are many.

supplier relationship management (SRM)   Focuses on keeping suppliers satisfied by evaluating and categorizing suppliers for different projects, which optimizes supplier selection.

supply chain   Consists of all parties involved, directly or indirectly, in the procurement of a product or raw material.

supply chain event management (SCEM)   Enables an organization to react more quickly to resolve supply chain issues.

supply chain execution (SCE) software   Automates the different steps and stages of the supply chain.

supply chain management (SCM)   Involves the management of information flows between and among stages in a supply chain to maximize total supply chain effectiveness and profitability.

supply chain planning (SCP) software   Uses advanced mathematical algorithms to improve the flow and efficiency of the supply chain while reducing inventory.

supply chain visibility   The ability to view all areas up and down the supply chain.

sustaining technology   Produces an improved product customers are eager to buy, such as a faster car or larger hard drive.

switching cost The costs that can make customers reluctant to switch to another product or service.

system availability Number of hours a system is available for users.

systems development life cycle (SDLC) The overall process for developing information systems from planning and analysis through implementation and maintenance.

systems development process The structure or means by which a software product is produced or enhanced. How software is developed by organizations.

system software Controls how the various technology tools work together along with the application software.

T

tacit knowledge The knowledge contained in people's heads.

telecommunication system Enables the transmission of data over public or private networks.

terabyte (TB) Roughly 1 trillion bytes.

test condition The detailed steps the system must perform along with the expected results of each step.

testing phase Involves bringing all the project pieces together into a special testing environment to test for errors, bugs, and interoperability and verify that the system meets all of the business requirements defined in the analysis phase.

threat of new entrants High when it is easy for new competitors to enter a market and low when there are significant entry barriers to entering a market.

threat of substitute products or services High when there are many alternatives to a product or service and low when there are few alternatives from which to choose.

throughput The amount of information that can travel through a system at any point in time.

time-series information Time-stamped information collected at a particular frequency.

token Small electronic devices that change user passwords automatically.

transaction Exchange or transfer of goods, services, or funds involving two or more people.

transaction processing system (TPS) The basic business system that serves the operational level (analysts) in an organization.

transaction speed Amount of time a system takes to perform a transaction.

transactional information Encompasses all of the information contained within a single business process or unit of work, and its primary purpose is to support the performing of daily operational tasks.

Transmission Control Protocol/Internet Protocol (TCP/IP) Provides the technical foundation for the public Internet as well as for large numbers of private networks.

transportation planning software Tracks and analyzes the movement of materials and products to ensure the delivery of materials and finished goods at the right time, the right place, and the lowest cost.

Trojan-horse virus Hides inside other software, usually as an attachment or a downloadable file.

twisted-pair wiring A type of cable composed of four (or more) copper wires twisted around each other within a plastic sheath.

U

unstructured collaboration (or information collaboration) Includes document exchange, shared whiteboards, discussion forums, and e-mail.

up-selling Increasing the value of a sale.

user documentation Highlights how to use the system.

utility software Provides additional functionality to the operating system.

V

value-added network (VAN) A private network, provided by a third party, for exchanging information through a high-capacity connection.

value chain Views an organization as a series of processes, each of which adds value to the product or service for each customer.

view Allows users to see the contents of a database, make any required changes, perform simple sorting, and query the database to find the location of specific information.

viral marketing Technique that induces Web sites or users to pass on a marketing message to other Web sites or users, creating exponential growth in the message's visibility and effect.

virtualization Protected memory space created by the CPU allowing the computer to create virtual machines.

virtual private network (VPN) A way to use the public telecommunication infrastructure (e.g., Internet) to provide secure access to an organization's network.

virus Software written with malicious intent to cause annoyance or damage.

voice over IP (VoIP) Uses TCP/IP technology to transmit voice calls over long-distance telephone lines.

volatility Refers to RAM's complete loss of stored information if power is interrupted.

W

waterfall methodology A sequential, activity-based process in which each phase in the SDLC is performed sequentially from planning through implementation and maintenance.

Web-based self-service system Allows customers to use the Web to find answers to their questions or solutions to their problems.

Web content management system (WCM) Adds an additional layer to document and digital asset management that enables publishing content both to intranets and to public Web sites.

Web log   Consists of one line of information for every visitor to a Web site and is usually stored on a Web server.

Web service   Contains a repertoire of Web-based data and procedural resources that use shared protocols and standards permitting different applications to share data and services.

Web traffic   Includes a host of benchmarks such as the number of page views, the number of unique visitors, and the average time spent viewing a Web page.

what-if analysis   Checks the impact of a change in an assumption on the proposed solution.

white-hat hacker   Works at the request of the system owners to find system vulnerabilities and plug the holes.

wide area network (WAN)   Computer network that provides data communication services for business in geographically dispersed areas (such as across a country or around the world).

wireless fidelity (wi-fi)   A means of linking computers using infrared or radio signals.

wireless Internet service provider (WISP)   An ISP that allows subscribers to connect to a server at designated hotspots or access points using a wireless connection.

wireless media   Natural parts of the Earth's environment that can be used as physical paths to carry electrical signals.

wire media   Transmission material manufactured so that signals will be confined to a narrow path and will behave predictably.

workflow   Defines all the steps or business rules, from beginning to end, required for a business process.

workflow management system   Facilitates the automation and management of business processes and controls the movement of work through the business process.

workshop training   Set in a classroom-type environment and led by an instructor.

World Wide Web (WWW)   A global hypertext system that uses the Internet as its transport mechanism.

worm   A type of virus that spreads itself, not only from file to file, but also from computer to computer.

PHOTO CREDITS

Chapter 2

Figure 2.33, page 64, Courtesy of the City of Hamilton.

Chapter 3

Opener, page 70, © Photodisc/Getty Images.

Figure 3.10, Courtesy of Visual Mining Inc.

Chapter 5

Opener, page 130, Courtesy of Fairmont Hotels & Resorts.

Page 131, left, Courtesy of Fairmont Hotels & Resorts.

Page 131, right, © Comstock/Jupiter Images.

Chapter 6

Opener, page 158, Ryan McVay/Getty Images.

Page 159, left, CP PHOTO/Adrian Brown.

Page 159, right, Royalty-Free/CORBIS.

Chapter 7

Opener, page 183, The McGraw-Hill Companies, Inc./John Flournoy.

Chapter 8

Opener, page 223, CP PICTURE ARCHIVE/Ryan Remiorz.

Page 224, left, Royalty-Free/CORBIS.

Page 224, right, Janis Christie/Getty Images.

Chapter 9

Page 255, left, Royalty-Free/CORBIS.

Page 255, right, © Photodisc/Getty Images.

Chapter 10

Opener, page 294, © image100 Ltd.

Page 295, left, Government of Canada.

Page 295, right, Digital Vision/Getty Images.

Apply Your Knowledge Projects

Business Driven Information Systems has 50 Apply Your Knowledge projects that students can use to drill-down into the material details. There are 25 business application projects, 20 Excel projects, and 5 Access projects. Excel projects come with multiple data and solution files that allow instructors to reuse the case while changing the data. Apply Your Knowledge projects, available in the Online Learning Centre, include:

- Capitalizing on Your Career ....Business
- Achieving Alignment ....Business
- Market Dissection ....Business
- Grading Security..........................Business
- Eyes Everywhere ....Business
- Setting Boundaries......................Business
- Contemplating Sharing................Business
- Dashboard Design.......................Business
- Great Stories ....Business
- Classic Car Problems ....Business
- Building Visibility ....Business
- Caring for Health ....Business
- Working Together.......................Business
- Different Dimensions..................Business
- Connection Components ....Business
- Internet Groceries ....Business
- Getting Personal ....Business
- Express Yourself ....Business
- Creating a Presence....................Business
- GoGo Gadgets ....Business
- Backcountry Skiing......................Business
- GEM Athletic Centre.................. Business
- Confusing Coffee ....Business
- Picking Projects..........................Business
- Keeping Time ....Business

- Controlling Your Spending..................Excel
- Gearing for Cash ....Excel
- Book Boxes.......................................Excel
- SplashEm ....Excel
- Talley's Purchases ....Excel
- Tracking Donations............................ Excel
- All Aboard..Excel
- In With the Out .... Excel
- Woods You...Excel
- Bill's Boots ....Excel
- Adequate Acquisitions ....Excel
- Formatting Grades ....Excel
- Moving Espressos ....Excel
- Reducing Transports ....Excel
- Better Business ....Excel
- Too Much Information.........................Excel
- Gizmo Turnover..................................Excel
- Managing Martin.................................Excel
- Mountain Cycle ....Excel
- Lutz Motors.......................................Excel
- Animal Relations ....Access
- Helping Animals ....Access
- iToys Inventory ....Access
- Call Around......................................Access
- MoveIt...Access